Advance praise for
The Rabbi Saved by Hitler's Soldiers

"Rigg's meticulously researched account of the wartime rescue of a Hasidic rabbi by German officers, working secretly with US intelligence, is a revealing look at the intricacies of diplomatic maneuverings and the complex, sometimes contradictory motivations of human actors."

Sue Fishkoff, author of *The Rebbe's Army: Inside the World of Chabad-Lubavitch*

"Rigg details one of the most interesting rescue operations of World War II. It is a complex tale with a fascinating cast of . . . characters, told against the tragic backdrop of World War II and the Holocaust. Rigg demonstrates not only a mastery of the politics and military operations involved but also a deep understanding of Jewish history and theology. This book is a must-read for students of Jewish history as well as the history of the Nazi regime."

Richard L. DiNardo, author of *Germany and the Axis Powers: From Coalition to Collapse*

"With all the death, pain, indifference, misery, suffering, and anguish associated with the great crime of the Holocaust, it is refreshing to see that there were people (from both sides) who were still able to exhibit humanity and work successfully to save human beings. This story adds names to similar heroic legacies such as Schindler, Sugihara, Winton, Fry, and Wallenberg."

Dr. Rick Halperin, director, Embrey Human Rights Program, Southern Methodist University

"Rigg has written a profoundly challenging book that exposes the ethical malaise that underlies modern society and its institutions. It deserves to be read as a warning of the danger humanity faces when the sanctity of the individual is sacrificed to either religious fanaticism or blind obedience to secular institutions."

Alexander B. Rossino, research historian at the Center for Advanced Holocaust Studies, United States Holocaust Memorial Museum

"Rigg has written another compelling book on the Holocaust—part action thriller and part indictment. Rigg not only narrates the incredible story of the rescue of the Lubavitcher Rebbe from almost certain death in wartime Poland, but also probes the Rebbe's much more problematic post-rescue role. Certain to generate controversy, his work demands to be read."

Robert M. Citino, author of *The Wehrmacht Retreats: Fighting a Lost War, 1943*

D0907834

"In itself a remarkable story of rescue—after all, Nazis aiding the escape of Jews from German-occupied Poland in cooperation with American authorities during a time of deep isolationism [reveals] complex motivations, on all sides, behind this mission. Thoroughly researched, detailed yet accessible, Rigg's book shows that, under certain circumstances and with much persistence, rescue efforts could be successful—a fascinating read and a timely reminder of the importance of choice and human agency in history."

Stephen G. Fritz, author of *Ostkrieg: Hitler's War of Extermination in the East*

"A fascinating study that expertly explores the roles of religious belief, political intrigue, racial prejudice, and the complexity of individual motivation in the incredible rescue of a Jewish mystic by German military intelligence officers from occupied Poland in 1940. A work that, more importantly, places this improbable rescue in the broader context of Jewish experience, the Holocaust, and US government policy during World War II."

Edward B. Westermann, author of *Hitler's Police Battalions: Enforcing Racial War in the East*

"A fascinating and superbly written book. Rigg's excellent research and brilliant storytelling make this work a great read."

General Anthony C. Zinni, USMC

*The Rabbi Saved
by Hitler's Soldiers*

The Rabbi Saved by Hitler's Soldiers

Rebbe Joseph Isaac Schneersohn and His Astonishing Rescue

Bryan Mark Rigg

UNIVERSITY PRESS OF KANSAS

Published by the University Press of Kansas (Lawrence, Kansas 66045), which was
organized by the Kansas Board of Regents and is operated and funded by Emporia
State University, Fort Hays State University, Kansas State University, Pittsburg State
University, the University of Kansas, and Wichita State University.

Library of Congress Cataloging-in-Publication Data

Names: Rigg, Bryan Mark, 1971– author.
Title: The Rabbi saved by Hitler's soldiers : Rebbe Joseph Isaac Schneersohn and his
astonishing rescue / Bryan Mark Rigg.
Description: Lawrence : University Press of Kansas, [2016] | Series: Modern war
studies | Includes bibliographical references and index.
Identifiers: LCCN 2016020351
ISBN 9780700622610 (hardback)
ISBN 9780700622627 (paperback)
ISBN 9780700622634 (ebook)
Subjects: LCSH: Schneersohn, Joseph Isaac, 1880–1950. | Rabbis—Poland—
Biography. | Hasidim—Poland—Biography. | Habad—Poland—History—20th
century. | Holocaust, Jewish (1939–1945)—Poland. | World War, 1939–1945—
Jews—Rescue—Poland—Warsaw. | BISAC: HISTORY / Military / World War II. |
SOCIAL SCIENCE / Jewish Studies.
Classification: LCC BM755.S285 R53 2016 | DDC 940.53/18092 [B] —dc23
LC record available at https://lccn.loc.gov/2016020351

British Library Cataloguing-in-Publication Data is available.

Printed in the United States of America

10 9 8 7 6 5 4 3 2 1

The paper used in this publication is recycled and contains 30 percent postconsumer
waste. It is acid free and meets the minimum requirements of the American National
Standard for Permanence of Paper for Printed Library Materials z39.48-1992.

Dedicated to my children: Sophia, Justin, and Ian.

They are my life.

Also dedicated to the late Christopher Hitchens (1949–2011),

a fighter for human rights.

The only thing necessary for the triumph of evil is for good men to do nothing.

—Edmund Burke

[The Lord] said to Cain, "Where is Abel your brother?" And he said, "I do not know. Am I my brother's keeper?" Then He said, "What have you done? The sound of your brother's bloods, they cry out to Me from the ground!" (Genesis 4:9–10). Many rabbinical scholars claim that this Bible story is used to declare a major tenet of Judaism: if you save a life, you save a world, but if you kill a life, you kill a world. When God claimed to Cain that the "bloods" cry out from the ground from his murdered brother Abel, He is stating that not only did Cain kill his brother, but he also killed his children, his grandchildren, his great-grandchildren, etc. In other words, he killed a world. Perhaps we should contemplate how many worlds will die today across this globe because we chose not to do enough.

CONTENTS

A personal word: About twenty years ago I was invited to speak on the Holocaust at Yale University's Slifka Center. After the speech a well-groomed and incredibly polite student came up to me and asked if I would read his senior thesis. I agreed, and he sent me the work on Wehrmacht soldiers who were of partially Jewish origin. As defined by the Nuremberg laws of 1935, they were *Mischlinge*, mixed breeds or mongrels, who faced persecution because they were of Jewish and "Aryan" ancestry; their Jewish parents and Jewish grandparents were often subjected not only to persecution but also to deportation and even annihilation because they were considered Jews by the state. Yet these men continued to serve in the German army, loyally, bravely, even heroically. Their superiors, some of whom were deeply anti-Semitic, often protected them. The material in the thesis was fascinating; the young student was indefatigable. I found him to be an "archives rat," which I meant as a compliment: he could ferret out valuable information from archive after archive. If it was there, he would find it.

The young student asked my advice: "Should I pursue this in graduate school?" I confidently answered, "No, seek a larger topic." But I added, "If you do pursue it further, do send me your work and I'll be happy to read it." Several years later Bryan Mark Rigg sent me what became the basis of his book *Hitler's Jewish Soldiers*, and he has been sending me book after book after book. He ignored my advice and now praises me as a mentor. Sometimes, it is gratifying to be wrong, very wrong.

A word about his early findings: Rigg showed that individuals—committed Nazis, German army officers who witnessed the annihilation of the Jews, and even some who participated directly in the "final solution" to the "Jewish problem"—had multiple loyalties. Sometimes they were bound by ties of comradeship, respect, friendship, and honor to those people the German state and German law considered Jews. These men were prepared to disregard, overlook, or even disobey the law of the land—at the risk of their careers and their standing—because of these personal loyalties. And the Jewish soldiers, whose families were in imminent danger, also had multiple, seemingly contradictory loyalties. While

German law considered them Jews, they thought of themselves as Germans and, more importantly, as German soldiers bound by a code of military loyalty. They may have loved their families, but they also loved their country, even a country that was persecuting their Jewish parents and grandparents. They loved the army and were loyal to the men with whom they served. Military ties run deep, and loyalty to comrades is essential to military discipline, bravery, and success. A soldier is often more willing to risk his life for his comrades than for the cause. These *Mischlinge* had a bifurcated identity that seemingly posed an indissoluble conflict, with each soldier resolving the tension differently, based on a sense of his German identity and Jewish origins and a distinct balance of loyalty to his family, the nation, the army, and his comrades.

Rigg brought to our attention the fact that Hitler was so consumed with identifying Jews that he personally decided which individuals were or were not Jewish even in 1942, when the war was at its peak and decisive battles were raging in the east, and even in 1944, when he faced advancing attacks from both the east and the west. One should never underestimate Hitler's obsession with Jews.

Almost by chance, Rigg uncovered the story of the rescue of the Lubavitcher Rebbe, Rabbi Joseph Isaac (Yosef Yitzchak) Schneersohn, and his family by Major Ernst Bloch, a decorated German army officer of Jewish descent. Bloch, who was in command of a group that included Sergeant Klaus Schenk, a "half-Jew," and Private Johannes Hamburger, a "quarter-Jew," had been assigned to locate the Rebbe in German-occupied Poland and escort him to freedom. They were working for German military intelligence under the leadership of Admiral Wilhelm Franz Canaris. I remember the first time I read an account of the rescue; my immediate reaction was, "Now that's a story!" Rigg has now told that story twice—several years ago in the initial version of this book, and again here, as new research and new information have sharpened his insight into what actually occurred.

Jews tell stories. Rashi (Rabbi Shlomo ben Yitzhak [1040–1105]), the most revered of all Jewish Bible commentators, notes that if the Torah were merely a book of laws, it would have begun with the twelfth chapter of Exodus, with the first commandment in the Bible. Yet imagine the Jewish narrative without the creation story, without Noah and the flood, without our biblical patriarchs Abraham, Isaac, and Jacob and the matriarchs Sarah, Rebecca, Leah, and Rachel. Imagine the biblical narrative without the paradigmatic Jewish story of slavery and the Exodus, wandering in the desert, the journey to the Promised Land, and standing at Sinai. The Torah would have been so much less interesting, less revered, less studied. The Gospels are the narratives of Jesus's life, a very Jewish way of transmitting the past.

Chabad tells stories of the rescue of the Rebbe, their exalted spiritual leader and master. Angels descended on Poland with the mission of saving him. They appeared in human form and gathered the Rebbe and his family, along with the sacred books, the holiest remnants of eastern European Jewry, and brought him into the heart of evil, into Berlin itself. From there, via Latvia, he made his way to the United States and rebuilt an entire universe, the remnants plucked from the fire. The story that Rigg has uncovered is no less miraculous and, at least to this non-Hasidic reader, perhaps even more so. Moreover, it is documentable, letter by letter, communication by communication, interview by interview, day by day. It requires no leap of faith to accept this narrative.

Chabad leaders in the United States were concerned about the fate of the Rebbe, whom they viewed as more than a holy man or a revered rabbi; he was God's emissary on earth, and he was imperiled in German-occupied Poland, confined to the Warsaw ghetto. They presumed that American officials, who were reluctant to receive refugees, might be persuaded to rescue the Rebbe because of his singular importance. To make his stature comprehensible to these Gentiles, he was portrayed as the Jewish pope. However, the Hasidim were not alone in pressuring the US government. Varian Fry and American consul official Hiram Bingham IV, working in Marseilles, were gathering poets, artists, philosophers, and scholars in Vichy France to bring the muses of Europe—Jews and political dissidents—to the United States. Similarly, Julian Morgenstern, president of Hebrew Union College, compiled a list of five promising rabbinical students and five prominent Jewish scholars to be brought to the United States to study and teach at the college so that a remnant of Reform Jewry would survive in the free world. Among those protected were the very non-Reform Jew Abraham Joshua Heschel, a scion of Hasidic royalty, and Guenther Plaut, who enjoyed a brilliant career as Canada's leading Reform rabbi. Zionists saved Zionists. Many were interested first and foremost in "their own"; only later—in some cases much later—did that interest extend to all Jews.

Chabad representatives in the United States hired a well-placed and dedicated lawyer to get them to the right desk, where they could pressure the right people. They did not promptly comply with his requests for hard information and financial forms, and they were parsimonious in paying his much-reduced fees and expenses. Yet he continued to work effectively and efficiently for the Rebbe's release.

At that time (1940), the United States still had diplomatic relations with the very undiplomatic Nazi regime, and two old friends who had been classmates at another time and in another place turned to each other. The US official requested of his German counterpart, "Rescue this leader, please." His motivation may have been less than altruistic. He may have mumbled to himself, "Please get these people off my back." Surely that was what he felt. Believing that Jews stuck together, German military intelligence assigned the task of finding the Rebbe to half-Jew Ernst Bloch and his team of *Mischlinge*. They searched throughout Warsaw for the Rebbe, who was hiding underground among his disciples. Historically, a *meshumad* (convert) is more dangerous than a non-Jew. For obvious reasons, there are few legends about heroic *meshumadim* in Jewish lore, but there are many stories of those who turned against their people. Nevertheless, Bloch was one of the rare heroes. He has been joined in the post-Holocaust world by Brother Daniel (Otto Rufssein) and Cardinal Lustiger of France. But identities in the contemporary world are much more fluid, much more complex.

Bloch not only had to worry about the Hasidim hiding the Rebbe. Once he found him, Bloch had to worry about the Gestapo in German-occupied Poland or even in Germany itself taking the Rebbe out of his hands. The struggle was between the Abwehr, which was determined to rescue the Rebbe, and the Gestapo, which was determined to capture him. Thus, Bloch also had to fear his own men. He had one more reason to be apprehensive: the Gestapo might discover his identity, putting his own freedom in jeopardy. Were this story a novel, it would have the character of an implausible fable, but as often occurred in the Holocaust, reality exceeded the imagination.

Chabad Hasidim will not be happy with this book. The historical enterprise is opposed to the process of mystification, and the analysis of documents can cast doubt on legends. Jews have become excellent historians. They have a long and exceedingly well-documented history, and the science of Judaism—*Wissenschaft des Judentums*—so prevalent in nineteenth- and twentieth-century Jewish scholarship, has subjected Judaism to rigorous historical analysis. Yet much of Judaism remains ahistorical. The Talmud recounts rabbinic conversations that stretched over five or six centuries, and the naïve Talmud student may feel that the rabbis he is reading about sat around the same table, even though they lived centuries apart. He senses himself part of that conversation, and the men he encounters seem to be present in the yeshiva house of study. Many sacred texts are attributed to authors who lived in other times, and Hasidism thrives on stories that seemingly breach the limits of time and space. Historical analysis may be anathema to them.

Rigg is quite respectful of the Rebbe's personal courage in confronting communism and its antireligious attitude. Joseph Isaac Schneersohn withstood torture and could not be broken. Military men understand what that takes. Rigg also admires the clandestine network the Rebbe built within the Soviet Union to preserve Judaism and Hasidism. Yet he is highly critical of the Rebbe's limited involvement in rescue once he came to the United States. More important, perhaps, he is less than admiring of three central elements that were essential to the Rebbe's mission and his very sense of being. First, the notion that religious practice and study can transform the world is difficult for a former US Marine Corps officer and a man of worldly action to understand or admire. Second, Rigg is dismissive of the messianic impulse, which was so central to the Rebbe's life and reached a crescendo in the work of his successor, the seventh Lubavitcher Rebbe, Menachem Mendel Schneerson, who was—and still is—regarded as the Messiah by many, perhaps most, within Chabad.

Messianism is deeply antiexistential. The here and now, the very nature of human experience, is regarded not as the domain of significance but as the antechamber to the world to come. Zionism secularized the messianic urge and transformed it into concrete political action. A century earlier, Hasidism tamed some of the more disruptive aspects of Jewish messianism; it pushed toward salvation rather than redemption. Yet in the aftermath of the Holocaust, with its world-shattering consequences, two full-fledged messianic movements burst forth in Judaism: the messianism of Rabbi Zvi Yehda Kook and his Gush Emunim followers in Israel, who believe—as do some Zionist Christians—that Jewish resettlement of the land is an indication of the hastening of the Messiah, and the messianism of Chabad. Rigg is a rigorous rationalist and simply does not comprehend the phenomenon. Messianism is driven by the tension between hope and despair, by hope triggered by despair, which was most plentiful in the world in which Rebbe Schneersohn lived.

I believe with complete faith that the Messiah has not yet come, and I tend to believe with equal faith the joke told in the ghetto about the watchman at the city's gate whose task was to herald the Messiah's arrival. He described his position: "The pay is not good, but the work is quite steady." Yet in Chabad, the messianic urge spurred action and sacrifice and gave its followers the sense that their solitary deeds were transforming the fate of the Jewish people, shaking heaven and earth. It may indeed be the secret of their enormous success under Rebbe Menachem Mendel Schneerson.

Third, Rigg does not understand the commitment to the Library, the assembly of sacred texts that have taken on a mythic life of their own after surviving Nazism and communism and even the attempt of the sixth Rebbe's last biological heir to claim them as his personal patrimony. Why would the Rebbe tarry when fleeing the Nazis to preserve his books? For the Rebbe, his task was that of Rabban Yochanan Ben Zakai, the ancient rabbi who fled Jerusalem in the year 70 CE, on the eve of its destruction, and reconstituted Judaism in Yavne with its wise men. He made Judaism portable; the synagogue became the substitute for the Temple that was set aflame. Torah study and prayer replaced sacrificial offerings, and the yeshiva became the new Jerusalem.

It will be difficult for any reader to comprehend how meager the resources of Chabad were then. Today, thanks in no small measure to the wise leadership of Rebbe Menachem Mendel Schneerson, Chabad is a global organization reportedly with a billion-dollar budget. Chabad emissaries are found wherever Jews are found. They are Jewish evangelists, seeking to proselytize Jews—only Jews—to fulfill one commandment at a time. It is inconceivable to those who did not know Chabad back then that a mere $4,000 or $5,000 would pose a problem or a burden. That, too, is a tribute to the success of the Rebbe Menachem Mendel and also to the vision of his father-in-law, Rebbe Joseph Isaac, who devoted the war years and the few years he was allotted thereafter to laying the foundation of what would become a global organization. Perhaps he intuited that there was little he could do to rescue individuals and that the very future of the Jewish people was dependent on the American Jewish community, which he saw as uninformed and assimilating, unlearned and impious.

My advice to pious readers is to be grateful for all the information Rigg has gathered, for the herculean work he has undertaken. The history he brings forth can only enhance the legends you tell. You may disregard his analysis, but don't allow your anger at his lack of understanding of your religious worldview to overshadow your appreciation of the sheer mastery of sources.

To those less pious readers: you will read in great detail about the many forces that came together to rescue one man and his family. You will read of his rescuers, their motivations, their fate, their frustrations, and their sense of dedication; you will read of the convoluted policies and people that empowered this rescue. You will encounter one hell of a story, and you may be struck by how sticking to the facts—in the *Dragnet* sense of "just the facts"—a miracle transpired. Even if you can't sense the divine, you may grasp the history as miraculous.

Michael Berenbaum
American Jewish University
Los Angeles, California

PERSONALITIES

Baal Shem Tov (Master of the Good Name), also known as the Besht—founder of the Jewish religious tradition called Hasidim

Michael Berenbaum—American historian

Rabbi Chaskel Besser—prominent Hasidic rabbi, Agudah leader, and survivor of the Nazi invasion of Poland in 1939

Alfred Bilmanis—Latvia's diplomat in Washington

General Johannes Blaskowitz—German general who protested Nazi atrocities in Poland in 1939

Major Ernst Bloch—German officer tasked to rescue Rebbe Joseph Isaac Schneersohn

Sol Bloom—US congressman from New York and chairman of the Foreign Affairs Committee

William Borah—US senator from Idaho and chairman of the Foreign Relations Committee

Louis Brandeis—first Jewish US Supreme Court justice and supporter of the rescue of Rebbe Joseph Isaac Schneersohn

Admiral Wilhelm Canaris—head of the Abwehr, the German military secret service

Neville Chamberlain—British prime minister (1937–1940)

Rabbi Mordechai Chefetz—head of the Lubavitcher movement in Latvia

Robert Citino—American historian

Benjamin V. Cohen—attorney and a member of FDR's "brain trust"; he helped author the New Deal

Eliot Coulter—second in command to Avra Warren in the Visa Department

Robert Divine—American historian

Rebbe Shalom Dovber—fifth Lubavitcher Rebbe

Mordechai Dubin—Latvian senator and strong supporter of Rebbe Joseph Isaac Schneersohn

Avrum Ehrlich—American historian

James A. Farley—postmaster general and an adviser to FDR

Roman Foxbrunner—American historian

Menachem Friedman—Israeli sociologist

Raymond Geist—American consul general in Berlin

Barry Gourary—Rebbe Joseph Isaac Schneersohn's grandson

Rabbi Samarius Gourary—Rebbe Joseph Isaac Schneersohn's son-in-
law and secretary

Arthur Green—American historian

Rabbi Meir Greenberg—one of Rebbe Joseph Isaac Schneersohn's
trusted students

Sebastian Haffner—German journalist

Sam Harris—American author and intellectual

Samuel Heilman—American sociologist

Heinrich Heine—German satirist and playwright

Holger Herwig—Canadian historian

General Reinhard Heydrich—head of the Gestapo and second in
command of the SS under Heinrich Himmler

General Heinrich Himmler—head of the SS

Major Johannes Horatzek—Warsaw's Abwehr chief

Cordell Hull—FDR's secretary of state

Rabbi Israel Jacobson—executive director of Chabad in America during
World War II

Rabbi Avraham Kalmanowitz—one of the main leaders of the Orthodox
rescue organization called the Vaad

Chaim Kaplan—distinguished Hebrew school principal in Warsaw in
1939

David Kertzer—American historian

Alexander Kirk—US chargé d'affaires in Berlin

Philip Kleinfeld—New York state senator and judge and a strong
supporter of the rescue of Rebbe Joseph Isaac Schneersohn

Rabbi Aaron Kotler—one of the main leaders of the Orthodox
rescue organization called the Vaad and founder of the yeshiva in
Lakewood, New Jersey

Hyman Kramer—president of US Chabad during World War II

Samuel Kramer—Chabad's legal counselor and one of its biggest
benefactors; he was also a close friend of Max Rhoade

David Kranzler—American historian

Harris Lenowitz—Hebraic studies specialist

Primo Levi—Holocaust survivor and writer

Rabbi Samuel Levitin—member of the Chabad rescue committee for Rebbe Joseph Isaac Schneersohn

Chaim Lieberman—Rebbe Joseph Isaac Schneersohn's personal secretary

Rabbi Menachem Mendel Leib Lokshin—US Chabad leader and associate of Israel Jacobson

Breckinridge Long—assistant secretary of state in charge of immigration

Earnest May—American historian

Marc E. McClure—American historian

Winfried Meyer—German historian

Robert T. Pell—assistant chief of the State Department's European Affairs Division

Clarence E. Pickett—executive secretary of the American Friends Service Committee in Philadelphia

Pius XI—Catholic pope (1922–1939)

Pius XII—Catholic pope (1939–1958)

Arthur Rabinovitz—Chabad US legal counsel and supporter of Rebbe Joseph Isaac Schneersohn

Rabbi Dovid Rabinovitz—US Chabad rabbi and a strong supporter of Rebbe Joseph Isaac Schneersohn

Fred Rabinovitz—Chabad US legal counsel and supporter of Rebbe Joseph Isaac Schneersohn

Max Rhoade—main Chabad lawyer and lobbyist for the rescue of Rebbe Joseph Isaac Schneersohn

Mark Roseman—American historian

Adolph J. Sabath—US congressman from Illinois and chairman of the House Rules Committee

Sergeant Klaus Schenk—subordinate of Major Ernst Bloch in the Abwehr

Rebbe Joseph Isaac Schneersohn—sixth Lubavitcher Rebbe (1920–1950)

Menachem Mendel Schneerson—seventh Lubavitcher Rebbe (1951–1994) and son-in-law of the sixth Lubavitcher Rebbe

Gershom Scholem—Israeli historian

Günter Schubert—German historian

Jonathan Steinberg—American historian

Nathan Stoltzfus—American historian

Karin Tiche—Warsaw citizen who witnessed the Nazi attack of the city in 1939

Michael Tress—president of Agudath Israel Youth Council of America and later of Agudath Israel of America

Harry T. Troutman—civil servant in the Visa Department

Henry A. Turner Jr.—American historian

Geza Vermes—British historian

Robert Wagner—US senator from New York

Gregory Wallance—American historian

Avra Warren—head of the Visa Department

Rabbi Alex Weisfogel—worked in the Vaad with Avraham Kalmanowitz

Sumner Welles—US undersecretary of state

Elie Wiesel—Holocaust survivor and writer

John C. Wiley—US minister in Riga

Joseph Wineberg—one of Rebbe Joseph Isaac Schneersohn's trusted students

Rabbi Stephen Wise—prominent US Jewish leader and friend of FDR

Helmuth Wohlthat—chief administrator of Göring's Office of the Four-Year Plan and an expert in international industry and economics

Rabbi Eliezer Zaklikovsky—Chabad historian

Schneur Zalman of Liadi—first Lubavitcher Rebbe

Efraim Zuroff—Israeli historian

Sabbetai Zvi—Jewish leader of the false Messiah crusade from 1665 to 1666

Introduction

Men never do evil so completely and cheerfully as when they do it from religious conviction.
—Blaise Pascal

By defending myself against the Jew, I am fighting for the work of the Lord.
—Adolf Hitler

I am proud of this book, which was first published ten years ago by Yale University Press as *Rescued from the Reich: How One of Hitler's Soldiers Saved the Lubavitcher Rebbe. Publishers Weekly* wrote: "This is great material—the stuff of Hollywood films." It is truly a remarkable story of how the US government, prior to entering World War II, used its influence with Nazi Germany to rescue the religious leader of a large Jewish community from the war zone in Poland. The director of the Israeli office of the Simon Wiesenthal Center, Efraim Zuroff, called this rescue "quite extraordinary in historical terms."[1] This new version is dramatically expanded, with additional primary source material and scholarship collected in the past decade. The enduring issues of humanity raised by this story are more deeply explored and analyzed, making this new work almost twice as long as and vastly different from the earlier book.

The history of this rescue is difficult to comprehend without a rudimentary understanding of the ultrareligious Hasidic sect called Lubavitch or Chabad and its former leader, the charismatic Rebbe Joseph Isaac Schneersohn. In eastern Europe in the early eighteenth century, this Hasidic group forged its own path within mainstream Judaism. In a time and place of discrimination against and oppression of Jews, this sect was characterized by mysticism, exclusivity, superstition, and dynasticism. Since this movement established its headquarters in the Russian city of

Lubavitch, its adherents came to be known as Lubavitchers. They are distinct from the larger Reform, Conservative, and Orthodox Jewish denominations, as well as from other Hasidic sects. This book delves into this group and its theology to help readers fully appreciate the significance of this story. Without such background, it would prove difficult to follow the nuances surrounding the rescue and the people involved.

Most people outside the Jewish world know nothing about this group. Any knowledge is largely a result of the revolution within Chabad initiated by Rebbe Menachem Mendel Schneerson, the charismatic successor of Rebbe Joseph Isaac Schneersohn who transformed Chabad into a global Jewish outreach movement with a presence in many countries throughout the world. We cannot perceive the movement in the 1930s and 1940s through the lens of our contemporary experience because there is a dramatic difference between Chabad then and Chabad now. Even though Chabad is worldwide, large numbers of Jews have had little or no personal contact with it, although many in the Jewish world have heard about its planting of "missionaries" and its outreach efforts. This is the only missionary-minded Jewish group similar to the Protestant sects that are well known throughout America, such as the Mormons and Jehovah's Witnesses. They do not seek to convert people of other faiths to Judaism, however; they try to convince Jews from other denominations and people of Jewish heritage with no religious beliefs to adopt their strict customs, beliefs, and practices, which they regard as the only correct way to practice Judaism. They stand on street corners or drive *mitzvah* trucks, mobile *sukkah* [temporary shelters used for meals during the Jewish holiday of *Sukkoth*] booths, and even *teffilin*-mobiles, asking passersby if they are Jewish and inviting them to perform acts of prayer and study right there on the spot.[2] I have met Chabadniks (as they are called) in places as varied as Jerusalem, Tel Aviv, Haifa, Berlin, Frankfurt, Krakow, Venice, New Haven, New York City, and Cambridge (England), and they have asked me if I am Jewish and whether I will put on teffilin (phylacteries) and pray with them.[3] In many respects, this worldwide movement would not exist if the rescue documented in this book had not happened. But we must forget what we now know about Chabad and its global presence to understand the nature of this rescue and the shape and scale of Chabad in 1940.

Even though Chabad has become one of the most visible Jewish com-

munities in the world due to this outreach, many of those who have heard
of the group or have spent time in one of the Chabad houses (places of
communal fellowship) have only an elementary understanding of its history and beliefs. The more one studies the members of this organization, the more one may question how they educate their children, view
non-Hasidic Jews, and deal with history.

The history of the Rebbe under the Nazis is much more than just
a rescue mission during the nightmare years of the Third Reich. It is a
story about how history is documented, how ideas shape action, and how
knowledge is preserved. Thus, this book explores why the rescue was
undertaken, how it was accomplished, and what the participants learned
from it. And that analysis includes the examination of a lot of religious
beliefs and ideology. I am neither a theologian nor a historian of religion;
I am a secular historian examining historical documents and interviewing eyewitnesses and others with an understanding of these events. I am,
by background and inclination, an outsider, and although my judgments
may be harsh, they reflect a careful reading of the documentation at my
disposal and the insights gained from oral interviews.

This was a strange rescue mission. The US government worked with
the Germans to rescue one of the most fundamentalist rabbis in the world
from Hitler's Europe. His religious sect is heavily focused on the Messiah. It condemns Reform, Conservative, and Modern Orthodox Jewish
movements; denies women's rights; and rejects secularists and atheists.
It perceives non-Jews as inferior to Jews, who are God's chosen people.
This makes it even more shocking that a rescue mission was ever undertaken, not to mention successful, since it took place in Nazi-dominated
Europe at the apex of Hitler's power. Had those few well-meaning bureaucrats in the State Department known what the Rebbe stood for, they
might have left him in Europe to his fate. The fact that in a sea of bigoted
and anti-Semitic civil servants the Rebbe had some good people working
on his behalf is a secular miracle in itself.

Also prominent in this story about the Lubavitchers, the rescue of
their Rebbe, and the religious themes involved are Nazi Germany and
the people in its government and military who helped Rebbe Joseph Isaac
Schneersohn. This is amazing, since the Third Reich was one of the most
evil regimes in the history of humankind. And during this horrible time,

as Nazi Germany rose to its full height, we find a fascinating story of a German secret agent, Ernst Bloch, who was ordered to find and rescue the Rebbe. Bloch was a "half-Jew" whom Hitler had Aryanized to allow him to serve in the military. His remarkable status in the German secret service presents some interesting insights into one of the darkest chapters of German history. This story provides a fascinating view inside the Wehrmacht, the SS, the war in Poland, and the Holocaust as it was gaining momentum. It shows that there were indeed good people within the Nazi hierarchy. Just as this book explores the Rebbe's life and thought in depth, it also examines Bloch's life, especially after the rescue, when he was involved in the brutal warfare on the Russian front. The juxtaposition of his thoughts and experiences with those of the Rebbe shows how random fate can be.

More specifically, this book explores in depth how the predominant Lubavitch belief that the only way to combat the Nazis was by spiritual and otherworldly means failed them during the Holocaust. Chabad beliefs discouraged the vast majority of its adherents from serving in the military and obstructed efforts to create coalitions with other groups to try to persuade the US government to rescue Jews. The Lubavitchers saw everything in religious terms, with divine intervention everywhere, so they had a religious explanation for the Shoah. Instead of condemning the fascists and those spreading hatred or decrying those whose inaction allowed the cancer of fascism to flourish, the Lubavitchers saw the persecution of the Jews and their ultimate annihilation through the classical religious lens of divine punishment. They condemned Jewish groups, which had reformed their religious convictions with Enlightenment ideas of reason, for causing the Holocaust by relinquishing proper religious practices. The Rebbe explained in 1941 that Nazi persecution was punishment for their "transgressions" and the "evil" they had done "in the eyes of G-d."[4] He elaborated that the Nazis were instruments of God's displeasure because many had violated the Lord's commandments, especially American Jews, who had brought this misfortune on the House of Israel with their "golden calf and the broken tablets."[5] He did not offer an explanation of why the catastrophe had occurred on European soil and why some of the most pious and devout Jews—his own followers among them—were the ones being slaughtered. Other Jews, especially the majority of American Jews, rejected this doctrine as blasphemous. The Rebbe failed to build coalitions and inspire people to do the right thing. His religious ideology prevented him from working with secular or non-Hasidic religious groups. He was an example of a spiritual leader who was victimized by intolerant fanatics, yet he spread another strain of intolerance, fanaticism, and inaction at a time when the world needed all good people to unite and take action to crush the evil bearing down on them.

Then there was Ernst Bloch and his Faustian trade-off. On the one hand, he loved his country and the army. On the other hand, to serve his country, he had to take an oath to follow Hitler and the Third Reich. At the height of the war with Russia, with all its brutality and death, he volunteered to go to the slaughterhouse of the front rather than remain at home with his family. Even at the end of the war, he chose to fight in the makeshift paramilitary unit called the *Volkssturm* to defend Berlin in a futile attempt to stop the Soviets. Although he apparently hated Hitler and knew the war was lost, he failed to act in his own interest. Like the Rebbe, one finds many problems with Bloch's convictions and his actions. And in the biggest irony of the story, although Bloch was able to save many others, from the Rebbe to many of his family members to countless men under his command, in the end, he was unwilling to save himself.

In the civic realm at the time, Americans took action against many US policies. The isolationists, such as those on the America First Committee (which boasted such luminaries as aviation hero Charles A. Lindbergh), fought every step the United States took or could have taken to intervene militarily against Germany or Japan, aid the Allies, and protect European Jews from persecution, right up to the time of the surprise attack on Pearl Harbor that brought America into the war. The State Department failed to actively pursue a policy of rescuing people, as demonstrated by the order to send the refugee ship *St. Louis* back to Europe, where almost one-third of its more than 900 Jewish passengers would die in the Holocaust.[6] Several Americans could have lobbied to make the United States a safe haven for the targets of Nazi persecution, but they did not.

This rescue of Rebbe Schneersohn also tells us that fighting genocide and religious totalitarianism should be a strong focus of enlightened and democratic societies. However belatedly, the United States did in fact become what Franklin Roosevelt called "the arsenal of democracy,"[7] beginning while it was still neutral, and it played a crucial role in bringing the Nazi regime to its knees once Hitler declared war against the United States. However, Germany probably would have been defeated earlier if the United States had acted expeditiously against the Nazis and other Axis powers instead of standing by as they rearmed, militarized, and threatened Europe. The United States waited for Germany to throw the first punch.[8]

Long before coming to power, Hitler revealed his murderous intolerance in his 1925 book *Mein Kampf* and in the frequent diatribes he made to anyone who would listen. The lack of any major international condemnation only emboldened him. In January 1939, just a few months before the invasion of Poland, Hitler said, "if international monied Jewry within Europe and beyond, again succeeds in casting the peoples into a world war, the result will not be the Bolshevization of the globe and a victory for Jewry, but the annihilation of the Jewish race in Europe."[9] The atrocities Germany committed in Poland in 1939 gave the world ample evidence that Hitler meant what he had "predicted" earlier that year and that a world war would bring about the destruction of the Jews.[10] William E. Dodd, the US ambassador to Germany, knew what Hitler had in store for the Jews when he announced at the Harvard Club in Boston in June 1938 that Hitler's goal was to kill *all* the Jews. Few believed it. It seemed few in the government were listening. As this book shows, the horrible crimes the Germans committed in Poland were ample proof of Dodd's claim.[11]

Fortunately for Rebbe Joseph Isaac Schneersohn, there were others like Dodd who saw the danger and were able to help him. Yet, as this rescue shows, it was difficult to get officials to act morally and save those suffering under Hitler. In the case of the Rebbe, many actually pushed the government to act for political, rather than moral, reasons, showing their self-interest at work. If morality had been at work instead, one could argue that more would have been saved. So even though the United States played one of the most important roles in defeating Hitler, it was dangerously slow to pick up the sword and did so not on moral grounds but with the goal of self-preservation.

However, the United States was not alone. British prime minister

Neville Chamberlain sold out Europe with his policy of appeasement when he signed the Munich Agreement in September 1938, ceding part of Czechoslovakia and announcing that he had achieved "peace in our time." This told Hitler that he held the political and military high ground. The years of Allied neutrality in the face of evil came at a tragically high price in blood and treasure, manifested around the world in events such as the Rape of Nanking, the Reich's November 1938 pogroms known as *Kristallnacht* (the Night of Broken Glass), the blatant takeover of Czechoslovakia and Austria, and the brutal attack on Poland, to name just a few. This fact must be a lesson to today's enlightened and democratic nations.

In conclusion, I hope readers think about the ideas and motivations that set the stage in 1939. Since the original book was published, I have often heard that the rescue of the Rebbe is one of the most astonishing stories of the war, but I have not heard people discussing why these men behaved the way they did. The story touched some of the highest levels of Hasidic and Orthodox Judaism, the German government and military, and the US State Department. History has rarely seen stranger bedfellows come together for the sake of good. Shakespeare notes in *The Tempest*, "misery acquaints a man with strange bedfellows,"[12] and the Holocaust was definitely a time of misery. During this period, few stories ended as well as this one did.

In addition to being intrigued by a conspiracy to rescue the Rebbe, I hope readers are challenged to think about how they live their lives and whether they would have the courage to stand up to evil and do the right thing. History shows us that we need more men (and women) like those who acted in this case with a high sense of moral integrity to save lives. Renowned Holocaust historian Michael Berenbaum wrote about a prisoner in the concentration camp at Sachsenhausen who would tell new arrivals about "the darkness that awaited them. He told them what was to be—honestly, directly, and without adornment." He would end with this admonition: "I have told you this story not to weaken you. But to strengthen you. Now it is up to you!"[13] This book will assault your senses and many ideas you have about history, religion, and justice. In the end, I hope it will make people more open-minded, stronger champions of justice, and better defenders of the helpless. We have a long way to go before we walk on such paths. We must constantly remind ourselves, as Socrates taught, that "the unexamined life is not worth living," and it is in the *pursuit* of truth (not its attainment) that we achieve enlightenment.[14] The rescue, in short, shows how high humanity can rise to take moral action, and how low society sometimes has to fall for one to see such goodness.

Prologue

In 1939 a group of Jews in Warsaw huddled in the corner of a building, saying prayers. The Nazis were combing the city for those they deemed threats to the occupation, and the Jews knew that many would meet their end, Jew and Gentile alike. As they chanted their ancient litanies, a loud bang echoed through the room; then came a quick succession of hard knocks at the door. All looked to their leader, Rebbe Joseph Isaac Schneersohn. "Should we let them in?" Many believed that only a few inches of wood stood between them and death. The Rebbe gave the nod to open the door. When they did, German soldiers rushed in and ordered them to stand with their faces against the wall. Several Jews said the Shema (Deuteronomy 6:4–9), a prayer uttered by pious Jews on the verge of death: "Hear, O Israel: The Lord is Our God, the Lord is One." They waited for the crack of rifle fire and utter darkness.

The Invasion of Poland and the Rescue Setup

We are bidden to "Remember the days of yore, ponder the years of each generation."
—Rebbe Joseph Isaac Schneersohn

Having remilitarized and de-democratized Germany, Adolf Hitler ordered the German army to reoccupy the Ruhr and to invade Austria and Czechoslovakia by subversion, intimidation, and false promises. Then he launched a campaign of military conquest by attacking Poland. In August 1939 he told his generals he would concoct a "propaganda reason" for the invasion, the plausibility of which should not concern them in the least. Declaring that the victors write the history books, he encouraged his commanders to close their "hearts to pity" and to "act brutally." Eighty million Germans, he explained, needed their *Lebensraum* (living space). He had written in *Mein Kampf*: "the Reich must again set itself along the road of the Teutonic Knights of old. . . . And so we National Socialists . . . take up where we broke off six hundred years ago. We stop the endless German movement to the south and west, and turn our gaze towards the land in the East."[1] The "messianic orator" felt destiny had called him to re-create the Germanic empire of old and avenge Germany's loss of territory under the Treaty of Versailles.[2] Yet, in focusing his attack against Poland, he had difficulty coming up with a legitimate excuse the world would accept. So he settled for a false pretext to launch his military forces against the antiquated army and poor defenses of the unprepared Poles.

In late August Hitler ordered SS general Reinhard Heydrich, head of the Gestapo, to stage an attack on German units stationed on the border with Poland, a mission requiring disguise and subterfuge. Heydrich and Heinrich Himmler, leader of the SS and Heydrich's boss, obtained 150 Polish uniforms from Admiral Wilhelm Canaris, head of the Abwehr (Military Counterintelligence Agency). Dressed in these Polish uniforms, SS soldiers assaulted the broadcasting station at Gleiwitz on the German border on 31 August. Heydrich then ordered his men to place several concentration camp inmates from Sachsenhausen, dressed in stolen Polish uniforms, within their ranks. These men, derisively referred to as *Konserwen* (tin cans), had been promised a "reprieve" if they cooperated. After the mock attack, the Germans machine-gunned the defenseless prisoners who had just helped them. The SS offered the bodies at Gleiwitz as proof to foreign journalists that Poland had attacked Germany. In "response," Hitler ordered the invasion of Poland and declared war. He knew he had to have a better reason than imperialism, and this provided him with an excuse. "Actual proof of Polish attacks is essential," Heydrich said, "both for the foreign press and for German propaganda."[3] The ruse would fool no one outside Germany, but Hitler didn't care. One wonders whether the Germans ever thought to ask why Poland, if it wanted to launch an attack against Hitler's Reich, would do so on such a small scale against a lonely radio station. The Nazis, however, were not interested in logical arguments. Hitler wanted at least some justification for his onslaught, even if it was built on a foundation of sand.

As part of his public relations campaign, at 5:40 A.M. on 1 September 1939, as his legions swarmed across the border, Hitler announced on the radio:

> The Polish state has refused the peaceful settlement of relations which I desired and has appealed to arms. Germans in Poland are persecuted with bloody terror. A series of violations of the frontier, intolerable to a great power, prove that Poland is no longer willing to respect the frontier of the Reich. In order to put an end to this lunacy I have no choice other than to meet force with force; the German Army will fight for the honor and rights of a new-born Germany.

He mentioned fourteen border incidents by the Poles that had left the Germans no recourse but to return fire.[4]

Hitler used the argument of saving "his people" in the seizures of

Austria, the Sudetenland (German-speaking territory in Czechoslovakia), and Memelland (in southern Lithuania), a total of roughly 44,000 square miles of new territory. It should come as no surprise that he used the same line to justify the attack on Poland. "Civilized" nations allowed the German dictator to get away with seizing Austria and the Sudetenland without retaliation. British prime minister Neville Chamberlain famously bragged in September 1938 that his policy of appeasement had ensured "peace for our time."[5] If anything, abandoning Czechoslovakia to Hitler had done the opposite, ensuring that the Allies ultimately fought a much stronger German army. Winston Churchill rightly noted that "the Government had to choose between shame and war. . . . They chose shame and will get war."[6] Hitler viewed the Allied leaders as weak, given their acquiescence to his demands throughout the 1930s, especially the dismantling of Czechoslovakia. He told his generals in August 1939 when preparing for war: "Our enemies are small worms. I saw them at Munich [Munich Conference of 1938]."[7]

In 1939, when Hitler resorted once again to imperial conquest based on trumped-up charges, the world was not prepared to stop him. He sent his panzers east. Even though the Germans living in Poland were only a small percentage of the overall Polish population, and even though Poland posed no threat to Germany, Hitler attacked to "protect" Deutschland. But why was Hitler so determined to destroy Poland? The real reason seems to be that, hungry for conquest and remembering the losses incurred in the west in World War I, he thought it would be easier to conquer the weaker countries to the east. Along with millions of Germans, he was angry that the Versailles Treaty of 1919 had split Germany in two, giving the Danzig corridor to Poland and separating Prussia from the mainland.[8] This, in itself, was an affront to German prestige and honor that Hitler could not tolerate. But instead of admitting the real reason, he made up a threat and then reacted to it.

Before the land invasion of Poland, the German navy drew first blood at 4:48 a.m. The battleship SMS *Schleswig-Holstein*, docked at the port city of Danzig on a prearranged "friendship visit," fired its fifteen-inch guns on the Polish defenses at the transit depot Westerplatte, pulverizing the garrison there. Though utterly surprised, the Poles fought tenaciously and defended the port from the German ground assault that followed.

For a whole week, against overwhelming odds, the garrison at Wester-platte held out, leading some to call this the "Polish Thermopylae," after the Spartans' famed resistance to Persian attack against hopeless odds. After the first salvos were unleashed from *Schleswig-Holstein*, the whole Polish-German border erupted in violence. Citizens on both sides struggled to understand the gravity of their situation.[9]

That day, twenty-year-old Karin Tiche, the daughter of a Jewish mother and a Christian father, walked onto her balcony in Warsaw. Observing two airplanes performing strange acrobatics in the air, she called for her mother to come see how their pilots were training for war. Then the aircraft fired their guns, and one suddenly fell from the sky, engulfed in flames. The plane, she realized, had Nazi markings. The Polish government immediately announced on the radio that the Germans had started a border conflict, which the Poles would readily win. "They told us this while they moved our government to the south of Poland away from Warsaw," Tiche said, "and we would soon find out that it was not just a border dispute, but a full-scale invasion and that we were losing everywhere." Germany's anti-Polish rhetoric and military maneuvers on the border had led many to expect war, but even so, its arrival surprised everyone. Once Hitler had completed the invasion of Czechoslovakia in March 1939, it seemed only a matter of time before he continued east to Poland, but many throughout the world had a difficult time keeping up with Hitler's quest for domination.[10] They did not take his writings and his threats seriously, which, in retrospect, seems like delusional wish fulfillment.

Today, we find the sneak attack on Poland shocking, but at the time, many Germans did not. The Versailles Treaty had been harsh, forcing Germany to cede territory to Poland, a country that had not existed for hundreds of years and had been re-created as a result of Germany's defeat in World War I. The Allies also appropriated other German territory and parceled it out to neighboring countries. Many Germans, not merely right-wing nationalists, were enraged at Poland's control over territories it had not conquered militarily and to which it had no apparent historical claim, such as the Wartheland. Writing in 1920, General Hans von Seeckt, head of the Reichswehr, declared Poland "Germany's mortal enemy," one that had to be destroyed. By the 1930s, the "overwhelming majority" of the Wehrmacht's officer corps supported an attack on Poland.[11] This indicates that Hitler's justification for war was intended not for German ears but for the outside world.

Hitler used overwhelming force to conquer Poland. On 1 September 1939, 1.5 million German troops crossed into the country, backed by 2,000 planes. Wehrmacht soldiers sliced through the ever-widening gaps in the unprepared and poorly equipped Polish army stationed along the border with Germany. Unlike Czechoslovakia, Poland lacked natural barriers, modern frontier fortifications, and state-of-the-art artillery, tanks, and aircraft. Poland had 2 million men under arms, many of whom fought bravely, but they were outmatched by the modern, motorized, highly trained, and disciplined German forces. Despite their passionate defense, the Poles did not last long. Their defeat was hastened when the Polish air force, comprising mostly outdated equipment, was almost entirely obliterated during the first few days of the campaign, leaving the Poles no air cover for their defense.[12]

Less than a week after the invasion, the Wehrmacht's northern advance had eliminated "an entire Polish army (Pomorze), mauled another one (Modlin)," and stood ready to penetrate deep into the center of Poland. In the south, the German army broke through "almost everywhere" it encountered the enemy. The final outcome was obvious by the end of the first week. "The Polish army was being pressed by two very heavy slabs of iron [the panzers]." By 8 September, those German tank forces had already reached the outskirts of Warsaw.[13]

As Germany swallowed Austria, Sudetenland, Czechoslovakia, Memelland, and Poland in 1938 and 1939, thousands of Jews throughout Europe tried to escape the Nazi juggernaut. Many sold their belongings to purchase passage out of Europe. Some were able to send their children to safety abroad but could not get out themselves; others abandoned their families and their possessions, following the motto "every man for himself." Few of them reached freedom. After Germany invaded Poland, the US government received pleas from Americans to help their relatives trapped in Europe, thousands of whom flooded American embassies and consulates with petitions for visas. Chicago had one of the largest Polish populations in the world, and many of these residents had fearful family and friends back in Europe. Most of their cries for help went unanswered. The US government was too busy with social issues, such as the massive unemployment resulting from the Great Depression (11 million unemployed in 1938, out of a population of 130 million [8.5 percent]), and it was too intent on maintaining diplomatic neutrality to get involved with refugee problems. Moreover, anti-Jewish sentiment peaked in the late 1930s, worsening an already difficult situation for Jews suffering under Hitler and for the American Jews trying to help them.[14]

In 1938 one poll found that 58 percent of Americans believed the Jews were at least partly responsible for Nazi persecution. For example, Gerald Winrod, a prominent Baptist minister and organizer of the group Defenders of the Christian Faith, traveled to Nazi Germany in the 1930s and "returned determined to expose the 'Jewish menace' to the American people." He derided President Roosevelt's social welfare program as the "Jewish New Deal" and "satanic." Many Americans were not as rabidly anti-Semitic as Winrod, but sadly, most did not see the Jews' plight as their own. Senator Robert Reynolds of North Carolina, the "arch foe of immigration liberalization," said, "Why should we give up those blessings to those not so fortunate? . . . Let Europe take care of its own people."[15] At the time, many in the US Immigration Department believed that Jews wanted preferential treatment. A staff person named Wilkinson expressed an opinion that was prevalent among many of these bureaucrats: "Experience has taught that Jews are persistent in their endeavors to obtain immigration visas, that Jews have a strong tendency—no matter where they are—to allege that they are the subjects of either religious or political persecution, that Jews have constantly endeavored to find means of entering the U.S. despite the barriers set up by our immigration laws."[16] The prevalence of anti-Semitism within the general public made the government less likely to take action on the problems of Jewish refugees.

Waves of immigrants often draw attention to serious global problems. But during the 1930s, the crisis creating so many refugees was ignored. This reality, plus the policies of appeasement in France and England and the indifference of the United States, enabled Hitler to consolidate his power in Germany and expand his reach abroad. Ignoring the suffering and Hitler's intentions only allowed the geopolitical problems to get bigger and harder to solve.

Even in the face of Hitler's aggression, American isolationists claimed that Europe was not their problem. Their resistance kept America from acting in the 1930s to prevent Hitler's rise to power. Shockingly, Republican senators Gerald P. Nye, William Borah, and Arthur Vandenberg and Democratic senator Burton K. Wheeler worked tirelessly to prevent America from aiding the Allies right up to 7 December 1941, the day Pearl Harbor was bombed.

There are many reasons for this behavior, and a few are explored here. After the hearings before the Nye Committee in the House of Representatives, which blamed arms dealers and bankers for getting the United States into World War I and called them the "Merchants of Death," Congress passed the Neutrality Act of 1935 over Roosevelt's opposition, prohibiting arms sales to belligerents. The Neutrality Act of 1936 also prohibited loans and extended the 1935 act. The 1937 act added restrictions on shipping, but Roosevelt was able to push through a two-year "cash and carry" provision, with an eye to aiding France and Great Britain. "Cash and carry" meant that belligerents could buy war materials if they paid for them promptly and transported them in their own ships. After the German invasion of Czechoslovakia in March 1939, Roosevelt lobbied to extend the "cash and carry" provision to allow sales to France and Britain. Yet, even in the face of such Nazi belligerence, America stood firm in its unwillingness to get involved. The isolationist America First Committee, established in September 1940 after the fall of France, grew to 800,000 members in 450 chapters. It fought passionately to prevent aid to the belligerents and any American involvement in Europe's crisis. According to historian Robert Divine, the neutrality legislation had "played directly into the hands of Adolf Hitler. Bent on the conquest of Europe, he could now proceed without worrying about American interference." In July 1939, two months before Germany invaded Poland, Roosevelt met with senators from both parties to try to persuade them to amend the neutrality acts. Yet many leaders failed to see the writing on the wall. William Borah, the Republican senator who had led the fight against Woodrow Wilson and the League of Nations, said, "There is not going to be any war in Europe this year. All this hysteria is manufactured and artificial." Today, it seems quite clear what the United States should have been doing before the invasion of Poland, but America had simply decided not to get involved in another mess started by the Europeans. Isolationists, however, would get their wake-up call when the German *blitzkrieg* (lightning war) erupted in Europe.[17] Discussion in the halls of Congress then shifted from *whether* to get involved to when America would *have* to get involved.[18]

When President Roosevelt heard about the German invasion of Poland on 1 September, he was far from surprised. "It has come at last. God help us all," he exclaimed. In his fireside chat on 3 September 1939, he said he wanted to keep the nation neutral but did not want his fellow Americans to remain neutral in thought: "Even a neutral cannot be asked to close its mind or conscience." Roosevelt knew America would have to help the Allies defeat Germany, but public opinion did not yet recognize the necessity of taking sides. The president, a skillful and inspiring political leader, would need to convince the people. In the early days of Hitler's aggressive expansion, many thought the German armed forces would be no match for the French military and the British navy and air force. The Japanese threat was also vastly underestimated prior to Pearl Harbor. American intervention would ultimately be triggered not by human rights violations but by the rapid conquest of the United States' democratic friends in Europe and Asia and recognition of the grave threat to the survival of its own democracy and Western civilization.[19] In retrospect, military weakness, appeasement, and neutrality only emboldened Hitler's aggression. Édouard Daladier, prime minister of France, said in October 1938, "If I had three or four thousand aircraft Munich would never have happened." France was eventually able to bypass restrictions on US arms sales, negotiating a huge order for American fighter planes in the spring of 1940. Most had not arrived by the time of the Battle of France, so they were diverted to Britain, where they were used in later battles against the Wehrmacht.[20] The Allies simply had not kept pace with German military production and aggression. One reason for this failure was the Great Depression and a lack of funds. Many have asked how Germany, which had lost the last war, was able to outperform the Allies in arms production. Although the Germans appeared much stronger than they were in reality, they succeeded in building a strong military simply by stealing money and resources from other people and other countries.

Rearming Germany, keeping people satisfied, and going to war required a tremendous amount of money. Hitler obtained the funds he needed by stealing the assets of millions of Jews and people from conquered nations, beginning with pilfering the possessions of hundreds of thousands of Jewish Germans. As part of the Aryanization process, Jews were forced to sell their interests in businesses they owned, along with their homes, art, and household goods, all at fire-sale prices.[21] Anything not sold was later confiscated. The Nazis took much of this stolen cash and put it into Swiss bank accounts. Likewise, some Jews stashed money in Swiss banks in an effort to hide some of their property from the Nazis. Many died without reclaiming that money. The Swiss banks never attempted to return the unclaimed money to family members—they just kept it and got rich. Swiss banks also profited from doing business with the Nazis (Credit Suisse, for example, had dealings with Himmler and Mussolini).[22] Hitler's "crimes against humanity. . . deprive[d] the banks from using the common assertion of just being neutral. There's no neutrality when you're dealing with crimes against humanity. You can't be the rock of Gibraltar for democracy when in fact you're feeding the very antithesis that is swallowing every other country around you." In other words, "the Swiss were the principal bankers [primarily Credit Suisse and Union Bank of Switzerland (UBS)] and financial brokers for the Nazis. Neutrality had collided with morality, and trade with Germany had the clear effect of supporting and prolonging Nazi Germany's capacity to wage war." Michael Hausfeld, one of the lawyers who worked on the case against the Swiss banks, said, "If, as it is said, that money is the root of all evil, then Hitler was the world's evil and the private banks of Switzerland were his root."[23] The "neutral" Swiss helped prolong Hitler's war by laundering money he stole from other countries and from murdered Jews. By some estimates, this extended Hitler's war effort by more than a year. To reiterate, "There's no neutrality when you're dealing with crimes against humanity," and for the Swiss banks, this neutrality led them to commit crimes against the Jews themselves.[24]

Likewise, by not intervening in Poland despite clear violations of national sovereignty and human rights, the United States allowed Hitler to extend the war. The fight would have ended much sooner if America had taken a stand against Nazi aggression in that critical year. In short, neutrality was not the answer when innocent lives were at stake.

Roosevelt lacked the political support to intervene militarily in 1939, but he and his administration condemned Hitler. The press chief in the State Department announced, "We only pity you people [Germans], your government already stands convicted; they are condemned from one end of the earth to the other; for this bloodbath, if it now comes to war between Britain, France, and Germany, will have been absolutely unnecessary. The whole manner of conducting negotiations was as stupid as it could possibly be." This statement enraged Hitler, who claimed that American hostility toward Germany stemmed from the "Jewish-controlled press" and the Jewish advisers surrounding the president, whom he derisively called "Rosenfeld."[25] Hitler believed that although the United States condemned the actions of his country, it would do nothing. Unfortunately, Hitler was almost right. Roosevelt worked with interventionists such as the Century Association in New York to build public support for helping the Allies and to come up with creative ways to aid the United Kingdom. For instance, he was able to swap old US destroyers for British bases in the Caribbean in 1940, and the Lend-Lease Act in March 1941 was an alternative to the cash-and-carry law, because Britain was running out of gold reserves. By then, a Gallup poll showed that 55 percent of Americans favored lend-lease without qualification, but most were still against going to war in any form or fashion.[26] In fact, "at no point did the United States choose to go to war against the Axis powers and Japan."[27] Japan had to attack the US fleet at Pearl Harbor and Germany had to declare war on the United States before the Americans were ready to fight. The United States got its nose bloodied and suffered a few broken bones before it struck back hard.

Many in Poland, as well as in the United States, expected the Allies to take action against Germany after hostilities broke out in 1939. After Hitler took Czechoslovakia, in violation of his assurances at Munich, the United Kingdom and France warned that they would go to war in the event of any further aggression by Germany. Chaim Kaplan, a distinguished Hebrew school principal in Warsaw and author of a memorable diary, wrote that he hoped the Allies would stick to their word and not leave Poland to the mercy of the Germans, as they had Czechoslovakia.[28] But a timorous world let Germany roll over the helpless Polish nation. Although France and Britain declared war on Germany and mobilized and deployed their forces in France, they failed to go on the offensive against Hitler, missing a golden opportunity to defeat the Wehrmacht quickly. The French did invade Germany, but they advanced only a few miles into the Saarland, across a narrow portion of the front, and withdrew their forces soon thereafter. It was a halfhearted and insincere attack. Would they ever act in force across the whole border? The only country that could help Poland in the east was the Soviet Union, but the USSR had signed the Nazi-Soviet Non-Aggression Pact in August 1939. Before making public guarantees to Poland, the British government had suggested that Poland and the USSR join in warning Germany against further aggression, but Poland refused to have any dealings with the Soviets. France had persuaded a reluctant Britain to negotiate with the USSR for an alliance in the spring of 1939, but this attempt also failed.[29] In fact, Stalin, like Hitler, was bent on Poland's destruction and hoped to gain vast amounts of land after its defeat. It is now known that Stalin was no less aggressive than Hitler when it came to seizing other nations' territory. He would soon invade Poland and other countries allotted to the USSR under the deal with Germany, once he saw that Hitler would obtain victory within his prearranged area of operations.[30]

With the blitzkrieg preventing most Polish Jews from fleeing, worried family members in the United States asked the government for help in getting their relatives out. They had good reason for concern: Hitler did not hesitate to kill anyone the Nazi ideology deemed "inferior." Almost immediately after the invasion, the SS began to murder undesirable elements of the population, including Jews, communists, Polish nobility, clergy, and intelligentsia.[31]

Almost 90 percent of the 3.5 million Jews in Poland in 1939, one-third of whom lived in poverty, would be murdered in the Holocaust. Lacking an organized plan of genocide at this point, the Germans initially killed Polish Gentiles with considerable frequency, focusing especially on the Polish elite.[32] The attack against the Jews was undifferentiated; peasants were attacked along with intellectuals, merchants, rabbis, farmers, and workers. "There was no way of knowing in 1939 that Hitler would be murdering us by the millions in a few years. No one would ever have thought this back then," observed Tiche. "The nation of Beethoven, Bach, and Goethe murdering people like they did was unthinkable." Historian Nora Levin writes that in the summer of 1940, no one, not even Polish Jews, could have foreseen the full extent of the Nazis' atrocities.[33] After all, many remembered that the Germans had treated the Jews in conquered eastern European nations relatively well during World War I, trying to win their support. This time would be different. Despite acts of persecution and isolated murders, the systematic shooting and gassing of millions was beyond human imagination. As Jonathan Steinberg notes, "Holocaust records show that Jews themselves often refused to believe what was happening in spite of the evidence of their own eyes."[34]

Hitler had given ample indication of his intentions, but few had taken him seriously. Moreover, he had predicted in a January 1939 address that if war came again, it would be the Jews' fault, and "the annihilation of the Jewish race" would be the result. Hitler aimed not only to reclaim lost territory and salvage national pride but also to eradicate supposedly inferior peoples, including Slavs and Jews. He had written about racial discrimination and world conquest in *Mein Kampf*, but few readers had taken him seriously. William Shirer notes, "Whatever other accusations can be made against Adolf Hitler, no one can accuse him of not putting down in writing exactly the kind of Germany he intended to make if ever he came to power, and the kind of world he meant to create by armed German conquest." A joke summing up people's difficulty understanding Hitler went as follows: "The difference between Bismarck and Hitler is that Bismarck said what he believed, but Hitler believes what he says." As Shirer correctly observes, although Hitler announced his plans, only when he started to put them into action did people take him seriously, and even then, many of the crimes he committed were still unbelievable in 1939.[35]

By way of illustration, on 5 September the Germans entered the town of Piotrkow and set fire to numerous Jewish homes. When the Jews ran out of the burning structures, the Germans shot them. On entering one building that had "escaped the flames, soldiers took out six Jews and ordered them to run." They shot five of them dead immediately; the sixth, Reb Bunem Lebel, later succumbed to his wounds.[36] Scenes like this took place throughout Poland.

A tiny minority saw the coming storm. Chaim Kaplan, who had heard Hitler speak on the radio in January 1939, wrote in his diary on 1 September that no Jew under Hitler's rule had any hope. "Hitler, may his name be blotted out," Kaplan recorded, "threatened in one of his speeches that if war comes the Jews of Europe will be exterminated . . . our hearts tremble at the future . . . what will be our destiny?" On 10 September

Reich Labor Service personnel en route to Poland in railcars emblazoned with large-nosed caricatures captioned "We're off to Poland—to thrash the Jews." (United States Holocaust Memorial Museum Archive of Photographs)

Kaplan again referred to the speech and questioned why God allowed Hitler to subject the Jews to such cruelty. Wondering whether they had sinned more than others to warrant this punishment, he concluded that they were "more disgraced than any people!"[37]

The persecution and killing of Jews in Poland, many of whom were conspicuous in their traditional garb, continued unabated. On 8 September the Germans rounded up 200 Jews at Bedzin, locked them inside a synagogue, and set fire to the building. One can only imagine their pleas for help and cries of terror as the fire reached its arms up to the sky and destroyed the place of worship. The screams died down as the wood crackled in the flames, and crossbeams broke as they were weakened by the inferno. The next day the Germans arrested 30 non-Jewish Poles, charged them with the murder of these Jews and the destruction of their property, and executed them in "one of the public squares."[38] The war in Poland unleashed the cruelty latent in the German ranks. As Henry A. Turner Jr. states: "To the everlasting shame of the German nation, Hitler found large numbers of lackeys eager to persecute, subjugate and slaughter people deemed dangerous or inferior by the perverted standards of his regime."[39]

Before war started in Poland, the Nazis knew about the ultrareligious Jews and simply did not want them in the German Reich. In the first days after the invasion, the Germans randomly destroyed hundreds of synagogues and murdered hundreds of Jewish civilians. At Czestochowa, they shot 180 Jews. In the village of Widawa, they burned Rabbi Abraham Mordechai Morocco alive when he refused to destroy the sacred scrolls. Other German soldiers took pleasure in hanging Jews from street lamps and watching them struggle to loosen the rope as they suffocated. During the first two months of the occupation, the Germans killed at least 7,000 Polish Jews and forced the rest into "resettlement" and harsh labor. Although there was still no organized plan of genocide, it became obvious that the Jews had no future under the German occupation.[40]

Poland in 1939 was a strange land for the German invaders, especially with its large Hasidic communities. In eastern Europe, many religious Jews spent their days in yeshivas, advanced academies for study of the Talmud (the ancient commentary of the Bible, called the oral Torah by religious Jews), or in *shtiblekh*, small houses of prayer. Many Polish Jews lived in *shtetls*, or small ghetto enclaves that were often no more than clusters of dilapidated shacks and the requisite synagogue and house of study. Since most Wehrmacht soldiers enjoyed relative prosperity and led secular lives, they were shocked at how tens of thousands of ultrareligious Hasidic *Ostjuden*, as the eastern Jews were pejoratively called—even by German Jews—lived their lives. The *Ostjuden* were strange looking, with their long beards and *peyes* (side locks), skullcaps, *gartlekh* (fancy silk belts), and long, dark coats, reminiscent of seventeenth-century Polish aristocracy and intelligentsia. The Germans, unable to understand how these Jews earned a living since they prayed and studied all day, regarded them as lazy. Even German Jewish soldiers stationed in the east during World War I had expressed disgust with the appearance, habits, and living conditions of *Ostjuden*.[41]

For decades before Hitler's rise to power, many assimilated German Jews had felt that the poor, culturally backward, and "dirty" *Ostjuden* gave the typically well-educated, socially integrated, and cultured German Jews a bad name.[42] A few German Jews helped the *Ostjuden*

Waffen-SS soldiers cutting off an elderly Polish Jew's beard. (YIVO and United States Holocaust Memorial Museum)

philanthropically, but by and large, they had no feelings of kinship. The *Ostjuden* lived in anachronistic ghettos and learned only "Polish Talmudic barbarism," in contrast to refined German *Bildung* (education). To self-conscious and proud German Jews, these "ghetto Jews" practiced an irrational, mystical, and superstitious religion that no longer had a place in a world based on reason and scientific knowledge. The *Ostjuden*, in turn, felt that their "heretical" *daitsch* (German) brothers had abandoned *Yiddishkeit* (Jewishness) by shaving off their beards, adopting modern ways, and desecrating the Sabbath. Primo Levi described an ultrareligious Jew in Auschwitz who viewed all "western Jews [as] Epicureans—*apicorism*, unbelievers."[43]

More secularized *Ostjuden* had rejected religion and embraced the tenets of communism, socialism, and Zionism, to name just a few. And even though they lacked the education and wealth of their German cousins, they were striving to enter the modern world by rejecting Orthodoxy or Hasidism, since they believed such a religious perspective did not address the very difficult social, political, and economic problems they faced. Some of their German counterparts may have looked down on them, but many other German Jews wanted to help the *Ostjuden* better themselves and fought to protect them. In general, though, the term *Ostjuden* conjured up images of ultrareligious Jews who were traditionally learned but lacked secular education and refinement. Germans in general, and German Jews in particular, tended to avoid these Jews and found them strange.

Due to this bias, many assimilated German Jews mistakenly regarded Hitler's anti-Semitism as a reaction to the culture of the *Ostjuden*. For some German Jews, the *Ostjuden* may have represented a part of themselves they wanted to deny. At one time, some of their ancestors may have resembled the *Ostjuden* they condemned, prompting them to reject their *Ostjuden* brethren even more vehemently. As the famous German author of Jewish origin Heinrich Heine (1797–1856) wrote about traditional Judaism: "The thousand-year-old family disease, / The plague dragged along out of the Nile Valley / The ancient Egyptian unhealthy faith." He blamed Orthodox and Hasidic Jews for inciting religious intolerance and hatred of foreigners and called them "unbearable hagglers and dirt-rags."[44] Heine's conversion allowed him to enter the mainstream of the German literary elite. Thus, the German Jews' prejudice against the ultrareligious eastern European Jews prevented them from seeing the real danger of Hitler's movement, causing them to think, to some extent, that the Nazis were disgusted only with *Ostjuden* and not with them. In *Mein Kampf*, Hitler often conjured up ultra-Orthodox or Hasidic Jew images and browbeat them.

Moreover, *Ostjuden* who remained ultra-Orthodox represented the undesirable stereotype dredged up by anti-Semites to show that Jews were not like "us." German Jews wanted to be like the Gentile society around them; they wanted to fit in comfortably and be accepted by their neighbors. For centuries, the church, guilds, universities, and civil authorities in most of Europe had restricted Jews to only the most undesirable jobs and the worst neighborhoods, if they were allowed at all. Now, German Jews in particular, and assimilated Jews in general, wanted their children to have an opportunity to get a first-rate education that would prepare them for life in the modern world. They wanted to choose the type of work they did and to go as far as their skills and hard work would take them. They wanted to live in nice neighborhoods. They wanted to wear contemporary clothes, speak the language and participate in the culture of their land, and socialize with people of other faiths. They wanted equal rights before the law. And they wanted to reform their religion, applying reason and challenging old customs and rules. The antimodernist Orthodox and Hasidic leaders of the *Ostjuden* wanted none of this. They were willing to have their people live in poverty, on the fringes of the economy and society; they shunned emancipation in order to maintain a closed society where Jews adhered to traditional practices and the true faith. The Enlightenment, science, and democracy threatened this world based on an ancient, revealed truth that they interpreted and applied.

Nonetheless, many eastern Jews knew there were better places to live, and multitudes left. More than 2.5 million *Ostjuden* had immigrated to the United States since 1880 and had largely assimilated into American society. Clearly, many *Ostjuden* wanted to break away from the world of oppression under the czars and the world of superstition and tradition under the rebbes and rabbis. When given a chance to better themselves in a free and democratic culture, many embraced the American dream and blended into the fabric of society.

If the majority of German Jews felt disdain for the *Ostjuden*, it is hardly surprising that most German Christians perceived them as primitive. Hitler wrote in *Mein Kampf* about an experience he had while walking in the streets of Vienna:

> [I] encountered an apparition in a black caftan and black hair locks. Is this a Jew? Was my first thought. . . . Is this a German? . . . The cleanliness of this people, moral and otherwise, I must say, is a point in itself. By their very exterior you could tell that these were no lovers of water, and, to our distress, you often knew it with your eyes closed. Later I grew sick to my stomach from the smell of these caftan-wearers. Added to this, there was their unclean dress and their generally unheroic appearance. All this could scarcely be called very attractive; but it became positively repulsive when, in addition to their physical uncleanliness, you discovered the moral stains on this "chosen people." . . . Was there any form of filth or profligacy, particularly in cultural life, without at least one Jew involved in it?

If you cut even cautiously into such an abscess, you found, like a
maggot in a rotting body, often dazzled by the sudden light—a kike![45]

Unfortunately, Hitler's grotesque anti-Semitism mirrors what many Germans, Austrians, French, and other western Europeans felt about Jews
from the east or ultra-Orthodox and Hasidic Jews. The caricature was
a throwback to how Jews had been viewed in the Middle Ages. Sadly,
Hitler had a large audience for such views. As Jonathan Steinberg observes about this passage from *Mein Kampf*, "Hitler attacks Jews for their
uncleanliness physically and by extension morally."[46] Hitler carried his
anti-Semitism "like a congenital hump," writes Sebastian Haffner. And
as described in *Mein Kampf*, "Hitler's antisemitism is an East European
plant." Haffner continues: "But in Eastern and South Eastern Europe,
where the numerous Jews were living, voluntarily or involuntarily, as a
separate nation within the nation, antisemitism was (and is?) endemic and
murderous, directed not toward assimilation or integration but towards
liquidation and extermination. And this murderous East European anti-
semitism, which allowed the Jews no escape, reached as far as Vienna
[where] the youthful Hitler picked it up."[47]

Hitler's writing against traditional Jews gave some German Jews the
mistaken impression that they were different and therefore acceptable.
Prejudice against this "type" of Jew was clearly illustrated by the forced
deportation of 12,000 Polish *Ostjuden* from Germany in October 1938.
As the Jews were pushed across the border, German citizens lined the
streets and yelled at them: *Juden Raus! Aus nach Palästina!* (Out with the
Jews! Off to Palestine!).[48] Because of these sentiments, German Jews were
even more eager to avoid being associated with this unpopular group
from the east. Thus, many of the "Aryans," as Hitler called them, went
along with the persecution and murder of these unfortunate people once
the government turned into a lawless killing machine in Poland.

Many Polish Jews felt helpless. Hasidic Jews, in particular, dedicated
their lives to learning the Torah, the five books of Moses, and other religious writings; they did not know how to fight or use weapons. Many
were physically weak from studying all day, and they had no endurance,
even if they had wanted to resist. Germans often expressed shock at how
passively these Jews accepted persecution, but they also grudgingly ad-

mired the Jews' dedication to God. When the Nazis torched a synagogue, it was common for Jews to brave gunfire and run into burning buildings to rescue the holy scrolls. These passionate Jews considered life meaningless without the Torah. For the Lubavitchers, the Torah was "Divine Reason," "G-d's Will," and a "light" to show humankind its way in life. The Lubavitch leader Rebbe Joseph Isaac Schneersohn wrote, "The Torah is G-d's only daughter, and the people of Israel are his only son." So in 1941, while the Nazis burned alive some of the leading scholars of Lubavitch in a Riga synagogue, these rabbis reportedly "spent their last moments together dancing with the Torah Scroll [and] singing the tunes of *Simchat Torah* [literal meaning: rejoicing in the Torah]." The Rebbe taught that "the Torah remains only with those who give their life for it." These Lubavitchers proved that they believed the Rebbe's creed.[49]

The atrocities against Jews were so shocking that even members of the armed forces protested. Wehrmacht general Johannes Blaskowitz complained to Hitler that "this state of affairs undermines order and discipline. . . . It is necessary to forbid summary executions forthwith. The German army is not here to give its support to a band of assassins."[50] He argued that atrocities by the SS would have a horrible effect on the German people because "unlimited brutalization and moral depravity [would spread] . . . like an epidemic through the most valuable German human material. If the high officials of the SS continue to call for violence and brutality, brutal men will soon reign supreme." Hitler ignored Blaskowitz's complaints. Even the notorious Nazi general Walter von Reichenau did not approve of the SS's actions. Hitler continued to disregard these misgivings, declaring that one cannot "wage war with Salvation Army methods."[51]

Admiral Wilhelm Canaris, head of the Abwehr, tried to influence those in power to remove SS units from Poland and end a situation that he believed disgraced the German people. He had struggled with the SS over jurisdiction throughout the 1930s, and now he regarded its involvement in domestic matters in occupied Poland as encroaching on his territory. Also, Canaris disapproved of wholesale murder. In response, Hitler asserted, "Our struggle cannot be measured in terms of legality or illegality. Our methods must conform to our principles. We must prevent a new Polish intelligentsia taking power and cleanse the Greater Reich of Jewish and Polish riffraff." He informed his generals the SS would intensify its work. As relations between the Wehrmacht and the SS deteriorated, Hitler removed the SS and the police from military authority on 17 October. On 19 October he decreed that by 25 October, the military administration of Poland (the government structure) would be replaced by civilian rule—that is, the SS and the Nazi government.[52] Unlike in some areas of western Europe, where native civilian officials continued to function during occupation, there would be no remnant of the former government in areas of eastern Europe occupied by the Nazis.

In retaliation for Germany's invasion, the Poles committed atrocities of their own. Fearing a fifth column, Polish officials gathered between 10,000 and 15,000 ethnic Germans for deportation to the center of the country. During these actions, enraged Poles murdered thousands of these Germans. The worst massacre occurred on 3 September at Bromberg, where Poles murdered more than a thousand Germans. As the Germans conquered more territory, they quickly discovered these mass graves, which the SS promptly used to justify its own, far worse crimes.[53]

Waffen-SS captain (later major general) Otto Kumm had his own opinions regarding these killings, which were shared by many of his fellow officers:

It was well known that special units, we called them *Einsatzgruppen*, were following behind the invasion forces and killing. This would later happen in the Soviet Union and be classified as anti-partisan or reprisal operations. I was not stupid, nor were the others. To my shame a few of my fellow officers saw no problem with "nipping this issue in the bud." This issue would come up again later, and when I later commanded my battalions and brigades, I gave my men strict orders. They were not to replicate the idiocy of others, and [SS lieutenant general Wilhelm] Bittrich supported me. That did not make us very popular with Himmler, or many of the other senior leaders. That was not my problem. I did not want my men going home as murderers. The war was bad enough. All this was going to do was create a partisan movement against us that would eventually drain our resources. This was simply common sense. But common sense was not in great abundance during those days.[54]

Kumm drew the right conclusions: these brutal actions against innocent people would make the SS a group of murderers. However, Kumm also showed his utter callousness toward many of the victims, the majority of whom were religious Jews, when he stated that the murders were bad because they would create partisans out of the native populations. Even though this interview was conducted four decades after World War II, there was no acknowledgment that these actions were inhumane and criminal. Kumm's opposition was entirely strategic. He was afraid it would put the wrong label on his men and create more enemies to fight. These were valid reasons, but not the most valid one, which speaks volumes about this man's mind-set during the campaign in Poland.

SS lieutenant general Karl Wolff, a close associate of Himmler, spoke more candidly about the killing of the Jews in the east in an interview in 1984:

> Poland was just as much a test of not only our will but also a test
> of how much our soldiers could take. I mean that we had orders
> to eliminate those who were a threat. Now, the identification and
> classification of what a "threat" actually was could be left to the
> imagination. No one was going to challenge a commander for killing
> suspected partisans even if they were sitting quietly in a church.
> Göring said it himself, "useless eaters needed to be removed for the
> greater good of Germany," and Hitler told me personally that "the
> more we remove today leaves much less to be removed tomorrow."
> This was to be the same program in all the occupied countries as the
> war progressed. So there you have it.[55]

Wolff's review of the war in Poland illustrates that months, if not years, of thought went into determining how Germany would wage war in Poland. Hitler and his closest followers, including Göring and Wolff, knew what was expected. However, it is interesting to note that even they were unsure how the soldiers and SS troops would handle these exterminations while carrying out their stated objectives. Although many in the Wehrmacht, such as Canaris and Blaskowitz, did not approve of *how* the "useless eaters" were being removed, there were enough other Germans, primarily in the SS, who supported Hitler's goals for the east and the extermination of Jews and other "undesirables."

On 3 September France and Britain followed through on their warning: they declared war on Germany and mobilized their forces. When that news reached Hitler, he "sat immobile, gazing before him."[56] He had not expected the Allies to respond, especially on behalf of a "pathetic" nation like Poland. He and his generals feared a two-front war, as had many leaders throughout German history, including Frederick the Great and General Count Alfred von Schlieffen.[57] Yet no massive Allied attack ever materialized in the west. Anglo-French actions were limited to blockading ports on the North and Baltic Seas, conducting scattered air operations, and fortifying the western frontier with Germany. With the declaration of war, celebrations took place throughout Poland, and Warsaw was adorned with French and British flags, but the Poles soon realized that Britain and France were not coming to save them. Colonel Józef Beck, Poland's foreign minister, informed the French that his nation felt betrayed. Back in May, General Maurice Gamelin, commander in chief of the French army, had promised General Tadeusz Kasprzycki, Poland's war minister, that "as soon as the main German effort against Poland begins, France will launch an offensive against Germany with the main bodies of her forces." But when the actual attack came, Gamelin ordered only a minor incursion in the Saarland, which caused the Germans no concern. The substantial French communist bloc, directed from Moscow, switched from an anti-Nazi to a strongly isolationist position with the signing of the Nazi-Soviet Non-Aggression Pact. King Leopold of Belgium was intent on maintaining neutrality so as not to provoke Hitler, and he refused to make even contingent defense plans with the French, much less allow them to establish forward positions in Belgium. The Dutch were also relying on their neutrality. Germany, in turn, gave worthless guarantees of neutrality to both Belgium and the Netherlands. Although the French had mobilized, they had no desire to undertake an offensive against a country that had demonstrated such "frightening destructive capabilities" in its campaign against Poland. The Germans' air superiority, autonomous tank formations, well-coordinated artillery, and mobile infantry gave them one of the most modern militaries the world had ever seen.

The French were wary of Germany's military might, even though its western borders were lightly defended, and many of the tanks and mechanized equipment used in the invasion of Poland had been damaged or had broken down. The British, still led by Neville Chamberlain, also worried about Hitler's new form of warfare and the possibility of an all-out attack on London. Should British forces be committed on the Continent, or should most of them (especially the air force) be held back in case of an attack on Britain? The British urged the French to take no military action; they wanted time to build up their military before the fighting started. The entirety of the West, in effect, deserted Poland. There would be no Allied reinforcements for Poland and no attack on Germany.[58]

"We are left abandoned and the shadow of death encircles us," wrote Chaim Kaplan. Germany had only a few divisions on its western border, and an Allied attack would have forced the Wehrmacht to withdraw a considerable number of its forces from the east to meet the assault. Practically all of Germany's planes were in Poland, and most of its tanks were engaged in the east. General Alfred Jodl, chief of Wehrmacht operations, wrote after the war: "If in 1939 we were not defeated, it was only because about 110 French and English divisions, which during our war against Poland faced 23 divisions in the West, remained completely inactive." The actual breakdown was seventy-six Allied divisions facing thirty-two German.[59] General Wilhelm Ritter von Leeb, who commanded the German defense forces on the western front, warned Walter von Brauchitsch, commander in chief of the army, that there was little he could do if France decided to attack. Leeb's troops lacked training and had little in the way of tanks, motor transport, and artillery. There were no reserves of supplies or ammunition. In short, whatever the exact numbers were, the Allies heavily outnumbered the Germans on the western front and would have won had they attacked in force. "Germany's strange victory occurred because the French and British failed to take advantage of their superiority" and neglected to formulate a plan to counter Hitler's moves in the east, notes Earnest May.[60]

Had the Allies honored their commitment to attack Germany once Hitler invaded Poland, the war might have taken a different course. However, France and Britain delayed for nine months, until Germany revised its plan of attack in the spring to include an armored Ardennes offensive through Luxembourg and Belgium and attacked France in May 1940. Against the advice of his top generals, Hitler had repeatedly given

A cartoon aptly depicts the feeling of the time: It shows a scantily clad female skeleton with "War" painted on her chest, luring a young man upstairs to her bedroom. On the back of the young man's jacket is written "Any European Youth." The deadly temptress says, "Come on in. I'll treat you right. I used to know your Daddy." (New York Daily/Getty Image)

orders for the attack on France to begin in October, but it was delayed by weather. In the United States, isolationist senator William Borah of Idaho termed the inaction of the French and British the "phony war," while the Germans called it the *Sitzkrieg* (sitting war).[61] France and England feared a massive war like the one they had fought in World War I. Their governments were led by men who had experienced the senseless, massive bloodshed of World War I and wanted to avoid large land battles again. They sought to avoid at all costs the murderous trench warfare that they feared would sacrifice another generation of young men.

In the atmosphere of Allied inaction, Germany destroyed Poland and could focus on its genocide of the Jews. In an effort to survive, many Polish Jews tried to pass themselves off as "Aryans" or joined partisan groups.[62] Others tried to escape the Nazis, but only a small number succeeded. Most needed assistance to flee, but few received such support—with one remarkable exception.

It was at this point that the neutral US government, hitherto seemingly indifferent to the plight of European Jewry, convinced some of the highest ranking officers and politicians in the Third Reich to carry out one of the most spectacular rescues of the war. The plan relied on assistance from the German military intelligence forces, the Abwehr. These German soldiers were ordered to find Lubavitcher Rebbe Joseph Isaac Schneersohn, safely escort him out of war-torn Warsaw, and send him to the United States. This daring operation required elaborate efforts by Abwehr agents and American officials and lawyers, and these unlikely allies worked together to rescue a most unusual victim. As the rescue plot crystallized, many wondered if the Rebbe could survive Hitler's inferno. Time was running out for him.

2

The Religious Climate during Hitler's Quest for Empire

> The Second World War inflicted even more grievous blows on the moral standing of the Christian faith than the First. It exposed the emptiness of the churches in Germany, the cradle of the Reformation, and the cowardice and selfishness of the Holy See. It was the nemesis of triumphalism, in both its Protestant and Catholic forms.
> —Paul Johnson, *A History of Christianity*

Europe and North America in 1939 were very religious continents. People in general looked constantly for divine answers to world affairs and natural phenomena. But it was, in general, a much different type of religious landscape than today's. Most denominations in Europe and America were full of hellfire and brimstone preachings bursting with anti-Semitic piffle. Today, most churches in North America, especially the nondenominational mega ones, preach the prosperity gospel (the Protestant movement in Europe is largely dead). Most of these churches are pro-Israel and send millions of dollars of aid each year to Jews in the Holy Land, which is dramatically different from the churches of pre–World War II Europe. The Catholic Church in 1939 preached the old doctrines of damnation, exclusivity, and Jew hatred. Since the reformations of Vatican II in the 1960s, Catholic leaders have often met with Jewish leaders. Today, the church is being led by Pope Francis, who preaches love and acceptance and counts an Argentine rabbi among his closest friends. Francis even made a special trip to Israel in 2014, expressing friendship and peace. Today, many people assume that Protestants and Catholics should have been fighting the Nazis and helping Jews in 1939. Unfortunately, the opposite was true in most cases. This is an important fact to acknowledge, because without an understanding of the religious climate in Europe at the time, one cannot recognize how remarkable the efforts to rescue Rebbe Joseph Isaac Schneersohn truly were. In short, his rescue went against many people's religious convictions.

People often ask why the followers of Rebbe Schneersohn didn't go to the Catholic Church or to some powerful Protestant denomination for help. The answer, quite simply, is that the vast majority of Christian leaders would not have been sympathetic to the Rebbe and would not have troubled themselves to effectuate his rescue. With the storm brewing in Europe, religious leaders were focused on taking care of their own flocks, who were scared by world events and concerned about their families' safety and financial security. Many would argue that people were still suffering from the effects of the last world war and the worldwide depression. They looked to their religious leaders for guidance and for help with their *own* problems as the world spun out of control. Some Americans thought they had entered the end-time and that the Second Coming was just around the corner. Many claimed Hitler was the anti-Christ. However, many Germans and Italians felt that God was on their side and that the Lord was blessing them with empire and riches. Germany was conducting land grabs all over Europe, and Italy had succeeded in taking over Ethiopia.

The invasion of Poland in 1939 met with the enthusiastic approbation of the German population, which was strongly Christian and divided between Roman Catholics and Protestants. One day after the attack, the Evangelical Church in Germany issued an official appeal "for Germans to support the invasion to 'recover German blood' for the fatherland." The Catholic hierarchy, whose flock made up about a third of Germany's population, encouraged and admonished "Catholic soldiers, in obedience to the Führer, to do their duty and to be ready to sacrifice their lives." Why was the Catholic Church inside Germany so supportive of Hitler? In short, the church had a history of backing fascist regimes.[1]

Pope Pius XI, an autocrat in his own right and plagued by scandals involving pedophile priests, had actively backed Benito Mussolini and his takeover of the Italian government in 1922. According to historian David Kertzer, the fascist movement became a "cleric-Fascist revolution." The pope felt confident that the fascists would restore the privileges and powers the church had lost under the democratic government. He hated "individual rights and religious freedom" and believed Mussolini would support him by suppressing these movements. Pius XI desired to bring about the "Kingdom of Christ on earth," and he intended to use Mussolini as a tool in his strategy. At rallies, priests would sing praises to Il Duce as the "Savior of our land." Any priest vaguely critical of Mussolini—for example, Giovanni Montini, who later became Pope Paul VI—was reported to Vatican authorities and disciplined. The church and the population cast Mussolini as a "Christ-like figure," and children in Catholic schools recited daily prayers that said: "I believe in the high Duce—maker of the Black Shirts—and in Jesus Christ his only protector."[2] The church hierarchy was just as supportive of Hitler as it was of Mussolini.

When Nazi Germany forcibly annexed Austria in 1938 (the *Anschluß*), Vienna's Cardinal Theodor Innitzer met with Hitler and supported the Nazi takeover. He had the church bells rung in celebration and swastikas displayed to greet the German army, and he had the following statement read in every church: "Those who are entrusted with souls of the faithful will unconditionally support the great German State and the Führer . . . obviously accompanied by the blessings of Providence." The statement ended with "Heil Hitler." The archbishops of Salzburg and Graz followed the cardinal's lead. This did not stop the Nazis from confiscating church property, closing Catholic organizations, and sending a number of priests to the Dachau concentration camp. "Pius XI was surprised, appalled and embarrassed by Mussolini's meek acceptance of the Nazi takeover." Furthermore, he was "furious" at Cardinal Innitzer, who seemed to be acting on his own, without papal approval. The Vatican daily newspaper and radio criticized the archbishops' statements, but Vatican state secretary Eugenio Pacelli (the future Pope Pius XII) told the German ambassador that the criticism was not official and the pope knew nothing about it. In other words, Pacelli encouraged Hitler to act with a free hand.[3]

As time passed, Pope Pius XI became more uneasy about Mussolini, and he acquired a much more critical view of Hitler, with whom he had signed a controversial and often violated concordat in 1933. One could argue that the pope's realization about Mussolini and Hitler came way too late—he should have seen their evil much sooner, before supporting them for years. But by the time the Germans invaded Poland, Pius XI was dead. Pope Pius XII (who, as papal nuncio in Germany, had actually negotiated the 1933 concordat) was in power, and he was a supporter of Hitler. He had gotten to know the Nazis well during his stay in Berlin.

Thus, the Catholic Church did not protest the invasion of Poland, an overwhelmingly Roman Catholic country. Instead, it later reaffirmed the pope's October 1939 encyclical *Summi Pontificatus*, which adopted a policy of strict neutrality in the face of the violence spreading across Europe. Inside Germany (a very religious nation), religious newspapers, both Protestant and Catholic, claimed the Germans were fighting for essential *Lebensraum*. Most Germans believed that God was on their side. As American journalist William Shirer wrote on 20 September 1939, while living in Berlin, "I have still to find a German [most of whom were Christians], even among those who don't like the regime, who sees anything wrong in the German destruction of Poland."[4]

This religious support for Hitler should not be surprising. Most religious leaders inside the Reich supported Hitler and considered him blessed by God. Lutheran bishop Hans Meiser prayed in 1937, "We thank you Lord, for every success . . . you have so far granted [Hitler] for the good of our people." Many churches extolled Hitler as the defender of Germany and, by extension, "Christianity from godless Bolshevism." Roman Catholic dioceses had church bells "rung as a joyful salute on Hitler's birthday on 20 April 1939 with prayers for the Führer to be said at the following Sunday mass." The Catholic primate, Cardinal Adolf Bertram, sent Hitler a personal greeting via telegram. Protestant scholars and leaders, including Gerhard Kittel, Paul Althaus, and Emmanuel Hirsch, supported Hitler and believed that God stood behind him. Hitler had carefully groomed many of these leaders from the beginning of his rule, appealing to God in a nationwide broadcast in 1933 that the rebirth of Germany would be founded on Christianity.[5] Hanns Kerrl, Reichsminister of Protestant church affairs, had been a Nazi Party member since 1923 and offered to donate all church property to the state "and make Hitler its 'supreme head' and *Summus Episcopus*."[6] There were a few brave dissenting Protestant leaders who resisted the Nazis, including Martin Niemöller and Dietrich Bonhoeffer of the Confessing Church, but unfortunately, they were a tiny minority. And many of them failed to see the danger at first. Pastor Niemöller was initially a Nazi Party member and supporter of Hitler. But after a few years of Nazi rule, he saw how dangerous Hitler was and changed his mind. Quite simply, most Christians in Germany, both Catholic and Protestant, supported Hitler and his regime. As SS general Otto Kumm said after the war:

> The great majority of us lived in great fear of a communist takeover of Germany. We had seen what the Bolsheviks did in Russia, and we to a man swore an oath to defend Germany against such a prospect. I for one joined the Party out of a sense of duty not only to Germany but also out of a sense of national self-preservation against such an outcome at home. History has proven that we were flawed, but you really had to live in those times to appreciate where our minds were. Poland was just another part of greater Germany in our mind. The division of Prussia was absolutely intolerable to every German, as many had families there beyond the corridor. In my mind then it was completely justified. Many of us were Catholics, and even the Protestants feared a Stalinist intervention using German communists as instigators to destroy our country. There could be no coexistence.[7]

The creation of a buffer zone between Germany and Russia, using Poland as a neutral zone, had many historical precedents in other times and other empires. There was some justification for establishing this zone: many Germans, including Hitler, had witnessed the civil war in Germany in 1919 and the chaos created by the communists in Germany's own backyard. Many Christians throughout Germany viewed the communists as "godless" and thus immoral. Moreover, many Germans, both Catholic and Protestant, felt that God had sent the Nazis to protect Germany from Bolshevism and to reclaim lands lost to other nations, like Poland, that they viewed as illegitimate.[8]

However, the overwhelmingly Catholic Poles had other ideas about God and Christianity in 1939. They hoped God and the pope would come to their defense. But Pope Pius XII remained silent, and God seemed to have turned his back on the embattled Polish nation. Pius XII had been elected pope in March 1939, and he supported much of what Hitler had been doing. "Believers are supposed to hold that the Pope is the Vicar of Christ on earth, and the keeper of the keys of Saint Peter. They of course are free to believe this, and to believe that God decides when to end the tenure of one Pope or (more important) to inaugurate the tenure of another." Based on this belief, it was apparently God's will that, a few months before the 1939 invasion, a pro-fascist but anti-Nazi pope (Pius XI) died with an unsigned encyclical condemning racism on his nightstand and was replaced by a more pro-Nazi pope (Pius XII). What was God telling Catholics in this moment?[9]

Among the SS, which persecuted the Poles so extensively, a significant number were practicing Catholics (25 percent), and the rest were largely Protestant. Most of the SS leadership, including Himmler and Heydrich, were Catholic. Another Catholic, Ernst Kaltenbrunner, replaced Heydrich after he was assassinated in 1942. The brutal commandant of Auschwitz, SS-Obersturmbannführer Rudolf Höss, had been raised in a strong Catholic family. Although he rejected his faith as a young man, he returned to his Catholic roots before his death. Right before his execution in 1947, he received the sacrament of penance and last rites. In the end, "Catholics engaged in the extermination processes were never told specifically by their clergy that they were doing wrong."[10]

Catholic priests also pursued power, implemented Nazi policies, and created fascist governments. For example, the head of the Nazi puppet state of Slovakia was a fascist in holy orders, Father Jozef Tiso. No Catholic has ever been "threatened with excommunication for participating in war crimes." Hitler proudly told his army adjutant Gerhard Engel, "I shall remain a Catholic forever." Since the Catholic Church has never excommunicated him, maybe he was right (the church could retrospectively declare that Hitler should have been excommunicated during his lifetime, but it has not done so). Interestingly, after Hitler's conquest of Austria in 1938, Mussolini, who was somewhat uneasy about Hitler's growing power, despite being allied with him, told a confidential Vatican go-between that the one man who could stop Hitler was the pope. "By excommunicating Hitler, he could isolate the Führer and cripple the Nazis. . . . [T]he Pope never seriously considered following the suggestion."[11] The only time the Vatican considered excommunicating Hitler was in 1932, one year before he seized power, for acting as a witness at the Protestant wedding of propaganda minister Joseph Goebbels, a Catholic, and Magda, a divorced Protestant. In the end, the church took no action against Hitler, but it did excommunicate Goebbels—not for his crimes against humanity, but for marrying a divorced Protestant.[12] As Paul Johnson tragically notes: "The Church excommunicated Catholics who laid down in their wills that they wished to be cremated . . . but it did not forbid them to work in concentration or death camps."[13]

In addition to making up the majority of SS and Nazi leadership, Catholics led most of the fascist totalitarian regimes of the twentieth century: Mussolini, Spain's Francisco Franco, Portugal's António Salazar, and Croatia's Ante Pavelić. They enjoyed support from the church and derived much of their childhood education from the church. "As for the Jews," Hitler told Catholic bishop Wilhelm Berning of Osnabrück, "I am just carrying on with the same policy which the Catholic Church had adopted for 1500 years." At no time were Catholics freed, "either by their own hierarchy or by Rome, . . . from their moral obligation to obey the legitimate authority of the Nazi rulers, which had been imposed on them by the 1933 directives of the hierarchy. Nor did the bishops ever tell them officially that the regime was evil, or even mistaken."[14]

The Catholic Church's refusal to confront the Nazis is part of a long history of complicity in horrible crimes, from the slaughter of the Crusades to the Inquisition and wars of religion, up to the more recent child-rape scandals[15] and the church's inaction against the Catholic leaders of the Hutu Rwandan genocide.[16] Sadly, during the Holocaust, the Catholic Church failed to follow the right line of morality, even though it told its people that it was infallible and its leader, the pope, was the Vicar of Christ in the world.

In the context of World War II, one is compelled to ask why so many Catholics were involved in killing the Jews, and why the Catholic Church in Rome did practically nothing to help the Jews or protest the German invasion of Poland—a predominantly Catholic country. The simple answer is that this was the church's modus operandi at the time. One might point to the church's educational and religious practices as the cause of the foundational conditioning of society that gave birth to genocidal maniacs in Germany. And unfortunately, not only Catholics but also many Protestants acquired their anti-Semitism from their religious traditions. "There was no explaining away," Donald L. Niewyk writes, "the contributions made by Christian antisemitism to the climate of opinion that made the genocide of the Jews possible in the European heartland of ostensibly Christian Western civilization."[17]

The reform of church doctrine to end liturgy and teachings that, for centuries, had incited and justified prejudice against and persecution of their Jewish neighbors did not come until the Vatican II Council (1962–1965), long after World War II. It finally declared that the "death of Christ cannot be charged against all the Jews then alive, without distinction, nor against the Jews of today." It reasoned that "Christ died for our sins," the crucifixion was salvation, and human sin was responsible for the crucifixion. Without sin, there would be no need for sacrificial atonement. It continued by stating, "the Gospel's spiritual love decries hatred, persecutions, displays of antisemitism, directed against Jews at any time and by anyone." One could argue that this pronouncement was 2,000 years too late, especially since the Catholic Church holds itself up as infallible.[18]

So, in the 1930s and during World War II, it was disappointing but not surprising that the Catholic Church and most Protestants not only turned a blind eye to Hitler's gruesome crimes but also openly supported his regime. Even though *Mein Kampf* had been publicly available since 1925, and Hitler's beliefs had been documented since the early 1920s in countless publications and speeches, the Vatican was the first sovereign to sign a treaty (*Reichskonkordat*) with the Nazis, which served to legitimize their rule in the eyes of other nations and of Catholics everywhere, just as Vatican approval and the Lateran Accords had done for Mussolini. It "ensured that Nazism could rise unopposed by the most powerful Catholic community in the world [Germany's]." It also encouraged Hitler's acts "against international Jewry." In keeping with the church's history of supporting atrocities or failing to speak out against such crimes, the pope remained silent during Hitler's invasion of Poland in 1939. One might have thought he would have at least revoked the 1933 treaty negotiated with Hitler, but he did not.[19]

Apart from his desire to preserve the Vatican, the pope's silence on Nazi behavior and war may have stemmed from his fear of losing control of the church inside Italy as well as in lands controlled by Hitler. Cardinal Eugène Tisserant witnessed Pope Pius XII's weak behavior up close in Rome and commented: "I fear that history will reproach the Holy See with having practiced a policy of selfish convenience and not much else!"[20] Protestant leaders also seemed to support or at least turn a blind eye to what Hitler was doing. Christian leaders' behavior during the Holocaust and World War II "exposed the emptiness of the churches in Germany, the cradle of the Reformation, and the cowardice and selfishness of the Holy See."[21]

It is clear that both Protestants and Catholics inside the fascist regimes of Europe were largely complicit in the crimes perpetrated by Hitler and his henchmen. There were few Christian leaders people could turn to for help in the fight against the Nazis because they were either Nazis themselves or sympathetic to the Nazi cause. Countless people have asked why Christians did not help rescue Jews in general and Rebbe Joseph Isaac Schneersohn in particular. But as this chapter shows, it was difficult to find the right Christians to help; in the lands dominated by the Nazis, Christians had for centuries been taught anti-Semitism as a divine preachment. Quite simply, those who were organizing the rescue of the Rebbe could not go to Protestants and Catholics for help because they would probably find not willing friends but prejudiced enemies.

3

The Lubavitchers and Their Rebbe

Superstition sets the whole world in flames. . . . Philosophy quenches them.
—Voltaire

The religious dynasty of Hasidic Jews called the Lubavitchers originated in Lubavitch, Byelorussia, in the late eighteenth century.[1] The Hasidim, as they are known today, began with the mystic Baal Shem Tov (Master of the Good Name), who mobilized a segment of eastern European Jewry that had suffered severe discrimination. Jews fleeing persecution in western and central Europe found refuge in Poland, where, from the sixteenth to eighteenth centuries, they enjoyed a form of self-rule. A large majority of Europe's Jews lived in Poland or lands claimed by it. Over the centuries, the Jews living in Poland experienced both good times and very bad times. Decades of persecution during the religious ferment of the sixteenth and seventeenth centuries, such as the Chmielnicki pogroms of 1648–1649 in the Ukraine (then eastern Poland), when tens of thousands of Jews were slaughtered by Greek Orthodox Cossacks, left the community impoverished.[2] This created a theological and emotional crisis for Jews and motivated many to look for a miracle or a new form of Judaism to lead them into the future. Moreover, the extreme poverty of the surviving Jewish masses prevented most of them from obtaining high status in a Jewish society that valued scholarship; this created a movement among those who wanted to learn more and gain respect within an educated elite. Finally, another galvanizing event that helped shape the Hasidic Jews was the 1665–1666 messianic crusade of a charismatic man named Sabbetai Zvi (1626–1676), which initially attracted many Jews. They thought he might be the promised Messiah, until his conversion to Islam. In many respects, the development of Hasidism was a reaction to Sabbateanism (Sabbetai Zvi's movement).

Sabbetai Zvi emerged as a leader while Europe was still recovering from the bloody Thirty Years' War (1618–1648). During this time, at least 10 million people suffered and died during a series of religious wars because they were Catholic or Protestant or because they were simply in the wrong place at the wrong time as the armies of God laid waste their crops and homes. While the Jewish world was obsessed with messianic movements like Sabbetai Zvi's, Christians were strongly focused on the second coming of their Messiah, Jesus.[3] Religious ferment does not occur in a vacuum, even among communities that seem to resist contact with one another. Thus, evangelical Christianity is flourishing today, while fervently Orthodox Jewish communities are experiencing a resurgence and liberal religious movements in both Protestantism and Judaism are in decline.

During Sabbetai Zvi's lifetime, there was plenty of religious turmoil and anti-Semitism. In this climate, the Jewish community hungered for a leader who would either end the persecution or help bring about the age of the Messiah. Sabbetai Zvi tapped into their extant fears and desires, with disappointing results. Like other putative Jewish Messiahs before and after him, Sabbetai Zvi devastated the Jewish community by dashing its hopes for a better future against the rocks of realpolitik. In his pursuit of a Jewish kingdom, he found many who were willing to embrace the movement, but once a religious crisis ensued—his conversion to Islam and his subsequent death—the messianic movement sputtered, and the history of his era was rewritten to expunge whatever support he had enjoyed.

Though quite unstable, Sabbetai Zvi could mesmerize audiences with his pronouncements of the coming kingdom of God. He promised to restore the kingdom of Israel and crown himself a Jewish king. This, in turn, would magically lead to a new age of peace and harmony. Believing he was on a sacred mission, he traveled to the Promised Land from Turkey to launch his self-described crusade. In 1665 many proclaimed him the Messiah, and Sabbetai Zvi seemed glad to take on the title and responsibility. As stories about him spread throughout Europe, the Middle East, and Africa, thousands proclaimed that God's reign on earth had commenced. According to some sources, Sabbetai Zvi's message captured the imagination of many eastern European and Sephardic Jews. Emboldened by his early success, Sabbetai Zvi and a group of fervent followers traveled to Turkey to ask the sultan, ruler of the vast Ottoman Empire, to surrender his throne. Sabbetai Zvi probably never actually met the sultan. But when the Sultan learned of this mission, he presented a counterproposal: convert to Islam or die. Sabbetai Zvi and many of his followers cynically chose the former. News of his conversion and his betrayal of Judaism devastated Jewish communities around the world. Some of his most devoted admirers developed a doctrine of the "Holiness of Sin," which posited that Sabbetai Zvi had descended into evil to redeem the divine sparks concealed in that realm. Many Jews might have accepted martyrdom, but a Messiah who converted—deemed by many a craven, cowardly act—shocked them into disbelief. Their long-awaited Messiah had turned out to be just another pretender.[4]

Although Sabbetai Zvi's escapade demoralized eastern European Jews and was quickly covered up, it did not discourage the general population from looking for another strong leader or from seeking a more personal relationship with the divine. They yearned, as had Jews throughout the ages, for a spiritual guru to help them learn the ways of God. And this desire continued to express itself in strange movements. Some Jews, called Sabbateans, continued to believe Sabbetai Zvi was the Messiah even after his conversion to Islam, and they spawned other movements. An eighteenth-century follower named Jacob Frank claimed to be the reincarnation of Sabbetai Zvi and the patriarch Jacob and said he received instructions from heaven. He rejected the Talmud and converted to Christianity in 1759, along with some of his followers, with much fanfare from the Catholic Church. However, Frank wound up being excommunicated by the Jews and was later jailed by the Christians as a heretic. After years in prison, he was released and eventually lived as a wealthy nobleman in Germany, supported by his followers.[5]

During the religious upheaval in Europe in the sixteenth, seventeenth, and eighteenth centuries, the movements of Luther, Calvin, Sabbetai Zvi, and Frank were just separate expressions of what had been going on in Christianity and Judaism since the beginning. After numerous disappointments, Hasidism arose to fill the needs of the desperate, downtrodden eastern European Jews who yearned for a stronger connection to God, and the Baal Shem Tov was their leader.

The Baal Shem Tov, also known as the Besht, wanted to empower individuals and inspired Jews to pray and sing and learn for themselves. He spiritualized the messianic yearnings and democratized access to the sacred. Unlike Sabbetai Zvi, who tried to connect people to himself personally as the Messiah, the Baal Shem Tov encouraged people to attach themselves to spiritual masters. Ironically, the Besht would give rise to generations of authoritarian mystagogues who were enthralled to their *wunder*-Rebbes. The Baal Shem Tov taught Jews to focus on personal prayer and song; rather than the traditional emphasis on books and study, he advocated a concentration on divine imminence. He told stories whose meaning was accessible to his followers. The Baal Shem Tov denied the powerful hierarchical religious establishment so that he could promote universal male literacy and religious study, which created mystical communities with different religious practices. This gave rise to the variety of Hasidic communities in existence today. The Baal Shem Tov is honored by Hasidic communities as a spiritual revolutionary, much as Luther and Calvin are honored by Protestants. Hasidim took off from the very areas where Sabbetai Zvi's movement had been the strongest.[6]

The Baal Shem Tov was born in 1698.[7] His life, according to Hasidic legend, started out like Isaac's. An angel visited his elderly parents and told them that God was going to grant them a child. Just as God had blessed Sarah and Abraham, the angel explained, God would bless them with a son who would take the Lord's message to mankind. The Besht's disciples described his ability to perform miracles, even as a young child. By the 1730s, he had gathered followers who were later known as the Hasidim, or "the pious ones."[8] Although the traditional Jewish leadership (*Misnagdim*) derided the Besht's movement, considering it a Zvi-like uprising, it attracted hundreds of thousands of eager followers. In fact, the *Misnagdim* might have been worried because so many jumped to join the Besht's movement.[9] He turned out to be a charismatic teacher who, wherever he went, inspired people to become more religious; miraculously, he even healed some of their ailments.[10] Although many of the stories surrounding the Besht are "possibly (or probably) completely fictitious," according to Avrum Ehrlich, they took on a life of their own and have become "the basis of Hasidic custom, theology and tradition."[11]

God, the Besht taught, is not an "infinite brain" (as many philosophers believed) grasped through intellectual creativity, but a distinct reality. God is the essence of life, the core of the soul, the depth of love, and the ultimate truth of every facet of the human condition. Although today these concepts sound like new-age spiritualism, they inspired the long-suffering, credulous, and poorly educated Jews of central and eastern Europe to discuss higher levels of thought and wisdom. For the most part, the people drawn to this movement, according to Gershom Scholem, were "simple and unsophisticated."[12] For the Besht, God ushered in a Jewish religious enlightenment that welcomed all Jews, not just the educated elite. As a result, the Besht's "message swept with torrential speed and power through the densely populated Jewish communities of Poland. People came by the thousands to hear him, to listen to his message, to receive his blessing, to join him in his frenzied and foot stomping prayer sessions."[13]

Similar movements were happening elsewhere. In the United States, the Great Awakening was taking place; in Germany, the rise of Pietism was occurring. Like the Hasidic movement, the preachers of the Great Awakening and German Pietism emphasized that an emotion-filled experience of God was the key to salvation, not intellectual contemplation. The Besht's movement could be viewed more as revivalist than novel, and it "drew its strength from the people."[14] And like the Great Awakening in America, with its doomsday preachers such as Jonathan Edwards, this new Hasidism gave birth to itinerant preachers like the Besht, who emphasized "the importance of fasting and penitence, threatening a demon-filled hell for the impure, and [promising] a physical heaven for the properly penitent."[15]

The Besht inspired his followers, teaching that everyone from unlettered peasants to the most punctilious of scholars had access to God. Contrary to what some Jewish leaders had taught in the past, even laypeople and nonscholars could learn about and discover God. Although the Besht encouraged study of the Torah, he also taught that one should look for God in the physical earth, echoing pantheism; refining and spiritualizing one's own life could help refine and spiritualize the world. According to Scholem, this focus would later be evident in the Chabad school, with its "striking mixture of enthusiastic worship of God and pantheistic, or rather acosmistic, interpretation of the universe on the one hand, and the intense preoccupation with the human mind and its impulses on the other."[16] The Besht urged his followers to believe that good deeds could hasten the coming of the Messiah, who would usher in a harmonious world free of disease, war, and suffering. The Messiah would create a world suffused with spirituality—as "filled with Divine knowledge as the waters cover the sea." Unlike Sabbetai Zvi, the Besht did not claim messiahship himself; he encouraged his followers to look toward the age when the Messiah would reveal himself and urged them to perform religious deeds that would hasten the Messiah's arrival. The Besht even claimed to have "ascended on high" in 1746, visited the "heavenly abode," and personally asked the Messiah when he was coming. It appears that many of the Besht's followers believed his spiritual powers were limitless.

When the Besht died in 1760, he was succeeded by one of his students, Dov Ber, known as the Magid of Mezeritch. The Magid is regarded as the educator of the largest class of Hasidic leaders and is considered the "supreme mystic, saint, and scholar who, by virtue of his reputed discipleship with the [Besht] became a legitimate interpreter of the new techniques of Hasidism." Upon his own death in 1773, the movement splintered into about thirty sects throughout eastern Europe. The Magid's disciples, called *Tzadikim*, or "righteous ones," continued the Baal Shem Tov's work of mentoring all Jews in the ways of God. The Hasidic movement might be called unique, in that each group centered itself around a Hasidic saint, which was "something entirely new."[17] Many of the splinter groups took their names from the birthplace, headquarters, or grave site of their leader. The Lubavitchers, named for the Byelorussian town where their movement began, were one such group. Their founder was Schneur Zalman of Liadi (1745–1812).[18]

More than other Hasidic groups, the Lubavitchers emphasized scholarship as well as worship. Like most Hasidic sects, however, they believed their Rebbe and his unique philosophy, Chabad, were incomparable. Chabad is an acronym of the Hebrew words *Chochmah*, *Binah*, and *Da'at*, meaning "wisdom," "understanding," and "knowledge"—the three levels of divine emanation in the Jewish mystical system (Kabala). Martin Buber, the Jewish philosopher and thinker who brought eastern European Hasidism to the German-speaking world, rightly notes that

Hasidism represents "Kabbalism turned Ethos."[19] Chabad demands of its followers comprehension, understanding, and appreciation of the message of Judaism and of Jewish mysticism. Questioning, debating, and contemplating the ideas of Judaism and Hasidism are intrinsic to the Lubavitch system. Chabad emphasizes that the true test of a person's spirituality becoming one with God is the believer's ability to love. According to their doctrine, Lubavitchers should strive to eliminate ego and vanity from their lives and cultivate a spirit of brotherly love and mutual assistance. If one is in touch with one's divine soul, the founder of Chabad wrote, one automatically falls in love with every single Jew, since all are "fragments of God." Schneur Zalman wrote in his book *Tanya* that he ardently believed in such spiritual growth and that all Jews should strive to do everything within their power to connect with God, to realize the purpose of existence.

Another fundamental part of Chabad culture is its heavy emphasis on the Messiah. Although messianism had been a constant theme of Judaism for more than 2,000 years, the Chabad movement emphasized the importance of yearning for the coming of the Messiah and the actions that could be taken to hasten his arrival. One contemporary of Schneur Zalman wrote of his book, "With the *Tanya*, the Israelites will go forth to meet the Messiah."[20]

Hasidic leaders often took the title *Rebbe*, a variation of the word *rabbi*, meaning "my teacher" or "my master." In these early days of the Hasidic movement, no formalized education was required to earn the title Rebbe; leaders were called by God to assume their roles, and their communities chose to follow them.[21] Shortly afterward, succession became dynastic, passing from father to son.

Schneur Zalman lived in a time of incredible upheaval and change in Europe. Besides warfare and murder (under the Terror of Robespierre), the French Revolution introduced the Enlightenment ideals of liberty, equality, and fraternity. Even though he created a police state, Napoleon instituted profound changes in the law to give Jews equal rights, citizenship, and greater opportunity within his expanding French empire, similar to what they purportedly enjoyed in America.[22] Meanwhile, to the east, Jews still faced pervasive discrimination, crushing poverty, violent attacks, and burdensome restrictions on employment, residence, and education. In Russia, Christians and Jews were not citizens; they were subjects of the czar, and most of them lived as serfs.

When Napoleon invaded Russia in 1812, Schneur Zalman firmly opposed the French and fled Liadi with sixty wagons of household goods and numerous followers. Zalman did not like the czar or feel any loyalty to Russia, but he feared that Napoleon's "enlightenment" would secularize Russian Jewry. That, in his mind, was a bigger threat than continued oppression under the czar. Zalman would rather die than live under Napoleon, and he wrote: "I was shown [from heaven] that, if Bonaparte would be victorious, the Jews would prosper and enjoy a more dignified position, but their hearts would become distant from their Father in heaven."[23] Ironically, the fanatic rabbis of Russia, like Zalman, "urged their flock to rally to the side of the very czar who had been defaming and flogging and fleecing and murdering them. Better a Jew-baiting despotism, they said, than even a whiff of the unholy French Enlightenment."[24] Rebbe Zalman died during his flight. After the Russians finally forced the French out of their country, the czar did not forget the Lubavitchers' loyalty, and the government's oppression eased. However, they enjoyed nothing close to the freedom, security, and equality of Jews in some Western countries.

Over the next 120 years in Russia, Chabad experienced ups and downs and the disruption of splinter factions, with several leaders competing for the position of Rebbe. Despite these hardships, it remained a vibrant Jewish community and a guiding light for many Russian Jews. At the start of the twentieth century, the Lubavitch movement, owing to its outreach efforts, had tens of thousands of adherents throughout Europe and North America. Most of them, though, lived in Russia, where the Bolsheviks would soon ridicule all religion as the opium of the masses and force atheism on everyone within their control.

By World War II, six generations of Schneersohn family members, descendants of Schneur Zalman, had guided the Lubavitch, or Chabad, movement. In 1939 the sixth Lubavitcher Rebbe, Joseph Isaac Schneersohn, was widely accepted as the unofficial leader of all Russian Hasidic Jews. Most Lubavitchers believed their Rebbe was endowed with mystical powers and considered him the unquestioned leader of world Jewry and the potential *Moshiach* (Messiah) of their generation. According to

Joseph Isaac Schneersohn (1880–1950), the sixth Lubavitcher Rebbe, at his desk in Brooklyn, 1949. (Eliezer Zaklikovsky)

Jewish theology, each generation of Jews is thought to have a potential Messiah, and the Lubavitchers believe that if the Messiah is going to appear, he will be their Rebbe. Many hold that because a *Tzadik* has succeeded in transforming his ego to allow his inner divine soul to pervade his entire consciousness, he is "without sin," and God blesses him with the *Ruach Hakodesh* (Holy Spirit). Lubavitchers' belief that theirs is the only truth is revealed by the high status claimed for their leader.[25]

Holocaust survivor and Nobel Peace Prize–winner Elie Wiesel wrote of the Rebbes: "He is what can be, what man wants to be, he is the chosen one who is refused nothing, in heaven or on earth. God is angry? He can make him smile. God is severe? He can induce him to leniency."[26] The Rebbe's followers assume he knows intellectually and feels emotionally the physical and spiritual needs of every Jew and recognizes how to connect each one to God. As a result, he has a special role as intermediary between God and his people. Moreover, his followers believed the Rebbe is able to feel the pain of the persecuted and suffer with them. "I feel each individual's hardships, and know more or less each individual's pain and suffering," Joseph Isaac Schneersohn wrote. "Each one of you is close to my heart, and each man's distress strikes deep." In other words, the Rebbe's relationship to his followers is emotionally profound and intimate. Schneersohn described the love a Rebbe has for his followers as stronger than the love a parent has for a child. As for his followers, they should say: "Rebbe, I am yours; I dedicate myself to you completely. It's only that the smart little fellow, who is wise to do evil—the Evil Inclination—is trying to fool me and ensnare me into a sack. Basically, that's not what I want. I'm yours: I want to be as I ought to be. Rebbe, have pity on me: take me out of where I am, and set me up where I ought to be!"[27]

The more one studies Lubavitch Judaism and its leaders, the more one is reminded of how the Christian movement grew out of Judaism 2,000 years ago. Geza Vermes even calls Jesus a "Hasidic rabbi" whose teachings mirror what we now find in Hasidism.[28] In fact, one can see parallels between the emergence of Lubavitch Judaism and the stories of Jesus's early followers in the Bible. Communities like Lubavitch give rise to messianic sects and supernatural explanations that override physical laws, such as when the seventh Lubavitcher Rebbe, Menachem Mendel Schneerson, died in 1994 and was proclaimed the Messiah by numerous people in the community.[29]

Knowing how his followers feel about him, the Rebbe is not only a human being but also an awesome prophetic figure worthy of total submission. Although there are many rabbis, there can be only one Rebbe in the Chabad community. His leadership is charismatic and typically dynastic. Elie Wiesel, whose grandfather taught him a love of Hasidism, states, "In Hasidism, the Rebbe by virtue of the strength he incarnates and the majesty he evokes . . . represents the father figure par excellence: someone good yet strict, charitable yet severe, tolerant with others but inflexible with himself. In other words, a singular human being in whom all attributes converge and in whom all contradictions are resolved." Chabad philosophy teaches that contradictions and paradoxes are innate to life itself and, indeed, to God himself (see Isaiah 45:7); consequently, for Lubavitchers, the Rebbe is the paradigm of how to embrace the paradoxes of life and use them as catalysts for deeper growth. Most Lubavitchers also believe that Rebbes, once dead, are closer to God in heaven, and they may ask deceased Rebbes to intercede with God on their behalf, similar to what Catholics do when they pray to saints.[30]

Born in Lubavitch in 1880, Rebbe Joseph Isaac Schneersohn assumed leadership of Chabad Hasidism in 1920. Although the Rebbe cherished and supported all sects of ultra-Orthodox Judaism, he believed that Chabad captured Judaism in its full majesty. Regarding the Reform and Conservative movements, he made a clear distinction between their individual members and the general groups. Every Jew, regardless of affiliation, the Rebbe taught, is as Jewish as Moses himself. But he felt that any reforms of Jewish law and tradition (according to his Halachic definitions) were historical errors and would increase assimilation in subsequent generations. Hasidim consider assimilation undesirable and take great pains to be different from other people in the clothes they wear, the way they cut their hair, the language they speak, the schools their children attend, the food they eat, and their manner of dancing and singing. They may drive cars and use mobile phones, and a few are very wealthy and successful in the modern world, but in some ways, the majority of Hasidim seem frozen in time—not biblical time in Israel, but about three centuries ago in eastern Europe. Many Hasidic leaders fear that once the old customs and religious laws are changed, a downward spiral will begin, resulting in complacency and total alienation from Judaism. Chabad is not unique in its views. Most ultra-Orthodox Jews, and especially Hasidic ones, hold that the beliefs and practices of Reform, Conservative, and even modern Orthodox Jews are at odds with Judaism's core beliefs.[31] They believe that only they have the "real" truth. This is problematic in terms of maintaining good relations with other Jewish groups. Under the seventh Lubavitcher Rebbe, Menachem Mendel Schneerson, a welcoming attitude toward all Jews became an essential part of his evangelism; however, he continued his predecessor's practice of accepting all Jews but not their versions of Judaism.

Rebbe Joseph Isaac Schneersohn believed that people who did not follow his ways were wrong, and they were disobeying God. He insisted that character could be improved only by occupying oneself with Hasidism; otherwise, one remained in a sinful state.[32] According to the Rebbe,

Chabad philosophy gave Jews an opportunity to experience the full richness of Judaism, to "suck the marrow" out of the Torah and its way of life. As the Rebbe said, "The ethical teachings and guidance in the service of G-d which are to be found in *Chassidus* are intended for all Jews, not only for Chassidim. *Every* Jew ought to listen closely to the voice of G-d which has been revealed through our forefathers, the Rebbes." The teachings "unfolded through our Rebbes and their tens of thousands of chassidim" could help unreligious souls "see and hear the plain truth about the life of man in This World." Through the study of *Chassidus*, the "divine level of wisdom," one drew "down the revelation of G-dliness in This World."[33]

Besides feeling confident that his brand of Judaism was superior to all other forms of Jewish observance, the Rebbe believed Jews were superior to Gentiles. Because Judaism comprises people of all races, and the full acceptance of converts goes back to biblical times, this seems an odd attitude for a Jew. As Rebbe Schneersohn's newspaper *Hakreah Vehakedusha* (Reading and Holiness), which he edited and approved, stated in December 1941, "But in general and as a nation, as a whole, we are always better than the other nations." Is this just high self-esteem or an attempt to build esprit de corps? Since Jews share a religion and have not been a nation for thousands of years, this description seems removed from reality. The Rebbe's newspaper further explained in June 1942 that the cause of anti-Semitism was often that people "begrudged the Jew his enviable higher position." Needless to say, claiming to be better than everyone else tends to arouse anger or envy, and it is not a good strategy to get others to treat you better.

Even more condescendingly, Chabad claims that Jews have both an "animal soul" and a "divine soul," whereas Gentiles have only an animal soul. Thus, according to this teaching, Jews are ontologically superior. This concept is found nowhere in the Bible and runs counter to the beliefs of most Jewish denominations. According to Judaic scholar Roman Foxbrunner, Lubavitchers believe that Gentile souls are of an "inferior order" and "totally evil with no redeeming qualities whatsoever." These souls "were created only to test, to punish, to elevate, and ultimately to serve Israel (in the Messianic Era)." In other words, Gentiles were destined to be eventual servants of the Jews.[34]

Lubavitch philosophy teaches that having a divine soul takes man closer to God, while the animal soul drags him down. Only Jews, according to Chabad founder Schneur Zalman, have divine souls, since they are the "descendants of the righteous patriarchs." Gentiles' souls die with their bodies, while Jewish souls are eternal. Most of these thoughts were expressed in Zalman's magnum opus *Tanya*, which states: "For in the case of Israel, this soul of the *kelipah* [animal soul] is derived from *kelipat nogah*, which also contains good, as it originates in the esoteric 'Tree of Knowledge of Good and Evil.' The souls of the nations of the world [Gentiles], however, emanate from the other, unclean *kelipot* which contain no good whatever. . . . 'The kindness of the nations is sin'—that all the charity and kindness done by the nations of the world is only for their own self-glorification."[35] The anti-Gentile doctrine of this Lubavitcher Rebbe is understood within the movement but is not widely proclaimed outside of it.

To be fair, although Chabad did not preach tolerance of other Jews and non-Jews, its members were not physically violent toward these people. Besides teaching that other forms of Judaism were inferior and espousing xenophobic beliefs about Gentiles, Rebbe Schneersohn and his followers focused on daily activities that included studying religious texts, performing *mitzvoth* (God's commandments), and preserving Jewish life in general and their Chabad practices in particular. Against incredible odds, he did his best to maintain yeshivas and synagogues throughout the world, primarily in the Soviet Union.

Today, many Lubavitchers would argue against these troubling Chabad teachings, saying they do not reflect the group's current beliefs. One could argue that their most recent leader, Menachem Mendel Schneerson, would not have focused on many of the messages his father-in-law, the sixth Rebbe did. But the movement's teachings in 1939 strike modern-day readers as problematic. In a historical context, many of Chabad's xenophobic tenets were written down when the sect lived in Russia, where people were generally anti-Semitic. So their hatred for Gentiles and others can be viewed as a response to the persecution they suffered at the hands of the local population. Although responding to racism with one's own form of racism is not necessarily a wise policy, it was at least understandable. The seventh Lubavitcher Rebbe changed this tradition. Menachem Mendel Schneerson's charismatic leadership and progressive form of Hasidism stamped the movement that most know today; hence, many readers who know something about Chabad will be surprised by much of its history and previous philosophy.

From the outset, Rebbe Joseph Isaac Schneersohn's life was shrouded in mystery—again, much like the biblical story of Isaac. In the late 1870s many Lubavitchers feared the end of the Schneersohn dynasty, since the fifth Rebbe had no children and his wife, Sara, had given up hope. According to Chabad sources, one night after crying herself to sleep, Sara had a dream in which three men revealed to her that she would have a son. One of them told her, "Don't cry, my daughter. I promise that this year you will give birth to a son—but only on one condition: immediately after [festival] *Yom Tov*, you must give eighteen rubles of your money to *tzedakah* [charity]." The other men nodded in agreement. Then the three blessed Sara and left.[36] Sara soon became pregnant with the only child she would bear. Thus began Joseph Isaac Schneersohn's life as a traditional Jewish legend, complete with angels, dreams, and divine ordination.

The Schneersohn family had a tradition of marriage among cousins that strengthened the network of alliances for future leaders. Historian Avrum Ehrlich writes that the inbreeding was so widespread "it can be seen as obsessive. The high degree of apparent infertility and other irregularities in the family might be linked to these practices." Since Joseph's parents were first cousins, his birth could also be seen as a genetic miracle.[37]

Shalom Dovber, the fifth Lubavitcher Rebbe (1860–1920), trained his son Joseph as his successor. He deeply loved all Jews but viewed as "God's enemies" Jewish atheists, Jewish socialists, and all other Jews who did not believe in God's commandments. The large number who became involved with the antireligious Communist Party as a way to counter the repressive and anti-Semitic forces in eastern Europe troubled him. Joseph was taught a strict interpretation of the laws and intolerance. His father spent hours teaching Joseph and other followers how to defend the movement from such people and how to inspire Jews in ways that would not be diluted by science, history, liberal education, social and political integration, or forces of assimilation. He trained them to be "'soldiers in the Rebbe's army' who would fight 'without concessions or compromise' to ensure that true Judaism would survive. Their struggle would pave the way for the coming of the Messiah."[38]

At an early age, Joseph regarded his father as one bestowed with unique powers. His father knew the truth before one spoke, and he could tell if someone were hiding information. Often, during prayers, his father would be moved to tears by the emotions he felt for his God. Knowing that he would follow in his father's footsteps, young Joseph assumed the burden of the expectations placed on him. At age eleven, for example, when his father was ill, he took it upon himself to go to the graves of his ancestors and ask them to take "pity [on] and arouse heaven's mercies" for his father. He returned to his father's bedside to find him recovered. "It was clear to me," he later said, "that it was my prayer at the resting place of my holy forebears that had aroused G-d's loving kindness and compassion." Even as a youth, he had great confidence in his spiritual abilities.[39]

It was also at the age of eleven, in late 1891, that Joseph Isaac first got into trouble with the law for defending his fellow Jews. According to Chabad sources, Joseph attacked a Gentile Russian policeman who was mistreating a Jew. The authorities arrested him for assault but quickly released him. This story, like many about the Rebbe, was probably embellished by later followers who wanted their Rebbe to mirror Moses's reaction to an Egyptian beating a Hebrew slave thousands of years before.[40] Had Joseph Isaac really attacked the policeman, he probably would not have been released without any consequences; or perhaps he got away with a warning, since he was so young and had inflicted no injury. Of all the stories about Joseph Isaac Schneersohn, this is the only one in which he may have resorted to physical force.

One day in 1893, young Joseph's father took him to the graveyard of his ancestors and told him that, just as Abraham had bound up his son Isaac for sacrifice, to honor his covenant with God, he now had to do something similar. He had to bind Joseph to the mission of dedicating his life to the Jewish people. Joseph seemed to understand what his father meant and accepted his responsibility to his people as best he could.[41]

So, at a young age, Joseph became involved with Lubavitch life and the traditions of his forefathers. Joseph spent countless hours walking with his father, discussing moral issues and how they related to the Torah. In 1895, at age fifteen, Joseph became his father's secretary, helping him answer letters and organize the distribution of literature, food, and clothes. He enjoyed these tasks. In addition to his work, he continued to pray and study with great passion. Joseph's father often reminded him that he was "a natural-born *chassid*, and that I must bear this in mind while I eat, talk, pray and study."[42]

At the age of seventeen, Joseph married his cousin Nehamah Dinah, the daughter of Abraham Schneersohn, a prominent rabbi in the Russian city of Khishinev.[43] They soon had three daughters. Joseph became the manager of Chabad schools and an important assistant in his father's organization. In 1904, with the outbreak of the Russo-Japanese War, he and his father led a campaign to provide Passover matzos for Jewish soldiers in the czar's army. After the war, Joseph's father sent him to Germany and Holland to persuade politicians there to intercede on behalf of persecuted Russian Jews. Both father and son spoke out vigorously against the czar's mistreatment of Jews, which often turned deadly, such as during the pogroms of 1905 and 1906.

During World War I, Joseph and his father secured the exemption of Lubavitcher rabbis from front-line military duty by aggressively petitioning the czar's ministers. Ultra-Orthodox and Hasidic Jews often try to avoid serving in the armies of the countries where they live, which is resented by other citizens and perceived as cowardly or unpatriotic by some, unfairly shifting the burden of defending the country to others. In some countries this causes anti-Semitism or, one might say, anti-Orthodoxy. The issue of military service was central to the rise of the Yesh Atid Party in Israel, which wanted ultra-Orthodox Jews to be required to perform their national service; thus, disputes of this nature are not restricted to non-Jewish countries. With this in mind, it was remarkable that the Rebbe got the czar to grant special status to rabbis in the army, given that other Jewish draftees had to serve for decades, if they survived that long. Joseph Isaac was raised, in other words, in an environment of political activism.

Joseph Isaac became the next Rebbe after his father's death in 1920. The dying man asked Joseph to risk his life for the sake of heaven, the Torah, and the preservation of Judaism. Having worked at his father's side for more than three decades, he did not need the admonition.[44] He had trained his whole life for this responsibility.

The new Rebbe, with his chest-length red beard, looked wise beyond his years. He had fiery blue eyes and, though middle-aged, moved with the energy of a teenager. He spent much of his day meeting with people, listening to their problems, and giving them advice. In addition, he answered countless letters from followers who lived too far away to visit. Every month he gave addresses to his cohorts, analyzing the struggles of the human condition from the Torah's perspective. Hundreds of thousands of Jews in Russia and throughout the world looked to him as their leader.

After the October Revolution of 1917, Russia fell into chaos and civil war. Against overwhelming odds, Rebbe Joseph Isaac Schneersohn devoted himself to preserving the Jewish community and religious life in Russia. Under the Bolsheviks, Russia and its successor, the Soviet Union, continued to oppress the Jews, whose fear of persecution, disease, and poverty was well justified. Russian peasants, jealous of the Jews' financial success in banking and business and indoctrinated with the idea that Jews were parasites on society, conducted pogroms that devastated several Hasidic communities. More than 2 million eastern European Jews—many of them afraid for their lives—immigrated to the United States in the late 1800s and early 1900s, seeking freedom, opportunity, and security. Most of them quickly learned that their eastern European Orthodoxy did not serve them well in the modern world, so they discarded their traditional ways and assimilated into American society, where modern Reform Judaism and later Conservative Judaism flourished as the predominant branches. A smaller, more ideologically driven group of Jews immigrated to Palestine to build the future Jewish state.

The Bolsheviks closed many churches and synagogues, seized religious property, and outlawed religious education. The Yevsektzia, which was the Jewish section of the Communist Party, went beyond the law to persecute religious Jews, including the Lubavitchers. Several Yevsektzia members were actually ex-Lubavitchers. Many of the Lubavitcher leaders were arrested on trumped-up counterrevolutionary charges, and in 1920 the Rebbe himself was apprehended. Immediately, a number of Jewish families in the United States urged government officials to intercede on behalf of the Rebbe and his international movement. Thanks to the intervention of prominent Americans, including Senator Robert Wagner of New York and Senator William Borah of Idaho, chairman of the influential Foreign Relations Committee, the Rebbe was eventually released.[45] Because the Soviet Union desired international acceptance, it could not ignore the requests of American politicians without unwanted consequences. Borah in particular was in favor of recognizing the Soviet Union in the international community, so the Russians could not dismiss his request lightly.

The Soviets opposed all religion. Initially they were anti-Judaism but not necessarily anti-Semitic. They had shut hundreds of synagogues and Jewish schools, so the Rebbe was forced to work clandestinely. He supported the "underground education of five thousand children" and dispatched emissaries to all parts of Russia to rebuild Jewish life. During the next two decades, the Rebbe and his followers opened approximately 600 schools throughout the Soviet Union. The Rebbe believed that Jewish education was the single most important guarantor of Jewish survival.[46] He also expanded his building program and set up schools in Poland, which had regained its independence at the end of World War I and had a large Jewish population until World War II. Because of the Soviets' hostility toward religion, the Soviet Union was no longer a safe home for his movement. A few years later the Rebbe founded his largest Lubavitcher yeshiva in Otwock, near Warsaw. Despite considerable anti-Semitism since World War I, Warsaw had become the leading center for Jews in Poland and, some would argue, the major center of Hasidism the world over.[47]

The Rebbe spent much of his time helping his persecuted brethren in the USSR from 1920 to 1927. The departure of most Jewish leaders had created a vacuum that the Rebbe quickly filled. He became head of the rabbinical council for Russian Jewry, and he was soon recognized as the leader of Russian Jews, whether Lubavitch or not. He received tens of thousands of dollars from the American Jewish Joint Distribution Committee, a secular humanitarian aid organization, to support his cultural work. Although he did a lot of good with these funds, he was criticized for "showing partiality toward Lubavitch institutions" and not distributing the money equally among the various religious sects he oversaw as

Chabad yeshiva in Otwock, Poland. (Chaim Miller)

head of the rabbinical council.[48] The Rebbe strongly denied these accusations. The Yevsektzia did not care about his focus; it simply disapproved of his receipt of funds to conduct religious activities. Because of the campaign against him, he was imprisoned multiple times in the USSR in the early 1920s, but each time he was eventually released, since there was no evidence to prove his anticommunist activities. As he saw it, he was not anticommunist but pro-Judaism. Upon his release, he would immediately resume his work. He believed he was a "true soldier for God," and his activities almost cost him his life on several occasions, but supportive friends and foreign politicians protected him.

In 1927 Soviet authorities arrested the Rebbe and charged him with operating an underground school and embezzlement. This detention would prove his most challenging struggle yet, as it carried a sentence of death. When the police came for him, his hysterical mother cried out, "What is this? Why have they come? Shall they extend their hands against innocent people, against my son who strives to help others? No! . . . I will not let them take my darling. I will go in your place. Take me. . . . Do not disturb my son, my only son who responds to others in their hour of distress. . . . Woe unto us, my dear departed husband . . . ! They are taking our son Yosef Yitzchak—your only son who sacrifices himself for others." The authorities ignored her. The Rebbe gathered several items to take with him, including some religious books. When asked what his followers should do, he told his son-in-law, Rabbi Samarius Gourary, "First let emissaries be sent to the graves of my father and my ancestors, in Rostov, Lubavitch, Nyezin, and Haditz to inform them of my plight. Also, ask all of the *chassidim* to recite Psalms during the first days."[49] This focus on communing with the dead demonstrates the community's adherence to the Hasidic concept that the answer to virtually all problems is religious. Their first thought, as usual, was not to seek a human solution to the problem but rather to plead for divine intervention. Is this because the Hasidic sect arose in a time and place where its members were oppressed, endangered, and utterly powerless, to the extent they believed any action they took would almost certainly be futile? One can only imagine what the antireligious authorities thought about this very strange man who, in his hour of need, pleaded for an audience with his dead grandfathers.

Interestingly, while the authorities were arresting the Rebbe, his middle daughter, Moussia, returned home from an unchaperoned date with Menachem Mendel Schneerson. This was unheard of for Hasidic couples, and it remains controversial to this day. The two young people had snuck away to enjoy some time alone, and they returned to find the Rebbe's court under siege. Seeing the commotion at the house, Moussia left Menachem Mendel and entered her home alone. Once she ascertained what was happening, she was able to go to a window and signal him to leave the area. As the Rebbe was being hauled off, his secretary Chaim Lieberman started to destroy incriminating correspondence and focused on doing everything he could to protect the treasures of the Rebbe's library.

In prison, the authorities beat the Rebbe horribly during his interrogations. According to Lubavitcher sources, one waved a gun in his face and said, "This little toy has made many a man change his mind." The Rebbe replied, "That little toy can intimidate only the kind of man who lives in only this world and indulges in worldly passions. Because I have only one God and two worlds, I am not impressed by your little toy." Despite his defiance, he was frightened when he heard other prisoners being taken outside the cell block at night and shot. Nonetheless, he kept his composure. When ordered to denounce his religion, the Rebbe told his interrogators, "I have already declared that I will not abandon my principles. No man or demon has been born, nor will be born that will make me budge even slightly." He was beaten for refusing to stand when the guards entered his cell. In quieter moments, he thought about his family and wondered whether the authorities had harmed them or his precious manuscripts.[50] Outside the prison, many thought the Soviets would kill him outright or send him off to Siberia, where he would die in a forced-labor camp.

Besides thinking of his ancestors and his family, in his darkest moments the Rebbe was often preoccupied with his books, which he considered necessary to the continuation of Chabad. Judaism had survived through the generations due to the preservation of the books of the Bible and other religious texts. For centuries, Jews had gone to great lengths to preserve the writings of the great masters, and Schneersohn carried on this sacred tradition. He felt that he represented the continuation of a movement that had gone on for one and a half centuries, and he was the embodiment of all its leaders and spiritual power. When asked his age, the Rebbe responded, "A hundred and fifty years old." He viewed himself as a reincarnation of all the Rebbes since the beginning of the movement and referred to them in the present tense. The Lubavitchers believed the Rebbe had inherited the patriarch Jacob's secret knowledge about the "dialectical relationship between life and death," giving him insights stemming directly from characters in the Bible. Such convictions must have given him strength to endure this trial.[51]

While Rebbe Schneersohn remained in prison, his future son-in-law and future seventh Rebbe, Menachem Mendel Schneerson, risked his own life, frantically destroying incriminating papers documenting the Rebbe's illegal religious activities in the Soviet Union.[52] Others, including his son-in-law Samarius Gourary, did everything they could to protect him.

When the authorities took his tefillin, prayer shawl, and religious books, Schneersohn went on a hunger strike. Without his tefillin and his books, he could not pray or study properly. Remarkably, and for reasons that remain unknown, his possessions were returned three days later. Equally remarkable was his guards' benign treatment, considering that he brazenly called his interrogator an "ignoramus" and a "vile creature." Making his imprisonment even more difficult, he refused to eat the unkosher prison food and depended on his family to deliver meals to him.[53]

In addition to the hundreds of people led by Schneerson and Gourary who were working for the Rebbe's rescue, a number of leaders around the world pressured the Soviets to free him. They included chief rabbi Abraham Isaac Kook of Palestine; modern Orthodox rabbi Israel Hildesheimer and Reform rabbi Leo Baeck of Germany; the Union of Orthodox Rabbis in the United States; Chabad of America and Canada; and Mordechai Dubin, a wealthy member of the Latvian parliament and of Agudah (or Agudath Israel), an anti-Zionist organization that represented Orthodox Jews. Under its president Hyman Kramer, US Chabad published numerous articles and announcements in newspapers to muster diplomatic support. Its legal counsel, Sam Kramer, worked tirelessly with politicians. Lawyers Fred and Arthur Rabinovitz, sons of Rabbi Dovid Rabinovitz, a fervent follower of the Rebbe, secured an appointment with Supreme Court justice Louis Brandeis, who approached several government officials, including Senators Borah and Wagner. Even President Calvin Coolidge eventually asked the Soviets to free the Rebbe.[54]

Under this pressure, the Soviets released Schneersohn from the notorious Spalerka prison in Leningrad and sent him into exile in Kostrama, in the Urals of eastern Russia. The Rebbe told his followers:

> We must proclaim openly and before all, that any matter affecting the Jewish religion, Torah, and its *mitzvot* and customs is not subject to the coercion of others. No one can impose his belief upon us, nor coerce us to conduct ourselves contrary to our beliefs. It is our solemn and sacred task to cry out and state with the ancient steadfastness of the Jewish people—with courage derived from thousands of years of self-sacrifice: "Touch not My anointed [Jewish people] nor attempt to do evil to my prophets." . . . We must remember that imprisonment and hard labor are only of this physical world and of brief duration, while Torah, *mitzvot*, and the Jewish people are eternal.[55]

His defiance of the Soviet Union made him well known throughout the Jewish world, and he became a hero for many ultrareligious Jews.

Commenting on the sixth Rebbe's time in prison, the seventh Lubavitcher Rebbe said of his father-in-law: "Indeed, this stance of heroic self-sacrifice in the face of great peril was an all-pervasive quality that characterized all of the Rebbe's activities, even prior to his arrest for the promulgation of Torah and the strengthening of Judaism in that land." Rebbe Menachem Schneerson continued, "Fulfillment of Torah and its commands was in the manner of 'hewn letters,' intrinsic to the essence of his identity. Therefore, his self-sacrifice was not a function of intellectual deliberation as to whether an action was obligatory or desirable. His response to existential challenge occurred naturally, because his service of G-d was the very core of his own existence."[56] The Rebbe viewed all good deeds as actions of God. He interpreted his liberation, including the political favors he received, as God's will.

Others did not have influential people to intercede on their behalf. Many Jewish leaders died in Siberian gulags, where the Soviets worked them to death; others died in front of firing squads. Often the Rebbe sent his students to act as emissaries throughout Russia, knowing full well that they were in grave danger. Almost like an officer going into battle, the Rebbe knew he would suffer casualties, but he regarded this as a necessary sacrifice in the battle for the spiritual welfare of Jews.[57]

Yet, in spite of the danger from Russian authorities, the Rebbe remained defiant. He cursed the Soviet authorities, saying that if they harmed Torah scholars, "may they be left without hands." In risking death to serve his people, he was doing what Chabad leaders before him had done. All the previous Rebbes, except for his father, had been thrown in jail at some point. The founder of Chabad, Schneur Zalman, had received a death sentence and spent fifty-three days in prison in St. Petersburg; his release is celebrated by Lubavitchers as the Festival of Liberation. The sixth Rebbe considered Zalman's liberation "a spiritual matter" in which the forces of good had triumphed over evil and "an episode that ultimately brought about a distinctive turn of good fortune upon the entire House of Israel." He even believed that Zalman had willed the whole event to create good out of evil, since *Tzadikim* rule "over all material matters."[58] His own imprisonment must have had profound meaning for him as well. How-

The Jacobson family: Israel Jacobson, executive head of
Chabad in the United States, with his wife, Shaina, and their
daughters (left to right) Rachel, Chaya Sarah, and Chava.
(Eliezer Zaklikovsky)

ever, it never occurred to him and his followers that if these men really
had "rule over all material matters," they would not have been arrested
in the first place.

In 1927, soon after he was exiled, the Soviets forced the Rebbe to
emigrate. They wanted him to leave immediately, but he refused to go
without his possessions, especially his sacred manuscripts and books; his
library had become part of the movement's reservoir of spiritual infor-

mation. The authorities, surprisingly, relented and allowed him to take his library. Needing a considerable sum of money to immigrate with his family and his possessions to Latvia (which had become an independent nation after World War I), the Rebbe enlisted the help of the executive head of US Chabad, Rabbi Israel Jacobson.

By 1927, Chabad had grown into a small but strong organization in the United States. In the early 1920s, when the Rebbe had asked for volunteers to go to America and set up a platform to help Lubavitchers immigrate there, Israel Jacobson had been the only one to raise his hand. Many thought him crazy, but Jacobson felt called to help the future of Chabad. He left Poland with his wife and three daughters and arrived in New York City in 1925, bringing the Rebbe's blessing with him. The Rebbe knew the Jews' days in the Soviet Union and even in Poland were numbered, and he believed the United States offered the best future home for their movement. Jacobson initially had a difficult time earning a living in New York, but he eventually found work as a rabbi and Torah teacher. Soon Jacobson was raising money for the Rebbe, and by 1927, he was sending thousands of dollars overseas each year to support the Rebbe's activities. Once the communist regime's antireligious economic policies resulted in the confiscation of most of Chabad's resources, America became a major source of funds for the Rebbe's movement.[59]

A word of historical caution is in order here. Today, Chabad is a global organization with significant resources. Although its total budget is unknown, it is generally assumed to be in the vicinity of $1 billion annually, so by today's standards, the sums Chabad sought to raise in 1927 were a mere pittance.

On receiving the Rebbe's appeal for funds to immigrate, Jacobson met with Lubavitchers Sam and Avraham Kramer and Rabbi Menachem Mendel Leib Lokshin and asked them to quickly raise $4,000 (comparable to $53,000 in 2015 dollars). They debated the possibility of raising that much money in such a short time, but Jacobson insisted it could be done. The Kramers were skeptical and thought Jacobson lacked an understanding of business, but Lokshin persuaded them to come up with the funds. Proving their resourcefulness, they managed to raise the money, and Jacobson wired it to the Rebbe. The Rebbe and his entire family, along with six followers, all his household possessions, and a large library, left Russia

Mordechai Dubin, Latvian senator and prominent Chabad leader. (Chaim Miller)

immediately, occupying four train cars. Two days later the Rebbe's party arrived in Riga, Latvia, a medium-sized, industrialized port city with wide boulevards and a renowned collection of Art Nouveau buildings.[60]

Once in Riga, the Rebbe began to transfer his vast library to Poland. With the help of Mordechai Dubin, an influential Jewish Latvian senator, he and his family became Latvian citizens.[61] It was a sad day when he realized he would never return to Russia, but he knew God's work was taking him elsewhere, and he had several representatives within the USSR to encourage the Lubavitchers there and address their needs. If a community needed clothes, food, or prayer books, he made sure it received them, and he continued to build a network of underground schools.[62] He felt his miraculous escape was a sign from God that he should continue his mission.

In 1929 the Rebbe traveled to Palestine and the United States. According to media sources, he talked to thousands of Jews at hundreds of gatherings to raise funds for the movement. He also wanted to explore the possibility of bringing Chabad's headquarters to the United States. Accompanied by Mordechai Dubin and son-in-law Samarius Gourary,

Two New York City policemen escort Rebbe Joseph Isaac Schneersohn off the SS *France* as he arrives in America on 17 September 1929 for a ten-month goodwill tour. Hundreds of people showed up to see him. During his stay, he would meet several prominent politicians, including President Hoover. (Author's collection)

he set foot on American soil on 17 September to start a ten-month tour of the United States. He was greeted by 600 Orthodox rabbis and thousands of Jews on Pier A at Battery Park in New York and hailed as a Jewish hero. It was the end of the Roaring Twenties, just a month before the stock market crash that ushered in the Great Depression. The police commissioner welcomed him on behalf of the mayor and provided a motorcycle escort. Because of his reputation as a great spiritual leader, the authorities took him seriously. He was especially touched by this warm reception, given the Arab pogroms against Jews that had occurred after his visit to the Holy Land. When asked about those events, he would cry. "The blood-spilling attacks on Jews which broke out one day after my departure from there [Palestine], have utterly devastated me," he said, "and I have still not recovered from the blow." The riots that led to the deaths of seventy Jews may have stemmed from the Rebbe's visit to a holy site in Hebron known as the Tomb of the Patriarchs. That place, holy to Christians, Jews, and Muslims because Abraham, Isaac, Jacob, Sarah, Rebecca, and Leah are thought to be buried there, was supposedly off-limits to Jews, and the Rebbe's visit enraged Muslim zealots.[63] In spite of his sorrow, he was "very happy to step upon this glorious country of freedom, liberty and opportunity for all, irrespective of race, color and creed." He continued, "May the Almighty bless this great country that has been a refuge for our Jewish people. I express my deepest appreciation to the Mayor and all public officials for extending this welcome."[64]

Shortly after his arrival, the Rebbe retired to a quiet room to pray and study his religious books. After a few days of rest, he turned his attention to generating support for Jews persecuted under the Soviets. The United States, which had broken off diplomatic relations in 1917, did not recognize the Soviet Union until 1933. The 2 million Jews living under Stalin, the Rebbe said, faced both economic and religious annihilation. Unless funds were raised for them, they would be poor in body and spirit, deprived not only of food and clothing but also of Torah study and instruction. Despite the Great Depression, the Rebbe collected tens of thousands of dollars. In Chicago alone, according to Lubavitcher sources, he raised $30,000. Speaking at Jewish gatherings, he also campaigned for the building of more yeshivas and synagogues throughout the United States and Europe. He also used this time in the United States to cement his lead-

In July 1930 Rebbe Schneersohn met President Hoover at the White House. He was accompanied by (left to right) Fred Rabinovitz, a lawyer for Chabad; H. Fogelman, vice president of Chabad; Hyman Kramer, president of Chabad in the United States; and his son-in-law Rabbi Samarius Gourary, Chabad's foreign secretary. (Eliezer Zaklikovsky)

ership of US Chabad. A breakaway group led by one of his teachers had turned against him, and it was important for the Rebbe to prove to all that he was the legitimate head of Chabad. Accompanied by Samarius Gourary and Hyman Kramer, he met with a number of dignitaries, including President Herbert Hoover, who had headed the program of US food aid to Europe during World War I, and Jewish Supreme Court justice Louis Brandeis, who had led the world Zionist movement during the war.[65]

On his return to Europe, the Rebbe continued his work in Poland, where he had moved from Latvia. By 1935, his yeshiva there had become internationally known for its Hasidic teaching of Chabad philosophy, the Torah, and the Talmud.[66] Throughout the 1930s he urged Jews everywhere to repent from their sinful ways and to become observant so that God would bless them rather than rebuke them with punishment. If they did, the *Mashiach* (Messiah) would come sooner.[67] In 1936, after living in Warsaw for two years, Schneersohn moved to the resort town of Otwock, fifteen miles south of the capital, where the fresh country air was better for his health.[68]

At age fifty-six, the Rebbe had already suffered a heart attack and a stroke. He also had multiple sclerosis, a degenerative disease of the central nervous system, with symptoms that can range from numbness and paralysis to incontinence. The disease affected the Rebbe's speech and his ability to walk; his teenage grandson Barry Gourary was often at his side to assist him.[69] The Rebbe's mind, however, was still sharp, and he refused to let the disease restrict his activities, which sometimes included smoking more than a pack of cigarettes a day (except, of course, on the Sabbath). Given that the Rebbe expected immediate, concrete expressions of divine favor for observant Jews, his own failing health might be seen as an indication of God's retribution. However, Chabad had interesting ways of rationalizing hardship: If the Rebbe could escape prison without harm, it was because he was able to control the physical world and secure God's blessing. If the Rebbe was ravaged by disease, it was because he had worked so hard for God. The followers never considered that the Rebbe's escape from Russia was attributable to some well-meaning people who had intervened on his behalf, or that his bad health was perhaps due to a lack of exercise, obesity, smoking, and his genetic makeup. At five feet eight inches tall and weighing more than 200 pounds, he did not cut an impressive figure. Yet most Lubavitchers thought him a giant. They were impressed not by his physical presence but by his spiritual aura.

4

The Rebbe in German-Occupied Poland

Si vis pacem, para bellum [If you want peace, prepare for war].
—Publius Flavius Vegetius Renatus, *De Rei Milittari*

Early on 1 September 1939, a hot Friday morning, many of the yeshiva students in Otwock, about fifteen miles southeast of Warsaw, awoke to the sound of explosions. No one knew what was going on. Only several hours later did they learn that Hitler had invaded Poland. "It was like thunder from the skies," wrote Joseph Wineberg, then a student. Barry Gourary, the Rebbe's grandson, remembered dressing in his room while the whole place shook as if there were an earthquake. The horrors of war quickly made their way to Otwock. The Chabad Jewish orphanage took a direct hit that killed ten children during the first bombardment. Another bomb struck the house where the Rebbe, his mother, his secretary Haskell Feigin, and many others, including Israel Jacobson's daughter and son-in-law, lived. No one was injured.[1]

As soon as the yeshiva students realized what was happening, they ran to the Rebbe for advice. Gazing at them with his clear blue eyes and stroking his gray beard, he asked his six American students to leave immediately for neighboring Latvia. "Do not be afraid of the bombs," he counseled them. "Every bomb has an address, and your address is not on any of them."[2] Rabbi Shmuel Fox remembered the Rebbe saying, "God will protect you wherever you will be and He will not let any harm be done to you."[3] After offering this encouragement, the Rebbe gave Rabbi Meir Greenberg, one of the departing students, a message for his Latvian friend Mordechai Dubin. He asked Dubin to do everything possible to bring him and his family to Latvia before it was too late, since they were Latvian citizens.[4] He also advised several of the remaining students to try to make their way to Vilna in independent Lithuania. Before night came, heavy curtains were placed over the windows in the Rebbe's house, and makeshift gas masks consisting of cotton and soda water were prepared in case the Nazis returned. Rabbi Samarius Gourary described the mood that Sabbath night: "The chandeliers hung unlit, shivering in the eerie atmosphere."[5] The future was uncertain for all.

Late that night the six American students, Meir Greenberg and Mordechai Dov Altein among them, left for the American consulate in Warsaw, where they were brusquely turned away. The consulate claimed it could not help. The students believed the consulate denied them assistance because they were Hasidic Jews.[6] The following day all six left Warsaw by train, heading for Riga. A journey that should have taken twelve hours took twelve days because of congested tracks and a breakdown in communications between train stations. The Rebbe relaxed only when he received the news that they had arrived safely. Once in Latvia, Rabbi Greenberg delivered the Rebbe's message to Dubin. A few days later he boarded a ship for the United States, along with his fellow students.[7]

Although most of the young Polish yeshiva students should have been in the army, only one of them, Hirsch Kotlarsky, had been deemed physically fit to serve. "Most of the other students," Kotlarsky said, "were not physically fit because of all the Torah study. I was of strong build and as a result I was drafted into the cavalry." According to available records, no Lubavitcher volunteered for military service. Most believed that God would save them, though they feared the authorities would draft them. As Wineberg said, "I was afraid that now that war had begun I would be mobilized." Like other ultrareligious Jews, the Lubavitchers did not feel obliged to fight for the country where they lived. On the contrary, they believed one should focus on Torah study and God and that such study would protect Jewish lives and guard Jewish souls. Even a few years later, according to a survivor of the Warsaw ghetto uprising in 1943, the remaining young Hasidic Jews refused to take up arms and fight; instead, they gave themselves over to prayer. "We, Jews, not having any sword at all, do not possess even this thin ray of hope," the Rebbe's newspaper declared, "and our fate does not depend at all upon anything material but is entirely reliant upon the heavenly mercy." War, the Rebbe declared, is the "greatest insanity."[8] This attitude is still present in Israel, where most ultra-Orthodox Jewish men seek religious exemptions from military service because of their Torah studies; religious women are exempt because military service is deemed incompatible with their role. Nonreligious women serve, as do religious women from the nationalistic Zionist camp.

War may be the "greatest insanity," but as history has repeatedly shown, nations that fail to prepare for war often disappear off the map. It is sad that cultures like the Lubavitchers expect others to fight for their freedom and safety while they pray to be delivered from danger by a miracle. The Lubavitchers in Europe might have done better if they had adhered to the loose interpretation of a phrase ascribed to the Russian Marxist Leon Trotsky: "You may not be interested in war, but war is interested in you," so you should prepare for it. Many Poles in 1939 found the ultra-Orthodox and Hasidic Jews' avoidance of military service unpatriotic. Some Polish soldiers even attacked Hasidic Jews, perhaps manifesting both anti-Semitism and frustration with this minority for shirking service. Lubavitchers did not understand this, and in 1939 the Rebbe apparently did not call on his community to protect the very nation that had given him refuge when he needed it most, after being expelled from Russia.[9]

The Rebbe's pacifism also shows an inherent weakness within his community. Deciding not to fight is not a good option in this world. As the intellectual Sam Harris writes, "The worst that is said of [pacifism], generally, is that it is a difficult position to maintain in practice. It is almost never branded as flagrantly immoral, which I believe it is. While it can seem noble enough when the stakes are low, pacifism is ultimately nothing more than a willingness to die, and to let others die, at the pleasure of the world's thugs."[10] In the face of immoral hooligans like Hitler, who wielded powerful forces against people who constituted much of the world in 1939, nonviolence and pacifism were generally enablers. In other words, the Rebbe should have encouraged his people to volunteer for the military in some free country and do all they could to help fight Hitler. Instead, the Rebbe talked of religion and uttered what nonbelievers perceived as idle curses against Hitler, refusing to see that only physical violence against the Nazis would turn the tide.[11]

Although many tried to convince the Rebbe to leave Poland, he wanted to stay with his family and his followers, believing God would soon defeat the "evil Germans."[12] When his followers urged him to leave, the Rebbe replied, "A Jewish Shepherd does not leave his flock alone especially in times of crisis."[13] There were obvious signs that he was not safe. Several officials in the Polish government had started to move south from Warsaw, intending to slip across the border into Romania if Poland lost the war. The Polish high command also announced plans to evacuate. These actions caused panic among the population. If the government and the military were leaving Warsaw, many felt the Rebbe should leave as well. Citing the verse "I (the Almighty) am with him (the Jewish people) in times of misfortune," the Rebbe stayed.[14]

With all Hitler's success over the past six years—politically, diplomatically, and now militarily—the Rebbe would have been wise to acknowledge that maybe God did not intend to intervene. A few years later, Auschwitz would turn the Rebbe's belief on its head. Given the lightning speed with which Hitler took over Poland and the 3.5 million Jews who lived there, it seemed that God had abandoned them altogether. Despite his bravado, the Rebbe sensed the danger and entertained other options; he was scared and considered choosing the path to safety rather than staying with his people. To leave or to stay was a dilemma facing both religious and political leaders. Leaving their people behind could be considered abandonment, yet political leaders could reconstitute their governments in exile, and religious leaders could rebuild their congregations in a safer environment and use their influence to save those left behind. Self-preservation was an obvious factor in these decisions, but it was seldom offered as the reason for leaving, and the Rebbe was no exception.

Late on 4 September, realizing how dangerous it was becoming in Otwock, the Rebbe traveled to Warsaw with his family and a group of students, hoping to escape from there to the Latvian capital of Riga. The Rebbe felt horrible about forsaking thousands of his fellow Jews, but he knew that only from Riga could he conduct rescue operations.[15] With tears streaming down his face, he told those who were staying behind, "Be well, everyone, and accept upon yourselves the yoke of Heaven. The king guards his subjects, and you, Jewish children, may Hashem [God][16] guard you wherever you will be, and us, wherever we will be." The Latvian consulate in Warsaw had sent a private car with foreign license plates to carry the Rebbe on his fifteen-mile trip to the capital. He took the most valuable Lubavitcher manuscripts, regretting that he could not take his "household effects and the entire Library," which numbered around 40,000 works.[17] Many have faulted the Rebbe for leaving his people in their hour of need and not being deported along with them, like the brave Rabbi Leo Baeck or the Hasidic Radomsker Rebbe. In fact, when his followers urged him to escape, the Radomsker Rebbe "cut everyone off with a prophetic statement: 'What will happen to three million Jews will happen to me. I'm not running away.'"[18] Yet, one can also argue that, just as General Douglas MacArthur obeyed orders and left his surrounded troops on Corregidor Island in the Philippines in 1942 so he could lead another army and fight another day, the Rebbe's escape allowed him to continue to lead his community during its worst days. At least he was not as bad as the Satmar Rebbe, who ordered his followers to remain in Hungary, where the Nazis exterminated almost all of them, while he secured a place on the Katzner transport to Bergen-Belsen and from there to neutral Switzerland.[19]

Mutilated bodies, dead horses, and the charred remains of buildings lined the road to Warsaw. The Luftwaffe continued to rain explosives on the highways leading to the capital, targeting civilians who were trying to escape.[20] One witness described helpless Poles hiding repeatedly in ditches and gutters from "Death on Wings."[21] Black plumes of smoke rose high on the western horizon as the Germans moved closer to Warsaw. Weary Polish soldiers and frightened citizens in search of protection and food hurried toward the capital in the vain hope of outrunning the Wehrmacht. The constant attacks of Stuka dive-bombers, with their high-pitched sirens, unnerved people as the sky and the earth were welded together in chaos. Robert Citino described the carnage during this campaign as "a truly apocalyptic moment in the history of modern military operations."[22] Polish general Wladyslaw Anders witnessed a Stuka pilot diving down on a group of children: "As he dropped his bombs and fired his machine guns, the children scattered like sparrows. The airplane disappeared as quickly as it had come, but on the field some crumpled and lifeless bundles of bright clothing remained. The nature of the new war was already clear." Besides attacking refugees, Luftwaffe pilots "brazenly attacked Red Cross aid stations." Hitler initially claimed his planes struck only military targets, but he later acknowledged that they bombed Polish cities to show the civilians the "pointlessness of their resistance."[23]

The journey to Warsaw seemed to take forever, but Rebbe Joseph Isaac Schneersohn assured his family and his followers they had nothing to fear. "God will provide safety to all of us," he said, and he told them that his father, Sholom Dovber, was interceding for them in heaven.[24] His faith calmed the group, and his words of comfort were welcome. Although most good leaders do not talk to the deceased in times of crisis, that is exactly what the Rebbe did. He believed the righteous can intervene before the throne of heaven and protect individual Jews. He was a charismatic leader, and his followers took comfort in his belief that he could commune with the departed. As Schneersohn reassured his flock, his car slowly made its way to the Polish capital, supposedly with legions of dead Jews in heaven on their side.

Although the Germans had not yet closed in, the atmosphere in Warsaw was that of a city under siege. Upon reaching a Jewish neighborhood in the north of Warsaw, Schneersohn decided to remain there to help his students escape to neutral countries and arrange for the safe transport of his yeshiva's precious documents. Many yeshiva students did not wait for help and departed on foot for Vilna, Lithuania. This was a smart move. In keeping with the secret provisions of the Ribbentrop-Molotov pact, the Soviets invaded and occupied eastern Poland on 17 September and would close the border with Lithuania in November. By then, around 2,500 Orthodox yeshiva students and numerous rabbis, many of them Lubavitchers, had managed to reach Vilna from Poland.[25] Unable to walk so far, the Rebbe could not escape after the Nazis bombed the train station and there were no more trains leaving for Riga. Trapped in Warsaw, the Rebbe stayed at the home of Rabbi Herschel Gurari on Bonifraterska Street, a dark apartment building in a remote area inhabited by a group of Lubavitcher Jews.

To enter the Rebbe's new neighborhood was to step back in time. The men wore the traditional black caftans and large fur hats typical of Polish noblemen in the seventeenth century, dressing nothing like their contemporary Polish neighbors. Following strict Hasidic customs, the women dressed modestly, covered their heads with wigs and scarves, and avoided eye contact with men.

By the time the Rebbe reached this part of Warsaw, few people dared to leave their homes. Germany, he quickly learned, had already seized

The Warsaw train station on 2 November 1939, after it was bombed. (National Archives)

large sections of the country. If he wanted to escape, he would have to hurry because the German Fourth Panzer Division had already reached the western outskirts of Warsaw.[26]

The "enemy is at the gates, and he sends his angels of death to proclaim his coming," wrote Chaim Kaplan. Many Jews probably had thoughts of the "vicious, destroying angel, the Angel of Death," since this supernatural creature, whose task is "taking the soul from the body," fills Orthodox and Hasidic literature. On 8 September Joseph Wineberg described the chaotic crowds in Warsaw as they ran "through the streets . . . crying and wailing" during the bomb attacks. His brother wanted to seize the opportunity and try to escape the city, but Wineberg told him they should put on tefillin, say their prayers, and ask God for guidance. His brother agreed, and they prayed together. Later, they learned the Germans had ambushed those who had tried to leave the city using their intended route, and Wineberg believed God had saved them. When he asked the Rebbe if they should attempt to flee anyway, Schneersohn replied, "If there is a sure way to escape, then escape, but if not, then we must trust that Hashem will take care of us."[27]

According to Lubavitchers, the suffering of the Warsaw Jews grieved the Rebbe. His bright eyes grew dull as he busied himself with prayers. Like Rabbi Wineberg, many others came to ask the Rebbe's advice, reciting the psalms, "shedding tears, [and] beseeching G-d to save them." One morning the Rebbe told his followers that his father had visited him in his sleep and declared that they should "fall at Hashem's feet and ask for mercy because Hashem will respect such a plea."[28] Many took his advice and prayed fervently.

As soon as the Germans attacked, Polish civil authorities instructed the population through newspapers and the radio to continue to dig trenches and build barricades and defense works. Jews came out in droves to help defend Warsaw, even on the Sabbath. But the Lubavitchers did not join in the defense of the city. Most believed that the best way for them to help was to pray constantly and to keep the Sabbath and other rituals sacred, even though Jews had recognized for thousands of years that saving lives takes precedence over the Sabbath. If the Lubavitchers had studied history more closely, they might have learned that the Jews' failure to defend Jerusalem on the Sabbath had allowed Roman general Pompey (Gnaeus

German soldiers and Polish citizens view the destruction of Warsaw from its outskirts. (United States Holocaust Memorial Museum Archive of Photographs)

Pompeius Magnus) to take the city in 63 BCE. The Polish police resented the Lubavitchers' intransigence and rounded them up from their homes, gave them a "generous helping of deadly lashes and beatings," and then forced them to join work details.[29] Prayer and Sabbath ceremonies were not stopping the Germans from conquering the city.

Thousands of refugees were entering Warsaw daily. On 9 September the commander of its garrison issued an order to the troops: "We have occupied positions from which there is no retreat. At this outpost we must die to the last soldier." By 11 September, thousands more terrified people had flooded into the already packed city, which was "not safe from disaster."[30] The consequences were devastating: when the Luftwaffe and the army bombarded the city, multitudes of innocent civilians perished, having no place to hide. The stench of burning skin and decomposing bodies trapped in the rubble filled the air. Public parks were used as makeshift graveyards to bury the dead. When the air-raid sirens sounded, people scrambled through the streets; those whose homes had already been destroyed searched for basements or ditches to jump into. Everyone feared death and likely felt as if they might be taking their last breath or seeing their last glimpse of life. A sense of helplessness came over them, for when the bombs were dropped, there was little they could do if one fell in their direction. The fate of so many could be summed up by the words of Herman Melville: "All men live enveloped in whale-lines. All are born with halters round their necks; but it is only when caught in the swift, sudden turn of death, that mortals realize the silent, subtle, ever present perils of life." Most residents of Warsaw, having no earthly idea when the war would end, felt like "dead men on leave."³¹

Fearing that the Nazis would target Jewish neighborhoods, many of the Rebbe's followers urged him to move to the Latvian consulate, which had expressed support for him as a distinguished citizen. The consul general invited the Rebbe to come, but he was unable to get there because city authorities had blocked off the streets. On 12 September, as the severest bombing of the Rebbe's sector of the city occurred, he took refuge in a cellar. Forty people suddenly occupied a room built for no more than twenty. The air became thick with the smell of unbathed bodies that had endured two weeks of war. Long, sleepless nights and warm, nerve-racking days had pushed the cowering occupants to the limits of human endurance. Late that afternoon, the cellar began to tremble from the explosions as the air-raid sirens blared throughout the city. Warsaw's streets erupted into flames. Tall buildings collapsed on their inhabitants, crushing some and burying others alive. As Schneersohn and the others looked to heaven through the dark ceiling, they feared that the cellar walls, "like the walls at Jericho," would fall down on them.³² As dust from the cracking brick and cement filled the room, many darted out and took refuge in another building nearby. The Rebbe had instructed several students to carry some of his most prized books with them during the attacks, but in the chaos of the bombings, several volumes were lost, causing the Rebbe much distress.³³

Despite everything, he continued to prepare for Rosh Hashanah, the Jewish New Year, on 14 September. He would not let a war interrupt his religious observances. Right before the celebration, air-raid sirens

Poles look through the ruins of a section of Warsaw destroyed by the Germans.
The German bombardment killed close to 40,000 civilians and severely damaged
25 percent of the city. (Jerzy Tomaszewski and United States Holocaust
Memorial Museum Archive of Photographs)

sounded throughout the city, followed by silence. Slowly, the roar of
hundreds of approaching planes echoed in the streets. As the bombs fell,
several hit the Rebbe's home, which erupted into flames. Remarkably,
he escaped the building and moved to another part of the city, where the
ceremony continued.

Rosh Hashanah represents a "time of trial and judgment," a time for
people to take "stock" of their "fulfillment of the Torah and its *mitzvot*."
During this time, the Rebbe emphasized, a person "takes account of the
fact that [in the Heavenly Court] the prosecuting angels . . . bring to mind
and verify the existence of all the sins . . . he was guilty [of] in the course
of the year, and demand that he be sentenced to harsh . . . punishment. He
further considers that if at this time he truthfully regrets his past, this will
alter things for him."[34] The Jewish New Year took on new significance as
the Lubavitchers searched their hearts to discover what they had done to

Drawing by Gerd Grimm, a "half Jewish" German soldier, of a
Polish town being attacked in 1939. (Author's collection)

cause such misfortune. According to the Rebbe's philosophy, when bad
things happened, it was God telling the Jews they needed to reform their
physical and spiritual behavior to counteract the negative events around
them.

As Rosh Hashanah began, according to Rabbi Samarius Gourary, a
thousand Jews came to the Rebbe's new quarters. They gathered in the
streets, in the courtyard, and in the building. They wanted to be close

to the Rebbe. To those who continued to urge him to move, at least to a non-Jewish area of the city, he explained, "My children are drowning, our brethren are in the greatest danger, and you want me to separate myself from them, hiding in another neighborhood? No, I will stay with the other hundreds and thousands of Jews, and my lot will be theirs." Rabbi Gourary himself had an opportunity to leave with his wife and son, but they all refused to abandon the Rebbe.[35]

During the two days of Rosh Hashanah, German planes bombed the Jewish section of Warsaw without mercy, and basement air-raid shelters often became mass graves. The Rebbe offered his followers the consolation that, even though they had had a bitter Rosh Hashanah, God would make it sweet for them. In other words, the trials they endured brought them closer to God.[36]

As more buildings were destroyed, the Rebbe moved from house to house. Because of his multiple sclerosis, his followers often had to carry him, but they considered it an honor to touch the Rebbe and transport him to safety. During one attack, an explosion threw the Rebbe from one side of a courtyard to the other. Remarkably, he was uninjured and merely asked for his things to be gathered and for help in finding shelter. His eighty-year-old mother, who was wheelchair bound and almost deaf, had to be carried through the chaos on a stretcher.[37]

The Rebbe had his students carry his prayer shawl and the Baal Shem Tov's prayer book wherever he traveled. Despite the hardships of war, he continued to study the Torah. On 14 September, when the Rebbe's house was bombed and a nearby wall collapsed, he sat at his desk studying his Torah while the place was showered with shrapnel.[38] As the air attack continued, Wineberg and a few others transferred the Rebbe's mother to safety. At her new location, she realized she had forgotten her eyeglasses and asked Wineberg to retrieve them so she could read her prayer book. He had to jump over several bodies and skirt several fires to get back to the old home, where he found both the glasses and a room full of Jews engaged in prayer. When he returned to Sara, he told her that things had calmed down and everyone who had stayed behind was praying. "Oh, I missed witnessing a *bracha*," she said, referring to the witnessing of an act of piousness.[39]

As the bombs rained down during the next attack, the air around the

Rebbe's dwelling became filled with a strange gray substance. Fearing the worst, some screamed hysterically, "Gas. Oh, no, gas!" Stories of the gassing of soldiers in the trenches of the western front during World War I were well known. When gas shells exploded, the deadly cloud might blister the skin and then irritate the lungs to the point that victims drowned in their own body fluids. So when the Lubavitchers thought the Germans had hit them with gas, panic broke out. Disregarding her own safety, the Rebbe's daughter Chana, the wife of Samarius Gourary, doused a cotton rag in soda water and placed it over her father's mouth to protect him from the fumes.[40] After a few moments, everyone realized the gray substance was only thick dust kicked up by the bombing. They were safe for the moment. As the bombers flew away, the survivors thanked God for sparing their lives yet again and emerged from the basement, where they were greeted by the terrible screams of helpless people trapped in burning buildings. The rank smell of burning flesh stung their nostrils, and they could hear the shouts of the elderly mixed with the squeals of babies.[41] People scurried through the streets, all in a state of terror. As the tired, scared Lubavitchers witnessed this horror, smoke and fire engulfed their building. The Rebbe and his followers looked up into the sky as the sun disappeared behind a wall of fiery smoke. But amazingly, they were alive.

His followers thought that if they remained close to the Rebbe, they would not be killed. They did not want to tempt fate by staying in the streets, however, so the Rebbe and a group of about twenty Jews rushed into a building that had been spared from the destruction. The Rebbe led them in a recitation of the Shema, the Jewish declaration of monotheism: "Hear, O Israel! The Lord is our God, the Lord is One." As they said this prayer, which is traditionally recited immediately before death, the whole building vibrated with bomb concussions from another attack; projectiles of earth, metal, and fire sprayed the area.[42] Hearts pounded, and breathing became heavy and rapid. Yet the death they expected passed them by, and the bombs stopped falling. Schneersohn and his group had survived another day. Most interpreted their survival as nothing less than a miracle.

Others were not so lucky. When the Rebbe heard that a building across the street had collapsed, burying many inside, he asked his students to dig out the victims. Most of those pulled out of the ruins were dead. They found a lifeless woman clutching her crushed baby girl; the child still had her thumb in her mouth. While they busied themselves with this task, several more bombs hit the area, sending shrapnel and broken concrete and brick through the air.[43] The Rebbe's followers behaved courageously when they thought they might be able to save a human life.

When it was clear that the attack was over, his followers transferred the Rebbe to the home of publisher and philanthropist Zalman Shmotkin at 32 Muranowska Street, where they thought he would be safer. The date was probably 15 September. They found a wagon, loaded the Rebbe and many of his loved ones in it, and transported them through the burning city. As they made their way through the streets, burning debris often landed on the wagon, only to be quickly removed by a zealous follower. Mangled, bleeding corpses lay in the streets, on the sidewalks, and in courtyards, and the rank smell of excrement, decaying bodies, and burned buildings filled the air.[44] It was as if they had all entered Dante's *Inferno* and had just crossed the River Styx to witness what was on the other side.

The horror of war brought the Jews of Warsaw together in terror. One day the Rebbe traveled along the ghetto's edge, where he intermingled with secular Jews. "Some of the people had beards and side curls, others were clean shaven," he said. "Some of the women wore wigs; others did not cover their hair at all. Despite their differences, everyone was united by fate, fear and despair."[45]

The Lubavitchers feared not only German bombs but also secret enemies among their neighbors. According to Samarius Gourary, as soon as the attacks started, certain "Nazi provocateurs" would dress up like Hasidic Jews and sneak into the Jewish parts of the city to murder them. Using terrorist tactics, they would throw boxes of dynamite into homes or other places where they thought they could kill the most people and then quickly escape.[46] This claim strains credulity, but it is interesting to note what some Lubavitchers were reporting from the war front.

On 16 September the Luftwaffe returned. "The Nazis targeted the Jewish neighborhood of Warsaw," Wineberg claimed. He remembers that when the Rebbe was encouraged to escape, he slammed his cane on the ground and said, "We will remain and he [Hitler] will escape." Yet despite his bravado, the bombs fell and his home caught fire. Several of the Rebbe's followers carried him down a flight of stairs in his wheelchair and out of the burning building. His mother, also wheelchair bound, became separated from the Rebbe, and Wineberg recalls her "crying, calling out, 'Why should my son have to suffer like this?'" The Rebbe remained placid and reportedly had his students recite a passage from the Mishnah. When they made a mistake, he corrected them. The Rebbe felt that the oral Mishnah recitation could create a sacred space "impenetrable to bombs."[47] But the Rebbe's predicament would soon get worse, and the bombs kept coming. Clearly, he was not creating that sacred space.

On 17 September the Soviet Union invaded Poland from the east, justifying the violation of its treaties with Poland by declaring that the country no longer existed and that it was "protect[ing] the inhabitants of western Byelorussia and western Ukraine."[48] The Molotov-Ribbentrop Non-Aggression Pact, which Stalin and Hitler had signed on 23 August 1939, had given them the ability to carve up Poland without becoming alarmed at the other's actions. The Soviets had also been given a free hand in Latvia, Estonia, Lithuania, part of Romania, and eastern Poland, which were among the areas in the Soviet sphere of influence under the terms of a secret protocol. Hitler had actually envisioned such a pact in 1925, when he wrote in *Mein Kampf*: "Let no one argue that in concluding an alliance with Russia we need not immediately think of war, or, if we did, that we could thoroughly prepare for it. *An alliance whose aim does not embrace a plan for war is senseless and worthless.*" This pact dictated that Hitler would receive western Poland and Stalin would receive eastern Poland. Before the war, the two dictators had agreed how much of Poland each would occupy and subject "to the unrestricted political engineering of their respective conquerors." Although Stalin claimed the Soviet Union's intervention was designed to protect his "fraternal" brothers, his reasons were purely imperialistic. When Germany started the war, Stalin had been slow to get involved, having just concluded a small war in August with Japan on his eastern border and not knowing how well the Wehrmacht would perform. Stalin quickly realized that Germany's blitzkrieg was overwhelming Poland, and he would have to invade soon to claim his portion. To divert international criticism, Hitler most likely encouraged Stalin to strike. Poland had expected Germany to attack, but the Soviet invasion shocked the Polish high command. Tragically, when the Soviet Union committed this "stab in the back" and started pouring over the eastern border, many Polish citizens mistakenly welcomed them, thinking they would fight the

Germans. In fact, some Russians apparently played up this misperception to gain easy access to the country. It did not take the Poles long to figure out the Soviets' true intention, however. It was only a matter of days before Poland would cease to exist.[49] Also, Stalin must have taken great pride in avenging what Poland had done to the Red Army at the battle of Warsaw in 1920, when the Poles, under the command of Józef Pilsudski, had soundly defeated the Bolsheviks and sent them back to Russia, humiliated.[50]

Sitting in the vise of two major powers whose militaries and populations dwarfed its own, Poland saw the handwriting on the wall. If the international community did not invade Germany quickly and declare war against the USSR for its blatant act of aggression, Poland would cease to exist within a matter of days. Norman Davies eloquently writes: "The Polish forces were caught in a trap, with no wall against which they could lean their backs and fight." The Soviet Union's actions took the whole world by surprise, not just the Poles. This act of aggression "prompted Churchill's famous remark that 'Russia is a riddle wrapped in a mystery inside an enigma.'"[51]

The Soviet invasion also posed a specific problem for Jews. For two centuries, Jews had been fleeing west to seek enlightenment and safety. Jews on the border between Soviet-held territories and German-held territories now had to decide which way to flee—east to the Soviet Union, or west to Nazi Germany. They had to go against the lesson of history and go eastward, where they faced starvation, disease, and an antireligious attitude, but not annihilation. In the postwar world, many Poles remembered how the Jews had welcomed the Soviet invasion, given the alternative of life under Nazi domination.

In front of a jubilant crowd "hysterical with joy," Hitler addressed the citizens of Danzig on 19 September, claiming that "Almighty God" had blessed the Wehrmacht with victory. He felt that destiny was on the Germans' side and spoke derisively of Britain and France, even more confident now of his military might and his leadership. From Danzig, Hitler moved on to the resort town of Zoppot, where he laid out his plan to euthanize the mentally handicapped in Germany and then backdated the order and told his underlings to get it done.[52] With each success, Hitler's diabolical plan against political adversaries, the unhealthy, Jews, Poles, and so on only increased in severity.

Commenting on Poland's tragedy, Winston Churchill, who had just been brought into the cabinet as First Lord of the Admiralty, noted that the world "has watched the vain struggle of the Polish nation against overwhelming odds with profound sympathy and admires their valor." On 20 September the London BBC sent a message of sympathy to Warsaw on its Polish news service. The Poles, however, wanted more than hollow words from the British. They wanted military action. The mayor of Warsaw, Stefan Starzynski, responded to the broadcast, asking, "When will the effective help of Great Britain and France come to relieve us from this terrible situation? We are waiting for it."[53] Although British and French forces fought Germany at sea and in the air, they did not mount a ground war, apart from France's abortive invasion of the Saarland. In the absence of such an assault, most of the German land forces could focus on battles in Poland, which would die essentially "deserted by [its] allies."[54]

The news of the Soviet invasion alarmed the Lubavitchers for a very personal reason: they feared that if the Soviets got their hands on the Rebbe again, no amount of international support could save him. In fact, as strange as it sounds, the Rebbe feared the Soviets more than he feared the Nazis at this time. Finally, in late September, the Rebbe agreed to leave Warsaw. He wavered, though, between wanting to be with his flock and wanting to save his life. According to Wineberg, for several days the Rebbe had even refused to believe that war had broken out. As Wineberg points out, even though Noah built the ark, it still took the rains for him to believe God's prophecy and board it. But just as the Rebbe began to plan his escape, the Wehrmacht encircled the city, and the perpetual bombing made leaving impossible. Nazi propaganda films captured Hitler watching through binoculars as the city burned. He turned to his military advisers, laughed, and then returned his gaze to the deadly effects of the Luftwaffe's bombs.[55]

Even as Warsaw was in its death throes, the Rebbe and thousands of Orthodox and Hasidic Jews continued their observance of the High Holy Days, especially the most sacred of all, Yom Kippur, the Day of Atonement. On 22 September, the evening of Yom Kippur, when they could have been searching for food or an escape route, the Lubavitchers instead turned their attention to their religious traditions. They were not alone, as many Jews sought solace in prayer that allowed them to give voice to their anguish. If Jews performed the rites required during Rosh Hashanah and Yom Kippur correctly and with the right heart, the Rebbe taught, angels would be dispatched from heaven. He believed that good deeds on earth are often performed by angels from heaven responding to the faithful acts of Jews. And if he was going to be rescued, the Rebbe needed angels, because "all missions which are related to the material world are carried out by [them]."[56]

The Nazis were cognizant of Jewish holidays, and as part of their program of humiliation and degradation, they chose these occasions to take anti-Jewish actions. In Jewish areas already under German occupation, the holiday became an opportunity for persecution. The Germans closed synagogues and took the worshippers to army barracks, forcing some of them to clean the floors and bathrooms with their prayer shawls. Others were forced to march around pointlessly and would be shot if they could not keep up the pace. The Germans even required Jews to bury their murdered compatriots—some of whom were not yet dead. One can only visualize the squirming, helpless souls trying to keep breathing as the soil covered them and they finally succumbed to suffocation.[57] In the face of severe Wehrmacht protests, the SS continued its unrestrained brutality. On 22 September the Germans arrived in Wloclawek, where they looted Jewish shops, blew up Jewish centers of worship, and executed several Jewish leaders.[58] Yom Kippur, for many, turned into a day of death, not of atonement. The Germans played God, choosing who would live and who would die.

The Rebbe made one concession to the dangers encircling him and his followers. Mindful of what might await the crowd if bombs fell, he violated the traditional way of ending the worship service. He had the shofar blown early, before nightfall, giving the sign that everyone could leave the service and take shelter before the bombing started again.[59] In Jewish law, if life is at risk, violation of the law is sanctioned and, in fact, mandated.

As the Holy Days drew to a close, the Rebbe blessed his followers, saying, "Good night, and may you always have happy occasions." But the holiday had brought joy to no one. Kaplan observed that "mourning is on every face. As our prophet said 'The whole head is sick and the whole heart faint.'"[60]

On 23 September the Germans began moving formations that were no longer engaged in combat in Poland to Germany's western border, where, as Field Marshal von Manstein later explained, "much to our surprise," the French and British "had looked idly on as their Polish ally was being annihilated."[61] That same day, the German guns began shelling Warsaw in earnest. Hitler was growing impatient. On 25 September he ordered intense bombing to force the city's capitulation. The Germans dropped more than 500 tons of high explosives and 72 tons of incendiary bombs and directed heavy artillery fire at the city, which erupted into flames. The Rebbe lamented: "houses burning, the piercing screams of the unfortunate victims, the terror-stricken people, especially the elderly, the women and children—all are beyond description." The previous day the city had lost its electricity, gas, and water.[62]

Few Americans can imagine what it is like to live in a war zone. After the bombs stopped falling, the screams of the wounded and the dying dominated the landscape. As an illustration of the horror: During the night of 25 September, in one of the city's hospitals, a doctor worked feverishly on a "young expectant mother, nineteen years of age, whose intestines were torn by the blast of a bomb. She was only a few days before childbirth." He was unable to save her. As she slowly bled out, her baby probably kicked and squirmed inside her as it was deprived of oxygen. Those nearby probably looked on in horror as her belly bubbled left and right as the nine-month fetus struggled for air. After both had died, they were dumped in a common grave with soldiers.[63] Along with the bombs, disease had begun to ravage the city. Dysentery, typhoid, and hunger plagued the inhabitants. As Churchill wrote, the Polish defense of their capital "was magnificent and forlorn."[64]

The Lubavitchers discussed what they would do with the Rebbe when the Germans conquered the city. The Nazis sought prominent rabbis and Jewish leaders, and they would consider the Rebbe a great prize. Whether his captors were Soviet or German, his demise seemed inevitable. Certainly, the Lubavitchers' fears were not unfounded.[65]

The Rebbe escaped death several times during the final bombardment of Warsaw, leading many to believe that a divine shield protected him, and surely reinforcing his own sense of invulnerability. On one occasion he left a building just moments before it tumbled to the ground after a direct hit from bombers. During this period, the Rebbe reportedly suffered shell shock.[66] However, a Lubavitcher rabbi who is a scholar of Chabad disputes this claim, arguing that a man of the Rebbe's stature and spiritual maturity would have no such mental weaknesses.[67] Most Lubavitchers find it extremely difficult to assess their Rebbes critically, and if a Rebbe shows any weakness or makes any mistakes, they try to find an appropriate exculpatory explanation, usually theological. During this intense bombardment, the Rebbe probably felt more fear than he had ever experienced while in prison under the Soviets in 1927. After the long hours of bombing, he simply succumbed to the fatigue caused by the ordeal. Noticing that his hand had started to shake when a shell exploded close to him, the Rebbe said, "I am not frightened, but the blast causes the flesh to tremble."[68] The fact that the Rebbe was physically incapable of running for cover probably added to his sense of helplessness at a time when a quick response was required whenever the sirens sounded. The trauma of the Nazi onslaught assaulted his theology, his physical endurance, and his understanding of the world. As a mortal human being, he probably felt out of control and confused—or, as his followers would put it, the mortal within him probably felt that way. Also, he was likely unable to smoke his usual twenty-five cigarettes a day and may have been experiencing the symptoms of nicotine withdrawal, which include anxiety, headache, fatigue, and irritability. The 500-pound bombs destroying his block and killing his neighbors probably heightened these side effects. Surely, he was also feeling grief for those who were dying and suffering all around him.

By now, his group was running out of supplies. Chaim Kaplan saw some people cutting meat from a rotting three-day-old carcass of a horse. The Rebbe would sometimes go days without eating. Yet hunger was a mild torment compared with the death that surrounded them. "Every morning," Karen Tiche says, "you would go outside and the dead would be piled up along the streets and the living would busy themselves carrying the bodies off to quickly dug graves in parks and courtyards to be buried."[69]

Warsaw could no longer defend itself. On 26 September General Juliusz Rómmel, commander of the Warsaw army, sent representatives to the Germans to discuss surrender terms. On 28 September Warsaw capitulated to the German. A few days later, Kaplan wrote bitterly in his diary that Rómmel "has made tens of thousands of people penniless and home-less; he has created widows and orphans without number." The Poles were enraged at their leaders; the Germans were ecstatic. When news of the surrender reached Germany, church bells tolled across the country to commemorate the Reich's victory in the east.[70] Obviously, the German ministers and priests sounding the celebration of victory from the houses of God felt the Lord was on *their* side.

"Beautiful Warsaw—city of royal glory, queen of cities—has been destroyed like Sodom and Gomorrah," wrote Kaplan. Interestingly, God destroyed Sodom and Gomorrah using fire and brimstone, so Kaplan's image of "death from the heavens" is an accurate one. But now the Almighty had willed the destruction of this city utilizing new weapons—artillery and Stukas and Heinkel 111 airplanes. But to this military historian, Warsaw's demise was caused by the "sin" of being unprepared and poorly equipped and lacking international support. The bombardment of Warsaw killed close to 40,000 civilians and severely damaged 25 percent of the city.[71] The Germans simply outmatched the Poles technically and strategically. For example, the Poles attacked the German panzers in one of the last cavalry charges in the history of warfare. They had allegedly been told that their lances would pierce the thin metal, but this was not the case, and these brave men were slaughtered. Most likely, they had attacked the Germans only in an "attempt to escape encirclement in the corridor" where they were trapped.[72] By this time, the Polish president and the commander in chief had escaped to Romania, and military units were ordered to disperse, bury their weapons, and "fend for themselves." Tens of thousands of soldiers would follow their president and commander into exile into Romania and Hungary.[73]

By October, Germany emerged victorious from the campaign. The Wehrmacht suffered 16,000 dead and 32,000 wounded, whereas the Polish armed forces suffered 100,000 dead, including 6,000 Polish Jews, and 133,700 wounded. On 5 October Hitler reviewed his victorious troops in Warsaw. Later, bursting with pride, he gave a speech in Berlin before the Reichstag, declaring, "In all history there has scarcely been a comparable military achievement." He assailed Poland's leaders and justified his war against their "ridiculous State," warning of the dark future that awaited this vanquished nation.[74]

Hitler reviews his victorious troops in the streets of Warsaw on 5 October 1939. (National Archives)

The war in Poland left the world stunned at how quickly Germany had conquered another country. No one had anticipated blitzkrieg warfare. The Germans had overwhelmed the Poles with three pincer movements—one from the north, from East Prussia, and two directly from the west, from Pomerania and Silesia—all headed straight for Warsaw. In less than a month, the Nazis had thrown their shadow over an additional 20 million people in eastern Europe. Immediately, thousands pleaded with the US government to help them escape Nazism.[75] While the United States considered how to react, Hitler established a murderous order in central Poland and systematically evicted Poles from the previously German territory known as the Wartheland.

The Nazis planned to settle Germans in the newly conquered territory and to turn Poland into a nation of serfs. In their eyes, Slavs were useful only as slaves; Polish Jews, of course, were seen as even lower than that. Colonel Eduard Wagner, the German quartermaster general, wrote on 9 September: "It is the Führer's and Goering's intention to destroy and exterminate the Polish nation. More than that cannot be even hinted at in writing." Many in Poland knew that Jews had no future under Hitler. The Nazis wanted to eliminate the Jews "physically through a slow choking process; through starvation, appalling living conditions, disease, and both capricious and organized murder." As Kaplan observed ironically in his diary, the country had fallen into the hands of the "sons of Ham," the people condemned by Noah to be Israel's slaves.[76]

The Nazis immediately put thousands of Poles to work clearing the destroyed capital of its rubble and dead. Bodies were decomposing everywhere, throwing off a thick stench of death, and they needed to be buried.[77] Throughout early October the Germans ran several soup kitchens in Warsaw to help feed the population, but when Jews came, the army sent them away.[78] The Lubavitchers, with their conspicuous dress, were easily recognized as Jewish and probably rarely obtained food at the distribution centers. Like other Warsaw Jews, they had to buy food on the black market, steal it, or trade other goods for it.

It was obvious that Jews would be persecuted under Hitler's regime and that the Rebbe must be hidden. The address Schneersohn had given to the Polish authorities when he arrived in Warsaw no longer existed; the building had been destroyed in the bombing. His followers speculated that the Germans might believe the Rebbe was dead and not pursue him. They prayed it would be so.[79]

On 5 October Hitler flew to Warsaw, where he reviewed a victorious army marching through the city's main streets. Swastika flags bedecked the roads, and serpentine rows of soldiers wound their way through the Polish capital. After saluting his victorious soldiers, Hitler returned to a nearby airfield and told foreign journalists there, "Take a good look around Warsaw. That is how I can deal with any European city."[80] With a swift shift in power, Warsaw was now under the absolute control of the Nazis. The future looked very grim.

5

A Plan Takes Shape

Those who can make you believe absurdities can make you commit atrocities.

—Voltaire

While the Lubavitchers in Warsaw tried to stay alive and keep their Rebbe hidden, their American coreligionists pressed the US government to rescue him. Rabbi Israel Jacobson, executive director of Chabad in America, felt lucky to have left Poland a few days before the war began. He was extremely close to the Rebbe and feared for the leader's life. Jacobson obtained information about Schneersohn through Rabbi Mordechai Chefetz, head of the Lubavitcher movement in Latvia. Chefetz, in turn, received regular updates from Chaim Lieberman, the Rebbe's private secretary, by telegraph, telephone, mail, and messengers. How Lieberman kept up the constant flow of information from war-torn Poland remains something of a mystery.

Lieberman escaped Warsaw on 21 September and arrived safely in Riga, the largest seaport in the Baltic states, a few weeks later. He made the 400-mile journey largely on foot; this was quite a feat, as he must have averaged around 20 miles a day. After Lieberman's departure, the flow of information about Schneersohn ebbed. "It is two weeks since I left Warsaw, and we in Riga are still unable to contact the Rebbe," he wrote. "The One Above alone knows what is happening to them there—pray that He protect them, and that we are reunited with them soon. It is impossible to describe the horrors of those first three weeks." A few days later Lieberman reported to Jacobson that the Rebbe's situation in Warsaw was "horrible, unbelievably and indescribably horrible. In addition to the worry over the Rebbe's poor health, we know they are under the pressure of real terror, for the Germans are inflicting terrible tortures, particularly on Rabbis."[1]

The Lubavitchers in the United States became increasingly concerned and intensified their pleas to government officials. Lieberman was now unable to confirm even whether the Rebbe was alive. Many felt their "whole existence was at stake if the Rebbe was not saved." He was the guiding force for the movement and a link between God and the community. His death would devastate the whole of Chabad.[2]

On behalf of many American Lubavitchers, state senator and judge Philip Kleinfeld of New York urged his friend Senator Robert F. Wagner to ask Secretary of State Cordell Hull (a devout Christian whose father-in-law was Jewish) to help ascertain the Rebbe's whereabouts.[3] Kleinfeld received most of his intelligence about the Rebbe from his dear friend and law partner Sam Kramer, Chabad's legal counselor. Together, they endeavored to find the Rebbe and get him out of Poland. Wagner, a German immigrant himself, was also from New York, home of the largest Jewish community in the United States. Wagner wrote to Hull on 22 September 1939 and enclosed several articles about the Rebbe and his movement, including reports of his 1929 visit to America, stressing his "high ecclesiastical position." Four days later Hull informed Wagner that communications with Poland had been suspended, and he offered to notify the senator when they were reestablished.[4]

Wagner was a good man to have on one's side in such circumstances. Besides his decade-long familiarity with the Rebbe, he had proved himself to be a man of action and conscience throughout the 1930s. In February 1939, after Britain had accepted 10,000 German refugee children, Wagner cosponsored a bill with Congresswoman Edith Rogers, authorizing 20,000 German children under the age of fourteen to enter the United States. Under this proposal, the children would be provided for by private organizations, not the federal government. Sadly, the isolationists in Congress torpedoed the bill before it ever got to the floor of either the House or the Senate. Persecuted, innocent children were not welcome in the country whose Statue of Liberty declares, "Give me your tired, your poor, your huddled masses yearning to breathe free." But Wagner's support of the bill identified him as a person who would try to save lives and help those in need. Among the large population of political officials and civil servants, he was one of the few who stood out as a moral voice of reason and compassion. Unfortunately, he was part of a tiny minority.

Cordell Hull and his wife, Frances (née Witz), in 1933, when President Roosevelt appointed him secretary of state. (National Archives)

Contrary to Hull's response to Wagner, and probably unknown to him, communications from Poland still existed. On 24 September Mordechai Dubin sent a cable from Riga, assuring Jacobson that Schneersohn was still in Warsaw at Zalman Shmotkin's house on Muranowska Street. Dubin had probably received this information from one of the Lubavitch messengers who traveled from Poland to Latvia. Exactly how these messengers made it in and out of the two countries remains unknown, but it is a testament to the Lubavitchers' resourcefulness. The next day Dubin sent word that the Rebbe's situation was critical and that "every hour counts." Dubin also thought it would be wise to contact Dr. Joseph Rosen of the American Jewish Joint Distribution Committee. Acting promptly on this information, Sam Kramer met with Rosen on 25 September, and Rosen sent a cable to John Cooper Wiley, the US minister in Riga, asking for his assistance with the Rebbe's rescue. Apparently, Wiley was then put in touch with Dubin to coordinate efforts.[5]

Wagner wrote to Hull again on 26 September to ask that the US minister in Riga gather "information as to the safety and whereabouts" of the Rebbe, emphasizing that many Jewish organizations in New York had expressed concern. Wagner informed Hull that the Rebbe had probably fled Poland for Latvia. In response to Hull's inquiry, the American legation in Riga reported on 30 September that the Rebbe was ill and was still in Warsaw, which proved to be correct.[6]

The Rebbe's case attracted the attention of a number of high-ranking officials, including Supreme Court justice Louis Brandeis and Democratic congressmen Adolph J. Sabath (Illinois), chairman of the House Rules Committee, and Sol Bloom (New York), chairman of the Foreign Affairs Committee. Brandeis received a report on 29 September from Arthur Rabinovitz, a lawyer and one of US Chabad's leaders, claiming that the Rebbe lay sick or wounded and trapped in Poland. Rabinovitz, who had arranged the Rebbe's meeting with President Hoover in 1930, urged Brandeis to act quickly.[7]

Stories of Nazi atrocities had begun to trickle into America. In his report to Brandeis, Rabinovitz reminded the justice that he had met the Rebbe nine years earlier, and he proposed that they demand permission from the German military authorities to arrange for the Rebbe's safe passage to Riga and then to Stockholm, in neutral Sweden. Rabinovitz suggested that Brandeis enlist the aid of attorney and FDR adviser Benjamin V. Cohen, characterizing the "pressure which Cohen might bring to bear" as "highly urgent." Rabinovitz knew that thousands had bombarded the US government with requests to save the Rebbe—some appealing directly to President Roosevelt himself. But he felt justified in troubling Brandeis with this matter because of the "extreme danger to Schneersohn's life and his great moral worth to Jewry."[8]

Brandeis took Rabinovitz's suggestion and consulted Cohen, part of Roosevelt's brain trust. The son of Polish Jewish immigrants, Cohen headed the National Power Policy Committee and belonged to several influential Jewish interest groups. He had been a member of the American Zionist movement's delegation at the 1919 Paris Peace Conference. He had also "drafted the New Deal legislation that transformed the financial markets of the United States." Although foreign policy was beyond Cohen's mandate, he wrote to Robert T. Pell, assistant chief of the State

Department's European Affairs Division, on 2 October 1939. Despite the war, Pell maintained contact with influential German officials. "I don't know just who in the State Department could help in a matter of this kind," Cohen wrote, "and consequently I am turning to you for advice."[9]

Pell agreed that "it would be a very great tragedy indeed if any harm befall" one of the "leading Jewish scholars in the world."[10] He thought Cohen had contacted him mainly because he knew the chief administrator of Göring's Office of the Four-Year Plan, Helmuth Wohlthat, an expert in international industry and economics and a Nazi Party member. Pell had met the ambitious and intelligent Wohlthat after the Evian conference in 1938, where representatives from thirty-two nations had addressed the plight of Jewish refugees from Germany and Austria. Sadly, Romania and Poland had formally requested to be considered "refugee producers" so that they too could "free" themselves of Jews. In other words, these countries wanted to force Jews out. Colonel Józef Beck, Poland's foreign minister, had actually said in 1937 that of the 3.5 million Polish Jews, "three million were superfluous and must emigrate." Earlier in his career, when Pope Pius XI had been the Vatican's nuncio to Poland (1919–1921), he had often heard priests and other church leaders express their hatred of the Jews, who were viewed as "enemies of Catholic Poland."[11] The US ambassador in Poland, Anthony Biddle, wrote to Secretary of State Hull that "'acute antisemitism' exists 'amongst the ranks of radical anti-Semitics . . . in Poland . . . where the Jewish problem [is] steadily becoming a more acute social-economic-political issue.'"[12]

Many Poles, the vast majority of whom were Catholic, were revolted by ultrareligious Jews and would have liked to see them leave. Since the Catholic Church preached that *all* Jews were guilty of crucifying Jesus (not just a few Jews back in ancient Palestine), anti-Semitism was an official church policy, and most Jews were looked down on in Catholic Poland, which was a conservative, somewhat authoritarian, poor, and backward country. So if Jews were looking to Poland for help in 1938, they were deluding themselves.

Unfortunately, most nations did not want to accept Jewish refugees. US representatives at the Evian conference refused to take a substantial number of Jews suffering under the Nazis or unwanted by Romania and Poland. Other nations followed suit. The Australian minister of com-

This cartoon appeared in many newspapers, including the *New York Times*. It depicts the horrible situation German Jews found themselves in, as many countries simply refused to help them emigrate from Germany. (United States Holocaust Memorial Museum/Express Newspapers)

merce, Lieutenant Colonel T. W. White, cynically explained, "As we have no real racial problem, we are not desirous of importing one." Given that Australia had originated as a British penal colony, White's statement reveals much about the xenophobic and anti-Semitic attitudes prevalent in 1938. One statement that circulated among Jews noted, "the world [is] made of two types of countries: the kind where Jews could not live and the kind where Jews could not enter." The "exultant Nazis crowed: *See, no one wants to take Jews off our hands.*" Hitler cynically commented that "antisemitism is merely a matter of degree."[13] Lending support to Hitler's statement, many of the Latin American countries, led by Brazil and Argentina, shut down Jewish immigration. After the conference, a number of South American governments immediately implemented new restrictions to prevent Jewish refugees from coming to their countries.[14]

In addition to antirefugee and anti-Semitic feelings in the United States, money issues may have prevented the government from helping

Helmuth Wohlthat worked in the Office of the Four-Year Plan under Hermann Göring. He was the point person in Germany for the US government's efforts to rescue Rebbe Schneersohn. (Author's collection)

Jews and putting pressure on Germany. Hull and other government officials were sensitive to public criticism of Germany because they worried that the Germans might not continue to pay their debts if the criticism became too harsh.[15] In the mid-1930s Hull had protested any boycotts against Germany, believing that "only good trade could lead to good political relations."[16] Unfortunately, money often trumps morality.

The problems raised at Evian were exacerbated by disunity among the twenty-one private Jewish delegations attending the conference, which the *Congress Bulletin* of the American Jewish Congress described as a "spectacle of Jewish discord and disruption."[17] Religious and political differences (Reform versus Orthodox, Zionist versus anti-Zionist) left many American Jewish groups confused as to how best to assist their persecuted brethren.[18] These problems would continue to plague American Jewry throughout the war. The infighting at Evian embarrassed these groups, and they accomplished little to address the plight of Jews under Hitler.

Despite the failure of the Evian conference, Pell succeeded in forging at least one decisive relationship. After the conference, the United States supported the Intergovernmental Committee on Refugees and sent officials to Europe to discuss the refugee problem with Germany. From late 1938 until the outbreak of war in September 1939, Pell (who eventually became vice director of the committee) met several times with Germany's representative, Wohlthat, who privately assured Pell that if a specific case arose in which American Jewry expressed interest, "he would do what he could to facilitate a solution." When Cohen contacted Pell about the Rebbe, Pell quite naturally forwarded his request directly to Wohlthat.[19]

As Günter Schubert notes, Wohlthat was probably the best person possible to get this rescue operation started and ensure its success. If Pell had contacted anyone in Germany's Foreign Office, the request would have ended up in the lap of the Reich's minister for foreign affairs, Joachim von Ribbentrop. Ribbentrop, a former wine merchant, was widely considered incompetent. When Göring was told that Ribbentrop knew a lot of influential people in the British government, Göring responded that he was more concerned about whether those people actually "knew Ribbentrop." Yet contrary to this low opinion of him, one could argue that Ribbentrop was good at building alliances with Latin American countries, and he had helped pull off the Nazi-Soviet Non-Aggression Pact of 1939. Regardless of his competence in foreign affairs, Ribbentrop was definitely an anti-Semite. So if Pell had brought the Rebbe's predicament to Ribbentrop's attention and asked for his help, it is highly unlikely that the rescue mission would have moved forward.[20]

In the meantime, the Lubavitchers in the United States continued their frantic efforts to rescue their Rebbe. Jacobson and Rabinovitz repeatedly reminded Brandeis, Pell, and Cohen of their leader's plight. Jacobson was a kind leader and a fine Torah teacher, but he was hardly a lobbyist. Although he had succeeded in helping Jews immigrate to America in the interwar period, the Rebbe's case was beyond his experience and abilities. In his dealings with Washington officials and immigration protocol, Jacobson proved to be a poor organizer who failed to delegate tasks to those around him. Chaskel Besser, a prominent Hasidic rabbi and Agudah leader, said of Jacobson: "He was very inefficient in his dealings with people. He would let things often slide that needed to be paid atten-

Benjamin Cohen, who was instrumental in establishing contact with Robert Pell of the State Department's European Affairs Division. (National Archives)

tion to." Even Jacobson's own grandson, Rabbi Leib Altein, admitted he was extremely disorganized. Jacobson, however, received no compensation for his efforts and lived primarily off a small salary and donations received from his Brooklyn congregation. He was motivated by his intense love for the Rebbe and for the cause. What he lacked in organizational and lobbying skills, he made up for with enthusiasm and religious observance. Jacobson himself was lucky to have escaped Europe. In August 1939 he had escorted the Rebbe's six American students to Otwock, and he had left Poland only a few days before the war started.[21]

Jacobson was deeply devout. While traveling to America in September, he and a few followers had attempted to conduct Rosh Hashanah prayers on the ship. Joseph Kennedy, ambassador to the United Kingdom and father of the future president, was a fellow passenger, and he complained that Jacobson was disruptive. Despite his personal friendships and business dealings with some Jews, Kennedy was a known anti-Semite and a fierce opponent of American involvement in the war. A furious Jacobson cursed Kennedy and all his male heirs.[22] Given the fate of the Kennedy men—one son died in combat, two were assassinated, and several grandsons died prematurely—the curse may have worked.

In the meantime, pleas to save the Rebbe, including those from Brandeis, Cohen, Pell, and Postmaster General James A. Farley (a politically influential adviser to Roosevelt), piled up on Secretary Hull's desk. Farley told Hull on 27 September that he had received many requests for help from the Lubavitch community, which comprised more than 200 congregations totaling 150,000 members in the United States and 10,000 in Canada. To put it mildly, these numbers were greatly exaggerated.[23] The total worth of the Chabad organization, according to Jacobson's sworn affidavit, was $500,000. Perhaps Farley thought the Lubavitchers included enough potential voters to make them worth listening to. Roosevelt would be running for an unprecedented and unpopular third term in 1940, and the stakes were high, given that his opponents would certainly not prepare America for war. Thus, the president may have been inclined to help the Rebbe because of the good it would do him in the Jewish community.[24]

For months, Chabad and other Orthodox Jewish leaders had been demanding the rescue of some 10,000 Hasidic and Orthodox Jews—considered the cream of Europe's Jewry. But once the US government indicated a willingness to rescue the Rebbe, Chabad apparently refrained from pressing for more. The group concentrated all its efforts on saving the Rebbe. On 2 October 1939 Hull informed Farley that the State Department would ask the American vice-consul in Riga to report on Schneersohn's situation, at the request of interested American citizens who were seeking to effect the Rebbe's rescue.[25]

On 2 October the Latvian embassy in Washington joined the chorus and telegraphed the Latvian Foreign Office in Riga, requesting assistance for the Rebbe. Latvia was a small, recently independent country, neither rich nor powerful, with a population of about 2 million. Approximately 70,000 of its citizens were Jewish, the vast majority of whom were neither Hasidic nor ultra-Orthodox. There were also thousands of Jewish refugees from Germany in Latvia. The Latvian embassy probably received information about the Rebbe from Dubin in Riga, who had regularly received messages from Chefetz in Warsaw. By 24 September, Dubin had already informed Jacobson of the Rebbe's most recent address and advised him that the Rebbe and his family should leave Warsaw immediately.[26] Toward this end, the Lubavitchers had enlisted the help of Rosen of the Joint Distribution Committee; he, in turn, had pressured Minister Wiley to help with the rescue. By 26 September, Chabad lawyer Max Rhoade was able to report that Wiley had been in touch with Dubin "and that he would try to do what he could in the Rabbi's behalf."[27] In short, Chabad was contacting everybody and anybody with political power. This chutzpah would get them to the highest echelons of power.

On 3 October 1939 Pell, authorized by Hull,[28] wrote to Raymond Geist, the American consul general in Berlin:

Rabbi Joseph Isaac Schneersohn known as Lubavitcher Rebbe, one of the leading Jewish scholars of the world and a Latvian citizen, has been trapped in Warsaw. The most influential Jewish leaders and others in this country, including the Postmaster General, Justice Brandeis and Mr. Benjamin Cohen, have asked our assistance in obtaining permission from the German Military Government of Warsaw for the safe egress of the Rabbi to Riga via Stockholm. While the Department does not wish to intervene in the case of a citizen of a foreign country you might in the course of a conversation with Wohlthat inform him as from me in view of our previous relationship of the interest in this country in this particular case. Wohlthat, who evidently wishes to maintain contact with the Intergovernmental Committee, might wish to intervene with the military authorities.[29]

Geist acted straightaway. Since he did not expect any support from the German Foreign Ministry, he decided to contact Wohlthat directly. "I turn to you," Geist told Wohlthat, "because I know you, and you may be assured of the absolute discretion of the American State Department. I am aware of the considerable risk to any German persons intervening in this matter." Geist then telegraphed Hull and Pell that he had met with Wohlthat, who had "promised to take the matter up with the competent military authorities."[30]

PREPARING OFFICE
WILL INDICATE WHETHER

Collect

Charge Department X
OR

Charge to
$

TELEGRAM SENT

TO BE TRANSMITTED
CONFIDENTIAL CODE
NONCONFIDENTIAL CODE
PARTAIR
PLAIN

Department of State

Washington,

October 3, 1939

AMERICAN EMBASSY

BERLIN

For Geist from Pell.

Rabbi Joseph Isaac Schneersohn, known as Lubavitcher Rebbe, one of the leading Jewish scholars of the world and a Latvian citizen, has been trapped in Warsaw. The most influential Jewish leaders and others in this country, including The Postmaster General, Justice Brandeis and Mr. Benjamin Cohen, have asked our assistance in obtaining permission from the German Military Government of Warsaw for the safe egress of the Rabbi to Riga via Stockholm. While the Department does not wish to intervene in the case of a citizen of a foreign country you might in the course of a conversation with Wohlthat inform him as from me and in view of our previous relationship of the interest in this country in this particular case. Wohlthat, who evidently wishes to maintain the contact with the Intergovernmental Committee, might wish to intervene with the military authorities.

Eu:RTP:AB

Enciphered by

Sent by operator M., 19

D. O. R.—No. 50

1—1462   U. S. GOVERNMENT PRINTING OFFICE

Robert Pell (authorized by Cordell Hull) asks Raymond Geist, the American consul general in Berlin, for help in rescuing Rebbe Schneersohn. This does not appear to be Hull's signature, but many people were authorized to sign for him, which is probably what happened here. (National Archives)

Wohlthat agreed that pressure from such influential sources warranted action. The United States had stunned German authorities by recalling Ambassador Hugh Wilson in November 1938 after the Nazis arrested some 30,000 Jewish men, burned hundreds of synagogues, and murdered more than a hundred people in the *Kristallnacht* pogrom. Roosevelt said, "I myself could scarcely believe that such things could occur in a twentieth-century civilization." After this pogrom, "panicky crowds of Jews formed long lines every day before the Berlin Embassy and the consulates in Germany." US relations with Germany had been strained as a result of Hitler's persecution of Jews, his hatred of freedom and democracy, and the invasion of Czechoslovakia and Poland. As Hitler moved forward with his plan to conquer Europe, it was important that Germany not have to fight everyone at once. Wohlthat therefore welcomed an opportunity to restore a modicum of goodwill between the two nations. Also, he might have thought that by helping the Rebbe he might be helping his own situation, just in case things turned out badly for the Nazis. We know that many military figures, including Generals Ludwig Beck and Walter Brauchitsch, believed that Hitler was leading Germany down the road to defeat. Although this was ultimately true by 1945, many thought Germany would be defeated in 1939 or 1940 if it attacked France—which Hitler wanted to do. Wohlthat had definitely been apprised of Hitler's next planned invasion, and he may have hoped to hedge his bets and improve his standing with the US government (indeed, after the war Wohlthat used this rescue to prove he was not a fanatical follower of Hitler).[31]

Back in the United States, Secretary of State Hull made sure that the Lubavitchers, not the government, would shoulder the cost of the rescue. The success of the mission did not, however, hinge on finances. It depended on Wohlthat. Regardless of his motivations, a high-ranking member of the Nazi Party had been charged with arranging the Rebbe's escape.

6

The Nazi Connection

A Nazi bigwig on holiday in Switzerland asked what a certain official building was. "That's our Admiralty," his Swiss companion told him. The Nazi laughed mockingly. "You mean to say you have an Admiralty—you, with your two or three ships?" The Swiss gave him a straight look and said, "In that case you'd better tell me what you Germans want with a Ministry of Justice."
—Anton Gill, *An Honourable Defeat*

Helmuth Wohlthat was well educated and had experienced the horrors of trench warfare in World War I. He had been injured twice: the first time when his horse was shot out from under him and he broke his arm, and the second time when a French sniper shot him through the throat. He survived, but his vocal chords were impaired. He had also engaged in hand-to-hand combat, bringing down a Frenchman with his dagger. He earned the Iron Cross Second and First Classes (roughly the US equivalent of the Bronze and Silver Stars) and became an officer. He often bragged that the famous artist Max Ernst had been one of his soldiers; recognizing the young man's talent, Wohlthat had made sure Ernst worked in the administration offices of his unit, behind the lines, instead of fighting in the trenches. This assignment likely saved Ernst's life. After the war, Wohlthat had a chance to work in the Ministry of War, but he refused, saying he had had enough of *Krieg* and bloodshed. He first pursued a career in international business and then, during the Third Reich, became a civil servant.[1]

By the time of the Rebbbe's rescue, Wohlthat was an ambivalent Nazi, despite his high office and party membership. According to his daughter Gisela Bauer, he had to join the party to "save his skin"—a claim made by many families as a postwar apology, so it might or might not be true.

But given his actions on behalf of Jews, there might be some truth to the statement. He had studied at Columbia University in New York from 1929 to 1930, graduating with a master's degree in economics. His time in the United States made him a logical contact for US officials seeking help in rescuing the Rebbe. Although it was dangerous to help Jews, there is evidence that Wohlthat did so during the 1930s. In 1974 he claimed he had allowed thousands of Jews to smuggle money and assets out of Germany. He also had friends in the German resistance. According to his daughter, Wohlthat may have had some Jewish ancestry himself, through a grand-parent, but this has been difficult to document. If so, he may have felt a kinship with those who were persecuted—something others in the same situation have claimed.[2]

Nevertheless, he also aggressively persecuted Jews, stealing money and assets from Jews who were officers, directors, shareholders, and key employees of a number of major German companies as well as many small businesses. On 22 July 1938, on Göring's orders, Wohlthat carried out the Aryanization (replacing Jewish owners with "Aryans") of the German properties of a Polish businessman named Ignaz Petschek, valued at 200 million reichsmarks ($500 million in 1938, and equivalent to $8.3 billion today). So with this in mind, why would Wohlthat agree to help the Rebbe? Presumably, he would not have acted to save the Rebbe without a direct appeal from the American government. It seems, too, that he had grown fond of State Department official Robert Pell and felt obligated to act on his request to the extent possible.[3] Some Lubavitchers have claimed that Göring was involved in the Rebbe's escape. If true, Göring's support obviously would have had a profound influence on Wohlthat. But given Göring's position at the pinnacle of the Nazi government, it seems unlikely that he actively participated in the rescue of the Jewish leader. There is no evidence of his involvement in the episode, but he may have known about it through his intelligence office, which tapped government phones and transcribed telephone conversations.[4]

Günter Schubert proposes that even if Göring and other high-ranking Nazi officials knew about the plan, they may have made no attempt to thwart it. At this stage (1939–1940), there was much talk about rendering Germany *Judenfrei* using emigration. Beginning in June 1940, Nazi bu-reaucrats discussed moving the Jews in Germany and in the conquered territories to Madagascar, a large island off the east coast of Africa. British and French control of the seas made this unlikely in wartime, however. So, if the Nazis learned of the US rescue plan, they might have done nothing simply because they wanted the Jews "out of their hair" and moved elsewhere anyway, and this was Germany's official policy at the time. Besides, the Rebbe was just one old Jew who had no particular value to Germany. If saving him would help keep America neutral while Germany conquered Europe, why not? Schubert believes that Göring most likely knew about the plan and even informed Hitler; if this is true, it means that Hitler did nothing to prevent Nazis like Wohlthat from helping the rabbi.[5] In any case, Wohlthat probably felt he was doing something unique and beyond his job description.

Although Wohlthat believed the Rebbe's release would serve Germany's best interests, he knew some Nazi authorities would object, so he felt compelled to carry out his mission discreetly.[6] Wohlthat knew of one man he could trust: Admiral Wilhelm Canaris, head of the Abwehr, the German military intelligence service. Despite being a high-ranking Nazi official, Canaris often helped Jews. He was a man of many faces, most of which were difficult to unmask. Undistinguished in appearance, Canaris stood five feet four inches tall and had something of a Napoleon complex. His clear blue eyes and silver hair earned him the nickname "Old Whitehead," a term of endearment; most of those who worked with Canaris considered him a "wise old man." He had a gift for languages, speaking fluent Spanish and possessing a working knowledge of English, French, Italian, and some Russian. He could memorize facts and foreign words with remarkable ease and loved history.

In his youth, Canaris apparently believed he was related to Constantine Kanaris (1790–1877), the naval hero of the Greek war of independence against Turkey and later the prime minister of Greece. He and his family visited their "relations" in Greece, and stories of Kanaris likely sparked his interest in pursuing a naval career. Early in his service, his superiors and comrades recognized his quick mind and admired his willingness to help those in need.[7]

During World War I, Canaris served on the warship SMS *Dresden*, which distinguished itself during the battle of the Falkland Islands. A few months later, in the battle of Más a Tierra, a British naval force trapped

Admiral Wilhelm Canaris,
head of the Abwehr,
the German military
secret service. (Eliezer
Zaklikovsky)

the *Dresden* at neutral Chile's Cumberland Bay, Robinson Crusoe Island, and he was taken prisoner after the Germans scuttled his ship. Interned at Valparaiso, Chile, in 1914, he soon escaped and made his way over the Andes to Buenos Aires, Argentina, using his language skills to pose as a young Chilean widower. In this disguise and with considerable acting skills, Canaris made it back to Germany in 1915. He then maintained his false identity to conduct undercover work in Spain. He also served as a U-boat commander, sinking four ships. After World War I, when Germany was swept by revolution, he detested what the socialists and communists were doing to his country and developed a passionate hatred for the Soviet Union. During this tumultuous time, Canaris continued to serve in the navy in several different capacities.

When Hitler took power in 1933, Canaris supported him. Soon after taking over responsibility for the Abwehr, he was promoted to admiral. A few years later, the admiral lectured his men about the "virtues of Nazism." Canaris explained at an Abwehr conference in 1938, for example, that "today, every German officer should unconditionally be a National Socialist" and feel bound by his oath to Hitler. Those who question Canaris's commitment to Nazism cite his later involvement in the plot to remove Hitler from power. But no one knows with certainty what Canaris thought of Hitler and the Third Reich. Initially, he, like many Germans, seemed enthusiastic about Hitler's plan to rebuild the military and his anticommunist stance. Canaris welcomed Hitler and his new movement as the best option for combating communism and restoring Germany's prestige.[8]

After the establishment of the Abwehr in 1935, Canaris started working with Heinrich Himmler, head of the SS. He also met frequently with General Reinhard Heydrich, head of the SS Reich Main Security Office, whom he had known since the early 1920s. Heydrich and Canaris lived near each other in Berlin; their families often dined together, and the two men enjoyed horseback rides.[9] After witnessing the mistreatment of military officers such as Generals Blomberg and Fritsch (Blomberg had married a former prostitute, and Fritsch had been wrongly accused of being a homosexual), as well as the Jews, Canaris allegedly started to distance himself from Nazism and later avoided Hitler, declining to dine with the Führer when invited. Yet he was able to hide most of his misgivings from those around him; Canaris had an amazing ability to adapt to his surroundings.[10] Given his skills, authority, and political outlook, he was an appropriate ally for Wohlthat to turn to in the search for the Rebbe. There is a good chance Wohlthat knew that Canaris had already helped many Jews and people of Jewish descent escape Hitler's Reich.

In 1935, when the Abwehr was just a small department in the War Ministry, Canaris's position gave him the opportunity to brief Hitler on international affairs. His power increased in 1938 when the Abwehr expanded to become a group of departments attached to the OKW (Supreme Headquarters of the German Armed Forces). By 1939, Canaris had developed the Abwehr into a highly respected intelligence-gathering agency.

The Abwehr functioned with unusual independence. Its mission was devoted to military intelligence, whereas the SS Reich Main Security Office dealt with internal threats to the party. Although their jurisdictions did not overlap, these organizations experienced much rivalry and friction over their responsibilities. Canaris made sure the SS had no authority over his personnel or operations. The men Canaris employed had impeccable professional credentials, operating with a freedom unknown to most government officials and army officers. They were better educated and had broader experience than the average Wehrmacht officer.[11]

Wohlthat and Canaris were well acquainted through their dealings in the government, and they were aware of each other's political misgivings. By 1939, Canaris, like Wohlthat, had demonstrated opposition to certain of Hitler's policies. Indeed, since 1935 he had been employing several men of Jewish background in his organization.[12] Hitler's acquiescence to Göring and Himmler's framing of General Werner von Blomberg, the minister of war, and General Werner von Fritsch, the commander in chief of the army, in 1938 shook Canaris's faith in the Führer, who took advantage of the generals' "disgrace" to remove many commanders from the military. This action diminished the traditional independence and power of the military, as Hitler replaced the head of the Wehrmacht and gave himself the power to "decide over war and peace." Hitler was determined to disable every individual and institution in Germany that could limit his absolute control over the Nazi Party and the state. Observing such moves, Canaris started to grasp "Hitler's perfidy and thirst for power." He also disapproved of the Nazi-Soviet Non-Aggression Pact signed in August 1939. After war broke out, Canaris told Field Marshal Wilhelm Keitel that the Wehrmacht would assume blame for the SS executions in Poland, as they had been carried out in its presence.[13] Keitel responded that Hitler had decided on this course of action, and if the army commander in chief did not want the Wehrmacht to perform these executions itself, Canaris would have to tolerate the SS. Although Canaris could not "officially" oppose this plan, he told Vice Admiral Leopold Bürkner a few days later in Vienna that "a war conducted in contempt of all ethics cannot be won. There is a divine justice even on this earth."[14] The Abwehr chief gathered documentary evidence of war crimes perpetrated by the SS and showed it to others, in the hope of convincing them to act against Hitler.[15]

After Wohlthat received information about the Rebbe from Pell in early October, he met with Canaris and told him about the case. Perceiving the favorable consequences of granting the request of highly placed officials in Washington, Canaris agreed to the rescue and promised to send officers to Warsaw for this purpose.[16] Another, more personal factor may have contributed to this remarkable decision. Canaris was demoralized. He apparently disagreed with Hitler's conduct of the war, and upon hearing that German divisions had crossed Poland's borders, he said, with tears streaming down his face, "This means the end of Germany." He expected France and England to declare war and Hitler to lead Germany to defeat. Nevertheless, he was elated at the success of the Polish campaign. Canaris was a complex person. On the one hand, he hated the fact that Hitler had launched Germany into another major European war. On the other hand, as a passionate officer and a patriot, he worked tirelessly on counterintelligence and espionage activities against Germany's enemies, even as he helped plan Hitler's overthrow. He knew that Germany would be better without Hitler at the helm.[17] So, helping a prominent person like the Rebbe escape this hostile environment was not out of character.

Canaris not only put his career on the line but also risked the lives of those he ordered to perform this task. He knew about the *Einsatzgruppen* (killing squads) that had been established by Himmler and Heydrich, who took all their instructions directly from Hitler. These squads followed the army and killed undesirables, particularly Jews and the Polish elite, under the operational name Tannenberg.[18]

Understanding that the rescue operation would be a delicate one, Canaris entrusted the job of escorting the Rebbe out of Poland to Major Dr. Ernst Bloch, a distinguished Wehrmacht officer who happened to be half Jewish. To prevent a paper trail, he probably gave all his orders orally. Canaris and Wohlthat had often dined with Bloch, who shared their animosity toward the Reich's anti-Semitic policies. Since the Abwehr was responsible for military information, it should not have engaged in such an operation, and Canaris knew he needed someone he could rely on. Perhaps he selected Bloch not only because he was an excellent soldier but also because of his Jewish background. It seemed logical to send a man of partial Jewish descent to save this important Jew, despite the deeper irony of Bloch's serving with distinction in the Wehrmacht.[19]

7

Bloch's Secret Mission

Kleider machen Leute [Clothes make the man].
—Gottfried Keller

Ernst Ferdinand Benjamin Bloch was born 1 May 1898 in Berlin, one of two sons of Dr. Oskar Bloch, a Jew, and his Gentile wife Margarete Schönberg. Margarete's first husband, also a Jew, had died in 1897, and she had two daughters with him. Mixed marriages were not uncommon in Germany; several thousand were taking place every year at the turn of the century.[1]

Bloch grew up in a wealthy home until his father died in 1910, and the family fell on hard times. Besides doing odd jobs to help support his mother and siblings, he worked hard at school and excelled in his studies. At the outbreak of war in 1914, sixteen-year-old Bloch left home without his mother's knowledge and tried to join the army. Several regiments rejected him because he was too young, but he eventually convinced Infantry Regiment 132 in Strasbourg to take him.[2] Like many other young Germans, he was thrilled at the prospect of serving his country and experiencing the adventures of war.

Bloch soon saw action. During the 1915 battle of Ypres in Belgium, an enemy soldier bayoneted Bloch through his lower jaw, destroying part of his chin and knocking out some teeth. Placing a boot on Bloch's shoulder, the soldier removed the blade and left him for dead. Bloch woke up in a field hospital. Remarkably, he returned to the front a few months later to fight at Verdun and the Somme in 1916, Champagne in 1917, and Flanders in 1918, where he was severely injured again, this time suffering shrapnel splinters in both legs, an arm, and his head.[3] Bloch recovered and returned to fight in the bloody trenches of the western front. By the end of the war he had been honored with two Iron Crosses, First and

Ernst Bloch as a Wehrmacht officer in late 1935 or early 1936. (Author's collection)

Second Class (similar to the US Silver and Bronze Stars), and the Wound Badge (akin to the Purple Heart). His brother Waldemar ("Waldi") was less fortunate, dying in 1919 from wounds suffered in battle. After the war, Bloch remained in the army.[4]

Bloch's heroism did not protect him from anti-Semitism. In 1921 he was rejected by a student fraternity for being Jewish.[5] His mother was shocked. She could understand why the fraternity would not want to take religious Jews, but the Bloch family had never been religious; in fact, she did not even consider her son Jewish. Moreover, being a Jew had not prevented her husband from becoming a successful medical doctor, and in his youth he had been a member of a distinguished fraternity. Enraged, Margarete wrote to her son: "I'm speechless and ashamed that even after the experiences since 1914 in the German Fatherland there are such narrow-minded people still around." But she also blamed her son for the humiliation: "Did you have to tell them that your father was a Jew? Why then? You don't have to advertise that information on your nose, and

Bloch with his sister after recovering from the severe wounds he received during World War I—probably 1916. (Author's collection)

besides, you have a Christian mother. . . . Your father didn't convert to Christianity, because he didn't want people to think that he did so simply to better his status. There are also Jews who have at least the same worth as the so-called Christians."[6] Bloch probably did mention that he was Christian, but his name likely provoked questions that he answered truthfully.

Bloch continued his studies at Friedrich Wilhelm University in Berlin, and in 1924 he received a doctorate in economics, graduating cum laude.[7] He remained on active duty as a Reichswehr officer throughout the Weimar Republic, and his Jewish background was not an issue. In 1930 Bloch married Sabine von Bosse, a Gentile. His father-in-law, Hans von Bosse, welcomed him into the family, writing tenderly:

My dear Son, for the first time I'm sending you my best wishes on your birthday. . . . You will see that you now belong to us and that our hearts are bound to you. We especially thank your parents for this day, and now we have taken their position [Bloch's mother had died 1922]. During this new year, you have committed yourself

to Sabine, and thus God bless you and make you both happy!
Happiness grows from the inside and cannot be hunted down but
rather must grow like a healthy fruit nurtured by sunshine and rain.
. . .

In True Love, Your Father[8]

Having lost his own father at an early age, Bloch must have been deeply
touched by these kind words. Not surprisingly, his union with Sabine
started out with a strong foundation. Throughout his married life, Bloch
dedicated himself to Sabine and never forgot his in-laws' kindness and
generosity in welcoming him into the family. Society at large did not share
the sentiments of his new family, especially after Hitler's assumption of
power in 1933, but Bloch would not encounter anti-Semitism again until
years after the fraternity episode.

In 1935 Admiral Canaris recruited Bloch to head the *I/Wirtschafts-
abteilung* (Foreign Economic Intelligence Department), tasked with
gathering data on the industrial capacity of foreign countries. Canaris
considered Bloch one of his most capable officers. Besides gathering intelligence on foreign industries, Bloch led German and foreign businessmen on industrial tours of the Reich and, after Germany's occupation
of the west in 1940, to Belgium, France, and the Netherlands. Canaris
praised Bloch on one occasion, writing, "[Your department] has accurately discerned its objectives: to keep watch on the enemy [Belgium and
France] munitions industry, discover its productive capacity and ascertain the local situation."[9]

The issue of Bloch's Jewish paternity surfaced again in 1935 with
passage of the Nuremberg racial laws, which decreed the segregation of
"Aryan" Germans from Germans of Jewish descent. On 14 November
1935 the Reich Interior Ministry issued a supplement to the legislation,
officially creating the "racial" categories of German, Jew, half-Jew (Jewish *Mischling* first degree), and quarter-Jew (Jewish *Mischling* second degree), each with its own regulations. Full Jews had three or four Jewish
grandparents or were members of the Jewish faith. Half-Jews had two
Jewish grandparents, and quarter-Jews had one Jewish grandparent.[10]
However, if a *Mischling* practiced the Jewish religion or was married to a
Jew, the Nazis counted that person as a full Jew (*Geltungsjude*). Accord-

Photograph taken for Bloch's military identification papers. The horrible wound on his face was quite pronounced, despite several surgeries to repair it. (Author's collection)

ing to Hitler, an individual who was more than 50 percent Jewish was evil (*übel*) and not worth saving. Ironically, the Nazis had to use religious criteria to define these "racial" categories, using birth, baptismal, marriage, and death certificates. These records, which were often stored in churches, temples, and courthouses, indicated what religion a person adhered to or had left. They also implicated churches in the process of proving one's Aryan heritage. Sadly, most German churches willingly turned over their archives to help document these *Untermenschen* [subhumans].[11]

The 1935 Nuremberg laws provided the substructure for additional anti-Jewish legislation aimed at maintaining the purity of the "Aryan" race. However, Article 7 of a supplementary decree of the Nuremberg laws authorized Hitler to "Aryanize" individuals who had been labeled Jew or *Mischling*. Applicants for Aryanization had to submit photographs taken from different angles (Hitler attached great importance to physical appearance) and detailed documentation about themselves; they

As head of the Abwehr's Foreign Economic Intelligence Department, Bloch often took foreign industrialists on tours of the Reich's factories, as he did with these Japanese businessmen in the spring of 1939. (Author's collection)

sometimes hired attorneys to help them prepare such files, which were then submitted to Hitler for his personal evaluation. Late in 1939 Canaris brought Bloch's case to the Führer, who signed documents declaring Bloch of "German blood" (*deutschblütig*), thus removing Bloch's "birth defect" with a stroke of his pen. Since there were many individuals of Jewish descent who were valuable to Hitler, he gave himself the option of keeping them around. Despite his desire to be able to tap into that talent pool, Hitler was stingy in bestowing Aryan status on people. Sometimes the families of those who had been Aryanized benefited from this clemency; in other cases it did nothing to help their relatives marked for extermination.

Canaris probably waited four years to seek the exemption for Bloch because his background had not been an issue until then. Many decorated veterans of World War I enjoyed several years of special treatment or indifference after the passage of the racial laws. It was not until 1939

This photograph of Bloch, taken in late 1938, was probably sent to Hitler in 1939 with his application for Aryanization. On the basis of his good military record and his "Germanic looks," Hitler declared Bloch of "German blood," allowing him to stay in the Wehrmacht. (Author's collection)

that Bloch's Jewish background caught up with him.[12] Bloch's application for Aryanization included his military records, high school and college transcripts, and recommendations from teachers and military superiors, as well as head-on and profile photographs. Bloch's official Aryanization document most likely followed the standard format: "I, Adolf Hitler, leader of the German nation, approve Ernst Bloch to be of German blood. His children may also claim this classification as long as Bloch does not marry anyone of foreign blood." Bloch and his descendants were thereby protected against racial discrimination.[13]

Bloch's son Martin later wrote, "My father felt he was German, and as a German he served his country. . . . Moreover, he felt protected by Canaris, in whose office he worked." Canaris described Bloch in a 14 March 1937 evaluation as a "reliable person . . . a diligent worker . . .

Nur für den Dienstgebrauch

im Heerespersonalamt

Liste von **a k t i v e n** Offizieren,
die selbst oder deren Ehefrauen jüdische Mischlinge sind
und vom Führer für deutschblütig erklärt wurden

Name u. Vorname	Dienstgrad u. R.D.A.	Dienststelle	Geburts- datum	Bluts- anteile
Adlhoch Franz	Gen.Major 1.11.42 (11)	Kdt. St.O.Kdtr. Rudnja	17. 6.93	Ehefrau 50%
Altmann Helmut	Oberst 1.2.42 (101)	Kdr. A.R.347	4. 1.97	selbst 25%
Andresen Hans	Major 1.1.42 (424)	b. Kw.Trsp.Abt.356 als/Kdr. Abt.	6. 8.07	selbst 25%
A. old Reinhard	Major 1.6.43 (6)	St. Gen.d.Pi. H.Gru.Nord	21. 5.12	selbst 25%
Aschenbrandt Heinrich	Gen.Major 1.12.41 (10)	Kdt. F.Kdtr.238	—	Sohn aus 1.Ehe, 25%
Behrens Wilhelm	Gen.Major 1.1.42 (5)	Kdr. Div. Nr.193	23. 8.88	selbst ?
Belli von Pino Anton	Oberst 1.4.58 (33)	F.Res.OKH, Dienst regelt Chef Kriegs- gesch.Abt.	13.12.81	selbst 25%
Bieringer Ludwig	Gen.Major 1.7.43 (1)	F.Res.OKH, kdt.zum Mil.Befh.i.Frkr.zur Einweis.i.d.G.eines Feldkdt.	12. 8.92	Ehefrau 50%
Bloch Dr. Ernst	Obstlt. 1.7.41 (45)	F.Res.OKH, kdt.zur 213.I.D. z.Verw.als Btls.Kdr.	1. 5.98	selbst 50%
Bonin Swantus	Oberst 1.4.42 (544)	Vorstand Bekl.Amt Erfurt	—	Ehefrau 50%
Borchardt Robert	Major 1.6.43 (32d)	Pz.Aufkl.Abt.7 Wiedereinberufung als akt.Offz.genehmigt, aber noch nicht arisiert	9. 1.12	?
Borowietz Willibald	Gen.Lt. 1.7.43 (7)	Pz.Jäg.Tr.Schule, hat Ritterkreuz, ist in engl.Gefangenschaft	17. 9.93	3 Kinder (50%) arisiert, Ehe- frau(Jüd)verstb.
Braune Günther	Oberst z.V.	z.Zt. Gehilfe beim Mil.Attaché Madrid	18.10.88	selbst 50%
Bruhnke Dr. Johannes	Oberst-Vet. 1.8.41 (1)	Wehrkr.Vet.IX	—	Ehefrau 25%
Colli Robert	Oberst 1.7.43 (36a)	Kdr. Gren.Rgt.547	27. 6.98	selbst 50%
Emmenthal Karl	Oberst 1.10.42 (50)	Bev.Trsp.Offz.beim AOK 1	26. 6.01	Ehefrau 25%

A 1944 list of "active officers who are either Jewish *Mischlinge* or
married to Jewish *Mischlinge* and whom Hitler has declared of
German blood." The "Blood Percentage" in the column on the far
right shows Bloch as 50 percent Jewish. (Author's collection and
Bundesarchiv)

**Jm Namen
des
Deutſchen Volſes**

erteile ich

dem Major (E)

Dr.Ernst B l o c h

die Genehmigung zur Annahme

des Ritterkreuzes

des Königlich Ungarischen Verdienstordens.

Berchtesgaden
~~Berlin~~, den   19. Oktober 1938

Der Führer und Reichsſanzler

D 31 ⓖ (5.38)

Hitler's decree awarding Bloch the Hungarian Knight's Cross Service Medal on 19 October 1938. The signature was a stamped facsimile. (Author's collection)

[who] does his duty well." In June 1938 Bloch was promoted to major. Later that year he was awarded the Hungarian Knight's Cross Service Medal.[14] Obviously, Bloch's Jewish ancestry did not matter to Canaris, but under Hitler's regime, Canaris had to be careful to protect Bloch, whom he clearly valued.

In addition to Bloch, Canaris chose other men of Jewish descent to help rescue Rebbe Schneersohn. One was Private Johannes Hamburger, a quarter-Jew who spoke French, Russian, and Polish and was familiar with Warsaw.[15] His grandfather had been a rabbi who converted to Christianity. Before the war, Hamburger had thought about becoming a priest, but instead he worked in the Abwehr, using his language skills and uncanny ability to get reluctant people to talk.[16] Sergeant Klaus Schenk, a half-Jew, was also recruited for the rescue mission.[17] He had a Jewish mother and thus, according to Jewish law, was a Jew; however, like most other *Mischlinge* in the Wehrmacht, he had been raised a Christian. Schenk had distinguished himself in battle in Poland and had received the Iron Cross for defending a position against attacking Polish infantrymen and snipers. One report claimed he killed more than twenty Polish soldiers and, when he ran out of ammunition, threw grenades to hold the enemy back until reinforcements arrived. He was the only survivor of his twenty-man unit.[18] Like Bloch, Schenk's face was scarred, but his injury was the result of a duel with a fraternity brother. In addition to being half Jewish, Schenk was homosexual, and he feared that someone would discover his secret. He had cause to worry, since the Nazis persecuted gays as sexual degenerates and would go on to kill thousands, using paragraph 175 of the German criminal code as legal justification. So with two strikes against him, Schenk knew that any transgression he committed would be viewed especially harshly under Hitler.[19]

The fourth man on this unusual mission was Major Johannes Horatzek, head of the Abwehr office in Warsaw. Because of his knowledge of Warsaw and Polish, he played a key role in locating the Rebbe. After the successful conquest of Poland, Canaris traveled around Warsaw with Horatzek, observing its destruction and confiding, "Our children's children will have to bear the blame for this." The Warsaw Abwehr chief was a rather fat man, with dark eyes and hair. Canaris apparently had a good working relationship with him.[20]

Bloch, Schenk, and Hamburger were not unusual figures in the Abwehr. Canaris employed a great many *Mischlinge*, including a quarter-Jew named Hans von Dohnanyi who, like Bloch, had been Aryanized.[21] Von Dohnanyi was one of the principal collectors of information on Nazi war crimes, as well as the brother-in-law of Pastor Dietrich Bonhoffer, a famous Nazi resister. In his biography of Canaris, Karl Heinz Abshagen writes that Abwehr personnel were often exempted from in-depth security checks of their family trees. As a result, although many were affected by the Nuremberg laws, they were allowed to remain. Thanks to Canaris, several Jews and half-Jews were protected from the Gestapo by their service in the Abwehr.[22]

Unlike Bloch, who was a career officer, many *Mischlinge* in the Wehrmacht had been drafted. The Nazis made military service mandatory for half-Jews and quarter-Jews. Although about 150,000 so-called *Mischlinge* served in the Wehrmacht,[23] most could not become noncommissioned officers or officers without Hitler's personal consent. The Jewish German population had a strong tradition of serving in the armed forces; during World War I, 100,000 Jews—almost one in five—had served in the German military.[24] Coming from military backgrounds, many *Mischlinge* hoped their service would protect them and their families from the rising tide of anti-Semitism. Thus, the presence of Bloch, Schenk, Hamburger, and von Dohnanyi in the Wehrmacht was not as strange as one might think.[25] Nor was it odd that they would be selected for the mission to find and rescue the Rebbe. Although it may have seemed logical to Canaris to send men of Jewish descent on this mission, ironically, they were the worst choice in terms of gaining the Rebbe's trust. For many religious Jews, those who turn away from Judaism or reject their heritage are considered *meshumadim* (converts)—dangerous people who have bent over backward to distance themselves from their sacred past and may be willing to betray old ties to prove new loyalties. So, for many reasons, this rescue mission was fraught with complications.

8

The Search Begins

All are fully aware of the teaching of the Ba'al Shem Tov that every
utterance and breath, everything one hears and sees, contains guidance in the
service of G-d.
—Rebbe Joseph Isaac Schneersohn

From late September into early October, the Rebbe and his followers
remained trapped in Warsaw, and despite the constant threat of arrest and
persecution, they continued to observe Orthodox tradition. On 25–26
September, at the height of the bombing, the Rebbe had a sukkah (small
hut) built for the upcoming holiday, inspiring his followers to believe that
the Jewish spirit would not be defeated.[1] He told them, "For Hashem to
do his part, we have to build a sukkah," and he promised "a long life to
whoever goes to gather the branches we need for the roof." The fragility
of this temporary dwelling—a sukkah has three walls and a roof composed of natural material that is partially open to the sky—may have been
a metaphor for the fragility of Jewish life in German-occupied Poland.
Ironically, it was a secular Jew who scurried off to do the Rebbe's bidding.[2] From 28 September until 5 October they celebrated Sukkot (Feast
of Tabernacles), which traditionally marks the end of the harvest. During
this holiday, Jews live in their homemade sukkot (plural of sukkah) to
commemorate the flimsy huts the Israelites lived in as they wandered in
the wilderness for forty years after their flight from slavery in Egypt (described in Exodus).

After Sukkot came Simchat Torah (Rejoicing of the Law) on 6 October. During the course of each year, the entire Torah is read in synagogues, and Simchat Torah marks the conclusion of these readings from
Genesis to the end of Deuteronomy. The Rebbe said that during Simchat
Torah, Jews seize the holy scroll and leap into dance. "[Men] dance with

the Torah—they are making the Torah happy. In the midst of this joy, however, one needs to do some thinking. True, we are happy with the Torah. But is the Torah happy with us?"[3] As the Nazis set up their administration in Warsaw, many Jews had difficulty focusing on the holidays, and the Rebbe may have felt the Torah was not happy with its people. In many communities throughout Poland, the *Hakafot*, the ritual marching and dancing with the Torah scrolls, was probably omitted in 1939 to avoid attracting unnecessary attention from the German authorities.[4] Chaim Kaplan wrote, "Never before have we missed expressing our joy in the eternal Torah—even during the Middle Ages. After 7:00 P.M. there is a curfew in the city, and even in the hours before the curfew we live in dread of the Nazi conquerors' cruelty. The Nazi policy toward Jews is now in full swing. . . . Midian and Moab [ancient enemies of the Israelites] have joined forces in order to oppress Israel."[5]

At the beginning of October, rumors circulated in Warsaw that the French had invaded Germany and taken twelve cities. In reality, the vaunted French army had remained idle, aside from its brief foray into the Saarland in September. The news services had shut down, and no one knew for sure what was going on in the outside world. In any case, most people had no time to think about politics and world events—they were too busy searching for food and drinking water. The Nazis rounded up Jews for forced labor, and a puzzled Kaplan exclaimed on 18 October, "Great God! Are you making an end to Polish Jewry? 'Your people' cannot understand: Why is the world silent?" Many in the Rebbe's group feared for their lives, and the Germans likely forced several of the younger men to join work details. Many Jews resigned themselves to a fate they believed would soon end in death.[6]

Back in America, Chabad continued to explore every option to help the Rebbe. Israel Jacobson had received information from the German vice-consul in New York that if they wanted to enlist the aid of German authorities, they should "try to send a prepaid cable to the German commanding General [Walter von] Brauchitsch in Warsaw."[7] Jacobson passed this on to Chabad's legal counsel Sam Kramer. Kramer's failure to act on this advice was wise; Brauchitsch, who had just helped defeat Poland and was part of planning the next invasion of France, Denmark, and Norway, was a strong supporter of Hitler and probably would have ignored a request to save the Rebbe. Thinking more practically, Kramer suggested the Lubavitchers ask his friend Max Rhoade, a brilliant lawyer, to start the paperwork to get the Rebbe and others out of Europe—namely, Rabbi Menachem Mendel Schneerson (the future seventh Rebbe) and his wife Chaya Moussia, and Rabbi Samarius Gourary and his wife Chana and son Barry.[8] The process was complicated by the absence of birth certificates. Many of the relevant documents were in the Soviet Union and therefore impossible to obtain.[9] Senator William Borah had been trying to help Gourary and his family leave Europe since early 1939, obviously without success.[10] Yet the fact that Borah wanted to help Gourary illustrates the Lubavitchers' connections in Washington, as well as the difficulty of obtaining entry visas for Jews.

Since Hitler's takeover in 1933, the number of rabbis seeking refuge in the United States had increased dramatically. Section 4(d) of the Immigration Act of 1924 allowed "ministers" of religion to enter the country on nonquota status.[11] But many had to prove they were employable, something officials in the Visa Department doubted. That department was headed by Avra Warren, a man who was not inclined to help Jewish refugees. In January 1940 Roosevelt would pick assistant secretary of state Breckinridge Long to oversee European refugee policy. For those hoping to help Jewish refugees enter the United States, the choice of Long was disastrous—the worst appointment made by Roosevelt in his four terms as president. Long was absolutely the wrong man to place in a position of power when so many lives hung in the balance. Long's self-avowed anti-Semitism and his ungenerous spirit would prove deadly for refugees. When he took over the department headed by Warren, he found a tradition of unwillingness to help those in need. One could argue that, to some degree, these officials were merely adhering to the spirit of the Immigration Act of 1924, which Marc E. McClure rightly describes as an "ethnically biased immigration quota system."[12]

After the war, diplomats who defied their governments and the law to save lives received well-deserved praise. But they were the exceptions. Swedish diplomat Raoul Wallenberg set up safe houses and saved thousands of Jews. The US vice-consul in Marseilles, Hiram Bingham, ignored US immigration law and issued travel documents to 2,000 Jews. The Nazi and German trade attaché Georg F. Duckwitz alerted the Danes to the

Avra M. Warren, head of the US Visa Department until January 1940. (National Archives)

planned deportation of Jews and helped arrange for the escape of 7,000 to Sweden. Chiune (Sempo) Sugihara, the Japanese consul in Kovno, Lithuania, ignored orders and issued thousands of Japanese visas, saving 1,000 Jews. German businessman and Nazi Party member John Rabe helped set up the Nanking Safety Zone, which saved more than 200,000 Chinese from the genocidal Japanese maniacs who took over the city in December 1937.[13] These individuals and a few others defied their superiors, bent or broke rules and laws, issued false identity documents and travel papers, and thereby saved many from death. But unfortunately, there were not enough of them. During these dark times, Long used his great intelligence, excellent education, charm, leadership skills, and political connections to thwart the efforts of refugees who were desperate to immigrate to the United States, even when American law would have permitted them to enter. He also worked to keep information about the Holocaust from government officials and the public.[14]

In the end, Long would not stop the Rebbe and his party from finding a new home in America because they had strong support in the halls of power in Washington, DC. Long's position, however, made the situation worse for the Rebbe and for others like him. In the early 1930s Long reportedly described *Mein Kampf* as "eloquent in opposition to Jewry and to Jews as exponents of Communism and chaos." He was also an "ardent fan of Italy's Fascist dictator Benito Mussolini." In the 1940s Long was adamant about restricting Jewish immigration to America. Although he mirrored to some degree the will of Congress and the American people, Long took it upon himself to keep foreigners out of America, especially Jews. He found himself in a constant struggle with refugee advocates and radicals, and he believed these people were motivated by personal animosity, not by a humane concern for those who were suffering under the Nazis. Long regularly fed the president false and misleading information, thereby exacerbating governmental inaction.[15] But in 1939, Long did not yet control immigration, and Warren, who was most involved with the Rebbe's case, was not yet serving directly under Long.

Given the indifference or hostility toward Jewish immigrants among some at the Department of State, it is hardly surprising that officials in the Visa Department made the application process as difficult as possible. Agents working under Warren and his second in command, Eliot Coulter, regularly questioned the sincerity of the rabbis they investigated. Believing that most of the rabbis would become public charges, they interpreted the immigration laws in the most restrictive way and rejected their applications. Needless to say, Max Rhoade faced incredible odds in his efforts to help the Rebbe reach the safety of the United States.[16]

The Lubavitchers in America had become increasingly worried about the Rebbe. A month had passed without any updates since the initial flurry of appeals to politicians. Nothing seemed to be happening. But good news would soon arrive. On 19 October US chargé d'affaires Alexander Kirk in Berlin informed Robert Pell at the State Department that an officer (Bloch) had been charged with finding the Rebbe and helping him escape. It appeared that Bloch was having difficulty finding the Rebbe, though.[17] On 24 October Jacobson telegraphed Chaim Lieberman, the Rebbe's secretary in Riga, informing him, "We received word through State Department Washington that German military authorities in Warsaw desirous of cooperating have dispatched officers to locate Rabbi and then accompany him to Riga."[18]

Soon Arthur Rabinovitz, Chabad's US legal counsel, informed Justice Louis Brandeis of the Rebbe's address. Brandeis relayed this information to Benjamin V. Cohen, who then told Pell. On 28 October Pell told Kirk in Germany that Schneersohn "may possibly be located at the Gourari home, Bonifraterska Street 29." Kirk seems to have taken a keen interest in the Rebbe's escape. Interestingly, Kirk was a homosexual and had to keep that fact a secret from his colleagues in the State Department, as it was grounds for dismissal and loss of his security clearance. Ironically, one of the key Americans involved in the Rebbe's rescue was a person the Rebbe would have disapproved of due to his sexual orientation.[19]

By November, Nazi persecution of Polish Jewry was becoming codified. The Germans required Jews in Poland to wear armbands with the Star of David, and many Jews feared being harassed and arrested.[20] Both Jewish converts to Christianity and religious Jews were compelled to wear the armbands. Some Jews took a perverse pleasure in observing the persecution of converts to Christianity. Kaplan wrote, "I shall, however, have revenge on our 'converts.' I will laugh aloud at the sight of their tragedy. These poor creatures, whose number has radically increased in recent times, should have known that the 'racial' laws do not differentiate between Jews who become Christians and those who retain their faith. Conversion brought them but small deliverance. . . . This is the first time in my life that a feeling of vengeance has given me pleasure."[21]

Many Jews believed that those Jews who renounced their faith weakened the body of Israel and betrayed their people. All too often, recent converts from Judaism demonstrated cruelty toward practicing Jews. The truth was that, although some Jews converted out of religious conviction, many others did so to better their social status and to avoid discrimination and persecution. For many centuries, the European churches, in league with civil authorities, had made being Jewish such a terrible disadvantage that no Christians would want to convert to Judaism, and Jews would be enticed to convert to Christianity. For instance, when German Jewish poet and writer Heinrich Heine was baptized, he claimed he had bought "an entry ticket to European culture" (*Der Taufzettel ist das Entrée Billett zur europäischen Kultur*).[22] The Rebbe looked down on such converts, calling them "apostates" and *nebbich* Jews (Jews to be pitied); he was even more repulsed by those "light-minded ignoramuses" who followed disbelievers and atheists. To observant Jews, abandoning Judaism, regardless of the reason, was wrong and a sin against God.[23] As the

Nazis started to lump together all those classified as Jewish on a "racial basis," regardless of religion, it created much confusion and dissension among the Jewish population, as illustrated by Kaplan's statement above.

Day after day, in the midst of all the chaos, Bloch combed the sections of Warsaw where Orthodox and Hasidic Jews lived, inquiring about the Rebbe. As might be expected, most Lubavitchers feared the German army major and told him nothing. On one occasion, Bloch confronted a Lubavitcher rabbi on the street and asked him to spread the word among the community that he had come to Warsaw to save Schneersohn. The Lubavitcher rubbed his eyes in disbelief, stood frozen, and finally stumbled away. Another time, Bloch approached a religious Jew and inquired after the Rebbe's whereabouts. The man's eyes widened, his mouth opened, and his shoulders slouched; then he slowly raised his hand, stroked his beard, and turned and disappeared down an alley.[24] The idea that German soldiers were seeking to help the Rebbe must have struck these men as incredible and absurd. Frustrated by his fruitless search, Bloch asked Hamburger what he should say to religious Jews when he met them. The major realized that the proper military greeting—name, rank, and mission—did not encourage the divulging of information. Smiling, Hamburger said, "To start with, say Shalom. Shalom is a good word."[25] Bloch grinned and repeated the word a few times.

Bloch and his men sometimes wore civilian clothes as they searched Warsaw. Protocol probably prevented them from discarding their uniforms entirely, and they certainly did not want to come under the scrutiny of the Gestapo. Their gray tunics provided anonymity among the thousands of Wehrmacht soldiers stationed in Warsaw. Since there had been long-standing friction between the SS and the Abwehr, especially in foreign intelligence activities, any help in disguising their activities was welcomed. Canaris had his men pay close attention to the SS in Poland. This was especially true after 17 October, when the army "lost its administrative control in Poland." On that day, at the Reich Chancellery, Hitler announced to an audience that included SS head Heinrich Himmler and commander of the armed forces General Wilhelm Keitel that Poland would henceforth be run by the general government set up by the German military and headed by his old party crony and lawyer Hans Frank. Frank was a rabid anti-Semite and gave the SS full reign in Poland to

An Orthodox Jew carrying a suitcase runs through
the wreckage of Warsaw in a photograph taken by the
German military on 4 October 1939. (National Archives)

implement its terror. Bloch would have a difficult time navigating in this
environment.[26]

Frank did not waste any time in issuing edicts that would dehumanize
the Jews in occupied Poland and strip them of their rights. On 25 October
Frank declared that Jewish males between the ages of fourteen and sixty
would be required to work at German-controlled public works projects.
They would be either placed in brigades and marched out to their stations
near the city or housed in special camps set up near the projects.[27] System-

atic persecution, ostracism, and ghettoization became the modus operandi of Frank's thugs throughout German-occupied Poland. This represented the beginning of the vortex of the Holocaust storm that would reach murderous velocity in two short years. If Bloch did not get the Rebbe out of the country, he and his followers would be separated from one another, forced to do hard labor, and segregated throughout Poland.

In the early days of the Polish occupation, many of these SS hooligans behaved as if they were crosses between sadistic fraternity brothers hazing their pledges and psychopathic serial killers playing with their prey before finally killing it. Gregory Wallance aptly describes them as "Caligula-like ghouls."[28] For instance, on 30 October a group of SS men entered the town of Turek, herded a group of Jews into a synagogue, and made them crawl like animals among the pews while the SS whipped them. Then, in a particularly humiliating act, the SS made the Jews pull down their pants and thrashed them on their bare buttocks. It reminds one of Shakespeare's *King Lear*, where he writes that the policeman who applies the lash to a whore has a need to use her for the very reason he is applying the lash. One poor Jewish soul, who had defecated in his pants, was forced to take a handful of his own excrement and smear it over the faces of his fellow Jews. Brave Wehrmacht general Blaskowitz once again protested these horrible actions, but to little avail. The German nation had been commandeered by a host of immature, sick-minded men consumed by hatred. The twisted road to Auschwitz was getting straighter every day. Blaskowitz's vehement condemnation brought the unwanted attention of Himmler. According to SS general Karl Wolff: "Himmler knew that there were many senior officers who were opposed to the policy, but that did not matter to him. He simply said, 'The Führer and I agree that if Blaskowitz, Guderian and others wish to oppose our Great mission, they would be well reminded of their position. . . . Müller [Heinrich Müller, head of the Gestapo] and his men do not differentiate between the weak and the traitorous.'"[29]

A number of Nazi leaders thought the Polish Jews should be killed en masse. Propaganda minister Joseph Goebbels visited Lodz on 2 November and called the 200,000 Jews in that metropolis "indescribable. They are no longer people, but beasts. There is therefore not a humanitarian, but a surgical task. Here one must make a radical incision. Otherwise Europe will be ruined by the Jewish sickness." On 22 November the Nazis rounded up fifty-three Jews at 9 Nalewki Street and executed them because a Jew from that district had killed a Polish policeman. This was "the first mass killing of Jews in Warsaw."[30] The life span of the typical Jew in Poland was about to be dramatically reduced.

On the basis of documents in Washington, it seems that Bloch and the others, probably including Warsaw's Abwehr chief Major Horatzek, discussed a strategy to convince the Rebbe of their good intentions. They were convinced that he was refusing, for obvious reasons, to reveal himself. Bloch and Hamburger agreed that instead of confronting men on the street, they should try going door to door. They did not know whether the Rebbe was alive or dead, and they had made little progress since their arrival. The direct approach was the only way, Bloch said.[31]

By that time, news of the soldiers' search must have reached the Rebbe, who sent someone, probably his son-in-law Samarius Gourary, to ascertain the Germans' intentions. This proved difficult, since most Polish Jews had every reason not to trust the Germans. The Lubavitchers were suspicious of the German soldiers who claimed to want to help them; Bloch and his men, for their part, probably felt little kinship with the Orthodox and Hasidic Jews of Warsaw. We know that Rhoade received information at the beginning of November that the Rebbe "apparently misunderstands or questions officer's motives."[32]

The Lubavitchers were justifiably skeptical of the Germans, even if they were *Mischlinge*. Many German *Mischling* soldiers serving in Poland—people just like Bloch—reacted negatively to *Ostjuden* or issues of Jewishness. In this respect and others, many *Mischlinge* had the same anti-Semitic feelings as non-Jews and were disgusted by the Hasidic Jews' appearance, habits, and living conditions. Obergefreiter Heinz-Günter Angreß, a half-Jew, noted that as his unit moved deeper into Poland, he found that *Der Stürmer* (a virulent anti-Semitic newspaper) had not exaggerated. The Jews there "looked simply horrible."[33] Unteroffizier Hans Mühlbacher wrote in his diary:

The Jews are dressed better on Saturday and go outside the ghetto (Ropczyce, Poland). I walk through the ghetto. It's awful what horrible people I see there. With grimacing faces they lean against the

doors of their homes and businesses and stare amazed at the tall officers walking by. . . . Truly two worlds stand opposite one another.
. . . The Jews give the impression of being the eternal Ahasverus.[34] . . .
The Jews make a much more decadent impression probably due to
centuries of inbreeding.[35]

Although Mühlbacher had a Jewish mother, he felt no connection with
the Orthodox Jews in the ghetto. He depicted them as weak and lacking
self-respect, noting they did not carry themselves upright like the Germans. His description of these Jews as "decadent" and products of "inbreeding" showed his utter contempt for them, and he derisively called
them *Ahasverus* (wandering Jew). Ironically, Mühlbacher's Jewish family
had "wandered" from the east before finally settling in Vienna.

Most *Mischlinge* could not believe that any of their ancestors looked
like the *Ostjuden*, and they found their poverty and archaic customs embarrassing. Half-Jew Gefreiter Friedrich Schlesinger, a *Landser* (common
foot soldier) during the 1939 invasion of Poland, was appalled to think
that his ancestors had looked like the *Ostjuden*.[36] Today, many believe that
such prejudice was felt only by non-Jewish Germans, but anti-Semitism
had spread to *Mischlinge* through years of virulent, pervasive propaganda
and assimilation. Two totally different cultures were colliding.[37]

Many *Mischling* veterans reported seeing other soldiers cut off Jews'
beards, force Jews in traditional garb to push military wagons, or prod
Jews with guns.[38] As Mark Roseman writes, "much of the violence against
Jews" during the campaign in Poland came "from ordinary soldiers,
whose antisemitism was aroused by the strange-looking eastern Jews."[39]
Many *Mischling* soldiers mistakenly believed the anti-Semitism directed
at *Ostjuden* would never affect them or their families.[40]

Because most *Mischlinge* did not look, act, or feel like the ultra-
Orthodox or Hasidic Jews they encountered in Poland, they misjudged
Hitler's true intentions. By the same token, the Lubavitchers would not
have accepted these children of converts, whom the Rebbe called apostates, as their religious brethren.[41] Even if the Lubavitchers had known
that Bloch and some of his team were *Mischlinge*, they were unlikely to
place their trust in any soldier of the Third Reich. In fact, they might have
trusted them less, not more.

A Lawyer's Work

Tut nichts! Der Jude wird verbrannt! [It doesn't matter, the Jew will be burned.]
—Gotthold Ephraim Lessing, *Nathan der Weise*

On 18 October 1939 American Lubavitchers held a fund-raiser for the Rebbe's rescue during the fifth annual *Malava Malke* at the New York City Jewish Center.[1] A letter from America's Chabad headquarters had gone out to several Jewish organizations at the beginning of October saying, "Every Jew, having a spark of Judaism within his breast, must conscientiously work to help save the Rabbi from the lurking peril, and thereby have a part in the merit of the great Mitzvah of *Pidyon Shvuim* [redemption of captives] and *Pikuach Nefashoth* [preservation of life] of our great Rabbi!" Sam Kramer and several others attended the fund-raiser, and although many turned out in moral support, only $2,000 was collected. The organizers had hoped to raise at least $10,000, and the lack of donations was demoralizing.[2]

Kramer, Chabad's legal counsel, was a close friend of the Rebbe and was primarily responsible for raising the money for his rescue. A World War I naval veteran, Kramer had helped found the Young Men's Hebrew Association (YMHA) and the Sons of Israel synagogue in Brooklyn, organize the first eastern board of directors for the Anti-Defamation League, and found Israel Zion Hospital; he also helped save a Swedish Protestant church from bankruptcy, in addition to supporting and running Chabad in America.[3] He was a busy man described as a *Macher* (one who makes things happen). Although a Lubavitcher, Kramer was clean-shaven and

Samuel Kramer, legal counsel for Chabad in the United States. He was responsible for contacting Max Rhoade, who helped organize the rescue. Kramer also provided much of the funding. (Debby Kramer Neumark)

wore modern clothes. He lived according to Torah values but wanted to bridge the gap between Jewish Orthodoxy and modern society. He felt that, as a religious Jew, he must not separate himself from the world but rather live within it and try to make it better, using the religious foundation he respected and loved. He honored his family's traditions and the leaders of the Orthodox community his forefathers had belonged to. Kramer's intimate knowledge of Chabad and his ability to operate in the real world made him indispensable to the Rebbe's rescue, since he knew how to translate the Lubavitchers' wishes into effective political action.

Realizing that the Lubavitcher rabbis had little experience dealing with governmental authorities, Kramer wrote to his close friend and distinguished DC lawyer Max Rhoade and asked for his assistance in October 1939. He believed Rhoade could link these two communities and achieve effective action. Born in 1897, young Max had come to America with his family in 1901 during the massive influx of eastern European Jewry at the turn of the century. When his father Joseph Zerach, an Orthodox Jew, disembarked the ship in Norfolk, Virginia, he saw a sign for "Rhoade Department Store" and decided to change the family name to Rhoade to make them seem more American. The family had arrived in the United States with counterfeit passports under the false name of Silverman, so the authorities could not trace where they had come from. Joseph had fled to avoid continued service in the Russian army; he wanted to live in the land of opportunity. The Rhoade family struggled initially, but Joseph eventually became a wealthy businessman and was able to send his children, a son and two daughters, to college. It had been a long journey for Joseph—from working in a cobbler's shop in an eastern European ghetto at age seven to living the American dream of education and good jobs for his children.

Max Rhoade knew the value of coming to America and took full advantage of the opportunities presented to him. Rhoade studied at George Washington University Law School and graduated in 1918. At the university he was editor of the *Hatchet*, the campus newspaper; deputy editor of the yearbook; president of the Menorah Society (similar to modern-day Hillels that promote Jewish life on college campuses); secretary of the Walter Clark Law Club; a member of Phi Alpha Fraternity; and an assistant law librarian for a year (students ran the library in those days). From

DEPARTMENT OF STATE
WASHINGTON

July 6, 1934.

To the American

    Diplomatic and Consular Officers.

Sirs:

    At the instance of the Honorable
Robert F. Wagner, Senator of the United
States from the State of New York, I
take pleasure in introducing to you
Mr. Max Rhoade of Baltimore, Maryland,
who is about to proceed abroad.

    I cordially bespeak for Mr. Rhoade
such courtesies and assistance as you
may be able to render, consistently
with your official duties.

        Very truly yours,

        Cordell Hull

Max Rhoade was well connected, as evidenced by this personalized letter
written on his behalf by Secretary of State Cordell Hull. (Author's collection)

Photograph of bearer

This passport is good for travel in all countries unless otherwise limited.
This passport is valid for two years from the date of issue unless limited to a shorter period.

PHOTOGRAPH ATTACHED
DEPARTMENT OF STATE
WASHINGTON

Max Rhoade's passport picture. (Author's collection)

an early age, Rhoade showed a willingness to get involved and to be a leader. Honing his skills as a thinker and a writer came in handy later for the long letters he would write about legal cases.

According to family members, Rhoade was a genius. He had an incredible memory and could follow any argument to its logical conclusion. Coupled with that genius, however, was his eccentric behavior. He was a pack rat and had difficulty connecting emotionally with others. He would obsess about an issue until it dominated his entire life, to the exclusion of personal relationships. He was a vegan long before there were vegans. At family gatherings, he always brought his own food, consisting mainly of raw fruits and vegetables. One niece recalled that Max would eat his nuts with a brown-skinned banana at the family table, but he never seemed to mind. Although there was no official medical diagnosis for Rhoade, it appears that he suffered from obsessive-compulsive disorder (OCD).

Once Rhoade took the Rebbe's case, it transformed his life. He would sleep during the day and work all night, conforming to European time so that he could deal with phone calls and telegrams that came in during those hours. His family must have thought he was a spy because he was so secretive about his work. He became obsessed with the success of the rescue, and without his services, the Lubavitchers would have had a difficult time navigating the legal labyrinth that was so familiar to Rhoade. Despite his eccentricities, Chabad could not have enlisted a better lawyer for its case. Rhoade employed his younger sister Cecelia as his assistant, and she typed up his letters and telegrams. Besides having the right mindset and a trusted colleague in his sister, Rhoade had developed great contacts in Washington. He had worked with Supreme Court justice Louis Brandeis throughout the 1920s and 1930s on various issues and had developed a warm and friendly relationship with him. A much-admired lawyer and Supreme Court justice, Brandeis had been chosen as head of the world Zionist movement during World War I. In addition, Rhoade had worked with the likes of Felix Frankfurter (a Harvard law professor and later a Supreme Court justice and adviser to FDR), Robert Szold (leader in the Zionist Organization of America), Emanuel Neumann (of the Jewish Agency in Jerusalem), Harold Loeb (writer and founding editor of *Broom*), Judge Louis E. Levinthal (president of the Zionist Organization of America), Congressman Leon Sacks, Senator Royal Samuel Copeland, Senator J. Hamilton Lewis, Senator Burton K. Wheeler, Rabbi Stephen Wise, Rabbi Eliezer Silver (president of the Union of Orthodox Rabbis), and Senator Sherman Minton, to name just a few. One passion shared by Rhoade and Brandeis was Palestine and Zionism, and it brought Rhoade into contact with numerous personalities in the government. Moreover, he had developed a reputation in the State Department, and on the recommendation of Senator Robert Wagner of New York, Secretary of State Cordell Hull wrote a letter in 1934 to all diplomatic and consular officers instructing them to assist Rhoade during his travels. Thus, Rhoade had the proper connections to bring attention to the rescue of Schneersohn.[4]

According to Rabbi Jacobson, he and Kramer instructed Rhoade "not to rest till the Rebbe had been saved." Jacobson wrote to Rhoade, "I need not emphasize the importance of the work we are doing because I understand that you are fully aware of the great and outstanding role the cele-

Max Rhoade, the Washington lawyer who helped organize the rescue. He was also successful in mobilizing political support for the Rebbe's cause. (Eliezer Zaklikovsky)

brated Rabbi Schneersohn has in the life of the Jewish people, and thus I am sure that you will please continue your excellent work and help us to bring about the speedy rescue of the Lubavitcher Rabbi." Rhoade agreed to take the case because of his "deep" friendship with Kramer, whom he could not turn down.[5] So in mid-October Rhoade took charge of the legal aspects of the rescue. He was a competent and rigorous attorney who believed that everything should be done according to regulations. He was well connected and well acquainted with the halls of government, and the fact that he spoke Yiddish, the main language of most Chabad rabbis, made him an excellent liaison between the Lubavitcher community and immigration authorities.[6]

Rhoade expressed to Kramer his concerns about the Rebbe's escape route, indicating that it would be best to approach the Swedish authorities, as there was fear of war in the Baltic states (Latvia, Estonia, and Lithuania). He discussed how Washington should support the immigration of this group of Jews and how information should be channeled to the Germans working on the case. Finally, he discussed money. Apparently, Rhoade had done legal work for the Lubavitchers on a pro bono basis in the past, but this time he felt compelled to request payment. He knew he would have to spend an unusual number of hours on the case. On 28 October, in a letter to Kramer and Jacobson, Rhoade insisted that his fees and expenses be paid on time as agreed to preserve his "peace of mind and ability to concentrate on the matter as you wish." An attorney who opens his own law office is dependent upon the fees he brings in each month not only to cover his rent but also to pay his legal staff and for his law library, utilities, furniture and equipment, travel expenses, and all other costs of operating his law practice, plus supporting his family and himself. In another letter a few days later, he told Kramer that he had talked to Jacobson and made "entirely clear my non-mercenary or rather non-profit motives in connection therewith."[7]

Jacobson made a special trip to Washington to discuss the situation with Rhoade and to deliver important documents. He encouraged Rhoade, telling him that rescuing the Rebbe would not "be solved in a day or so, with a call or letter here and there, all on a charitable basis. You have done many favors for us till now, let us make an arrangement so you can work for us on a permanent basis and expedite the whole affair and bring it to a quick and successful conclusion."[8] Although this sounded as if Jacobson intended to pay Rhoade for his services, the attorney remained skeptical. On 25 October he wrote to Jacobson to say he had enjoyed meeting him; then, putting pleasantries aside, he emphasized that, regardless of the honor involved in working on such a case, he needed to be paid: "it is only too obvious that the situation demands enormous concentration and time, with resulting serious impairment of my current income. . . . I therefore hope, to enable me to continue tackling this job with some sort of mental comfort and freedom from undue distraction, that you will carry out your own plan promptly regarding myself. I wish I could afford otherwise."[9] Both the tone and substance of Rhoade's letter suggest he was worried about the Lubavitchers' willingness to pay. Based on his past experience with Chabad, he probably feared that its representatives would not honor their promises, and he often reminded Kramer and Jacobson of their financial commitment to him. Despite these concerns, Rhoade began to prepare the applications for US residency visas for the Rebbe and his group.

According to Chabad historian Eliezer Zaklikovsky, Jacobson probably knew his organization could not afford to pay Rhoade's fees and was less than candid with the attorney. Jacobson and his followers were desperate, and they knew the plan stood little chance of success without a high-powered lawyer like Rhoade. They may have believed that once they hired Rhoade to rescue the Rebbe, God would provide the means to pay him. Or they may have hoped that Rhoade would come to realize the Rebbe's importance and change his mind about payment.[10] This was a less than scrupulous way of doing business, but for the Lubavitchers, cutting corners was justified if the Rebbe's safety depended on it. Unlike Zaklivkovsky, Rabbi Avraham Laber believes the Lubavitchers had the money to pay Rhoade; Jacobson was just late making the payments. Laber maintains that Jacobson made the trip to DC to meet with Rhoade in person because this would be more efficient than communicating through the mail or over the telephone, and if he had the disposable cash to travel, he surely had the money to pay the lawyer.[11]

To obtain visas, Rhoade needed to prove to the US Immigration Service and the State Department that the Rebbe and his group were rabbis and thus "professors" of Jewish theology who could find employment as teachers. Providing sufficient proof would be difficult, however, as there was a strong anti-immigration bias in the "visa decision machinery," and the State Department showed little sympathy for the Jews suffering under Hitler.[12] Rhoade would have to work exceptionally hard to open America's gates for the Rebbe and his associates.

The entire plan was contingent, however, on the Germans finding Schneersohn and keeping him out of the clutches of the SS. With each passing day, hope dwindled that the Rebbe had survived, and the whole of Chabad prayed for him. With no word from Europe, several Lubavitchers expressed their frustration with Rhoade, even though he had been working on the case for only a few weeks. Jacobson wrote to Kramer on 30 October 1939, "I have not seen anything tangible about the Rabbi's affairs as yet." Though he understood their distress, Rhoade found the Lubavitchers' constant inquiries and complaints distracting, if not annoying. On 4 November he wrote to Kramer (who also doubted Rhoade's diligence), assuring him that he was "work[ing] at top speed to close this case."[13] Rhoade's tone indicated his irritation.

On 4 November Rhoade also wrote to Benjamin V. Cohen, noting that those interested in the Rebbe's welfare were in a state of "the greatest anxiety" and "perturbed over the lack of word from the German authorities." Rhoade encouraged Cohen to have the American consulate in Warsaw "urge Rabbi Schneersohn to cooperate with the German military officer [Bloch] assigned to facilitate his safe egress to Riga, and to notify them of the Rebbe's condition and needs." Rhoade realized that Bloch would probably have difficulty winning the Rebbe's trust, as no independent authority had informed the Rebbe of Bloch's intentions. Rhoade believed that if the American consulate could communicate with the Rebbe, he would follow Bloch. By now, Lubavitchers in Riga and Vilna knew about the German plan (probably from the American telegrams) and had sent secret messengers to Warsaw to convince the Rebbe of the Germans' sincerity.[14]

Rhoade still had to convince US immigration authorities that the Rebbe was worthy of their help. Believing that the case warranted the involvement of the State Department, Rhoade bombarded it with letters, confident that "the Department will gladly make an exception in the case of Rabbi Schneersohn, consistent with the extraordinary action already taken upon Secretary Hull's instructions at your [Cohen's] request. . . . It seems logical, that if the State Department went out of its way in one phase of this matter, it might just as well complete the job."[15] Rhoade's strategy of presenting the State Department's action on behalf of the Rebbe as a fait accompli was surprisingly effective in getting it to do what he believed should be done.

The scope of the rescue expanded to include additional members of the Rebbe's family and close associates numbering well over a dozen. Rhoade hoped Jacobson had arranged for various synagogues to employ the rabbis in the Rebbe's entourage, because he needed proof of that as soon as possible. The fact that most members of the Rebbe's group were born in Russia made Rhoade's job easier, since that country's quota remained open. But he still needed detailed information about Chabad "to give a clear picture to the American Consulate of the past and present earning capacity of the Rebbe and the other heads of the families who wish to come to America, as indicating a source of future income."[16] Despite the goodwill of many in the government, the fact remained that if the Rebbe could not support himself, he would not be welcomed. Under the law, if someone were likely "to become a public charge," he or she would be denied a visa. An applicant required "an American sponsor to have $5,000 or more in a bank account" to prove that he or she would not be a drain on society.[17]

Rhoade asked Jacobson to provide him with a lot of details: the number of Chabad members throughout the world, the number of Lubavitch synagogues, the estimated total income of the Chabad organization for the last five years, the source of Chabad's income, the organizational structure of Chabad, the name and address of its chief financial officer, the estimated total and nature of the Rebbe's personal income for the past several years, and similar information for the rabbis accompanying the Rebbe.[18] Obviously, Rhoade had no knowledge of Chabad's infrastructure. Jacobson was an energetic leader, but he had no real office and did not speak English well (his primary language was Yiddish); his young daughter often had to translate letters he received.[19] He had no financial staff in his organization. Although it is difficult to believe today, given the complexity of the Chabad organization, Jacobson's office was not organized or operated as a corporation, and he could not provide the detailed information Rhoade required. By their nature, charismatic religious leaders like the Rebbe make no distinction between personal assets and institutional property, even though such distinctions are important in secular law. All this greatly hampered Rhoade's efforts to prove that Chabad could support the Rebbe. Frustrated with Jacobson, Rhoade wrote to him on 4 November, "I hope you will not mind my impressing upon you the necessity of reading my letters carefully and answering me on every point, because I cannot constantly keep track of these things and necessarily depend upon you to carry out anything I suggest and unless all of this is done very promptly we shall find ourselves delayed at various junctures." Jacobson constantly disappointed Rhoade in these matters, even though as far back as February 1939, the Rebbe, fearing that war might break out, had asked him to obtain visas for him, his family, and his inner circle.[20]

The Rebbe's escape route also troubled Rhoade. He feared that Sweden might enter the war on the German side (it would stay neutral), that the Soviet Union might invade the Baltic states (which it did a few months later), and that the Rebbe's host countries might prevent him and his group from leaving without the proper papers. He also feared that the Gestapo would intervene if the Rebbe and his family received emergency visas in Berlin. Since the acting chief of the Visa Department in Washington, Eliot B. Coulter, had advised Rhoade that "it was impossible for either emergency visitors' visas or immigration visas to be prearranged," it seemed best for the Rebbe to travel to Riga and wait there until the United States could complete the necessary paperwork. Helmuth Wohlthat had informed Robert Pell that he planned to evacuate the Lubavitchers to Sweden but needed more time. Wohlthat also reserved the option of sending Schneersohn to Riga via Vilna, if necessary—a route Rhoade objected to because of the looming threat of a Soviet invasion.[21]

Rhoade continued to worry about his client's failure to pay his fees—an issue no one wanted to discuss. He wrote to Kramer on 6 November, "I had already indicated that because of the monkey wrench which this matter has thrown into current income for weeks past, I prefer remittance now, rather than at the conclusion of the matter." Perhaps the reluctance to pay Rhoade stemmed from the fact that Kramer was bearing the brunt of the expense personally and was struggling with this burden. Rhoade knew this and suggested that Jacobson, together with the Lubavitcher community, relieve Kramer of this obligation. Rhoade expressed the hope that "Jacobson and his colleagues will be able to effectuate a 'catch up' plan this week, for any further allusion to the subject is quite embarrassing."[22] On 8 November Rhoade protested that Jacobson had "not yet forwarded the check payable to the Swedish Legation for the amount of $4.82" and that his fee of $48.27 ($809 in today's dollars) from October was still outstanding. Jacobson's reluctance to pay is difficult to understand. He had access to discretionary funds to cover these expenses, and $2,000 had been raised specifically for the Rebbe's rescue. If Chabad in America possessed assets worth $500,000, it could have taken out a loan or mortgaged real estate to pay its legal fees.[23]

The same day, Rhoade received a letter from Jacobson that failed to answer Rhoade's questions about Chabad's resources or to explain why his bills remained unpaid. The lawyer replied angrily, "As I understand your letter, you do not have, and apparently do not care to secure from Lieberman any concrete, factual information on the past of Rabbi Schneersohn and the other prospective immigrants." Rhoade informed

Jacobson that the absence of this information would be "a definite hand-icap in obtaining even quota visas for these people." Jacobson's failure to comply perplexed Rhoade. "Despite the greatest good will and pre-arranged friendliness," he explained to Jacobson, even "ordinary rabbis" accompanying the Rebbe had to demonstrate an ability to support them-selves; "mere generalities" about Schneersohn's "importance as a spiri-tual figure and the spiritual importance of Chabad" would not suffice. Although this type of theological argument might convince Lubavitchers, US immigration officials would not be impressed. No one disputed the Rebbe's spiritual authority, but it did not prove his ability to earn a living in America. Furthermore, the rest of the Rebbe's entourage had no such claim to greatness. Rhoade needed data from Jacobson that would prove the "*bona fide* nature of the synagogue contract-affidavit material."[24] He refused to take responsibility for failing to bring the Rebbe safely to the United States if Jacobson did not provide what he needed. "I just want to record for future reference," he said, "that I asked for this information and could not get it." He would not be doing his job, he continued, "if I failed to warn you about this problem, which is very apt to arise."[25]

Rhoade likely complained to Kramer about the difficulty of work-ing with Jacobson. However, Jacobson knew the players in Europe, and regardless of his obvious lack of experience, he was the top person in the United States working for Chabad. Nevertheless, instead of getting good translators and listening to Rhoade's advice, Jacobson was sloppy and often seemed to be flying by the seat of his pants in his dealings with the authorities, perhaps thinking that the religious importance of saving the Rebbe would result in divine intervention to make everything right. After taking several days to try to come up with information on the Reb-be's income, Jacobson finally admitted to Rhoade on 10 November, "in principle we have no system and control of the income of the Lubavitcher Rabbi, and thus cannot furnish such a statement of income."[26] Rhoade knew this acknowledgment would not be well received at the immigra-tion office, but he soldiered on.

Jacobson notwithstanding, Rhoade made progress with the State De-partment. Cohen thought Rhoade should discuss the situation with Pell, who was handling the case under Hull's oversight.[27] After meeting with Rhoade on 8 November, Pell described the Rebbe as "a sort of modern St.

Francis of Assisi" who was deserving of aid and succor.[28] Since St. Francis was a mystic, this was an apt analogy.[29] The following day Rhoade made two requests of Pell: ask Wohlthat whether the Germans had discovered Schneersohn's whereabouts, and cable the Warsaw consulate and instruct its staff to locate the Rebbe and inform him of Bloch's mission.[30]

Rhoade felt it was important to pass along information about Bloch's intentions, since it appeared that neither the Rebbe nor his followers were willing to reveal themselves to the Abwehr officer.[31] On 9 November Rhoade asked Pell to send Bloch the Rebbe's old address, "since we suspect that the Rabbi is in hiding and fears to entrust himself to the German officer." He then expressed his appreciation for everything Pell had done and mentioned that he had informed Brandeis and Cohen of Pell's "continued generous and whole-hearted cooperation." Mentioning Brandeis and Cohen in the same sentence was surely a tactic to encourage Pell to get the Rebbe and Bloch together by any means necessary.[32] The Rebbe certainly knew about the search by now, but he had probably had difficulty verifying Bloch's credibility. Knowing that the Rebbe was understandably "cynical regarding the officer's mission," Rhoade wanted Pell to find a way to help the Rebbe verify which Germans he could really trust.[33] And Rhoade believed that passing along this confidential information about the Rebbe's address might convince him to trust Bloch—after all, how would a German know this information if not from Lieberman, whose cables had reached Pell and, by extension, Wohlthat? With stories of German atrocities becoming more widespread in Warsaw, it was critical to persuade the Rebbe to let Bloch help him. After receiving Hull's authorization, Pell sent the relevant information to the US embassy in Berlin.[34]

With the help of Congressman Sol Bloom, whose district on the West Side of Manhattan was home to many recent German Jewish immigrants, Rhoade also talked to Latvian diplomats. In addition, he wrote to Alfred Bilmanis, Latvia's diplomat in Washington, on 8 November, reminding him that a German officer had been assigned to facilitate the Rebbe's escape and asking him to instruct his people in Latvia to reassure the Rebbe of Bloch's trustworthiness. Rhoade also needed Bilmanis's cooperation to ensure that the Rebbe would not be detained at the Lithuanian or Latvian border, given that these countries had been reluctant to admit more

Jewish refugees.[35] The Rebbe would be traveling without his passport and other necessary documents, which had been lost, and the route through Lithuania might be better than the one through Königsberg, Germany, where the "danger of molestation by anti-Jewish elements" was greater. In addition to helping the Rebbe, who was one of Latvia's "distinguished citizens," Rhoade had to persuade the Latvian diplomat to help his entourage of seventeen people. Although Bloch had not yet located Schneersohn, Rhoade insisted that Bilmanis have visas ready for the speedy departure of these Lubavitchers. He feared the Soviet Union would invade the Baltic states any day, and if the Soviets caught the Rebbe, he would be as good as dead. The Soviet threat, combined with Latvia's apparent inaction, seemed to justify Rhoade's curt tone with Bilmanis. He could only hope that Dubin and other friends of Chabad in the Latvian government would pressure their officials to issue the appropriate documents.[36]

Meanwhile, Bloch and his group were scouring Warsaw for the Rebbe. Using the information passed from Rhoade to Pell to Wohlthat, they soon found the building Schneersohn had given as his original address. Bloch's team reported to Wohlthat that the building had been "completely demolished during the bombardment at the end of September," and it was impossible to determine whether the Rebbe had been "in the building at the time of its destruction." Bloch assumed the Rebbe might be dead, but he continued his search.[37] Walking from house to house, Bloch's team asked scared and hungry Hasidim, some of whom were Lubavitchers, about the Rebbe, but no one dared to talk. On one occasion, a little girl opened the door and asked what the soldiers wanted. Suddenly, a woman's arm reached out, pulled the child away from the entryway, and slammed the door. Another time, a young man opened the door and, at the sight of the officers, lost control of his bladder. Bloch and his men nonetheless continued their door-to-door search, explaining to the residents that they wanted to help the Rebbe, not harm him.

No doubt, the Lubavitchers "all felt that if the Nazis ever captured the Rebbe, that would have been a great prize for them." Many were convinced, understandably, that "the Nazis were after him."[38] The Lubavitchers were terrified, and the atmosphere in the city had become horrific. As one Jew wrote, "Darkness rules the streets of Warsaw [and] dominates our minds."[39] Time was running out for the Rebbe. Soon the borders would be closed, and no Jews would be able to leave Poland.

Back in Washington, Rhoade continued to fear that Schneersohn would never entrust himself and his followers to a German officer. On 9 November Rhoade cabled Lieberman and wrote to Kramer, emphasizing the need to convince the Rebbe to trust Bloch. Rhoade was counting on Lieberman to accomplish this task, since he had lost hope that the rather apathetic representatives of the Latvian government would ever locate the Rebbe. Indeed, the Latvians had other worries that took priority; there were war clouds on the horizon as the neighboring Soviet giant looked menacingly at their country. Rhoade and Kramer were nonetheless perturbed by the Latvian government's inaction. Rhoade found it strange that the Latvian Foreign Office had failed to act on information from Bilmanis or in response to the presumed efforts of Dubin. He suspected "that Latvia is displeased with the Rebbe—only a naturalized Latvian citizen—for having overstayed in Poland with something akin to a presumption of expatriation."[40] Rhoade and some of the Lubavitchers in the United States agreed that, unfortunately, Dubin and Lieberman had little influence with the Riga Foreign Office. Rhoade worried that the State Department might lose interest if it discovered that the Lubavitchers lacked strong Latvian support.[41] "Perhaps the Latvian Foreign Office has done its best," Rhoade speculated, "but failed for reasons of its own (unless we are to assume gross negligence), to apprise Bilmanis of the nature of its action." While voicing concern for the Rebbe, Bilmanis had told Rhoade he could go no further without embarrassing himself and his government, and he suggested that Senator Dubin deal with Latvian officials on the Rebbe's behalf. Rhoade did not tell Bilmanis that Dubin had only minimal influence with the Latvian government, fearing that this information might discourage Bilmanis from continuing his efforts. Bilmanis might have done more, Rhoade felt, but the many competing demands from others in dire straits probably discouraged him. To impress and influence Bilmanis, Rhoade arranged for the two of them to meet Justice Brandeis, which, he told Kramer, "gratified [Bilmanis] a great deal."[42]

The lawyer urgently needed an ally with some political clout in Riga, but he did not know where to turn. His one remaining tactic was to pressure American Jews to change the "lukewarm" attitude of the Latvian Foreign

Office. Rhoade feared, however, that Dubin and other friends of the Rebbe assumed that once the United States had become involved, they could fold "their hands in total inaction." But he did not want to "believe that they were such saps." Because of the confusion, Rhoade insisted that Kramer help him obtain approval from the authorities to call Dubin or Lieberman in Riga as soon as possible to find out what was going on. Rhoade also wanted to talk with the American ambassador to Latvia, who was supposed to prepare the visas for the Rebbe and his group. Rhoade commented that the Latvian government should be contacting the US government, not vice versa. He continued to worry that Latvia might be upset with the Rebbe, who, despite his Latvian citizenship, had chosen to live in Poland for years. If the Latvians believed the Rebbe had rejected their country, which at least seemed to be the case, they might not be willing to help him.[43]

Many Lubavitchers feared the Rebbe had been killed. When they met in the synagogue or on the streets of Brooklyn, no words were needed to express what was in their hearts. It is difficult to describe to modern readers how the Lubavitchers felt about their Rebbe, because that type of unquestioning devotion is rare today. They thought their whole world would be destroyed if the Rebbe were to die. Although many leaders seek such absolute devotion, few achieve it. The Rebbe was one of those few, and his followers would do anything he ordered. In 1939, when the Chabad community thought it might lose its leader, members were racked with such worry that it often made them physically sick.

In the ongoing search for news of the Rebbe, Rhoade soon received information that the German authorities had obtained his new address. Rhoade immediately asked Pell to get Wohlthat to confirm that this address was not the "demolished building."[44] The next few days were filled with arrangements for the Rebbe's escape. Despite his financial concerns, Rhoade worked diligently on the case, primarily because of his friendship with Kramer. He attempted to open channels of communication with Latvia, even though Pell had advised him that the American embassy in Berlin could not, for diplomatic reasons, establish contact with the Latvian legation there. Rhoade suggested to Kramer that they inform Lieberman of this fact. Unless something changed quickly with Latvia, Rhoade felt, they would never get the Rebbe out, and he suggested that they contact the American embassy and solicit its help.

On 15 November Pell reassured Rhoade of his interest in the case and promised he would leave no "stone unturned" to discover the Rebbe's whereabouts. Pell also informed Rhoade that the American embassy was impressed with the international interest the case was attracting, and he was communicating information about the Rebbe's situation to the Warsaw consulate. Although Latvian support had diminished, Rhoade found increasing support in the United States, primarily from Pell and, through him, Hull.[45]

Concerned about the Abwehr team, Rhoade wrote to Kramer on 16 November and expressed his "misgivings about reposing too much confidence in the German [soldiers]."[46] He warned that "no one can depend on the German attitude, particularly under the present regime, and in war time."[47] However, Rhoade had no choice but to trust the Germans, who seemed to be acting in good faith.

Lieberman echoed Rhoade's concern that the Lubavitchers in Latvia were having trouble securing the government's support for the Rebbe's escape. With the help of the Red Cross, Rhoade hoped to put the Latvian Foreign Office "on the spot," forcing it to take action and assist in the Rebbe's rescue.[48] Dealing with politicians domestically and internationally, Rhoade was fighting a two-front battle. On the one hand, he had to fight anti-Semitism from non-Jews, as well as ignorance about secular law and immigration procedures among the ultra-Orthodox Jews. On the other hand, he had to fight the ignorance of certain politicians and convince them that the Rebbe and his entourage were significant enough to be worth saving. It was no easy task, and the fact that Rhoade was able to continue the dialogue and keep people engaged was quite a testament to his ability.

On 20 November Rhoade and his wife, Helen, joined Bilmanis at the Latvian embassy for a reception, where Latvian officials gave the impression that they would cooperate.[49] Despite the efforts of the United States, the Abwehr, Latvia, and the International Red Cross, no one had been able to locate the Rebbe. One would think that finding an elderly, wheelchair-bound rabbi and his group of devoted followers in a major city like Warsaw would have been easy. However, keep in mind that it took the United States more than a decade to find Osama bin Laden—a six-foot-six-inch-tall radical Muslim terrorist who was often hooked up to a dialysis machine and followed by numerous disciples, wives, and children—in an age of modern technology, satellites, and cameras. So it is not surprising that locating the Rebbe in a recent war zone occupied by the Germans was a difficult task in the age of letter writing, telegrams, and telephones. Even if the Rebbe could be found, the Lubavitchers had hardly paved the way for his arrival in the United States. They had refused to honor their financial obligation and failed to provide important documents. Chabad's leadership in America often had a difficult time focusing on the mechanics that would have allowed them to achieve their goal.

By way of illustration, the Lubavitchers continued to fall behind in paying their bills. Rhoade protested to Kramer yet again on 21 November, saying he had tried to keep costs to a minimum, "but in a matter like this," cables, telephone calls, and large expenditures of time were inevitable. Rhoade repeated that he had received neither his fee for the previous week nor payment of his last expense statement. He would have been deeply offended, he explained, "except for my knowledge of the sacrifices you [Kramer] are making yourself." He then made it absolutely clear that working on the Rebbe's rescue had resulted in a "heavy personal loss."[50] Apparently, Kramer was paying most of Chabad's expenses personally. One wonders why Jacobson and the American Chabad leaders, who had raised $5,000 for the Rebbe by this time, allowed their bills to remain unpaid. Rhoade was aware of this fund, and it is strange that he never mentioned it. Perhaps he thought its purpose was to convince government officials that the Rebbe could support himself in the United States.[51] However, his letters to Kramer indicate his belief that the Lubavitchers were more than capable of paying their bills.

On 25 November Rhoade wrote to Kramer again, requesting payment of his fees and expenses.[52] Kramer's response seemed to be preparing Rhoade for the inevitable reality that the Lubavitchers would never pay him, and, consequently, he should take solace in the good deeds he was performing and the appreciation he would receive. The Lubavitchers probably felt that since Rhoade was Jewish, he should work to save the Rebbe whether they paid him or not; they likely viewed it as an honor to be chosen to rescue Schneersohn. Earlier, Kramer had written to Rhoade about reaping spiritual rewards: "As I have already indicated, compensation for your services will have to come from heaven, with the hope that the blessings from the Lubavitcher [Rebbe] and the numerous other rabbis interested in his welfare will be reflected in the happiness and prosperity of yourself and your dear Helen. I am confident that what you have done and will continue to do in this matter will be 'spreading bread upon the water' which, in due time, will bring its own compensation to you."[53] Rhoade did not appreciate such arguments. Blessings from ungrateful rabbis who were playing the guilt card did not pay his rent.

Rhoade was also frustrated because he was spending significantly more time on the Rebbe's case than anticipated. As a perfectionist, he was intent on exploring every avenue that could help with the rescue, but in doing so, he neglected other cases that would have netted more cash. As a result, he became resentful, yet he felt obligated to complete the case out of friendship and a sense of duty. Although Chabad did not pay nearly enough for his services, and although he doubted it would ever pay him in full, he could not, without losing face, just drop the case, which had brought him in contact with some of the highest officials in the US government.

The issue of Rhoade's payment is perplexing. On the one hand, given that the Rebbe's life was in danger and the Nazis were persecuting millions, one is taken aback by Rhoade's oft-repeated mention of his fees. On the other hand, one would suppose that a dedicated follower like Jacobson would have been willing to pay any amount to save the Rebbe. If Chabad were so big and powerful in the United States, with tens of thousands of followers, it should have been easy to raise a few thousand dollars—if those claims were true. Interestingly, and luckily for the Lubavitchers, neither Rhoade nor others bothered to verify Chabad's influence, membership, or economic power base. Had they been more inquiring, they might have been surprised to find how much perceptions differed from reality. Of course, Lubavitchers today claim that this reality just adds to the miraculous nature of the event. In the end, their religious beliefs did not prevent them from exaggerating their size and strength in order to increase their influence when such misrepresentations could save their Rebbe.

10

The Angel

There is a time to kill and a time to heal.
—Ecclesiastes 3:3

Acting on promising new information from Wohlthat, on 25 November Bloch and his team inspected an apartment house where they thought the Rebbe lived. An old man greeted them at the door, a look of hostility and fear on his face. When Bloch explained that they had been ordered to help the Rebbe escape occupied Poland, the old man denied any knowledge of the Rebbe's whereabouts and closed the door. After Bloch left, however, Schneersohn instructed his staff and family that if the officer returned, they should give him "truthful information."[1] Perhaps the Rebbe had finally been informed that Bloch could be trusted. Messengers had been going back and forth between Riga and Warsaw, and Riga had received several telegrams from the United States, where information was being obtained from Wohlthat. It seems that someone had finally accomplished the task of convincing the Rebbe that Bloch's men meant no harm, for he "would never have left with German soldiers unless they had some way of proving their intentions."[2]

The Rebbe dispatched Samarius Gourary, his most trusted son-in-law and de facto foreign secretary, to inform the soldiers that he would accept their help. The tall, stocky Gourary was a Torah scholar and a learned Hasid of the old Lubavitch world, and he often handled political situations for the Rebbe. Many believed that Gourary was in line to become the next Rebbe. Gourary found a group of Germans, probably Bloch's group, and passed along the Rebbe's message. On his way home, several soldiers, obviously non-Abwehr personnel, cut off half his beard, vertically dividing his face. When Gourary returned, his colleagues told him he should consider himself lucky, since some Jews had lost not only their beards but a few ears as well.[3]

It is unknown whether Gourary's message actually reached Bloch. However, convinced that the old man had been hiding something, Bloch decided to return to the apartment house. He was sure the Rebbe was there. Bloch ordered several of his men to dress in full battle gear and prepare for any contingency. He needed to get to the Rebbe quickly (before the SS could reach him), secure the perimeter, and then assess the situation. When he and his soldiers returned to Herschel Gurari's house, where the Rebbe lived, they broke down the door and entered a dark hallway that smelled of sewage. The bombing had destroyed the plumbing, and the household used buckets for toilets. A small child's cries echoed down the corridor, and a woman's soft voice could be heard comforting the baby.

In the chaos that ensued, the Rebbe tried to maintain his composure. Loud German voices yelled orders. The dozen or so Lubavitchers turned white and remained silent.[4] Four German soldiers ordered everyone to stand and face the walls. The Jews obeyed, putting their hands in the air. Many shook as they turned their backs to the Germans. The Rebbe's grandson, Barry Gourary, expected to feel the cold steel barrel of a gun against his neck. Many started to pray. The Germans' hobnail boots clattered on the wooden floor, and the holster straps of their swinging rifles jangled. If the Jews could have seen the Germans' belt buckles, they would have read the inscription *Gott mit uns* (God is with us). If they felt anything, it was not God's presence—it was fear. A few started to cry. Some thought of their families; others thought of God and death. They heard one German counting: "*eins, zwei, drei, vier. . . .*" Another was calling out names. As each person's name was called, he or she was asked to turn and face the Germans. One by one, they turned, eyes gravitating to the swastikas on the men's uniforms. When all the names had been called, another German handed the Jews their travel papers, explaining that they would need the documents for their escape. The Lubavitchers stared blankly at the men and their papers. Once the initial shock wore off, some of the Lubavitchers apparently became distressed that so few of them had been chosen to leave.

According to Rabbi S. Gourary, there were actually three German officers and two detectives who arrived at the Rebbe's residence. After they had identified the Jews to be rescued, they rounded them up into one room, locked the door, and then discussed their plan with the Rebbe. One of the officers—it is unknown whether it was Bloch or Horatzek— explained that they were there to rescue the Rebbe and his "hierarchy," but the Rebbe had to decide whether or not to trust the Germans. They pressed him to respond immediately, and the Rebbe declared, "I am going."[5]

Soon thereafter, Wohlthat reported to Washington that Bloch had found the Rebbe and that he should be able to leave Warsaw by 1 December under the protection of a "German staff officer."[6] The Rebbe was exhausted. His cheeks were sunken, his eyes were hollow, and his complexion was yellow. He needed time to recover his strength before beginning his journey.

Bloch's mission was not yet complete. He now faced the daunting challenge of spiriting the Rebbe past the SS and the Gestapo. Escorting ultra-Orthodox Jews through German-occupied territory was not the usual task of a military officer. No one could have envisioned a more absurd scene than the one facing the Rebbe, his entourage, and their German savior.

11

The Rebbe's Escape Route

Do not stand idly by while your neighbor's blood is being shed.
—The Torah

On 25 November, the very day Bloch met with the Rebbe, US charge d'affaires Alexander Kirk informed Pell that Schneersohn had been located. On 27 November Pell passed on the wonderful news to Rhoade: the German soldiers had found the Rebbe alive, and he was now under the protection of a staff officer. Pell also told Rhoade that, in response to the Rebbe's plea for funds, he had sent $250 through the State Department.[1] A great burden must have been lifted from Rhoade's shoulders—the Rebbe had finally been located.

The Rebbe, remarkably, seemed most concerned about his library. On 27 November he sent Lieberman a telegram explaining that he had "no dwelling now, and find myself in the home of friends with the whole family in one room, and therefore have no place for the books." The Chabad library seemed as sacred to the Rebbe as his own life, and in fact, the importance of that library would endure well beyond the Rebbe's life. He specifically asked Lieberman not only to rescue his staff and his family but also to save his "valuable library" consisting of some 40,000 volumes, valued at "about $30,000." The Lubavitchers wanted the United States to obtain permission from the German consul to take the books with them.[2]

Given everything the Rebbe had been through, one wonders why he devoted so much time and influence to saving his books rather than saving some of the millions of Jews whose lives were in danger. The Rebbe's concern with his sacred books blinded him to the critical mission of helping others escape Nazi-controlled Europe. He was obsessed with his books and suffered from tunnel vision. As Jonathan Steinberg astutely writes, "Acts, even acts of virtue, depend on what the clock says."[3] Here, the Rebbe's focus on his books was the wrong focus at the wrong time.

Two things were crucial for a successful escape: visas to enter the United States, and a safe route from Warsaw. Rhoade renewed his efforts to prepare immigration affidavits, but he still lacked proof that the Lubavitchers could support themselves. Julius Stulman, a wealthy Lubavitcher in New York, agreed to support Schneersohn and some of his family members and applied for visas for the Rebbe, his wife, and his mother. A few weeks later, Jacobson wrote to Stulman and asked for more help, saying, "I am sure that you will kindly comply with my request and the merit of this great Mitzvah will sustain you and your family, and you will be blessed by G-d."[4] Even with Stulman's support, Rhoade still had to convince the authorities that the other seventeen people with the Rebbe would not become public charges.

Pell and Rhoade were well aware that they were dependent on Wohlthat for the Rebbe's safe passage out of Poland. They had previously decided that the best route would be from Warsaw to Berlin to Riga, but Rhoade now favored an escape route through Italy, a fascist state that had not yet joined Germany in the war. Pell pointed out that Wohlthat had already accomplished the extraordinary feat of arranging a military escort for foreign Jewish citizens into Germany, sidestepping the Gestapo. Although the Gestapo usually respected military authorities—which included Wohlthat, as a member of Göring's staff—it might "butt in" if a situation looked unusual. (Göring had handed control of the Gestapo over to Himmler in 1934; it was now out of the army's chain of command and answered only to Hitler.) Pell therefore advised staying with the original plan, since changing the route to go through Italy or Switzerland would attract the attention of the Gestapo and put the Rebbe in grave danger if he were caught.[5] Ultimately, Pell and Rhoade left the decision to Wohlthat.

Pell also advised Rhoade that although he had no direct influence on the granting of visas, he would do his best to convince Visa Department chief Avra M. Warren and his assistant Eliot Coulter to help the Rebbe and his group. Coulter had told Pell that his department's "hands are tied respecting procedure," but Pell believed exceptions could be made, and it appears that Coulter helped when he could.[6]

Harry T. Troutman of the Visa Department worked diligently to get the rabbis in the entourage nonquota visas, probably after receiving proof that they were "ministers." Troutman argued that these "ministers" were unique because they represented the heads of a religious body, and he carefully prepared the paperwork required by the legation in Riga for their emigration.[7] The Rebbe was fortunate to have men like Troutman and Coulter on his side, because a few months later their boss made a special trip to Europe to instruct consular officials to curtail the entry of refugees.[8] The Visa Department's "increased stringency was difficult to understand in the face of a much worsened crisis."[9]

Those advocating on behalf of the Rebbe kept his multiple sclerosis and strokes a secret. Health issues had prevented others from receiving visas, for fear they would become public charges. The Visa Department rejected one person because he had a contagious fungal disease called favus and flat feet. Although these conditions would not have stopped him from earning a living as a rabbi, the department stood firm.[10]

Up to this time, most official discussions had focused on Schneersohn, with only brief mention of his followers and family members. The Rebbe's group included his wife, Nehamah Dinah; his mother, Sara; his son-in-law Samarius Gourary; his daughter Chana Gourary; his grandson Barry Gourary; his son-in-law Mendel Horenstein; his daughter Sheina Horenstein; and his secretary Haskell Feigin, Feigin's wife Sonya, and their five children (two sons and three daughters). Soon, more would be added. Rhoade appealed to Pell on 28 November, asking that Wohlthat guarantee safe passage to Riga for all of them. Rhoade also asked permission to warn Warren of the problems that would arise when members of the Rebbe's group could not produce proper identification. In a letter to Warren, Rhoade encouraged him to deal "liberally with the situation," noting that "the Rabbi's world prominence" justified such a generous attitude.[11] On 30 November Rhoade asked that the US consulate in Warsaw issue visitors' visas to the Rebbe's group. To prove that Stulman had agreed to support Schneersohn, his wife, and his mother, Rhoade enclosed copies of financial documents. Rhoade also promised to provide affidavits for the other people in the group as soon as possible, which Stulman sent shortly thereafter.[12]

Although it looked as if the Rebbe and his entourage could lawfully enter the United States, they still had to escape the watchful eyes of the SS, which had begun to move Jews into camps and ghettos throughout German-occupied Poland. Extracting the Rebbe and his group from a secured ghetto would have been quite difficult, so Bloch had to get them out of Warsaw before the ghetto walls were closed.[13] The struggle between the SS and the Abwehr was intense, and the SS was gaining the upper hand.

Anxious about the Rebbe's safe passage out of Germany, Rhoade got involved in the details of the plan. Stalin seemed to be on the verge of conquering the Baltic states, making travel through them dangerous. Rhoade therefore preferred that the group go to Sweden and await their ship to the United States. If Wohlthat knew the United States had provided "prearranged transit visas," he might approve travel through Königsberg, Berlin, and the port of Sassnitz, where the group could catch a ferry to Sweden. Rhoade had arranged for the Swedish transit visas to be picked up in Berlin, but he feared the group would have to wait too long for the documents, so he requested that Wohlthat arrange for the visas to be stamped on board the Sassnitz-Tralleborg ferry. Rhoade now regarded this route as more advantageous than the one through Lithuania. However, if Wohlthat opted for the route through Vilna to Riga, someone at the American embassy in Berlin would have to officially approve the plan, with a caution to avoid Soviet-occupied territories at all costs.[14]

When Jacobson and one of his colleagues on the Chabad rescue committee, Rabbi Samuel Levitin, learned that Rhoade was proposing different escape plans, they became irritated and told Kramer that "approaching influential people every day with new plans" left them "exasperated." Jacobson and Levitin thought it had been agreed that if no alternative plan could be carried out quickly, the Rebbe would proceed to Riga.[15] They obviously wanted Kramer to reel Rhoade in. Tempers were rising, and the Lubavitchers were getting impatient. They also expressed resentment at Rhoade's fees. When Kramer questioned Rhoade about his charges, the lawyer answered, "While I don't blame you for being sensitive to the expenses, it is very difficult to exercise normal conservatism. Whenever I am in doubt, I resolve it in favor of the Rabbi, as time is of the essence."[16] The long days of work and anxiety had started to take their toll, and people's nerves were on edge.

Although he had received no official response, Rhoade hoped the

Germans' silence meant they had agreed to guarantee safe passage to the seventeen individuals accompanying the Rebbe. He wrote, "The silence of Berlin on the request for enlargement of the escort to include the entire group consisting of the Rabbi's relatives . . . indicates that no objection has been made. . . . All the adult males are Rabbis, thereby entitling the entire group to non-quota status."[17]

On 30 November the world was shocked to learn that the Soviet Union had invaded Finland after the Finns had refused to concede territory north of Leningrad that Stalin claimed was vital to the Soviet Union's security.[18] Many Lubavitchers feared that once the Soviets had forcefully seized the Finnish territory, Stalin would turn his military might against the Baltic states, and the Rebbe would fall into Soviet hands in Riga. Given the speed with which the USSR had crushed Japan in August 1939 and helped Nazi Germany conquer Poland in September, how long could sparsely populated Finland and the little Baltic states hold out against the might of the Soviet Union?

Meanwhile, in the Visa Department, Coulter urged Rhoade and Pell to send the American consulate in Berlin evidence of adequate financial provision for the Rebbe and his followers once they arrived in the United States. Rhoade protested that sending such information to Berlin was not only impractical but also dangerous because of the Gestapo. Nonsecret cables containing such financial information might precipitate a Gestapo extortion plan and take the matter out of Wohlthat's hands.[19] Rhoade asked Pell for assurance that the Berlin consulate would provide the Rebbe and his followers with emergency visitors' visas "without going into the details." Rhoade had little faith in his ability to convince the consulate that the Rebbe and his entourage fell under the nonimmigrant clause, because the group's "entire condition contradicts the 'tourist' idea." In other words, they had to get visas to enter the country on a permanent basis.[20] Rhoade officially labeled the members of Schneersohn's group as the Rebbe's "dependents" to avoid an extensive investigation into their financial resources and those of the Chabad organization, thereby expediting the granting of visas for the entire group. In a further attempt to get the Visa Department to act, Rhoade compared the Rebbe's situation "to what might happen if war conditions in Italy compelled the Pope and his associates at the Vatican to seek temporary refuge in the United States for the purpose of carrying on the world affairs of the Catholic Church."[21]

In the meantime, Wohlthat and the Abwehr had decided on an escape route from Warsaw via Berlin and Riga to Stockholm, and then on to the United States. Rhoade needed Pell to help "secure American visitors' visas for the Rebbe and his group upon their arrival in Berlin." Rhoade hoped Pell could convince Wohlthat to instruct the military escorts to take the Rebbe and his group to the American embassy to receive their travel documents. To get their visas, the group would have to give the proper answers to American officials "regarding their intentions" upon arrival in Berlin.[22]

As a backup plan, Rhoade had contacted a well-connected Cuban lawyer about obtaining Cuban visitors' visas for the group. Cuba demanded $5,000 per person, so it would have cost around $100,000 to send the entire group there. Rhoade told Kramer that Cuba might be their only option to secure safe passage to North America, even though the Cuban authorities were more than willing "to financially exploit the opportunity presented by refugees in distress." Rhoade advised that they "should avoid these 'gaslonim' [thieves] if possible." Nevertheless, Cuba was like a "'Schwester im Dorf' [a sister in the village] though . . . a mightily punk 'Schwester.'"[23] For now, everything hinged on the Germans, who had to get the Rebbe and his entire group out of German-occupied Europe.

In a letter to Pell written on 29 November, Rhoade reasoned that the German officials who seemed willing to help "would not wish to do things half way and certainly would not wish to deprive the Rabbi, who is a sort of Pope, of his immediate disciples." He insisted that Pell at least request that the group be escorted to safety. Pell thought their entry into the United States would not pose a problem, since the Rebbe and most of his followers were Russian born, and the quota for Russia remained open. The others could possibly receive nonquota visas because they were rabbis, although that approach might prove difficult. Rhoade expressed the hope that the German authorities might be willing to arrange for the group's transportation to Italy instead of Lithuania, obviously because of fear of the Soviet Union. Rhoade claimed that if Wohlthat did this, "it would be a fine feather in the German's cap." Annoyed by the long list of new demands, Pell advised Rhoade that the Germans were unlikely to consider so many options.[24]

Rhoade now foresaw another danger: the use of international cables, albeit in diplomatic code, to transmit sensitive information. He feared the Gestapo might intercept the cables, "develop an extortion plan, and take the matter out of Wohlthat's hands."[25] Although Pell had far more experience with such matters, the lawyer urged the utmost secrecy regarding financial support for the Rebbe.

On 5 December Rhoade changed his request to Pell yet again. He asked Pell to cable the embassy in Berlin and have it instruct the group to proceed to Riga via Lithuania, citing the "unwillingness to risk further delay because of a possibly better, but delay-involving plan, as there is much anxiety." This must have frustrated Pell to no end, and it is a testament to his humanity and understanding that there is no record of his exasperation with Rhoade's sudden and frequent change of plans. Rhoade ended his letter by saying, "I am sure the feelings of the Rabbi's associates have your fullest sympathy."[26] And in fact, Rhoade's assessment seems accurate, because Pell passed on this new request to his contacts in Berlin.

12

Flight

It is taught in the *Mishnah*: "Therefore every man is obliged to say, 'For me was the world created.'"
—Rebbe Joseph Isaac Schneersohn

Having gone to such extraordinary lengths to locate and rescue the Rebbe, Bloch was shocked to learn that the Lubavitchers expected him to arrange for the escape of more than a dozen additional Orthodox Jews, rather than the few family members he had been ordered to help. Bloch told Schenk that although the Rebbe was a "great leader" in his own community, he lived a life "totally divorced from reality."[1] The Rebbe failed to see that he was not in command of the situation, and his refusal to leave unless his entire family and all his closest followers could accompany him jeopardized the whole rescue. He simply did not understand the danger to himself, as well as to the soldiers sent to protect him, if Bloch tried to escort a large group of Orthodox Jews through German-occupied Poland, much less Germany itself. Bloch was also surprised by the Lubavitchers' irrational complaints. For instance, when he brought them cheese, bread, and sausages, they refused to eat the food because it was not kosher. Bloch was dumbfounded. "These crazy people," he grumbled, "are hungry and sick. Indeed, [they are] a strange people—they don't even know when somebody is trying to help them."[2] The Lubavitchers, in contrast, admired the Rebbe's refusal to eat nonkosher food, despite being plagued by hunger. To them, such an act was an example of his godliness.[3]

There had been confusion about the size of the group in the United States as well. For example, in late November, Pell expressed surprise when he learned of Rhoade's assumption that the Germans would save everyone in the Rebbe's entourage. Pell explained, "Up to the present there had been only the question of the Rabbi. My request to Herr

Wohlthat was made on behalf of the Rabbi and in his reply he had extended that to include the Rabbi's wife and child ... a request to extend Wohlthat's action to include a large number of people might prejudice the whole affair." Rhoade pleaded with Pell to at least ask about the rest of the group, but Pell initially refused, fearing that it might cause Wohlthat to "react unfavorably against the Rabbi."[4] However, soon after this conversation with Rhoade, Pell started to push for the rescue of the entire group, which Wohlthat agreed to.

Bloch procured a truck and a wagon to transport the Lubavitchers to a railroad station outside of Warsaw, where they would board a train for Berlin; from there, they would take another train to Riga.[5] Wohlthat's office had already received funds for Schneersohn's travel, and by 13 December, it had arranged for him and his dependents, except for Mendel and Sheina Horenstein, to travel directly to Riga. Since the Horensteins were Polish citizens, they could not leave Europe owing to US restrictions.[6] This operation required the coordinated efforts of a number of people. Bloch needed a truck, fuel coupons, and train tickets. He also had to arrange clearances to pass through Wehrmacht and SS checkpoints and special approval for "foreigners" to enter Berlin.

Only two months after the initial rescue requests to Wohlthat, the US embassy in Berlin reported on 22 December 1939 that Rebbe Schneersohn, his family, and some of his followers had left Warsaw for Berlin and Riga.[7] The report failed to describe the difficulties encountered by Bloch and his team in transit. On 14 December, the last day of Chanukah, the Rebbe and his group left with Bloch for Berlin. Bloch had advised the Lubavitchers that they would have to follow his exact instructions, warning them that he might have to handle them roughly to prevent the SS or other Germans from becoming suspicious. He explained that in a dire emergency he might have to touch some of the women, although he would do his best to avoid that insult to their beliefs.[8]

As they left the building, the Lubavitchers must have felt a nervous excitement at finally escaping Warsaw. Passersby must have wondered where these Germans were leading this group of Hasidic Jews. Would they be killed? Although life in Warsaw had returned to a semblance of normalcy, it was an occupied city dominated by the Nazis. As the Jews stepped into the waiting vehicles, Polish children watched them and ran their index fingers along their necks to signify execution. Schenk shooed the children away and reassured his charges they had nothing to fear. They carried their suitcases and religious books and cast their gaze downward. A few of them held hands and whispered to one another.

Only yards away, the clanging sound of marching troops echoed through the streets. It was an SS unit, armed with rifles and sidearms. The skull-and-crossbones insignia sparkled on their black uniforms. As the group approached, Bloch considered the possibilities. If the SS was after the Rebbe, he and his men could not defend their charges. Suddenly, Bloch yelled, "OK, you pigs. Get in the truck and wagon. I said now." Schenk roughly herded the Jews into the vehicles as quickly as he could, yelling, "Faster."[9] The SS unit marched past without paying much attention.

Bloch rode in the truck with the Rebbe. Along the road they observed the charred remains of Polish armored trucks and troop carriers, the carcasses of horses, and the fresh graves of civilians caught in the maelstrom of war. Schenk later recalled that as the Rebbe looked out at this horror, he shook his head, put his old, wrinkled hand to his face, and rocked back and forth, mumbling to himself.

When they reached the first checkpoint outside the city, the SS asked Bloch to step out of the truck. Bloch presented his papers and carefully viewed his surroundings. He scolded one SS soldier for not saluting properly. Schenk heard the man apologize halfheartedly. Bloch immediately took out his notebook and asked for the man's name and that of his superior. Suddenly, the soldier's eyes widened. He knew he was in trouble.

As two soldiers busied themselves with Bloch, another two walked up to the wagon and the group of strange-looking people on it. In one of the young soldier's blue eyes, Schenk saw not hate but a fierce curiosity. He asked Schenk who these people were. Schenk told him to direct his questions to Bloch, his superior. "What unit are you with?" the SS man demanded. Schenk replied, "We are members of the Abwehr." The young man's eyes opened wider; he turned his face to the ground and returned to his post.

Bloch walked back to the truck, breathing heavily. He looked at Schenk and said, "We made it through this one. I told them these Jews were prisoners and sent for by special authority in Berlin. They seemed to want no further explanation. Anyway, the Wehrmacht should be at these checkpoints, not SS."[10] Bloch looked back at the guards as the truck started up and moved slowly through the opened field gate. His eyes narrowed, and he instinctively placed his hand on his pistol.

During the journey, the Rebbe asked Bloch why he was rescuing them. When Bloch revealed his ethnicity, the Rebbe asked him if he felt Jewish. Bloch must have been taken aback by the question, and he probably hesitated. What did this man, who looked like a character out of seventeenth-century Poland, mean by such a question? The "half-Jewish" Wehrmacht officer answered that he did not, but admitted he had always been intrigued by his Jewish past. "You have a strong Jewish spirit," the Rebbe responded. The fact that Bloch was rescuing them seemed to verify his Jewish loyalty in the Rebbe's eyes, and he saw Bloch's brave act as a "return" to his roots. The Rebbe's strong feelings of kinship with Bloch were most likely unnoticed by the German officer, who was simply performing his duty to the best of his abilities. However, the Rebbe believed that God was conducting this whole event, and what better instrument than a fellow Jew.

During the journey, they passed countless columns of soldiers and military trucks, some of them with large, white SS runes painted on their sides. Despite the horror and danger surrounding them, the Lubavitchers remained focused on their faith. Some tried to convince Schenk that their method of worshipping was the best way to observe God's laws. As Schenk understood their argument, a harmonious world would arise only when all Jews recognized their Rebbe and his doctrine. Once this unity was achieved, the Messiah would come. The Lubavitchers thanked Schenk and the other Germans for ensuring that the world would not lose the greatest living leader who held "mankind's destiny in his hands."[11] This seemed to be a general theme among the Lubavitchers. According to a special report to the State Department, Chabad, using articles from the *Jewish American*, had rated the Rebbe "among the ten greatest Jews in the *world*."[12]

One checkpoint right outside Warsaw proved particularly difficult. As they started the inspection process, one SS soldier shouted at Bloch and pointed his finger at the Rebbe. Several SS men raised their rifles and directed them at the Rebbe's face; Schneersohn's hands visibly shook.

Although the sky was a light gray, the shadows of the soldiers danced around the Jews, who kept their eyes focused on the ground. Bloch told the commanding officer, a tall, ordinary-looking man in a jet-black uniform, that he had special orders to take these Jews to Berlin. The SS officer sniffed, blinked, and shook his head, saying he had not been informed about this cargo. He threatened to detain the Jews and hold Bloch and his men at his headquarters until he received authorization from Berlin, noting that the whole thing "smelled rotten" to him. "Why does the Abwehr care about Orthodox Jews?" he asked, gesturing to the group. "They are ignorant scum who should be shot." Then he turned his cold eyes back toward Bloch and asked, "What are you really doing?"

For a moment, Bloch feared the SS had learned of the mission. In the next few minutes, he might lose the entire group and possibly his own Aryanization status. A cold sweat broke out across his shoulders, and his breathing became more rapid. He later told Schenk that if the Berlin SS knew that he, a "half-Jew," had helped more than a dozen Orthodox Jews escape Warsaw, they would have "my head delivered on a platter."[13] Bloch's fear was not unwarranted. People who had helped Jews escape from the Third Reich were punished with imprisonment and even death. One soldier who had helped some Jews cross the border into Romania was executed because his action "dishonored the Wehrmacht."[14] So Bloch had every reason to feel nervous.

"I don't understand why these Jews are being taken to our capital," the SS officer insisted, his face reddening with frustration. "Secondly, I don't like taking orders from an army officer who is incapable of telling me why these creatures are being escorted to Berlin or who has ordered him to do so." The SS man ended his diatribe with a rascally grin. Bloch's fists clenched and the blood rushed to his cheeks as he shouted that Admiral Canaris had issued his orders. He went on to say that he had been in contact with several regiments in the area, naming them and their commanding officers. Bloch told the SS officer that if he did not let the group through, he would personally see to it that the officer was arrested and "properly dealt with." The SS officer stared at Bloch, summing up the gravity of his threat. After some uneasy hesitation, he ordered the roadblock opened for Bloch's group. The bluff had worked. A few miles past the roadblock, Bloch reassured the Rebbe that everything would be all right, adding, "The SS is not Germany."[15] The Rebbe did not look persuaded. Schenk registered the deep irony of their situation: there were SS personnel who wanted to kill the Jews, and Wehrmacht soldiers who wanted to help them—and both groups were German.

In fact, many of the Lubavitchers believed that Bloch was not a real German officer but a Jew disguised as a soldier. Chaim Lieberman later wrote: "German soldiers were bloodthirsty like wild animals to hurt our group of Jewish men with beards and side locks as soon as they saw us. . . . A German Jew, who had served in World War I and wore a uniform covered with medals, helped the Rebbe and his family escape this danger."[16] Bloch had obviously told the Lubavitchers about his Jewish father to calm their fears; perhaps he even felt akin to them in some strange way. The fact remains that they believed a fellow Jew was rescuing them. Some saw Bloch as a guardian angel sent by God, which perhaps struck them as more plausible—and less miraculous—than a "friendly Nazi." The belief that these unusual Germans were acting under God's command was not uncommon for the Lubavitchers, for the Bible portrays God as using both good forces and bad for his own purposes, including to reward, to protect, to punish, or simply to demonstrate his awesome power. By way of illustration, Rabbi Nisson Mengel, a survivor of Auschwitz, described a Nazi soldier who had helped him during a death march near the end of the war. This German had shown him kindness and protected him, and he referred to the soldier as the prophet Elijah in disguise. But how much greater the miracle, he observed, if the man were just an ordinary Nazi soldier.[17]

On arriving at the train station, Bloch's group again attracted the attention of the authorities. An army officer questioned why Jews had been issued first-class train tickets. Bloch or one of his men may have told him that the Jews were traveling under diplomatic protection, or they offered some other explanation that prompted the officer to leave without further questioning.[18] The Jews looked and felt out of place sitting in a train full of Nazi officials and military personnel. As the train rolled through the countryside, the Jews must have seen the destruction in countless Polish towns and cities where the Wehrmacht had conducted its blitzkrieg. The landscape of war likely evoked an overwhelming sense of helplessness among these rabbis, yeshiva students, and religious women.

For most Lubavitchers, handling any type of weapon was alien to their world. A lifetime devoted to religious observance and a lifestyle that placed no value on exercise or physical labor left the Lubavitchers of 1939 physically weak. Even today, Lubavitcher society values scholarship over physical fitness, and physical fights are roundly condemned. These ultrareligious Jews might praise Joshua for destroying Jericho, Moses for eradicating the Midianites described in Numbers, or even King David and his armies for annihilating the Philistines during their constant wars against these "idolaters," but they abhor violence and brutality. Any invader of a society controlled by Lubavitchers in particular, and Hasidic Jews in general, would find the inhabitants easy prey, as the Holocaust would unfortunately prove.

As the train continued west toward Germany, the Lubavitchers likely experienced a variety of strange thoughts. On the one hand, they probably felt helpless, having no choice but to depend on these Germans who seemed to be acting in good faith. Outside of these men, they undoubtedly felt disdain and hatred from most of those around them. On the other hand, given the Lubavitchers' typical overestimation of their own importance, they most likely worried that the Germans were really taking the Rebbe to Berlin as an impressive prize to be paraded around. Regardless of the goodwill Bloch had shown them, traveling *toward* Nazi Germany, rather than away from it, must have caused them great unease, as if they were entering a house on fire instead of running away from it as fast as they could.

One can only imagine what they thought and felt as they crossed the border into the Greater German Reich and passed through towns bedecked with swastika flags. Due to the ongoing military operations, tanks, trucks, motorcycles, and cannons must have been visible everywhere they traveled. Armed soldiers in battle dress would have been marching through the streets or transferring men and equipment to trains and lorries headed west in preparation for war with the French, Belgians, Dutch, and English. As the train entered the Third Reich, it must have been clear that this was not their world. As one Lubavitcher described it, they were now in the "very heart of the evil Nazi kingdom."[19]

On 15 December the Rebbe and his group arrived in Berlin. They stayed one night at the Jewish Community Center (*Jüdische Gemeinde*), a charity similar to the United Way, sleeping in its dining hall. Rhoade had been deeply worried about the Rebbe traveling to Berlin, exposing himself and others to "antisemitism, Nazi variety, on its home ground." He warned that "Jews, especially [those] as Jewish looking as these Rabbis, should get out of Berlin as quickly as possible," even though he knew the military escort would "reduce molestation to a minimum." Luckily for the Lubavitchers, as well as for Bloch, they apparently had no problems while in the German capital. US chargé d'affaires Alexander Kirk probably met with the Rebbe and his group at the Jewish Community Center to give them additional information as well as the documentation they would need for their journey. The next day, the Lubavitchers boarded another train for Riga, again in a first-class cabin and accompanied by their German escorts and delegates from the Latvian embassy.[20]

When questioned again why Jews were traveling in the first-class section of the train, a "German officer," most likely Bloch, reportedly gave the same response from a few days earlier: they were traveling on diplomatic orders and should be left alone.[21] At the Latvian border, the German soldiers bade the Jews farewell. It was probably the last time Bloch saw the Rebbe. As they left German soil, the Rebbe and his group rejoiced. "We felt so good once we reached the Latvian border," Barry Gourary said. En route to Riga, the train stopped at Kovno (Kaunas), Lithuania, where several of the Rebbe's followers met the train and danced with joy as he arrived.[22] He had returned to his world.

13

Waiting in Riga

> It is a fantastic commentary on the inhumanity of our times that for
> thousands of people a piece of paper with a stamp on it is the difference
> between life and death.
> —Dorothy Thompson (US journalist), 1938

When news reached America that Schneersohn, his family, and his
staff had reached Riga safely, Jacobson left a meeting and ran out into
the streets, where he jumped up and down, did "handsprings on the sidewalks," and shouted ecstatically. "I could not contain my joy," he said.
He then returned to his office to continue planning the next leg of the
Rebbe's journey. That day, Jacobson also received a phone call from the
Rebbe himself, thanking him and the American Lubavitchers for all their
efforts on his behalf.[1]

On 20 December Rhoade telephoned Pell at the State Department and
then immediately wrote him a letter expressing his appreciation for Pell's
"wonderful efforts." But the case was not yet closed. The Rebbe's group
still lacked US entry visas. Foreseeing a bureaucratic roadblock—"insuf-
ficient proof" of guaranteed employment in the United States—Rhoade
asked Pell to help him obtain exemptions for the group. He emphasized
once again their special status:

[This is] a novel and perhaps even a non-precedented situation and,
therefore, requires unusual handling. The situation, in principle, is
analogous to the problem that would result if forced evacuation of
the Vatican occurred as a result of war and the Catholics in America
desired to bring all the ordained ministers of religion (priests) of the
Vatican to the United States for the purpose of transferring the seat
of the Catholic hierarchy to this country. In such a situation, the

[179]

status of the Pope and other high prelates of the Catholic hierarchy as ministers of a religious denomination, even though not officially affiliated as priests of any particular congregation, could not be properly [authenticated]. That is likewise true of Chabad hierarchy.

Rhoade repeatedly invoked the analogy to the pope, to great effect. He explained that section 4(d) of the Immigration Act of 1924 defined the Rebbe and his rabbis as "clergymen" worthy of nonquota status. To drive home his point, Rhoade quoted the Department of Labor on the subject of section 4(d): "The intent of the law is to enable religious bodies . . . to bring needed ministers . . . from foreign countries." Rhoade insisted that although the members of Schneersohn's group did not have congregations to take care of them, they would find sufficient support from US Chabad. He concluded that American Lubavitchers should not be deprived of the "spiritual welfare" provided by the hierarchy.[2]

In case this argument did not persuade Pell and the Visa Department, Rhoade also worked on securing quota visas. Here, the burden of proof fell on US Chabad headquarters. For all of Rhoade's eloquent pleading, and for all the time Pell devoted to the case, the simple fact remained that their efforts would be futile if Jacobson could not obtain the necessary information to procure the "life-saving" visas. Besides proving that the men could support themselves, he had to prove that they would "qualify as Rabbis within the meaning of the law." Without such documentation, the whole case would be jeopardized.[3] Unlike Reform, Conservative, and Reconstructionist rabbis, who are expected to graduate college and then spend several years attending a rabbinical seminary, ultra-Orthodox and Hasidic rabbis shun formal higher education and get their rabbinical certification after serving an apprenticeship with other rabbis. Of course, a college diploma and a seminary degree are not required for many Christian ministers either, especially among the evangelical faiths (e.g., Church of Christ denominations). But the lack of such formal education can make it more difficult to document that a person is a minister to a skeptical or hostile bureaucrat.

Rhoade continued to experience problems with Jacobson—the very person whose cooperation was most vital. He wrote to Jacobson on 21 December about the lack of "sufficient concrete details and financial information" and his fear that the affidavits he had would be inadequate for the issuance of visas. He also complained that the US Chabad rabbis were pestering him about his work. The case, he said, was "without precedent," in view of the "legal technicalities involved in connection with the Immigration Act, which I cannot possibly take the time to explain by letter or expect you gentlemen to understand. Therefore, you will please restrain your impatience and assume that I am moving heaven and earth to accomplish the desired result. Don't expect the impossible just because such unusual things have already been accomplished."[4]

Besides dealing with Jacobson, Rhoade continued to struggle with the State Department. On 22 December he wrote to Kramer, "Our Rabbis are not the conventional type so even if we regard them as superior we had to anticipate difficulties with a goyish [Gentile] mentality by carefully formulating the facts."[5] They had to persuade the Visa Department that these men were not only invaluable to Chabad but also beneficial to American society.

Rabbi Judah Gourary, under Jacobson's guidance, had developed the strategy of focusing solely on the "hierarchy" angle to bypass the quota system, as reflected in Rhoade's letters from December.[6] In the relevant documents it was often argued that, under section 4(d) of the Immigration Act of 1924, the Rebbe could be classified as a "minister" because he had practiced his religion for at least two years and wished to enter the United States "solely for the purpose of . . . carrying on the vocation of minister" of his religious denomination. Referring to the members of the Rebbe's group as the "hierarchy" helped classify them as ministers of an entire movement, thus taking advantage of a critical loophole in the Immigration Act. If this tactic were successful, Rhoade would no longer have to depend on Jacobson, as there would be no need to secure affidavits to prove the existence of separate supporting congregations.[7] Jacobson had failed to procure those affidavits after three months, not to mention the documentary proof that the Rebbe and his group were indeed rabbis. Starting in mid-December, Rhoade discussed this idea with the State Department, which seemed to be open to it.

Rhoade wrote to Hull on 23 December, "Inasmuch as these Rabbis, as a hierarchy, are even superior to ordinary Rabbis, their non-quota status both with respect to their past vocation as ministers of a religious denomination and their purpose to continue their vocation of discharging their high religious functions after admission to the USA is obvious." The lawyer had done all he could with the information he had. He wrote to Kramer, "Pell is our man 100% and has done everything possible with the Visa Division. I don't think anyone can do more." He reminded Kramer not to "minimize the technical difficulties at this end. As an old, and may I add rather successful, hand at immigration matters, I am not a bit ashamed of the progress so far and it is almost impossible (and a terrible waste of time) to justify and explain everything that is being or not being done."[8] Rhoade had so much confidence in Pell that he took the Lubavitchers' request about their library to him. On 23 December he wrote to Pell, "As the Nazis have quite a record for destroying literature, and in view of the plans now in progress to transfer the seat of the world hierarchy to the United States, I have been asked by . . . Chabad to request you to please [help.] . . . I understand that some of the manuscripts are priceless. The value of the collection alone is sufficient to render immediate action imperative."[9]

Rhoade was correct to worry about the Nazis burning the Lubavitchers' books. In May 1933 Nazi propaganda minister Joseph Goebbels organized a nationwide book-burning campaign that took place in public squares and towns throughout Germany, destroying the works of Heinrich Heine, Moses Mendelssohn, Franz Kafka, Albert Einstein, Sigmund Freud, and numerous others. At *Opernplatz* in Berlin, 20,000 books went up in flames in a "vast *auto-da-fé*" as Goebbels yelled out to the nearby crowd, "German men and women! The age of arrogant Jewish intellectualism is now at an end! . . . You are doing the right thing at this midnight hour—to consign to the flames the unclean spirit of the past. This is a great, powerful, and symbolic act."[10] The Nazis also burned the books of non-Jewish authors who were deemed "unGermanic," including Ernest Hemingway, Jack London, and even Helen Keller. During the Polish campaign, the Nazis burned the entire library of Lublin's Jewish Religious Academy simply because the books belonged to this "detested race." "It was a matter of special pride," a German eyewitness later reported, "to destroy the Talmudic Academy [the *Yeshiv Chachei Lublin*, the Wise Men of Lublin], which was known as the greatest in Poland." The Lublin Orthodox Jews circled the bonfire and wept loudly and bitterly. The manuscripts and books burned for twenty-four hours.[11] The Nazis were continuing a tradition of burning Jewish books that had started in the Middle Ages and involved the Catholic Church.[12] One is reminded of Heine's famous line: "Where books / Are Burned, in the end people will be burned as well" (*Dort, wo man Bücher verbrennt, verbrennt man am Ende auch Menschen*).[13]

Since the Rebbe's library helped preserve the movement's entire culture, and given the Nazis' eagerness to destroy Jewish books, Rhoade's request was not unreasonable. But, as Pell explained to Rhoade, he would have to prove that the library was American property—a daunting task. Even though the Rebbe could argue that the books were essential to the movement, he could not make the same case for his jewelry, silverware, and other household items, which he also wanted to take with him.[14] The Rebbe's unrestrained requests indicate that he did not understand the precariousness of his own situation and the herculean efforts being made on his behalf. Most of his followers, however, were not critical of these requests; they thought the Rebbe should have whatever he wanted. He was God's chosen, so what right did they have to question him? But when his appeals were put to the US government, the cogs of the political machine ground to a halt.

Back in Riga, the Rebbe remained agitated about the status of his precious library. He wrote to Jacobson on 26 December 1939:

> Surely I will receive within a few days a detailed letter about all that has been done for the saving of my library and about taking it out from there. . . . There are about a hundred and twenty boxes of books and three boxes of manuscripts of our revered and holy parents, the saintly Rabbis . . . and you will surely do all you can to bring them to your country. There are also the remainder of our other valuables that was left over after the great conflagration . . . the jewelry etc. . . . I have already advised several times by telegram, and also my son-in-law (Gourary) has spoken with you several times over the telephone about the books and the manuscripts and you have as yet not answered anything. I repeat and say again and request most earnestly that you kindly hasten this matter as soon as possible.[15]

Since some of these manuscripts documented Lubavitch history, the Rebbe considered them essential to the preservation of the traditions of "his people."[16] He may have been thinking of the famous rabbi and leader of the Pharisees during Roman times, Rabban Yohanan Ben Zakkai, who is credited with rebuilding and thus saving Judaism after the Jewish revolt that started in 66 CE. After sneaking out of Jerusalem to meet with Roman authorities, Ben Zakkai requested only that the town of Yavneh, a center of Torah study, be spared from destruction. He believed that religious observance was the primary reason God had created mankind. So instead of pleading with the Romans to spare Jerusalem, Ben Zakkai concentrated on saving scholars and carrying on the religious traditions of study and worship, which he considered essential to Jewish survival. The Rebbe shared Ben Zakkai's convictions about the importance of studying the Torah and ancient Jewish texts. In his mind, his library was essential for saving his Jewish community's way of life, which was based on observing God's laws.[17]

Some of the Rebbe's books were sacred remnants that had, like the Rebbe, survived the Soviets and, it was hoped, would survive the Nazis as well. However, several of the manuscripts were not religious at all; some were actually antireligious books published by the Yevsektzia (the Jewish section of the Communists Party) or secular ("heretical") books such as Dante's *Inferno*. Hundreds of the books were still in print and could have easily been replaced. The Rebbe had collected books avidly for years. "He collected anything having to do with Judaism or if the book was written in Hebrew," according to Arthur Green. "He was fanatic in collecting anything he could put his hands on and frequently petitioned publishing houses and authors for books." Throughout the 1920s and 1930s the Rebbe "publicly appealed for book donations."[18] The Rebbe hated the thought of parting with any of these books.

Why, in the midst of the chaos and horror of war, was the Rebbe so worried about not only his books but also his household goods? One must remember that Chabad had suffered horrible persecution under the czars and Stalin, and the Nazis were viewed as just another group to be endured. The Rebbe had not experienced ghettos or concentration camps, so he did not recognize the need to focus exclusively on saving lives; he just wanted to be free of Nazi persecution. Only in hindsight do the Rebbe's efforts to save his personal possessions seem perplexing. His actions should not be construed as shortsighted or selfish; he believed he was taking the necessary steps to ensure the continuation of his work. He did not think the money and effort expended for his books and possessions would interfere with his ability to help people in need. He had paid $300 for a lawyer in Poland and probably several hundred dollars for packaging, storing, and shipping his belongings. It is unlikely that he viewed saving his library and saving Jews as mutually exclusive efforts. Yet there is no documentary evidence of comparable efforts by the Rebbe to save the lives of his community members or other Jews. Likewise, as pointed out by the famous Jewish sage Rabbi Akiva, Ben Zakkai's mistake was not asking the Romans to save Jerusalem and all its inhabitants, in addition to his students and library.[19]

The Rebbe's obsessive quest to save his library has unsettled many. Historian and Orthodox Jew Efraim Zuroff asks, "How can one justify expending even a small amount of resources and energies to try and save the rebbe's library at a time when the rescue of lives should have taken precedence?" One wonders why the Lubavitchers never discussed using their funds and political contacts to save more Jews, but as Zuroff writes, Lubavitchers "do not consider such a set of priorities controversial or in any way problematic."[20] In other words, if the Rebbe wanted something to be done, no one questioned his authority. According to Rabbi Shalom Dovber Levine, the head of Chabad's library and archives, "There was something very secret and holy in building the Library from the start . . . in the worse times of depression in Russia and Europe, he gave his life for it. He viewed it as part of the rebuilding of the Lubavitch movement."[21]

This focus on saving the books was premature, however, as visas for the group had not yet been issued. To convince those in Riga of the Rebbe's status, Rhoade asked Senator David Walsh of Massachusetts and Secretary of State Hull to forward requests to the American consulate in Riga. Their cable requested that the Rebbe and his hierarchy be given "favorable consideration" for nonquota visas. It also requested quick action due to the threat of an expanding war and assured the recipients that any information provided by the Rebbe could be trusted.[22] Upon receiving a request for help, Postmaster General James A. Farley responded on 28 December that obtaining a temporary visa would not be an easy thing to arrange, but he would do whatever he could.

Rhoade continued to urge his contacts to pressure the Visa Department, as those involved in the rescue obviously felt that department head Avra Warren needed prodding. Rhoade probably asked Senator Wagner to contact Warren directly, which he did on 29 December, asking Warren for an update.[23] Warren's assistant, Coulter, replied to Wagner a few days later, telling him the Riga legation had already received information about the visa applications of the "aliens." Coulter assured Wagner that although several issues still needed clarification, "the applications of the aliens in question will be given every consideration consistent with the immigration laws."[24]

On 29 December Rhoade asked Cohen to appeal to Hull again to obtain the Visa Department's "more rapid and definite cooperation." Recognizing that "ordinary cases" did not merit such extraordinary action, Rhoade argued that it was a "matter of life and death" for the "recognized world spiritual head of a whole orthodox Jewish denomination, numbering hundreds of thousands of adherents." Rhoade reasoned that since Cohen had been partly responsible for the Rebbe's successful escape to Riga, he had a vested interest in "seeing the job completed. . . . Otherwise, all the weeks of immense effort may prove in vain."[25] Cohen advised Rhoade to be patient with the overworked Visa Department, where things had slowed down because of the Christmas and New Year celebrations.[26] On 2 January 1940 Rhoade replied to Cohen, noting that although they had "to reckon with certain limitations, this is the sort of case where it is proper to cut the red tape. There is unquestionably enough evidence in the hands of the American Consulate in Riga to warrant immediate issuance of the non-quota visas to the rabbis comprising the *hierarchy* of this religious denomination."[27] In response to the lawyer's plea, Coulter stated on 3 January that making an exception for the Rebbe "would, of course, be inconsistent with the Immigration Laws and established practice."[28]

Concerned by the delay and by the increasing hostilities in Europe, Rhoade wrote to Adolph J. Sabath—in Rhoade's opinion, the most important Jewish member of Congress—that Riga was unsafe "because of the possible spread of the present Baltic conflict and the danger of Russian domination of Latvia."[29] Rhoade continued to pressure every high-ranking official he knew, characterizing his crusade as a "general bombardment." State senator and judge Philip M. Kleinfeld promptly responded to Rhoade's request and sent a cable to Latvian officials.[30] Sabath, Farley, Wagner, and Walsh, among others, also sent cables to Riga.[31] They were all similar to the following:

> Will deeply appreciate favorable action on application World Chief Rabbi Joseph Isaac Schneersohn and associate Rabbis of World Chabad Hierarchy for non-quota visas in compliance with desire American Branch Chabad denomination for removal of this hierarchy to America due to coming war peril and evacuation from Poland. My request is prompted by assurance from distinguished American friends of Rabbi and his associates that representations can be relied upon.[32]

On 4 January Coulter informed Rhoade in bureaucratic style that he could not ask the consular officer in Riga to act outside the immigration laws. He explained that Rhoade should send the requisite information to Riga because "the burden of proof is placed by law upon an alien applying for a visa to establish his eligibility." Coulter ended his letter by saying, "The cases of the aliens concerned will receive every consideration consistent with the immigration laws."[33] Rhoade responded on 6 January: "Pell had referred to your Division the visa phase in the hope that an acceleration plan could be devised in view of the urgency and importance of the hierarchy aspect." Rhoade reminded Coulter that the Rebbe was the celebrated world leader of Chabad, and his followers were "not merely ordinary Rabbis of individual congregations." He challenged the need for identification, which the Rebbe and his group could not possibly provide. Since "the reputation of applicants is such as to render their claims entirely trustworthy, there is no need of extremely exacting and time consuming requirements, especially in time of war danger." He also warned that if the Soviet Union conquered Latvia, the Rebbe and his hierarchy would be *subject to the extreme penalty of death as counter revolutionists*, for former proscribed religious activity in Russia."[34] Given the threat posed by the Soviet situation, Rhoade wrote to Congressman Sabath that very day, asking him to take up the issue of nonquota status with Secretary of State Hull.[35]

Rhoade's fear was warranted, for in June 1940 the Red Army would occupy the Baltic states, and many Jewish leaders would disappear, along with thousands of others in Latvia.[36] Unbeknownst to those involved with the rescue (but perhaps not unsuspected), they had a few months to get the Rebbe out of Riga before the Red Army's invasion. But at the time, these US-based rescuers felt like they had only days. The mounting tension strained the friendship between Rhoade and Kramer. Kramer criticized Rhoade for making suggestions to politicians before consulting the Lubavitchers; Rhoade was feeling the pressure of time, and from his point of view, it was better to try too hard rather than not hard enough.[37] In a particularly bold effort, Rhoade attempted to gain the ear of Pell's boss, Myron C. Taylor, a former US Steel executive who was in charge of refugee work for President Roosevelt and his personal representative to the Vatican.[38] Rhoade argued in a letter to Kramer that if Taylor would dedicate "himself to the humanitarian refugee work" of rescuing the Rebbe, it would be "a concrete illustration of Christianity's efforts on behalf of stricken Jewry."[39] But if Rhoade was hoping that Taylor might obtain help from the Vatican, he would be sorely disappointed.

The Roman Catholic Church, with its enormous moral influence in Germany, Austria, Italy, Spain, France, Hungary, Poland, and other countries with large Catholic populations, was a force to be reckoned with. Stalin had once arrogantly asked, "How many divisions has the Pope?" As Christopher Hitchens rightly notes, "The true answer to [Stalin's] boorish sarcasm was, 'More than you think.'"[40] But the Catholic Church did not utilize these masses for moral action against the evil spreading across Europe; in fact, it seemed to turn a blind eye to Hitler and even supported him.[41]

After becoming pope in 1939, Pius XII discouraged attacks against Hitler and did little to fight the Nazis' anti-Semitic policy. Pius XII had even shown sensitivity to German needs, drafting the concordat with Nazi Germany and giving Hitler badly needed recognition early in his regime. Although the pope did not rouse the Roman Catholic Church to mount an aggressive or high-profile campaign in opposition to Hitler and

Mussolini, some priests and bishops acted heroically, such as Bishop Clemens von Galen, whose sermons helped halt the brutal Nazi euthanasia program. So if the Catholic Church was having a difficult time standing up to Hitler (and was in fact standing with him), and if the church failed to stand up for its own members, there was little chance that it would help a Jew.[42] Rhoade, however, hoped that Taylor would at least call the embassy in Latvia and persuade the office to issue immediate visas to the Rebbe and his group. Rhoade also suggested asking Judge Samuel I. Rosenman, who often advised the president on Jewish matters, to appeal directly to Roosevelt.[43]

Rhoade discussed with Kramer another matter that was still weighing heavily on his mind: his fees.[44] He complained that hundreds of dollars in bills remained outstanding, and he needed his friend's support to rectify the matter. "Because frankly," Rhoade wrote, "this thing has reached a point where it is absolutely pulverizing me, though for your sake and the sake of the cause, I am still grimly carrying on."[45] This situation is related to the psychology of business—that is, clients know what the *fees* are, but they rarely consider the *cost* in human capital, expertise, and time.[46] In short, the Lubavitchers showed their lack of appreciation (to say the least) of Rhoade and his talents by not paying him in full for his services, as they had promised.

The fact that Rhoade continued to work for the Lubavitchers is remarkable. Most lawyers would have fired such clients. Although documenting Rhoade's motivation is somewhat difficult, I spent a significant amount of time with Rhoade's family and his correspondence, and I believe he thought the Rebbe and his entourage would die if he did not act. His humanitarianism speaks volumes, for at this stage of the game, no one would have faulted him for walking away. Ironically, Rhoade—a secular Jew—was behaving more morally than a sea of Hasidic Jews whose entire lives were consumed by religion. The Lubavitchers failed to acknowledge that this man who had rejected both Hasidism and monetary profit was acting with incredible kindness and self-sacrifice by offering competent and even zealous representation. They probably did not fully understand how much other work Rhoade had sacrificed to focus on the Rebbe's case or how unique Rhoade's expertise was. The Hasidic scholars were concerned with the most minor details of religious law, but they remained ignorant of the civil laws and political processes of the countries where they lived. This is just one example of the severe handicaps resulting from their self-imposed isolation and shunning of modern education, a practice the community perpetuates even today. They trusted God to provide, and they believed that reward awaited them in heaven. So they prayed—and ignored Rhoade's bills.

As Rhoade was trying to collect his fees, the US embassy in Riga asked the government to conduct a special investigation of Chabad to verify the information it had received. The embassy actually sent the request to Hull, who apparently forwarded it to Troutman or Warren in the Visa Department.[47] Rhoade knew this investigation was important, and he eagerly awaited the findings. Special agents from the Visa Department were assigned to meet with American Chabad leaders at the beginning of January. The glacial progress made Rhoade nervous, so he asked Troutman to do his best to "accelerate" the investigation:

> Owing . . . to the impracticability of establishing the new seat of
> the hierarchy at Riga or in any country other than the U.S.A.,
> each day lost results in great damage to the denomination. I refer
> particularly, of course, to the American branch of that denomination.
> . . . You know from the file of the great efforts expended by the
> State Department through diplomatic channels in bringing about the
> evacuation, with the consent of the military authorities. Under these
> exceptional circumstances, I am sure you will not regard our constant
> insistence upon exceptionally speedy handling as unreasonable.[48]

He also informed Troutman: "This particular denomination is extremely religious. The Jewish Sabbath commences at sundown Friday and at this time of the year it is necessary for the offices to close at 3:00 P.M. Friday (through Saturday) in order to permit preparations for the Sabbath. It will be appreciated if you will kindly call this to the attention of the investigator."[49]

But when Special Agent Tubbs showed up for the appointment in the late afternoon of 5 January, no one met him at the office. Although it was permissible to violate the Sabbath to save a human life—especially the lives of the Rebbe and his disciples—the leaders of Chabad did not wait around for a visit that might never materialize. There was also some confusion caused by Chabad's use of multiple addresses, and the agent had been given the wrong one. Once again, Jacobson's sloppiness had messed things up. Rhoade corrected the mistake with the State Department as quickly as he could, and another appointment was rescheduled for 9 January. This time, Tubbs met with a delegation from Chabad, including Jacobson and Sam and Hyman Kramer, and verified much of the information. The delegation assured him that $50,000 would stay in the United States as salary for the hierarchy.[50] Sam Kramer, according to Jacobson, "launched into a brilliant exposition of what the Chabad movement is" and "the important work they accomplish for the Jewish community." Chabad likely provided proof that the Rebbe had a contract to act as the rabbi of congregation Anshe Lebovitz in Chicago, with an annual salary of $4,000 for at least five years. After several hours, the agent left with the information he needed for his report.[51]

In his report, Tubbs expressed skepticism about the Lubavitchers' intention to invest their assets in the United States, in light of the importance they placed on outreach and maintaining communities overseas. Since most followers of the Rebbe lived overseas and "will permanently continue to remain in Europe . . . the greater portion of the influence and efforts of this organization will certainly continue to be in that direction." Tubbs believed the hierarchy was seeking sanctuary in the United States not because they wanted to become Americans but because of their precarious situation in war-torn Europe. It is clear that Tubbs had doubts about the hierarchy's potential contributions to America as a whole.[52] It seems, however, that his damning report was ultimately disregarded, presumably in deference to the large number of high-ranking officials already invested in the case.

American politicians seemed to think the Rebbe's case was worthy of their time, but it was still proving difficult to rescue him. Even true intellectuals and artists such as Hannah Arendt and Marc Chagall would struggle with Washington politics and would have to rely on others to push their cases. Varian Fry, an American who traveled to German-occupied and Allied Europe in 1940, helped rescue these talented individuals and many more through the privately run Emergency Rescue Committee. Recent scholarship has shown that some civil servants in the State

Department, such as Vice-Consul Hiram Bingham in Marseille, exercised incredible courage by disregarding US immigration laws to rescue these talented Jews. Along with Fry, Bingham worked on Chagall's case as well as that of anti-Nazi writer Lion Feuchtwanger and brilliant Nobel Prize–winning physiologist Otto Meyerhof. He saved hundreds by bypassing the red tape and issuing visas. He may have helped thousands escape the Nazis using his contacts throughout Europe, and he even hid a few Jews in his personal residence.

In general, the wheels of bureaucracy moved very slowly to procure the necessary documents for these "new citizens." It seemed that if one wanted quick action, one had to proceed illegally or extralegally, as Bingham did. In 1940 Hull actually reprimanded the staff at the embassy in France, and Bingham in particular, for helping too many Jews escape.[53] In short, without a strong advocate, applicants were refused entry into the United States as a matter of course. The Rebbe was lucky he had influential people supporting him.

Finally, on 9 January, Rhoade received confirmation that visas would be issued to the Rebbe and most of his entourage as soon as officials had completed their investigation.[54] He started making arrangements for the Lubavitchers to travel from Sweden to France and then Italy, where they could board an Italian American ocean liner. Alternatively, they could have traveled through Germany if Wohlthat had helped them, but many feared a route through the "land of Hitler." After much debate, and with Wohlthat probably having the final say, it was decided that the Rebbe's group would fly from Riga to Stockholm and take a train from there to the port of Göteborg, Sweden, for the transatlantic voyage.

In the meantime, agents assigned to review the Rebbe's case identified some additional problems with the information provided by Chabad. The civil servants discovered that the Lubavitchers had lied about the balance in the bank account of the Chicago synagogue that would support the Rebbe. Instead of almost $2,000, the account had only $343. It seemed that every time one looked below the surface, more problems were found.[55]

At the same time, Green Haywood Hackworth, a legal adviser in the State Department, requested further legal clarification. He asked his assistant, R. W. Flourney, to review the case with regard to the law.

Flourney examined the investigations; the information provided by Chabad; the personalities involved, such as Wagner; and the 1924 Immigration Act. In the end, Flourney found no reason to reject the hierarchy justification to approve the visas for the Rebbe and his group. He even used many of Rhoade's arguments, such as comparing Catholic governing bodies to the Rebbe's case. After reviewing all the facts, Flourney concluded that the Schneersohn case "will set a precedent of some importance." This was the first case to claim that a Jewish group had a hierarchical administrative structure and could therefore take advantage of nonquota visas allowed for "ministers"—a finding that, in the end, made proof of finances irrelevant. "Minister" was basically defined as someone who had been practicing as a religious leader for at least last two years—a criterion met by the Rebbe and most of his group. Whereas most rabbinical arrangements are nonhierarchical—that is, rabbis are hired by their congregations, enjoy equal authority, and do not necessarily report to one another—Hasidic arrangements are hierarchical, with the Rebbe and his court exercising authority and ruling by preeminence. Hackworth knew that the issuance of nonquota visas was likely to be questioned, since so many Americans were unemployed and suffering, so Flourney included a draft of a telegram to be sent to Wiley in Riga, instructing that the visas be issued, and initialed it for approval.[56]

Interestingly, had Flourney (or Hackworth, for that matter) wanted to reject the Rebbe and his group, he could have cited many things wrong with the case. For instance, they could not provide birth certificates, rabbinical degrees, or bank statements. Flourney could have questioned the "hierarchy" angle, since many of the group were members of the Rebbe's family, including three sons-in-law. One son-in-law, Menachem Mendel Schneerson, could not even be classified as a minister, since for the last two years he had been studying secular subjects in Paris and had not been working as a rabbi, even though he was ordained. Flourney could have claimed that the so-called governing body had been thrown together at the last minute to take advantage of the hierarchy angle, since it seemed that these men had never acted as a governing body before. Had he used these arguments, the rescue might have delayed or even prevented. However, in a clearly argued four-page letter, he concluded that the hierarchy and their families should be allowed into the United States. Given the climate of anti-Semitism and xenophobia within the State Department, this act seemed truly extraordinary, if not miraculous.

On 13 January 1940 the State Department finally approved the visas (but the embassy in Riga still had to issue them). The Horensteins, who were Polish citizens, were not granted visas, and there were problems with the Feigins' paperwork, so they would have to remain in Europe for the time being.[57] A few weeks later, the embassy in Riga informed Hull that evidence of the hierarchy's ability to support itself had been submitted, and the visas would be forthcoming.[58] The Rebbe and most of his entourage were fortunate because, in 1940, they were among tens of thousands of Jews who hoped to leave Europe for the United States.[59] Over the next four years, hundreds of thousands of desperate, persecuted Jews would suffer and die because they were denied permission to enter the country.[60] As Gregory Wallance wrote, "The refugees desperately hoped for salvation that would never come as they waited patiently with gloomy faces in long lines outside American consulates."[61] A large percentage of them would be slaughtered in the Holocaust. Pell became so disgusted with Breckinridge Long's immigration policies that he resigned from the Intergovernmental Committee in March 1941. He wrote to his boss, Myron Taylor, that Long "indulged in an unrelenting attack on the work and the officers . . . connected with [their duties]. There is just no use going on."[62] The Jews would lose one of their strongest supporters, as evidenced by the help he gave the Lubavitchers.

The United States allowed 105,000 refugees from Nazism to enter the country between 1933 and 1940, but this was only a small percentage of those who tried to immigrate (between 1940 and 1944, the record was even worse).[63] US leaders condemned Nazi atrocities but took little action.[64] The United States sent Undersecretary of State Sumner Welles to Berlin in early 1940, and he pleaded the Jews' case during an audience with Field Marshal Hermann Göring. In typical Göring fashion, he insolently responded that the whole world had racial problems and noted that the United States treated blacks just like the Nazis treated Jews. Welles acknowledged that the United States had its racial problems, but unlike Germany, it was not exterminating its own citizens. Göring refused to pursue the issue.[65] Welles could have pushed for the United States to increase its immigration quotas, and he probably did broach the subject

Breckinridge Long (left) with Representative Sol Bloom of New York. As director of immigration matters from 1940 until 1944, Long was responsible for keeping hundreds of thousands of refugees out of the country. (National Archives)

with the State Department. However, the United States was unwilling to help these desperate immigrants. The tragic story of the ocean liner *St. Louis*, which set out from Germany for North America in the spring of 1939 with 930 Jewish refugees, is a case in point. When the US government refused refuge to the Jews on board, the ship was forced to return to Europe, where more than one-quarter of the passengers died under the Nazis. Similar fates befell refugees on the *Ordina*, *Quanza*, and *Flanders*.[66] In late 1941, almost 800 desperate Romanian Jews fleeing a fascist government chartered a broken-down ship called the *Struma* and sailed for Palestine. Britain refused to admit them to Palestine. The ship, which had broken down off the coast of Turkey, was towed out to sea, where it exploded and sank, possibly torpedoed by the Soviets. There was only one survivor, David Stoliar. Eleanor Roosevelt complained to Welles about Britain's closing of Palestine. Welles, the highest ranking official in the State Department who was sympathetic to the Jews, wrote to Ray Atherton in the Division of European Affairs (who was decidedly unsympathetic): "If the British government did not wish this shipload of refugees to go to Palestine, some arrangements should have been made, purely from humanitarian considerations, to have found shelter for them during the war among the East African colonies."[67]

Supply ships routinely returned empty from Europe, and they could have been filled with refugees. Roosevelt received many requests to use these ships for that purpose, but he apparently passed them off to the Visa Department. The callous leadership of Warren and his successor Long reflected the State Department's reluctance to pursue a policy of active rescue.[68] Long was behind many of the decisions not to help rescue refugees. In June 1940 the Battle of France had been lost, and the British Expeditionary Force and more than 120,000 French troops had been evacuated at Dunkirk, but much of the army's equipment had been left behind. England was bracing for nightly bombing raids and a German invasion, and Franklin and Eleanor Roosevelt supported an effort to evacuate British children to the United States and Canada. Isolationist Long was aghast when the president and Congress approved the rescue effort. He was disturbed by this emotional reaction to the plight of the refugees, saying that many Americans suffered from "'an enormous psychosis' which he attributed to 'repressed emotions about the war.'"[69] Long therefore formulated a diabolical plan in a memo dated 26 June 1940: "We can delay and effectively stop for a temporary period of indefinite length the number of immigrants into the United States. We can do this by advising our consuls to put every obstacle in the way and to require additional evidence and to resort to various administrative devices which would postpone and postpone and postpone the granting of the visas."[70]

In the summer of 1942, when the opportunity arose to rescue 5,000 orphaned Jewish children stuck in Vichy France, Long actively prevented it. Most of the children had lost their parents in the Holocaust and were trying to avoid the same fate. Even though Eleanor Roosevelt pushed hard for their rescue, Long's efforts delayed any action; before any of the children could leave, the Germans occupied France, loaded most of the helpless little ones in boxcars, and sent them to their death in the east.[71]

Many of these children could have been saved with one or two ships. As Roosevelt's close adviser, attorney Benjamin V. Cohen, said after the war, "Things ought to have been different, but war is different, and we live in an imperfect world."[72] *Imperfect* is quite an understatement.

James McDonald, chairman of the President's Advisory Committee on Political Refugees, protested angrily. Mrs. Roosevelt complained to the president, who in turn talked to Welles; Welles advised the president to talk to Long, which he did. But although Long made some nice, sympathetic-sounding statements from time to time, he saw his actions as justified and continued to use his high position and knowledge of the bureaucracy to keep refugees out and to hide any evidence of the Nazis carrying out their "final solution." Eleanor told her husband that Long was a fascist.[73]

Albert Einstein, one of the earliest and most famous Jewish refugees to be welcomed into the United States, used his influence a few months later to alert FDR to the bureaucratic measures designed to keep other refugees from immigrating to the United States. Einstein also played a key role in convincing the US government to undertake the Manhattan Project, leading to the development of the atomic bomb and saving countless lives in the Pacific theater.[74] As the most prominent scientist of his generation, Einstein was widely respected and used his influence on behalf of his fellow refugees. Yet try as he might, he could not overcome the forces that were committed to keeping American shores closed.

Since most American Jews admired Roosevelt and were greatly impressed with his New Deal, they could not fathom the president's refusal to help people in need. Roosevelt, who took office in 1933, during the depths of the Great Depression, had done much for the country: implementing the Federal Deposit Insurance Corporation (FDIC), protecting investors and providing funding for businesses through new securities laws and the Securities and Exchange Commission, creating jobs for the unemployed, setting up the National Labor Relations Board, generating a safety net for workers that included Social Security, and adopting other programs to bolster the economy and give hope to those struggling to survive. In 1936 he won reelection by a landslide. Then he made the biggest political blunder of his career. Hoping to outmaneuver the conservative Supreme Court justices who had ruled some of his New Deal laws unconstitutional, he came up with the Court-packing plan, whereby Congress would enlarge the Supreme Court and authorize the president to appoint several new, more liberal justices. The plan was unpopular with both Democrats and Republicans; even Vice President John Nance Garner opposed it. Consequently, the plan failed, and Roosevelt's opponents were suddenly reinvigorated. As a result, Roosevelt became more cautious politically; he was unwilling to buck public opinion at a time when war clouds were gathering in Germany and his leadership to rearm America and build support for the Allies was crucial to preserving US freedom and peace in Europe. Until America's entry into the war in December 1941, Roosevelt was hesitant to act in the absence of public support, and no one was pushing him to rescue the Jews from Hitler.[75] Another consideration was his plan to run for an unprecedented third term in 1940.

In fairness, the full extent of the Nazis' war plans and the atrocities they would commit was not well known. Moreover, Roosevelt was heavily engaged in building up the small, poorly equipped, and poorly trained American armed forces and in getting public and congressional support to amend the Neutrality Act and send aid to the beleaguered Allies, over the strong objections of the isolationists. In addition, 1940 was an election year. Until the summer of 1940—when hundreds of thousands of British and French troops were evacuated at Dunkirk, and France, Belgium, and the Netherlands fell—it appeared highly likely that the Republican candidate for president would be an isolationist. Instead, Roosevelt would face the courageous, interventionist dark horse Wendell Willkie, who refused to play politics with the issue of military preparedness in order to win the isolationist vote in this close election. Given these facts, it is clear that the political and international climate was chaotic and ever changing.

With the president's attention focused elsewhere, and with the anti-Semitism prevalent in the State Department, it is remarkable that the Rebbe and his group received visas at all. Long was a well-educated, high-ranking, career State Department employee who had lost two bids to represent Missouri in the Senate. He did not want eastern European Jews coming to America and justified his position by citing (1) the restrictive Johnson-Reed Immigration Act of 1924, passed by Congress and signed by President Coolidge to limit immigrants from eastern Europe (many of whom were Jewish), southern Europe, Africa, and Asia; and

(2) his concern that large numbers of spies and saboteurs might slip into the country among the refugees. If these were truly his motivations, he could have sought changes in the immigration law to save more of those being hunted down by Hitler and his genocidal minions, he could have devised methods to screen applicants (many of whom were young children and clearly posed no threat) to eliminate potential spies and saboteurs, or he could have restricted their movement after entry. He did none of these things. Long played a key role "in obstructing both Jewish refugee immigration to the United States and rescue initiatives." Refugee aid organizations protested Long's obstructionism, but the president did not remove him. By the middle of 1940, Long had cut immigration by 50 percent. By some estimates, 90 percent of the quotas for immigrants from countries under German and Italian control (some 190,000) went unfilled. Long was later accused of misleading Congress in secret testimony he gave about Jewish immigration. Roosevelt could have replaced Long or ordered him to alter his tactics, but he did not.[76]

Under these circumstances, it was extraordinary that the State Department issued visas for the Rebbe's group, allowing the next phase of immigration to begin. The US government may have been spurred to act because of political pressure, but it also seemed satisfied that it had finally received enough documentation pertaining to Chabad's financial resources. Chabad reported that its US operation received $35,000 annually, and it projected that it would obtain $50,000 if the leaders of the movement were granted admittance to the country. Bank statements showed that the Rebbe had $5,000 in his personal accounts.[77] This information was apparently enough to convince the State Department. Philip Kleinfeld wrote to Cordell Hull on 17 January to thank him and Robert Pell on behalf of Chabad. He also acknowledged Eliot Coulter's important role in the Rebbe's escape.[78]

But the Lubavitchers were not satisfied with merely saving the lives of the Rebbe, his family, and his staff. Their next priority was to rescue the Rebbe's books and household goods. On 22 January 1940 Rhoade told Kramer that unless Chabad could prove that it held "title to the library," there was nothing he could do.[79] These documents never materialized, and even if they had, retrieving the books from the Nazis would have been a tall order.

The Rebbe, however, refused to give up the fight. On 7 February, while waiting in Riga, he hired a lawyer in Warsaw to arrange for Schenker & Company to ship 135 to 145 cases of books from his library and 11 cases of household goods from Poland to New York via Italy.[80] By this time, Rhoade had resigned as the Lubavitchers' lawyer, so Jacobson wrote to the new lawyer, Henry Butler, on 14 February and explained that the Rebbe had "the right" to bring his "books and things" to the United States. After working with Rhoade for months, Jacobson had clearly learned little from him, as evidenced by his next request. He wanted Butler to contact the US consul in Berlin and have him ask the US consul in Warsaw to gather some of the Rebbe's personal items that had been left in Otwock, take "said things under his care and send them here. The Lubavitcher Rabbi can advise the American Consul at Riga as to the whereabouts and existence of the said things."[81] Butler apparently never responded to this request, and Rhoade was no longer available to present it to the government through the proper channels. Jacobson's focus on trivial items such as books, prayer shawls, and cutlery shows an utter lack of understanding of events taking place in the world, where the shadow of death hung over so many.

During this time, the Nazis became aware of the Rebbe's personal items, which they refused to return to him. The SS commander in Warsaw notified the commissioner for the Warsaw ghetto that "Rabbi Schneersohn's cases, which included his crystal, china, and silver, were considered unregistered Jewish property" and therefore subject to forfeiture. Yet remarkably, in the summer of 1941, the Lubavitchers received a large number of cartons from Europe. David Edelman, a yeshiva student at the time, remembers the great excitement when two big trucks showed up at Chabad's Brooklyn headquarters and delivered thousands of books as well as some of the Rebbe's household goods, all rescued from Europe.[82] The arrangements made by the Rebbe through his lawyer in Warsaw had apparently been successful, regardless of the Nazis' intentions.[83]

Once his work was largely done, Rhoade had resigned as the Rebbe's lawyer on 29 January and turned the assignment over to Butler, who dealt with the few remaining legal matters and worked for a lesser fee.[84] Rhoade's reasons for resigning were probably financial, and his exit was quite abrupt and final. He never participated in the discussions of what to

Chabad's headquarters at 770 Eastern Parkway in Brooklyn, New York. (Chaim Miller)

do next, nor was he consulted about access to his contacts. Throughout December and January he continually reminded Jacobson and Kramer of his unpaid invoices. According to Rhoade's family, Chabad never paid him his full fee and never thanked him for his help. So Rhoade washed his hands of Chabad and never dealt with it again.[85]

Despite the resolution of the visa issue, the Rebbe did not leave Riga immediately. On 20 February 1940 he notified Jacobson that their departure would have to be delayed to allow his mother to recuperate from a stomach operation. In addition, the Rebbe had fallen and broken his arm, so he would need time to heal as well.[86] He also was "loath to leave Riga for America without" his daughter Sheina and son-in-law Mendel Horenstein.[87] During this time, the Rebbe was supported by charity and loans from friends in Riga. Fortunately, his daughter Chana Gourary had hidden a large sum of money in her clothes and underwear, and they lived off that for several weeks. But their funds were drying up.[88]

In the meantime, things had gotten worse in Warsaw. Twice in February 1940, Assistant Secretary of State Adolph A. Berle tried to get Hull to take some action after receiving reports of the brutal deportation of Jews. He encouraged the US government to object directly to the German government: "We should register a protest. We did so during the far less significant, though more dramatic, riots of a year ago November [*Reichskristallnacht*]; and I see no reason why we should not make our feelings known regarding a policy of seemingly calculated cruelty which is beginning to be apparent now." But Hull did not follow Berle's recommendation, and the fate of the Jews in Warsaw continued to drift toward the abyss of the Holocaust.[89] It is unknown whether the Nazis would have changed their policies had the United States protested. However, the failure to even make the effort speaks volumes about US policy at the time. Riga was no longer safe either. If the Rebbe did not leave soon, he faced danger from both the Soviets and the Nazis—whichever moved first to take over Latvia.

14

Crossing the Perilous Ocean

As has been said above, Chassidim [Hasidim] ought to always seek the truth in any matter, to understand its essence clearly.
—Rebbe Joseph Isaac Schneersohn

On 6 March 1940, after a valiant defense against incredible odds, Finland sued for peace and surrendered the territory the Soviet Union had demanded in November 1939. Although the Soviet victory had come at a high price—the loss of 200,000 men to Finland's 25,000—Stalin's quest for expansion was not over.[1] He seized the Baltic states a few months later, in June 1940. Had the Rebbe and his group still been in Latvia, they probably would have died.

On 4 March 1940 the Rebbe's group left Riga, catching one of the last flights from Latvia to Sweden and crossing the Baltic Sea on an eighteen-seat airplane. Supposedly, thousands gathered around the Rebbe that day to say good-bye.[2] He was accompanied by his wife, his mother, his son-in-law Samarius Gourary, his daughter Chana, his grandson Barry, his secretary Chaim Lieberman, his nurse Seina Locs, and three other Lubavitchers. Haskell Feigin and his family, along with a few other Lubavitchers, were scheduled to leave for Sweden soon, but they never made it out.[3] Several other members of the hierarchy and their family members remained under the Nazi jackboot. Only Rabbi Mendel Schneerson and his wife were relatively safe living in France.[4] During his time in Riga, Schneersohn had tried to rescue twenty-one others in that city, thirty-five in Warsaw, and thirty-three in France, most of whom had to remain in Europe.[5] The Rebbe was pained to leave his brethren, and during the journey he muttered remorsefully: "Now we are orphaned!"[6]

From Stockholm, Schneersohn's party traveled by train to Göteborg, arriving at 8:00 a.m. on 5 March. Two days later they boarded the Swedish

The Swedish liner *Drottningholm*. (Eliezer Zaklikovsky)

liner *Drottningholm*, which was full of refugees bound for New York. There were 253 passengers, and the Rebbe stayed in stateroom 13.[7] It was a dangerous passage. German submarines prowled the North Sea and the North Atlantic—the ship's exact route. German torpedoes had already sent hundreds of vessels, along with their passengers, to the bottom of the ocean. The German U-boats struck with such surprise and in such a devastating fashion that few survived.

Passenger liners were not immune to war. On 3 September 1939 Germans torpedoed the SS *Athenia*, killing 120 people, 28 of them Americans. Between 5 and 6 September German submarines also sank the merchant ships *Bosnia*, *Royal Sceptre*, and *Rio Claro* off the coast of Spain. Only the crew of the *Rio Claro* survived. A few days later the British aircraft carrier HMS *Courageous* went down with 500 men, including its captain, William Tofield Makeig-Jones. In September 1939 alone, the Germans sank approximately fifty ships.[8] A month later they sank another prestigious English vessel, the battleship *Royal Oak*, taking 833 officers and men with it.[9] By the time the *Drottningholm* set sail, the Germans had spent six months honing their U-boats' hunting skills.

No ship was safe from German attack—not even those of neutral countries. The Germans had already sunk ships belonging to Norway, Holland, Spain, and Sweden (often due to the difficulty of identifying ships). As the war progressed, neutral countries' losses from German U-boats increased. Indeed, there was a distinct possibility that the Germans would mistake the *Drottningholm* for an Allied ship, even though it was painted white, had a large circle painted on the funnel, and had the word *Sverige* (Sweden) prominently displayed on its side. At 538 feet long and 60 feet wide, the ship presented a fine target.[10] In addition, several German pocket battleships and other warships roamed the seas, ready to sink or capture Allied vessels. Many on the *Drottningholm* must have wondered what would happen to the Jewish passengers if the Germans boarded the ship. In September a ship carrying Rabbis Altein and Greenberg had been stopped by a U-boat and searched, but fortunately, it had been released.[11] There was a chance the Rebbe would not share their luck.

Mines were another danger. They had caused extensive damage to Allied and neutral shipping. Many mines were magnetic and could explode without contacting the vessel. The Luftwaffe and the German navy had dropped thousands of these magnetic mines over hundreds of square miles of the Baltic Sea, North Sea, and Atlantic Ocean.[12]

The Rebbe's ship sailed along the coast of Norway and docked at Bergen after only two days at sea. It had encountered mechanical problems and needed to be repaired.[13] Although the group was not aware of it at the time, even a short delay could have been disastrous. Only one month later, Germany invaded Denmark and Norway. By early March, the German navy had already sent thirty-two submarines to Norway's coast, in preparation for the invasion.[14] Four were positioned near Bergen. Repairmen worked on the *Drottningholm* all night, and to the relief of all aboard, the ship resumed its journey on 9 March. Soon, however, heavy fog caused the captain to shut down the engines, and the ship bobbed lazily up and down in the ocean—a sitting duck. Although it was late at night, many passengers got out of bed and nervously walked the hallways. The fog lifted the next day, and the ship continued its journey.

Before they made it to the open Atlantic, German submarines stopped them twice. One can only imagine what the passengers felt as the submarines surfaced and unfurled their red flags with black swastikas. Each time the Germans boarded the ship, searched it, and questioned the captain before allowing it to go on its way. They were trying to ascertain the ship's neutrality by checking for any military cargo.

On 13 March, after four days at sea, a warship stopped them. It turned out to be British, and after some intense moments of uncertainty, the *Drottningholm* was permitted to proceed. According to the Lubavitchers, they were stopped two more times by British warships, but they were always released and allowed to continue their journey. In April, having conquered Norway and Denmark, the Germans would block off the Baltic Sea's access to the Atlantic.[15]

While all this drama was taking place, Sam Kramer wrote a note to Harry Troutman in the Visa Department, thanking him for his efforts. He informed Troutman that the Rebbe "and his group have embarked for America" and noted that the rescue was "due in great measure to your splendid efforts and cooperation."[16] Schneersohn was one of the few Jewish leaders who received American help; many other rabbis did not get the support they needed to escape Europe. In October 1940 two members of the President's Advisory Committee on Political Refugees, chairman James G. McDonald and executive secretary George L. Warren, issued a memorandum stating that several rabbis living in the Baltic countries had been put on lists by the immigration office but were not rescued because "action on their behalf was never from the start more than a gesture of sympathy." The majority of Hasidic leaders in eastern Europe, as well as the leaders of other Jewish denominations, did not escape and died in the Holocaust.[17]

Once he made it past the German U-boats and mines, the Rebbe still had one more obstacle to clear: the health examination that would be performed at Ellis Island, New York, in compliance with the immigration laws. Under normal circumstances, the medical officials would likely deny Schneersohn entry due to his multiple sclerosis, strokes, and obesity. Jacobson decided they needed to put pressure on James L. Houghteling, the US commissioner general of immigration. By now, Chabad had learned that it was easier to get things done when one had a strong advocate. Jacobson therefore suggested that they ask Congressman Adolph J. Sabath to intervene with the authorities and communicate with Houghteling, advising his department to "avoid all difficulties for the Rabbi and his group in [getting] off the boat." Kramer had already applied pressure to one of Houghteling's subordinates, Commissioner Reimer, at Ellis Island, but they knew they needed more.[18] Sabath complied and wrote to Byron Uhl, the director of immigration at Ellis Island, and told him, "For months I have been cooperating and aiding in bringing Rabbi Joseph Schneersohn and his family to the U.S." He then gave specific details about the ship carrying the Lubavitchers and its arrival time. He continued: "I understand that the Rabbi has suffered a great deal before he was relieved and permitted to leave Poland. Therefore I will greatly appreciate it if he will be [shown] such courtesy as is possible to facilitate his entry into this country."[19]

Strategically speaking, it was a wise move by Chabad to warn immigration officials that the Rebbe was not in the best shape. Moreover, it was smart to have a distinguished man like Sabath contact these officials directly and encourage them to turn a blind eye to an obviously sick immigrant in a wheelchair. The whole operation would turn into a tragic comedy if the Rebbe were rejected at the feet of the Statue of Liberty. Even healthy people could be rejected, so the pressure applied on behalf of the Rebbe was necessary and, in fact, critical. Whether the Rebbe would be able to navigate this last minefield of bureaucracy was still in question, as no one knew how the officials at Ellis Island would respond to this strong-arm tactic.

15

The Rebbe and the Holocaust: Chabad in America

"The kindness of the nations is sin"—that all the charity and kindness done by the nations of the world is only for their own self-glorification.
—Rabbi Schneur Zalman, *Tanya*

If you will not listen to me [God] and carry out all these commands [*mitzvot*], and if you reject my decrees and abhor my laws and fail to carry out all my commands and so violate my covenant . . . then I will set my face against you so that you will be defeated by your enemies; those who hate you will rule over you. . . . And I will bring the sword upon you to avenge the breaking of the covenant.
—Leviticus 26:14–15, 17, 25

On hearing that the Rebbe was on his way to the United States, Chabad sent a notice to several rabbis saying, "If our mouths had the sea's capacity for song, it would not suffice to praise and thank G-d for the miracles and wonders He has performed for us and for the entire House of Israel by salvaging for us this teacher of his people, this leader of *his* nation, the Rebbe." Their prayers for God to save the Rebbe were indeed answered. The Rebbe's ship arrived in New York harbor late in the evening on 18 March, but the passengers had to wait until the next day to disembark, since the authorities had already closed the port.[1] In February and March the Germans and their allies sank seventy-six ships; luckily, the Rebbe's vessel was not one of them.[2]

On 19 March a boat carrying immigration officials and a committee of the Rebbe's supporters, including Hyman and Sam Kramer, Philip Kleinfeld, and Isaac Jacobson, met the *Drottningholm* before it entered port.

Rebbe Joseph Isaac Schneersohn on 19 March 1940, waiting in his stateroom on the *Drottningholm* to step ashore in America. (Eliezer Zaklikovsky)

A representative from Mayor Fiorello La Guardia's office was also on hand to greet the Rebbe. Having apparently passed his medical exam, Schneersohn was allowed to step onto American soil. The Swedish captain asked the Rebbe whether he wanted to be the first to leave the ship, but the Rebbe replied no, he wished to leave last. Through those who disembarked ahead of him, he requested that his followers waiting at the pier recite the benediction "Blessed is he who gives life to the dead" when they first caught sight of him.[3] Although he deeply regretted the suffering of those left behind, he felt relieved to be alive and in the United States, where he would be able to help his yeshiva students and other Chabad leaders still in Poland, Russia, and the Baltic.

Before being rolled onto American soil in his wheelchair, the Rebbe told Jacobson, "The sufferings I endured in prison in Russia do not compare to the torments of the 12 weeks I spent under *their* rule."[4] The day was cold and rainy, but that did not stop a crowd of supporters from

Rebbe Schneersohn's arrival in New York in March 1940 (accompanied on his right by his son-in-law Samarius Gourary and grandson Barry Gourary). (Chaim Miller)

coming out to welcome the Rebbe. Before he appeared, his eighty-year-old mother was carried off the ship on a stretcher, sending a hush through the crowd. Eager eyes watched for the Rebbe to emerge. When he was wheeled off the ship dressed in traditional Hasidic garb, including a *Shtreiml* (a large, round fur hat), several hundred people, most of them Lubavitchers, erupted with cheers, prayers of thanksgiving, songs of "Heveinu Shalom Aleichem" (Peace unto You), and joyful dances. His followers saw his escape as an act of "mystical significance, leadership and heroics."[5] The Rebbe's face was pale, "tormented and terrified," that "of a man rescued from a fire." Rabbi Zalman Posner, one of the onlookers, later said that seeing the "legendary" Rebbe step foot on US soil was "a tremendous event in my life."[6] Many of his followers truly believed the Rebbe was God's chosen leader for all Jews and had a direct line to God, making him worthy of absolute obedience.

A few hours later, at a special reception at the train station, the Rebbe asked those present to pray for the Jews trapped in Poland. In a slow, slurred, but passionate voice, he said:

> We should begin with a *brachah* [prayer of thanksgiving], thanking God for saving us from a very troubling situation and bringing us out of distress to abundance. To my great sorrow, I will have to interrupt the joy which we are all feeling right now. The great pain which our brothers and sisters are enduring without mercy at this moment does not let me rest. The cries of our brothers and sisters in Poland, and of the many *yeshivah* students in particular, haunt me wherever I go, and I cannot rest until *Hashem* has helped and saved them.[7]

He went on to say, "Jews are being mercilessly massacred, there exists in Europe a holocaust which defies description. America's conscience must be awakened, and above all, American Jewry must alert itself to the life-saving mission now on its hands as never before in the history of mankind."[8] He hoped American Jews would intensify their efforts to help their brethren, whom the Nazis were killing in large numbers. Rabbis and communal leaders were in the greatest danger of extermination, he said, naming several of his students who should be at the top of the list of those saved. If American Jewry did its part, the US government would follow suit.

As he spoke, the tears of those standing above him dripped down on his shoulders and hat. Although he did not grant any interviews, the Rebbe later issued a statement through Rabbi Gourary, appealing for the rescue of "3,500,000 Jews in Poland who are 'on the verge of annihilation.' . . . You of our brethren in America, who cannot imagine what modern warfare is like . . . should create a vast fund to alleviate the lot of your Polish brethren, who have been made to suffer for all Israel," a "communal sin offering for the Jewish people."[9] This declaration seemed to be in keeping with the times and an appropriate plea for someone who had just been saved himself. The Rebbe showed much honor, empathy, and solidarity here. The mission was clear: save Jews. And the people who should do the saving was clear: American Jews and government officials.

I am struck by the theology the Rebbe offered. He saw the events that were transpiring through the theological lens of sin and divine punishment. He referred to the Jews as a "communal sin offering." Why were they being sacrificed? Was God really exterminating them as punishment for people's sins? How did the Rebbe know God's motivation? And was Hitler an instrument of God? The latter part of his statement illustrates a tunnel-vision philosophy whereby only heavenly causes could account for the good and bad things happening on earth and only religious solutions were possible. As always, he ignored social, political, historical, medical, or scientific causes and remedies. But in general, his plea to rescue those trapped in Europe was a good start to his time in the United States.

Equally painful to the Rebbe upon his arrival was his followers' caution not to expect too much from American Jews, who were members of other denominations and did not live what the Hasidic Jews considered "observant" lives. Ironically, having just arrived in the freest and most prosperous, successful, and secure Jewish community in the history of the world, the Rebbe set out to "salvage" the American children of the "lost generation" and give them back their Jewish identity. He was saddened by how far American Jewry had fallen from Jewish observance. "The endless tears that accompanied my first [bedtime prayers] on American soil," he said, "shall remain undescribed."[10] The Rebbe had been told that American Jews would not follow him. They had assimilated and integrated into American society and would not respect a Yiddish-speaking, Torah-educated mystical rabbi who knew nothing about their society or their country. Prosperous, secure people are seldom attracted to radical philosophies. His followers knew this revelation would shock and distress him, and it is a testament to their courage that they briefed the Rebbe on this matter. Maybe they were trying to persuade him to start looking at America in a more open-minded, middle-of-the-road way. However, he was not receptive to that type of change. In July 1941 he would start pleading for Jews to stop their idolatry and turn away from their sins so that Hitler's persecution would stop and the Messiah would come.[11] In August 1941 he said that American Jews' "coldness and indifference . . . towards Torah and religion" were just as destructive as the fire in Europe that threatened "to annihilate more than two-thirds of the Jewish people."[12]

It is challenging for most people to comprehend how deeply the Rebbe lived his life according to the Torah (the Pentateuch, the first five books of Moses) and the Tanach (what Christians call the Old Testament)—the cornerstone of literature, philosophy, and law dominating both Jewish and Christian life for centuries. The Reform movement that swept through the United States, Canada, and parts of Europe (principally western and central Europe) beginning in the early 1800s changed the face of Judaism, turning away from the ancient customs and Talmudic laws that constituted the Rebbe's reality. In place of the old theology and way of life, Reform Jews emphasized ethics as laid out by the prophets and scholars in the Bible, but adapted to modern, pluralistic, democratic societies. For that reason, Reform Judaism is also known as Ethical Judaism or Prophetic Judaism. Other streams of Judaism, such as Conservative Judaism, retained more of tradition but made major reforms as well. Those who did not participate in the reformation included the Hasidic Jews and the ultra-Orthodox Jews. Prior to the Enlightenment, there were no Orthodox Jews; that designation arose to differentiate Jews who were resistant to change from those who accepted the modernized version of Judaism created by reexamining the old rules and customs and identifying those that were meaningful and reasonable in modern society.

When the Rebbe came to America, he found these new forms of Judaism abhorrent, and he forbade the Lubavitchers to attend American schools or colleges, fearing that such institutions would lead them away from true belief. He thus created an insulated culture, which neither helped promote knowledge nor encouraged American society to find new truths. When the Rebbe pointed his finger from his wheelchair and condemned non-Orthodox Jews, he did not further the causes of tolerance and freedom of religion. He wanted his people to stay focused on Jewish sacred literature, as interpreted and supplemented in ancient times; he wanted them to be kept in the dark as far as modern knowledge was concerned, compelling them to put on the "heavy coat of ignorance and fear."[13] As Heinrich Heine wrote, "In dark ages people are best guided by religion, as in a pitch-black night a blind man is the best guide; he knows the roads and paths better than a man who can see. When daylight comes, however, it is foolish to use blind, old men as guides."[14] The Rebbe wanted his people to follow him, even though he shut his eyes to the vast storehouse of knowledge outside of the religious texts he considered authoritative. He insisted that his flock also close their eyes to that knowledge, lest they begin to question his teachings. The Hasidic doctrine was formed not in an atmosphere of scientific inquiry and critical reasoning but in one of revealed truth. In the Rebbe's mind and that of other Hasidic leaders, faith preceded, shaped, and controlled the means of acquiring knowledge. St. Augustine espoused the principle, "I believe in order to understand."[15] In the world of faith, nothing to the contrary was admissible for consideration.

The majority of Jews in the world have thrown off the chains of ultra-Orthodox traditions. The likes of Martin Buber, Baruch de Spinoza, Moses Mendelssohn, Heinrich Heine, Albert Einstein, Robert Oppenheimer, Louis Brandeis, and countless others would never have achieved greatness if their families had remained in Hasidic or ultra-Orthodox communities and accepted the constraints placed on their education and employment. Because they left, they were able to contribute to society in remarkable ways.

Given his beliefs, the Rebbe had a difficult time adjusting to life in America. He was no lover of Thomas Jefferson's freedom of religion and separation of church and state, of the Reform ideals of equality and full integration into American society, or of the nascent movement for women's rights. Within his little empire in Brooklyn and Crown Heights, he wanted to create a theocracy that would build a center for "true" Judaism. Ignoring many of his critics, the Rebbe struggled to find a spiritual explanation for and response to Hitler. He believed absolutely that his religious efforts were just as important as, if not more important than, America's all-out war effort. Both would bring victory to the just, but in the Rebbe's world, God could achieve far more than any military or political strategy.

The Rebbe also believed that the Holocaust challenged humanity to root out evil at its source. This led him to focus on the concept of the Messiah and on preparing the Lubavitchers, the Jews, and the rest of humanity for his imminent arrival. In his view, only when every Jew worshipped like he did would the Messiah come and bring peace on earth. Unsurprisingly, his followers enthusiastically embraced this urgent and affirmative spiritual mission.[16]

In the Rebbe's opinion, American Jewish leaders who believed that the only recourse was to defeat Hitler militarily were "wrong" and "leading their followers astray by uttering false prophecies" and not focusing on the *Mashiach*. Such leaders, he explained, had "traded our proved method of pleading for [God's] intervention for politics and diplomacy." They had forgotten the great hope and "joyous news" of God's promise of a Messiah, who was "about to arrive—he is already standing within reach of us!" Only with the proper focus on living righteously and preparing for the "final deliverance" would circumstances improve. At a time when the "Jewish people [were] drowning in [their] own blood," Schneersohn condemned as irresponsible those Jewish leaders who focused on a "diet of worldly prospects, ignorant of the real cause of the world catastrophe," which was the lack of penitence and prayer. These spiritual leaders, like the world press, were "abysmally ignorant" of the "truth in the developments of the war." Without an announcement from these leaders that the Jews were on the "eve of the era of redemption" and that "the present Jewish sufferings are pre-messianic travail," all efforts with the government would be fruitless. The Rebbe felt abandoned by Jewish organizations that ignored his call for redemption. He was saddened that they had given up on the promise of the Messiah and instead worked solely in the secular world to accomplish their goals. Only his own message, he felt, was "true and timely."[17]

The Rebbe interpreted the war, the democracies' inability or unwillingness to rescue Jews, the infighting among Jewish groups, and Hitler's
persecution as the fulfillment of prophecies about the Day of Reckoning.
The Jews were now entering the stage of redemption from exile that they
had experienced after the destruction of the Second Temple in 70 CE;
thus, the time of the Messiah was imminent. The Rebbe wished to awaken
Jews to this reality and to teach them how to make the Messiah's arrival
as painless as possible.[18] At the same time, he could advocate "drastic"
spiritual action. To ensure that even the children understood that something was dreadfully wrong, he directed that, as long as Hitler slaughtered Jews, Lubavitcher children should not eat candy. He also called for
a worldwide fast in 1941 so that "our brothers and sisters," who by the
"hundreds and thousands . . . are being tormented by deadly terrors,"
would return to God "in wholehearted repentance," thus encouraging
the Messiah's arrival.[19]

Since the Jews had not remained faithful to God's commandments,
said the Rebbe, their "sins have kindled a fire under our feet. We forgot
to be Jews; now we are being reminded by the powers above that we
must return. . . . Only penitence can save us from the consequences." If
they did not repent, Satan and his human agents ("professional atheists")
would win by deceiving them into relying on secular means rather than
God and the Messiah.[20] In October 1941 he claimed:

> Our brothers and sisters overseas now find themselves in a most
> perilous and frightful situation. . . . Hundreds and thousands of
> congregations and entire communities of our brothers and sisters are
> being persecuted and tortured to extermination. Those remaining
> alive are exposed to famine, imprisonment and exile. . . . Maimonides
> tells us, apropos of the laws on Fast days, that on the occasion when
> a great calamity befalls our people, it is incumbent upon us to offer
> prayers to the Almighty and acknowledge that the trouble is in
> punishment for inobservance of the Torah, and thereby bring about
> G-d's mercy upon us . . . we behold in all these trials and tribulations
> the approach of Messiah . . . brothers and sisters, HAVE COMPASSION
> UPON YOURSELVES, UPON YOUR SONS AND DAUGHTERS, so that you
> be not destroyed in the birth pangs of the coming Messiah. Forsake

your evil ways. . . . Entreat our FATHER IN HEAVEN for forgiveness for
the past misdeeds.[21]

An article in the Rebbe's newspaper explained, "Our Sages have said:
'When disaster comes upon the world—look forward to salvation!'"[22]
The Rebbe had some justification for using Jewish texts to claim that the
Messiah would come only after horrific events had occurred. For example, the ancient Talmudic sage Rabbi Nachman said it would be a terrible
time for humanity. The prophets Ezekiel and Isaiah described the destruction of the world right before the coming of the Messiah, and from
his writings, it is clear the Rebbe thought humanity was approaching Ar-
mageddon.[23] Just as Moses had been sent by God to lead the Jews out of
bondage in Egypt under Pharaoh, the Messiah would now deliver the
Jews from the Holocaust.[24] The Rebbe wrote in June 1941 that Chabad
had "been rousing American Jewry to become aware that we are living
in the last days before the Redemption." God caused all events, and the
slaughter of Jews under Hitler was a "pre-messianic travail" that would
give them their "final deliverance!"[25]

Soon after his arrival in the States, the Rebbe purchased hundreds of
dollars' worth of religious books. He then spent long hours reading at his
desk amid huge stacks of them. Some have argued that he was searching
for an explanation of the violence sweeping across Europe.[26]

A few days after his arrival, the Rebbe again spoke publicly and asked
everyone to help those in Europe. On 24 March 1940 he gave a talk at the
Greystone Hotel on the Upper West Side of New York City, where he
said:

I cannot recover from my experiences in Warsaw, the fearful, life-
threatening twenty seven days of war . . . as well as the pain-filled,
cruel eighty-one post-war days . . . days lived in dread of death. The
horrible life conditions of our brothers and sisters, the oppressive
fright, the pitiless deeds of (today's) Haman[27]—thoughts of these
give me no rest. I must cry out—American Jews—of every kind,
every description: Save Your Brethren Now![28]

Unfortunately, his pleas reached no farther than the Lubavitchers and some other Orthodox communities. Once again, the Rebbe said exactly what needed to be heard. However, it seemed that no one was listening.

In 1880 a quarter of a million Jews lived in the United States, and most of them were very Americanized in appearance, behavior, and attitude. Some could trace their American roots back for many decades if not centuries. After massive waves of eastern European immigrants at the turn of the twentieth century, there were 4.5 million Jews in America by 1925.[29] The new arrivals from eastern Europe—most of them poor, downtrodden, and non-English-speaking—were particularly unpopular, and their strangeness provoked disapproval and prejudice on the part of many Americans. This prejudice was not unlike that experienced by other ethnic immigrants, including Irish, Italians, Mexicans, and Chinese.[30] There was concern among the older, more established American Jews from western and central Europe that they too would suffer from the backlash against the recently arrived Jews from eastern Europe. Although these new immigrants were hardworking and eager to put down roots, they had not yet assimilated. This spurred efforts by the more integrated Jews to speed up the acculturation process.

The prejudice against Jews was widespread. Sixty percent of Americans polled by Roper in the late 1930s thought Jews had "objectionable qualities." According to Michael Berenbaum:

> Nearly half believed Jews had "too much power" in the United States; and as many as 20 percent said they would sympathize with an anti-Semitic campaign at a time when antisemitism was running riot in parts of Europe like Germany, Austria, and Italy where it was official government policy and backed by some influential church officials. In virtually every poll, Jews were cited as posing a major threat to the country.[31]

So it is remarkable that a group of Jews led by Max Rhoade, a Jewish lawyer, was able to convince the US government to undertake a protracted effort to get the Rebbe out of Europe.

During the first few years of his ministry in the United States, the Rebbe often talked about his experiences in Poland and his escape, but he never mentioned the Germans publicly. The paradox of German army officers helping him in the face of the atrocities committed primarily by the SS was confusing at best. Also, although most historians know the difference between the Wehrmacht and the SS, the Rebbe most likely lumped them together. What Bloch, Wohlthat, Canaris, Schenk, and a host of others did for him did not make sense because they seemed to be standing shoulder to shoulder with the likes of Himmler, Heydrich, and Hitler. How could these people work together? The story of a miracle seemed more plausible to the Lubavitchers. And the more we explore the actual history of what happened, the more miraculous it seem to be. To the Lubavitchers, it made sense that angels in human form had saved the Rebbe because, in Chabad's opinion, only God could have choreographed the disparate cast of characters who worked together to extract the Rebbe and his party from a mass of killers.

Although the Rebbe never mentioned Bloch or the team that helped him escape, he thanked Cordell Hull on 25 March 1940 for his support: "You can imagine how delighted and happy we are to set foot again on the friendly soil of the United States . . . after the dreadful experiences we had in Poland of the war under the Nazi regime."[32] He also sent a letter overflowing with appreciation to Justice Brandeis. In April the Rebbe asked to meet with President Roosevelt to express his gratitude, but the president's busy schedule made a meeting impossible. In August the Rebbe repeated his request through Massachusetts congressman John W. McCormack, who had helped many Jews. The Lubavitcher who corresponded with McCormack on Schneersohn's behalf wrote that the Rebbe was the "head of the Protestant Jews," who numbered "3,000,000 in this country and 8,000,000 in the world. This man got out of Poland through the kindness of the President and he wants to thank [him]." These figures were grossly exaggerated, and the Reform Jews certainly did not consider the Rebbe their leader. One of Roosevelt's secretaries replied to McCormack, telling him that although the president had no time at the moment, "I do hope that things will ease up so Rabbi Schneersohn may see the President at some not too future date."[33] A meeting with the president would have been a good opportunity to plead for the rescue of more Jews. Also, a meeting with Roosevelt would have added to the prestige of the Rebbe's movement, and to him and his followers, it seemed appropriate to his status.

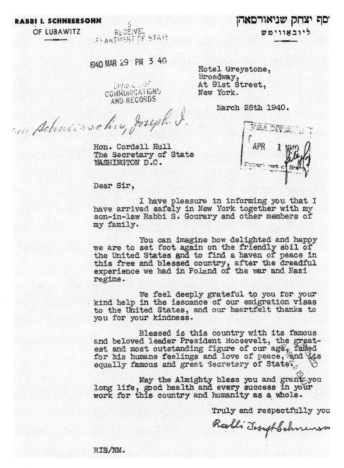

The Rebbe thanks Secretary of State Cordell Hull for
rescuing him. (National Archives)

After staying at the Greystone Hotel for several months, the Rebbe
moved in the summer of 1940 into a converted abortion clinic and medical office at 770 Eastern Parkway in the Crown Heights neighborhood of
Brooklyn. Due to his poor health, he rarely ventured outside and relied
on newspapers and his followers to inform him of current events. His
new home was quite modern for the time; it had wheelchair access and an
elevator, making it ideal. Here the Rebbe set up his headquarters, which is

still considered deeply sacred to the Lubavitchers.[34] Replicas of the building have been built in Israel and throughout the world.

Throughout 1940 and 1941 the Rebbe sent food packages to Torah scholars and their families in Poland and Russia. He relied on Rabbi Mordechai Chefetz in Riga to funnel the packages to Poland via Latvia, often breaking the British blockade to do so. The Soviet Union forcibly annexed Latvia, Lithuania, and Estonia in June 1940, executing thousands and shipping thousands more to the USSR. The Lubavitchers in America received reports that several of the families had received this aid. But after the German invasion of Russia in the summer of 1941, these shipments of food stopped.[35]

On his arrival in 1940, the Rebbe immediately made efforts to rescue his students who had remained in Poland. He requested funds from the American Jewish Joint Distribution Committee, a rescue and relief organization comprising precisely the type of assimilated Jewish leaders he had railed against. He also asked his American students to write letters to the authorities and worked tirelessly to secure visas and safe passage.[36] His students, he said, were "the very kernel of the existence and establishment of the [movement] in America." He obtained visas for thirty students and made arrangements with the Russian company Intourist for their travel from Vilna to the east coast of Russia, China, or Japan. Once in these foreign lands, they had to wait for the money and the necessary documents to board ships for America. On 13 January 1941 the Rebbe expressed his disappointment at the amount of money raised. His rescue fund had accumulated $5,040 for the thirty students (probably for their travel), but he needed another few hundred dollars for two more students. He had taken out so many loans that he did not know where to turn anymore. Meanwhile, the thirty who had already received documents and money traveled to Kobe, Japan, where they patiently awaited further instructions. The Rebbe pleaded for funds through his newsletter in March 1941. He appealed for assistance in saving "Jewish treasures that the greatest amount of gold" could not replace, and he urged rabbis to impress on their congregations "that every hour is dear not only in this life but also in the life to come. We must save Torah scholars and in doing so save ourselves."[37]

It appears that in 1941 the Rebbe's *Pidyon Shvuim* (Redeeming Those Imprisoned) fund obtained 500 to 600 visas for rabbis and students stranded in Poland, Lithuania, Latvia, Estonia, Finland, Sweden, Bulgaria, and France, but it is unclear whether they had enough money to leave. It is likely that most of them did not escape before the United States canceled their visas, out of fear that saboteurs would exploit the open immigration policy (an absurd theory promulgated by Breckinridge Long and others in the State Department). The State Department did not differentiate between Jews who were oppressed by the Nazi regime, and therefore among its most ardent opponents, and others who might have given the Nazis their allegiance. By the time a visa was granted, it was often too late to save the individual. A report on the department's shameful record submitted to Secretary of the Treasury Henry Morgenthau stated, "It takes months and months to grant the visas and then it usually applies to a corpse."[38]

The Rebbe seemed to focus only on Lubavitchers. In fairness, other groups also concentrated on rescuing their own. Varian Fry, for example, rescued artists, scholars, and musicians, men and women with special gifts who would fit in well with the American cultural elite who were sponsoring their rescue. Rabbi Julius Morgenstein, the president of Hebrew Union College, rescued five Reform rabbinical students and five distinguished scholars. He offered the students admission to the college and the scholars academic appointments to its faculty. Rabbi Abraham Joshua Heshel was among those rescued. With the situation in Europe getting more desperate by the minute, Schneersohn concentrated his efforts on those Jews with the best chance of being rescued—specific individuals he could identity and to whom the authorities might respond. One Chabad rabbi explained that, according to Jewish law, one is supposed to save one's family first in any crisis, and all Lubavitchers were the Rebbe's children. Other Orthodox Jewish organizations in America also focused exclusively on rescuing their rabbis and yeshiva students—a controversial policy bitterly debated among American Jews.[39]

Unfortunately, in June 1941 the United States canceled the visas of those students stuck in Japan. The "close relatives edict" prevented refugees who had relatives under German occupation from entering the United States. "For Jews, of course, no exception was made if the relative was starving to death in a concentration camp," observes Henry L. Feingold.[40]

RABBI I. SCHNEERSOHN
OF LUBAWITZ
770 EASTERN PARKWAY
BROOKLYN, N. Y.
SLocum 6-2919

יוסף יצחק שניאורסאהן
ליובאוויטש

By the Grace of G-d,
Elul 20, 5701.

(Sept. 12, 1941.)

His Excellency,
The President of the United States of America,
Honorable Franklin Delano Roosevelt,
The White House,
Washington, D.C.

Peace and Greetings !

In the name of the Chabad-Lubavitz adherents throughout
the wide world, whose teacher and spiritual leader I have been
destined to be, following in the path of my forefathers, the Heads
of Chabad for six generations, and

In in behalf of the Agudas Chasidei Chabad of the United
States and Canada, with several hundreds of Congregations in the
United States, comprising some 150,000 members, Chabad adherents,
citizens and legal residents of this country,

I wish to convey to your Excellency our profound gratitude
for all you have done and are doing in the cause of Justice and
righteousness in this land and other lands, and for the protection
of all that is sacred and dear to all right thinking human beings.

Millions of Jews throughout the world, in addition to all
Jewish subjects of this land, feel certain that your Excellency who
has been invested by the grace of Almighty G-d with the leadership
of the United States under the banner of freedom, justice and equality, recognize with the purity and wisdom of your heart, the worthy
traits of the People of Israel, and have given thought, which with
the help of G-d you will also materialize, to ensure lasting benefit,
both spiritually and materially, to the people of Israel in all lands.

I have the honor of enclosing herewith the text of the
special Prayer which I have composed for Rosh Hashana (New Year) and
Yom Hakipurim (Day of Atonement), the Days of Judgment when the
Lord of the Universe takes to account all human beings; this Prayer
to be recited in all the Synagogues throughout the land where our
people shall congregate during these coming Solemn Days, a prayer
for the success and welfare of this land, for the triumph of justice
and truth in all lands and that the Almighty bless your Excellency
with long life and many happy years, that you may lead your subjects
in the path of justice, equity and peace.

With heartfelt blessings,

Respectfully yours, Rabbi I Schneersohn

On 12 September 1941 the Rebbe wrote to President Roosevelt
to express Chabad's support for all he was doing for humanity.
(Franklin Delano Roosevelt Library)

In public, the Rebbe praised President Roosevelt, and on 12 September 1941 he wrote to him, "I wish to convey to your Excellency our profound gratitude for all you have done and are doing in the cause of Justice and righteousness in this land and other lands, and for the protection of all that is sacred and dear to all right thinking human beings . . . [and] to ensure lasting benefit, both spiritually and materially, to the people of Israel in all lands." The Rebbe had composed a prayer for the president to be recited in synagogues throughout America; it read in part: "We beseech Thee, O Merciful God! Inscribe our gracious President [and his ministers who] are fighting in the cause of justice and righteousness, unto a happy, blessed and successful New Year."[41] In the Rebbe's efforts to develop a relationship with the president, he was always careful to affirm his allegiance and emphasize his praise. There was nothing unique about the Rebbe's words, which echoed thousands of letters FDR was receiving at the time. The fate of the free world rested on the shoulders of the American president, so even those who wanted greater action on behalf of the Jews supported the president and the war effort that was about to begin.

On 7 December 1941 Japanese naval and air forces launched a sneak attack on the Pacific Fleet at Pearl Harbor, sinking or badly damaging a number of battleships, destroying many planes on the ground, and killing 2,400 "Americans in a matter of minutes."[42] Japan attacked other British and American forces at the same time, including in the Philippines (then an American territory with a sizable army contingent). Congress declared that a state of war existed with Japan. Germany, Italy, and other Axis countries then declared war on the United States. The isolationist movement evaporated almost instantly. In January 1942 the United States, Great Britain, the Soviet Union, and twenty-two smaller or exiled governments signed a declaration by the United Nations pledging not to sign any separate peace agreements.

From the end of November into the first part of December 1941, the Nazis, who had wrested control of Latvia from the Soviets, marched virtually the entire Jewish population of Riga about eight miles out of town to the Rumballa Forest and shot them dead—more than 36,000 men, women, and children. One of them was the eighty-one-year-old doyen of Jewish historians, Simon Dubnov. Due to his age and sickness, he was unable to move out of the Riga ghetto quickly enough, causing a Latvian collaborator to pull his gun and shoot him in the back. Dubnov's dying words were *Schreibt un farschreibt* (Write and record). Among those murdered were the Rebbe's personal secretary Haskell Feigin, his wife Sonya, and their five children.[43] Theses Riga citizens died a couple of months before the Nazis' Wannsee Conference, where they coordinated their efforts to murder all the Jews—the "final solution" (*Die Endlösung*).[44] The decision on the final solution had undoubtedly been made by Hitler months before, making the Rebbe one of the last to leave Riga.

On 11 December 1941, just days after the United States entered the war, Schneersohn wrote to Roosevelt, "In this grave hour, when the security of America has been challenged by a wicked treacherous enemy, we desire to express our unqualified solidarity with our president, government and the people of the United States, and our solemn determination to selflessly do our duty and privilege in the defense of our land."[45] The next day the president's secretary replied, "Permit me, in the President's name, to thank you for your telegram. . . . For the splendid assurance conveyed in your message he is more appreciative than he can say."[46] One wonders how Roosevelt would have responded if the Rebbe had asked him to ease the restrictive immigration policies. Perhaps the Rebbe was reluctant to offend those responsible for saving his life. Or perhaps he believed that Jews already relied too much on governments for salvation. Or he might have thought that asking the president to save European Jews would be futile, even though Roosevelt had played a small role in his own rescue. Undoubtedly, the Rebbe and all Jews understood how important it was for the United States to triumph in this epic battle.

Even if the Rebbe had raised the issue of rescuing Jews, Roosevelt and his administration had far more pressing issues. The surprise attack on Pearl Harbor had embarrassed the US government. Then Germany and Italy had declared war against the United States. Roosevelt thus faced a two-front war spanning more than half the globe and a military that could barely conduct defensive operations along the US borders. As Lyne Olson notes, the United States could not even repulse Mexican bandits coming across the Rio Grande. At the time, the United States had the world's seventeenth largest military, sandwiched in rank between the armies of Bulgaria and Portugal—a not very proud position among not very respected company. The United States had only 175,000 men in the armed forces, many of whom could not even handle a weapon.[47] Things would soon change, though.

Although the Rebbe's letter of support for Roosevelt was well intentioned and probably appreciated, it deserved no more than a polite reply from a secretary. The president needed to deal with his generals and admirals and the defense of the nation as World War II erupted in all its fury. Instead of looking upward toward power, the Rebbe might have considered how to motivate his own followers, especially if they numbered in the millions, as his propaganda machine had claimed. He had seen how badly the utterly helpless Orthodox Jews suffered under the ruthless Nazi onslaught in Poland. Many moderate and secular Jews had fought bravely and patriotically for Poland; at least half a million American Jews would fight bravely for the United States, and 40,000 would give their lives.[48] As a testament to the United States' pluralistic society—by no means perfect, but better than most—Rabbi Roland B. Gittelsohn gave a eulogy for the fallen Marines at Iwo Jima in March 1945: "Here lie officers and men, Negroes and whites, rich men and poor—together. Here are Protestants, Catholics, and Jews—together. Here no man prefers another because of his faith or despises him because of his color. Here there are no quotas of how many from each group are admitted or allowed. Among these men there is no discrimination. No prejudices. No hatred. Theirs is the highest and purest democracy."[49] Chaplain Gittelsohn knew what he was talking about, for he had been in the thick of battle, ministering to the Marines during the hard days of combat. Such wisdom and solidarity were rare at this time. Gittelsohn was the first rabbi appointed to the Marine Corps, and he was but one of many American Jewish men who served their country valiantly during this conflict. Many other Jews throughout the world served bravely in Australian, Soviet, British, Canadian, and other Allied armies.

True leaders consider every angle of an argument, but the Rebbe did not see the world from other perspectives and believed his view was the only one that mattered. If he had not suffered from tunnel vision, perhaps the Rebbe would have encouraged his rabbis and yeshiva boys to put down their Bibles and siddurim (prayer books) and pick up their rifles and fight. He failed to understand what it would take to stop Hitler and Tojo and free his fellow Jews in Europe—military violence. Studying the

The sixth Lubavitcher Rebbe, Joseph Isaac Schneersohn (left), with the future
seventh Lubavitcher Rebbe, Menachem Mendel Schneerson, in Austria in
February 1935. (Eliezer Zaklikovsky)

Torah and building religious schools did little to halt the rampaging Nazis
and the imperialistic Japanese. Interestingly, Menachem Mendel Schneerson (Schneersohn's son-in-law and successor) was a trained engineer who
worked on the war effort at the Brooklyn Navy Yard. But in terms of
participating in the war effort directly, he was an exception among the
Lubavitchers.

In September 1942 the news of Nazi atrocities started to reach the United
States in detail and in force. Jacob Rosenheim, president of the Orthodox
Agudath Israel World Organization, received a cable from Isaac Sternbuch, its representative in St. Gallen, Switzerland, through the Polish embassy. It read in part: "According to numerous authentic information from
Poland, German authorities have recently evacuated Warsaw Ghetto and
bestially murdered about one hundred thousand Jews. [The murdered
corpses are used in] manufacturing soap and artificial fertilizer. Similar
fate is awaiting the Jews deported to Poland from the occupied territories. . . . Do your best to arouse such American intervention appealing
to statesmen, press, and public opinion." Sternbuch then requested that

Stephen Wise, Lubavitcher headquarters, Eliezer Silver, Albert Einstein, Jacob Klatzkin, Thomas Mann, and others be informed of this development. Rosenheim complied and immediately informed Roosevelt of this information as well.[50] The next day Rosenheim met with James G. McDonald, chairman of the President's Advisory Committee on Political Refugees, to discuss the Sternbuch cable. McDonald was "terrified by the news from Poland"; he dictated letters for Justice Felix Frankfurter and Eleanor Roosevelt and promised to get the information in front of the president. Many of those whom Rosenheim contacted pushed for some type of action to help the Jews under Hitler. Curiously, Chabad did not follow up on Rosenheim's request to approach all its contacts. Rosenheim also held a high-level meeting on 5 September with the following Jewish groups: Agudath Israel, Agudas Harabbonim, World Congress, Labor Committee, and Misrachi. Chabad was conspicuously absent.[51]

In December 1942 Rabbi Stephen Wise wrote to Roosevelt about the tragedy: "Do you know that the most overwhelming disaster of Jewish history has befallen Jews in the form of Hitler mass-massacres? Hitler's decision was to exterminate the Jewish people in all Hitler-ruled lands, and it is indisputable that as many as two million civilian Jews have been slain." Wise asked Roosevelt to meet with a group of Jewish leaders, which the president agreed to do. The meeting took place on 8 December and included representatives from B'nai B'rith, the Union of Orthodox Rabbis, the American Jewish Committee, and the Jewish Labor Committee.[52] Once again, neither Chabad nor any other Hasidic group was there. In discussing this troubling fact with an archivist at the Kleinman Holocaust Education Center, I was told that the Rebbe did not follow up on Rosenheim's request or take part in Wise's meeting because, quite simply, he did not take orders.[53] Instead of writing to officials or meeting with Rosenheim, Rebbe Schneersohn and his son-in-law Rabbi Gourary wrote to Roosevelt in the name of Chabad, praising him and asking God to grant him and the armed forces strength against the "enemies of mankind."[54] Although the Rebbe's letters acknowledged the president's great responsibility, the Lubavitcher community made it known through its newspaper that it felt like the government was ignoring the tragedy of the Jews. These letters, which continued from 1940 until 1942, were basically the extent of Schneersohn's interaction with the government and with Roosevelt.

Soon after his arrival in the United States, the Rebbe had told his followers that he could not blame "democratic countries" for ignoring the Jews' horrible situation, "because self-preservation is the first rule of nature." He felt powerless against a government that did not care about the "cruel treatment meted out to us everywhere." In February 1942 an article in his newspaper explained: "We haven't anyone to champion our cause and intervene on our behalf with our torturers, though it would not do any good if such a champion were available . . . we were warned against awaiting any salvation from our surrounding world other than that from our G-d, blessed be He." The Rebbe and his sect seemed to reject the quintessentially American concept held by most Jews, Protestants, and Catholics: God helps those who help themselves. The problem was not that he and his followers were praying for an end to Nazi tyranny, to war, and to the persecution of Jews. Good people all over the world were echoing those prayers. The problem was that by forbidding access to the great storehouse of modern, scientific knowledge; rejecting reasoned, enlightened inquiry; and refusing to integrate into the modern world, the Rebbe and his sect were both ill equipped and disinclined to take the actions that could have helped save the free world and rescue Jews from the Holocaust.

The United States, the United Kingdom, and the British Commonwealth countries were at war with the Axis powers. Even the Soviet Union was fully engaged against Germany. Rather than standing on the sidelines and blaming the American government, the Rebbe could have urged his people to gird themselves for war, just like the Jews in biblical times and, more importantly, like the people of all faiths in America. He could have taken more action by working with lobbying groups and with the people in the US government who had saved him. He could have turned to Max Rhoade to mobilize a Chabad lobbying group, but the records show he never tried to rehire this highly skilled and well-situated lawyer.

Once the Rebbe decided that diplomacy would not work with the Nazis and that the US government was unwilling or simply not in a position to do more, he focused on the spiritual survival of the Jews. Jewish history and Torah philosophy, he said, always saw war on two fronts: first, people must do everything possible to save their lives and the lives of all innocent people; second, they must pray to God for salvation. Ultimately, a combination of the two was the key to survival. Even after their own efforts had been exhausted, the Rebbe declared, Jews must never forget that their survival was guaranteed by their commitment to God and to spiritual integrity, which he felt they had failed to maintain at this critical time.

For the Rebbe, knowledge of and commitment to the values and practices of the Torah were essential to Jewish survival and endurance. Schneersohn argued, citing classical Torah texts, that the Jews' present difficulties meant they should examine their own lives, searching for what needed to be improved or repaired. Chabad believed the Jewish world was being tormented because it had been "flooded with all sorts of idol worship known as Reform, Assimilation, World Culture, Socialism, and various other isms." The Jews were at the forty-ninth stage of impurity (if they reached the fiftieth, they would disappear), the tenth plague had afflicted the world, and the end was in sight. The organization warned that those Jews who "stubbornly persist in their proclamation of and their adherence to . . . truly earthen idols, civilization and democracy, risk the loss of their lives." The Rebbe announced in August 1941 that if every Jewish home did not cleanse itself of the forty-nine stages of impurity, the Jews would be stricken by the "destroying angel."[55]

Threatening the Jews with the destroying angel was like telling born-again Christians that Satan was in their presence. The Rebbe had a sharp tongue and pen. Messages to his close aides and disciples were often conveyed with razor-sharp candidness, bolstered by images of spiritual warfare. Of course, speculation as to why God was causing these afflictions was the Rebbe's exclusive domain. Other American religious groups also offered their interpretations. Many Christians saw Hitler as the anti-Christ and believed that only if people (especially Jews) turned to Jesus would there be world peace. In fact, many Christian missionaries cruelly claimed that Jews "were drowning in blood" because they had rejected Jesus as the Messiah.[56] So, in his theological pursuit of an explanation for what was happening in the world, the Rebbe was joined by a host of other religious leaders trying to understand God's actions.

Discouraged by the US government, the Rebbe explored other options for his thirty stranded students, who had left Japan for Shanghai, China, owing to the outbreak of the Pacific war.[57] He needed the students because, without a strong Lubavitch Torah center, the world would suffer even more. Eventually, he secured visas for nine of them to go to Canada. The other twenty-one students remained in China for the rest of the war.[58]

In addition to his students, the Rebbe was especially anxious to get his daughters Sheine Horenstein and Chaya Moussia Schneerson out of Europe. Sheine and her husband were Polish citizens, and because Poland was occupied by Germany, they were ineligible for US visas. Back in January 1940, Rhoade had discussed a clever ploy to have "Rabbi" Horenstein[59] and Rabbi Juda Eber listed as the "custodians" of Chabad library, allowing them to escort the books to America. However, before the plan could be implemented, Rhoade dismissed Chabad as a client. Sheine, her husband Mendel, and the entire Horenstein family were murdered in Treblinka in 1942. Eber died in the Nazi extermination action at Riga during the fall of 1941.[60]

The Rebbe appointed Samarius Gourary to arrange for the escape of Chaya and her husband Menachem, even though the two brothers-in-law disliked each other and were rivals to succeed the Rebbe. According to Samarius's son Barry, the relationship between the two men resembled that of Cain and Abel, without the murder. When Samarius started his efforts to rescue his brother-in-law, his wife Chana asked, "Why are you doing this? Don't you know Menachem hates you?" Samarius replied, "Yes, I know he probably will do me [political] harm if he comes to the U.S., but I have been given my orders." Although Samarius disliked Menachem, he would not want any Jew to die under the Nazis. As a result, he obeyed the Rebbe and rescued his "ungrateful brother-in-law," who, according to Barry, was conducting "underhanded dealings" to become the next Rebbe.[61]

Thanks to the emergency visitors' visas Samarius helped them obtain, Chaya and Menachem fled Vichy France for the United States in 1941. Remarkably, Breckinridge Long actually wrote a personal letter authorizing the issuance of Menachem's visa.[62] The Schneersons were among the fortunate few. Many of the Jews who remained in France were soon herded onto trains headed for the death camps.[63] It seems that Rebbe Schneersohn managed to convince officials at the US consulate that Menachem was a "great Torah scholar" who was invaluable to the Chabad hierarchy and would contribute to America.[64] Besides his desire to save a great rabbi who was also his son-in-law, the Rebbe may have wanted to ensure that the Lubavitcher movement had proper leadership after his death. When Menachem arrived in America in the summer of 1941, the Rebbe appointed him head of the educational department, "the movement's social-service organization and its publishing house." The Rebbe was clearly grooming Menachem to be influential in Chabad, if not the next Rebbe.[65]

It has been argued that while the United States was still neutral, Schneersohn should have urged Brandeis, Pell, or even Hull to work for the rescue of all Jews under Hitler. For a while, Hitler was intent on keeping America neutral until he had defeated the Allies; he even rejected requests from German naval officers to attack US shipping that was aiding Great Britain under the Lend-Lease Act so as not to provoke the Americans. Some Jews were allowed to temporarily escape death if the Nazis saw some benefit in it. Conceivably, the Rebbe could have met or at least corresponded with influential Americans to discuss rescue efforts, but the record shows he did nothing of the sort. Some Lubavitchers familiar with the history counter that the ailing Rebbe did everything he could to rescue his followers, and meeting or petitioning government officials would have accomplished nothing.[66] Yet other Orthodox leaders who met with officials in Washington and pleaded for their brethren in Europe accomplished a great deal. They focused on saving lives in Europe, whereas, according to David Kranzler, the Rebbe focused on saving Jewish souls in the United States.[67] Efraim Zuroff writes that, compared with their actions on behalf of the Rebbe, Lubavitch "activists invested proportionally . . . little effort in saving the rebbe's students, who were also stranded in the Warsaw area." But in war, when a general and several of his men are captured, the greatest effort is made to rescue the leader. Certainly, Lubavitch activists were not unique, and other Hasidic groups in the United States gave top priority to saving their rebbes as well.[68]

In an act of great solidarity, the Rebbe made several public pleas for the Gerer Rebbe, who, remarkably, was also rescued (along with several family members) by German soldiers. According to Chaskel Besser, an officer fitting Bloch's description also helped the Gerer Rebbe escape, although no corroborating evidence has been found. However, coordination between German military personnel and American politicians did

The elderly Gerer Rebbe, resting on his cane, may have been rescued by Major Ernst Bloch as well. (Kleinman Holocaust Education Center)

take place. Bloom, Brandeis, Hull, and Wagner were involved in the rescue; it is not clear whether those connections were established by Chabad, but one can assume they were. Schneersohn also worked for the rescue of Rabbi Aaron Rokeach, the well-known Rebbe of Belz, and Rabbi Ben Zion Halberstam, the Rebbe of Bobov. In April 1941 he wrote to the Belzer Hasidim, asking for information about the Belzer Rebbe's location and the names of all his family members, promising "I will do whatever I can" for him. The Rebbe wrote to several people on behalf of the Belzer Rebbe. Senator Wagner also wrote on behalf of Rokeach, who made it out of the Bochnia ghetto in 1943 with the help of a Hungarian officer. Interestingly, just as Schneersohn and his followers believed he was rescued by supernatural powers, Rokeach thought divine intervention had saved him, too. In fact, he believed his deceased father, grandfather, and great-grandfather had masqueraded as Hungarian generals to save him from the Nazis at a critical point in his escape. Unfortunately, efforts to save the Rebbe of Bobov were unsuccessful, and he was murdered in July 1941 in Lemberg.[69]

These efforts are only some of those undertaken by the Rebbe to rescue non-Lubavitchers. He also wrote to the American Jewish Joint Distribution Committee, begging for money to obtain visas and pay transportation expenses for Polish Jews. After he arrived in the United States, he pleaded for funds to pay for food and transportation for the many Jews stranded in the Baltic. These efforts continued throughout the summer of 1940. He even sent emissaries to meet with committee representatives and request financial aid. In 1940 the Rebbe wrote, "I am melting away from the pain of our brothers . . . from all sides I hear cries of oppression and hunger. What can I do when the fund is empty?" Beginning in April 1941 he turned to the Quakers, headquartered in Philadelphia; they had extensive contacts with humanitarian services throughout Europe, and he asked them to help save as many Jews as possible.[70]

With the Nazis tightening their grip on millions and the doors of the United States virtually closed, the Rebbe exerted his strongest efforts for those he might actually be able to save. In a letter to the Jewish community in Australia, the Rebbe wrote, "Let us not divert our minds even for one moment from the fate of our brothers, the Jewish people, who find themselves in crisis and captivity, and from the tremendous responsibility that lies upon us now. From the moment I arrived in the US, I could not relax, knowing the tremendous calamity that has befallen our brothers, the Jewish people, in Europe." But the Rebbe felt there was only so much he could do. Sadly, a sense of impotence was common among Jewish leaders in the United States. David Wyman writes, "American Jews lacked the unquenchable sense of urgency the crisis demanded." In 1940, death camps, gas chambers, and genocide were still unimaginable. Even in 1944 and 1945, people still had difficulty understanding the scope of Hitler's destruction.[71] General Dwight D. Eisenhower, who certainly knew more about the Holocaust than the average American due to his position as supreme Allied commander, was shocked in April 1945 when he visited the Ohrdruf concentration camp after it had been liberated by US soldiers.[72] Unfortunately, seeing is often the only way to believe.

Even though the Rebbe did not take advantage of the political contacts that had helped him escape Europe, he did use the *Pidyon Shvuim* to help rescue people, running ads in his newspaper and asking readers to donate to the fund. In addition to rescuing a few Lubavitchers, the fund was used to build schools and support study; according to Rabbi Shalom Dovber Levine, a large portion of it supported those suffering under the Soviets throughout the war.[73] Since most of the Rebbe's followers were located in western Russia, this latter focus was understandable. Hundreds of thousands of Russian Jews were starving and, after Hitler's invasion in June 1941, dying on the front fighting the Nazis or being gassed by the SS in the camps. The Rebbe never forgot the plight of Russian Jewry.

One of the key players in organizing the Rebbe's escape, Latvian senator and fellow Lubavitcher Mordechai Dubin, endured terrible hardships. After the Soviets occupied the Baltic in June 1940, they deported Dubin and other Lubavitchers, along with tens of thousands of non-Jewish Latvians, from Riga to the Soviet Union, where many of them disappeared. When Dubin eventually returned to Riga, he was in poor health. The Soviets sent many Lubavitchers to Siberian concentration camps, where they suffered from starvation, malnutrition, disease, and cold. The situation in the Soviet Union was difficult, but at least the Soviets did not engage in systematic murder.[74] Almost all the Jews who remained in Latvia at the time of the German conquest in mid-1941 had been murdered by the end of the year.

With Dubin and others in mind, the Rebbe sent a delegation to the White House in March 1941 to obtain emergency visitors' visas.[75] The Soviet authorities had apparently sent most of those named by the Rebbe to concentration camps. Because they were Soviet citizens and had opposed the communist regime, their rescue would prove difficult, despite the Soviets' close diplomatic ties with the United States. With the help of Clarence E. Pickett, executive secretary of the American Friends Service Committee in Philadelphia, the Lubavitchers arranged a meeting with Eleanor Roosevelt. Ironically, it was not the Rebbe's political contacts but a Christian who was willing to help them get inside the White House.

Pickett wrote to Mrs. Roosevelt on 5 March, saying, "Three distinguished rabbis of the bearded sort pled with me to ask you to see them." She agreed to a meeting, and on 18 March 1941 Judge Philip Kleinfeld, Rabbi Samarius Gourary, and a few others visited her at the White House. Although they mentioned many names, their primary focus was Mordechai Dubin, who had done so much to help the Rebbe over the years. The Lubavitchers presented her with a two-page memorandum. The first page appealed to the "First Lady of the Land, famous for her kindness and great humanitarian work, to kindly intervene in behalf of a distinguished public worker and humanitarian, Senator Mordechai Dubin, through the above mentioned channels, with a view to securing the early release of . . . Dubin, and his deportation together with his family to this country, where asylum and refuge are awaiting him." Others, mainly yeshiva students, were listed on the second page. The memorandum concluded by stating, "Intercession is earnestly appealed for in behalf of the above mentioned victims of intolerance with the view of procuring their release and deportation from the Soviet Union to this country, where hospitality and refuge has [sic] been offered to them." Although the Rebbe had made a public statement in 1940 on behalf of all Jews in Poland, his organization was not requesting help for Jews living under German oppression or asking that Hitler's atrocities be made more public. As David Kranzler says, "Chabad focused on its mission to rescue American Jews from assimilation and rebuild its community working against incredible odds. It focused on its own mission."[76] This meeting with Mrs. Roosevelt and the document presented to her clearly show that when Chabad had a chance to plead for rescue, it was interested in saving only its own people. It is amazing that the First Lady even met with the Lubavitchers, since at the time, the United States was not interested in helping any Jews, whether they suffered under Hitler or Stalin.

It is not clear what the Lubavitchers' meeting accomplished. As usual, Mrs. Roosevelt tried to be helpful.[77] She presented the matter to Undersecretary of State Sumner Welles, her husband's friend, and asked him to approach the Soviet ambassador. Welles responded on 31 March that he had brought the matter to the ambassador's attention but could not intervene for non-American citizens, "since the Soviet Government consistently refuses to entertain representations from this Government on their behalf." After receiving a copy of Welles's letter, Pickett thanked the First Lady on 22 April and noted, "It looks as if nothing further can be done. I have sent copies of this letter on to the persons who visited you in Washington." Mrs. Roosevelt often had difficulty convincing those in power to help people in need, but that did not stop her from trying; unfortunately, she was powerless to change the situation for many desperate Jews.[78] Her relationship with her husband was not good, and many of those in the president's inner circle did not take her seriously. As Holger Herwig notes, "Roosevelt allowed Eleanor to bring information, but he usually ignored her requests."[79] Pressure from a source Roosevelt respected would be required to get him to act.

Documents show that the Rebbe also tried to save 3,000 Jews in France, pleading their case in a number of letters to government officials. Chabad leaders had a second meeting with Eleanor Roosevelt to discuss the issue, and this time she suggested they deal directly with Secretary of State Hull. According to the available records, they never approached Hull. It seems that despite having access to the First Lady, in the end, they accomplished little.[80] The Lubavitchers' efforts to save these 3,000 Jews were futile. Many of those who did not make it out of France by late 1940 were murdered in the Holocaust.[81]

Before the war, France had a sizable Jewish population of more than 300,000. Many of them were refugees from eastern Europe during the 1920s and from Germany, the Netherlands, and Belgium in the 1930s; about 190,000 were French citizens. Most of them were neither ultra-Orthodox nor Hasidic (unlike Menachem Schneerson, who had been in France pursuing secular studies—very rare in Chabad society). From

1939 to 1941 the Jews experienced anti-Semitism from French nationals, especially under the collaborationist Vichy regime. Had America opened its borders, more of them could have been saved.[82] One wonders why the Rebbe did not pursue the plight of the Jews in France more aggressively. Quite often, the Lubavitchers showed a lack of diligence when it came to political action on behalf of Jews in need. Whereas the actions undertaken on the Rebbe's behalf fill hundreds of documents in the National Archives, that level of effort was never expended for anyone else.

Throughout 1942 and 1943 the Rebbe tried to help Jewish refugees in the Soviet Union by working with Rabbi Jacob Rosenheim at the Agudath Israel World Organization. He wanted the Soviets to allow telegraphic communications between the Jews in the Soviet Union and their relatives in the United States. He also asked the Soviets to allow representatives from America to travel to the Soviet Union and "make direct contact" with the refugees, to fix a favorable exchange rate between the pound and the dollar "for relief purposes," and to allow Chabad to deliver siddurim, calendars, and prayer shawls. Rabbis Shemaryohu Gurary and Jacob Rosenheim and a few others met with Welles on 8 February 1943 with this petition in hand.[83] It is unclear from the historical record what happened to their requests, but if Welles had been unable to help back in 1940, it is probably safe to say that he could do even less now, in the middle of a full-scale world war. In any case, the Russians had just won a brutal battle for Stalingrad and were preparing for a counteroffensive north and south of that city. Moreover, their country was still occupied by forces from Germany, Finland, Romania, Hungary, and Italy; they had many enemies and much land to reconquer. Obviously, the Soviets had more pressing concerns than delivering prayer books to Chabad refugees. In fact, on numerous occasions the Soviets had been inclined to imprison or even kill Chabad leaders. The fact that Chabad bothered Welles with this relatively trivial request showed how little its members understood political realities. But at least they were doing more than just praying and studying.

When the Rebbe's rescue efforts failed in 1940 and 1941, he began to concentrate on his spiritual mission. Primarily, he wanted to make American Jewry more observant by Hasidic standards. He might have continued his quest to save those stranded in Europe if he had thought there was a chance of success, but after encountering so many obstacles, he believed

Rabbi Avraham Kalmanowitz, one of the most prominent leaders of the Orthodox Jewish rescue organization Vaad. His efforts, along with those of Rabbi Aron Kotler, helped save thousands of lives. (Agudath Israel of America)

it would be unproductive to keep going. As a result, he turned his energies to what he perceived as the attainable goal of rebuilding Jewish life in America.

The Rebbe's attempts to rescue European Jews might have been more successful had he joined the Vaad Hahatzalah—the Orthodox Jewish rescue agency—or other groups working to save Jews, but he had no interest in sharing power or building alliances. Unfortunately, Chabad's relationship with the Vaad was less than friendly. In the fall of 1940 Chabad had asked the Vaad to help 156 rabbis emigrate from Lithuania to the United States, a request the Vaad apparently ignored. According to Rabbi Alex Weisfogel, who worked with one of the Vaad's greatest leaders, Avraham Kalmanowitz, "The reason why the Vaad probably did not act on their request as they would have liked is that the Vaad focused on all Jews, not just Lubavitchers. The problem with Chabad then was that it focused just on what it needed." David Kranzler has a different perspective. He believes that because it was difficult to help anyone, and because doing so required a lot of money and influence, the Vaad used its meager resources to save its own members first (it was able to rescue only a handful of yeshiva students initially). In other words, the conflict had less to do with ideology than with finances. Many in the Lubavitcher community, however, thought the Vaad was anti-Hasidim and, as Yosef Jacobson claims, did not accept "the Rebbe's reputation and fame as one of the foremost leaders of his day." It therefore ignored Chabad's needs. Whatever the reason, the lack of help from the Vaad upset the Rebbe deeply.[84]

According to Rabbi Moshe Kolodny, director of the Orthodox Jewish (Agudath Israel) Archives of America, the problems between the Vaad and Chabad arose from strong differences in theology. Many in the Vaad, according to Kolodny, viewed the Lubavitchers as too absorbed in the claim that they had found the only way to live a Jewish life. The Vaad also disagreed with Chabad's focus on the Messiah and their Rebbe. And, as Kolodny explained, since Chabad apparently did not offer the Vaad any reciprocal support for its endeavors, it was unreasonable for Chabad to expect the Vaad to help the Lubavitchers. Rabbi Weisfogel said, "With Chabad, it was always a one-way street always favoring them." But according to Milton Kramer, president of Chabad's National Committee for the Furtherance of Jewish Education, Kolodny's and Weisfogel's claims are untrue. Kramer points out an inherent contradiction, asking rhetorically how Kolodny and Weisfogel could say that Chabad would not work with the Vaad when it was clearly the Vaad that considered Lubavitchers pariahs? In the end, the Vaad simply found Chabad a nuisance and difficult to work with and ignored its demands.[85]

The religious bickering that took place both then and now makes one shake one's head. While all of European Jewry was going up in flames in Hitler's crematoriums, Jewish groups argued about the Messiah, about theology, about Halacha, and about status. These issues, which cannot be proved or disproved either way, seem incredibly frivolous, given the number of people being slaughtered by Hitler. Even though the true horror of the Holocaust was not completely known at this time, one would have hoped that these petty rabbis could put aside their religious differences and work together. But not even Hitler's persecution—which some of them, including the Rebbe, had experienced personally, could bring them together in a united front.

The Rebbe seemed to be willing to work with the Vaad, if its members had shown him more respect. In a letter to Rabbi David Rabinovitz, a close friend and confidant, Schneersohn mentioned that the Vaad was raising money for all yeshivas, including those of Chabad, yet he had not received any funds. The Rebbe asked Rabinovitz to obtain "the $1,000 they owe me," saying he felt deeply hurt by the Vaad's ill treatment of him. He claimed that throughout a lifetime of fund-raising, he had never made a distinction between Chabad and non-Chabad schools or institutions and had given hundreds of thousands of dollars to non-Chabad schools. "If I were to demand from them to pay me back for the money I spent in order to support and save their yeshivahs over the years," the Rebbe continued, "they would have to give up even their girdles." According to Chabad, the Vaad refused to give the Rebbe the $1,000.[86] The Rebbe's failure to gain the Vaad's trust and cooperation shows yet another aspect of his weakness as a leader.

In July 1944 Rabbi Aaron Kotler (founder of the yeshiva in Lakewood, New Jersey), Rabbi Baruch Korff (later known as President Nixon's "rabbi"), and Michael Tress (president of the Agudath Israel Youth Council of America and later Agudath Israel of America) petitioned President Roosevelt to help rescue Jews in Hungary on behalf of the following Jewish organizations: Vaad, Agudath Israel of America, Rabbinical Council of America, Union of Orthodox Jewish Congregations of America, Young Israel of America, and Emergency Committee to Save the Jewish People of Europe. The Rebbe's name and Chabad were missing from this petition because he refused to build an alliance with these organizations (in fact, he condemned them for their tactics). Rabbi Kotler, a refugee himself, was relentless in his pursuit of rescuing Jews. Korff had seen his mother shot dead during a pogrom in 1919 in the Ukraine; he knew what was going on under the Nazis and felt a visceral sense of urgency. Tress was a prominent businessman who was willing to spend his fortune and even mortgage his house to rescue Jews (it appears that Chabad's headquarters in Brooklyn was never mortgaged to either save Jews or pay Rhoade). Kotler, Korff, and Tress and the organizations they represented sent the following statement to Undersecretary Edward R.

Stettinius (who had replaced Sumner Welles after allegations of a homosexual overture to a porter on the presidential train):

> A cold, terrifying horror has gripped the approximately one
> million Jews of Hungary [have already been reduced by 500,000
> through extermination] by the enemy. The spectre of the horrible
> sadistic torture and death is increasing by the hour. . . . We refuse
> to resign ourselves to the idea that humanity is really so helpless
> that nothing can be done to come to the rescue of those who need
> it most urgently. We refuse to resign ourselves to building a new
> world freely and happily for everyone but with one people, old and
> civilized and peace-loving, *annihilated*. To this day all avenues of
> rescue open to the United States and Great Britain brought meager
> results. For every Jew purportedly saved from occupied territory, ten
> thousand or more are put to death.[87]

They pleaded with Stettinius and Roosevelt to contact Pope Pius XII and urge him to intervene in Hungary, since it was a largely Catholic country. Kotler, Korff, and Tress got their message heard at the White House, and the Rebbe could have been there shoulder to shoulder with them, but he was not. Instead, he had petitioned the government in 1943 to send siddurim, calendars, and prayer shawls to the Jews in the Soviet Union.

Chabad did contact Tress in November 1944, but its purpose was to solicit funds for its schools, at a time when Tress and Agudath Israel were desperately trying to raise money to save Jews in Europe. Illustrating its ignorance of Agudath's true mission, Chabad asserted that by affiliating with Lubavitch, Agudath would enhance its prestige "to its proper and deserving position." It made this bold statement despite the fact that Chabad almost never affiliated with any other organization when rescue was the goal. In the end, Chabad's own mission and the building of schools seemed to be its only undertakings. Of course, even during wartime people must keep learning and building schools if they can, but with Chabad's stated budget of $250,000 a year, one wonders why Rhoade remained unpaid and why some of these funds were not turned over to aid the rescue efforts of Agudath.[88]

Most disturbingly, instead of finding a way to work with Agudath Israel, the Vaad, and other Jewish groups, Schneersohn went out of his way to condemn their leaders for working with non-Orthodox and Christian organizations. Ironically, for years the Rebbe had attempted to work with the Quakers and non-Orthodox Jews, such as the American Jewish Joint Distribution Committee, on behalf of suffering Jews in Russia, yet he condemned such behavior by others. According to Jewish law, one must violate almost every commandment—except for idolatry, murder, and forbidden sexual relations—in order to save lives, but the Rebbe believed that violating the commandments actually took lives. The Rebbe felt that when God's decrees were broken unnecessarily, especially by those who were working with Reform Jews and Christians, God would condemn those actions.

Rabbi Kotler of the Vaad, an Orthodox rabbi, worked with both non-Orthodox and secular leaders. Many other Orthodox rabbis criticized him for his willingness to work with such people. Kotler's response was that he was willing to "work with the Pope" and even prostrate himself before the Catholic leader "if it would save . . . one Jewish child."[89] Kotler's colleague Rabbi Avraham Kalmanowitz agreed with him and worked with Reform Jews and even atheists. These courageous Orthodox rabbis helped rescue thousands.[90] Even though their educational and theological backgrounds were similar to the Rebbe's, they were able to build bridges between different theological, ideological, and ethnic communities. Despite their Orthodox ways, they were able to adapt to current events in such a way that allowed them to do so much more than the Rebbe, who remained isolated in his Brooklyn headquarters.

Stephen Wise, a Reform rabbi and prominent Jewish leader, was a longtime supporter of President Roosevelt. Wise had backed FDR in his successful run for governor of New York against a Jewish opponent. The rabbi based his support on the character, programs, and ability of the candidates, not their religion. FDR valued Rabbi Wise's opinion and kept in touch with him over the years. He was perhaps "the most politically powerful rabbi in American history."[91] Wise believed that people of different faiths should work together to promote understanding. He "always felt . . . the holy duty of urging the establishment of such fellowship between Jew and Christian as would be worthy of both faiths." Wise wrote, "Often I saw fit to remind Christian congregations of the truth about Jesus, that he was above all a Jew in faith and life and practices alike." Wise went on to explain the importance of Jew and non-Jew meeting "from time to time in the spirit of common worship of the universal Father." He observed that if "mutual respect" were nurtured "between those of different faiths, of religious viewpoints however divergent or even conflicting," it would create a stronger civilization for both Jew and Christian alike—something needed during the Holocaust.[92]

When Rabbi Wise first received evidence of the Holocaust—in an August 1942 telegram from Gerhard Reigner via Samuel Silberman, and in November 1942 from Undersecretary of State Sumner Welles—he took action to win the support of Protestants, Catholics, and Jews "to intervene and protest the horrible treatment of Jews in Hitler's Europe." He contacted 500 newspapers. He organized a National Day of Mourning and Prayer in the United States, and twenty-nine foreign countries held ten-minute work stoppages and memorial services. Wise claimed, "I am almost demented over my people's grief." Rabbi Wise contacted Roosevelt and arranged a meeting at the White House that included representatives of the American Jewish Committee (the nation's oldest human rights organization), the B'nai B'rith, the Union of American Orthodox Rabbis, and the Jewish Labor Committee. Roosevelt told them, "We are dealing with an insane man—Hitler and the group that surrounds him represent an example of a national psychopathic case." The president told his visitors that he would issue a statement and asked them to draft it for him.[93]

In the United Kingdom, requests by Jewish groups (including the World Jewish Congress) prompted the government to issue a statement denouncing "in the strongest possible terms the bestial policy of cold-blooded extermination." The US and British governments responded positively and issued a joint declaration promising that war crimes would be prosecuted after the war. Members of the House of Commons stood in silent respect as the declaration was read—an act previously done only to mourn "the death of a sovereign." All this was front-page news.[94]

Many of the methods used by people like Wise and Kotler troubled the Rebbe, particularly their working so closely with Christians. He said in 1943:

These false prophets and iniquitous rabbis have brought our people to the ludicrous state in which rabbis have themselves photographed with clergymen; rabbis are invited to officiate at a Seder in a church and Christian clergymen are invited to synagogues to listen to the Sounding of the Shofar and to [hymns sung at the table during Sabbath], to [prayers for Yom Kippur]. Genuine rabbis, Torah scholars, stand abashed. They cannot lift their eyes out of shame— for the Destruction that is being brought upon the Jewish street.[95]

Ironically, when Chabad needed help in 1939, it had reached out to Rabbi Wise for assistance. Four years later it condemned him. The Rebbe certainly did not object to working with Christians if they could further his goals; he had done so himself with the Quakers. But behind their backs, he derided their traditions and denounced interfaith religious gatherings; sharing in the worship of God and mixing among their communities should be avoided. In short, the Rebbe was quite parochial.

The Rebbe preached during the war that it was actually a mitzvah to denounce those who had transgressed by "desecrating the practical *mitzvot*, such as *tefillin* and the prayers, by irresponsibly spurning the restrictions of kosher dietary laws and the family purity laws; by giving their children an irreligious education in *treifah* Talmud Torah schools whose men and women teachers are godless, and in *yeshivos* that match; and by attending temples with their faithless rabbis." The Rebbe's organization claimed in September 1941 that, if the Jews had been better educated and "lived according to the precepts of the Torah," the present "catastrophic situation would not have developed." In other words, he believed the Holocaust was God's punishment for the Jews' abandonment of their faith. Only renewed obedience to God and belief in the prophets would end the punishment—continued disobedience and disbelief constituted "perverse Jewish Nazism." Political action to end the Holocaust or save lives was futile as long as the Jews failed to follow the commandments. Given this ideology, the Rebbe could not seek the help of those who, in his mind, were violating God's laws. This attitude would have made the Rebbe quite difficult to work with, since he would cooperate only with those willing to accept his dictates and support his policies.[96]

Using the term "Jewish Nazism" to describe Jewish groups that were noncompliant with Chabad doctrine showed his utter contempt for them. Likening the enlightened, freedom-loving American rabbis to the Nazis showed how deluded the Rebbe was and how fanatical and full of hatred he could be. He believed these Jews were leading people away from God and killing their souls, and he would be their judge and jury, ensuring that they were punished for their sins and for causing the Shoah.

Once the Rebbe started down this path of condemnation, he never stopped. He became obsessed with pointing the finger at others to explain what Hitler was doing and why God was allowing it to happen. Reading through his newspaper, talks, and writings, it merges into one long rant that repeats the same theme. In a speech he gave in 1943, the Rebbe attacked secular, Reform, and Orthodox Jewish leaders who organized events and protests that took place on holy days and the Sabbath:

> These leaders brazenly defy God and scoff at Him. Even their mournful demonstrations—which the godless leaders of certain Jewish parties believe are going to save Jews in peril, and for which they have cooperation of unprincipled rabbis—are called for Friday evening. This planned desecration of *Shabbos* is a rebellious response to the commandment from the G-d of our fathers to keep this day holy, and a senseless and shameful affront to their fellow Jews. This they do while our brothers and sisters are being slaughtered, murdered, buried alive, with a cruelty that the world has never witnessed; while the blood of Jewish old and young, fathers, mothers and tiny toddlers, is flowing in rivers throughout all the occupied countries.[97]

The Rebbe viewed their tactics as damaging to the plight of Jews, rather than useful in raising public awareness. It is a sad commentary that the Rebbe did not take all that hatred and energy and focus it on political action to achieve something good in this world.

Those demonstrations the Rebbe condemned actually accomplished a lot. And conducting such activities on the Sabbath and on holy days was in fact permitted—indeed, required—by Jewish law to save lives. In the minds of the organizers, they were fulfilling a mitzvah to save life at any cost and thereby obeying God's law. Although it is clear that the Rebbe encouraged certain actions to save human lives, he wanted Jews to focus on the bigger picture. In 1942 he said it was incumbent on Jews to use "natural [political] means" and "self-sacrifice" to save "our brothers and sisters." But those actions, according to the Rebbe, had to follow Jewish law and practice. He believed Jews had been distracted from 3,000 years of proof of what had sustained Israel—namely, spiritual activism—and that spiritual revitalization was needed at this time. Demonstrations would not help, in his opinion.[98]

Thus, it is not surprising that the Rebbe discouraged mass demonstrations when others saw a need for them.[99] In 1941, for example, the mere threat that 50,000 to 100,000 African Americans were going to march on Washington prompted President Roosevelt to issue an executive order that would increase employment opportunities for blacks.[100] A march on Washington by more than 400 members of the Union of Orthodox Rabbis of the United States and Canada on 6 October 1943, in the sacred days between Rosh Hashanah and Yom Kippur, helped create the War Refugee Board, which saved thousands of lives in 1944 and 1945 and finally took refugee matters out of the hands of the anti-Semitic Breckinridge Long.[101] Likewise, the *Rosenstraße* protest illustrates that demonstrations can have a real effect. In February 1943, in the heart of the Nazi empire in Berlin, hundreds and sometimes thousands of women and children protested the arrest of their Jewish husbands and fathers. These brave citizens defied Goebbels, Hitler, and Himmler at the height of their power in their own backyard. Many of the women yelled, "Give back our husbands." Even though the SS threatened them with gunfire, they continued to protest for more than a week. Remarkably, the Nazis eventually gave in to the protesters' demands and released the 2,000 men.[102] The Rebbe supposedly had more than 160,000 followers in North America (according to other sources, millions!). Think of the demonstrations he could have staged if he had not viewed them as offensive and counterproductive. One wishes he had shown half the courage of the brave women and children in Berlin during the dark days of 1943.

Many did not agree with the Rebbe's tactics. Philosopher Jacob Klatzkin wrote to the Rebbe on 8 March 1943 and said his heart ached because Jewish leaders were not taking to the streets of America, dressed in

On 6 October 1943 more than 400 Orthodox rabbis marched on Washington to protest America's inaction in helping Jewish victims of Hitler. President Roosevelt refused to meet with them when they arrived at the White House. (Agudath Israel of America)

mourning, to protest the lack of government effort and to awaken Americans to the "murder of tens of thousands of our brothers." He asked, "Why are our Orthodox leaders silent?" He begged the Rebbe to lead Hasidic and ultra-Orthodox Judaism in this cause.[103]

The Rebbe responded on 31 March, expressing sadness at Klatzkin's sentiments. Never in all his years of communal service, he said, had there been a time like this, when righteous Gentiles willing to protect Jews were nowhere to be found. There were groups to protect "cats, dogs, maybe even mice, but no groups to protect Jews." The countries and governments that benefited from "our wisdom and wealth are now turning their backs and eyes away. These people a few years ago treated us nicely, but now their eyes are shut and ears closed to the spilling of the blood of Israel in the conquered areas under evil Nazism." To "our embarrassment and shame," Schneersohn explained, "and to the shame and embarrassment of all humanity," the government tells "us to calm down and rest assured that when the war is over, then they 'will see what we can do for you.' Until then, we are, God forbid, disowned crumbs on the eve of *Pesach*."[104] At the time, Americans of all faiths had joined the armed forces by the millions and, with their Allies, were engaged in pitched battles against the Axis powers in North Africa and the Pacific, in the air above Europe, and at sea. On the home front, in what was now the arsenal of democracy, Americans were working around the clock to turn out the planes, tanks, trucks, ships, and other equipment, as well as food and clothing, for the Allies.

Demonstrations aimed at inspiring the Jewish people were no use, according to the Rebbe: Jews already knew what was going on. "We see so clearly that they [the government] are sitting behind a diplomatic curtain. We do not know if they are laughing or gloating on the evil deeds, but what we do know is that they are pretending all is in order. If demonstration is for the government's benefit, the world sees that their ears are closed to the screams of our 'corpses' and their eyes are closed to the river and streams of blood. . . . The one thing that we can do, should do, must do is to awaken the compassion of our Father, our King in Heaven. In order to awaken the compassion of Heaven, why do we have to make a demonstration?" The Rebbe's strategy in this titanic struggle against evil was to seek God's help, since humans appeared to be unable or unwilling to save the Jews. He believed God had sent the Germans to "collect on His debts," since the Jews had not been following his commandments. The chutzpah of secular and nonobservant Jewish leaders was "leading Jews to sin." When "our brothers and sisters are being murdered with the greatest cruelty in fire and water and burned alive," and when hundreds of thousands of Jewish men were serving in the armed forces, Jews around the world should humble themselves before God and return to Judaism. "Precisely in the time when the dark clouds of antisemitism are covering this country and the haters of Israel are sharpening and shining their weapons to kill Jews (may their swords go into their own hearts and may their bodies fall into their own pits)," Jews needed to pray to God for forgiveness and study the Torah. According to the Rebbe, nonobservant Jews, or *kofrim* (apostates), needed to do the most to stop Hitler's genocide. Instead of bothering him with letters, Klatzkin should go to his *kofrim* brothers and protest that they were not keeping the Sabbath holy, not wearing tefillin, not eating kosher food, and not obeying God.

If they returned to the way of life they knew was right, things would get better. God, the Rebbe explained, had brought him to America to build his yeshiva and keep the "Holy Torah alive." Having witnessed how far the Jews had strayed from God, he had published a newspaper about their coming destruction. He had foreseen the terrible things to come and "the birth pangs of the Messiah"—all "very serious topics and secrets of our sages."[105] Once again, the Rebbe spoke from the conviction that he was perfect and everyone else was defective. This incredible hubris shows that religious leaders are not necessarily the most enlightened, democratic, tolerant, and sane among society.

Perhaps the most puzzling aspect of the Rebbe's political inertia is the fact that, unlike most other Jewish leaders, he had experienced Nazi atrocities firsthand (albeit for only a short time). Some have argued that this political inaction was due to the Rebbe's lack of experience with a democratic government; the governments he had known in Europe, primarily under the Soviets, had often been brutally intolerant toward Jews.[106] He therefore did what he had been taught and what he had always done—pray and study—which made him a saint among the Lubavitchers. They thought that watching him pray allowed them to observe ultimate holiness, especially during times of extreme hardship. Most religious leaders would agree about the power of prayer, but few would suggest that prayer should be one's only action in the face of danger. Political action had saved the Rebbe's life, yet he condemned that tactic and focused only on his spiritual battle against mainstream Jews in the United States.

Even before leaving the ship that had brought him to America, the Rebbe had told Jacobson, "Our work is Torah, and the strengthening of *Yiddishkeit* here, and Torah and *Yiddishkeit* overseas." Once he had turned the Jews toward strict observance of the Torah and fortified their "fear of Heaven," God would drive their tormentors "to the gallows."[107] The Rebbe pleaded with God to send his angels to welcome "thy people Israel" and end persecution and war.[108] During countless events, his followers saw him break down in uncontrollable tears. In part, he may have been lamenting the fact that in Russia and Poland he had been one of the top Jewish leaders, but in the United States his stature was significantly reduced.

Avrum Ehrlich argues that the Rebbe's move to the United States can be viewed as tantamount to a commander who leaves his troops in a losing battle and retires to safety, perhaps to fight another day. Yet most of the Rebbe's followers saw his escape "as part of a larger mystical-military mission." The expansion of Chabad in America, a country viewed by most Hasidic and ultra-Orthodox Jews as heretical (the impure country—the *treife medina*), was the beginning of the "final struggle" that would usher in the redemption of the nation of Israel. For centuries, Hasidic and Orthodox rabbis had discouraged or prohibited Jews from moving out of anti-Semitic and despotic Europe to lands of freedom and unlimited opportunity, where these rabbis would lose control. Millions had disregarded their warnings. Now, Jews who had obeyed these leaders were suffering terribly and paying with their lives. Despite the fact that America was the safest place in the world for Jews and the only place the Rebbe could go, his followers saw his actions as a brave effort to fight assimilation in the Western world.[109]

Given the Rebbe's chronic health problems, it was remarkable that he was functioning at all. He could not walk on his own, and he had difficulty even picking up a pencil. He needed help eating, washing, defecating, urinating, and dressing. He mostly remained in his room and relied on newspapers, radio broadcasts, and his followers to keep him informed of outside events, as he did not speak English. Even in this fragile state, his mind was sharp. He retained authority over the movement, and his ideas served as the guiding light for his followers. Illness tends to make people more introspective, which may partly explain his turn away from the political and his deep plunge into eschatological theories.

In many respects, the Rebbe probably felt powerless to effect political change. The world seemed to be spinning out of control as Hitler continued his conquest of Europe. Schneersohn knew that Jews were dying, and many of them were his Jews—Torah-observant Hasidic Jews. After Poland, Hitler had continued his military buildup and invaded and conquered Denmark, Norway, France, the Netherlands, Yugoslavia, Greece, Crete, North Africa, and large swaths of Russia between 1940 and December 1941, when his expansion was finally checked outside of Moscow. By the fall of 1941, Germany controlled most of Europe and much of North Africa. It seemed that God favored not the Rebbe but Hitler. Given the Rebbe's religious framework, the period from 1939 onward must have seemed like the final battle between God and Magog that would usher in the arrival of the Messiah. What was unclear to the Rebbe was who would win that epic battle. Given his personal experience with the Soviets and the Nazis, one can perhaps understand why the Rebbe felt that God's wrath was ushering in the last days. Less understandable is why the Rebbe believed that only he could see things clearly. For instance, his newspaper boldly claimed to be the "only publication that interprets our times from the genuinely Jewish standpoint. . . . Learn the truth, and be prepared to guide yourself according to your own best interests."[110] The Rebbe in particular and the Lubavitchers in general never suffered from false modesty.

Perhaps the reason the Rebbe had been saved, according to his theology, was his exceptional faithfulness to God's commandments. He stated:

> With G-d's help, and in the merit of my holy forebears, I have
> remained faithful, regardless of my shattered physical condition,
> to the principles governing communal activity that I was taught by
> my Rebbe—the great self-sacrificing leader and mentor, my father,
> of blessed memory. With self-sacrifice I fulfill his holy testament,
> by disseminating Torah study inspired by the awe of heaven, by
> furthering authentic Jewish education, and in general by working for
> the public welfare.[111]

Like most religious leaders, the Rebbe was struggling to find meaning for his movement during a changing, troubling, and awesomely depressing time. However, many of the Rebbe's conclusions are disquieting. But as several Lubavitch scholars, including Simon Jacobson, have pointed out, his words of condemnation and redemption reflect a Jewish approach that is rooted in Torah sources, including Maimonides, the great twelfth-century theologian and physician, who writes: "When a calamity strikes the community we must . . . examine our lives and correct our ways. To say that the calamity is merely a natural phenomenon and a chance occurrence is insensitive and cruel."[112]

Contemporary Lubavitchers are particularly sensitive about the Rebbe's views on the Holocaust, and they prefer to emphasize a radically different angle espoused by his successor, Rebbe Menachem Mendel

Schneerson.[113] According to Schneerson: "To say that those very people were deserving of what transpired, that it was a punishment for their sins, heaven forbid, is unthinkable. We cannot *explain* the Holocaust, for we are limited by the earthbound perspective of mortal understanding. As G-d says, in a prophecy of Isaiah, 'For My thoughts are not your thoughts.' No scales of judgment could ever condemn a people to such horrors." He went on to explain, "So awesome was the cruelty to which our people were subjected that Satan himself could not find sins to justify such suffering." Later he added, "To say that the Jews were punished for their sins with the Holocaust is a desecration of God's name. It is not us who have to repent after the Holocaust, but rather it is God who has to" repent for allowing so many to suffer and to lose their faith.[114] This is controversial because Rebbes are not supposed to contradict one another. Yet here is Menachem Mendel Schneerson claiming that his father-in-law's assessment of the Holocaust was dead wrong: it was not the Jews' fault. We should note that the seventh Rebbe's works were written a generation later, after the Holocaust had become a subject of theological debate and after the writings of Elie Wiesel, Emil Fackenheim, Richard L. Rubenstein, Eliezer Berkovits, and Irving Greenberg, among others.

Schneerson's father-in-law also challenged God, but with a different focus. In a letter from 1945, Rebbe Schneersohn cried out:

Oh, G-d, where are your holy and precious children? Left rolling naked [in the streets], devastated physically and spiritually, starving orphans and widows, ill and broken. Oh, Master of the Universe! To whom have You done this? Jews have been punished many many multitudes of times more than their sins. Jews, a nation of Torah, keepers of the law, men and women living a life of Torah and mitzvot with an inner love, rabbis, Torah sages, righteous people, people of piety, Hassidim, servants of G-d, were murdered in the most horrific and barbaric ways.

It seemed the Rebbe could not understand why, instead of just the secular and Reformed Jews being punished for not following the Torah, it was disproportionately the Hasidic and Orthodox Torah followers whom

God "murdered." The Rebbe's theology was unable to explain historical events; it was overwhelmed by the Holocaust.

Ironically, the Rebbe's view of the Holocaust turned men like Hitler into instruments of divine will. The Rebbe's newspaper explained in July 1941 that American Jews had to realize that God ruled the world and caused all events; they were wrong to think that only "an energetic effort on the part of the democracies can and will annihilate" Hitler. The Rebbe believed that, as the Talmud says, "God sets up a wicked ruler like Haman so that he shall make His people return to the good way." Hitler had been sent as "a plague of God, in order to cause the Jews to return to the good, and the only salvation for the Jews is to repent of their sins."[115]

The Rebbe truly believed that his message to the Jews was a compassionate one. Because he "loved" the Jews so much, it pained him to acknowledge that the pious were dying for the others during this premessianic travail.[116] He thought this "bloodbath" should inspire all Jews to return to the Torah and thus clear the path for the "Righteous *Mashiach*." The "suffering of world Jewry today is a voice from heaven calling" all Jews to "*teshuvah* [repentance] of unfaithful ways," and if they heeded the call, a "beautiful and luminous world will arise." God "sends hardships to cleanse us of our sins. They should be received with true affection, because their purpose is our benefit. . . . Whom G-d loves He afflicts."[117]

The view that God had orchestrated the Nazi slaughter and that Hitler was working on God's behalf is a troubling one for most people. Distinguished rabbi Ken Roseman, former dean of the Hebrew Union College–Jewish Institute of Religion, says, "That one believes the Holocaust comes because the victim merits it is obscene."[118] Interestingly, such a view of the Holocaust raises several delicate issues about God and his actions. The concept of a God living above us and intimately involved with our daily lives is challenging to the faithful. As Karen Armstrong, a teacher at the Leo Baeck College for the Study of Judaism, notes, "If God is omnipotent, he could have prevented the Holocaust. If he was unable to stop it, he is impotent and useless; if he could have stopped it and chose not to, he is a monster."[119] If God actually ordered the Holocaust, as the Rebbe claimed, how should we interpret his actions? Conservative rabbi Harold Kushner writes:

The idea that God gives people what they deserve, that our misdeeds cause our misfortune, is a neat and attractive solution to the problem of evil at several levels, but it has a number of serious limitations . . . it teaches people to blame themselves. It creates guilt even where there is no basis for guilt. It makes people hate God, even as it makes them hate themselves. And most disturbing of all, it does not even fit the facts.[120]

Prominent Hasidic rabbi Chaskel Besser believes that a true understanding of God and why he allows bad things to happen is beyond human comprehension: "I'm not in Heaven and I'm not a prophet so I cannot comment on why God did what he did. . . . I only know that the Holocaust makes me want to be a better person every day. . . . The Rebbe was wrong to say he knew what God wanted for everyone." In Besser's opinion, documenting these stories of the Rebbe would prove difficult for historians because the "Lubavitchers will conduct a smear campaign if you don't praise them."[121] The truth is often difficult to swallow.

In analyzing the actions of men like the Rebbe, Orthodox rabbi Norman Lamm, chancellor of Yeshiva University, goes so far as to charge them with blasphemy. Such views, Lamm says, are "repugnant to me and bespeak an insufferable insensitivity." He adds that pointing a finger at others, as the Rebbe did, "is an unparalleled instance of criminal arrogance and brutal insensitivity. . . . How dare anyone, sitting in the American or British or Israeli Paradise, indict the martyrs who were consumed in the European Hell?" He fails to see why God would order the Nazis to kill anyone to punish the Jews for their transgressions, and he speaks from a position of pain, since the Nazis murdered his grandmother. Saying such a thing is "unforgivable," Lamm explains. One should not forget, Lamm continues, that Moses was punished by God for "making offensive statements" against his people. In the end, he concludes, "small-minded people blame others, not themselves."[122]

It is difficult for Lubavitchers to accept the Rebbe's limitations, yet history shows that Schneersohn made mistakes. Focusing on a theology of condemnation, the Rebbe missed opportunities to save lives and offended many. Consequently, according to Rabbi Alex Weisfogel, the Rebbe was a "moral failure." In the end, the Rebbe's messianic preaching led to little positive action and failed to alleviate the plight of Jews in Europe. As Harris Lenowitz writes: "While the messiah idea stirs up passionate hope and faith, betrayal and failure lie at its roots. . . . No messiah succeeds in leading his followers and the world to a harmonious existence."[123] One Holocaust survivor claimed that when Zyklon B poison gas was thrown into the death chambers and the Jews trampled one another to escape it, they must have felt that God had abandoned them.[124] Others claimed that the Jewish Messiah or God himself was murdered in Auschwitz, or at least he was shown not to exist, since he neither stopped Hitler's crimes nor answered the prayers of his victims. When the SS hanged a young child, Elie Wiesel heard someone ask, "Where is God now?" As he witnessed the child's slow death, taking thirty minutes to expire, Wiesel reflected: "Where is He? Here He is—He is hanging here on this gallows."[125]

The Rebbe was not alone in his opinion of why God allowed Hitler to do what he did, but a discussion of this theological process raises more questions about life and the world than it solves. The Rebbe's belief touches on one of the more complex issues in Jewish theology and that of other faiths as well: the simultaneous belief in the concepts of divine providence and free will. One is led to conclude that God and his actions are truly beyond human comprehension, just as Rebbe Menachem Mendel Schneerson said.[126]

After his arrival in the United States in 1940, the Rebbe focused on building up the Lubavitch community. This desire, notes Michael Berenbaum, "in and of itself was a response to the destruction of European Jewry." The Rebbe believed that "the survival of the Jewish people depends on the Torah." On many occasions between 1941 and 1943, he pleaded with the religious community for funds to build a central yeshiva, the Tomchei Temimim. He chastised his followers for not contributing enough to Chabad schools, admonishing them to "support these Yeshivahs more generously and thereby free yourselves from the shame of not paying the rightful dues which the Torah expects a Jew to honor." He believed a central Lubavitcher yeshiva would cure many of the ills that had befallen the Jews and would save Jewry from "religious annihilation."[127]

The Rebbe also defended his group's freedom of religious expression (of course, he did not defend Reform, Conservative, or Reconstructionist Judaism). He appealed to his followers to help Jews in the Soviet Union who were prevented from practicing their religion, and he attacked secular Jewish leaders in Israel for not providing a religious education for the orphaned children of Orthodox victims of the Holocaust. Such neglect was a "shameless effrontery," he said; teachers had "set up an 'apostasy corner' for the children entrusted in their care."[128] His language was aggressive:

> In German-occupied territories Hitler set up lime-kilns in order to torture and cremate Jewish bodies; in [Israel] a certain group has set up houses of apostasy in order to torture and cremate Jewish souls. . . . These people are teaching the children to desecrate the *Shabbos*, to eat *treifah* [nonkosher] food, to eat on *Yom Kippur* [a day of fasting], to eat *chametz* [leavened products forbidden on Passover]. They do not even allow them to say *Kaddish* [the prayer for the dead] in memory of their parents who lost their lives in sanctification of the Divine Name, and they teach them to scoff at the notion of G-d and Jewish religious observance.

He asked Jewish leaders to help in the campaign against the secular education of these children. Although they had failed to rescue the Jews under Hitler, he urged them to "rescue their orphans from apostasy." Withholding a religious education was "a despicable moral violation" that had to be "utterly uprooted from the Jewish people."[129] For the Rebbe, failing to follow God's laws was the worst sin one could commit, and he devoted his life to making Jews observant, according to his definition. As George Bernard Shaw states, "No man ever believes that the Bible means what it says. He is always convinced that it says what he means."[130]

During the ten years from his rescue in 1940 until his death in 1950, the Rebbe energetically built up the Lubavitch community in the United States from his home at 770 Eastern Parkway in Brooklyn, New York, now the headquarters of Chabad. He founded several schools for boys and girls, summer camps, and a publishing house. After the war ended in 1945, he set up his Refugee Relief and Rehabilitation Organization in Paris, which helped secular and religious Jews in displaced-persons camps get kosher food and eventually immigrate to Israel. He apparently stopped talking about the Holocaust being punishment for the sins of the Jews and focused strictly on his spiritual mission and the coming of the Messiah. In 1949 he became a US citizen, saying on that occasion, "I recall with gratitude the humanitarian act of the American Government in those critical days in 1940, when it intervened to help rescue me from Hitler's clutches and bring me to these American shores." Now, instead of raging against democracies, and in a rare declaration of gratitude, the Rebbe thanked the land responsible for his escape. Other than letters to Hull, Roosevelt, and Brandeis, this seems to be the only document in which the Rebbe expressed his thanks. He never thanked the Germans, which was understandable, but he also never thanked Max Rhoade, who was instrumental in saving him.

The Rebbe never publicly described the details of his escape. Nor did he do so in his private memoirs. Perhaps it was too painful to be reminded of those people, including his daughter and son-in-law and many other relatives, who were now dead. Most Lubavitchers believe that the mechanics of the miracle are immaterial. All that matters is that it allowed the Rebbe to strengthen Chabad around the world. Likewise, the Belzer Rebbe "adamantly opposed" publication of the story of his rescue by Hungarian officers. Quoting the French sage Rashi, he said it "is forbidden to publicize personal miracles."[131]

The Rebbe's tenure came to a close early one Sabbath morning. On 28 January 1950, at 7:45 a.m., his faithful daughter Chana Gourary informed those gathered at Chabad's headquarters that the Rebbe had taken a turn for the worse. On this occasion they broke the Sabbath law—as they were obligated to do to save a human life—and called the doctor to come at once to attend to their leader. The doctor came and checked on the Rebbe, but there was nothing he could do. At 8:07 a.m. the doctor pronounced the Rebbe dead. His daughter was distraught and frantically pleaded with the doctor to "save her father." Throughout the day there was great mourning within the Lubavitcher community. All recited the psalms to "ease their leader's soul on its final journey." One Lubavitcher described the scene as follows: "With every second that went by the crowd swelled in number [at Chabad headquarters], sounds of

Rebbe Joseph Isaac Schneersohn's grave in Cambria Heights, New York. His followers leave messages asking him to pray for them in heaven. (Author's collection)

sobbing and wailing were heard from every quarter . . . under the sheet, lay our crown, our splendor. Oh, how the heart was wrung!" The Rebbe's followers, led by Menachem Mendel Schneerson, prepared him for burial as if he were an ancient high priest of Israel.

Menachem Mendel declared that the Rebbe had been a prophet, the Moses of his generation, and even the Messiah. He believed he was able to commune with the Rebbe, even in death. Several in the community were disappointed that the Rebbe's predictions of the Messiah had not come true, and some briefly claimed that the Rebbe was the Messiah and had not really died and that they should be patient and wait for him to reveal himself. Jews dealt with their disappointment over the belated arrival of the Messiah in a number of ways, including prayer and good deeds, but also with humor. When a Jew in the ghetto was questioned about his assignment to look out for the Messiah, he simply replied, "The pay is not good but the work is steady." Interestingly, the Rebbe had alienated so many American Jewish groups that few, if any, rabbis from other sects attended his burial. Nor did the politicians and secular advocates responsible for the Rebbe's rescue, such as Wagner, Kleinfeld, Cohen, and Rhoade, attend the Rebbe's funeral. Their nonattendance may have been due to the Rebbe's attitude or to disappointment in his leadership. Also, it may have been due to the Orthodox tradition of burying the dead virtually immediately, on the same day if possible. Even in the absence of such leaders, about 3,000 people reportedly "jammed the streets and sidewalks" in front of Chabad headquarters.

Soon after the death of Rebbe Joseph Isaac Schneersohn, some in the Chabad community urged Menachem Mendel Schneerson to accept the position of Rebbe. Menachem Mendel "protested vehemently," saying, "the Rebbe lives." Like many others, it seems that he could not accept that such a great man had actually left them. Chabad therefore remained leaderless for one year until Schneerson assumed the position of Rebbe in 1951, on the anniversary of his father-in-law's death. Even so, some still believed that Schneersohn was the Messiah and that he would soon return, take back the mantle of leadership, and guide them into the promised age he had so often spoken about. Not surprisingly, this did not happen—or, as some might say, at least not yet. Spinoza eloquently sums up Schneersohn's misguided preachings: "As a consequence of human gullibility, faith has become 'nothing now but credulity and prejudices,' and true religion a tissue of 'absurd mysteries.'"[132]

Menachem Mendel embraced his role as Rebbe and energetically led his people. He often talked to his dead father-in-law and claimed to receive answers. Rabbi Herschel Greenberg said, "Rebbe Joseph Isaac Schneersohn is the Messiah just as Rebbe Menachem Mendel Schneerson is the Messiah." He explained, "The Rebbe [Menachem Mendel Schneerson] is the Messiah of our generation who inherited this position from his predecessor the Rebbe Joseph Isaac Schneersohn, who, in a certain sense, share the same soul." This creative reasoning illustrates the mental and verbal gymnastics the Lubavitchers had to perform when it became clear that the Rebbe's messianic predictions were false. As Menachem Friedman and Samuel Heilman rightly note: "Jewish history is littered with messianic disappointments," just as Christianity is full of disappointments about the Second Coming.[133]

Joseph Isaac Schneersohn's vision of making Chabad one of the most important organizations for *Yiddishkeit* in the world has largely been realized, thanks to the dedication, perseverance, and leadership skills of his son-in-law, the seventh Rebbe. Chabad is one of the largest Hasidic communities globally, comprising approximately 200,000 committed adherents plus hundreds of thousands of non-Hasidic Jews who attend Chabad schools, synagogues, and study groups. There are more than 3,800 emissary couples in forty-five states and sixty-one foreign countries, and the movement has 2,766 institutions worldwide and an operating budget of close to $1 billion a year. The Rebbe's view—strengthened and greatly enlarged on by the seventh Rebbe—has motivated thousands of Lubavitchers to set up communities. This is, in essence, Chabad's mission, and it has been highly successful. They are the missionaries to Jews throughout the world, offering free study, free food, and free lodging at many of their centers—always with a smiling face and always with the hope of encouraging every Jew who crosses their threshold to become more of a Hasidic Jew.

In the summer of 1994 Rebbe Menachem Schneerson died without leaving an heir apparent, and Chabad suffered another crisis of leadership. Many in the community proclaimed that Schneerson was now the Messiah and that he would return from the dead to lead the Jews to Israel and establish God's earthly kingdom. Harris Lenowitz, an expert on messianic movements, says that even Schneerson "made it clear he was the messiah." Large signs declaring him the Messiah were erected on the George Washington Bridge linking New York and New Jersey, as if to convince the rest of the world. This controversial belief split the community, and many thought the movement might collapse. Some contend, however, that the debate is merely tactical; in other words, most believe that the Rebbe—Menachem Mendel—is the Messiah, but they question the wisdom of proclaiming it to those who might deny it. Two decades have now passed without a resurrection, and despite the crisis in leadership, the Lubavitchers remain the strongest Hasidic group in the world, and it continues to grow. Many claim the seventh Rebbe is still alive and that his spirit and influence are stronger than ever—some even claim that he speaks to them. In the building next to his grave, nonstop videos play his services and speeches. Despite the current divisions, if Rebbe Joseph Isaac Schneersohn could see what his movement and disciples have created, he would be proud and feel vindicated. Even though he could not save all the Jews of Chabad, he saved Chabad and raised a new generation of Jews. He would probably say that God had rescued him from Poland to make Chabad one of the most powerful Hasidic groups ever and to build a strong house of Torah in America.[134]

16

The Fate of the Rescuers

The evil that men do lives after them; / The good is oft interred with their
bones.
—William Shakespeare, *Julius Caesar*

While the Rebbe was conducting his activities in the United States,
Bloch had a dramatically different experience during World War II. To
give the reader a better understanding of the war on the Russian front
and the effort it took to roll Germany back, defeat Hitler, and liberate
the death camps, here I provide a detailed description of Bloch's life from
1943 to 1945. An understanding of his fate, as well as that of Canaris and
Wohlthat to some extent, gives one a better feel for how complex Nazi
Germany was and how varied the wartime experiences of the participants
could be. In addition, this chapter examines what ultimately happened to
the Germans who helped rescue the Rebbe.

If the Rebbe never alluded to his rescue, neither did Bloch. Indeed,
since he was in the secret service, he had been trained never to discuss his
work—not even with his wife.[1] Had he survived the war, Bloch might
have been more open. After rescuing Rebbe Joseph Isaac Schneersohn
and his entourage, he returned to his industrial espionage work, and in
late 1940 he was promoted to lieutenant colonel.[2] He commanded more
than forty officers and staff members. Bloch dined on occasion with industrialists such as Gustav Krupp von Bohlen and Max Schlenker; he
enjoyed the confidence of important executives, including those of the
giant IG-Farben cartel, which produced thousands of products for the
Third Reich (among them Zyklon B) and built a big factory at Auschwitz
(using slave labor and literally working them to death). Bloch provided
the military with information about the industrial capabilities of various
countries, and his corporate contacts helped him place spies abroad. His

[263]

job brought him into regular contact with both Canaris and Wohlthat. Early in 1941 he was ordered to assess the industrial capacities of the British Empire, the United States, and the Soviet Union—no small task. For his accomplishments in the Abwehr, Bloch was awarded the War Merit Cross Second and First Class with Swords.[3]

Bloch was so highly skilled and respected that in 1941 Field Marshal Walter von Reichenau wanted him to join his staff and advise Army Group South on economic matters, but the request was denied.[4] For a staunch Nazi like Reichnenau to request a half-Jew for such a critical job seems incredible. Obviously, he was familiar with Bloch's work and valued his expertise, which overrode his status as a *Mischling*.

Bloch served in the Abwehr until his petition to be sent to the Russian front as a battalion commander was granted in April 1943, and he was posted to the area around Kiev.[5] The army had denied Bloch's earlier requests for a combat command because of his age. His personnel file states no reason for the official change of heart, but several Abwehr officers were sent to the front at this time. One can assume that in the spring of 1943, as the Wehrmacht prepared for the battle of Kursk—the largest tank battle in history, with thousands of tanks on both sides—combat officers were in greater demand than industrial spies. Also, the Gestapo began investigating the Abwehr for antigovernment activities in April 1943 and arrested several of its members. Canaris himself came under suspicion, and his secret service ceased to function effectively. One of its alleged crimes was smuggling Jewish refugees out of Germany. Perhaps Bloch saw the handwriting on the wall and decided to get out of a situation that could turn dangerous for him.[6]

During the battle of Kursk, Bloch commanded troops in the rear, keeping the lines of communication and supply open for the soldiers at the front and for the combating partisans. After the disastrous defeat at Stalingrad during the winter of 1942–1943, Hitler had focused on a new offensive at Kursk. He hoped to regain the initiative and straighten his defensive lines in the east. By 5 July 1943, the day the battle began, the Germans had deployed 2,700 tanks, 2,500 planes, and almost 1 million men against Kursk, "the largest concentration of force against such a confined area yet seen on the Eastern Front." The Russians countered with more than 3,300 tanks, 2,650 planes, and close to 1.5 million men. The

Ernst Bloch (far right) on the Russian front, 1943. (Author's collection)

engagement was the biggest clash of armor to date and would be sur-
passed only by the First Gulf War.[7] Eleven days later, on 16 July, Hitler
ordered a withdrawal. Despite vicious fighting to penetrate the layers of
defensive works and minefields around Kursk, the Germans could not
break through.

One may wonder why Bloch left the Abwehr to participate in such horrible battles, but many German officers would not have found the move
strange. Bloch's son and his secretaries contend that he left because of his
ambition: his only opportunity for promotion was at the front, where he
felt he belonged.[8] Moreover, by 1943, Germany's recently expanded borders had begun to shrink, limiting the need for industrial espionage. Bloch
apparently preferred life on the front to life in the office. Adolf Ratjen, one
of Bloch's former subordinates, wrote to Bloch in September 1943: "I am
happy to hear from you, Herr Lt. Colonel, that things are going well with
you and can imagine that life out there is more satisfying for you than the
desk work that goes on here. We *I-Wi* [International Economic Intelli-
gence] people . . . often think of our earlier father [i.e., boss]." It was true

that Bloch hated desk work and preferred being out in the field with his men, reveling in the fraternity of warriors. He had grown up in the bloody trenches of World War I between the ages of sixteen and twenty. By now, Bloch was in charge of 1,000 men, and he was in regular contact with the enemy. He constantly monitored the positions of his men and advised them on their defensive works. Whenever his men engaged in combat, he immediately went to where the battle raged and took part in fighting Ivan (the Germans' nickname for the Russians).[9]

During the chaos of the loss at Kursk, the Germans were trying to secure their lines and stop the Soviets from pushing them back. Bloch led his battalion in numerous skirmishes and conducted an organized retreat as the Russians shoved the Germans backward. He constantly fought the cold, filth, hunger, and death that confronted him daily. In three months, Bloch's division had retreated more than 250 miles to an area around the town of Zhitomir (Zhytomyr) in the Ukraine, seventy miles west of Kiev. There, Bloch busied himself placing infantry units, artillery batteries, and specialized weapons units throughout his defensive lines. He described these diverse activities as managing a "Piccadilly Circus" (*Taubenschlag*). Each night, he slept in a different sector of the front, alongside his men. He worried that they might have to engage in guerrilla warfare (*Bandenkrieg*), which they were not really trained for. It was a horrific type of fighting in which no prisoners were taken. As one German soldier wrote: "Partisans were not eligible for the consideration due to a man in uniform. The laws of war condemned them to death automatically, without trial." But the partisans took no prisoners either and often mutilated any German who fell into their hands, decapitating them, cutting off their genitals, or forcing them to disrobe and submerging them in troughs of water in subfreezing temperatures. Antipartisan warfare was foreign to Bloch, but he believed that if he kept his eyes and ears open, he could quickly learn how to fight in this manner. Thinking of these matters, Bloch quoted Goethe's *Faust*: "Understanding and good sense find utterance with little art" (*Es trägt Verstand und rechter Sinn mit wenig Kunst sich selber vor*). Goethe's next line is: "And when you have seriously anything to say, is it necessary to hunt for words?" In other words, Bloch would eventually master this new form of fighting, but until then, he admitted that he was struggling.[10]

As a battalion commander, and due to his contacts from his Abwehr days, Bloch often met with several of the commanding generals in the area of operations. They sought him out either because of prior work they had done together or because of Bloch's important responsibilities. In September he met with General of the Artillery Ernst-Eberhard Hell, who was conducting rearguard operations for their sector of the front after the defeat at Kursk. Bloch found him to be an "excellent man" and a pleasure to be around, and Hell apparently approved of what Bloch had done with his men. In October he met with General of the Infantry Anton Dostler, whom he knew from the Abwehr. Dostler was also pleased with Bloch's work. Dostler was temporarily in command of the 213th Security Division while its commander, Lieutenant General Alexander Göschen, was on vacation. Bloch was on friendly terms with Göschen as well. He also corresponded regularly with Rear Admiral Otto Schulz and Vice Admiral Leopold Bürkner, who had worked in the Abwehr and took over the military intelligence office after Canaris left. Bloch's commanding officer, Colonel Mielke, was continually amazed at how many people Bloch knew.[11]

During the retreat from Kursk, Bloch had been ordered to destroy and burn everything so it would not fall into the enemy's hands. His men destroyed houses, food supplies, train tracks, streets, bridges, factories, and radio stations. There were fires everywhere. In carrying out their orders, they had to be careful to avoid being ambushed by *Kommandos*, who would be eager to "burn their camp around their ears" (*die Bude über dem Kopf anstecken*). In a letter to his wife, Bloch described the horizon, aglow with flames, as gruesomely beautiful. "One reluctantly thinks of the Thirty-Years War," he wrote. Morally, he struggled with the pain and suffering being inflicted on civilians, yet he knew his actions would help his men, and besides, he was obeying orders. Moreover, he thought of the hundreds of thousands of Germans who had lost their possessions or their lives, and this justified, in a way, what they were doing.[12] Living in this environment desensitized the German *Landser*, and the soldiers "fought from simply fear, which was our motivating power. The idea of death, even when we accepted it, made us howl with powerless rage."[13] Pressure by the Soviets probably caused Bloch's troops to do things they normally would not have done. In another sector, one *Landser* described the rear action as follows: "I remember two villages stripped of every scrap of food, and more than one massacre. Men were ready to commit murder for a quart of goat's milk, a few potatoes, a pound of millet. Starving wolves on the run don't have time to stop and talk."[14] Whether Bloch's men behaved this way is unknown, but this was probably not an uncommon scene on the Russian front.

Bloch often had to retreat, build new defensive positions, stay there a few days, and then, under attack, withdraw. Sometimes, he said, he had to march for six hours a day. On average, each man probably carried about eighty pounds of gear, including food, water, ammunition, weapons, books, sleeping bag, first-aid kit, compass, overcoat, knife, rope, and so forth. For a man who was forty-five years old, Bloch was in incredible physical shape. Just marching ten to twenty miles while carrying heavy gear would have been challenging. Bloch probably transported many things in his staff car when they moved from one town to the next, but as vehicles broke down and there was less gasoline to go around, Bloch probably had to carry much of his own gear.

In addition to all the movement, Bloch and his men had to fight the Soviets. As Bloch explained, "We defend ourselves on Russian soil, using Russian methods and with Russian brutality." Most of the Reds they fought were poorly trained, poorly fed, poorly equipped, and poorly led, but in the end, there were just too many of them. If they had just a few more panzer divisions, Bloch lamented, they could turn the tide. Despite the horror of war, Bloch enjoyed what he was doing. "I feel very good," he wrote to his wife, "that I have been able to experience a real piece of this war." On 2 October Bloch's men were able to hold their position, even though they had been hit hard. He described the difficulty of holding off the masses of Russians, and in some respects, he was overwhelmed by the sheer numbers the Soviets were putting in the field.[15]

German soldier Guy Sajer wrote about his Soviet counterparts: "Even the blindest saw that the Russian soldiers were moved by a blind heroism and boldness, so that even a mountain of dead compatriots wouldn't stop them. We knew that under such circumstances combat often favors simple numerical superiority, and much of the time we felt desperate." But when the communist horde came at them, they threw themselves "back into battle" and tried to "ward off the red monster about to devour us."[16]

Bloch must have witnessed the same events and had the same thoughts himself.

In November 1943 his regimental commander wrote that Bloch had adjusted quickly to life on the front. He had already been awarded the Iron Cross Second Class in October, and by December, the general of the division noted that Bloch was ready to command a regiment.[17] He was well on his way to becoming an accomplished leader of men in combat. During this time, the Soviets attacked the Zhitomir area in force. In preparation for this attack, Bloch had strategically placed his machine guns, antitank cannons, and mortars. Although the Ivans had increased in strength, the Germans made the Russians pay dearly for their offensive, although they too suffered casualties. The enemy used their tanks to good effect and surprised Bloch's men in many sectors.[18]

When Bloch withdrew his battalion to find another defensive position, he joined a column of armored trucks and started heading southwest. Suddenly, several Soviet tanks and infantry opened fire on them as they passed through a village. Bloch and his men instinctively jumped from their vehicles and took cover in the nearby ditches. Then they escaped to some neighboring woods, where the Russians pursued them for hours. That night, the Germans, who had "scattered like rabbits," came back together. Luckily, only a few had been killed.[19]

Soon thereafter the Germans counterattacked, but they failed to retake the area around Zhitomir. By 12 November, the Soviets had responded to their counteroffensive, and the Germans could hear the bombs exploding all around them. Bloch complained that the men in the security units were not first-rate troops, and they needed a strong leader to stay on top of them to make sure they kept their lines. Many of them were new to combat. Nonetheless, Bloch managed to find good leaders (*Beherzte*), and these men held it together. Moreover, his men had good camaraderie; they showed him great respect and willingly followed his orders.[20]

To embolden his men, Bloch read them the text of a speech Hitler had given on 8 November at the twentieth reunion of the Beerhall Putsch in Munich at the Löwenbräukeller:

We are fighting the fifth year of the greatest war of all time. As
it began, the enemy in the east was barely a hundred and fifty

kilometers away from Berlin. In the west, his fortresses threatened the Rhine; the Saar region was under fire from his artillery. And now . . . the National Socialist state has crushed this ring of encirclement in historically unique blows. The heroism of its soldiers pushed the fronts nearly everywhere over a thousand kilometers from the borders of the Reich. . . . You shall also leave here with fanatical confidence and the fanatical faith that there can be nothing other than our victory. We fight for this.

According to Bloch, this speech was full of "confidence and security and noteworthy conclusions about the glory of what is to come."[21] An SD (secret service) report claimed that this speech "had revived morale and confidence in victory."[22] Bloch thought his men needed such words of encouragement because, when one is waiting for battle in the front lines, one's thoughts can wander and morale can waver. As one *Landser* wrote:

Abandoned by a God in whom many of us believed, we lay prostrate and dazed in our demi-tomb. From time to time, one of us would look over the parapet to stare across the dusty plain into the east, from which death might bear down on us at any moment. We felt like lost souls, who had forgotten that men are made for something else, that time exists, and hope, and sentiments other than anguish; that friendship can be more than ephemeral, that love can sometimes occur, that the earth can be productive, and used for something other than burying the dead.[23]

Given such thoughts, Bloch was wise to try to embolden his men, to convince them that victory could be obtained and that they were fighting a just war.

By mid- to late November, Bloch's division was forced to move seventy miles south to the area around Winniza (Vinnitsa), a town in the Ukraine. Days of marching in the cold and damp, without food or water, took a toll on Bloch and his men. Their muscles ached, their feet turned bloody, and they were covered with lice. However, he assured his wife, "I am good, just sometimes exhausted and limping."[24]

As Guy Sajer wrote, the war was "smoking chaos, a wellspring of continuous fear, alarm and rumor, and thousands of explosions." He described what Bloch and his men must have felt: "The sound of firing and the groans of the wounded incited us to massacre the Russians, who had inflicted us with so many horrifying wounds."[25] The extreme cold only made the situation worse. Many of Bloch's letters mentioned the fight with the elements. When it turned dark, temperatures would drop thirty-five to forty degrees below freezing. Gasoline would freeze; oil would become gel and "then glue," blocking the mechanisms in cannons and rifles. "Many men died while performing their natural functions, as a result of a congelation of the anus." The woods rang out with bizarre noises as the bark on trees exploded under the pressure of freezing; even stones cracked when temperatures fell low enough.[26] Bloch was right to call this "the brutality of Winter" (*Brutalität des Winters*).[27]

In the letters to his wife, Bloch was often very forthright in his descriptions of war and its trials and tribulations. But words must have been inadequate to explain the realities of war in the east, where the men rarely had leave, fought hard on a daily basis, lost their friends, and experienced incredible hardships. The Wehrmacht in general, and Bloch and his men in particular, were deployed more widely and engaged in constant combat for longer periods than any other modern armed force. "For the *Landser*, combat consisted of a thousand small battles, a daily struggle for existence amid terrible confusion, fear, and suffering," writes Stephen Fritz. "Combat meant fighting in small groups, in sinister blackness or in the cold lonely bunkers, in crowded houses from room to room on windswept steppes against steel monsters, with each unit and each man—confused men with a need for one another—fighting for their lives, longing to escape their fate, leaving a trail of torn, mutilated, and dead flesh in their wake."[28]

During the retreat south, the earth shook from the artillery, and Bloch's men continued to fight off the Russians on their right and left. In fact, many forces were encircled at Zhitomir, but luckily for the Germans, one corridor remained open, allowing most of them to retreat. As Bloch moved his troops south toward Vinnitsa, he encouraged them along the way. As a good officer, he made sure he knew his men's names, their weapons, and their placements. By way of illustration, on 12 November, once they had settled into their foxholes and defensive positions, Bloch made his rounds as usual, but this time, he brought some cognac and made sure the men got a few sips from his makeshift bar. Such random acts go a long way toward building unit cohesion and loyalty. According to his secretaries Ursula Cadenbach and Bettina Motz, Bloch was good at this kind of thing at the Abwehr office, and he continued the practice on the eastern front with his *Jungs* (boys). The Soviet counterattack must have taken them by surprise, because Bloch lost a lot of his personal items, especially his books. Amazingly, Bloch often found time to read, and he quoted from the books and explored their meaning in letters to his wife.[29]

As the war dragged on, Bloch started to long for the comforts of home: showers, clean clothes, tables full of food. However, as soon as these thoughts invaded his mind, they immediately turned sour because everything was so "uncertain." Life for Bloch became a continual push-pull between doing his duty with absolute professionalism and preventing his men from dying, on the one hand, to wishing the war would end and he could return to his family, on the other. Paradoxically, although he loved the front and the adventure, he also wanted it to be over. Many veterans have expressed the same feelings: war was hell, and it took them away from their families, but it was also the only time they felt alive and experienced true friendship. Bloch eloquently described these strong emotions in letters to his wife: "You see from this letter in what type of arena my thoughts move, primitive and mindless. Perhaps the soul places a lot of worth on the possibility that exploring such musings will later bear much fruit." As Fritz rightly notes, "The *Landser* lived in a complex world, one both physically unstable and emotionally chaotic."[30]

Bloch witnessed the turning point for the Wehrmacht in the retreats he was conducting. When he first arrived on the front in the summer of 1943, he observed the last significant German offensive against the Russians. Unlike the invasion of the Soviet Union in 1941 (Operation Barbarossa) or Stalingrad in 1942, when the Germans had been able to push forward, the Russians would now stay on their heels until the final destruction of the heart of Nazi territory: Berlin. The Wehrmacht still had much punishment to inflict on the Red Army, but as Bloch's men did so, they were backing up almost daily.

In the face of these hardships, he wrote: "Familiarity breeds contempt. As a result, the soldier must continue to keep his goal in mind to overcome this reality. Times like this [make] one stronger and this is good [Bloch seems to be alluding to Nietzsche here: *Was mich nicht umbringt, macht mich stärker* (What doesn't kill me makes me stronger.)]. Later, I will be happy to claim these experiences as my own. As I walk through the hills, valleys and fields in the moonlit nights, I become calm and only the occasional firing of bullets interrupts my peace." Although Bloch candidly described his experiences, he was always mindful of what his wife Sabine was going through, especially the Allied bombing attacks on the capital. He reminded her that she "embodies Home and everything that is precious that I love."[31]

What was Bloch actually fighting for? One can glean from his letters that he was defending his homeland against communism. Bloch did not like Hitler, but he feared the Soviets more, as strange as this seems now.

At one point, Bloch picked up a book about German language and literature in one of the buildings near Vinnitsa. It was a "Bolshevik" propaganda piece, which Bloch mocked. He said the book proved that the Russians were corrupt and uneducated. He quoted from it, noting that the Soviets thought the ideas of Heinrich Heine had helped them construct a new nation; that Wolfgang von Goethe was a fighter for the progressive, communist concept of a "free land and free people"; and that Friedrich Schiller and Thomas Mann warred against the oppression of the feudal system. Bloch concluded that the Russians obviously considered themselves examples for everyone in the world and thought that other lands were primitive and backward. "One can only laugh," Bloch exclaimed, when reading such garbage. Bloch praised Germany's superior spiritual and cultural life, which the Russians had "no clue about" (*keine blasse Ahnung*) and no desire to understand. He was thankful that class warfare and ignorance in Germany had been vanquished 100 years before (he is probably referring to the Revolution of 1848). In other words, he viewed the system under Stalin as lacking culture, education, and a government worthy of a literate and educated people.[32]

So, in effect, Bloch fought to bring about the rise of German culture and to defend Deutschland against Soviet ideologues and uneducated thugs. Even though Bloch was fairly balanced in his approach to Hitler and the Nazis, maybe due to his Jewish background or his relationship with Canaris, he also viewed the war as a major clash of ideologies. Today, we know that Stalin was no better than Hitler, but Bloch did not see that. Bloch recognized that the Soviet Union was evil, but he failed to see that serving in Hitler's army and doing his bidding were not the best ways to get rid of Stalin.

Germany's focus on its archenemy in the east was summed up well in 1941 when religious leaders in Germany got behind Hitler's invasion and praised him. Protestant clerics sent Hitler the following telegram on 30 June 1941:

> You, my Führer, have banished the Bolshevik menace from our own land, and now summon our nation, and the nations of Europe, to a decisive passage of arms against the mortal enemy of all order and all western-Christian civilization. The German nation, including all its Christian members, thanks you for this deed. The German Protestant Church accompanies you in all its prayers, and is with our incomparable soldiery who are now using mighty blows to eradicate the source of this pestilence, so that a new order will arise under your leadership.[33]

Bloch was not alone in viewing Stalinized Russia as a major threat to civilization. This belief, as well as his loyalty to the army, gave his service meaning.

Even though the Germans had been rousted from the region around Zhitomir, Bloch wrote on 20 November about his excitement that the city had been retaken by the German Fourth Panzer Army. It would not last long, as the counterattack "petered out in the rain on the 26th."[34] The activities of the tanks to the north took some pressure off Bloch and his men, and they were able to have a church service. On this *Totensonntag* (Sunday before Advent, when the dead are commemorated), six evangelical preachers attached to the 213th Security Division addressed hundreds of men. Their sermons inspired the *Landser*, and they engaged in animated conversations. One of the main scriptures they discussed was the parable of the rich man and Lazarus (Luke 16:19–31).[35] A beggar named Lazarus lived at a rich man's gate. He ate the trash of the rich man and was so weak that as he lay in pain on the ground, "dogs came and licked his sores." When both men died, the rich man went to hell (*Hades*) and Lazarus went to heaven, where he was placed next to Abraham. The rich man looked up from the underworld and pleaded with Abraham to allow

Religious service held for some of Bloch's men on the Russian front, 1943.
(Author's collection)

Lazarus to dip his finger in water and cool the rich man's tongue with
it, "because I am in agony in this fire." Abraham denied the rich man's
request, saying that no one in heaven may go to hell, and vice versa. Then
the rich man pleaded with Abraham to have Lazarus raised from the dead
so that he could go to his father's house and tell his family the truth so
they would not end up in hell, like he has. Abraham coldly told the rich
man that if they did not listen to Moses and the prophets, whose teachings they already had, they would not listen to Lazarus.

Bloch did not specify what lessons the Protestant minister, probably
Rudolf Harney,[36] offered to those in attendance, but four possibilities
stand out. The first is that Jesus was using this story to warn people what
would happen if they did not believe in him. Since he had come to preach
the good news that salvation comes only through him, they had better
listen in this life, because if they did not, they would suffer "agony in . . .
fire" in the next life (Luke 16:24). As one religious commentator notes,
"Jesus made a poignant prophecy, although his listeners at the time probably missed the point. Many of them, especially the Pharisees, refused
to believe him even after he rose from the dead."[37] So, if the minister

was focused on salvation, he would have espoused the theology that only those who believe in Jesus will have eternal life. Those who refuse Jesus will burn in hell for eternity. This likely would have led to an animated debate among the Wehrmacht troops, especially since many of them were Christian and they faced death daily. They probably wondered what had happened to their countless friends who had died and what would happen to them if they fell. Perhaps the men in Bloch's unit debated who was going to hell and who was not. Those who were religious most likely believed that they would be saved, like Lazarus. Observant people tend to think that only others will go to hell, never themselves.

Why would the ministers preach hellfire? Fear can be a powerful motivator, and scaring people back to their faith is an age-old tactic. Some of the soldiers may have been doubting God. One German chaplain even described losing his faith, "now that he'd seen god's creatures tearing each other to pieces without the slightest trace of remorse."[38] So, the preachers may have used this lesson to bring some of the believers back into the fold, so to speak.

The second possible lesson of the parable concerns the danger of lusting for material goods and money. There is more merit in this lesson than in that of hellfire and damnation, but on the Russian front it seemed to have little relevance. Why would the ministers stress the evils of riches and wealth when most of the men just wanted a good meal, dry clothes, a woman's touch, and the war to end?

The third lesson involves the necessity of acting on information one knows to be true. Knowledge without action is futile and stillborn. In the military setting, this would have been the most appropriate lesson. In combat, complacency and lack of awareness of one's surroundings can be lethal. So the lessons of remembering one's training, checking and rechecking one's position and equipment, and following orders can help ensure survival and success in war. This would have been the most powerful lesson for these infantrymen.

The fourth lesson from this parable relates to what may have been a damning critique of the Nazis. This parable is a direct attack on the ancient "leaders of Judaism for their attitude to outcasts, and by implication the Gentiles."[39] Ironically, this story was being preached to *Landser* about a Jew (Jesus) condemning the leaders of Pharisaic Judaism for their racism and inability to embrace goyim. Moreover, these Pharisees do not even realize that those goyim will have a seat at the table of God and Abraham and that they, who practiced exclusion and discrimination, will rot in hell.

Harney, who was probably the lead preacher at the service, may have picked this theme to gently explore this tough issue. He was a member of the Confessional Church, which was in opposition to the dominant Protestant church that supported the Nazis, called the German Christians (*Deutsche Christen*). This parable claims that "the unpardonable sins are Inhumanity and Implacability." "It declares love to be the supreme duty, and it declares the disregard thereof to be, without exception, a deadly damning sin, because it is a duty which shines in the light of its own self-evidence. . . . 'Ye have the voices of conscience, hear them.'"[40] In the end, this parable teaches that kindness should rule the day and that those who are suffering should be helped and cared for. That millions of Jews were dying all around these men as they listened to this sermon strikes one as farcical. But if they knew about the Holocaust, they probably did not give it much thought. They were being attacked by the Russians, and they probably thought the brotherly love in this Bible story pertained to their own comrades. Bloch curtly noted that the lesson of the parable was urgently needed by his men (*eindringlich*).[41] He does not specify what that lesson was, but one hopes it was this last one.

Regardless of the discussions that took place that day, the most absurd thing about the whole event was that if Jesus had been there in their midst, he would have been arrested by the Nazis, placed on a train to Auschwitz, and exterminated. Nazi leaders and officers, regardless of their convictions, had taken an oath to Hitler and were fighting his war. Yet they were learning about the "King of Jews" and his teachings, many of which stood in direct opposition to Nazism.

On 24 November 1943 Bloch wrote to his wife and asked whether the raids (*Terrorangriffen*) on Berlin over the previous two days had harmed their family. He constantly worried about their welfare and the bombing attacks. His family lived in Potsdam, however, so he had less to worry about than men who had families in Berlin, like Wohlthat. He made a tongue-in-cheek comment to his wife that if Potsdam—a Mecca for Prussian militarism—were hit by bombs, Frederick the Great would rise from the dead and exact revenge. On this day he described the front as quiet and admitted that he was miserable with the rain and cold. The muddy earth was "grotesque," he said, making movement difficult and destroying boots. A few days later they continued their slow movement to the south. Bloch was troubled by the misery of the mothers and small children, who had little food and few possessions, standing out in the cold and the wind. "How the people everywhere are suffering," he noted. By the end of November, the cold and the deep snow forced Bloch to bundle up so heavily that he could barely move. Sometimes the temperature dropped to forty-five degrees below zero. "Some men fainted as the cold struck them, paralyzed before they even had a chance to scream." They covered their hands and faces with engine grease.[42]

During the struggle with the elements, Bloch continued to declare his love for Sabine. On 28 November he wrote: "Your letters bring much happiness and confidence and they give me a sincere and deep joy as I read them. When two people, like us, have declared their love to one another and built up a life together, then [one can handle anything that comes his way]."[43]

As they settled into new positions and new villages, partisans harassed their positions and the Soviet air force bombed and strafed their columns. Bloch did not lose any men, but the attack created much chaos, and people went a little crazy (*Kopflosigkeit*). In the harsh winter, the front stabilized somewhat, and Bloch settled in to adjust his lines and build up defense works. As he made his rounds, he constantly looked through his binoculars and made fun of himself, saying he was behaving like a General Staff officer. Things were quiet for now, but he knew that combat would soon return in all its fury (*wird schon wieder losgehen*).[44]

During this downtime, Bloch dealt with a mass of paperwork. Especially hard were the eight letters he had to write to the wives of fallen officers. If his battalion lost that many officers, at least 150 to 200 men must have died in the past several months of battle. Every place Bloch left, he also left a graveyard of men. Such was the reality of war on the Russian front. The matter-of-fact way he wrote about these men showed that Bloch had no fear for his own life.[45] As one *Landser* wrote, "In fact, none of us could imagine his own death. Some would be killed—we all knew that—but each one imagined himself doing the burying."[46] After Bloch wrote to these widows, he compiled his reports on the wounded officers, the recommendations for medals of valor, and the after-action reports. Through all the tough fighting, he and his men had become incredibly bonded. After finishing his paperwork, he found time in the evenings to read Theodore Fontane's *Stine*. Then, in April, he received wonderful news from his wife: she was pregnant with their fourth child (he must have had leave in August 1944, although the documents are silent on this point). He took great pleasure in discussing names for the baby and told her he was very happy (*Ich freue mich schon sehr*).[47]

Bloch soon began to wonder why he had not yet been promoted or received a regimental command. It is interesting to note that Bloch was concerned about his career and obviously believed that Germany would continue to exist in its present state, though somewhat battered and bloodied. He had run out of patience and started writing to his contacts because he worried that the Army Personnel Department had "forgotten him." His commander Colonel Mielke even called headquarters in Berlin to inquire about Bloch's promotion to full colonel. Bloch also asked his friend Vice Admiral Leopold Bürkner to look into the matter. As the Promotion Board dragged its feet, he and his wife fretted that his Jewish background might be holding him back. In the end, he did not think his "purification" (*bereinigte Sache*) had anything to do with it. However, he did suspect that something was happening; the head of the Reich Main Security Office, SS-Obergruppenführer Ernst Kaltenbrunner, had combined the Abwehr with the SD, and he thought this might have something to do with his delayed promotion.

Bloch was right to be concerned. Kaltenbrunner, Heydrich's successor, had already written on 3 March 1943 that traitors, homosexuals, half-Jews, men married to Jews, and Gypsies could not serve in special military units. Besides Kaltenbrunner, Bloch had another Nazi to worry about: Colonel (later Major General) Rudolf Hübner in the Army Personnel Department. This man was a fanatic Nazi, and Hitler would promote him in August 1944 to head the National Socialist Guidance Staff of the Supreme Headquarters of the Army. He was not someone Bloch wanted to have in control of his future prospects. Hübner wrote to Bloch and was noncommittal about his case. Bloch was disappointed and wrote to his wife: "I will, like so often, now follow your advice—'Stay where you are.'" So Bloch continued with his duties, trained his men, and practiced making them in his image (*Wie der Herr, so das Geschirr*—A slave resembles his master). In the spring his division was transferred to Kovel, about seventy miles northwest of Vinnitsa.[48]

As life under the Nazis became more difficult for Jews and *Mischlinge*, Canaris tried to protect Bloch. In 1943 Canaris added a statement in Bloch's files that he was "positive about Nazism." Canaris did all he could to shield his subordinates from potentially harmful Nazi officials. In 1944 Bloch's superiors described him as a "National Socialist," but a censor added a question mark next to this description. One of Bloch's secretaries had reported that he detested Hitler and told jokes about him. Ever mindful of the censors, he sarcastically wrote that when Mussolini was rescued by the Nazis and brought to Hitler's headquarters in Obersalzberg, he would be able to make new plans for the war. Bloch never belonged to the party, and both his son and his secretary claim he detested the Nazi regime, although he served the army loyally. There is no conclusive evidence either way: did Bloch became a "positive Nazi" on the surface, just to protect himself, or did he truly believe in National Socialism? Most likely, his commanders described him as a loyal Nazi without his knowledge, to protect him.[49] And in the short term, it kept the Nazi hard-liners from impeding his career.

In 1944 Bloch was finally, and surprisingly, given command of Regiment 177 of the 213th Security Division (*Sicherungs-Division*), which had more than 3,000 soldiers fighting on the Russian front around Kovel. He wrote proudly that now there was nothing standing in the way of his promotion, and he signed the letter to his wife "Regimental Commander."[50] Frau Rotraut Nonnemann wrote to Bloch's wife on 19 July 1944 to congratulate her on his promotion: "I have heard from some old *I-Wi* comrades that your husband finally received a regiment. I am terribly happy for him and hope that he has enough time to familiarize himself with his new task before the Russians are inside our region."[51] A family friend told Frau Bloch that he hoped she had good news from her husband because "he must be having a hell of a time fighting the Russians."[52] The friend was right. Bloch wrote on 27 June 1944 that they were in full contact with the enemy and continued to shell *Banditen* and destroy their bunkers. Quite often, when they went out on patrols, the Soviets ambushed his men. Bloch was in the thick of combat.[53]

Throughout June and July, Bloch and his men fought the enemy and were continually pushed westward. Bloch noted on 30 July that they were now in a region with paved roads, something the Ukraine and Russia generally did not have. Everyone was suffering from the long marches, the heat, and the dust. They were headed to their next position—a Polish town called Baranow, on the Vistula south of Radom and about 150 miles southwest of Kovel. In this last phase of the war, Bloch reflected:

> One thinks of the Thirty-Years War where the torch of destruction moved from one end of the land to the other. Sometimes there were a few years of peace, but then back to murder, robbery and plunder. Somehow, life blooms again from the ruins. People start over again and rebuild and expand. Life comes full circle between building and destruction. The person who has not understood and overcome this is to be pitied.[54]

For all intents and purposes, the war was lost, and many soldiers fighting for Germany knew it. But most, including Bloch, fought on. For his exemplary service, the army promoted Bloch to colonel on 1 June 1944. By 1945, Bloch's regiment had been devastated, and only a handful of the men were still alive. The Soviets were closing in on Germany's heartland. By then, Bloch was no longer in the army.[55]

On 2 January 1944 Hitler ordered one of his generals to compile a list of *Mischling* officers and officers married to Jews or *Mischlinge* who had received Hitler's *Deutschblütigkeitserklärung* (German blood declaration).[56] Bloch was one of the seventy-seven officers on that list. Hitler intended to discharge these officers, although that did not happen for several months.

After the failure of the 20 July 1944 plot to kill Hitler, he and many of his cronies declared *Mischlinge*, among others, the scapegoats.[57] Hitler no longer deemed *Mischlinge* worthy of living in the Reich and earmarked them for extermination. Bloch was possibly closer to death than he realized.

Martin Bormann, Hitler's right-hand man, wrote on 2 November 1944 that the "event of 20 July has shown the necessity to remove all people in positions of authority, who, owing to their ancestry, could be seen as a liability to the National Socialist ideology and its *Weltanschau-ung*." Even *Mischlinge* declared *deutschblütig*, Bormann believed, should be deprived of the rights of "Aryans." During the war's final days, Hitler discharged several dozen battle-tested officers, despite their prior Ary-anization.[58] The release of these officers was counterproductive at a time when Hitler needed every experienced soldier available.

The SS helped hunt down *Mischlinge* the Wehrmacht could not im-mediately locate, including Bloch. In September 1944 Heinrich Himmler, the Reichsführer of the SS, requested Bloch's discharge because of his Jewish ancestry, even though Bloch's commander had described him on 1 March 1944 as a "National Socialist . . . who has shown himself brave in the face of the enemy." Despite such positive reports, on 15 September 1944 Oberststurmbannführer Willy Suchanek wrote to General Wilhelm Burgdorf in the Army Personnel Department and requested Bloch's dis-missal and immediate deportation to a forced-labor camp.[59] On 26 Sep-tember Burgdorf confirmed that Bloch had been dismissed, but he noted that Bloch had previously received Hitler's "German blood" declaration and had asked to be "sent to the front despite his several wounds from the first world war." In spite of Burgdorf's halfhearted efforts, the army relieved Bloch of his command in October 1944. On 15 February 1945 Burgdorf signed the order officially discharging him.[60] The document read as follows: "The Führer has decided as of 31 January 1945 to dis-charge you from active duty. It is an honor to thank you on behalf of the Führer for your service rendered during war and peace for our people and Fatherland. I wish you all the best in the future. Heil Hitler."[61]

That Burgdorf, a sycophant of Hitler, actually tried to help Bloch is shocking. Burgdorf was the man who delivered the poison to Field Mar-shal Erwin Rommel in 1944, along with the ultimatum from the Führer to commit suicide.[62] He was no friend to enemies of the state, making his support of a half-Jew even more surprising. This proved how well respected Bloch was.

The discharge stunned Bloch, but when ordered to leave his regiment, he likely obeyed without question. He sent a copy of Burgdorf's letter to his life, along with a note: "Even though this is very difficult for me to take, at least the letter was written in a friendly manner." Walther Brock-hoff, a close friend of Bloch's, wrote to Sabine on 31 October 1945 to ask

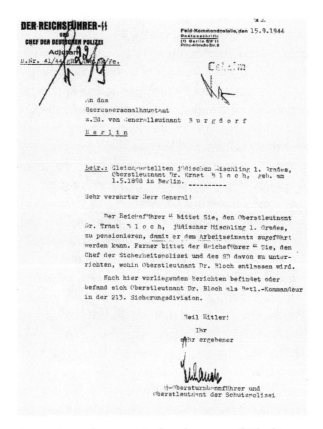

On 15 September 1944 Suchanek requested Bloch's
dismissal and deportation to a forced-labor camp.
(Bundesarchiv/Militärarchiv)

why her husband had been discharged. He could find no logic in it and
observed: "One does not dismiss a brave and battle tested officer away
from the front during the hour of the greatest danger. There have been
and will be few officers of his caliber."[63]

Returning home as a retired officer, Bloch was lucky not to be deported and sent to a forced-labor camp, as the SS had demanded. As the
war drew to a close, *Mischlinge* stood at the edge of the Holocaust's gap-
ing jaws, and tragically, many of them did not even know it. Even men
like Bloch, an ex–military intelligence officer, failed to see how dangerous
it was for them and their children to live under Hitler. At the close of

1944, Himmler ordered the execution of *Mischlinge* in camps before the enemy could liberate them. According to Harald Ettheimer, after the war, a fellow half-Jewish inmate discovered in camp documents "Himmler's order" to execute them.[64] Luckily for them, it was not obeyed. If such an order was given, SS commanders of Organization Todt (OT) camps did not enforce it.[65] Contrary to normal behavior in the Nazi camps, *Mischlinge* were free after their guards deserted their posts.

At the war's end, control over the OT camps disintegrated, leaving each camp commander to decide what to do with his prisoners. Some in the OT camps were offered the opportunity to fight in the Wehrmacht against the invading Allied armies. Horst Schmechel remembered that of the approximately 200 half-Jews in his camp, 3 chose this option when their commander, OT-Frontführer Bauer,[66] presented it to them.[67] Klaus Budzinski remembered that his SS camp commander gave the half-Jews weapons, addressed them as "my dear *Mischlinge*," and told them they would be fighting the Allies.[68] The Jews and *Mischlinge* who served in such units presented a confusing picture to the Allies. In September 1944 the *Miami Daily News* reported the bewilderment of US Army chaplain Martin M. Perley when twenty Wehrmacht prisoners of war requested "Jewish prayer books, Jewish scriptures and mezuzahs" after arriving from the battlefields of Normandy. All of them were half-Jews except for one, who was a full-Jew. Some had spent "months in German concentration camps [most likely OT camps], but when the manpower shortage in Germany became acute," the Nazis gave these men "uniforms, arms and ammunition and absorbed [them] into the German army." The fact that many of these men were taken from forced-labor camps and put back in the military shows that certain elements within the Nazi leadership were pragmatic in their approach to racial laws. The need for able-bodied fighting men overrode any eugenic conviction that these men should be removed from the population. This last-ditch effort by the Nazis was not uncommon. Gypsies and Gypsy *Mischlinge* were drafted at the beginning of 1945 into the ill-famed SS Special Regiment Dirlewanger and were given weapons to fight at the front.[69] Bloch would be drafted into a similar makeshift unit, but at the time of his discharge, he could not know this.

On 3 January 1945, probably under party pressure, the Wehrmacht issued one of its last orders regarding *Mischlinge*. It stated that employing "Jewish-*Mischling*" officers, even those with exemptions, in key positions and promoting them above the rank of colonel should be avoided.[70] This last order showed that the party was tired of "discovering" so many *Mischling* colonels and generals like Bloch, most of whom had been discharged in the fall of 1944. Discharging men in such high positions negatively affected both morale and the Wehrmacht's ability to fight efficiently.

It seems that only active-duty officers were discharged. Most reserve *Mischling* officers served until the war's end. Bloch probably would have been left alone if he had not been an Abwehr officer. Since the SS had taken over the entire military intelligence department, fanatics were in control of Bloch's personnel files from his Abwehr days, which did not bode well for his security. He is the only *Mischling* officer I have found whose personnel file included orders from the SS dictating his future. It is amazing he was not treated even more harshly, given that Himmler had taken an interest in his case. Roughly half the half-Jews documented in my research spent the last months of the war in concentration camps or OT forced-labor camps. The others continued to work, study, or serve, either because they were not found or because they had received exemptions.

Hitler's preoccupation with race, particularly his desire to discharge high-ranking and experienced officers like Bloch from their posts, targeted not only *Mischlinge* but also those married to *Mischlinge*. Few active officers escaped Hitler's discharge order. An exception was General Gotthard Heinrici, who was spared because of his exceptional military acumen. He was married to a half-Jew, and his quarter-Jewish son served with an "Aryanization" exemption, similar to Bloch's. Heinrici finished the war as an army commander and conducted the final battle of the Oder and the defense of Berlin.[71] In January 1945 Himmler repeated the order to send half-Jews to forced-labor battalions.[72]

By this time, Hitler was a physically sick man. Although he was only in his mid-fifties, his head and hands shook visibly (probably from Parkinson's disease), his eyes were bloodshot, and saliva sometimes trickled from his lips.[73] But even in this state of poor health, he was still obsessed with the Jews. His decision to send thousands of half-Jews, many of whom were Wehrmacht veterans, to forced-labor units instead of to the front showed his obsession with race. These thoughts were still on his mind just a few hours before he put a pistol to his head and pulled the trigger on 30 April 1945, saying, "Above all, I charge the leadership of the nation, as well as its followers to a rigorous adherence to our racial laws and to a merciless resistance against the poisoner of all people—international Jewry."[74] A few days later, the war ended.

Instead of going to an OT camp or a forced-labor assignment in late 1944, Bloch sat at home in Babelsberg, contemplating his future. He talked to various bankers and industrialists about employment after the war.[75] But a few months later, the Volkssturm (a paramilitary organization for civilian fighters) drafted Bloch into its ranks. He busied himself with digging trenches and setting up machine gun positions in the Michendorf forest, five miles south of Potsdam and twenty-five miles south of Berlin. As Bloch carried out his duties, he became irritated with many of the men there; they did not take their activities seriously, even though they could hear the bombs raining down on Berlin. A bizarre apathy seemed to have set in among the men of the Volkssturm as the end drew near.[76] Even so, Bloch was probably fortunate that he had been forced to leave his regiment, where the death toll was high. On 10 April 1945 Bloch wrote to his wife: "Unfortunately our whole regiment is decimated. Almost all the officers are dead, wounded, or missing. . . . However, the regiment has fought bravely to the bitter end holding its ranks excellently."[77] The Wehrmacht lexicon writes that the Russians "annihilated" (*vernichtet*) Regiment 177.[78]

In the Volkssturm, Bloch trained men and then fought next to them against the Soviet troops. These units were usually made of up boys aged thirteen to fifteen and old men over the age of fifty. Wehrmacht officers derisively referred to these units as "casseroles" because "they were a mixture of old meat and green vegetables." Although numbering 60,000 in Berlin, the Volkssturm could hardly be called an effective fighting force; it basically represented only a speed bump for the few million Soviets massed at the trenches. Bloch must have had mixed emotions—disgust that the Nazis would send such an unprepared and physically weak force into battle, and a profound sense of duty to protect the men and serve as their leader. As historian Anthony Beevor writes about the Volkssturm, it was "the Nazi Party's most flagrant example of useless sacrifice."[79]

Bloch wrote sarcastically of these units in 1944, ever mindful of the censor:

We have just received news of the creation of the Volkssturm. What an uplifting time. Necessary. A justifiable action, full of unshakable confidence. I am extremely happy that the leadership of the Reich has proven its strength, certainty and confidence. May our efforts be successful. I am certain that this way of conducting the war holds many promises. Obviously, our Christian belief does not rule the day right now. Christians would do the right thing even without an order from the state.[80]

Bloch knew he could not express his real opinion—that this was an insane idea—but his wife knew exactly what he meant. Even though he was sure this eleventh-hour effort would accomplish nothing, he busied himself with distributing supplies and teaching others how to set up defensive positions. By the end of the war, he had become less circumspect, writing in one of his last letters to his wife, "One could not imagine how insane things have become."[81]

The last time Bloch saw his family was at the christening of his fourth child, Maria, on 14 January 1945 at the Garrison Church in Postdam. On that day, he felt demoralized and worried about the future. From all his letters, it is quite obvious that he was a devoted father and adored his wife. To be unable to attend the christening himself must have caused him great anguish. Many in the capital saw the writing on the wall and looked toward the future with horror. Berliners often gave in to dark humor, telling one another during the Christmas season of 1944: "Be practical: give a coffin."[82] Bloch knew the Russians were getting closer to the capital, so he arranged for his family to take a passenger train to Wrisbergholzen, just south of Hildesheim, to be captured by the Americans. He decided to stay in Berlin and help defend the city. His oldest child, thirteen-year-old Martin, was in the Jungvolk and wanted to stay with his father and fight the Russians, but Bloch convinced him to go west with his mother. Bloch knew he probably would not survive, and he did not want his son to suffer the horrors of war.[83]

For the most part, only the World War I veterans in the Volkssturm, like Bloch, remained at their posts. They had been conditioned by their experiences in the trenches to maintain their positions until relieved. Also, the men in these makeshift units feared the military police (*Kettenhunde*), who were hanging "traitors"—those who had left their units without permission—throughout the city and along the routes to the front. Placards were placed around the suspended corpses that read: "Here I hang because I did not believe in the Führer." It is estimated that during the battle for Berlin, at least 10,000 German soldiers were executed as deserters. In the end, Bloch probably felt like the German soldier who said in January 1945, "We are lost, but we will fight to the last man."[84]

By late March 1945, Allied forces moving in from the west had taken the initiative and were advancing toward Berlin. More than 350,000 Wehrmacht troops were encircled in the Ruhr, the industrial heartland, with Ninth Army pressing in from the north and First Army from the south. "Hitler had ordered the 350,000 Germans trapped in the pocket to organize into small groups and escape to the east. A few did, but most lost their will to resist." Allied troops overran concentration camps as they advanced, liberating the few emaciated and ill survivors they found living like animals in the appalling conditions; many of the inmates did not know about the Allied invasion of Europe. The camps contained Jews, political prisoners from various countries, and suspected Allied collaborators. General Dwight D. Eisenhower ordered that the remains of the victims of the camps be buried in public places, with crosses or stars of David marking each grave. Engineers precisely laid out the graves, which were dug by leading citizens from nearby towns, and local residents viewed the remains before burial. Jewish, Protestant, and Catholic chaplains participated in the funeral services.[85]

On 12 April 1945 Franklin D. Roosevelt, the only president many of the American fighting men had ever known, died, and Harry S. Truman succeeded him. By 16 April, organized German resistance had ended in the Ruhr pocket, and most of the remaining 325,000 troops had surrendered. More than 200,000 slave laborers and 5,600 Allied prisoners were liberated. German troops were aware that the end was near, and they were anxious to surrender to American, British, Canadian, or French troops rather than become prisoners of the vengeful Soviets. In early May an entire German army of about 150,000 men, including ten generals accompanied by their wives or mistresses and aides, surrendered to an American division of 10,000 troops.[86]

At this time, as the movie *Downfall* depicts so well, Berlin lay in ruins, largely destroyed by Allied bombs and Soviet artillery. For the 3 million German citizens who remained in the metropolis (120,000 of them infants), there was no water, no electricity, no supplies, and no hope for the "thousand-year Reich." Civilians and soldiers alike were covered with lice and suffered from dysentery due to the unclean drinking water. As a result, streets and soldiers' "trenches became squalid."[87]

Most lived in fear not only of the impending Russian onslaught but also of the constant Allied bombing. On 3 February Allied bombs left 22,000 dead in the German capital; on 13 March an additional 2,500 citizens died in another air raid, and 120,000 found themselves homeless. Suicides increased dramatically as the enemy neared the city's gates. Hitler's thousand-year Reich, barely more than a dozen years old, would soon end. Wild dogs roamed the streets looking for food and rotting bodies in the piles of rubble. Two and a half million Soviet soldiers were laying siege on the urban landscape, while Hitler remained holed up in his bunker. Lines of trenches zigzagged through the city parks, especially the large one called Tiergarten Zoo, and makeshift barriers along the streets were all that remained of the mighty German defenses. Young boys in the Hitlerjugend and old men in the Volkssturm manned the battlements and offered minimal resistance to the Soviets and their 6,250 tanks and self-propelled guns. Stalin must have taken great satisfaction in knowing that his mechanized force deployed to capture Hitler's capital dwarfed the force Hitler "had deployed to invade the whole of the Soviet Union." Even so, it was painstaking work; the Russians had to clear the city street by street and block by block, killing all those who offered opposition. In the process, the Russians would suffer 78,291 killed and 274,184 wounded.[88]

The Soviets, enraged by the brutal killing of 20 million of their citizens, including the cruel murder of over three million Red Army POWs in German custody, rarely took prisoners, and the Germans seldom surrendered to them. One Soviet army slogan read: "There will be no pity. They have sown the wind and now they are harvesting the whirlwind."[89] The Nazis had whipped, raped, and murdered countless women during the war. In one instance, the notorious Dirlewanger Brigade burned down three hospitals with patients inside, then, as was the custom, took the nurses back to the camp to be gang raped before being hanged naked alongside the doctors to the accompaniment of flute music. Now it was the Russian

soldiers who often brutally raped German women and girls, sometimes repeatedly. Some estimate that more than 100,000 Berlin women were raped
during and after the siege, 10,000 of whom later died of internal bleeding
or suicide. About 2 million rapes occurred, with Soviet military approval,
in East Germany (Prussia, Pomerania, and Silesia) and Berlin. The Soviets
boasted that at least they did not kill the women, as the Nazis had their
citizens. One Russian major claimed the "grandmothers" probably liked
the sex—their first "action" in years (one cannot imagine a more grotesque
and misogynistic response to these crimes). In the night, the screams of
young girls and women echoed in the streets of the German cities occupied by the Soviets. Even women freed from concentration camps and
forced-labor plants did not escape the Soviet army of sexual criminals,
who justified their crimes as punishment for Nazi atrocities. Some women,
knowing what awaited them when the Russians arrived, murdered their
own children by cutting their wrists and then committed suicide themselves. Sometimes, like at Masada, men killed their wives and children and
then took their own lives to prevent them from falling into the hands of
the Soviets. Desperate civilians trying to run from the invading Soviets
would sometimes be overtaken by T-34 tanks and killed. As Guy Sajer described it: "Cruelty has never been more fully realized, nor can the word
'horror' ever adequately express what happened."[90] This "horror," albeit
criminal, was nothing like what happened at Auschwitz, but as many psy-
chologists will attest, abuse begets more abuse. Sergeant Albert Kerscher,
a Tiger tank commander and Knight's Cross holder, recalled:

> My unit was caught behind the Russian lines so we were in a fighting
> retreat. We would often look at the road signs identifying the east
> Prussian and other German towns as we were forced back. We
> finally stopped reading the signs to mark our retreat. We simply
> counted hundreds of women who had been raped, killed and nailed
> to the doors of homes, barns and businesses. Some were tied to
> lampposts naked showing their abuse.[91]

In this scene of purgatory, Bloch must have felt confused, angry, and
lost. One can only guess what he told his men to encourage them to keep
the integrity of their lines, or what hope he gave them for the future. Ger-

man soldiers often told each other, "Enjoy the war because the peace will be terrifying" (*genießt den Krieg der Frieden wird fürchterlich*). Churchill described the situation perfectly when he wrote, "You may have to fight when there is no hope of victory, because it is better to perish than live as slaves." General Heinrici did all he could to defend Berlin, but he had little to work with.[92]

In late April 1945 the Soviets closed in on the German capital. From 21 April to 2 May, Soviet artillery fired 1.8 million shells against the city. Explosions, shrapnel, death, and destruction were hourly experiences.[93] Just a couple of weeks earlier, a comrade from Bloch's regiment in Russia, Captain Pfeiffer, had written him an emotional letter describing the sad state of the troops facing the war's imminent end: "We have become poor and insignificant. Now it is our responsibility to clean up everything which this short-sighted government has destroyed."[94] Bloch continued to fight just outside of Berlin at Nikolskoe, near Wannsee. After repelling several Russian attacks, he reportedly led a counterattack against Soviet lines, throwing grenades into their midst and firing his submachine gun as he advanced. A mortar shell landed right behind him, and he died when a piece of shrapnel blew a hole in his neck.[95] It was 30 April 1945—one day before his forty-seventh birthday, and just a little more than a week before Germany's final defeat. On the same day, Hitler would commit suicide with his new bride, Eva Braun, accelerating the Götterdämmerung.

It seems like Bloch was buried near where he died in battle. Historian Anthony Beevor describes the circumstances of the Germans defending Berlin: "Too badly wounded to be moved [they] were left to suffer where they lay. Few had any strength left to bury the dead. At best bodies were rolled into a ditch or shell crater and some sandy soil thrown over them."[96] This was probably what happened to Bloch.

After the war, a childhood friend of Bloch's, Karl Pries, honored Sabine Bloch's wish that he find her husband's body or grave so that she could get a pension to support her four children. He reported the results of his search in a letter dated 24 October 1946:

My dear Sabine . . . we have finally been able to find Bloch's body. . . . I believe that we can be certain that this corpse is Bloch's because of its obvious features. The corpse . . . is in unbelievably good

condition. One can still see the scar on his mouth. The lower and
upper jaw showed the horrible wound inflicted on his teeth with
their gold crowns. The color of the hair was most definitely that of
Bloch's. . . . Bloch had a large wound in the neck which certainly
killed him instantly. The face was for all intents and purposes very
peaceful without any signs of trepidation, and his mouth was closed.
As a result, it is my opinion that Ernst had a fast and beautiful
soldier's death which many would have envied.[97]

The family was lucky to find Bloch. Most men ended up in unmarked
graves and were forever forgotten. Even today, around 1,000 bodies are
found each year inside the city limits, to the south in the pine forest, and
along the Seelow Heights approaching Berlin from the east. Most were
Germans who gave their lives for their country in 1945.[98]

Once the body of her husband had been found, Frau Bloch had the
evidence required to receive a widow's pension. Some of Bloch's children
were upset with their father for staying in the Volkssturm when he could
have escaped. His actions do seem strange, but as an officer trained in the
Prussian tradition, he regarded duty to his country as his highest calling.
Like Canaris, he lived in a schizophrenic world, condemning Hitler and
his regime but, because of his upbringing and training, loyally serving his
commander in chief and his country.

Canaris, unlike Bloch, continued his Abwehr activities, collecting
intelligence for the Wehrmacht but also pursuing his goal of persuading
high-ranking officers to oppose Hitler. As a result, his Abwehr became
a haven for men like Hans Oster, who planned to kill Hitler. Oster hated
Hitler and his Nazi elite "from the very depth of his soul" for their "lying demagogy" and "moral corruption." Other men in Canaris's Abwehr
continued to rescue Jews, and Canaris often used his power to "get victims of Nazi persecution safely across the German frontiers."[99] Besides
the Jews Bloch rescued, the Abwehr helped several hundred others escape "over the frontiers of the Third Reich."[100] Canaris did his best to
uphold the honor of the Wehrmacht and often ordered sabotage measures
against Hitler's orders. Unfortunately, the Nazis arrested many of Canaris's men, including Oster, in 1943 and placed Canaris under surveillance.
Consequently, in February 1943 Canaris was dismissed from his post, and

the SS eventually took over the Abwehr. The authorities gave Canaris an unimportant job in the summer of 1944 in the Special Staff for Mercantile Warfare and Economic Combat Measures, where the Gestapo kept a close watch on him. After the attempt on Hitler's life in July 1944, the Nazis arrested Canaris, although they had no proof of his involvement in the bomb attack that almost killed Hitler.[101] After months of interrogation and imprisonment at the Flossenbürg concentration camp, the Nazi court convicted Canaris of treason in April 1945 and sentenced him to death. Before he died, he told a fellow prisoner: "I die for my country and with a clear conscience. You, as an officer, will realize that I was doing my duty to my country when I endeavored to oppose Hitler and to hinder the senseless crimes by which he has dragged Germany down in ruin. I know that all I did was in vain, for Germany will be completely defeated." On 9 April the SS hangmen came to his cell, stripped him naked, marched him to the gallows, and hanged him. On the Führer's instructions, those who were hanged "were suspended from hooks on an iron girder . . . by a thin cord." Consequently, they died a slow and painful death. Hitler ordered all executions filmed, and for quite a time thereafter, on an almost daily basis, he watched the films of the men dying "in his private cinema at the Wolf's Lair."[102] Hans Baur, Hitler's pilot, commented on this bizarre ritual: "Hitler would leave after lunch and watch many hours of these executions. I asked him why, what purpose did it serve. He said, 'Baur, a soldier must savor every victory. In watching my enemies die I see that I am truly protected by a special being, perhaps God for a greater purpose.'"[103]

After Canaris succumbed, his corpse was placed on a wood pile in the camp and incinerated. The smell of burning flesh filled the air as Canaris's bodied shriveled up and then slowly broke apart and turned to ash. Hitler would later claim that it was traitors like Canaris who had prevented him from conquering the world, and he blamed them for the fact that he was forced to live in a "gray bunker where he scuttled like a rat beneath the rubble of the city that was to have been the crown of his kingdom of a thousand years."[104]

Helmuth Wohlthat had a totally different ending. Soon after the Rebbe was rescued, Wohlthat was part of an economic delegation sent to Japan in late 1940 or early 1941, where he remained until the war's end. Once war broke out between Japan and the United States, he was unable to bring his family to Japan. This may have been a relief, since his marriage was on the rocks. It had started out on the wrong foot: his second wife, Margarethe, had taken Wohlthat away from his first wife, Cläre née Hesemann (Margarethe's cousin), after a torrid affair. For obvious reasons, this led to a strained family dynamic that only worsened over the years. So being sent to the Far East for work gave Wohlthat an acceptable excuse to absent himself from an unpleasant—albeit self-created—situation. After Japan surrendered to America, he was interned by the US Army and remained in Japan for another two years. On his release in 1947 he returned to Germany, where he went through a de-Nazification process that he quickly passed. Robert T. Pell even wrote a recommendation for Wohlthat, praising his courage for staying in touch despite being pressured by people like Himmler to break off contact with the Americans. Such an endorsement surely helped Wohlthat's case.

He was not successful on all fronts, however. Margarethe immediately divorced Wohlthat upon his return. She was enraged that he had abandoned his family for so many years—not only her and their daughter but also his three children by his first wife. Fortunately, they all survived the war in the Rhineland. Margarethe's home had been destroyed in October 1943, and she moved to a small village in Pomerania called Lychen, about fifty miles north of the German capital. Interestingly, she was able to avoid the brutality of the Russians because, for the last two years of the war, she had hidden the famous Jewish music professor and composer Siegfried Borris, his Indonesian wife Condoo, and his half-Jewish daughter Kaja. After the war, Borris explained to the authorities that Margarethe had saved him and his family, giving her and her daughter some temporary protection from the raping, pillaging Soviet conquerors.

After the de-Nazification process, Wohlthat set up an office in New York City and started a consulting business that kept him traveling between the United States and Germany for the next three decades. He remarried in 1956. His third wife, an American woman named Madeleine Fischer, was German by birth. She had fled Nazi Germany in 1933 with her Jewish husband and was a widow when she met and fell in love with Wohlthat. He died in Germany in 1982, having never discussed this story with his family.[105]

What Would Have Happened if Hitler Had Won the War?

Historians are reluctant to answer hypothetical questions, but there is significant evidence to suggest the outcome if Hitler's Germany had won the war. For one thing, the Nazis' "mechanism of destruction" would have engulfed the half-Jews like Bloch. As Ursula Büttner wrote, "It was only a question of time when [half-Jews] too should share the fate of the 'full Jews.'"[1] Quarter-Jews, like Bloch's four children, would have faced further discrimination, selective sterilization, and possible extermination. The elimination of *Mischlinge* had already been conceived in the 1930s. According to article 5, section 2, paragraph (c) of the first supplementary decree to the Nuremberg Laws, issued 14 November 1935, any half-Jews born after 15 September 1935 would be considered Jews.[2] Also, as state secretary Wilhelm Stuckart and minister adviser (*Ministerialrat*) Hans Globke wrote in their 1936 commentary on the racial laws, the disappearance of the *Mischling* race was the aim of the legal solution to the "*Mischling* Question."[3]

The Nazis continually betrayed their true plans for the *Mischlinge*. For example, when the Nazis discovered that a half-Jew had not left the Jewish community and had tried to marry his pregnant Aryan fiancée, the SS sent him to Auschwitz and commented, "We'll do everything we can so that not only the full-Jews, but also the *Mischlinge* will disappear."[4] The Nazis believed this would eliminate the disguised Jew, whom they considered the most dangerous of all Jews.[5] They were obsessive about "Jewish blood."

In 1943 Himmler informed state secretary Hans Heinrich Lammers, head of the *Reichskanzlei*, that the *Endlösung* would include half-Jews.[6] Dr. Richard Hildebrandt, head of the SS Main Office for Race and Resettlement, wrote to Himmler on 17 March 1943 about the final solution of the "Jewish *Mischling* question" (*Endlösung der Judenmischlingsfrage*). He said that SS-Standartenführer (SS Colonel) Dr. Bruno Kurt Schultz had recommended further testing of quarter-Jews in the future to determine whether they looked racially inferior. Those who "looked Jewish" should be treated like half-Jews. To justify this policy, he argued that a quarter-Jew could have inherited more than 25 percent "Jewish blood" from his half-Jewish parent.[7] Himmler notified Bormann on 22 May 1943 that he wanted the children of *Mischlinge* tested "just like plants and animals," and those who were racially inferior would be sterilized, thus safeguarding the German gene pool.[8] Himmler believed that "*Mischlinge . . .* were particularly unpleasant occurrences" and implied they were "freaks" of nature.[9] If it had been up to Himmler, he would have included half-Jews in the *Endlösung* from the beginning. In the summer of 1944 Himmler's office issued a statement that if any *Mischlinge* were still alive in 100 years, they would be only "*Mischlinge* of the third, fourth and fifth degrees." The hope was that half-Jews and quarter-Jews would be extinct by then. "The removal of Judaism from our German Reich," the memorandum continued, "and the purification of our German *Volk* from Jewish-*Mischling* blood is the greatest racial-political task presently."[10] But before the systematic deportation and total expulsion of *Mischlinge* could be carried out, German society would have to be desensitized to *Mischling* persecution. The decision to deport half-Jews to OT forced-labor camps in 1944 was a big step in that direction. Until then, the plan to deport and exterminate *Mischlinge* had been largely theoretical.

However, German *Mischlinge* were fortunate compared with their non-German *Mischling* counterparts. In the eastern territories, non-German *Mischlinge* had already been marked for extermination. The Reich Main Security Office for the Eastern Territories wrote in the summer of 1941: "In view of the Final Solution . . . it appears necessary both from a political and a racial standpoint, in order to avoid a later recovery of the Jews, to define the concept of a Jew as broadly as possible. . . . Anyone who has one parent who is a Jew will also count as a Jew."[11] The meaning of this policy was clear: all half-Jews in the eastern territories would be deported to death camps; there would be no segregation of half- and full-Jews, as there was in Germany. Hans Frank, the governor general of occupied Poland, included *Mischlinge* in his extermination scheme, writing in a report dated 16 December 1941:

> The Jews are for us also very parasitical eaters. We have in the General Government an estimated 2.5 million, maybe together with *Mischlinge* and all that hangs on, 3.5 million Jews. We can't poison them, but we will be able to take some kind of action which will lead to an annihilation success and I am referring to the measures to be discussed in the Reich. The General Government will be just as *judenfrei* as the Reich.[12]

Frank believed the Nazis would be free of the "Jewish disease" only when the *Mischlinge* were exterminated as well.

The policy implemented in Poland and other areas would follow this line of thinking. For example, in the summer of 1940, *Mischlinge* in Poland were already being pushed into ghettos.[13] Half-Jews there were included in the plans for deporting Jews to concentration camps. Some *Mischlinge* from Greece, Hungary, and Italy were deported as well.[14] Viktor Klemperer, professor of Romance literature at the Technical University of Dresden, had met Danish *Mischlinge* who had to wear the Jewish star, in accordance with the law decreed after Heydrich's assassination on 4 June 1942.[15] Half-Jewish Danes felt compelled to leave Denmark; of the 5,919 refugees of Jewish ancestry who fled Denmark for Sweden, 1,310 were half-Jews.[16] The Nazis also forced half-Jews to identify themselves as Jews in Luxembourg, Holland, northern France, Vichy France, Belgium, Poland, the Baltic states, and the Soviet Union.[17] One can safely conclude that hundreds of thousands of non-German *Mischlinge* ultimately died in the Holocaust.

The Nazis treated German *Mischlinge* better than non-German *Mischlinge* in an effort to maintain popular support among Aryan Germans, particularly relatives of *Mischlinge.* Non-German *Mischlinge*, especially those in the east, had no such lobby group.[18] From the racial scientists' point of view, a German half-Jew was still half-Aryan, and since all things Aryan were to be preserved and encouraged, the policy regarding German *Mischlinge* was problematic at best. This ideological dilemma took so long to resolve that the war ended before the Nazis could deport the German half-Jews to the death camps.

Nonetheless, Himmler wanted German half-Jews and Jews who were married to Aryans destroyed.[19] Several brutal acts against German *Mischlinge* had already been committed, and an institution had been set up specifically to exterminate *Mischlinge*.[20] Wilhelm Kube, general commissar for Belorussia, wanted to know in 1941 whether German Jews and *Mischlinge* should be given exemptions. Apparently, he felt uncomfortable exterminating "part-Jews (*Mischlinge*), Jews with war decorations, or Jews with 'Aryan' partners."[21] Based on the documentary evidence, it seems that Germans of Jewish descent were not given preferential treatment and were earmarked for murder. In 1942 Gestapo chief Heinrich Müller ordered that Jewish and half-Jewish inmates of concentration camps be sent to the extermination camps.[22] In 1943 some German half-Jews and Jews married to non-Jews were sent to the Warsaw ghetto.[23] Hauptsturmführer (SS Captain) Alois Brunner, a deportation expert, deported some German *Mischlinge* to the east in 1942–1943. During an investigation of one *Mischling*'s papers, he crossed out the word *Mischling* and wrote "Jew," saying: "What? Y'er a *Mischling*? . . . Y'er a dirty Jew."[24] Between 1943 and 1944, *Mischling* children from welfare institutions were sent to Hadamar's euthanasia center, where they were poisoned.[25] On 9 November 1944 an article in *Der Stürmer* stated: "The Jews that we still have aren't as dangerous as the half-Jews because these half-Jews can mix in with the German population. . . . Hopefully the time will quickly come, when this dangerous pack of people won't be allowed to do what they want to. If the half-Jews aren't taken care of, then the Jewish-question will only be partially solved."[26] The article reflected what many Nazis desired. They believed that the destruction of European Jews would be final only when all the half-Jews were eliminated.

By late 1944 and early 1945, the Nazis had deported some *Mischlinge* from the Reich to Theresienstadt.[27] During the evacuation of Auschwitz in late 1944, the SS transferred the *Mischlinge* there to Ravensbrück.[28] Hans Kirchholtes, who served in an OT camp near Hamburg, remembered that many half-Jews were interned in the Neuengamme concentration camp.[29] Wolf Zuelzer's mother, a half-Jew who was married to an Aryan, had to wear a Jewish star and was forced to work in a munitions factory; she was later deported to Theresienstadt.[30] My earlier studies documented that some German half-Jews were deported to Auschwitz, Buchenwald, Minsk, Groß-Rosen, Sachsenhausen, and Dachau.[31] Presumably, many were sent to these camps because they had disobeyed Nazi orders or escaped from OT camps.

The alternative to exterminating half-Jews was to sterilize them. The Nazi regime sterilized some 400,000 people during its twelve years in power.[32] Hans-Oskar Löwenstein de Witt, a *Geltungsjude*, claimed he knew a young *Mischlinge* couple, ages eighteen and nineteen, whom the Nazis forcibly sterilized.[33] Half-Jew Gerhard Bier recalled one half-Jew who volunteered for sterilization because he had been promised he would be spared deportation.[34] Holocaust historian Yehuda Bauer notes that although "no clear policy was adopted, experiments in sterilization were made and undetermined numbers of *Mischlinge* were thus crippled."[35] Fritz Steinwasser, a quarter-Jew, claimed that his uncle found SS documents outlining plans to sterilize the Jews and *Mischlinge* in their family and then send them to the east.[36] However, universal sterilization of German *Mischlinge* was not implemented because Hitler never gave his approval.

Surviving *Mischlinge* ultimately owe their lives to Hitler's inability to decide whether to execute them like Jews, sterilize them, or deport them. Hitler probably feared social unrest if he exterminated half-Jews. The backlashes against the government that occurred after *Reichskristallnacht* in 1938,[37] after the discovery of the euthanasia program in 1939–1941,[38] and during the *Rosenstraße* protest outside Goebbels's office in 1943[39] indicated that unrest was likely if too many Germans were personally affected by the persecution. Historian Mark Roseman notes that Hitler was "intensely sensitive to issues of morale and public opinion."[40] According to Hannah Arendt, a "'forest of difficulties,' in SS-Obersturmbannführer Adolf Eichmann's words, surrounded and protected them [the *Mischlinge*]—their non-Jewish relatives, for one, and for another, the disappointing fact that the Nazi physicians, despite all their promises, never discovered a quick means of mass sterilization."[41] As a result, Hitler repeatedly said he would deal with the half-Jews after the war. Many *Mischlinge* today have little doubt about their fate if Hitler had continued to rule. Reiner Wiehl said, "[Had Hitler won], my mother, my sister, myself—all dead!"[42] Robert Braun asked, "After Hitler killed six million Jews, what would it mean to him to kill several thousands of *Mischlinge* to keep German blood pure?"[43] Wilhelm Dröscher wrote in 1946 that had Germany won the war, "that would have meant the end of me."[44]

Interestingly, Hitler condemned others for their softness on the Jewish question and rejected those who treated anyone of Jewish descent leniently. Yet he often made exceptions to his own ideology. Nonetheless, the *Mischlinge* situation was on the verge of turning into a nightmare, and given Hitler's track record, it is clear how it would have turned out.

Conclusion

Man is oblivious to his own shortcomings; more, he fails to recognize his
personal fault.
—Rebbe Joseph Isaac Schneersohn, *On the Teachings of Chassidus*

Do not condemn your fellow man until you have stood in his place.
—Hillel

All too often, the history of Nazi Germany is depicted as a morality
play, a story of good and evil, victims and perpetrators. Such a dichot-
omous view fails, however, to account for the complexity of the Third
Reich, not to mention the complexity of human motivation and behavior.

In this polarized view, on one side stand the courageous, altruistic
American liberators of oppressed Europe. But the truth is that heroic
America was reluctant to act for a dangerously long time. American of-
ficials failed to respond not only to the pleas of thousands of desperate
European Jews who wished to escape to the United States but also to
Germany's request at the 1938 Evian conference to let Jews emigrate.[1] It
took a group of extremely influential politicians—including Secretary of
State Cordell Hull; assistant chief of the State Department's European
Affairs Division, Robert T. Pell; Postmaster General James A. Farley;
Supreme Court Justice Louis Brandeis; Senator Robert Wagner; attorney and member of FDR's "brain trust," Benjamin V. Cohen; and several
others—to steer Rebbe Schneersohn's case through the bureaucratic Ber-
muda Triangle. As Max Rhoade wrote, "The size of the task and its maze
of angles are only too obvious."[2] Without such a powerful and persistent
lobby in Washington, the chances of an average European Jewish refugee
reaching America were slim to none.

As this story shows, anti-Semitism was by no means unique to the

Third Reich. Anti-Semitic, anti-immigrant sentiments and a lack of com-passion for refugees had infected the European Division on the third floor of the State Department, especially during the tenure of Breckin-ridge Long. A small group of experienced, well-educated bureaucrats that included Long, Avra Warren, and others was able to thwart the will of the president of the United States, Secretary of State Hull, Undersecretary of State Sumner Welles, and Treasury Secretary Henry Morgenthau, as well as hampering rescue efforts by dedicated lawyers, officials, and bureau-crats at various levels of the government; the First Lady; and numerous Jewish groups. Knowing this, one is shocked that the Rebbe's case got the attention it did and that he made it out of Nazi Europe.

Anti-Semitism was prevalent in American society as well, although in a far less virulent form. Father Edward Coughlin, an Irish Canadian priest, came to Detroit and began religious radio broadcasts in opposition to the Ku Klux Klan, which had burned a cross on his church lawn in 1926. After CBS took his broadcasts national, the priest became increasingly political and antisocialist in the 1930s. At first, Coughlin was strongly in favor of the New Deal and capitalism; later, he was strongly opposed. Although CBS eventually dropped him, he raised enough money to cre-ate a thirty-six-station radio network that reached tens of millions of lis-teners each week. After 1936, Coughlin backed Hitler and Mussolini as antidotes to communism, espoused isolationism, and spewed anti-Semitic rants to an audience of as many as 30 million. Not until May 1942, six months after American GIs were fighting fascists on the battlefield, did Coughlin's bishop order an end to his broadcasts.[3] He is a dramatic exam-ple of what many Americans probably felt during this time.

One would think that those in power, whether Jews or Gentiles, would be interested in saving human beings, but the simple fact remains that most people were interested only in themselves and their own, re-gardless of the moral issues involved. In general, Jews in the United States did not do enough for those suffering under Hitler. Most of the Jews close to Roosevelt, according to historian David Wyman, "did very little to encourage rescue action."[4] The efforts of Brandeis, Cohen, and Philip Kleinfeld were unusual. According to Saul Friedman, other American Jewish leaders in government "opted for mendicancy rather than lead-ership. . . . Insecure themselves, constantly wary of raising the specter of double-loyalty which was the grist of antisemites, these persons over-exerted themselves to display their Americanism, their concern for this nation's welfare to the exclusion of all others, even when doing so meant the deaths of loved ones in Europe."⁵ Unfortunately, this statement mirrors some of the Rebbe's behavior during the Holocaust. He feared his actions would accomplish nothing with the government. Moreover, his paramount concern was for the Jews' spiritual welfare. Rather than combining that concern with strong political action, he gave in to delusions of messianic prophesies and condemnations of American Jews.

Roosevelt was susceptible to political pressure, but American Jews were uncertain what they wanted him to do. Breckinridge Long, who committed himself to halting the flow of refugees to America, wrote in his diary in 1944, "The Jewish organizations are all divided amid controversies . . . there is no cohesion or any sympathetic collaboration—rather rivalry, jealousy and antagonism." Moreover, as Henry L. Feingold observes, many Jewish organizations were "traumatized by domestic antisemitism and reluctant to accept responsibility for [their] European brethren."⁶

Even though the Jewish community was not united, many in the Roosevelt administration wanted to avoid the perception that the president was controlled by Jews and doing their bidding.⁷ Also, Roosevelt had to consider the labor unions, which were apt to see an influx of refugees as a threat to American jobs, given that the United States was just emerging from the Great Depression. Even if that fear were driven by anti-Semitism rather than any real threat to the job market, Roosevelt needed the unions' support. Finally, most Americans simply did not want the immigration quotas eased.⁸ Anti-Semitism played a large part in Americans' desire to limit immigration. Steven Early, Roosevelt's press secretary, wrote to the president in July 1941:

> A very grave problem, apparently being entirely ignored, is the quiet and persistent growth of anti-Jewish feeling in our larger centers. I see it and sense it here there and elsewhere, where the plain folks are beginning to resent the pro-Jewish attitude at Washington and also locally. The great and mysterious influx of Jewish refugees, most of whom seem to have ample funds and immediately go into business.

The great number of the Jewish faith placed in high position where their own lack of tolerance is immediately paraded to the masses. . . . Pray God we never have religious outrages here but it seems to me that official Washington would do well to recognize this growth, and by care and tact, calm it down.[9]

Roosevelt was walking a delicate tightrope: he wanted to help the Jews under Hitler, but he was afraid of alienating Congress and voters whose support he needed to prepare for war and save Great Britain, whose help he realized would be vital when Hitler turned his wrath on the United States. And in the early years, he needed that support not only for New Deal programs but also for the crucial effort to build up America's national defense and aid the Allies over the strong objections of isolationists. Luckily for the Rebbe, he was one of those the Roosevelt administration decided to help.

Roosevelt hated anti-Semitism and appointed more Jews in his administration than any president before him, but it affected his political career. While Jews made up only 3 percent of the US population, 15 percent of FDR's senior appointees were Jewish.[10] State Department records show that some vital information about the Holocaust was kept from FDR and the public by those in the European Division, which neither Hull nor Welles controlled. Although Roosevelt was "genuinely free from religious prejudice and racial bigotry," he was either unaware of or sometimes turned a blind eye to officials' anti-Semitism, as dramatically demonstrated with the handling of Jewish refugees under Warren and Long. Since Long ran the show in some key areas of the State Department from 1940 until 1944, this spelled death for thousands.[11] The bright, determined, self-righteous Long was completely lacking in empathy and was absolutely the wrong man in this crucial position at the worst possible time. He "enforced barriers to refugees with a zeal born from an unholy marriage of antisemitism, self-pity, and paranoia."[12] When Long's actions came to light, Congressman Emanuel Celler made this damning statement: "The State Department [under Long] has turned its back on the time-honored principle of granting havens to refugees." Lawyers working with Morgenthau went further and wrote that Long was actually an accomplice to Hitler and a war criminal "in every sense of the term."[13]

In light of these facts, the efforts of American politicians and Jews on Schneersohn's behalf were remarkable. Roosevelt was certainly informed of Rebbe Schneersohn's plight, and he allowed Jewish leaders and government officials to pursue his rescue.[14] This behavior was uncharacteristic, given Roosevelt's other actions with respect to the Holocaust.

Roosevelt had many other matters on his mind in 1939 and 1940, including the war in Europe, tension with Japan, the grave threat of totalitarian countries to freedom in the world, getting the votes he needed in Congress, the lingering effects of the Depression, his reelection, and his failing health. But none of them justified inaction. In 1943 Secretary Morgenthau, in a gross overstatement, complained: "When you get through with it, the [US] attitude to date is no different from Hitler's attitude."[15] Everyone knew that Hitler was virulently anti-Semitic, that he defamed and persecuted Jews, deprived them of their livelihood, stole their property, isolated them from their friends and neighbors, sent goons to humiliate them and beat them up, and threw some in concentration camps, where they were cruelly treated and some died. But it was still inconceivable that Germany would set out to murder every Jewish man, woman, and child on earth. During the first six and a half years after Hitler seized power in Germany, he killed no more than about ten thousand Jews. While Jews had made important contributions to German science, medicine, law, culture, and business, less than one percent of Germany was Jewish in 1933, and about one quarter of one percent was Jewish by the start of World War II. After the Nazi invasion of Poland and the Soviet Union in 1939 and 1941 respectively, things got quickly worse as rabidly anti-Semitic Germany suddenly controlled the countries with the largest share of Europe's Jews. Countries that were friendly to Germany, such as Hungary and Romania, were pressured to persecute Jews and kill them or turn them over to Germany. But Hitler still kept hidden what was happening to those shipped east, so as not to alarm the intended victims or engender any public sympathy that might interfere with his scheme. Karl Wolff provided an explanation for this secrecy, which eventually became a direct order from Himmler to senior SS leadership:

We were having a late lunch with Hitler when the issue arose of Jews being sent east. The relocation program had really just started.

Göring had mentioned that it may be a good idea to let German Jews know that there would be new opportunities for them if they voluntarily left. Himmler seemed to think it was a good idea. It would make things easier. As this was 1940, there really was no final decision made. Hitler said he would think about it. Then in 1942, just after Heydrich's conference [the Wannsee conference], Himmler said that "nothing will be said or mentioned about the deportations east. We should keep the German people oblivious to any of this. They would not completely understand our mission, but in time, they will. Secrecy is the issue at hand now."[16]

As a result, the SS did everything possible to hide what it was doing. Concentration camp inmates might be forced to write postcards to family back home, saying they were alive and well, before they were executed. An entire camp was set up at Theresienstadt in German-occupied Czechoslovakia as a model Jewish settlement. The Red Cross was taken to visit the camp in 1944, and a propaganda film was made. In reality, tens of thousands of people died of malnutrition, disease, and sadistic treatment there, and it was used as a stopover to the death camps.

After America entered the war in December 1941, there were limited options for the Allies to save Jews in German-occupied Europe. We now know that as many as 1.5 million were shot to death before the death camps (at Belzec, Sobibor, Chelmno, Treblinka, Auschwitz, and Majdanek) became fully operational. West of the Molotov-Ribbentrop line that divided Europe between Hitler and Stalin in 1939, Germans generally preserved secrecy about the fate of the Jews who were often shipped by rail to concentration camps or death factories they had built in occupied Poland. To the east of the Molotov-Ribbentrop line, most Jews were exterminated close to their homes, often shot over pits or ditches. Almost the entire Jewish population of Latvia was killed during a two-day period. The Jews of Riga were not shipped to concentration camps. They were not gassed. They were awakened early in the morning, marched eight miles out of town, and shot to death at Rumballa. The door through which the Rebbe had escaped had closed. At that point, most US government leaders simply focused on winning the war as quickly as possible.

Even after receiving convincing evidence in 1942 that the Nazis were systematically killing Jews by the hundreds of thousands, Roosevelt had only hollow words for American Jewish leader Rabbi Stephen S. Wise: "We shall do all in our power to be of service to your people in this tragic moment."[17] Roosevelt would not force immigration authorities to help the oppressed seeking refuge; moreover, he would not pursue the diplomatic and military options necessary to prevent, or at least slow, the systematic killing of Jews under Hitler. In Wyman's judgment, "Roosevelt's indifference to so momentous a historical event as the systematic annihilation of European Jewry emerges as the worst failure of his presidency."[18] But realistically, what could Roosevelt have done? Short of defeating Nazi Germany, the United States and its allies had no means of rescuing the Jews who were eventually murdered in concentration camps like Auschwitz or were shot in places like Ukraine, Belarus, Latvia, Lithuania, or the occupied western part of the Soviet Union. With much of its Pacific Fleet destroyed or badly damaged at Pearl Harbor, with its army in the Philippines cut off and under siege, and with German submarines sinking its ships carrying desperately needed food, arms, and men to Great Britain, the United States was making an all-out effort to draft, train, and equip a vastly expanded army for combat overseas while fighting in the Pacific. The Soviet Union was invaded on 22 June 1941 by more than 4 million soldiers from Germany and its allies, and within weeks, millions of Polish and Soviet Jews were under Nazi control. Within half a year, the Nazis had murdered half a million with their death squads in the *Einsatzgruppen*. The Soviet Union had conducted a scorched-earth retreat and had moved many factories to the east, beyond the Ural Mountains. They would soon be falling back much further to the Volga and the Caucasus Mountains.

Jews could have been rescued before the war, if America had opened its doors to European immigrants during the Great Depression—a tragic loss of an opportunity. As much as one-third of the workforce was unemployed in 1933 when both Hitler and FDR came to power, and the safety net Americans now take for granted (including unemployment insurance, Social Security and Medicare for retirees, and federal deposit insurance) did not yet exist. Getting Congress to open up the United States to immigrants would have been next to impossible, with so many Americans unemployed and so many losing their homes and farms. Getting Jews to leave their homes in countries that had not been conquered by Hitler also would have been a problem before the war. Perhaps the hardest to convince would have been the Hasidic and ultra-Orthodox Jews, whose leaders had instilled negative images of the United States and who were fearful not only of moving to the United States but also of abandoning their traditional roots and communities. In December 1938 Roosevelt wrote to Mussolini, asking the Italian leader to set up a refugee camp in Ethiopia for Jews forced out of their homes by the Germans. Mussolini refused and suggested that the United States set up the camp itself.[19] The Dutch and Belgians were relying on neutrality to keep them out of another war, and the French were depending on their armed forces. The Czechs had a defense treaty with the French. The Italian fascists did not adopt anti-Jewish laws until later. Would the Jews have left these countries? The best time to take in refugees would have been before the United States entered the war. By 1942, diplomacy was no longer an option. Hitler's motivation to cooperate with America, and thereby keep it neutral, no longer existed. But to say that there was no practical way for the Allies to save the Jews, short of defeating Nazi Germany, does not mean that none of the Jews could have been saved.

The most realistic opportunities would have been working with neutral countries such as Switzerland, Sweden, Portugal, and Turkey to establish refuges for persecuted noncombatants and applying pressure on Axis countries that were not so committed to genocide and feared what the Allies would do to them after the war. When the tide had turned and Hitler's forces were bogged down and losing to the Red Army in the east and losing to American, British, and Commonwealth forces in North Africa, Italy, and later France, the handwriting was on the wall. Hitler was willing to sacrifice vital military resources to kill more Jews, but fascist anti-Semites like Admiral Miklós Horthy in Hungary had other priorities. Horthy dragged his feet when ordered to exterminate Hungarian Jews. In fact, Horthy was removed from power and the Nazis took over his country in 1944, before any serious deportation of Jews started. Romania had a coup in 1944, replacing the virulently anti-Semitic Prime Minister Ion Antonescu with King Michael and switching sides and supporting the Allies. The Allies could have prevented many of the Romanian and Hungarian Jews from being killed, but it was simply not a main focus of their militaries. It would have been possible to save tens of thousands in certain places and hundreds of thousands overall, but it was no longer possible to save millions.

There were numerous other opportunities to defeat Hitler before 1940, which could have saved not only 6 million Jews but also tens of millions of others who died in the war. Those opportunities slipped away one by one. Before Hitler took over, the Soviet Union let Germany conduct secret military training and war exercises on its territory, in violation of Germany's obligations under the Treaty of Versailles.[20] The better-trained German army, which had learned much about maneuver warfare in the Soviet Union, would return, uninvited, in 1941. In 1936 Nazi Germany was allowed to reoccupy the Rhineland and remilitarize it, in violation of the Versailles and Locarno treaties. At the time, France and Great Britain were much stronger than Germany and could have stopped it, but there was no military response, and Hitler grew stronger as a result. When Hitler occupied and annexed Austria in 1938, in violation of the Treaty of St. Germain, France and Britain made only a mild verbal objection. In 1939, at the urging of the appeasement-happy British prime minister Neville Chamberlain, Czechoslovakia was dismembered and laid open to Nazi Germany, despite French treaty obligations to defend Czechoslovakia. Some of the finest artillery, machine guns, and tanks were produced at the Škoda Works there; there were also steel and chemical factories, which Hitler utilized against others. Czechoslovakia was a democratic country prepared to fight for its freedom with a well-trained, modern army of thirty-five divisions, good natural defenses in its mountain range, and reliable man-made frontier fortifications. It could have made an effective ally, but instead, it was sacrificed in exchange for empty promises. When Great Britain and France finally declared war against Germany in 1939, following the invasion of Poland, the Allies delayed any substantial attack on Germany, which had much of its army in the east, and many of its tanks and trucks had broken down or been damaged or destroyed in Poland.

The fact that so few US leaders recognized that Hitler "was deeply, inescapably and destructively mad" and did nothing to stop him is one of the Allies' biggest mistakes.[21] President Roosevelt had to fight American isolationism and American indifference to events overseas. Only an attack against the United States brought an end to US isolationism. By

1942, it was reasonable for Roosevelt to believe that the best way to help Jews under Hitler was to defeat Germany as soon as possible. The Allies had settled on a strategy of liberating Europe first and then beating Japan. Some of those who could have been saved during the war were ignored and left to their fate. Although FDR was "well aware of the catastrophic situation," according to Wyman, he seemed indifferent to their fate.[22]

Maybe Roosevelt and those in the State Department thought the Jews were trying to gain preferential treatment over the Russians, Poles, Slavs, Jehovah's Witnesses, and others who were dying in the war. There was, after all, no shortage of innocent victims around the world. After the war, President Truman, though a big supporter of the state of Israel, expressed what may have been a common attitude among American politicians: "The Jews, I find are very, very selfish. They care not how many Estonians, Latvians, Finns, Poles, Yugoslavs or Greeks get murdered or mistreated as DP [displaced persons] as long as the Jews get special treatment. Yet when they have power, physical, financial or political neither Hitler nor Stalin has anything on them for cruelty or mistreatment to the underdog."[23] Truman's statement makes it clear why few American politicians took action to help the Jews suffering and dying under Hitler.

Gregory Wallance's assessment of responsibility in *America's Soul in the Balance* is much more nuanced and focused. He assigns blame to those in the European Division of the State Department: Breckinridge Long, Borden Reams, Ray Atherton, John Hickerson, Eldridge Durbrow. They stalled visa requests, delayed the approval of rescue plans, or kept vital information about the Holocaust from the president, Congress, the Jewish community, and the public. At the same time, he lauds the dedicated individuals in the government who did their utmost to save refugees: Sumner Welles, Randolph Paul, John Pehle, Josiah E. Dubois Jr., Henry Morgenthau.[24]

Many condemn Jewish leaders for not fighting harder against Roosevelt's apparent inaction. Famous Holocaust writer and survivor Elie Wiesel says, "They should have shaken heaven and earth, echoing the agony of their doomed brethren; taken in by Roosevelt's personality, they, in a way, became accomplices to his inaction."[25] A number of Jewish leaders, including the Rebbe, made mistakes in their dealings with the government. Lubavitchers may say this was impossible, since the Rebbe was a perfect being, but history illustrates that this was not the case.[26] "Orthodox leaders, and even prominent and learned rabbis, are capable of making serious, and in some cases fatal, mistakes," observes Efraim Zuroff. "Any attempt to portray the *gedolim* [great Jewish leaders] as perfect human beings, incapable of error, is not only inaccurate but an affront to our intelligence and an insult to the memory of those whose lives were not saved during those terrible times."[27] As shown throughout this book, the Rebbe did not exercise any leadership with regard to the rescue of Jews. The Rebbe's failure to support the Vaad or public demonstrations, his ongoing rebuking of non-Orthodox and secular Jews, and his focus on messianic visions were black marks on his record as the head of Chabad during the Holocaust. His behavior prevented him and his followers from playing a more productive role in uniting the Jewish population in the United States and putting more pressure on the Roosevelt administration. One sees clearly why the Rebbe failed in his dealings with the White House, but why did the Jews in general not put more pressure on Roosevelt? As already seen, most Jews in America were not waiting on the Rebbe for guidance.

Many American Jews greatly admired Roosevelt; some even compared him "to their great biblical heroes, Abraham, Moses, Isaiah . . . because of his concern for the common man and the poor, his optimism for the future, his hatred of all forms of exploitation, and his ever-insisting pleas for education, secular and religious [which] indicated his conviction that democracy and humanitarianism could not function without knowledge, as well as his faith." They also understood the heavy burden he bore. The fate of the free world was on his shoulders. The cause of American "Jewry's 'political impotence,' was the Jews' worship of Roosevelt."[28] A few leaders, such as Rabbis Kalmanowitz, Silver, and Kotler of the Vaad and Peter Bergson, head of the Emergency Committee to Save the Jewish People of Europe, saw the urgency of the situation. Although they were foreigners with limited financial resources, they got the US government to move at its highest levels and helped save thousands of lives. Henry Morgenthau, the only Jew in the Roosevelt cabinet, is another notable example; he took convincing information about Long's obstruction and crimes, compiled by Treasury attorney Josiah E. DuBois Jr., and confronted the president, who immediately agreed to create the War Refugee

Board (WRB) in early 1944, stripping authority from Long and basically ending his government career.[29] The WRB, according to Wyman, saved between 100,000 and 200,000 lives.[30] Unfortunately, these men were rare among civil servants and political leaders, and even though their actions were amazing compared with what other Jewish leaders did (or did not do), they were not enough. John Pehle, executive director of the WRB, said candidly, "What we did was little. . . . It was late. Late and little, I would say."[31] He needed more support, which the American Jewish population did not provide. Rebbe Joseph Isaac Schneersohn could not be counted among American Jewish leaders at that time.

A lack of imagination and aggressiveness, as well as an unwillingness to go against Roosevelt, prevented many from meeting the situation head-on. Most people knew things were bad for the Jews under Hitler, but they could not fathom how bad. This makes the Rebbe's attitude even more problematic because he had seen what the Nazis were capable of, yet he failed to turn this knowledge into productive action. Roosevelt might have been prodded into action if he had been threatened with political retaliation, but apparently, this was not attempted.[32] Even Morgenthau, Kalmanowitz, Kotler, and others missed opportunities to rescue people. Certainly, many Jewish leaders failed to take radical action to mitigate or prevent the crimes being committed.

Only in late 1943, when the true scope of the Holocaust dawned on Morgenthau, the Vaad leadership, and Bergson and his dissident group, did they aggressively pursue the rescue of Jews under Hitler.[33] At that point, a clear warning was issued by the Allies to Hitler and his Nazi underlings. This *Statement on Atrocities*, signed by Roosevelt, Churchill, and Stalin in October 1943, addressed the reports of "atrocities, massacres and cold-blooded mass executions" and warned that German officers and men as well as Nazis who "have been responsible for or have taken a consenting part in the above atrocities, massacres and executions will be sent back to the countries in which their abominable deeds were done in order that they may be judged and punished" or punished elsewhere by the Allies. No one can know how many Nazis heard this warning, or exactly what effect it had, but at a time when the defeat of Nazi Germany was becoming increasingly certain, it may have done some good. After the war, Allied military tribunals who prosecuted war criminals at

Nuremberg cited the *Statement on Atrocities* as the lawful authority for their trials. Unfortunately, the only aggressive action the Rebbe took was to rescue his library, which he succeeded in doing. Yet even Kalmanowitz, who pursued rescue efforts with a passion, wrote to Assistant Secretary of State Adolf A. Berle in August 1944 and asked him to send prayer books and Bibles to the Jews in the USSR, rather than using the requisite funds for lifesaving efforts.[34] By August 1944, the rabbi should have known that America had more important matters on its plate, such as General Omar Bradley's forces in Operation Cobra breaking out of Normandy and sweeping across France toward the Nazi Reich. The Rebbe was not the only person obsessed with books, but at least Kalmanowitz wanted to send books to others, not rescue his own. Even so, both men should have focused on saving lives.

It is clear that many Jewish leaders failed to take radical action to mitigate and perhaps prevent one of the most horrendous crimes to befall humanity—industrialized genocide. The types of radical action they could have taken, especially between 1939 and 1941, were manifold. For instance, they could have pushed the United States to open its borders or use empty cargo ships returning from Europe to bring refugees to America. Bergson worked with playwright Ben Hecht to produce the play *We Will Never Die*, which helped raise awareness of the destruction of European Jews in 1943. More than 100,000 people saw the production, including Eleanor Roosevelt, six Supreme Court justices, 300 senators and congressmen, and numerous military officers. In her column "My Day," Mrs. Roosevelt praised the play as one of the most "impressive and moving pageants I have ever seen. No one who heard each group come forward and give the story of what had happened to it at the hands of the ruthless German military, will ever forget those haunting words: 'Remember us.'" Wallance writes that this play "was the single most effective attempt to bring the Nazis' scheme to murder European Jewry to the attention of the American public."[35] In short, there were many things Chabad could have done to help the Jews in Europe, other than praying and studying the Torah.

To Rebbe Schneersohn and others, taking care of the soul was just as important as, if not more important than, saving the body. On the one hand, religion prevented them from taking practical action; on the other hand, a lack of imagination prevented them from understanding what the Nazis were really doing. Despite the evidence, people had a difficult time understanding that Hitler was using bullets, starvation, and gas chambers to slaughter millions.

The motives of the politicians involved in the Rebbe's rescue must be examined before we hold them up as heroes. Max Rhoade, who lobbied successfully for the Lubavitchers, explained his strategy for manipulating these politicians:

> In dealing with government officials here in Washington, it is particularly important to handle the individual in accordance with his personal psychology. . . . I might add that everything here in Washington, contrary to public impression, is not done on the basis of "getting friendly." There are peculiar types of bureaucratic officials who are absolutely rigid, and it would ruin a matter not to harmonize with their own personalities. That is a large part of the technique of getting favorable action in Washington. You must first of all know something about your man and size him up properly. With some, the "friendly basis" is the "ticket," with others, it is poison. It might be just right to use political influence with one individual and suicide to use it with another, and so on.[36]

Rhoade constantly emphasized the Rebbe's significance to Jews all over the world and compared him with the pope to convince American officials that their intervention would benefit them on many levels. They could proudly cite their contribution to world Jewry, prove their humanitarian concern for European Jews, and gain the support of a large group of voting American Lubavitchers. Yet even Rhoade did not let his sincere belief in the necessity of saving the Rebbe completely distract him from his campaign to get paid for his legal services. Still, Rhoade is one of the main heroes in this story (besides Bloch). For all the goodwill shown by politicians and diplomats on the Rebbe's behalf, without Rhoade, all their efforts would have been wasted. Without him coordinating and finessing the entire situation, the plan would have broken down. Rhoade is worthy of our respect for his professionalism and his brilliance. Without the vital paperwork procured by him, the bureaucrats would not have had the proper documentation to rubber-stamp. As American journalist Dorothy Thompson wrote about the immigration process: "It is a fantastic commentary on the inhumanity of our times that for thousands and thousands of people a piece of paper with a stamp on it is the difference between life and death."[37] Rhoade's superb attention to detail is what ensured the Rebbe's rescue.

A number of high-ranking American officials rose to the occasion when approached about rescuing the Rebbe. Hull's intervention is remarkable because, according to Wyman, he "paid almost no attention to his department's policies concerning the destruction of the Jews."[38] Rather than taking an interest because his wife, Frances, was of Jewish descent, Hull worried that her background "would cause controversy and keep him from the Presidential nomination he so passionately desired."[39] Another potential problem was the fact that her father had fought for the Confederacy during the Civil War.[40] Nonetheless, Hull took positive action on behalf of the Rebbe in 1939 and 1940, and the Jewish leader acknowledged Hull's help, writing to him on 25 March 1940:

> We feel deeply grateful to you for your kind help in the issuance of our emigration visas to the United States, and our heartfelt thanks to you for your kindness. Blessed is this country with its famous and beloved leader President Roosevelt, the greatest and most outstanding figure of our age, famed for his humane feelings and love of peace, and its equally famous and great Secretary of State. May the Almighty bless you and grant you long life, good health and every success in your work for this country and humanity as a whole.[41]

But the "famous and great" Hull acted under pressure. According to Wallance, "Hull generally shunned Jewish issues such as the plight of refugees from Nazi Germany," and almost nothing about the plight of the Jews "appears in the voluminous Hull files in the Library of Congress."[42] It seems that this was the *only* time Hull stepped in to help a Jew.

Ironically, Hull worried that Americans would be overwhelmed by the scope of the devastation facing Jews in Europe. At an October 1939 meeting of the Inter-Governmental Committee on Political Refugees, he said, "I think it would be most unfortunate if future historians should be called upon to say that civilized man confessed his inability to cope with this harrowing problem and let the undertaking die at its most critical period."[43] The "inability to cope" was the very excuse used by many in the government. According to the Rescue Commission of the American Jewish Conference, "the number [of refugees using different visas] amounted to about 5.9 percent of those who could have been admitted if one considered the entire quota rather than the effective one" from 1933 to 1944. What was needed was a commitment to save lives, and that commitment was absent.[44] Donald L. Niewyk writes, "Many of the victims might have been saved had other countries opened their doors to Jewish refugees. The time to aid the targets of racial bigotry is before their situation becomes untenable."[45]

Sadly, America's inaction confirmed to the Nazis the Western powers' apathy. The lack of an international response during the Evian conference and the absence of diplomatic pressure after *Kristallnacht* in 1938 further demonstrated that indifference. Hitler said on 30 January 1939, "It is a shameful example to observe today how the entire democratic world dissolves in tears of pity, but then, in spite of its obvious duty to help, closes [its heart] to the poor, tortured people."[46] The failure to rescue passengers on the refugee ship *St. Louis* in May 1939 only substantiated the world's uncaring attitude. The Nazi newspaper *Der Weltkampf* wrote in August 1939, "We are saying openly that we do not want the Jews, while the democracies keep on claiming that they are willing to receive them—and then leave the guests out in the cold! Aren't we savages better men after all?"[47]

Hitler's and *Der Weltkampf*'s statements, unfortunately, contained elements of truth. The inaction of the Allies, writes Henry L. Feingold, "allowed the Nazi regime to claim that the world at large shared their revulsion to Jews as well as guilt in their death."[48] One can only speculate whether the Nazi regime would have altered its extermination plans if international pressure had been applied as early as 1939. One thing is certain: had the United States simply altered its immigration policies starting in 1938 or 1939, hundreds of thousands of Jews would have been saved by 1941. But in fairness to American leaders, few could imagine that the consequence of not admitting these refugees would be genocide. Moreover, the United States had no legal obligation to these people, and most governments are amoral by definition.[49]

One sees examples of this "amoral" approach throughout history, such as the brutal rape of Nanking by the Japanese. Imperial Japan in the 1930s looked down on the Chinese as subhuman. From the end of 1937 into the early months of 1938, the Japanese slaughtered about 300,000 and raped at least 20,000 Chinese citizens, starting with their march from Shanghai and ending with their conquest of Nanking. In this sadistic orgy, the Japanese "went beyond rape" and sliced off women's breasts, cut open pregnant women's bellies, killed infants, and buried people alive. They castrated many of the captured Chinese prisoners before using them for bayonet practice or dousing them with gasoline and lighting them on fire. The Japanese press reported on contests among the Japanese soldiers to see who could kill the most Chinese civilians in an occupied territory over a given period. These events were reported in American newspapers and periodicals, but the US government did nothing. Yet, the question must be asked, should it have?[50]

Throughout history, those in the comfort of America have said of events in Cambodia, Rwanda, Bosnia, Sudan, or ISIS-controlled Iraq, "That is horrible," yet do next to nothing. The United States typically does more than other nations to get involved, sending armed forces to fight genocidal regimes in faraway places, but it often acts only when US trade routes or energy resources are threatened, US citizens are captured, or US territory is attacked. In the end, as Iris Chang writes, "civilization itself is tissue-thin."[51] We need to do more, because evil men continue to do much harm. Hitler unfortunately expressed a prophetic view of genocide when he said in August 1939, "Who speaks today of the extermination of the Armenians [by Turkey]?"[52] The sad answer to his question, then as now, was not as many as there should be. A more proactive (as opposed to reactive) approach to genocide and crimes against humanity should be part of US and other nations' national strategy. As an observer of the French Revolution, Edmund Burke purportedly said, "for evil men to triumph, good men must do nothing." In short, the story of the rescue of Rebbe Schneersohn shows us that much more can and should be done. This includes a continuation of the post–World War II policy of creating and strengthening international organizations and treaty obligations for as many countries as possible, so that the heaviest burden is not borne entirely by the United States and its closest allies, the United Kingdom, Canada, France, Belgium, the Netherlands, and Australia, to name just a few.

On the other side of a two-dimensional view of this rescue stand the villainous Germans. Although the fiction that all German citizens were equally evil may have held up at a great distance, any closer interaction with German society would have shattered that illusion. Even Hitler drew a distinction between the respective roles of the Wehrmacht and his elite SS troops. In August 1939 he informed Himmler: "Poland will be wiped off the map of nations. What will happen behind the Wehrmacht front may not meet with the approbation of the generals. The army is not to take part in the elimination of the Polish cadres and the Jews. This will be the task of the SS."[53] General Blaskowitz's brave protests against the SS prove that some Germans were willing to speak out against violations of human rights and Nazi brutality. Everything was not black and white in the Third Reich. If Hitler did not expect officers and men in the German military to support the extermination of the Jews, why should we assume that they approved of or participated in the slaughter? The fact that Helmuth Wohlthat, chief administrator of Göring's Four-Year Plan; Wilhelm Canaris, head of the Abwehr; and Bloch and others in the Wehrmacht risked their careers and their lives to escort a group of Hasidic Jews out of Poland, through Germany, and on to Latvia under the Gestapo's nose was astonishing. Primo Levi could have been describing them when he wrote: "In telling this story after forty years, I'm not trying to make excuses for Nazi Germany. One human German does not whitewash the innumerable inhuman or indifferent ones, but it does have the merit of breaking a stereotype."[54] These men do indeed counter what we have come to believe about high-level Nazi civil servants and Wehrmacht officers.

After the Evian conference, Wohlthat informed Pell of his willingness to intercede for particularly important Jews; saving the Rebbe suited his personal ideology and offered an opportunity to foster goodwill in Washington. Given the international climate of hostility, Germany welcomed any goodwill it could get. It was clear that the German Foreign Office was keenly interested in Roosevelt's opinions about Nazi policies and that Wohlthat was an important player in maintaining good relations with the United States. Germany was not yet at war with the United States, and it still hoped to convince Britain to ignore its actions in Poland and join it as an ally. Germany was promoting a program of forced Jewish emigration at this stage, and the Rebbe and his group leaving Europe fit with this strategy. Canaris, too, had expressed reservations about Hitler's regime to Wohlthat and others long before the Rebbe's case landed on his desk. He had used his office to protect several "half-Jewish" officers, including Bloch, and promoted them according to their abilities, regardless of racial policies. Bloch simply followed orders. Or did he? Given his Jewish father and other Jewish relatives, saving the Rebbe and his followers may have been a duty he carried out with pleasure. Perhaps that is why he refused to give up when locating the Rebbe proved so difficult. After Bloch succeeded at this assignment, Canaris allowed or ordered him to conduct other missions to rescue other Jews, possibly including the Gerer Rebbe. Bloch's secretary claimed that he later helped two Jewish families escape to Switzerland.[55]

Some may find Bloch's decision to continue his active military service puzzling. He may have kept fighting because he regarded the Soviets as "no better than the Nazi loser," as James Tent observed. Perhaps he had become so brutalized by two world wars and so apathetic about life and his uncertain future that he actually looked forward to dying "with the last bullet in the last battle of the war and be done with it."[56] As Anton Gill notes, many soldiers struggled with their loyalty oath to Hitler and chose to kill themselves or deliberately seek death in battle rather than violate that promise. So if Bloch became fatalistic in the last days or hours of his life, he was typical.[57] After the horrible battles around Zhitomir in November 1943, where he experienced much death and hardship, he wrote to his wife: "One lives from day to day because one never knows what the next hour will bring."[58]

Bloch does not fit neatly into the category of either hero or villain, victim or perpetrator. His motivation for both serving in the army and helping the Rebbe brings into sharp relief the complicated and often conflicting loyalties of Germans in the 1930s and 1940s. Why did Bloch want to serve Hitler's state? Bloch was a career soldier, wounded and decorated in World War I, and in the army he found his beloved calling.[59] Bloch wore the German uniform and swore an oath first to Germany and then, after 1933, to Hitler. He gathered valuable data on enemy countries for the Nazi war machine, and he fought on the Russian front against one of Germany's archenemies. He saw Germany and the Nazi state as distinct entities; he could serve Germany without serving Hitler. Only this explanation can account for his volunteering in 1943 for the Russian front and later fighting and dying in the Volkssturm, rather than escaping with his family to the west and surrendering to the Americans, like thousands of other Germans did. Although he may have been delusional, Bloch felt bound by his oath to remain loyal to his comrades and his nation.[60] He was no Oskar Schindler, but he was certainly no Adolf Eichmann either, much to his credit.

Maybe Bloch knowingly sent himself on a suicide mission to hold off the vengeful Red Army soldiers who were destroying cities, raping girls and women, and enslaving the survivors. He might have thought that, somehow, his death would protect his family, who had just left for the west.

Had Bloch known about the genocide, would he have continued to fight? Everyone in Germany had been steeped in a witch's brew of anti-Semitic propaganda and hate-filled rants since 1933. The everyday abuse of Jewish Germans was open and obvious, as were special occasions such as *Kristallnacht* and the roundups of Jews to be sent to the camps. As a high-ranking Abwehr intelligence and combat officer, he must have known more than the average German soldier.[61] He had fought over the very ground where Hitler's Holocaust had slaughtered thousands of souls, especially in the Zhitomir district. However, most soldiers do not spend their days philosophizing or discussing politics when they are surrounded by death and fearful for their own lives.

If Bloch saw firsthand evidence of what we now call the Holocaust, he may not have understood the full meaning of what he witnessed. He had to concentrate on surviving, and the systematic extermination of the entire Jewish population of Europe may have been unbelievable from his point of view. The tragic paradox is that Bloch fought for a regime that exterminated people like his father, eventually would have annihilated him, and, at best, would have degraded his children to second-class citizenship or subjected them to sterilization.[62]

Bloch was not alone. Tens of thousands of so-called *Mischlinge* fought in the Wehrmacht, and many of them did so as high-ranking officers, including half-Jew Field Marshal Erhard Milch and quarter-Jew Admiral

Bernhard Rogge.[63] They served because they were drafted or were career soldiers. Some volunteered, hoping to survive by hiding in uniform. Some enlisted because they wanted the adventure and glory of a military career; they trained for war, and when it came, they did their duty. Some were committed Nazis. Most were German patriots serving their country.

Bloch was a creature of war, and his desire for a combat command attests to this fact. He knew how to save others, but ultimately he did not save himself. The real question is whether Bloch was unable or unwilling to save himself by escaping to the west. He certainly knew the fate that awaited the Rebbe and the other Jews he helped if they stayed in German-occupied territory. Bloch knew that Hitler was aware of his own Jewish background. But did he know what was going to happen to him? Sadly, he drew the wrong conclusion, believing that Hitler made a distinction between *Ostjuden* and assimilated Jews like his father and Jewish *Mischlinge* like himself. Did Bloch ever understand this? The answer is buried in the battlefield where Bloch gave his life defending his country.

The rescue of Rebbe Joseph Isaac Schneersohn illuminates the complexity of life in Germany; it is not just a curious anomaly. It suggests that American officials might have been able to rescue more Jews, but it also reveals the enormous difficulties involved in such efforts. It shows that many Jewish leaders in the United States, even those who experienced Hitler's extermination policies firsthand, like the Rebbe, failed to understand the urgency of helping those Jews still stranded in Europe—Jews who, with an easing of immigration restrictions, could have been rescued from Hitler's hell. The story of Bloch and the Rebbe shows the moral complexity of war.

Today, what could or should have been done seems obvious. "Nothing is easier than to apportion praise and blame, writing many years after the events," Walter Laqueur observes. "It is very easy to claim that everyone should have known what would happen once Fascism came to power. But such an approach is ahistorical . . . [and] few come out of the story unblemished. It was a story of failure to comprehend, among Jewish leaders and communities inside Europe and outside, a story of failure among non-Jews in high positions in neutral and Allied countries who did not care, or did not want to know or even suppressed the information."[64] The Rebbe's followers worked hard to put a name, a face, a great reputation, and a large following in front of powerful politicians. Although those politicians might have been able to ignore the faceless masses without feeling too much guilt, leaving a revered leader in Hitler's clutches was unthinkable. Thus they worked tirelessly to rescue the Rebbe while nameless and ordinary Jews—teachers, students, tailors, farmers, factory workers, housewives, doctors, lawyers, businessmen, retirees, and little children—were left to suffer and die. Hopefully, civilized humanity will be quicker in the future to recognize the signs of genocide and intervene to save lives. Too many countries are not doing enough to save the innocent. A recent *Wall Street Journal* article described the US response to ISIS in a way that could be applied to most responses to genocide: "Without question the U.S. was behind the curve, and with dire consequences."[65] Nonetheless, at least the United States gets involved. Many countries rarely do.

This story reveals how much good can be achieved when a small group of people stand together to do the right thing. In the Talmud it is written, "If you save a life you save the world."[66] This remarkable rescue saved more than a dozen lives. All it took was letter writing, a few thousand dollars, and the courage to speak up.[67] Maybe in the future, this story will encourage others not to stand idly by when a little effort could produce a dramatic result. How sad that the 6 million Jews who died in the Holocaust were not afforded the treatment the Lubavitcher Rebbe received in 1939.

Rescue stories like Schneersohn's were rare during the Third Reich. Yet it shows that some lived by a moral code to save lives when they could. Moreover, it illustrates that opportunities did exist to save people from the dark cloud of Nazism, even after war erupted in 1939. Bloch, Canaris, Pell, Rhoade, and others had different motivations, but ultimately, they all found ways to help people in mortal danger.

Rhoade, in particular, went out of his way to rescue Schneersohn, even though he was neither paid in full nor acknowledged by Chabad. One only wishes there had been more like him. Rhoade had honed his skills in 1937, working with the US Immigration Office to help two cousins, Helen and Aron Groer, emigrate from Europe. Ironically, the Groers did not think it would get that bad, but Rhoade knew it would. As soon as he got their visas, he made it clear that they were to get the hell out of there. He had even traveled to France beforehand to double-check their documents and avoid any delays.[68]

Remarkably, if the men who rescued him had known the Rebbe's true personality and what he stood for, they probably would not have worked so hard to save him. There was no shortage of people in extreme danger. In this respect, the Rebbe's followers and his lawyer skillfully portrayed him as "one of the leading Jewish scholars of the world, a paramount figure in Jewry."[69] There was little to admire about Schneersohn unless one was a devout Lubavitcher, and Schneersohn obviously had little use, love, or respect for those who rescued him or for mainstream Jews. The Jews he denounced for causing the Holocaust were the very ones who saved his life, yet the Rebbe failed to see this irony.

Since the Rebbe believed that God was behind the operation, he dismissed the incredible risks taken by Bloch, Canaris, and Rhoade. Neither during nor after the war did the Rebbe thank the families of his rescuers. He did thank Roosevelt, Hull, and Brandeis, but these were powerful men whose help he still needed and whose response would add to the Rebbe's prestige. It appears that writing to the men who did all the grunt work was beneath his dignity, and they received not even an approving nod. Sadly, when Max Rhoade, who lived just down the street from the Rebbe in New York City, died in 1964, he was a recluse of modest means. Not one Lubavitcher ever raised a finger to help him. He collapsed on the street suffering from cancer and was taken to Bellevue Hospital. The medical staff notified his sister, who visited him shortly before he passed away. He died with no one by his bedside, and a rabbi at the hospital informed the family of Rhoade's passing. Soon thereafter, the family gave him a proper but modest Jewish burial in the family plot in Mt. Pleasant, New York. Only a handful of people attended the funeral. According to the family, Rhoade's experiences with the Lubavitchers during the rescue turned him off to the movement and its leader. The fact that Chabad never paid him for his services drove his wife Helen "crazy," and it was one of the reasons she divorced him. Max adored Helen, and he was devastated when she left him. In short, he came to disrespect the very people he had worked so hard to save. Yet he worked tirelessly, diligently, and skillfully to accomplish the rescue, not allowing his disgust with the lifestyle, the prejudices, or the mystical theology of these Hasidic Jews dissuade him from saving their lives. Rhoade was the true *Tzaddik*, or righteous person, in this story.

Rhoade never bragged about all the good deeds he had done. In fact, until this work, not even the Rhoade family knew about the rescue. He never breathed a word about it. Perhaps he never spoke of it because he ultimately felt that all his time and effort on behalf of the Rebbe and his inner circle had been wasted on individuals who did not deserve it. Most Lubavitchers were unwilling to integrate into American Jewish society, contribute to American culture, or serve in the military; they refused to attend secular universities or take traditional jobs. Thus, Rhoade may have felt that he had saved the wrong people, that there were so many others who were more worthy of his skills and would have been more appreciative of his services.

The Chabad organization has never acknowledged any of these heroes; nor has it ever criticized the Rebbe for condemning other Jews from the safety of the United States or for focusing on his books and his messianic campaign rather than saving lives. It was his religious fervor in Russia under an oppressive and intolerant government that got him enough notoriety to justify the involvement of American officials in 1939, but it was also that fervor that prevented the Rebbe from taking action to rescue others in Europe once he had arrived safely on American shores. His religion made him famous in the world's eyes, but the Hasidic tendency to value only religious explanations and solutions blinded him to reality. In hindsight, how important was the Rebbe? He showed that his brand of Orthodox Judaism was divisive and at odds with modernity.

Paradoxes abound in this rescue story. A Jewish lawyer (Rhoade) worked with an anti-refugee government; German secret service agents rescued a prominent and fanatical rabbi. This story also offers an opportunity to examine why people do good things. Schneersohn and his group of Jews were helped because he was a prominent holy man. Many others were in imminent danger, but they did not attract the attention of the State Department. Should only people with celebrity status receive special consideration? His worthiness was based on his fame and on the claims of his disciples, admirers, and friends, not his intelligence, kindness, or wealth. Many aspects of the Holocaust can be categorized as right or wrong, good or bad; however, the morality of this story is more complicated. Viktor Frankl, a survivor of Auschwitz, wrote that the people who survived Hitler's Holocaust quite often "lost all scruples in their fight for existence; they were prepared to use every means, honest and otherwise, even brutal force, theft, and betrayal of their friends, in order to save themselves. We who have come back, by the aid of many lucky chances or miracles—whatever one may choose to call them—we know: the best of us did not return."[70] Frankl suggests that survivors felt guilty about what they had to do to save their own lives. However, one gets the impression that the Rebbe never truly reflected on the details of his rescue or the complicated questions it raised about his and others' behavior. The Rebbe did not spend much time examining his own life. And as Socrates said, "The unexamined life is not worth living."

Finally, the Rebbe's rescue raises the controversial issue of immigration policy and the path to citizenship. America's screening process in 1940 was flawed, as shown by how the Rebbe and his followers were able to deceive the system. He was rescued because people thought he was a leading scholar of Judaism—something he was not. He was saved because government officials thought his stature among Orthodox Jews was similar to that of the pope among Catholics, which may have been true of his successor but not of him. He was allowed into the United States because officials believed he could support himself at a certain level, which he could not. He was given a visa because he was thought to be healthy, which, given his multiple sclerosis and numerous strokes, he was not (medical facts Rhoade and others kept secret, for obvious reasons).[71] The Jewish leader American officials thought they had rescued did not exist. But as Frankl points out, dishonesty was often necessary to survive.

This story shows how flawed the US immigration system was during World War II. Has the situation improved? Even now it seems fame, power, and wealth are still the most desirable qualities in immigrants. Green cards are awarded to those who invest $500,000 into a business and can prove that the investment will create at least ten jobs.[72] Those with other qualities might make better citizens, namely, those who are honest, hardworking, tolerant, educated, employable, kind, open-minded, smart, and so forth. As former president Bill Clinton, President Barack Obama, and former presidential candidate Mitt Romney have repeatedly said, it is incredibly shortsighted and unwise that the US government does not

Puck cartoon "Looking Backward" shows fat, well-dressed, and obviously very wealthy men standing with their arms outstretched against a downtrodden foreigner attempting to gain entrance to the United States. The ancestors of these rich and powerful men, displayed in large shadows behind each of them, are clearly recent arrivals in a strange land. The caption below this cartoon reads: "They would close to the newcomer the bridge that carried them and their fathers over." (Billy Ireland Cartoon Library & Museum, Ohio State University)

attach a green card to every advanced degree awarded to foreign students by American universities.[73] The result is that the United States is actually exporting thousands of well-educated and hardworking people. The United States needs to work on its immigration policies. In 1939 and 1940 it should have welcomed the thousands who wanted to leave Nazi Europe, especially if they were well educated and of sound mind. If education had been a qualification back in 1940, most Jews would have been granted visas. Even the Rebbe should have been granted asylum in this land of freedom of religion, leaving it up to him to figure out how to make a living once he got here. People should not be forced to lie, to create an image with no basis in reality, just to get ahead of others who followed the rules and in many cases were more deserving.

One can only imagine how many are kept out of safe places like the United States because they are unknown and poor. America was built on the backs of immigrants and on the promise that if one worked hard, one could get ahead. Ironically, immigrants often work harder than those who have lived here for several generations. We all too often forget the blessings bestowed on our grandfathers and grandmothers as we tighten the borders of the United States. Yes, there should be a procedure in place to ensure that immigrants are worthy, but they should not be excluded or forced to lie and cheat because they are not famous.

One could argue that the United States is missing out on an incredible opportunity to strengthen its universities, its workforce, its future, and, most important, its democratic ways by restricting immigration. In short, even though the Rebbe may not have been the most deserving, he should never have had such a difficult time gaining entrance to the United States. There are thousands today who should be given the same consideration, just as our ancestors were given at some point in the nation's relatively short history. Any study of US history would prove this.[74] If we do not repay the kindness shown to our ancestors, we are hypocrites and we will fail as a nation. The rescue of the Rebbe teaches us to practice kindness to the less fortunate on a daily basis, especially those who are persecuted because of their beliefs, ethnicities, and cultures. Hiram Bingham, who defied US immigration law in 1937–1941 to save hundreds, allegedly said that if one knows the right thing to do but does not act on it, then one does not really believe in it. Unfortunately, history shows that many lack the courage to do the right thing.[75]

Genocide is occurring today throughout the world, and we could do much more to stop it. We should fight against the desire to earn more money, obtain more fame, or acquire more things and pursue goals that would make this world a better and safer place. It is fine to acquire wealth and have a nice life—in fact, that is the American dream that many have fulfilled and for which many still strive. But in pursuit of such materialistic goals, we often become so dazzled that we "forget our essential fragility, forget that all of us are in the ghetto, that the ghetto is fenced in, that beyond the fence stand the lords of death, and not far away the train is waiting."[76] Life is short, and life is fragile; death is a reality. "Now it is up to you" to make a difference.[77] What are you going to do today that will make this world better than it was yesterday?

Afterword

The past is the teacher of the present and the guide of the future.
—Rebbe Joseph Isaac Schneersohn

In 1992 I began investigating the phenomenon of soldiers of Jewish descent who fought in the Wehrmacht; the result was the book *Hitler's Jewish Soldiers: The Untold Story of Nazi Racial Laws and Men of Jewish Descent in the German Military*. During my research I came across the story of Ernst Bloch and the Rebbe, a story that seemed too fantastic to believe.

Historians and journalists have looked at the rescue of Rebbe Joseph Isaac Schneersohn from various angles, but to the best of my knowledge, this is the only historical study that synthesizes Lubavitcher sources, German and American archives, and oral and written testimonies. Much of the information was published by Yale University Press in 2004 under the title *Rescued from the Reich*. Since then, new documents and information about the rescue, Rhoade, and Bloch have surfaced and are included in this current work.

The short section on the rescue in Rolf Vogel's *Ein Stück von Uns* particularly sparked my interest in 1994. I also learned of Alan Abrams's book *Special Treatment*, which mentions the story. I examined documents in the National Archives in Washington, DC, and in the Bundesarchiv-Militärarchiv in Freiburg, and I interviewed several members of Bloch's family in the United States, France, and Germany, including his son Martin, who gave me 250 pages of primary documents and almost 200 photos. In 1996 I received a copy of Winfried Meyer's book *Unternehmen Sieben* from Martin Bloch, who directed my attention to the sections that deal with his father and the rescue. Although Meyer devotes only a few pages to the story of the rescue, his research proved most helpful. After my first meeting with Martin Bloch in 1996, I interviewed one of Ernst Bloch's secretaries, Ursula Cadenbach, in Hamburg. She provided me with valuable background on Bloch's character, and with her help, I was able to locate his subordinate Klaus Schenk. I was also introduced to his other secretary, Bettina Motz. In 2014 Bloch's grandsons Max Obenaus and Felix Bloch alerted me to several letters written by Bloch during the war that had recently been discovered with a family member in Paris. They proved most useful in piecing together Bloch's war experiences. To examine Helmuth Wohlthat's de-Nazification file, I visited the Hauptstaatsarchiv in Düsseldorf. Shortly thereafter, I asked the Lubavitchers in Latvia for information about Mordechai Dubin, the Latvian diplomat who was a key informant about the Rebbe for US officials. They led me to Chabad headquarters in the United States.

Lubavitcher rabbi Avraham Laber of Troy, New York, provided me with documents about the Lubavitcher community's interactions with lawyers and politicians in Washington and its religious activities in 1939–1940. From Gershon Jacobson, editor in chief of the *Algemeiner's Journal* in New York City, I obtained information about Dubin. With the help of Rabbi Shalom Dovber Levine and Rabbi Leib Altein, I found additional documents in the Lubavitcher Library in Brooklyn, New York. A number of Lubavitchers gave eyewitness accounts, including the Rebbe's grandson Barry Gourary and one of the Rebbe's students, Joseph Wineberg, who were both in Poland when Hitler invaded. Gourary was an actual eyewitness to the rescue and was one of those who escaped with him. Although he had grown distant from his Lubavitch origins and had in fact been sued by the Lubavitchers over his grandfather's library, he was an indispensable source. I also spent many hours discussing the rescue with Lubavitch historian Rabbi Eliezer Zaklikovsky. In addition to being generous with his time, he provided several documents about Chabad and the Rebbe. Also, Yossef and Simon Jacobson met with me on several occasions and offered advice on my manuscript throughout 2003–2004, and both were very generous with their time. Between 2002 and 2004 I met with Milton Kramer, the son of Hyman Kramer and historian of the family, and Debby Kramer Neumark, the daughter of Sam Kramer.

To learn more about the Lubavitchers' interaction with the Roosevelt administration, as well as about US policy toward refugees, I visited the Roosevelt Institute and Library in Hyde Park, New York. I also used the Agudah Israel Archives of Orthodox Judaism and the Vaad collection at Yeshiva University, both in New York City. I have also received much help and support in finding documents from the Kleinman Holocaust Education Center in Brooklyn, New York. Archivist Dovid Reidel was especially helpful.

Rachel Altein and Eliezer Zaklikovsky's *Out of the Inferno*, a compilation of documents and eyewitness accounts, was a wonderful resource, even if it does not tell the story in full. Since 2014 I have been in touch with Wohlthat's daughter Gisela Bauer and numerous family members of Max Rhoade, including Bruce Blumberg, Annie Groer, and Barbara Baron. All these people were most helpful.

Almost simultaneous with the publication of my first book on the rescue, German historian Günter Schubert published a book on America's actions during World War II, *Der Fleck auf Uncle Sams weißer Weste*, which includes a short chapter on the rescue of the Rebbe. All his sources were known to me, but he explores several interesting insights about the rescue that I incorporated into this updated book.

The Lubavitchers and their documents were obviously essential to the story of the Rebbe's rescue. However, my dealings with them were complex and sometimes frustrating, not dissimilar from the experiences of Susan Fishkoff and Avrum Ehrlich. In researching her book *The Rebbe's Army*, Fishkoff came to many of the same conclusions I did, writing, "There's much about Chabad I don't like. . . . The messianism. The excessive veneration of the Rebbe. The refusal to recognize Reform or Conservative Judaism. The arrogance of a theology that teaches that only Jews have a godly soul and are thus privileged, above other people, to make the world a holy place."[1] Ehrlich, in his book *Leadership in the HaBaD Movement*, claims that to combat such criticism, many Lubavitchers develop private and public theologies about the Holocaust, Gentiles, and messianic strivings. In other words, they seem to speak out of both sides of their mouths to avoid being labeled parochial and exclusive.[2]

Working with the Lubavitchers on the interpretation of documents was frustrating, to say the least, since they are an ahistorical group. As

Lubavitcher rabbi Herschel Greenberg explained about Hasidic and ultra-Orthodox Jews: "Religious Jews look at history as a secondary matter to the primacy of belief. The Torah and Talmud come before history." Their ahistorical approach is dramatically revealed whenever the record of events detracts from the image of their organization or their Rebbe. If something might be construed as negative, they often say it is false or an incorrect interpretation of the documents, or they claim it is the interpretation of those who hate them or do not understand their movement. For them, questioning the Rebbe is "worse than sin." Moreover, when they find something in the documents they do not like, they often censor the material or alter it. They have even been known to fabricate documents to prove a point or to hide an unpleasant fact about their history.[3] One Lubavitch rabbi explains that finding Lubavitch sources "is easier said than done, since Lubavitch looks to the future much more than to the past. This is also why much of what you've learned by speaking to me [and others?] has been hard to document."[4] Moreover, as historian David Myers observes, modern critical thought has challenged traditional Judaism by encouraging Orthodox Jews to depart from the "tenets of inherited faith. The more one knew about the past, the more reasons there were for abandoning it."[5]

Even though some Lubavitchers were difficult to work with, many others took the time to speak with me, feed me, and read my manuscript. I am deeply thankful for all their help and kindness.[6] Yet, if they thought I might say something critical, some immediately withdrew their help, regardless of the evidence before them. Their friendship seemed to be based on the hope that I would believe what they wanted me to believe, and when that proved incorrect, they rejected me. Some went out of their way to rebut what I was writing, not by challenging the facts or the logic but by saying that I was on a mission to destroy Chabad. Although I would like to mention the Lubavitcher rabbis who helped me, I fear that they would be reprimanded by the Chabad community, so I have purposely left their names out.

The Lubavitchers resist the task of documenting the past. They live in a sacred time and celebrate sacred events, and at least some of them believe they are living at the end of history. My work as a historian is to find the best evidence of what happened, interpret the documents, and tell the story they reveal. Some (perhaps most) of my conclusions may be incompatible with the core of Lubavitcher beliefs. Furthermore, by its very nature, history situates people in a specific time and place, and events must be understood within that context. Lubavitch Hasidim want to situate the Rebbe outside of time; they want to believe that his teaching and even his spirit and presence will endure forever. I, however, am convinced that the Rebbe is dead and cannot interact with people today. I have no reason to conclude that he has some special influence on God in heaven. As a historian, I want to see the Rebbe as a man of his time, and so we may clash. Lubavitchers are what they are—worthy of our interest and admiration to some degree, but not uncritically. I am what I am—a scholar and a thinker working in accordance with his task and his discipline and preserving a piece of their history. Yet, in the end, many of the Lubavitchers are unable to see past their community. They are taught from an early age not to question their leadership or their past. As a result, instead of reflecting on critiques or engaging in healthy debate, they lash out at those who question their way of life. I came to their community with an open mind, intent to report on history as it happened, to the best of my ability. I have done my best to remain faithful to that goal.

In the last decade, I have given hundreds of talks about the Holocaust and the Rebbe. Knowing that some of what I uncovered was unflattering, I did not expect the Lubavitchers to be happy; however, I was shocked by the response of some individuals. I was offered money to remove everything negative about the Rebbe. I was promised that if I only praised the Rebbe, I would be rewarded with a book tour with honorariums from hundreds of Chabad communities, making me a rich man. I was even threatened with lawsuits if I talked derisively about the Rebbe. Nevertheless, I chose to tell the truth as I saw it. During many of my talks, Lubavitch rabbis would stand up and exclaim that I was defaming one of the greatest Jewish leaders. Who was I, they would ask, to question Joseph Isaac Schneersohn? Some Hasidic rabbis have heckled me at my lectures and claimed *Lashon Hora* (evil tongue). Yet many of them do not shy away from harshly criticizing others, including Jews of the more liberal denominations. Some of these rabbis would openly deride Jesus, calling him not just a false Messiah but one of the most despicable Jews ever. They often hold themselves out as beyond reproach when condemning other religious figures, but they become extremely defensive whenever their leaders are questioned.

Chabad has often tried to prevent me from talking, exerting pressure on those that invited me to their communities to speak. Chabad struggles in the public domain when the facts of its history and its ultimate goal for society—to convince the world that it is the only true form of Judaism—are revealed. Authors who have only positive things to say about the Rebbe (such as Edward Hoffman and Joseph Telushkin) were actually commissioned by Chabad to write their books. I would advise Chabad to be more open and objective about its history and its true intentions. Having grown up in an evangelical Christian environment, I see some of the same problems in the Chabad community that I now recognize from my childhood: the shunning of reason and scientific inquiry for blind faith, exclusivity, denial of historical truth, intimidation, and brainwashing. There is plenty of room for improvement, and I hope for that.

Today, we look back at the ancient Philistines, Aztecs, Tunisians, Greeks, and Egyptians and wonder why they worshipped their idols or performed their elaborate rituals. One day, we will probably relegate the Lubavitchers and similar ultrareligious groups to the superstitious "infancy of our species."[7] As the great transcendentalist Ralph Waldo Emerson said: "The religion of one age is the literary entertainment of the next."[8] Unless they embrace the modern world, the Lubavitchers will become like the old Jewish cults known as the Essenes or Ebionites from thousands of years ago that no longer exist. Democratically minded societies will continue to struggle with groups that claim women, Gentiles, and non-Chabad Jews are inferior. Such trivial contentions are a waste of time when we have larger issues such as fanatic Islamic groups, world hunger and poverty, North Korean and Iranian nuclear threats, and violence against women, to name just a few of today's pressing problems. Preserving some radical, eighteenth-century Jewish cult does not add to our understanding of how to create peace, how to further science, and how to heal the world (*Tikkun Olam*).

After being involved with this story for more than twenty years, I often find myself questioning why so many innocent people died in the Holocaust. If there really is a loving and just God who can and does intervene in human affairs, why did he not save millions of Jews from the

Holocaust? Why did he allow Adolf Hitler to be born, seize power, and cause such immense suffering, destruction, and death in the world? If anything, the rescue of the Rebbe shows us that if there is a God, he is a strange one indeed.

As I walked the streets of Auschwitz in 2014, I realized that 400,000 of the 1.3 million souls murdered by the Nazis there were children. I often think that they were the ones who should have been saved, rather than a zealous rabbi and his closest cohorts. While touring this death camp, I watched my two sons, aged seven and eleven, throwing rocks and running around the lone train car left at Auschwitz Birkenau, right by the selection ramp. I thought: my sons are standing on the graves and ashes of so many innocent people who deserved to be rescued. The Rebbe, in hindsight, was not the most deserving of rescue. As Michael Berenbaum writes, "The ultimate crime in the Holocaust was the murder of children. A poet has said that the death of a child is the loss of infinite possibility."[9] These "infinite possibilities" would have benefited American society much more than a fanatical religious leader. America needs fewer religious misfits, not more of them, because the fewer religious fanatics any society has, the more harmony it is likely to experience. As John M. Barry clearly illustrates in his book on the early Protestant settlers, it was religious misfits who came to this country and inflicted incredible persecution on one another. This persecution led the great founding fathers to set up a system of separation of church and state.[10] They saw that it takes secular systems to discipline religious organizations. Conversely, the very fact that America, with its secular tradition, was willing to open its borders to a person like the Rebbe shows the strength of the system that honors freedom of religion and freedom of speech. This is something about the United States that should be cherished.

ACKNOWLEDGMENTS

I have so many people to thank for their contributions to this work that it would be difficult to name them all, yet several deserve special mention. Foremost on the list is Jonathan Steinberg, my adviser at Cambridge University, where I wrote the foundation for this book under his guidance in 1997. His support and encouragement helped me through some of the most challenging experiences of my academic career. He also read the manuscript twice in 2003. I thank him from the bottom of my heart.

I would also like to mention my professor at Yale University, Paula Hyman. While taking her course on the Holocaust in the spring of 1996, I wrote a short essay about the Rebbe's rescue. At the time, she encouraged me to continue to research the subject and explore the larger issues of politics, war, and genocide surrounding this event. Her insightful comments about this work have been incredibly helpful. Her constant support throughout the years has been an inspiration, and I miss her since her untimely death in 2011.

Over the past decade and a half, distinguished Holocaust historian Michael Berenbaum of the University of Judaism honored me by reading my work several times, giving invaluable advice and criticism. His support means more to me than he will ever know. He constantly encouraged me to tell this story, and since the publication of *Hitler's Jewish Soldiers*, he has been my strongest advocate and supporter. He has been a wonderful *Doktorvater* [doctorate dissertation adviser].

I would also like to thank Larisa Heimert, my editor at Yale University, for her dedication to the 2004 version of the book. Her constant attention to detail and insightful criticism were greatly appreciated. I am also grateful to my current editor, Michael Briggs of the University Press of Kansas. This is my third book with him, and he is a pleasure to work with. Kansas is not only my publishing house but also a place where I have found several friends who are incredibly supportive and very professional.

Special thanks to the late historian David Kranzler, director of the Holocaust Archives at Queensborough Community College, who took the time to meticulously read my work and offer invaluable feedback and suggestions. This man possessed a wealth of knowledge and was a real mensch. He is also missed.

Martin Bloch, the son of the man largely responsible for the Rebbe's rescue, entrusted me with hundreds of documents about his family. I spent time at his home discussing his father and those documents on various occasions in 1996, 1997, 1998, and 2002. Without his help, I would have had a difficult time reconstructing the history of his father. Bloch was also responsible for putting me in touch with Ursula Cadenbach, Ernst Bloch's secretary. In turn, Cadenbach put me in touch with Klaus Schenk and Bettina Motz, both of whom helped me tremendously. Bloch's other children, Cornelia Shonkwiler, Maria Obenaus, and Christian Bloch, also supported this project with encouragement and information, as did Bloch's grandson Felix Bloch and his daughter-in-law Maria Bloch. These members of the Bloch family have shown incredible enthusiasm for and interest in my work, not to mention spending countless hours proofreading. Martin saw the original work published in 2004, but unfortunately, he died in 2009. Recently, Felix Bloch and Max Obenaus have been very helpful in proofreading my work and providing newly discovered primary sources on their grandfather.

Special thanks to Milton Gustafson, who assisted me in the search for documents in the National Archives. Despite being a high-ranking civil servant, he personally went into the stacks and retrieved difficult-to-find documents. Also, for his constant support and advice, I am indebted to former director Günther Montfort of the Bundesarchiv-Militärarchiv in Germany. His meticulous editing was essential for both the earlier work and this one. For his insights into Jewish and Lubavitch history, I thank Arthur Green of Brandeis University for his assistance and comments. I also thank Milton Kramer, son of former Chabad president Hyman Kramer and a former Chabad president himself, and Debby Kramer Neumark, daughter of Chabad's legal counsel Samuel Kramer. Both were invaluable in helping me reconstruct the history of their family—a family that proved instrumental in rescuing the Rebbe. Milton Kramer was very generous with his time and his willingness to help.

After getting to know many of the Lubavitchers at their Brooklyn headquarters, I found them extremely helpful and more than willing to discuss the rescue with me, in particular Leib Altein, Mordechai Dov Altein, Rachel Altein, Shmuel Fox, Zalman Gurari, Meir Greenberg, Hirsch Kotlarsky, Shalom Dovber Levine, Elie Shmotkin, Zalman Shmotkin, and Joseph Wineberg. Special thanks to Yoseph Yitzchak Jacobson, Avraham Laber, Zalman Posner, and Eliezer Zaklikovsky. These men are resident experts on Lubavitch history, and without their thoughtful suggestions and feedback, I would not have been able to piece together the story of the Rebbe's background and escape. In addition to their guidance, Laber and Zaklikovsky provided me with hundreds of pages of invaluable documents that helped me reconstruct the roles played by the US government and the Lubavitchers in the rescue. Both these men went beyond the call of duty in giving me their time and advice. Although they did not always agree with my conclusions, they remained willing to discuss the issues and debate the facts with me. Their dedication is a testimony to their sincere generosity and their devotion to Chabad and Rebbe Menachem Mendel Schneerson. They are indeed a minority among the Lubavitchers, and Zaklikovsky was subjected to derision and scorn from some of his fellow Chabad adherents for helping me. For his courage, I am thankful.

Special thanks to the late grandson of Rebbe Joseph Isaac Schneersohn, Barry Gourary, for reading my manuscript and allowing me to interview him. Although he was very old and sick, he generously shared his experiences and knowledge. He also answered many follow-up questions by telephone. He was the only living eyewitness to many of the events in this book, and he provided a counterhistory to the formal history of the Lubavitch movement. Since he was no longer part of the movement and was persona non grata with the Chabad community (owing to a fight over the ownership of his grandfather's library), he showed much courage by talking about these events. For his continued support and guidance, I thank Rabbi Dovid Gottlieb of Ohr Somayach Yeshiva in Jerusalem. I also appreciate the interview provided by the late Karin Falencki, a survivor of the 1939 attack on Poland. Her insights were truly helpful in understanding this invasion from a Warsaw resident's perspective.

I thank Winfried Meyer for his insights and research into this story, which is briefly discussed in his excellent book *Unternehmen Sieben*. Also, special thanks to David Wyman, whose scholarship about the United States during the Holocaust is unmatched. I could not have reconstructed much of the historical background without his works. For his insights into Hasidic life and for his incredible support in reading my work, I thank prominent Hasidic rabbi and Agudah leader Chaskel Besser of New York. For their advice on theological issues, special thanks to Eva Fleischner of Montclair State University, Rabbi David Lyon of Temple Shalom in Dallas, and Joe Errington, a Methodist minister who was the chaplain supervisor of the Program Review Division in the Federal Bureau of Prisons. American Military University professor James Leonard Abrahamson, whose knowledge of American history is impressive, did me the great service of reading my manuscript and offering detailed comments and criticism about its content and structure. His time spent on my behalf is greatly appreciated. For their insights into Jewish history, special thanks to distinguished Reform rabbi Kenneth Roseman; Kip Lombardo, Hillel program director at Boston University; and Bernhard Klein, chair of the History Department of Kingsborough College. The late, distinguished Holocaust historian Raul Hilberg of the University of Vermont must be acknowledged for his help, including the search for documents. During a conference in California in February 2004, he also spent time discussing possible titles and historical techniques with me, and his advice was greatly appreciated. Special thanks to Holocaust historian Donald Niewyk at Southern Methodist University for his tough criticism and helpful suggestions. And last, Professor Henry Feingold, director of the Jewish Resource Center of Baruch College in New York, did me the great service of reading the manuscript and providing several valuable suggestions.

I would like to thank my friend, the late Peter Schliesser, for his editorial comments. He suffered under the Nazis as a "half-Jew" and provided insights that enriched my research tremendously. For her insight into Judaism and her careful reading, thanks to Roseanne Schnoll, a professor at Brooklyn College. Special thanks to historian Alex Rossino of the US Holocaust Memorial Museum for his careful reading of my work and his invaluable criticism. I thank the highly decorated Loach pilot (three Distinguished Flying Crosses) and Vietnam veteran Jim Wood for his helpful comments. For their constructive criticism and advice, I thank former Yale professor Mark Shulman and Hugh Corbet, president of the Cordell Hull Institute. My agent Rob McQuilkin went beyond the call of duty and read my work twice, offering valuable feedback. Rabbi Moshe Kolodny, director of Agudath Israel of America Archives in New York, not only helped me find documents but he also read the manuscript and gave me useful feedback. I also appreciate Grace Roosevelt of the Roosevelt family, whose suggestions strengthened the book.

The following people deserve special thanks for their professionalism and help in finding documents for this book: Sam Anthony, special program director at the National Archives in Washington, DC; Kate Flaherty, archives specialist in still pictures at the National Archives in College Park, Maryland; archivist Robert Clark of the Franklin D. Roosevelt Library in Hyde Park, New York; Misha Mitsel at the Joint Distribution Committee Archives in New York; and Shulamith Berger, curator of the Special Collection at Yeshiva University in New York.

I must thank Frank Hytken, JD, who spent countless hours helping me revise and edit this new edition. He is a former Marine Corps officer and a voracious reader, and his historical insights were invaluable. Also, Reid Heller, JD, adjunct professor of Jewish studies from the University of North Texas, provided excellent insights into Jewish thought and Hasidic history. One of the smartest people I know, Kevin Murphy, JD, helped me tremendously with historical sources. These dear friends, along with Gracie Golonka and Michael Scholten, made this book better. Historian Colin Heaton was generous with his time and primary sources, helping me strengthen this book. Also, my former Yale professor and good friend Jeffrey Sammons did me the great honor of reading this second version. His comments made the book both stronger and shorter. To everyone mentioned here, thank you all again. A good book is never written alone. It takes the help and support of many, and I thank all these people from the bottom of my heart.

ORIGINAL FOREWORD FOR
Rescued from the Reich

The stories of rescue of Jews from Nazi slaughter, though regrettably limited in number, are inherently compelling. They usually involve individuals who, for one reason or another, chose to defy authority, breaking with the dominant indifference of their societies to what was happening to the Jews in their midst.

Some, like the Huguenots of Le Chambon-sur-Lignon in France, who hid thousands of Jews in their village and smuggled others to Switzerland, were motivated by religious conviction, a charismatic and influential pastor, and suspicion of the state honed by their experience as a small Protestant minority in a Catholic land. Others, like Sempo Sugihara, the Japanese consul general in Kovno, Lithuania, were true bystanders who seem to have been offended by state persecution of innocent civilians. On his own authority, and in direct violation of his government's policy, in 1939–40 he issued some sixteen hundred Japanese transit visas to Jews so that they could escape from Soviet-occupied Lithuania.

Equally offended was Varian Fry, but he did not chance to encounter a problem close by. He chose to confront it, leaving the security of America in 1940 to rescue German and East European refugees. A Harvard-educated Protestant anti-Fascist raised with a liberal social conscience, he represented the privately funded Emergency Rescue Committee, established after the fall of France to aid prominent figures in the arts and sciences, Jews and non-Jews, to escape from Europe. During his year in Marseille, he incurred the wrath of American officials for his dedication to his task. Before he was expelled from Vichy France in August 1941, he succeeded in smuggling more than a thousand refugees, among them Hannah Arendt, Marc Chagall, Jacques Lipchitz, and many less famous people, to safety. And then there were mavericks like Oskar Schindler, who disliked being told what to do. A man who relished taking risks, he risked his life to save the Jews who worked in his factory.

Even among these rare accounts, the story of the rescue of Joseph Schneersohn, the leader, or Rebbe, of the Lubavitch Hasidic sect, his family, and his entourage and their relocation in early 1940 to the United

States stands out. Indeed, the Lubavitch Hasidim understand this event, and the survival of their Rebbe, as a mark of divine providence. This rescue was not an act of providing shelter to, or hiding, Jews in Nazi-occupied Europe. Most of the few Jews who survived the Holocaust in Eastern Europe without spending time in concentration or death camps were assisted in some way by local Gentiles, sometimes out of compassion, sometimes in exchange for money. Schneersohn's daring rescue was carried out not by religiously committed individuals, not by political dissidents, and not by those seeking financial gain. An unlikely combination of high officials in the U.S. government and members of the Nazi army and government cooperated to implement it.

Pursuing every clue, amassing the archival evidence, and interviewing persons with relevant information, Bryan Mark Rigg recounts what reads like a political thriller. His assiduous research, which carefully reconstructs the different stages of the rescue plan, connecting the dots of what may seem like a fantastic scheme, provides what will be the definitive narrative of this striking episode.

What is truly remarkable in Rigg's account is his evidence of the active collaboration of Nazi soldiers and officials, who presumably cared little for the survival of any Jews, in carrying out the rescue. Here he draws upon the research he presented in his first book, *Hitler's Jewish Soldiers*, a study of Germans with some Jewish ancestry who served in the Wehrmacht, the Nazi armed forces. A key figure in ensuring that the rescue went as planned was Major Ernst Bloch, a Nazi officer who had a Jewish father but who had been officially "Aryanized" by order of Hitler. Other men of Jewish descent were also selected for the mission, perhaps with the presumption that they might see their participation as a protest against the racist policy that demeaned them and endangered members of their families.

Yet the highest Nazi officer who took charge of the rescue plan, Admiral Wilhelm Canaris, head of the Abwehr, the Nazi military intelligence service, was not of Jewish origin. His agreement to participate might be seen as an early sign of his later disaffection with Hitler. Similarly, another Nazi, Helmuth Wohlthat, chief administrator of Göring's Four Year Plan, who was in charge of organizing the rescue, fully met Nazi racial criteria. He was known to some American diplomats, having met with them to discuss the problem of refugees from Germany. The involvement of these men in the project provides additional evidence for the arguments of many scholars of the Third Reich that Nazi antisemitism was not monolithic. Not every Nazi was a fanatic antisemite nor did every member of the Nazi government place the solution of the "Jewish problem" at the top of the regime's priorities. There were members of the Nazi Party and the government, not to mention the army, who did not fully endorse Nazi racism, even if they often kept their reservations to themselves. Moreover, some Nazi officials may have thought that the release of a few prominent Jews might provide some much needed positive public relations, given the regime's violations of treaties, annexation of Austria, and invasion of Poland.

The initiative for the plan, however, did not come from the Germans. Without pressure from the U.S. State Department, the rescue of the Lubavitcher Rebbe would not have occurred. Yet this same State Department had demonstrated no interest in saving Jews from Nazi persecution before the outbreak of war. As numerous studies have documented, the State Department followed an obstructionist policy that prevented the vast majority of Jewish refugees from Germany and Austria from entering the United States during the thirties. The international conference on the refugee problem convened in Evian in 1938 announced in advance that no country would be required, or expected, to accept more refugees as a result of participating. Along with virtually every other country represented at the conference, the United States shed crocodile tears for the victims of Nazi persecution but did not change its restrictive policies.

The involvement of Secretary of State Cordell Hull in the mission that successfully rescued the Lubavitcher Rebbe from Poland and brought him to the United States raises questions that this book cannot definitively answer. Why did the U.S. government engage in diplomatic contacts with Nazi political and military figures to ensure the safety of a Jewish religious leader when antisemitism, as measured by polls, was at its height in the United States? Why the concern for one rabbi when the Nazis had not yet decided to solve the "Jewish problem" in the East through mass murder? Jews in Poland seemed to be in no more danger for their lives than other civilians in an occupied war zone. To be sure, in 1939–40 the United States was not at war with the Germans and therefore had some diplomatic leverage. Further, an impressive roster of Jewish politicians and prominent public figures lobbied on behalf of the beleaguered Rebbe. They ranged from Congressman Sol Bloom of New York to Attorney General Benjamin Cohen to Justice Louis Brandeis of the Supreme Court. They secured the intervention of other politicians, including Senator Robert Wagner of New York and Postmaster General James A. Farley. It is likely that American officials' ignorance of the social topography of American Judaism, when combined with the political pressure exerted by well-placed politicians, may have persuaded them that the rescue of the Rebbe, described as an important spiritual leader, could yield good publicity at a minimum risk. Certainly the Roosevelt administration did not have to worry about its domestic Jewish support. But the administration may have presumed that the high-profile rescue would deflect Jewish pressure for the entry into America of many more Jewish refugees.

What appears most significant in the decision to go forward with the rescue was the concerted efforts of Lubavitch Jews themselves. Dedicated to their Rebbe, without whom they could not envision the survival of Lubavitch Hasidism, they used every contact they and their supporters possessed to get their pleas heard. They seem to have persuaded American politicians and diplomats that Rabbi Schneersohn was a very impor-tant spiritual leader and that Lubavitch Hasidism was a major component of world Jewry. This was ironic, for there were numerous Hasidic sects in Eastern Europe, and the Lubavitcher Rebbe was not the most prominent European rabbi. Nor did Lubavitch Hasidism occupy a preeminent place within the American Jewish community of the time; it was a far less visible group than it subsequently became, and it has always remained small. Within Orthodoxy in America, in fact, Hasidism as a whole played a minor role. Even now, after the post–World War II influx of Hasidim, it has been estimated to account for only 5 percent of American Orthodoxy. In 1939, most American Jews who aspired to, or had reached, middle-class status were affiliating with Conservative and Reform Judaism, while Orthodoxy was associated with immigrants who had not yet Americanized. There were fully acculturated Orthodox Jews in America, but the followers of Lubavitch Hasidism were not among them. Mainstream Orthodoxy in America found its sources of authority in the newly built Yeshiva

College and in non-Hasidic *yeshivot*, academies of Talmudic learning, not in Hasidic institutions.

Lubavitch Hasidim, however, were conscious of the importance of political power and had maintained contacts within the American Jewish community and with influential politicians. Senator Wagner, in appealing to Hull, commented that many Jewish organizations in New York were concerned about Schneersohn. The Lubavitch Hasidim may have retained cultural markers associated with Jewish immigrants from Eastern Europe, but they were aware of the sites of political power in America. And some of their supporters were prosperous businessmen and lawyers. Their president was the CEO of a successful manufacturing company. He and his family had close ties with the American Jewish Joint Distribution Committee, a major philanthropic institution that provided assistance to Jewish communities in Europe and had great influence there. The Lubavitch leadership in America also recognized the importance of the press in spreading information about the Rebbe and his preeminence. Schneersohn's 1927 arrest in the U.S.S.R. and his threatened death sentence and subsequent expulsion from that country had attracted international press attention, and he had even traveled to the United States in 1929–1930. During that visit he had a meeting with President Hoover. Indeed, press coverage of his American trip was cited by Hull as tending to establish his "high ecclesiastical position."

The focus on one prominent person, a spiritual leader and great scholar, as he was described, proved successful. Even politicians and diplomats appreciated the power of the story of a single victim, with a name and a biography, as opposed to anonymous throngs of equally deserving victims. Schneersohn's rescue did not challenge the quota system that governed U.S. immigration policy in the way that the unsuccessful Wagner-Rogers Bill, which sought in 1939 to bring 20,000, mostly Jewish, refugee children from Germany to the United States over two years, did. The coming together of pious Hasidim, American diplomats, and German soldiers and government officials at the beginning of the Second World War to rescue a rabbi and his entourage is an example of the contingency that is a part of every historical incident. Had the Lubavitch Hasidim waited until late 1940, the Schneersohns would have faced the horrible conditions of ghettoization. Had the United States entered the war at its inception, the rescue would have become impossible. Had the numerous contacts between Germany, Poland, and the United States broken down, the plan would have been stymied.

We will never know just what motivated the various players in this dramatic episode, except to note that altruism seems not to have played a central role. Bryan Mark Rigg enables us, however, to follow the complex negotiations that fueled the rescue of the Lubavitcher Rebbe and to take stock of the innumerable threads that had to mesh to save even a handful of Jews from the Holocaust.

Paula Hyman
Yale University, 2004

NOTES

ABBREVIATIONS

BA-B	Bundesarchiv, Berlin, Germany
BA-MA	Bundesarchiv/Militärarchiv, Freiburg, Germany
BMRS	Bryan Mark Rigg Sammlung [Collection], BA-MA
CLD	Chabad Library Documents
IfZ	Institut für Zeitgeschichte, Munich, Germany
KHEC	Kleinman Holocaust Education Center, Brooklyn, New York
NARA	National Archives and Records Administration, Washington, DC
RGBL	Reichsgesetzblatt, BA-MA
WNRC	Washington National Records Center, Suitland, Maryland
YU-VHC	Yeshiva University Archives, Vaad Hatzala Collection 1939–1963, New York, New York

INTRODUCTION

1. Efraim Zuroff, review of Rachel Altein and Eliezer Zaklikovsky, eds., *Out of the Inferno, Jerusalem Post*, 15 December 2002.

2. According to historians Menachem Friedman and Samuel Heilman, when the Lubavitchers do their missionary work, they spend time only with people who are Jews according to the Orthodox definition. They "will not work with 'half-Jews' or 'Jews by choice.' Even Gentiles, for whom the Noahide laws could be invoked, were easier populations than the children of mixed marriages." Thus, anyone not meeting the Halachic definition of a Jew is usually ignored by Lubavitchers. Menachem Friedman and Samuel Heilman, *The Rebbe: The Life and Afterlife of Menachem Mendel Schneerson* (Princeton, NJ, 2010), 257.

3. Phylacteries are small boxes, usually made of leather, that contain Hebrew scriptures on vellum and are worn by Jewish men during prayers to remind them to keep Halacha (Jewish law).

4. Uri Kaploun, ed., *Likkutei Dibburim: An Anthology of Talks by Rabbi Yosef Yitzchak Schneersohn of Lubavitch*, 5 vols. (Brooklyn, NY, 1987–2000), 3:40, 5:315.

5. Ibid., 3:41–42, 56–57, 62–63, 4:71; Chaim Dalfin, *The Seven Chabad-Lubavitch Rebbes* (New York, 1998), 109.

6. Paul Johnson, *A History of the American People* (New York, 1997), 769–777; Gerhard L. Weinberg, *A World at Arms: A Global History of World War II* (New York, 1994), 85–86; Yehuda Bauer, *A History of the Holocaust* (New York, 1982), 130; David M. Kennedy, *The American People in World War II: Freedom from Fear Part Two* (Oxford, 1999), 46.

7. Gregory Wallance, *America's Soul in the Balance: The Holocaust, FDR's*

State Department, and the Moral Disgrace of an American Aristocracy (Austin, TX, 2012), 201.

8. This is indeed a complicated argument that deserves more exploration. For an excellent book on what could have happened had the Allies stood up to Hitler in 1939 and 1940, see Ernest R. May, *Strange Victory: Hitler's Conquest of France* (New York, 2000).

9. Martin Gilbert, *The Holocaust* (New York, 1985), 84; Ian Kershaw, *Hitler 1936–1945: Nemesis* (New York, 2000), 152–153.

10. Kershaw, *Hitler 1936–1945*, 152–153.

11. Erik Larson, *In the Garden of Beasts: Love, Terror, and an American Family in Hitler's Berlin* (New York, 2011), 137, 351.

12. William Shakespeare, *The Tempest*, act II, scene 2, lines 33–41.

13. Michael Berenbaum, *The World Must Know: The History of the Holocaust as Told in the United States Holocaust Memorial Museum* (Baltimore, 2007), xxi.

14. Plato, *The Trial and Death of Socrates: Apology* (Cambridge, 1975), 39. Joseph Campbell states it even more dramatically: "The person who thinks he has found the ultimate truth is wrong. There is an often-quoted verse in Sanskrit, which appears in the Chinese *Tao-te Ching* as well: 'He who thinks he knows, doesn't know. He who knows that he doesn't know, knows. For in this context, to know is not to know. And not to know is to know.'" Joseph Campbell with Bill Moyers, *The Power of Myth* (New York, 1991), 65.

CHAPTER 1. THE INVASION OF POLAND
AND THE RESCUE SETUP

1. Nicholas Bethell, *The War Hitler Won: The Fall of Poland, September 1939* (New York, 1972), 13, 140.

2. Gregory Wallance, *America's Soul in the Balance: The Holocaust, FDR's State Department, and the Moral Disgrace of an American Aristocracy* (Austin, TX, 2012), 22.

3. Heinz Höhne, *Canaris* (New York, 1979), 338–339; Bethell, *War Hitler Won*, 2–3; Yisrael Gutman, *The Jews of Warsaw, 1939–1943: Ghetto, Underground, Revolt* (Bloomington, IN, 1982), 3; Victor Madej and Steven Zaloga, *The Polish Campaign 1939* (New York, 1985), 106–107; Martin Gilbert, *The Second World War: A Complete History* (New York, 1989), 1; William L. Shirer, *The Nightmare Years 1930–1940* (New York, 1984), 448–449; André Brissaud, *Canaris* (London, 1986), 141; Norman Davies, *God's Playground: A History of Poland*, vol. 2, *1795 to the Present* (New York, 1982), 435. For a detailed report on the "Tin Cans" operation, see Leonard Mosely, *On Borrowed Time: How World War II Began* (New York, 1969), 417–443.

4. Bethell, *War Hitler Won*, 2; Höhne, *Canaris*, 353. Although Germany had signed a nonaggression pact with Poland in 1934, when its military was dramatically smaller than that of Poland, it now blatantly violated that agreement. John

Keegan, *The Second World War* (New York, 1990), 44. Hitler never kept his promises.

5. Ian Kershaw, *Hitler 1936–1945: Nemesis* (New York, 2000), 122–123; Winston S. Churchill, *The Second World War*, vol. 1, *The Gathering Storm* (Boston, 1983), 318; Wallance, *America's Soul*, 197. Chamberlain did everything he could to avoid war, even things that seem naïve and foolhardy to a modern reader, such as thinking he could trust and work with Hitler. He had been so profoundly influenced by the horror of World War I that he said: "I am myself a man of peace to the depths of my soul. Armed conflict between nations is a nightmare to me." Churchill, *Second World War*, 315. With respect to the sacrifice of Czechoslovakia, it is interesting to note that when the Western powers were slicing up this country in the "interest" of peace, Poland took advantage of the situation and demanded the frontier called Teschen. As Churchill wrote, the Poles swooped in to "grasp their share of the pillage and ruin of Czechoslovakia." So, despite its destruction by the Germans in 1939, one must remember that when Poland had power over others, it behaved very poorly and showed its own "villainy." Ibid., 322–323, 347–348.

6. Wallance, *America's Soul*, 197.

7. Kershaw, *Hitler 1936–1945*, 123. Shockingly, no Czechoslovakian government official "was invited to the meeting that dismembered the country." David Kertzer, *The Pope and Mussolini: The Secret History of Pius XI and the Rise of Fascism in Europe* (Oxford, 2014), 325.

8. Interestingly, when one studies the Brest-Litovsk Treaty between Germany and Russia to end the war in the east in 1917, it was much harsher on Russia than the Versailles Treaty was on Germany. So, when Germany had the upper hand, it proved to be less moderate than those nations that ultimately defeated it in 1918. One is reminded of the old truism that Germany "is either at your throat or at your feet." See Anton Gill, *An Honourable Defeat: A History of German Resistance to Hitler 1933–1945* (New York, 1994), 3; Sheila Fitzpatrick, *The Russian Revolution 1917–1932* (Oxford, 1990), 65.

9. Davies, *God's Playground*, 435; Jerzy Jan Lerski, *Historical Dictionary of Poland, 966–1945* (Westport, CT, 1996), 646; John Toland, *Adolf Hitler* (New York, 1976), 569; Mosely, *On Borrowed Time*, 436. The reference to Thermopylae comes from a battle between the Spartans under King Leonidas and the Persians under Xerxes in 480 BCE. Supposedly, a small band of Spartans held off the Persians for several days and killed many more than their own number before they all died. See Peter Green, *Ancient Greece: A Concise History* (New York, 1973), 111–115.

10. Interview with Karin Falencki (née Tiche), 3 January 2003, BMRS, BA-MA. The story about the planes fighting above Warsaw is confirmed by others. See Hania Warfield and Gaither Warfield, *Call Us to Witness: A Polish Chronicle* (New York, 1945), 25. See also Rachel Altein and Eliezer Zaklikovsky,

eds., *Out of the Inferno: The Efforts that Led to the Rescue of the Rabbi Yosef Y. Schneersohn of Lubavitch from War-torn Europe in 1939–1940* (Brooklyn, NY, 2002), 305; Gutman, *Jews of Warsaw*, 4; Bethell, *War Hitler Won*, 4.

11. Kershaw, *Hitler 1936–1945*, 190, 200; Alexander B. Rossino, *Hitler Strikes Poland: Blitzkrieg, Ideology, and Atrocity* (Lawrence, KS, 2003), 5–7, 225; Erich von Manstein, *Lost Victories: The War Memoirs of Hitler's Most Brilliant General* (Novato, CA, 1982), 24.

12. Keegan, *Second World War*, 44–47; Churchill, *Second World War*, 443–445; Bethell, *War Hitler Won*, 27–28; Matthew Cooper, *German Army 1933–1945: Its Political and Military Failure* (New York, 1978), 169–171.

13. Robert M. Citino, *The German Way of War: From the Thirty Years' War to the Third Reich* (Lawrence, KS, 2005), 262–263.

14. Gutman, *Jews of Warsaw*, 4; Saul S. Friedman, *No Haven for the Oppressed: United States Policy toward Jewish Refugees, 1938–1945* (Detroit, 1973), 39, 43. The unemployment rate at this time was 15 percent. Rafael Medoff and David Wyman, *A Race against Death: Peter Bergson, America, and the Holocaust* (New York, 2002), 1; Yehuda Bauer, *American Jewry and the Holocaust: The American Jewish Joint Distribution Committee, 1939–1945* (Detroit, 1981), 39. Even President Franklin Roosevelt was somewhat prejudiced against Jews. See Ted Morgan, *FDR: A Biography* (New York, 1985), 508–509; Doris Kearns Goodwin, *No Ordinary Time: Franklin and Eleanor Roosevelt—The Home Front in World War II* (New York, 1994), 102; David Wyman, *The Abandonment of the Jews: America and the Holocaust 1941–1945* (New York, 1989), 6; Walter LaFeber, *The American Age: United States Foreign Policy at Home and Abroad since 1750* (New York, 1989), 367–368.

15. Friedman, *No Haven*, 174; Bauer, *American Jewry*, 39; Deborah E. Lipstadt, *Beyond Belief: The American Press & the Coming of the Holocaust 1933–1945* (New York, 1986), 92–93, 129; David Wyman, *Paper Walls: America and the Refugee Crisis 1938–1941* (New York, 1985), 10; Karen Armstrong, *The Battle for God* (New York, 2000), 216; Hasia R. Diner, *Jews in America* (New York, 1999), 89. Many of FDR's critics called the New Deal the "Jew Deal" because he had several Jewish Americans advising him at the time, including Benjamin V. Cohen and Henry Morgenthau.

16. Neil Rolde, *Breckinridge Long: American Eichmann* (Solon, ME, 2013), 139–140.

17. The term *blitzkrieg* was first used in a 1939 issue of *Time* magazine to describe the amazing German victories in Poland. It later came to denote a combined-arms action using planes, tanks, and infantry in coordinated attacks against an enemy's center of gravity. Robert M. Citino, *Quest for Decisive Victory: From Stalemate to Blitzkrieg in Europe, 1899–1940* (Lawrence, KS, 2002), 181.

18. LaFeber, *American Age*, 364–366, 369, 373; Robert A. Divine, T. H. Breen, George M. Fredrickson, and R. Hal Williams, *America: Past and Present*

(London, 1987), 783–784; Jacob Heilbrunn, "War Torn: 'Those Angry Days' and '1940,'" *New York Times*, 25 July 2013; Wallance, *America's Soul*, 198.

19. James MacGregor Burns, *Roosevelt*, vol. 1, *The Lion and the Fox* (Norwalk, CT, 1956), 394; David M. Kennedy, *Freedom from Fear: The American People in Depression and War, 1929–1945* (New York, 1999), 425; George McJimsey, *The Presidency of Franklin Delano Roosevelt* (Lawrence, KS, 1999), 193–194, 203. Roosevelt said almost the same thing about Americans not remaining "neutral" in the "mind of conscience" when Japan invaded Indochina in 1940.

20. W. F. Keylor, "France and the Illusion of American Support, 1919–1940," in *The French Defeat: Reassessments*, ed. Joel Blatt (Providence, RI, 1998), 204–244.

21. Marc Eric McClure, *Earnest Endeavors: The Life and Public Work of George Rublee* (Westport, CT, 2003), 256.

22. Jane Schapiro, *Inside a Class Action: The Holocaust and the Swiss Banks* (Madison, WI, 2003), 47, 114, 129, 131, 137, 157–159. The Swiss banks continued to do business with some of the most despicable people in the world, including Yasir Arafat, Vladimir Putin, and Kim Jong-il. See Luke Harding, "Putin, the Kremlin Power Struggle and the $40 Billion Fortune," *Guardian*, 20 December 2007; Paul Roderick Gregory, "Want Putin's Attention on Ukraine? Follow His Money," *Forbes*, 3 March 2014; Issam Abu Issa, "Arafat's Swiss Bank Account," *Middle East Quarterly* (Fall 2004): 15–23; Oliver Arlow, "Kim Jong-il Keeps $4 Billion 'Emergency Fund' in European Banks," *Telegraph*, 20 February 2015.

23. Schapiro, *Inside a Class Action*, 202; Matthew Allen, "Ten Years after Swiss Banks Agreed to Pay Back Assets to Holocaust Victims, One of the Deal's Chief Architects Said It Helped Lift a Cloud over the Country," *Swiss News*, 11 August 2008; "Banks and the Holocaust; Unsettling," *Economist*, 17 August 2000. Credit Suisse's bad behavior has continued throughout the years, and it has not learned from its mistakes. For instance, Credit Suisse received the largest fine levied by the United States for violating economic sanctions against Iran (2009), and it was fined again for "bundling mortgage loans with securities [and] misrepresenting the risk" of those "mortgages during the housing boom" (2012). Its most recent fine was a staggering $2.6 billion levied by the Justice Department for violating US tax laws (2014). John Eligon and Claudio Gatti, "Iranian Dealings Lead to a Fine for Credit Suisse," *New York Times*, 15 December 2009; Aaron Lucchetti and Jay Solomon, "Credit Suisse's Secret Deals," *Wall Street Journal*, 17 December 2009; "New York Sues Credit Suisse over Mortgages," *New York Times*, 29 November 2012; Tom Braithwaite, "Credit Suisse Pleads Guilty to Tax Evasion," *Financial Times*, 19 May 2014. Besides Schapiro's *Inside a Class Action*, which details how poorly Credit Suisse and UBS behaved with respect to Holocaust victims' assets, see Tom Bower's *Nazi Gold: The Full Story of the Fifty-Year Swiss-Nazi Conspiracy to Steal Billions from Europe's Jews and Holocaust Survivors* (New York, 1997).

24. Schapiro, *Inside a Class Action*, 114.

25. Toland, *Adolf Hitler*, 572. Anti-Semitic attacks against Roosevelt were common from German and Italian sources. In 1938 *Il Popolo d'Italia* called FDR "a Jew by race" and the "Pope of World Jewry" and claimed that the US government was controlled by Jews. Kertzer, *Pope and Mussolini*, 352. On one occasion Hitler called Roosevelt a "petty-fogging Jew" and then commented that his wife was "completely negroid" in appearance and clearly a "half-caste." Wallance, *America's Soul*, 120.

26. "Bill to Aid Britain Strongly Backed," *New York Times*, 9 February 1941; Wallance, *America's Soul*, 198–200.

27. Paul Johnson, *A History of the American People* (New York, 1997), 769. General Keitel reportedly claimed that the Allies would do nothing when Germany attacked Poland because "France was too degenerate, Britain too decadent, America too uninterested to fight for Poland." Gill, *Honourable Defeat*, 115.

28. Chaim A. Kaplan, *Scroll of Agony: The Warsaw Diary of Chaim A. Kaplan* (New York, 1965), 19; Keegan, *Second World War*, 40–41.

29. Ernest R. May, *Strange Victory: Hitler's Conquest of France* (New York, 2000), 197.

30. Keegan, *Second World War*, 43, 47; Max Hastings, *All Hell Let Loose: The World at War 1939–1945* (London, 2012), 11; Gerhard L. Weinberg, *A World at Arms: A Global History of World War II* (New York, 1994), 34–52.

31. Kershaw, *Hitler 1936–1945*, 240–244; Rossino, *Hitler Strikes Poland*, 1. See also Martin Gilbert, *The Holocaust* (New York, 1985); Arno J. Mayer, *Why Did the Heavens Not Darken: The "Final Solution" in History* (New York, 1988).

32. Although the Germans had not undertaken systematic extermination at this point, they had been conducting programs within Germany to euthanize those classified as subhuman or degenerate.

33. Yehuda Bauer, *A History of the Holocaust* (New York, 1982), 142–143; Bauer, *American Jewry*, 31, 67; Davies, *God's Playground*, 264; Falencki interview; Nora Levin, *The Holocaust: The Destruction of European Jewry, 1933–1945* (New York, 1973), 207. See also Bethell, *War Hitler Won*, 13.

34. Jonathan Steinberg, *All or Nothing: The Axis and the Holocaust 1941–1943* (New York, 1991), 50–51.

35. Gilbert, *Holocaust*, 84; Todd Brewster and Peter Jennings, *The Century* (New York, 1998), 213; Wolfgang Benz, *The Holocaust: A German Historian Examines the Genocide* (New York, 1999), 61; Kershaw, *Hitler 1936–1945*, 152–153; Gutman, *Jews of Warsaw*, 11; Paul Johnson, *A History of the Jews* (New York, 1987), 492; Wyman, *Abandonment of the Jews*, 4, 19; Bethell, *War Hitler Won*, 13; Gilbert, *Second World War*, 4; Gill, *Honourable Defeat*, 231. In regards to Wolfgang Benz, his sources need to be used with caution. Due to recent controversies where he invited anti-Semites like Sabine Schiffer to speak at his center and it being discovered that he had kept secret the fact that his professor and mentor was a Nazi named Karl Bosl, his sources need to be used with care. Even when

confronted with the fact that the public knew about Bosl, Benz surprisingly refused to distance himself from his "Nazi doctoral supervisor" or condemn the
man who was a "high-level member of the Nazi party and an energetic ideologue
of the Hitler movement." Also, it seems like he has failed to recognize the danger
of Islamic fanatics in the world. He has even equated anti-Semitism with "Islam-
ophobia," an argument Dr. Clemens Heni at Yale University totally refutes and
shows to be in error. Even Rabbi Meir Lau, chairman of the Yad Vashem Board of
Directors and chief rabbi of Tel Aviv, criticized Benz for such arguments. When
the controversy heated up, Benz tried to pass blame onto others as being behind
it, but in the end, it turned out he had made up the story about those people actually being the instigators. The head of the German American Jewish Committee
Office, Deidra Berger, said that Benz has proved to be a big disappointment to
the Jewish community inside and outside of Germany for his lack of courage and
latent prejudice (interview with Deidra Berger, 20 June 2014). Supposedly due to
these controversies and because he has de-legitimatized his own center, he had to
leave the Center for Research on Anti-Semitism at the Technical University in
Berlin, which he has led for years. It is sad to see what many had once thought
to be such a great scholar fall from grace with such horrible revelations. See Clemens Heni, "Why Prof. Wolfgang Benz Is Headed in the Wrong Direction,"
Wissenschaft und Publizistik als Kritk, 1 May 2009. Dr. Heni wrote this article
while he was a researcher at the Yale Initiative for the Interdisciplinary Study
of Anti-Semitism (YIISA), Yale University. See also Benjamin Weinthal, "Berlin
Professor Slammed for Defending Nazi," *The Jerusalem Post*, 31 January 2010.

36. Gilbert, *Second World War*, 5.

37. Kaplan, *Scroll of Agony*, 20–21, 28.

38. Gilbert, *Second World War*, 7.

39. Henry Ashby Turner Jr., *Hitler's Thirty Days to Power: January 1933*
(London, 1996), 182–183.

40. Levin, *Holocaust*, 149–150; Gilbert, *Holocaust*, 87–108; Mayer, *Why Did
the Heavens Not Darken*, 182. See also Chaim Shlomo Friedman, *Dare to Survive* (New York, 1991). For more information about General Heydrich's policies about resettlement, see Nuremberg Trials Document PS-3363, Heydrich's
Schnellbrief, 21 September 1939. Special thanks to Raul Hilberg for providing
this document.

41. Edward Hoffman, *Despite All Odds: The Story of Lubavitch* (New York,
1991),15; Shimon Huberband, *Kiddusch Hashem: Jewish Religious and Cultural
Life in Poland during the Holocaust* (New York, 1987), 178; Levin, *Holocaust*,
150; Steven E. Aschheim, *Brothers and Strangers: The East European Jew in
German and German Jewish Consciousness, 1800–1923* (Madison, WI, 1982),
143–145, 150–151; Jürgen Matthäus, "German *Judenpolitik* in Lithuania during
the First World War," *Leo Baeck Yearbook* 43 (1998): 162–164; Trude Maurer,
Ostjuden in Deutschland, 1918–1933 (Hamburg, 1986), 26–28. The term *Ost-*

juden must be used carefully, as it has been employed throughout history in a very derisive way. The literal translation of *Ostjuden* is simply "Jews from the East," and many Jews in eastern Europe at this time were neither ultrareligious nor primitive in their thinking. But as noted by Reid Heller, an adjunct professor at the University of North Texas, this term can be a horrible epithet similar to "nigger" or "kike."

42. Aschheim, *Brothers and Strangers*, 3; Peter Noa file, Bl. 9, BMRS, BA-MA.

43. Aschheim, *Brothers and Strangers*, 3–5, 13–14, 152; Noa file, Bl. 9; Primo Levi, *Moments of Reprieve: A Memoir of Auschwitz* (New York, 1995), 20.

44. Carl J. Rheins, "Verband nationaldeutscher Juden 1921–1933," *Leo Baeck Yearbook* 25 (1980): 255; Aschheim, *Brothers and Strangers*, 15; Jeffrey L. Sammons, *Heinrich Heine: A Modern Biography* (Princeton, NJ, 1979), 25, 39, 97.

45. Adolf Hitler, *Mein Kampf* (Boston, 1971), 56–57. In the original German, Hitler used the term *Judenlein*, which some would translate not as "kike" but as "little Jew" or "Jew boy." Regardless of the translation, Hitler was obviously using a derisive term.

46. Steinberg, *All or Nothing*, 194. Steinberg writes that for Hitler, "Jews became maggots, germs, dirt, rottenness, putrefaction. In Hitler's disordered fancy, he must wage a constant war against infection. In April 1943 he told Admiral Horthy: 'They had to be handled like tubercular bacilli which could infect a healthy body. That wasn't horrible when one thought about the fact that innocent creatures of nature like hares and deer had to be killed to prevent damage.' The basic argument behind Hitler's madness was pure social Darwinism." Ibid., 195.

47. Sebastian Haffner, *The Meaning of Hitler* (Cambridge, 1979), 9. Haffner is a journalist, not a historian, so his use of the term "extermination" to describe actions carried out before Hitler came to power may strike one as exaggerated. There was indeed oppression, marginalization, exclusion, and the occasional pogrom in eastern Europe before 1939, but "extermination" is probably too extreme a term for anything predating Hitler.

48. Hannah Arendt, *Eichmann in Jerusalem: A Report on the Banality of Evil* (New York, 1964), 228. Herschel Grynszpan's family was one of those forcibly deported to Poland with these *Ostjuden*. He was living in Paris at the time. Enraged at this injustice, he got a gun and assassinated a low-level German diplomat named Ernst vom Rath on 7 November 1938. The Nazis used this to launch their nationwide pogrom called *Kristallnacht* on 9–10 November 1938. Johnson, *History of the Jews*, 485; McClure, *Earnest Endeavors*, 264; Wallance, *America's Soul*, 44.

49. Huberband, *Kiddusch Hashem*, xii–xiii; Uri Kaploun, ed., *Likkutei Dibburim: An Anthology of Talks by Rabbi Yosef Yitzchak Schneersohn of Lubavitch*, 5 vols. (Brooklyn, NY, 1987–2000), 2:82–83, 89. The Torah means "instruction."

Chaim Miller, *Turning Judaism Outward: A Biography of the Rebbe Menachem Mendel Schneerson* (Brooklyn, NY, 2014), 136; Menachem Friedman and Samuel Heilman, *The Rebbe: The Life and Afterlife of Menachem Mendel Schneerson* (Princeton, NJ, 2010), 101.

50. Brissaud, *Canaris*, 157.

51. Levin, *Holocaust*, 154–155; *The Von Hassell Diaries 1938–1944: The Story of the Forces against Hitler Inside Germany as Recorded by Ambassador Ulrich von Hassell—A Leader of the Movement* (New York, 1947), 79; Nicolaus von Below, *Als Hitlers Adjutant 1937–1945* (Mainz, 1980), 72–73; Brissaud, *Canaris*, 157; Kershaw, *Hitler 1936–1945*, 248.

52. Brissaud, *Canaris*, 157; Kershaw, *Hitler 1936–1945*, 247.

53. Rossino, *Hitler Strikes Poland*, 62, 124–128, 203; Mayer, *Why Did the Heavens Not Darken*, 181. Kershaw believes that around 4,000 ethnic Germans were killed. Many of these figures are yet to be determined. See Kershaw, *Hitler 1936–1945*, 241–242.

54. Interview with Otto Kumm by historian Colin Heaton, 1985.

55. Interview with Karl Wolff by historian Colin Heaton, 1984.

56. Shirer, *Nightmare Years*, 453.

57. To learn more about how German leaders viewed their position in Europe and the fear of two fronts, see Citino's excellent book *The German Way of War.*

58. Sources used for this paragraph and the preceding one are: Bethell, *War Hitler Won*, 9–15, 61, 84, 101, 119–120, 123; Weinberg, *World at Arms*, 51, 65–66; Kaplan, *Scroll of Agony*, 23; Warfield and Warfield, *Call Us to Witness*, 27; Falencki interview; Madej and Zaloga, *Polish Campaign*, 122; Gordon A. Craig, *Germany 1866–1945* (New York, 1978), 716; Manstein, *Lost Victories*, 45; Keegan, *Second World War*, 47, 61; May, *Strange Victory*, 188, 205, 278, 290, 292, 301–303, 371–374.

59. Kaplan, *Scroll of Agony*, 25; Bethell, *War Hitler Won*, 27, 169; Craig, *Germany*, 716. Jonathan M. House, *Combined Arms Warfare in the Twentieth Century* (Lawrence, KS, 2001), 113–114; James S. Corum, *The Roots of Blitzkrieg: Hans von Seeckt and German Military Reform* (Lawrence, KS, 1992), 203; Barry Watts and Williamson Murray, Military Innovation in Peacetime," in *Military Innovation in the Interwar Period*, ed. Allan R. Millett and Williamson Murray (New York, 1998), 372. The Allies had a 1.2-to-1 advantage in manpower and 3,000 tanks to the Germans' 2,200 to 2,800 in total—in 1939 most of the German troops and tanks were in Poland. These numbers are probably at the lower end of the true figures. Corum states that in 1940 the French Char B tank was probably the best in the world. Special thanks to graduate student Lieutenant Colonel Jeffrey Scott of American Military University for these sources. According to French general Maurice Gamelin, the French had a 3–4-to-1 advantage as of 5 September 1939. May, *Strange Victory*, 278.

60. May, *Strange Victory*, 10, 17, 272, 277–278.

61. Madej and Zaloga, *Polish Campaign*, 158; Brewster and Jennings, *Century*, 215.

62. See Rossino, *Hitler Strikes Poland*; Davies, *God's Playground*, 264. For an amazing story of a family living as "Aryans," see Robert Melson, *False Papers: Deception and Survival in the Holocaust* (Chaimpaign, IL, 2000).

CHAPTER 2. THE RELIGIOUS CLIMATE DURING HITLER'S QUEST FOR EMPIRE

1. Ian Kershaw, *Hitler 1936–1945: Nemesis* (New York, 2000), 190–200, 240; Alexander B. Rossino, *Hitler Strikes Poland: Blitzkrieg, Ideology, and Atrocity* (Lawrence, KS, 2003), 27; Arno J. Mayer, *Why Did the Heavens Not Darken: The "Final Solution" in History* (New York, 1988), 183.

2. David Kertzer, *The Pope and Mussolini: The Secret History of Pius XI and the Rise of Fascism in Europe* (Oxford, 2014), xxx, 4, 48–49, 68, 80–81, 84, 94–95, 110, 127, 147, 157, 164–165, 178–180, 185, 192, 231–232. The accounts of the pedophile priests advising Pope Pius XI are sickening to read. These foul men were Caccia Dominioni, the prefect of the papal household; Father Ricardo De Samper; and Father Tacchi Venturi, the secret go-between for the pope and Mussolini. See ibid., 92–95, 231–232, 382–383, 428 nn. 22, 23, 31, 461 n. 21, 495 n. 34. Kertzer writes that had it not been for Mussolini's secret service, which reported these crimes against children, the Vatican would have destroyed all the evidence. See ibid., 95. This seemed to be a trend. When evidence against pedophile priests was about to be seized by secular authorities in Breslau in 1937, the archbishop there had the files destroyed. Ibid., 260.

3. E. B. Buckley, *Hitler's Austria: Popular Sentiment in the Nazi Era, 1938–1945* (Chapel Hill, NC, 2000); Kershaw, *Hitler 1936–1945*, 413; Kertzer, *Pope and Mussolini*, 276–278; Ernest R. May, *Strange Victory: Hitler's Conquest of France* (New York, 2000), 60.

4. Kershaw, *Hitler 1936–1945*, 190–200, 240; Ian Kershaw, *The Hitler Myth: Image and Reality in the Third Reich* (Oxford, 1990), 145; Rossino, *Hitler Strikes Poland*, 27; Mayer, *Why Did the Heavens Not Darken*, 183; Christopher Hitchens, *God Is Not Great: How Religion Poisons Everything* (New York, 2007), 4, 240; Richard Dawkins, *The God Delusion* (New York, 2006), 274; John Cornwell, *Hitler's Pope: The Secret History of Pius XII* (New York, 1999), 84–87, 90–93, 96–98, 114, 233–234, 273.

5. Kershaw, *Hitler Myth*, 105, 111, 116; Robert Ericksen, *Theologians under Hitler* (New Haven, CT, 1985), 25; Cornwell, *Hitler's Pope*, 137; Paul Johnson, *A History of Christianity* (New York, 1995), 489. The famous Protestant minister Martin Niemöller of the Confessional Church (*Bekennende Kirche*), a small denomination that opposed Hitler, was right to "formulate a Declaration of Guilt by the Church for not having opposed Hitler sooner and more strenuously" after the war. Niemöller had been a Nazi Party member at the beginning of Hitler's

rule, so even he did not see the danger at first. See Anton Gill, *An Honourable Defeat: A History of German Resistance to Hitler 1933–1945* (New York, 1994), 50.

6. Johnson, *History of Christianity*, 490.

7. Interview with Otto Kumm by historian Colin Heaton, 1985.

8. For more on how Germans felt about religion and the Nazis, see Kershaw, *Hitler Myth*.

9. Cornwell, *Hitler's Pope*, 199–215; Kertzer, *Pope and Mussolini*, 373, 376, 386–387; Johnson, *History of Christianity*, 490; Hitchens, *God Is Not Great*, 4, 239–240.

10. Cornwell, *Hitler's Pope*, 215; Johnson, *History of Christianity*, 491; Steven Paskuly, ed., *Death Dealer: The Memoirs of the SS Komandant at Auschwitz Rudolf Höss* (New York, 1996), 186, 192, 196–197, 205; "Rudolf Hoess Converted in Wadowice," *Wadowice* 24 (16 April 2012); Hitchens, *God Is Not Great*, 240. Cornwell says the SS was 25 percent Catholic, while Johnson says 22.7 percent. Since Cornwell's scholarship is more recent, I use his figure.

11. Kertzer, *Pope and Mussolini*, 280; Dawkins, *God Delusion*, 274; Hitchens, *God Is Not Great*, 240.

12. Kertzer, *Pope and Mussolini*, 205, 280; Hitchens, *God Is Not Great*, 4, 240. The Catholic Church still views cohabitation, remarrying without annulment, and unions with non-Catholics as mortal sins, akin to murder. See David Gibson, "Cardinal Raymond Burke: Gays, Remarried Catholics Are Just as Sinful as Murderers," Religion News Service, 27 March 2015. In courting the Vatican in 1933, Hitler's ambassador Eugenio Pacelli (later Pope Pius XII) made assurances that Hitler wanted "good relations with the Holy See," especially since he was a Catholic. See Kertzer, *Pope and Mussolini*, 200.

13. Johnson, *History of Christianity*, 490.

14. Ibid., 490, 487.

15. Hitchens, *God Is Not Great*, 4, 240. Concerning the horrific behavior of the Catholic Church in the child-abuse scandals throughout the world, see Laurie Goodstein, Nick Cumming-Bruce, and Jim Yardley, "U.N. Panel Criticizes the Vatican over Sexual Abuse," *New York Times*, 5 February 2014. This article rightly notes that "Church officials have proved they cannot police themselves." See also Anthony Faiola and Michelle Boorstein, "U.N. Panel Blasts Vatican Handling of Clergy Sex Abuse, Church Teachings on Gays, Abortion," *Washington Post*, 5 February 2014; John L. Allen Jr., "Second UN Panel Criticizes Vatican on Sex Abuse," *Boston Globe*, 23 May 2014; Jonathan Freedland, "Pope Benedict Has to Answer for His Failure on Child Abuse," *Guardian*, 15 February 2013.

16. Chris McGreal, "The Catholic Church Must Apologise for Its Role in Rwanda's Genocide," *Guardian*, 8 April 2014; Moni Basu, "Arrest Highlights Clergy's Role in Rwanda Genocide," CNN, 30 November 2009; Chris McGreal, "Hiding in Plain Sight in France: The Priests Accused in Rwandan Genocide,"

Guardian, 7 April 2014; Hitchens, *God Is Not Great*, 190–193; René Lemarchand, "The Rwanda Genocide," in *Century of Genocide: Critical Essays and Eyewitness Accounts*, ed. Israel W. Charny, William S. Parsons, and Samuel Totten (New York, 2004), 395–412.

17. Donald L. Niewyk, "Holocaust: The Genocide of the Jews," in Charny et al., *Century of Genocide*, 136.

18. See Johnson, *History of Christianity*, 492–493.

19. Hitchens, *God Is Not Great*, 4, 240; Sam Harris, *The End of Faith: Religion, Terror, and the Future of Reason* (New York, 2004), 103–105; Cornwell, *Hitler's Pope*, 7; Victor J. Stenger, *God the Failed Hypothesis: How Science Shows That God Does Not Exist* (Amherst, MA, 2007), 249; Gill, *Honourable Defeat*, 74; Kertzer, *Pope and Mussolini*, 50–51, 58, 106, 109, 404. See also Thomas Childers, *A History of Hitler's Empire*, 2nd ed. (Chantilly, VA, 2001). With regard to the availability of *Mein Kampf*: by 1940, more than 9 million copies had been sold. Gill, *Honourable Defeat*, 65. For the Catholic Church's tradition of preaching that Jews were cursed because they had killed Jesus, see Kertzer, *Pope and Mussolini*, 12. For example, in 1555 Pope Paul IV announced in a papal bull, *Cum nimis absurdum*, that Jews should be forcibly moved into ghettos and shunned by Christian society. He argued that Jews had been cursed by God to "eternal slavery" for their crime of murdering "Jesus and refusing his teachings." Ibid.

20. Johnson, *History of Christianity*, 492–493.

21. Ibid., 493.

CHAPTER 3. THE LUBAVITCHERS AND
THEIR REBBE

1. Lubavitch means "City of Love" in Russian.

2. Gershom Scholem, *Sabbatai Sevi: The Mystical Messiah 1626–1676* (Princeton, NJ, 1973), 1; Paul Johnson, *A History of the Jews* (New York, 1987), 259–260; Max I. Dimont, *Jews, God and History* (New York, 1964), 245–246. Both Johnson and Dimont quote the Jewish chroniclers as claiming that around 100,000 Jews were slaughtered during the Chmielnicki pogroms, which continued for several years after the initial violence in 1648. Steven Katz disputes this figure, saying it was 42,500 at most. Steven T. Katz, *The Holocaust in Historical Context*, vol. 1, *The Holocaust and Mass Death before the Modern Age* (Oxford, 1994), 157 n. 106. Interestingly, the Rebbe felt that the massacres of 1648–1649 were a result of God's doing. See Uri Kaploun, ed., *Likkutei Dibburim: An Anthology of Talks by Rabbi Yosef Yitzchak Schneersohn of Lubavitch*, 5 vols. (Brooklyn, NY, 1987–2000), 1:83.

3. J. Michael Allen and James B. Allen, *World History from 1500* (New York, 1993), 15–16. Historian Edward McNall Burns writes that half the population in Germany and Bohemia died due to famine, disease, and war during this conflict. Brutal soldiers on both sides committed torture, rape, and murder. Edward Mc-

Nall Burns, *Western Civilization: Their History and Their Culture* (New York, 1954), 465. It is difficult to ascertain the total number who died in the Thirty Years' War, but many historians consider 10 million a likely figure. Many people, it must be noted, died of starvation and disease rather than as a direct result of warfare. For an excellent work exploring people's obsession with Christ-like figures, see Norman Cohn, *The Pursuit of the Millennium: Revolutionary Millenarians and Mystical Anarchists of the Middle Ages*, revised and expanded ed. (Oxford, 1970).

4. Johnson, *History of the Jews*, 267–272; Dimont, *Jews, God and History*, 282–284. Zvi created a new religion called the Donmeh, and his followers elevated conversion and assimilation while secretly worshipping Zvi as the Messiah, similar to the Christian worship of Jesus. Donmeh still exists in modern Turkey. For an excellent work on Zvi, see Scholem, *Sabbatai Sevi.* Ironically, these messianic campaigns drove many Jews throughout the centuries to move to Israel, building communities that had been there for several generations before the founding of the state in 1948. Aaron Jacob, *The Campaign against Israel's Legitimacy: Answers to Israel's Critics* (New York, 2010), 6.

5. Dimont, *Jews, God and History*, 284–285; Johnson, *History of the Jews*, 273–274.

6. Gershom G. Scholem, *Major Trends in Jewish Mysticism* (Jerusalem, 1941), 330.

7. For the sources used in this section on the Baal Shem Tov (Besht), see note 18.

8. The opponents of Hasidism, the *Misnagdim*, were responsible for naming the Besht's followers Hasidim, although this term had been around for centuries before the Besht arrived on the scene. Interview with Rabbi Elie Shmotkin, 31 December 2003; Zalman to Rigg, 8 January 1996, Schneersohn folder 6, BMRS, BA-MA. For information about the name Besht, see Avrum M. Ehrlich, *Leadership in the HaBaD Movement: A Critical Evaluation of HaBaD Leadership, History, and Succession* (New York, 2000), 22; Johnson, *History of the Jews*, 295. According to Rebbe Schneersohn, the Besht was born on the eighteenth of Elul in 1698. *Likkutei Dibburim*, 1:71–72.

9. Scholem, *Major Trends in Jewish Mysticism*, 331, 346. Later, many opponents of Hasidism tried to convince the Russian government to take action against this group. Even with this opposition, Hasidism grew rapidly. According to historian Howard Sachar, "Much as the rabbis, the defenders of traditional Judaism, protested against this revivalist 'heresy'—even persuading the *Va'ad* of Four Lands to issue a *herem* against it in 1772—Hasidism continued to draw hundreds of thousands of new followers each year." Howard M. Sachar, *The Course of Modern Jewish History: The Classic History of the Jewish People, from the Eighteenth Century to the Present Day* (New York, 1990), 68. The famous Rabbi Elijah, the Gaon of Vilna, wanted to kill one of the Chabad leaders in his hometown. After the Gaon's death, one of his followers even tried to get the

czar's government to execute the founder of Chabad. Joseph Telushkin, *Rebbe: The Life and Teachings of Menachem M. Schneerson, the Most Influential Rabbi in Modern History* (New York, 2014), 10. I am quite disappointed by Rabbi Telushkin's lack of critical analysis of the Rebbe. Moreover, according to Chabad scholar Chaim Miller and Holocaust historian Michael Berenbaum, Telushkin was paid by Chabad to write this book. As a result, it is more propaganda than serious scholarship and must be used with caution.

10. Sachar, *Course of Modern Jewish History*, 67–68.

11. Ehrlich, *Leadership in the HaBaD Movement*, 21–26, 113–114.

12. Scholem, *Major Trends in Jewish Mysticism*, 347.

13. Sachar, *Course of Modern Jewish History*, 68.

14. Scholem, *Major Trends in Jewish Mysticism*, 343, 346.

15. Sachar, *Course of Modern Jewish History*, 67.

16. Scholem, *Major Trends in Jewish Mysticism*, 341.

17. Scholem wrote the following about Hasidic *Tzadikim*: "Hasidism as a whole is as much a reformation of earlier mysticism as it is more or less the same thing. You can say if you like that it depends on how you look at it. The Hasidim were themselves aware of this fact. Even such a novel thing as the rise of the Zaddikim and the doctrine of Zaddikism appeared to them as being, despite its novelty, well in the Kabbalistic tradition. So much seems clear, that the followers of these Hasidim became genuine revivalists." Ibid., 338. For the novelty of Hasidic leadership, see 344.

18. Ehrlich, *Leadership in the HaBaD Movement*, 21–26, 113–114; Sue Fishkoff, *The Rebbe's Army: Inside the World of Chabad-Lubavitch* (New York, 2003), 17–18; Yaffa Eliach, *Hasidic Tales of the Holocaust* (New York, 1982), xv–xvi; George Robinson, *Essential Judaism: A Complete Guide to Beliefs, Customs, and Rituals* (New York, 2000), 384–391; Edward Hoffman, *Despite All Odds: The Story of Lubavitch* (New York, 1991), 15, 17; Dimont, *Jews, God and History*, 288–290; Johnson, *History of the Jews*, 295–298; Louis Jacobs, *The Jewish Religion: A Companion* (New York, 1995), 456; Harris Lenowitz, *The Jewish Messiahs: From the Galilee to Crown Heights* (Oxford, 1998), 4, 149–165; Karen Armstrong, *The Battle for God* (New York, 2000), 26–30; Sachar, *Course of Modern Jewish History*, 67–72; *Likkutei Dibburim*, 1:71; Joseph I. Schneersohn, *Lubavitcher Rabbi's Memoirs: The Memoirs of Rabbi Joseph I. Schneersohn, the Late Lubavitcher Rabbi*, vol. 1 (Brooklyn, NY, 1961), 30–31, 41, 205; *Likkutei Dibburim*, 2:227, 266–273, 296–299; Joseph I. Schneersohn, *Saying Tehillim: Selected from Letters by the Late Lubavitcher Rebbe Rabbi Yoseph Yitzhak Schneersohn on the Subject of Reciting Psalms* (Brooklyn, NY, 1975), 9–10. For concepts of the Messiah that the Baal Shem Tov probably thought about, see Isaiah 2 and 11 and Micah 4. Also, thousands of Torah scholars at the time recognized in his teachings the mystical truths passed down through the generations, especially via Rabbi Isaac Luria, the Arizal who taught it was a *mitzvah* to teach

the mystical wisdom of God. The Besht was continuing this tradition by revealing to all the inherent godliness of their souls and their lives.

19. Scholem, *Major Trends in Jewish Mysticism*, 342. Moses picked Bezalel to build the ark of the covenant (Exodus 31, 37) because of the traits he had, which Chabad also stands for.

20. *Tanya* means "It has been taught." See note 21 for sources of additional information on the *Tanya*.

21. Ehrlich, *Leadership in the HaBaD Movement*, 12, 73, 93, 113–117; Harry Rabinowicz, *Hasidism: The Movement and Its Masters* (New York, 1988), 90; Naftali Loewenthal, *Communicating the Infinite: The Emergence of the Habad School* (Chicago, 1990), 9; interview with Eliezer Zaklikovsky, 4 June 2003; Hoffman, *Despite All Odds*, 18–19; *Likkutei Dibburim*, 2:104–107. Rebbe Schneersohn wrote that "Chabad Chassidus, especially, is a Divine philosophy that opens the portals of wisdom and understanding, to know and recognize with intellectual comprehension 'Him Who spoke and the world came into being.' It indicates the path for every individual, according to his capabilities, to approach Holiness and to serve G-d with his heart and mind." Joseph I. Schneersohn, *On the Teachings of Chassidus (Kuntres Toras Hachassidus)* (Brooklyn, NY, 1965), 18; Arthur Green, "Early Hasidism: Some Old/New Questions," in *Hasidism Reappraised*, ed. Ada Rapoport-Albert (London, 1996), 441–443. Rebbe Schneersohn felt that Rebbe Zalman (the Alter Rebbe) was like Moses, in that his soul came from the world of *Atzilus* (emanation), or the world closest to creation; he believed people like Moses and Zalman were "all embracing souls, leaders of Israel." *Likkutei Dibburim*, 1:54; Armstrong, *Battle for God*, 102–103.

22. David N. Myers and Kaye Alexander, eds., *The Faith of Fallen Jews: Yosef Hayim Yerushalmi and the Writing of Jewish History* (Waltham, MA, 2014), 261.

23. Aviezer Ravitzky, *Messianism, Zionism, and Jewish Religious Radicalism* (Chicago, 1996), 181.

24. Christopher Hitchens, *God Is Not Great: How Religion Poisons Everything* (New York, 2007), 272–273.

25. Ehrlich, *Leadership in the HaBaD Movement*, 27–33, 46, 51, 87, 95, 100, 160–161, 202, 232, 239, 241; Laber to Rigg, 22 April 2001, Schneersohn file, BMRS, BA-MA; interview with Bernhard Klein, 9 September 2003; interview with Avraham Laber, 8 May 2003; Hoffman, *Despite All Odds*, 20, 24; interview with David Kranzler, 24 January 2004; Joseph I. Schneersohn, *The "Tzemach Tzedek" and the Haskala Movement (Ha "Tzemach Tzedek" Utenaus Hahaskolo)* (Brooklyn, NY, 1962), 3; Rabinowicz, *Hasidism*, 90; Aaron Wertheim, *Law and Custom in Hasidim* (Hoboken, NJ, 1992), 27; Green, "Early Hasidism," 444–445; *Likkutei Dibburim*, 1:x, 33, 35. Schneersohn believed that although every generation had had Rebbes, they had remained hidden until God started to reveal them beginning with the Besht. *Likkutei Dibburim*, 1:138. For the Lubavitchers' conviction that their leaders are indeed potential Messiahs, see Menachem Friedman

and Samuel Heilman. *The Rebbe: The Life and Afterlife of Menachem Mendel Schneerson* (Princeton, NJ, 2010), 277.

26. Quoted in Ehrlich, *Leadership in the HaBaD Movement*, 31. See also Wertheim, *Law and Custom in Hasidim*, 230.

27. *Likkutei Dibburim*, 1:105, 116–117; 4:21; 2:92.

28. Vermes writes, "It would appear, rather, that the logical inference must be that the person of Jesus is to be seen as part of first-century charismatic Judaism and as the paramount example of the early Hasidim or Devout . . . Jesus of Nazareth takes on the eminently credible personality of a Galilean Hasid." Geza Vermes, *Jesus the Jew: A Historian's Reading of the Gospels* (Philadelphia, 1981), 79, 83. See also Ira Tick, "Jesus the Hasid: A Review of Geza Vermes' 'Jesus the Jew,'" *Beacon*, 24 October 2011.

29. Friedman and Heilman, *Rebbe*, 276; David Berger, *The Rebbe, the Messiah and the Scandal of Orthodox Indifference* (Oxford, 2001), 26–29, 129–130. According to Friedman and Heilman (278), Chabad is probably in the process of developing "a new sort of Judaism." Some people in Chabad argue that the belief that Schneerson was the Messiah is still very controversial and that those who hold this belief are marginalized within the movement. However, other evidence indicates that this is not the case.

30. Quoted in Hoffman, *Despite All Odds*, 29. For Chabad's ancestor worship, see Ehrlich, *Leadership in the HaBaD Movement*, 106–111. For Chabad's difficult relationship to the claim that Rebbe Menachem Mendel Schneerson was the Messiah, see Berger, *Rebbe*. Friedman and Heilman describe this practice of communing with the dead: "This [speaking with the dead] was part of a process called *yihudin* (unification), mystical procedures by which the living continue to be attached to the soul of the departed saint. It is based on the assertion of the *Zohar*, the primary text of kabbalah, that the *zaddik* is more present 'in all the worlds' after his death than during his life. Indeed, the Talmud (B. T. *Hulin* 7b) in its assertion that '*gedolim tsaddikim be-mitatan yoter mi-be-hayyeyhen*' (saints are even grander in their death than in their lives) provided perhaps the ultimate basis for the notion that a rebbe could achieve more for his followers after his passing than during his lifetime. Accordingly, part of the responsibility of the dead *zaddik*—and of course a rebbe is a *zaddik*—involves his petitioning on behalf of the living (particularly those with whom he is unified) after his passing." Friedman and Heilman, *Rebbe*, 16. Also, many Lubavitchers believe their leaders can have more of an influence among the living once they are dead. One leader said, "a *tsaddik* lives more today than yesterday." Ibid., 21. With regard to the inherent contradictions of God in the Bible, Isaiah 45:7 reads: "I form the light, and create darkness: I make peace, and create evil: I the Lord do all these things" (King James Version).

31. Rebbe Schneersohn was also called Rebbe Maharyatz, which is an acronym for *Moreinu Ha Rav Rebbe Yosef Yitzchok* (Our Master, the Rabbi, Rebbe

Yosef Yitzchok). In addition, he was known as the Frierdiker Rebbe, which means the "previous Rebbe," since he was the sixth out of seven. Chaim Dalfin, *The Seven Chabad-Lubavitch Rebbes* (New York, 1998), 105; *Likkutei Dibburim*, 1:194, 201; Efraim Zuroff, *Response of Orthodox Jewry in the United States: The Activities of the Vaad Ha-Hatzala Rescue Committee, 1939–1945* (New York, 2000), 36. According to historian David Kranzler, Zuroff's book needs to be used carefully because his claims are "baseless and irresponsible." David Kranzler, "Orthodoxy's Finest Hour: Rescue Efforts during the Holocaust," *Jewish Action* 63, 1 (Fall 2002): 32. Zuroff responded to Kranzler's attack in "Orthodox Rescue Revisited," *Jewish Action* 63, 3 (Spring 2003), and in a letter to the editor of the *Jerusalem Post*, 2 September 2003.

32. *Likkutei Dibburim*, 1:31.

33. Ibid., 1:91, 128, 194, 307; 2:48; Ehrlich, *Leadership in the HaBaD Movement*, 261–262. Many Orthodox Jews believe that, out of respect, they should not write the name of God. According to Rebbe Menachem Schneerson, even when writing, "we must feel a sense of awe, a sense that G-d is above and beyond our words." Simon Jacobson, *Toward a Meaningful Life: The Wisdom of the Rebbe Menachem Mendel Schneerson* (New York, 1995), x. Rebbe Jospeh Schneersohn also felt that the best way to bring God into the world was through commandments. He wrote, "*Mitzvah* means attachment, becoming one with G-d. The soul is, as we have been taught, part of G-d above. The mitzvah is the power to bring G-d down into this world through doing what G-d commands us to do. In this way man becomes one with the One, with G-d who is One, and besides whom there is nothing else. Man becomes a vehicle for the holiness of G-d." Schneersohn, *The "Tzemach Tzedek,"* 102. He further explained, "this drawing down (*hamshachah*) of G-dliness into the world can take place only by means of *avodah* [Hebrew for 'work,' which basically means prayer, study, and following the commandments]." *Likkutei Dibburim*, 2:4–5. If one does not study, "one becomes coarsened and ignoramus'd, and does harm thereby to all of Israel." Ibid., 1:147.

34. Roman A. Foxbrunner, *HABAD: The Hasidism of R. Shneur Zalman of Lyady* (Tuscaloosa, AL, 1992), 108–109.

35. Schneur Zalman, *Tanya* (Brooklyn, NY, 1969), 23–24; *Hakreah Vehakedusha* [Reading and Holiness], December 1941, June 1942; Foxbrunner, *HABAD*, 108–109; Hitchens, *God Is Not Great*, 207.

36. Yosef Y. Kaminetzky, *Days in Chabad* (Brooklyn, NY, 2002), 218; *The Rebbes: Rabbi Yosef Yitzchak Schneersohn of Lubavitch*, vol. 2 (Israel, 1994), 16–17. According to Chabad legend, this story mirrors the biblical story of Abraham and Sarah being told by God that they will have a child (Genesis 18:1–19). According to Professor Arthur Green of Brandeis University, one must realize that many of the stories about the Rebbe's childhood "are Hasidic legends, not historical accounts." Green to Rigg, 27 July 2003, Rebbe Schneersohn file,

BMRS, BA-MA. Also, one must use *The Rebbes* carefully; it is written for a young audience, and its sources are not listed in notes. Nonetheless, the information is taken from Lubavitch sources and tells the story that most Lubavitchers accept.

37. Ehrlich, *Leadership in the HaBaD Movement*, 108, 242.

38. Armstrong, *Battle for God*, 148; *Likkutei Dibburim*, 4:255; Ehrlich, *Leadership in the HaBaD Movement*, 244–5; Steven Smith, *Spinoza, Liberalism, and the Question of Jewish Identity* (New Haven, CT, 1997), xiii.

39. *Likkutei Dibburim*, 4:244–255.

40. Interview with Rabbi Zalman Posner, 3 May 2003; Alter B. Metzger, *The Heroic Struggle: The Arrest and Liberation of Rabbi Yosef Y. Schneersohn of Lubavitch in Soviet Russia* (Brooklyn, NY, 1999), 189; Eliezer Zaklikofsky, *America Is No Different* (New York, 1999), 69. For the story of Moses killing an Egyptian for beating a Hebrew, see Exodus 2:11–12.

41. Menachem Mendel Schneerson, *Sichot Kodesh* (unpublished transcript of the rebbe's talks from 1958), 282.

42. *Likkutei Dibburim*, 1:179–180; Charles Rader, ed., *Challenge: An Encounter with Lubavitch-Chabad* (Brooklyn, NY, 1970), 49.

43. Rader, *Challenge*, 49; Ehrlich, *Leadership in the HaBaD Movement*, 247–248.

44. Rader, *Challenge*, 50; Hoffman, *Despite All Odds*, 23–24, 31; *The Rebbes*, 12; Geoffrey Hosking, *Russia: People and Empire 1552–1917* (Cambridge, 1997), 395; Zaklikofsky, *America Is No Different*, 68; Ehrlich, *Leadership in the HaBaD Movement*, 252, 257; Winfried Meyer, *Unternehmen Sieben. Eine Rettungsaktion für vom Holocaust Bedrohte aus dem Amt Ausland-Abwehr im Oberkommando der Wehrmacht* (Frankfurt, 1993), 128; Zaklikofsky, *America Is No Different*, 74. Winfried Meyer did a wonderful job with his book *Unternehmen Sieben*. However, sometimes he was sloppy with his source material. For example, on page 493, footnote 197, he thanks Rabbi Avraham Laber for translating the source for Chaim Lieberman's quote, but then fails to give the source this quote came from: Rabbi Raphael N. Cohen, *Shmuos Vsipurim*, Israel, 1977. So his sources sometimes need to be checked.

45. News clipping attached to telegram from Riga to Secretary of State Hull, 18 March 1940, General Records of Department of State, Itinerary 705, Visa Case Files 1933–1940, 811.111, Joseph Schneersohn, Record Group 59, NARA; Metzger, *Heroic Struggle*, 144; Zaklikofsky, *America Is No Different*, 68; Posner to Rigg, 8 January 2004, Bloch file, Schneersohn folder 6, BMRS, BA-MA; Ehrlich, *Leadership in the HaBaD Movement*, 248, 252; Kranzler interview; Friedman and Heilman, *Rebbe*, 79. For information on the Yevsektzia, see Yaacov Ro'i, ed., *Jews and Jewish Life in Russia and the Soviet Union* (New York, 1995); *Likkutei Dibburim*, 1:144. For the number of eastern European Jews coming to America during the eighteenth and nineteenth centuries, see Jack Rischel and

NOTES TO PAGES 62–65 [365]

Sanford Pinsker, eds., *Jewish American Culture and History Encyclopedia* (New York, 1992), 267. From 1881 to 1924, approximately 2.5 million Jews emigrated from Russia, Romania, and Austria-Hungary; more than 2 million of them came to the United States. Special thanks to David Kranzler for this information. Kranzler, who is quoted throughout this book, was an amazing scholar whose collection was recently bought by the Yad Vashem museum for $100,000—a rare feat for a scholar. However, archive specialist Henri Lustiger recently found that Kranzler's citing of sources can be sloppy, so his work should be double-checked when used. Henri Lustiger, personal communication, 30 December 2014.

46. Hoffman, *Despite All Odds*, 23; Metzger, *Heroic Struggle*, 307–308; Ehrlich, *Leadership in the HaBaD Movement*, 263–265; Aryeh Solomon, *The Educational Teachings of Rabbi Menachem M. Schneerson* (Lanham, MD, 2000), 6.

47. Yehuda Bauer, *American Jewry and the Holocaust: The American Jewish Joint Distribution Committee, 1939–1945* (Detroit, 1981),31, 67; Yisrael Gutman, *The Jews of Warsaw, 1939–1943: Ghetto, Underground, Revolt* (Bloominton, IN, 1982), xv.

48. Hoffman, *Despite All Odds*, 23; Ehrlich, *Leadership in the HaBaD Movement*, 254–258, 262; David E. Fishman, "Judaism in the U.S.S.R., 1917–1930: The Fate of Religious Education," in Ro'i, *Jews and Jewish Life*, 253–258. Fishman notes that the Lubavitchers censored some of the criticism leveled at the Rebbe for favoring Lubavitchers with Joint Distribution Committee funds.

49. Metzger, *Heroic Struggle*, 34, 35; Shmotkin interview; Zaklikofsky, *America Is No Different*, 7, 10, 23; Ehrlich, *Leadership in the HaBaD Movement*, 262, 266; Günter Schubert, *Der Fleck auf Uncle Sams weißer Weste: Amerika und die jüdischen Flüchtlinge 1938–1945* (Frankfurt, 2003), 123. Even though Schubert's work here is a nice piece of history, it must be viewed as incomplete and even sometimes sloppy. He primarily used just the sources in the National Archives in the United States for the rescue, which gives a very incomplete view of this history. Moreover, he is sometimes sloppy or his English is not that good. He claims the United States awarded Rebbe Menachem Mendel Schneerson the Congressional Medal of Honor (Schubert, 145). This award is only given to military personnel, and it is the highest decoration given for valor. Most often, this is awarded to the person posthumously for incredibly brave actions in battle. The Rebbe received the Congressional Gold Medal, which is one of the highest decorations for civilians the US government can bestow on an individual for contributions to American society (the person need not be a citizen although this is often the case). For a supposedly seasoned scholar to make such an elementary mistake must make one question his overall scholarship. His sources should be double checked.

50. Rader, *Challenge*, 52; Metzger, *Heroic Struggle*, 19, 53–54, 105–107, 111, 146–147; interview with Barry Gourary, 8 May 2003, BMRS, BA-MA; Friedman and Heilman, *Rebbe*, 79; Special Agent Tubbs, Department of State, to Fitch,

10 January 1940, 3, General Records of Department of State, Itinerary 705, Visa Case Files 1933–1940, 811.111, Joseph Schneersohn, Record Group 59, NARA.

51. Shmotkin interview; Metzger, *Heroic Struggle*, 138; Schneersohn, *Lubavitcher Rabbi's Memoirs*, 1. After the Rebbe's death, many of his followers claimed he was still with them. Translator Uri Kaploun wrote that the Rebbe "is present with us here and now." *Likkutei Dibburim*, 1:xii; Gershon Greenberg, "Menahem Mendel Schneersohn's Response to the Holocaust," *Modern Judaism* 34, 1 (20 February 2014): 86.

52. Hoffman, *Despite All Odds*, 37. See also Metzger, *Heroic Struggle*, 167, n. 3. According to Barry Gourary, this is revisionist history. At the time, Menachem was not active in Hasidic causes; he was studying electrical engineering, which his father-in-law did not approve of; the Rebbe thought secular studies would pollute Menachem's mind. Gourary to Rigg, 4 August 2003, Schneersohn 2003 folder, BMRS, BA-MA. See also Ehrlich, *Leadership in the HaBaD Movement*, 274, 297, 315–316.

53. Metzger, *Heroic Struggle*, 104–105, 131–133, 139–140; Zaklikofsky, *America Is No Different*, 23. Interestingly, the Rebbe said that "prayer is the foundation of all of Torah and Mitzvot" and therefore an incredibly important foundation for a Jew's soul. Schneersohn, *On the Teachings of Chassidus*, 21.

54. Propaganda tract distributed by the Lubavitchers about this event, General Records of Department of State, Itinerary 705, Visa Case Files 1933–1940, 811.111, Joseph Schneersohn, Record Group 59, NARA; Tubbs to Fitch, 10 January 1940, 3; Metzger, *Heroic Struggle*, 143–144; Milton Kramer, ed., *The Kramers: The Next Generation* (Brooklyn, NY, 1995), 15, 68; Zaklikofsky, *America Is No Different*, 10; Ehrlich, *Leadership in the HaBaD Movement*, 258, 262, 266; Edelman to Rigg, 23 February 2004, Schneersohn folder 6, BMRS, BA-MA; Schubert, *Der Fleck auf Uncle Sams weißer Weste*, 123.

55. Nissen Mindel, *Rabbi Joseph I. Schneersohn, the Lubavitcher Rabbi* (New York, 1947); brief biographical sketch and outline of the activities of Rabbi Joseph Isaac Schneersohn, 360 C.60P, 15/1, Records of the United States Theaters of War, World War II, WNRC; interview with Rabbi Meir Greenberg, 18 August 1996, BMRS, BA-MA; Hoffman, *Despite All Odds*, 24; Meyer, *Unternehmen Sieben*, 128; "This Is Your Life," essay written by son-in-law Melvin Neumark and daughter Debby Kramer Neumark for Sam Kramer's sixtieth birthday, Schneersohn folder 6, BMRS, BA-MA; *Likkutei Dibburim*, 1:vii; Metzger, *Heroic Struggle*, 153; Posner to Rigg, 8 January 2004; Ehrlich, *Leadership in the HaBaD Movement*, 258; Schneersohn, *Saying Tehillim*, 1, n. 1. Making his own time in prison more significant, the Rebbe wrote, "Even if an ordinary person is imprisoned he becomes refined by the experience." He went on to say how great it was that Rebbe Zalman had risked his life for the Torah, which, in Rebbe Schneersohn's mind, was the reason for his own imprisonment as well. *Likkutei Dibburim*, 1:94.

56. Metzger, *Heroic Struggle*, 325, 328.

57. Hoffman, *Despite All Odds*, 25; Yehuda Bauer, *A History of the Holocaust* (New York, 1982), 285; Shmotkin interview; Rabbi Eli S. to Rigg, 6 January 2004, Schneersohn folder 6, BMRS, BA-MA. The following sixty-seven Lubavitchers were murdered by the Soviets (it is by no means a comprehensive list): Yitzchak Alperovich, Pinchas Althaus, Eliyohu Balkind, Mordechai Brusin, Avraham Budnav, Shmuel Chanin, Yekutiel Chanin, Yona Cohen, Shmuel Aba Dulitzky, Feivish Estrin, Meir Friedman, Shaul Friedman, Yehosua Friedman, Hendel Galprin, Meir Gansburg, Yosef Garfinkel, Eliyohu Gitlin, Yehoshua Gold, Dober Grinpes, Yehoshuah Gurary, Nateh Hanzburg, Kherson, Eliezer Katz, Michoel Katzeneleboigen, Sarah Katzeneleboigen, Dovber Kuznitzav, Zalman Kuznitzav, Dovid Labak, Shimon Lazarov, Menachem Mendel Lein, Yehoshua Lein, Dober Levertov, Simcha Levin, Elchanan Dovber Marazov, Pinchas Marazov, Shmuel Marazov, Yehuda Medalia, Yaakov Zecharya Meskolik, Shmuel Natik, Shmuel Nimotin, Avrahamn Baruch Pevsner, Nachum Yitzchak Pinson, Nason Nateh Rabinov, Ben Tzion Chaim Raskin, Yaakov Yosef Raskin, Yehuda Leib Raskin, Yitzchak Raskin, Yitzchak Rivkin, Shmuel Rozenbaum, Schnuer Zalman Schneerson, Yochanan Schneerson, Schnuer Schneur, Yitzchak Elchonan Shagalov, Skveerki, Avraham Levik Slavin, Chaim Sosonkin, Itah Sosonkin, Moshe Sosonkin, Aryeh Spaznikov, Betzalel Spivack, Avraham Swerdlov, Aaron Eliezer Tzeitlin, Meir Tzinman, Yaakov Wangreen, Shneur Zalman Weinshtak, Feivel Zalmanav, Hershel Zuben.

58. *Likkutei Dibburim*, 1:56, 66, 89, 91, 173, 176; 5:10. The Festival of Liberation is known as *Chag Hageulah* by the Lubavitchers. Rebbe Shneur Zalman was also arrested on trumped-up charges of antigovernment activities, and when he was released, his followers rolled in the streets of Petersburg with joy. Jacobs, *Jewish Religion*, 464; *Likkutei Dibburim*, 1:98.

59. Israel Jacobson, *Zi Koron L'Beis Yisrael: Memories of Rabbi Israel Jacobson 1907–1939* (Brooklyn, NY, 1996), 97–125; Zaklikofsky, *America Is No Different*, 41; Ehrlich, *Leadership in the HaBaD Movement*, 268.

60. Jacobson, *Zi Koron L'Beis Yisrael*, 150–151; "This Is Your Life"; Metzger, *Heroic Struggle*, 166; *Likkutei Dibburim*, 1:1.

61. B. Gourary interview.

62. Hoffman, *Despite All Odds*, 37; Dalfin, *Seven Chabad-Lubavitch Rebbes*, 114; Ehrlich, *Leadership in the HaBaD Movement*, 257.

63. Pogroms occurred in several cities in 1929, including Hebron and Jerusalem. There were many reasons for them, but the main one was the nationalistic antagonism between the Arabs and the Jews. The Palestinians' anger was fueled by false rumors that the Jews wanted to build a place of worship at the Wailing Wall. Some Jews were killed, and thousands had to leave their homes in the old city of Jerusalem. Ironically, a few days before these events, the Rebbe had spent several hours praying at the Wailing Wall. See Friedman and Heilman, *Rebbe*, 108.

64. Propaganda tract prepared by the Lubavitchers about the Rebbe's 1929 visit to the United States, General Records of Department of State, Itinerary 705, Visa Case Files 1933–1940, 811.111, Joseph Schneersohn, Record Group 59, NARA; Ehrlich, *Leadership in the HaBaD Movement*, 266, 277; Zaklikofsky, *America Is No Different*, 6, 7 n. 1, 8, 10, 17, 20; Friedman and Heilman, *Rebbe*, 108. Many have asked why the Rebbe's other son-in-law and future seventh Rebbe, Menachem Mendel Schneerson, did not accompany him on this trip. At the time, Menachem Mendel was in charge of all Chabad affairs in Europe—a very important position. Zaklikofsky, *America Is No Different*, 29. However, he also found plenty of time to study in Berlin and Paris and live a very secular and non-Chabad life (see Friedman and Heilman's biography of Schneersohn). It appears that Samarius Gourary, who had been the Rebbe's aide for almost forty years, was being groomed to be the next Rebbe. See Ehrlich, *Leadership in the HaBaD Movement*, 253–257, 325.

65. Propaganda tract about the Rebbe's 1929 visit; Jacobson, *Zi Koron L'Beis Yisrael*, 205–206; biographical sketch of Schneersohn; Charles Rader, ed., *Challenge: An Encounter with Lubavitch*, (Brooklyn, 1970) 53; Rabbi Israel Jacobson, "Journey to America," *Di Yiddishe Heim* (1956), 3; Meyer, *Unternehmen Sieben*, 128; Kramer, *The Kramers*, 15, 68; Zaklikofsky, *America Is No Different*, 11, 13, 15–16, 18, 34–35; Ehrlich, *Leadership in the HaBaD Movement*, 269–271; Schubert, *Der Fleck auf Uncle Sams weißer Weste*, 123.

66. The Talmud comprises the Mishnah, edited in 200 CE, and the Gemorah, compiled in 500 CE; their task is to interpret the written Torah. The Chabad yeshiva was called the Tomchei Tmimim, which means "supporters of righteousness."

67. *Likkutei Dibburim*, 5:10, 27–28, 33, 46, 50, 94. The Rebbe often talked about the Messiah. See ibid., 1:13, 82, 87, 93, 149–150; 2:1, 16–18, 131, 227, 266–273, 275–276, 279–280, 288–290, 296–298; Schneersohn, *Saying Tehillim*, 47. For a Chabad perspective of the Messiah, see Shmuel Boteach, *The Wolf Shall Lie with the Lamb: The Messiah in Hasidic Thought* (Lanham, MD, 1993).

68. Rader, *Challenge*, 53; Zaklikovsky interview.

69. B. Gourary interview; interview with Joseph Wineberg, 4 May 2003, BMRS, BA-MA; Hoffman, *Despite All Odds,* 24. Starting in the early 1930s, the Rebbe's health steadily declined. Zaklikofsky, *America Is No Different*, 41; Chaim Miller, *Turning Judaism Outward: A Biography of the Rebbe Menachem Mendel Schneerson* (Brooklyn, NY, 2014), 110; Friedman and Heilman, *Rebbe*, 30.

CHAPTER 4. THE REBBE IN GERMAN-OCCUPIED
POLAND

1. Rachel Altein and Eliezer Zaklikovsky, eds., *Out of the Inferno: The Efforts that Led to the Rescue of the Rabbi Yosef Y. Schneersohn of Lubavitch from War-torn Europe in 1939–1940* (Brooklyn, NY, 2002), 298, 303; interview with

Joseph Wineberg, 4 May 2003, BMRS, BA-MA; interview with Barry Gourary, 8 May 2003, ibid.; Rabbi Isarel Jacobson, "Journey to America," *Di Yiddishe Heim* (1956), 3–4.

2. Interview with Rabbi Meir Greenberg, 18 August 1996, BMRS, BA-MA; Eliezer Zaklikofsky, *America Is No Different* (New York, 1999), 49.

3. Interview with Rabbi Shmuel Fox, 14 January 2003.

4. Greenberg interview.

5. Altein and Zaklikovsky, *Out of the Inferno*, 303; interview with Avraham Laber, 6 January 2004; Zaklikofsky, *America Is No Different*, 49.

6. Interview with Rabbi Mordechai Dov Altein, 14 January 2003.

7. Greenberg interview; Jacobson, "Journey to America," 4; Zaklikofsky, *America Is No Different*, 50.

8. Charles Rader, ed., *Challenge: An Encounter with Lubavitch-Chabad* (Brooklyn, NY, 1970), 53; interview with Rabbi Hirsch Kotlarsky, 3 January 2003; Wineberg interview; interview with Rabbi Elie Shmotkin, 31 December 2003; interview with Adam Boren, 9 December 2003; *Hakreah Vehakedusha* [Reading and Holiness] 13 (October 1941), 15 (December 1941).

9. Rabbi Chaskel Besser, who is cited and mentioned often in this book, was in Warsaw in August 1939. He eventually escaped to Palestine via Romania, but he almost did not make it. While on the train heading south, several young men boarded, on their way to join the army. On learning that he was a Jew and trying to leave the country, they got very aggressive and threatened him. Luckily for Besser, a Catholic priest stepped in and may have saved his life. This is just one example of how young Polish males felt about religious Jews and their unwillingness to serve. Besser, who was a very kind man and a good rabbi, simply did not want to fight for the country where he lived. This attitude naturally created much resentment. Warren Kozak, *The Rabbi of 84th Street: The Extraordinary Life of Haskel Besser* (New York, 2004), 43–47. See also Saul S. Friedman, *No Haven for the Oppressed: United States Policy toward Jewish Refugees, 1938–1945* (Detroit, 1973), 39–40.

10. Sam Harris, *The End of Faith: Religion, Terror, and the Future of Reason* (New York, 2004), 199. Even though it is the opinion of many, including myself, that the pacifism of Quakers and Jehovah's Witnesses is immoral, it must be noted that in Germany, these two religious groups "were especially courageous" in resisting the Nazi regime by protecting persecuted Jews. Anton Gill, *An Honourable Defeat: A History of German Resistance to Hitler 1933–1945* (New York, 1994), 106.

11. There were others like the Rebbe who promoted pacifism in the face of extreme violence. Unitarian reverend John Haynes Holmes, one of the founding members of the NAACP and ACLU, promoted pacifism in confronting Hitler. He wrote in 1939: "To me, Hitler is all that is horrible, but as such he is the product of our world, the veritable incarnation of our nationalistic, capitalistic and

militaristic era. Whatever is worst in our civilization seems to have come to a vile head in him. He is our own sins sprung to life, to confound us, scourge us and perhaps destroy us." Carl Hermann Voss, *Rabbi and Minister: The Friendship of Stephen S. Wise and John Haynes Holmes* (Buffalo, NY, 1980), 306. Owing to his pacifism, Holmes was shunned by most of society. Roosevelt wondered what was wrong with him, and even Holmes's close friend Rabbi Stephen Wise expressed surprise at his pacifism in the face of such evil. Ibid., 306–310.

12. B. Gourary interview.

13. Wineberg interview.

14. Robert Kee, *1939: In the Shadow of War* (Boston, 1984), 310; Yisrael Gutman, *The Jews of Warsaw, 1939–1943: Ghetto, Underground, Revolt* (Bloomington, IN, 1982), 7; Chaim Kaplan, *A Scroll of Agony: The Warsaw Diary of Chaim A. Kaplan* (New York, 1965), 26; Hania Warfield and Gaither Warfield, *Call Us to Witness: A Polish Chronicle* (New York, 1945), 29; Nicholas Bethell, *The War Hitler Won: The Fall of Poland, September 1939* (New York, 1972), 102; Victor Madej and Steven Zaloga, *The Polish Campaign 1939* (New York, 1985), 139; Altein and Zaklikovsky, *Out of the Inferno*, 298.

15. B. Gourary interview; Jacobson, "Journey to America," 4.

16. *Hashem*, Hebrew for "the name," is another way for religious Jews to refer to God without using his name.

17. Altein and Zaklikovsky, *Out of the Inferno*, 298; *The Rebbes: Rabbi Yosef Yitzchak Schneersohn of Lubavitch*, vol. 2. (Israel, 1994), 149; Pell to Rhoade, 13 November 1939, Schneersohn folder 1, BMRS, BA-MA; interview with Zalman Gourary, 18 May 2003, BMRS, BA-MA; Jacobson, "Journey to America," 4; US District Court, Chabad against Barry and Hanna Gourary, CV-1985-2909, 6, Schneersohn folder 6, Kramer files, BMRS, BA-MA; Zaklikofsky, *America Is No Different*, 49.

18. Kozak, *Rabbi of 84th Street*, 41.

19. Harris Lenowitz, *The Jewish Messiahs: From the Galilee to Crown Heights* (Oxford, 1998), 264.

20. Gutman, *Jews of Warsaw*, 4–5; Altein and Zaklikovsky, *Out of the Inferno*, 298–299; Madej and Zaloga, *Polish Campaign*, 116, 122; Warfield and Warfield, *Call Us to Witness*, 31–32; Martin Gilbert, *The Second World War: A Complete History* (New York, 1989), 2.

21. Warfield and Warfield, *Call Us to Witness*, 32. See also Bethell, *War Hitler Won*, 27.

22. Robert M. Citino, *The German Way of War: From the Thirty Years' War to the Third Reich* (Lawrence, KS, 2005). 263.

23. Bethell, *War Hitler Won*, 27, 122; Alexander B. Rossino, *Hitler Strikes Poland: Blitzkrieg, Ideology, and Atrocity* (Lawrence, KS, 2003), 1; William L. Shirer, *Berlin Diary: The Journal of a Foreign Correspondent 1934–1941* (New York, 1941), 209.

24. B. Gourary interview; Altein and Zaklikovsky, *Out of the Inferno*, 298; *The Rebbes*, 149.

25. B. Gourary interview; Efraim Zuroff, *Response of Orthodox Jewry in the United States: The Activities of the Vaad Ha-Hatzala Rescue Committee, 1939–1945* (New York, 2000), 44–45, 47; Yehuda Bauer, *A History of the Holocaust* (New York, 1982), 283. According to Zuroff, there were 43 Lubavitcher yeshiva students in Vilna at this time. Zuroff estimates there were 2,100 Orthodox refugees, and Bauer puts the number at 2,611. To keep it simple, I have used 2,500.

26. Altein and Zaklikovsky, *Out of the Inferno*, 298; Madej and Zaloga, *Polish Campaign*, 138; Kaplan, *Scroll of Agony*, 26; Bethell, *War Hitler Won*, 113.

27. Altein and Zaklikovsky, *Out of the Inferno*, 298; Kaplan, *Scroll of Agony*, 27; Wineberg interview; Lewis D. Solomon, *The Jewish Book of Living and Dying* (New York, 1999), 55, 103.

28. Altein and Zaklikovsky, *Out of the Inferno*, 298–299; Wineberg interview.

29. Kaplan, *Scroll of Agony*, 20; Altein and Zaklikovsky, *Out of the Inferno*, 304. For information about Pompey, see Titus Flavius Josephus, *The Jewish War*, trans. G. A. Williamson (New York, 1981), 46, 161; Paul Johnson, *A History of Christianity* (New York, 1995), 9.

30. Kee, *1939: In the Shadow of War*, 310; Kaplan, *Scroll of Agony*, 29.

31. Herman Melville, *Moby Dick* (Oxford, 2008), 254; Christopher Hitchens, *Hitch-22: A Memoir* (New York, 2010), 3; Gilbert, *Second World War*, 10.

32. Altein and Zaklikovsky, *Out of the Inferno*, 299; Greenberg interview.

33. Altein and Zaklikovsky, *Out of the Inferno*, 306.

34. Ibid., 299; Jacobson, "Journey to America," 4; Uri Kaploun, ed., *Likkutei Dibburim: An Anthology of Talks by Rabbi Yosef Yitzchak Schneersohn of Lubavitch*, 5 vols. (Brooklyn, NY, 1987–2000), 1:119. On angels and Hasidim, see Norman Lamm, *The Religious Thought of Hasidism: Text and Commentary* (New York, 1999), 202, 522. Angels are often mentioned in the Rebbe's talks. See *Likkutei Dibburim*, 2:29, 42, 178, 214, 283; 1:5–7, 20, 118–119, 159.

35. Altein and Zaklikovsky, *Out of the Inferno*, 303, 305; Jacobson, "Journey to America," 4.

36. Gutman, *Jews of Warsaw*, 6; Wineberg interview.

37. Altein and Zaklikovsky, *Out of the Inferno*, 304; Wineberg interview; B. Gourary interview.

38. Altein and Zaklikovsky, *Out of the Inferno*, 299, 304–305; Wineberg interview; Zaklikofsky, *America Is No Different*, 50.

39. Wineberg interview.

40. Zaklikofsky, *America Is No Different*, 49; Altein and Zaklikovsky, *Out of the Inferno*, 299–300, 303.

41. Kaplan, *Scroll of Agony*, 29.

42. *The Rebbes*, 151; Nosson Scherman and Meir Zlotowitz, eds., *The Complete Artscroll Siddur* (Brooklyn, NY, 1984), 90–91. The Shema is the Jewish

profession of faith. Karen Armstrong, *A History of God: A 4,000-Year Quest of Judaism, Christianity and Islam* (New York, 1993), 52; Altein and Zaklikovsky, *Out of the Inferno*, 300–301.

43. Wineberg interview; Altein and Zaklikovsky, *Out of the Inferno*, 304; Zaklikofsky, *America Is No Different*, 50.

44. Matthew Cooper, *The German Air Force 1933–1945* (New York, 1981), 101; Gilbert, *Second World War*, 18; Altein and Zaklikovsky, *Out of the Inferno*, 300–301; Kaplan, *Scroll of Agony*, 29; *The Von Hassell Diaries 1938–1944: The Story of the Forces against Hitler Inside Germany as Recorded by Ambassador Ulrich von Hassell—A Leader of the Movement* (New York, 1947), 79. Zaklikofsky gives Shmotkin's address as 31 Mirinovska Street (*America Is No Different*, 50). According to a relative of Shmotkin, he lived at 32 Muranowska Street.

45. *The Rebbes*, 150–151.

46. Altein and Zaklikovsky, *Out of the Inferno*, 302.

47. Wineberg interview; Gershon Greenberg, "Menahem Mendel Schneersohn's Response to the Holocaust," *Modern Judaism* 34, 1 (20 February 2014): 90.

48. Gerhard L. Weinberg, *A World at Arms: A Global History of World War II* (New York, 1994), 56; Norman Davies, *God's Playground: A History of Poland*, vol. 2, *1795 to the Present* (New York, 1982), 437; Andrew S. Weiss, "The Improviser," *Wall Street Journal*, 21–22 February 2015.

49. Winston S. Churchill, *The Second World War*, vol. 1, *The Gathering Storm* (Boston, 1983), 392–395; Madej and Zaloga, *Polish Campaign*, 152–153; Weinberg, *World at Arms*, 51–52, 55; Davies, *God's Playground*, 437, 440; Kozak, *Rabbi of 84th Street*, 40; John Toland, *Adolf Hitler* (New York, 1976), 583; Adolf Hitler, *Mein Kampf* (Boston, 1971), 660 (emphasis added). Special thanks to Alex Rossino for information about the German documents proving that the Nazis were pressuring Stalin to invade from the east.

50. Churchill, *Second World War*, 390; Sheila Fitzpatrick, *The Russian Revolution 1917–1932* (Oxford, 1990), 63.

51. Churchill, *Second World War*, 449; Davies, *God's Playground*, 437, 439.

52. Gilbert, *Second World War*, 11.

53. Kee, *1939: In the Shadow of War*, 316.

54. Davies, *God's Playground*, 439.

55. Wineberg interview; *The Rebbes*, 149; Kaplan, *Scroll of Agony*, 35; Ian Kershaw, *Hitler 1936–1945: Nemesis* (New York, 2000), 236; Rhoade to Kramer, 3 (point 2—Warsaw to Riga), Schneersohn folder 3, Bloch file, BMRS, BA-MA.

56. Shimon Huberband, *Kiddusch Hashem: Jewish, Religious, and Cultural Life in Poland during the Holocaust* (New York, 1987), 46–48; Altein and Zaklikovsky, *Out of the Inferno*, 301; *Likkutei Dibburim*, 1:5–7, 20. See also Solomon, *Jewish Book of Living and Dying*, 71, and *Likkutei Dibburim*, 2:42, 48. The prayer the Rebbe gave is common among observant Jews at this time.

57. Nora Levin, *The Holocaust: The Destruction of European Jewry, 1933–1945* (New York, 1973), 152; Fox interview.

58. Gilbert, *Second World War*, 12. According to Gilbert, the Germans who committed these crimes were part of the SS Brandenburg Division. However, Brandenburg was a special formation until 1943, when it became a division. Also, it was a Wehrmacht unit, not SS.

59. This horn was also sounded as a reminder of "fearful days." Friedman, *No Haven*, 155.

60. Altein and Zaklikovsky, *Out of the Inferno*, 301–302; Kaplan, *Scroll of Agony*, 35–36.

61. Erich von Manstein, *Lost Victories: The War Memoirs of Hitler's Most Brilliant General* (Novato, CA, 1982), 58.

62. Kaplan, *Scroll of Agony*, 36; Cooper, *German Air Force*, 101; Gilbert, *Second World War*, 13; Madej and Zaloga, *Polish Campaign*, 140; Altein and Zaklikovsky, *Out of the Inferno*, 290, 300–301; Gutman, *Jews of Warsaw*, 7; Stanislaw Strzetelski, *Where the Storm Broke: Poland from Yesterday to Tomorrow* (New York, 1942), 87; Bethell, *War Hitler Won*, 139.

63. Gilbert, *Second World War*, 13.

64. Churchill, *Second World War*, 447.

65. Levin, *Holocaust*, 150; Gilbert, *Second World War*, 8; Huberband, *Kiddusch Hashem*, xvi; Altein and Zaklikovsky, *Out of the Inferno*, 295; interview with Chaskel Besser, 15 July 2003, BMRS, BA-MA.

66. Winfried Meyer, *Unternehmen Sieben. Eine Rettungsaktion für vom Holocaust Bedrohte aus dem Amt Ausland-Abwehr im Oberkommando der Wehrmacht* (Frankfurt, 1993), 136; "1,000 Rabbis Greet Rabbi Schneersohn, Exiled Polish Leader," *New York Herald Tribune*, 20 March 1940; "Rabbi from Warsaw," *Time*, 1 April 1940; interview with Rabbi Zalman Gurary, 19 January 1997, BMRS, BA-MA.

67. Ibid.; interview with Eliezer Zaklikovsky, 4 June 2003.

68. Altein and Zaklikovsky, *Out of the Inferno*, 301.

69. Gutman, *Jews of Warsaw*, 7; Kaplan, *Scroll of Agony*, 27, 35, 38; Altein and Zaklikovsky, *Out of the Inferno*, 306; interview with Karin Falencki, 3 January 2003, BMRS, BA-MA. See also Todd Brewster and Peter Jennings, *The Century* (New York, 1998), 215.

70. Madej and Zaloga, *Polish Campaign*, 141; Cooper, *German Air Force*, 103. Brewster and Jennings, *Century*, 215; Kaplan, *Scroll of Agony*, 39; Arno J. Mayer, *Why Did the Heavens Not Darken: The "Final Solution" in History* (New York, 1988), 183.

71. Kaplan, *Scroll of Agony*, 38; Gutman, *Jews of Warsaw*, 8; Madej and Zaloga, *Polish Campaign*, 141.

72. Citino, *German Way of War*, 259; Davies, *God's Playground*, 438–439;

Gordon A. Craig, *Germany 1866–1945* (New York, 1978), 715; Brewster and Jennings, *Century*, 216; Richard M. Watt, *Bitter Glory: Poland and Its Fate 1918–1939* (New York, 1979), 422; Max I. Dimont, *Jews, God and History* (New York, 1964), 245; Churchill, *Second World War*, 443; William L. Shirer, *The Nightmare Years 1930–1940* (New York, 1984), 457. However, Victor Madej and Steven Zaloga dispute this claim. According to them, the Poles had been familiar with armor for a long time and would not have conducted such a suicidal charge. Italian journalists who visited the battlefield were told that the dead Polish cavalrymen had been killed by attacking German tanks. Madej and Zaloga, *Polish Campaign*, 110. See also Thomas Childers, *A History of Hitler's Empire*, 2nd ed. (Chantilly, VA, 2001), for his take on the cavalrymen attacking German tanks.

73. Davies, *God's Playground*, 437–438.

74. Madej and Zaloga, *Polish Campaign*, 156; Matthew Cooper, *German Army 1933–1945: Its Political and Military Failure* (New York, 1978), 169; Martin Gilbert, *The Holocaust* (New York, 1985), 91; Weinberg, *World at Arms*, 57; Mayer, *Why Did the Heavens Not Darken*, 178; Kershaw, *Hitler 1936–1945*, 236; Alan Bullock, *Hitler: A Study in Tyranny* (New York, 1983), 556.

75. Churchill, *Second World War*, 443; General Records of Department of State, Itinerary 705, Visa Case Files 1933–1940, 811.111, Joseph Schneersohn, Record Group 59, NARA; brief biographical sketch and outline of the activities of Rabbi Joseph Isaac Schneersohn, 360 C.60P, 15/1, Records of the United States Theaters of War, World War II, WNRC; John Keegan, *The Second World War* (New York, 1990), 44–47.

76. Kershaw, *Hitler 1936–1945*, 243–245; Strzetelski, *Where the Storm Broke*, 107–127; Simon Segal, *The New Order in Poland* (New York, 1942), 56–58; Bethell, *War Hitler Won*, 147; Rossino, *Hitler Strikes Poland*, 141; Gilbert, *Second World War*, 6; Kaplan, *Scroll of Agony*, 10, 43. Kaplan is being ironic here. He is using his diary to express his frustration with the situation. Noah cursed Ham for seeing his nakedness and condemned Ham's sons to be Israel's slaves. According to biblical legend, Ham became the father of Africa. Now Kaplan sees the irony of the Jews serving people who should actually be under them. See Genesis 9:21–27 (New International Version). Wagner would later join the resistance against Hitler. After the failed assassination attempt against Hitler on 20 July 1944, Wagner committed suicide at Zossen, where he was stationed. Gill, *Honourable Defeat*, 254.

77. Kaplan, *Scroll of Agony*, 38.

78. Ibid., 43.

79. B. Gourary interview.

80. Gilbert, *Second World War*, 19.

CHAPTER 5. A PLAN TAKES SHAPE

1. Interview with Joseph Wineberg, 4 May 2003, BMRS, BA-MA; Rebbe Joseph Isaac Schneersohn, *Igrois Koidesh*, vol. 5 (Brooklyn, NY, 1983), 5; Rabbi Israel Jacobson, "Journey to America," *Di Yiddishe Heim* (1956), 4–5.

2. Interview with Rabbi Meir Greenberg, 18 August 1996, BMRS, BA-MA.

3. David Wyman, *The Abandonment of the Jews: America and the Holocaust 1941–1945* (New York, 1989), 184; Saul S. Friedman, *No Haven for the Oppressed: United States Policy toward Jewish Refugees, 1938–1945* (Detroit, 1973), 225; Gregory Wallance, *America's Soul in the Balance: The Holocaust, FDR's State Department, and the Moral Disgrace of an American Aristocracy* (Austin, TX, 2012), 74. Hull was not proud that his wife Frances (née Witz) was of Jewish descent. Michael Beschloss, *The Conquerors: Roosevelt, Truman and the Destruction of Hitler's Germany 1941–1945* (New York, 2002), 53; Henry L. Feingold, *The Politics of Rescue: The Roosevelt Administration and the Holocaust, 1938–1945* (New Brunswick, NJ, 1970), 19; Irwin Gellman, *Secret Affairs: Franklin Roosevelt, Cordell Hull, and Sumner Welles* (Baltimore, 1995), 98; Wagner to Hull, 22 September 1939, 360 C.60P, 15/1, WNRC; Kleinfeld to Wagner, 24 September 1939, Schneersohn folder 3, Bloch file, CLD, BMRS, BA-MA. Kleinfeld seems to have been on very good terms with Wagner, referring to him as "Bob" in his letters. Rhoade was deeply impressed with the contacts Kleinfeld and Kramer had in Washington, DC, and believed the Rebbe was "very fortunate" to have men so "deeply interested in him." Rhoade to Jacobson, 29 September 1939, Schneersohn folder 3, Bloch file, BMRS, BA-MA. Hull apparently got involved even in insignificant cases to help people. See General Records of Department of State, Itinerary 705, Visa Case Files 1933–1940, 811.111, Ida Schmuckler, Record Group 59, NARA.

4. Milton Kramer, ed., *The Kramers: The Next Generation* (Brooklyn, NY, 1995), 76; Wagner to Hull, 22 and 26 September 1939, 360 C.60P, 15/1, WNRC; Dept. of State to American Legation in Riga, 13 January 1940, General Records of Department of State, Itinerary 705, Visa Case Files 1933–1940, 811.111, Joseph Schneersohn, Record Group 59, NARA; Michael Berenbaum, *The World Must Know: The History of the Holocaust as Told in the United States Holocaust Memorial Museum* (Baltimore, 2007), 53. Hull seemed to be getting pressure from many areas. For example, Henry Monsky, national president of B'nai Brith, asked Hull to take action on the Rebbe's behalf. Monsky had been contacted by the Lubavitchers in Chicago. Kramer to Rhoade, 12 October 1939, 4, point 17, Schneersohn folder 3, Bloch file, CLD, BMRS, BA-MA.

5. Kramer to Rabinovitz, 24 September 1939, Kramer to Rhoade, 25 September 1939, Kleinfeld to Wagner, 25 September 1939, Kramer to Rosen, 25 September 1939, and Memorandum of Activities regarding Rabbi Schneersohn, 26 September 1939, all in Schneersohn folder 3, Bloch file, CLD, BMRS, BA-MA; Wineberg interview.

6. Wagner to Hull, 26 September 1939, and telegraph from Hull to American Legation in Riga (John C. Wiley), Latvia, 360 C.60P, 15/2, WNRC; Packer to Hull, 30 September 1939, ibid., 15/7.

7. Paul Johnson, *A History of the Jews* (New York, 1987), 460; James MacGregor Burns, *Roosevelt*, vol. 1, *The Lion and the Fox* (Norwalk, CT, 1956), 230. Bloom also helped insignificant people when he could. See General Records of Department of State, Itinerary 705, Visa Case Files 1933–1940, 811.111, Martha Schmul, Record Group 59, NARA; Arthur Rabinovitz to Justice Louis D. Brandeis, 29 September 1939, 360 C.60P, 15/6, WNRC.

8. Telegraph from Rabinovitz to Brandeis, 29 September 1939, 360 C.60P, 15/2, WNRC; Rabinovitz to Brandeis, 29 September 1939, ibid., 15/6; Jacobson, "Journey to America," 3.

9. Benjamin V. Cohen to Robert T. Pell, 2 October 1939, 360 C.60P, 15/3, WNRC; William Lasser, *Bengamin V. Cohen: Architect of the New Deal* (New Haven, CT, 2002), 7–8, 26–27; Wallance, *America's Soul*, 256. In addition to Rhoade working various government offices in Washington, Rabinovitz spent time in Washington meeting with his contacts to help Schneersohn. Jacobson to Rissman, 25 September 1939, Schneersohn folder 3, Bloch file, BMRS, BA-MA.

10. Memorandum from Pell about his telephone conversation with Cohen, 2 October 1939, 1, 360 C.60P, 15/4, WNRC.

11. Robert Wistrich, *Hitler and the Holocaust* (New York, 2001), 57; David Wyman, *Paper Walls: America and the Refugee Crisis 1938–1941* (New York, 1985), xiii, 45, 48; Stephen Wise, *Challenging Years: The Autobiography of Stephen Wise* (New York, 1949), 221; David Kertzer, *The Pope and Mussolini: The Secret History of Pius XI and the Rise of Fascism in Europe* (Oxford, 2014), 12; Marc Eric McClure, *Earnest Endeavors: The Life and Public Work of George Rublee* (Westport, CT, 2003), 248. Although the Evian conference was called primarily because of the Jews in Europe, they were referred to as refugees, not Jewish refugees. Ironically, the conference wanted to avoid drawing too much attention to the Jews.

12. McClure, *Earnest Endeavors*, 255.

13. Wistrich, *Hitler and the Holocaust*, 57; Wyman, *Paper Walls*, 50; Friedman, *No Haven*, 56, 60; Henry L. Feingold, *Bearing Witness: How America and Its Jews Responded to the Holocaust* (Syracuse, NY, 1995), 77; Neil Rolde, *Breckinridge Long: American Eichmann* (Solon, ME, 2013), 140–141; Günter Schubert, *Der Fleck auf Uncle Sams weißer Weste: Amerika und die jüdischen Flüchtlinge 1938–1945* (Frankfurt, 2003), 45.

14. McClure, *Earnest Endeavors*, 249.

15. Erik Larson, *In the Garden of Beasts: Love, Terror, and an American Family in Hitler's Berlin* (New York, 2011), 137, 231–233.

16. Walter LaFeber, *The American Age: United States Foreign Policy at Home*

and Abroad since 1750 (New York, 1989), 368. See McClure, *Earnest Endeavors*, 253, for further details on Hull and his economic concerns in 1938.

17. Wyman, *Paper Walls*, 49.

18. Friedman, *No Haven*, 144, 154; Feingold, *Politics of Rescue*, 280–283.

19. Memorandum from Pell, 2 October 1939, 2; Wyman, *Paper Walls*, 51, 56; Feingold, *Politics of Rescue*, 54, 58–63, 71; Winfried Meyer, *Unternehmen Sieben. Eine Rettungsaktion für vom Holocaust Bedrohte aus dem Amt Ausland-Abwehr im Oberkommando der Wehrmacht* (Frankfurt, 1993), 130–132; Feingold, *Bearing Witness*, 76.

20. Schubert, *Der Fleck auf Uncle Sams weißer Weste*, 132.

21. Interview with Chaskel Besser, 15 July 2003, BMRS, BA-MA; discussion with Jacobson's grandson, Rabbi Leib Altein, September 1997; interview with Rachel Altein (Jacobson's daughter), 14 January 2003.

22. Edward Klein, *The Kennedy Curse: Why America's First Family Has Been Haunted by Tragedy for 150 Years* (New York, 2003), 15. This story is well known in Lubavitcher circles and originates from that community. Interview with Eliezer and Chanie Zaklikovsky, 25 December 2003. Though they are not often used, curses are a part of Judaism. For example, the Rebbe cursed Soviet officials who dared to harm Torah students. Uri Kaploun, ed., *Likkutei Dibburim: An Anthology of Talks by Rabbi Yosef Yitzchak Schneersohn of Lubavitch*, 5 vols. (Brooklyn, NY, 1987–2000), 5:10. See also Louis Jacobs, *The Jewish Religion: A Companion* (New York, 1995), 55.

23. Department of State, Office of Special Agent in Charge, 360 C.60P, 15/6, WNRC; General Records of Department of State, Itinerary 705, Visa Case Files 1933–1940, 811.111, Joseph Schneersohn, Record Group 59, NARA; Kleinfield to Farley, 27 September 1939, and Irwin S. Chanin to Bloom, 27 September 1939, Schneersohn folder 3, CLD, BMRS, BA-MA; Schneersohn to Roosevelt, 12 September 1941, box 7, OF 76c, Franklin D. Roosevelt Library, Hyde Park, NY. Tens of thousands of Russian Jews had emigrated in the late 1800s and early 1900s, and according to Rabbi Avraham Laber, a historian of the Lubavitcher movement, this number may be a conservative estimate. Rabbi Eliezer Zaklikovsky agrees with Laber. See also affidavit of Rabbi Israel Jacobson, January 1940, Schneersohn folder 3, CLD, BMRS, BA-MA; Edward Hoffman, *Despite All Odds: The Story of Lubavitch* (New York, 1991), 23; Meyer, *Unternehmen Sieben*, 129. However, Paula Hyman, professor of history and head of Judaic studies at Yale University, believes that 160,000 Lubavitchers in North America is an inflated number; it was probably closer to 40,000. Professor Bernhard Klein of Kingsborough Community College of Brooklyn concurs with Hyman. Professor Henry Feingold, director of the Jewish Resource Center of Baruch College in New York, puts the figure even lower—probably no more than 20,000. According to Lubavitcher sources, the population was 40,000 in 1929; see Eliezer Zaklikofsky, *America Is No Different* (New York, 1999), 19. If this number is

accurate, then 110,000 Lubavitchers must have entered the United States between 1929 and 1939. It remains unclear exactly how many Lubavitchers were in the United States at the time; even today they do not keep records of their membership. Lubavitcher rabbi Zalman Posner agrees with Professors Hyman, Klein, and Feingold that the 160,000 figure is "nonsense"; Posner to Rigg, 8 January 2004, Schneersohn folder 6, BMRS, BA-MA. However, he is in the minority among those I have talked with, and the fact remains that back in 1939–1940, this is the number the Chabad leadership was claiming. Historian David Kranzler says Chabad had maybe 10,000 members. Interview with Kranzler, 24 January 2004. Rabbi Moshe Kolodny, head of the Agudah Archives of Orthodox Jewry in New York, puts the number at 2,000. Interview with Kolodny, 21 January 2004. Based on all these different figures, it seems clear that the number was smaller than claimed; however, determining an exact number is probably impossible. Even Rabbi Telushkin's recent propaganda piece for Chabad admits that in 1950 Chabad "was a relatively small movement centered in one borough of New York City (with small outposts elsewhere) and that it was in danger of going under or becoming so small as to be insignificant." Joseph Telushkin, *Rebbe: The Life and Teachings of Menachem M. Schneerson, the Most Influential Rabbi in Modern History* (New York, 2014), 32. With this admission, it is obvious that the claim of 150,000 members in 1939 was a flat-out fabrication.

24. Jacobson affidavit, January 1940; Deborah E. Lipstadt, *Beyond Belief: The American Press & the Coming of the Holocaust 1933–1945* (New York, 1986), 2.

25. Feingold, *Politics of Rescue*, 139, 330 n. 44; Hull to Farley, 2 October 1939, 360 C.60P, 15/6, WNRC.

26. State Department, Division of European Affairs, telephone conversation with Mr. Smits from the Latvian embassy, 2 October 1939, 360 C.60P, 15/6, WNRC; Wineberg interview; Kramer to Rabinovitz, 24 September 1939, 1, Schneersohn folder 3, Bloch file, CLD, BMRS, BA-MA. At this stage, there was incredible activity and energy directed toward meeting with anyone who could possibly help the Rebbe.

27. Kramer to Rabinovitz, 24 September 1939, 2. Kramer met with Rosen on 25 September and reported that he and the Joint Distribution Committee were "very much interested in Rabbi Schneersohn's welfare." Rosen then wrote a recommendation for the Rebbe, which was sent to US minister John Cooper Wiley. Kleinfeld to Wagner, 25 September 1939, Kramer to Rhoade, 25 September 1939, cable from Rosen to Wiley, 25 September 1939, and memorandum of activities regarding Rabbi Schneersohn, 26 September 1939, 2, point 6, all in Schneersohn folder 3, Bloch file, BMRS, BA-MA. By 16 October Kramer was confident that Wiley would do everything in his power "to extend his full cooperation." Kramer to Rhoade, 16 October 1939, 2, ibid.

28. Günter Schubert notes that even though Hull's name appears at the bottom of this document, he probably did not actually sign it. There was so much

correspondence being sent on a daily basis, it would have been difficult for Hull to sign each one. Even so, Hull certainly knew what was going on. Assistant Secretary of State George S. Messersmith initialed this document, indicating that it was legitimate. See Schubert, *Der Fleck auf Uncle Sams weißer Weste*, 126. Gregory Wallance documents that "eighteen people in [Hull's] area of responsibility alone had authority to sign [his] name to diplomatic cables." Wallance, *America's Soul*, 81.

29. Pell to Geist, 3 October 1939, 360 C.60P, 15/3, WNRC.

30. André Brissaud, *Canaris* (London, 1986), 158; Karl Heinz Abshagen, *Canaris* (London, 1956), 150; Meyer, *Unternehmen Sieben*, 134; telegram from Geist and Kirk to Hull, 360 C.60P, 15/5, WNRC. Alexander Kirk was chargé d'affaires in Berlin at the time, and he took a keen interest in helping Schneersohn. Interestingly, he was a homosexual, and the Rebbe would not have approved of his lifestyle. See Schubert, *Der Fleck auf Uncle Sams weißer Weste*, 129–130.

31. Hull to Robert Wagner, 26 September 1939, and Hull to James Farley, 2 October 1939, 360 C.60P, 15/6, WNRC; Robert Edwin Herzstein, *Roosevelt & Hitler: Prelude to War* (New York, 1989), 233; Ian Kershaw, *Profiles in Power: Hitler* (New York, 1991), 149; Alexander B. Rossino, *Hitler Strikes Poland: Blitzkrieg, Ideology, and Atrocity* (Lawrence, KS, 2003), 90; Feingold, *Politics of Rescue*, 19, 42–43; Wyman, *Paper Walls*, 56; Ernest R. May, *Strange Victory: Hitler's Conquest of France* (New York, 2000), 45, 68–79; memorandum from Pell, 2 October 1939, 2; Wallance, *America's Soul*, 124; e-mail from Marc Eric McClure, 2 March 2015.

CHAPTER 6. THE NAZI CONNECTION

1. Interview with Gisela Bauer, 28 September 2014; letter from Gisela Bauer to Bryan Mark Rigg, 13 September 2014, Bloch file, BMRS, BA-MA.

2. "War Front: Capitalism in Germany," *Time*, 7 April 1941; Helmut Metzmacher, "Deutsche-englishe Ausgleichsbemühungen im Sommer 1939," *Vierteljahrshefte für Zeitgeschichte* 14, 4 (1966): 407; Karl Heinz Abshagen, *Canaris* (London, 1956), 45–47, 57; Winfried Meyer, *Unternehmen Sieben. Eine Rettungsaktion für vom Holocaust Bedrohte aus dem Amt Ausland-Abwehr im Oberkommando der Wehrmacht* (Frankfurt, 1993), 130–131; testimonies by several Jews Wohlthat helped in the 1930s, Hessisches Hauptstaatsarchiv, Düsseldorf, Germany; interview with Helmuth Wohlthat by Rolf Vogel, 17 December 1974, Bonn, Germany, BMRS, BA-MA. Some of the men in the resistance that Wohlthat was in touch with were Ulrich von Hassell, Carl Goerdeler, and General Ludwig Beck. Bauer to Rigg, 13 September 2014; Bill W. Santin, Registrar Services Columbia University, to Rigg, 14 January 2015, Bloch file, BMRS, BA-MA.

3. Raul Hilberg, *Destruction of the European Jews* (New York, 1961), 76–80; Meyer, *Unternehmen Sieben*, 128–139.

4. Rabbi Israel Jacobson, "Journey to America," *Di Yiddishe Heim* (1956), 3; Heinz Höhne, *Canaris* (New York, 1979), 411; Abshagen, *Canaris*, 99; Günter Schubert, *Der Fleck auf Uncle Sams weißer Weste: Amerika und die jüdischen Flüchtlinge 1938–1945* (Frankfurt, 2003), 126–127. According to Rabbi David Edelman, Göring was involved; he had told foreign representatives that for $100,000 he would help anyone get a Jew out of Europe. Edelman to Rigg, 23 February 2004, Schneersohn folder 6, BMRS, BA-MA. However, if Göring had been involved, he most likely would have used this in his defense during the Nuremberg trials in 1945. The fact that he did not mention it once indicates that if he did know what Wohlthat was doing, he did not pay it much mind. See http://avalon.law.yale.edu/imt/judgoeri.asp.

5. Schubert, *Der Fleck auf Uncle Sams weißer Weste*, 9, 58, 128–130; Marc Eric McClure, *Earnest Endeavors: The Life and Public Work of George Rublee* (Westport, CT, 2003), 274; Donald L. Niewyk, "Holocaust: The Genocide of the Jews," in *Century of Genocide: Critical Essays and Eyewitness Accounts*, ed. Israel W. Charny, William S. Parsons, and Samuel Totten (New York, 2004), 128; Thomas Childers, *A History of Hitler's Empire*, 2nd ed. (Chantilly, VA, 2001).

6. Abshagen, *Canaris*, 150; letter from Generalfeldmarschall von Mackensen to Generaloberst von Blomberg, 11 January 1936, RW 6/73, BA-MA; letter from Reichsminister und Chef der Reichskanzlei Lammers to Generalfeldmarschall von Mackensen, 3 February 1939, N 39/62, BA-MA.

7. Höhne, *Canaris*, 7, 15, 167–169, 362; André Brissaud, *Canaris* (London, 1986), 5–6; Abshagen, *Canaris*, 19–20, 23, 44; Anton Gill, *An Honourable Defeat: A History of German Resistance to Hitler 1933–1945* (New York, 1994), 82.

8. David Kahn, *Hitler's Spies: German Military Intelligence in World War II* (New York, 1977), 226, 229; Abshagen, *Canaris*, 12, 21, 71, 73, 229; lecture by Admiral Canaris at the conference at the military high command, 3 March 1938, Bl. 400–402, RW 6/56, BA-MA; Höhne, *Canaris*, 34, 45–47, 51–52, 131–134, 213, 216, 247; Brissaud, *Canaris*, 7, 10.

9. Kahn, *Hitler's Spies*, 231–232; Abshagen, *Canaris*, 75; Meyer, *Unternehmen Sieben*, 14; Höhne, *Canaris*, 86, 162, 177–178; Brissaud, *Canaris*, 12–13, 50.

10. Kahn, *Hitler's Spies*, 234–235; Meyer, *Unternehmen Sieben*, 134; Höhne, *Canaris*, 212.

11. Höhne, *Canaris*, 212; Brissaud, *Canaris*, 28; Abshagen, *Canaris*, 25–36, 74, 76, 83, 94, 157.

12. Rolf Vogel, *Ein Stück von uns* (Bonn, 1973), 306–307; *Nachhut*, 15 February 1971, Heft 11, S. 12; Msg 3-22/1, BA-MA; Michel Bar-Zohar, *Hitler's Jewish Spy: The Most Extraordinary True Spy Story of World War II* (London, 1985). See also Meyer, *Unternehmen Sieben*.

13. Brissaud, *Canaris*, 89, 155; Meyer, *Unternehmen Sieben*, 134; Höhne, *Canaris*, 250, 258, 276, 360; Alan Clark, *Barbarossa: The Russian-German Con-*

flict 1941–1945 (New York, 1965), 14; Gordon Craig, *The Politics of the Prussian Army 1640–1945* (New York, 1964), 495; RGBL, II, 4 February 1938; Militär-geschichtliches Forschungsamt, ed., *Germany and the Second World War*, vol. 1, *Build-up of German Aggression* (Oxford, 1998), 521; Ian Kershaw, *Hitler 1936–1945: Nemesis* (New York, 2000), 57, 188; Robert O'Neill, *The German Army and the Nazi Party, 1933–1939* (New York, 1966), 72; Ernest R. May, *Strange Victory: Hitler's Conquest of France* (New York, 2000), 216–217.

14. Brissaud, *Canaris*, 156; Kahn, *Hitler's Spies*, 235; Höhne, *Canaris*, 364; Martin Gilbert, *The Second World War: A Complete History* (New York, 1989), 8.

15. Brissaud, *Canaris*, 156; Meyer, *Unternehmen Sieben*, 26, 30, 31; Gill, *Honourable Defeat*, 87.

16. Bürkner to Wohlthat, 15 January 1948, 100021/49193, Bl. 55F, Hessisches Hauptstaatsarchiv; Brissaud, *Canaris*, 158; Abshagen, *Canaris*, 150.

17. Höhne, *Canaris*, 296, 298, 303–304, 331–332, 335, 352; John Wheeler-Bennett, *The Nemesis of Power* (New York, 1980), 455; Brissaud, *Canaris*, 151. See also *The Von Hassell Diaries 1938–1944: The Story of the Forces against Hitler Inside Germany as Recorded by Ambassador Ulrich von Hassell—A Leader of the Movement* (New York, 1947), 75. After witnessing one of Hitler's outbursts against Britain in the spring of 1940, Canaris declared him "mad." Höhne, *Canaris*, 331.

18. Brissaud, *Canaris*, 153; Norbert Frei, *National Socialist Rule in Germany* (Cambridge, 1993), 125; Paul Gordon Lauren, *Power and Prejudice* (London, 1988), 126–127; George Victor, *Hitler: The Pathology of Evil* (Dulles, VA, 1998), 196; Yehuda Bauer, *A History of the Holocaust* (New York, 1982), 147; Ian Kershaw, *Profiles in Power: Hitler* (New York, 1991), 152; Yisrael Gutman, *The Jews of Warsaw, 1939–1943: Ghetto, Underground, Revolt* (Bloomington, IN, 1982), 12–15; Robert Wistrich, *Hitler and the Holocaust* (New York, 2001), 73; Nora Levin, *The Holocaust: The Destruction of European Jewry, 1933–1945* (New York, 1973), 150, 204; Alexander B. Rossino, *Hitler Strikes Poland: Blitzkrieg, Ideology, and Atrocity* (Lawrence, KS, 2003), 10, 14, 22; Höhne, *Canaris*, 363.

19. Meyer, *Unternehmen Sieben*, 134; Abshagen, *Canaris*, 197; Bürkner to Wohlthat, 15 January 1948; interview with Martin Bloch, 13 October 1996, BMRS, BA-MA; Pers 6/9887, Bl. 1a, BA-MA; Brissaud, *Canaris*, 23.

CHAPTER 7. BLOCH'S SECRET MISSION

1. Pers 6/9887, Bl. 1a, BA-MA; Ernst Bloch file, Bl. 96-9, BMRS, BA-MA; Bryan Mark Rigg, *Hitler's Jewish Soldiers: The Untold Story of Jews and Men of Jewish Descent Who Served in the German Military* (Lawrence, KS, 2002), 56–57.

2. Interview with Martin Bloch, 13 October 1996, BMRS, BA-MA; Bloch file, ibid.

3. Interview with Ursula Cadenbach, 15 October 1996, BMRS, BA-MA; Bloch interview; Pers 6/9887; Bloch file.

4. First draft of a collection of materials for the Bloch family history by Martin Bloch, 3 November 1962, Bloch file, BMRS, BA-MA.

5. Frau Bloch to Ernst Bloch, 8 February 1921, Bloch file, BMRS, BA-MA.

6. Ibid.

7. Doctorate, 2 August 1924, Bloch file, BMRS, BA-MA.

8. Hans von Bosse to Bloch, 29 April 1930, Bloch file, BMRS, BA-MA.

9. Cadenbach interview; David Kahn, *Hitler's Spies: German Military Intelligence in World War II* (New York, 1977), 90; Heinz Höhne, *Canaris* (New York, 1979), 200; Pers 6/9887; silver plate given to Bloch by Japanese industrialists (J. Kihara, K. Oka, N. Tamura, H. Ishihara, T. Kawabe, K. Iwakami, S. Niimi, M. Sasao, M. Numaguti, and A. Arima), "In commemoration of our trip throughout Greater Germany May/June 1939," Bloch file, BMRS, BA-MA; photo album outlining the journey led by Bloch, "Trip of the German Armed Forces High Command with German Business Leaders through Belgium and France from 16 to 21 November 1940," ibid.

10. Verordnung zum Reichsbürgergesetz, 14 November 1935, RGBL, I (1935), Nr. 135, 1333–1336; Raul Hilberg, *Destruction of the European Jews* (New York, 1961), 48; *The Holocaust*, vol. 1, *Legalizing the Holocaust—The Early Phase, 1933–1939* (New York, 1982), 31; H. G. Adler, *Der Verwaltete Mensch. Studien zur Deportation der Juden aus Deutschland* (Tübingen, 1974), 280. If a Jewish woman had a child out of wedlock and the father's identity could not be determined, the Nazis classified the child as a full Jew. See *Akten der Parteikanzlei der NSDAP: Rekonstruktion eines verlorengegangenen Bestandes* (Munich, Bundesarchiv, Microfiches, hrsg. v. Institut für Zeitgeschichte, 1983), 107-00404; *Heeresadjutant bei Hitler 1938–1943. Aufzeichnungen des Majors Gerhard Engel*, hrsg. u. kommentiert v. Hildegard von Kotze, Schriftenreihe der Vierteljahreshefte für Zeitgeschichte Nr. 29 (Stuttgart, 1974), 32. If a person was three-eighths Jewish, he or she was most often classified as a quarter-Jew. Countless men and women documented in this study were actually 37.5 percent Jewish, and the majority were classified as quarter-Jews by the Nazis. See *Akten der Parteikanzlei der NSDAP*, 107-00389-390. When a person was more than 37.5 percent Jewish but less than 50 percent Jewish, he or she was usually classified as a half-Jew. Likewise, those who were more than 12.5 percent Jewish were usually classified as quarter-Jews.

11. Hilde Kammer and Elisabet Bartsch, eds., *Nationalsozialismus. Begriffe aus der Zeit der Gewaltherrschaft 1933–1945* (Hamburg, 1992), 39–40; Ian Kershaw, *Hitler 1889–1936: Hubris* (New York, 1999), 572; Norman Rich, *Hitler's War Aims* (New York, 1974), 1–2; Nathan Stoltzfus, *Resistance of the Heart: Intermarriage and the Rosenstrasse Protest in Nazi Germany* (London, 2001), xxv; Marion A. Kaplan, *Between Dignity and Despair: Jewish Life in Nazi Germany* (New York, 1998), 191.

12. Martin Gilbert, *The Holocaust* (New York, 1985), 45–47; Rolf Vogel, *Ein*

Stück von uns (Bonn, 1973), 238; Winfried Meyer, *Unternehmen Sieben. Eine Rettungsaktion für vom Holocaust Bedrohte aus dem Amt Ausland-Abwehr im Oberkommando der Wehrmacht* (Frankfurt, 1993), 128; Bloch file; Kahn, *Hitler's Spies*, 91.

13. Rigg, *Hitler's Jewish Soldiers*, 186–187; Pers 6/9887; Bloch file; Vogel, *Ein Stück von uns*, 308–309; Kahn, *Hitler's Spies*, 91.

14. Martin Bloch to Bryan Rigg, 29 August 1996, Bloch file, BMRS, BA-MA; Pers 6/9887, report from Canaris about Bloch, 14 March 1937, and Bl. 13, BA-MA; certificate of award from Hitler to Bloch, 19 October 1938, Bloch file.

15. Hamburger is a pseudonym. At the request of the family, their whereabouts and their name have been kept secret.

16. Interview with Mrs. Johannes Hamburger, BMRS, BA-MA.

17. Interview with Klaus Schenk, 18 November 1996, BMRS, BA-MA.

18. Schenk had lost his *Wehrpaß* (military passport), so it is difficult to determine where he was when attacked by the Polish army. It most likely happened when the Posnan Army, entrapped by the Wehrmacht west of the Vistula, "turned and attacked the German Eighth and Tenth Armies from the rear, inflicting heavy casualties on the surprised 30th Division in the first impact." John Keegan, *The Second World War* (New York, 1990), 46. According to Schenk, he was transferred from the infantry to the Abwehr so quickly because of some contacts he had there. In addition, his commanding officer had recognized Schenk's bravery and intelligence, which may have contributed to his selection to the Abwehr. Since there are no files on Schenk in the Bundesarchiv, it is difficult to ascertain exactly why he was chosen for this duty.

19. Schenk interview; Gilbert, *Holocaust*, 824. Renowned Holocaust historian Donald Niewyk disputes Gilbert's claim that tens of thousands of homosexuals were killed. According to Niewyk's files, around 10,000 were murdered by the Nazis. See also Rigg, *Hitler's Jewish Soldiers*, 26. For an interesting case study, see James F. Tent, *In the Shadow of the Holocaust: Nazi Persecution of Jewish-Christian Germans* (Lawrence, KS, 2003), 128–130. The website of the Holocaust Museum notes, "In 1935, the Nazi regime revised Paragraph 175 of the German criminal code to make illegal a very broad range of behavior between men." For Hitler's relationship with homosexuals and his attitude toward them, see Lothar Machtan, *The Hidden Hitler* (New York, 2001).

20. Meyer, *Unternehmen Sieben*, 135–136; Höhne, *Canaris*, 361.

21. Meyer, *Unternehmen Sieben*. See also Höhne, *Canaris*, 265–266; Anton Gill, *An Honourable Defeat: A History of German Resistance to Hitler 1933–1945* (New York, 1994), 215.

22. Höhne, *Canaris*, 489, 507; Karl Heinz Abshagen, *Canaris* (London, 1956), 101. See also Meyer, *Unternehmen Sieben*.

23. Rigg, *Hitler's Jewish Soldiers*, 51–67.

24. Yehuda Bauer, *A History of the Holocaust* (New York, 1982), 54; Rigg, *Hitler's Jewish Soldiers*, 72.

25. For more on *Mischlinge* in the Wehrmacht, see Rigg, *Hitler's Jewish Soldiers*.

CHAPTER 8. THE SEARCH BEGINS

1. Charles Rader, ed., *Challenge: An Encounter with Lubavitch-Chabad* (Brooklyn, NY, 1970), 53. For background on this holiday, see Leviticus 23:42–45.

2. Interview with Joseph Wineberg, 4 May 2003, BMRS, BA-MA.

3. Uri Kaploun, ed., *Likkutei Dibburim: An Anthology of Talks by Rabbi Yosef Yitzchak Schneersohn of Lubavitch*, 5 vols. (Brooklyn, NY, 1987–2000), 1:120. In the Rebbe's form of Judaism, women are not allowed to dance with the Torah. This dancing, the *Hakkafos*, was a very spiritual act for the Rebbe. He described it as follows: "During the *Hakkafos* the doors of heaven are open, because the Torah's happiness throws open the doors and gates of all the chambers of heaven." Ibid., 2:81. See also 2:89, 172–173.

4. Shimon Huberband, *Kiddusch Hashem: Jewish Religious and Cultural Life in Poland during the Holocaust* (New York, 1987), 53–54.

5. Chaim A. Kaplan, *Scroll of Agony: The Warsaw Diary of Chaim A. Kaplan* (New York, 1965), 45. Midian and Moab were the leaders of ancient tribes that wanted to destroy Israel. Midian was the son of Abraham by Keturah. Moab was Lot's grandson through incest with his daughter. Merrill C. Tenney, ed., *Pictorial Bible Dictionary* (Nashville, TN, 1966), 532, 549.

6. Kaplan, *Scroll of Agony*, 44, 46, 48, 54–56, 59.

7. Jacobson to Kramer, 10 October 1939, Schneersohn folder 3, Bloch file, CLD, BMRS, BA-MA. In Jacobson's sloppiness, he misspelled Brauchitsch's name.

8. Jacobson to Kramer, 30 October 1939, ibid. See also Rhoade to Kramer, 27 October and 4 November 1939, Schneersohn folder 1, ibid.; Rhoade to Hull, 2 November 1939, General Records of Department of State, Itinerary 705, Visa Case Files 1933–1940, 811.111, Samarius Gourary, Record Group 59, NARA (hereafter cited as Visa Case Files 1933–1940 and the case name).

9. See Rhoade to Hull, 2 November 1939; letter to American consular officer in Warsaw, Poland, 14 January 1939, Visa Case Files 1933–1940, Samarius Gourary; Hodgdon to Yellen, 21 May 1940, Visa Case Files 1933–1940, Rubin Halberpsohn.

10. Visa Department memorandum about Mr. Rhochkind, secretary to Senator Borah (who called about Rabbi Gourary's case), 12 January 1939, Visa Case Files 1933–1940, Samarius Gourary.

11. Visa Case Files 1933–1940, Bernhard Hamburger, Rubin Halberpsohn, Moses Rokach, Yoel Halpern, and Joseph Isaac Schneersohn. Nonquota status

was given to certain people, such as the wives and minor unmarried children of US citizens, nonimmigrants, and natives of Western Hemisphere countries. The law also allowed others outside these classifications to be given such status.

12. Marc Eric McClure, *Earnest Endeavors: The Life and Public Work of George Rublee* (Westport, CT, 2003), 249. For a detailed analysis of Long, see Gregory Wallance, *America's Soul in the Balance: The Holocaust, FDR's State Department, and the Moral Disgrace of an American Aristocracy* (Austin, TX, 2012).

13. Martin Gilbert, *The Holocaust* (New York, 1985), 117, 124, 701–702, 752–754, 761–762, 766–767; Bryan Mark Rigg, "Where They Are Now: Civil Disobedience (Issuing of the U.S. Postal Stamp in Honor of Robert Kim Bingham)," *Yale Alumni Magazine*, May–June 2006; Leni Yahil, *The Holocaust: The Fate of European Jewry* (Oxford, 1990), 575; Iris Chang, *The Rape of Nanking: The Forgotten Holocaust of World War II* (New York, 1997), 109–121, 188–197.

14. Wallance, *America's Soul*, 16.

15. David Wyman, *The Abandonment of the Jews: America and the Holocaust 1941–1945* (New York, 1989), 105; David Wyman, *Paper Walls: America and the Refugee Crisis 1938–1941* (New York, 1985), 212; Rafael Medoff and David Wyman, *A Race against Death: Peter Bergson, America, and the Holocaust* (New York, 2002), 41; Henry L. Feingold, *The Politics of Rescue: The Roosevelt Administration and the Holocaust, 1938–1945* (New Brunswick, NJ, 1970), 15, 17–18, 38, 135–136, 209; Irwin Gellman, *Secret Affairs: Franklin Roosevelt, Cordell Hull, and Sumner Welles* (Baltimore, 1995), 232; Wallance, *America's Soul*, 67, 170. For information about diplomats who helped save Jews, see "Diplomats Who Saved Jews" at the University of Minnesota's Center for Holocaust and Genocide Studies, http://chgs.umn.edu/museum/exhibitions/rescuers/saving Diplomats.html.

16. Tubbs to Fitch, 10 April 1939, Visa Case Files 1933–1940, Bernhard Hamburger; Kinsey to Fitch, 1 September 1938, Visa Case Files 1933–1940, David Rokeach; Visa Case Files 1933–1940, Joseph E. Gottlieb; Kinsey to Burr, 11 July 1934, Visa Case Files 1933–1940, Moshe Levin; Visa Case Files 1933–1940, Rabbi David Cohen.

17. Telegram from Kirk to Pell, 19 November 1939, 360 C.60P, 15/7, WNRC.

18. Telegram from Jacobson to Lieberman, 24 October 1939, Schneersohn folder 3, CLD, BMRS, BA-MA; Pell to Cohen, 28 October 1939, 360 C.60P, 15/9, WNRC.

19. Rabinovitz to Brandeis, 24 October 1939, Neumark folder, Bloch file, BMRS, BA-MA; Cohen to Pell, 26 October 1939, 360 C.60P, 15/9, WNRC; Günter Schubert, *Der Fleck auf Uncle Sams weißer Weste: Amerika und die jüdischen Flüchtlinge 1938–1945* (Frankfurt, 2003), 129–130.

20. Nora Levin, *The Holocaust: The Destruction of European Jewry, 1933–1945* (New York, 1973), 206; Yisrael Gutman, *The Jews of Warsaw, 1939–1943:*

Ghetto, Underground, Revolt (Bloomington, IN, 1982), 29; Hania Warfield and Gaither Warfield, *Call Us to Witness: A Polish Chronicle* (New York, 1945), 117; Kaplan, *Scroll of Agony*, 71, 73, 78–79; Arno J. Mayer, *Why Did the Heavens Not Darken: The "Final Solution" in History* (New York, 1988), 189.

21. Kaplan, *Scroll of Agony*, 78–79.

22. Manfred Windfuhr, ed., *Heinrich Heine, Historisch-kritische Gesataus-gabe der Werke* (Hamburg, 1973–1997), 10:313; Ruth Gay, *The Jews of Germany* (New Haven, CT, 1992), 141; Marvin Lowenthal, *The Jews of Germany: A History of Sixteen Centuries* (Philadelphia, 1936), 234.

23. *Likkutei Dibburim*, 4:73, 5:314; interview with Paula Hyman, 20 September 2003.

24. Interview with Klaus Schenk, 18 November 1996, BMRS, BA-MA.

25. Interview with Mrs. Johannes Hamburger, BMRS, BA-MA.

26. Ibid.; Martin Gilbert, *The Second World War: A Complete History* (New York, 1989), 22. Photographs in the Bloch family archives confirm that, when on assignment, Bloch was often in civilian clothes.

27. Gilbert, *Second World War*, 23.

28. Wallance, *America's Soul*, 24.

29. Interview with Karl Wolff by historian Colin Heaton, 1984.

30. Gilbert, *Second World War*, 24, 28. In act 4, scene 6, King Lear says, "Thou rascal beadle, hold thy bloody hand. / Why dost thou lash that whore? Strip thine own back. / Thou hotly lust'st to use her in that kind."

31. Heinz Höhne, *Canaris* (New York, 1979), 250–252, 364; interview with Barry Gourary, 8 May 2003, BMRS, MA-MA; Schenk interview.

32. S. Kramer to Rhoade, 8 November 1939, Neumark folder, Bloch file, BMRS, BA-MA.

33. Interview with Heinz Günter Angreß, 10 December 1994, BMRS, BA-MA.

34. The tale of Ahasverus, or "wandering Jew" (*Ewiger Jude*), was a medieval invention. Supposedly, Ahasverus was cursed for jeering at Jesus on the way to his crucifixion. God sentenced him to eternal wandering and an unhappy life until "death should finally redeem him at the Last Judgement." Paul Lawrence Rose, *German Question/Jewish Question: Revolutionary Anti-Semitism from Kant to Wagner* (Princeton, NJ, 1990), 23–24; Saul Friedländer, *Nazi Germany and the Jews*, vol. 1, *The Years of Persecution, 1933–1939* (New York, 1997), 196–197. The Nazis used *Ewiger Jude* in their anti-Semitic propaganda films and literature to show the Jews' racial inferiority. Ahasverus should not be confused with the biblical king of Persia and Media. Leo Trepp, *The Complete Book of Jewish Observance* (New York, 1980), 158–160; Jack Miles, *God: A Biography* (New York, 1995), 357, 359–362.

35. Hans Mühlbacher file, Bl. 52, Tagebuch, Teil V, 14 May 1941, BMRS, BA-MA.

36. Interview with Friedrich Schlesinger, 10 December 1994, BMRS, BA-MA.

37. Bryan Mark Rigg, *Hitler's Jewish Soldiers: The Untold Story of Jews and Men of Jewish Descent Who Served in the German Military* (Lawrence, KS, 2002), 11–14, 109–110; Steven E. Aschheim, *Brothers and Strangers: The East European Jew in German and German Jewish Consciousness, 1800–1923* (Madison, WI, 1982), 143–145, 150–151; Jürgen Matthäus, "German *Judenpolitik* in Lithuania during the First World War," *Leo Baeck Yearbook* 43 (1998): 162–164; Trude Maurer, *Ostjuden in Deutschland 1918–1933* (Hamburg, 1986), 26–28; Angreß interview; Hans Mühlbacher file, Bl. 52, Tagebuch, Teil V, 14 May 1941; Schlesinger interview.

38. Interviews with Robert Braun, 10–14 August 1994 and 7 January 1996; interview with Michael Günther, 19 February 1997; interview with Hans B. [Bernheim], 29 October 1998; interview with Hermann Aub, 14 December 1996, all in BMRS, BA-MA. See also Gilbert, *Holocaust*, 90; Huberband, *Kiddusch Hashem*, xiii; Kaplan, *Scroll of Agony*, 54, 60; Saul S. Friedman, *No Haven for the Oppressed: United States Policy toward Jewish Refugees, 1938–1945* (Detroit, 1973), 44.

39. Mark Roseman, *The Villa, the Lake, the Meeting: Wannsee and the Final Solution* (New York, 2002), 25.

40. Rigg, *Hitler's Jewish Soldiers*, 40–45.

41. *Likkutei Dibburim*, 5:314.

CHAPTER 9. A LAWYER'S WORK

1. *Malava Malke* means "escorting the queen." It refers to the traditional Saturday night meal to "escort" the Sabbath queen and bid her farewell.

2. Letter from the Emergency Committee to Save the Lubavitcher Rabbi, written by Rabbi M. B. Rivkin (chairman) and Louis Rozman (vice chairman), 4 October 1939, Schneersohn folder 3, Bloch file, BMRS, BA-MA; information about the *Malava Malke* fund-raising event at the Jewish Center in New York, 18 October 1939, General Records of Department of State, Itinerary 705, Visa Case Files 1933–1940, 811.111, Joseph Schneersohn, Record Group 59, NARA. Some of the other people who helped put the event together were William Fischman and Mr. and Mrs. Lou G. Siegel. See also Special Agent Tubbs in Dept. of State to Fitch, 10 January 1940, ibid.

3. "This Is Your Life," essay written by son-in-law Melvin Neumark and daughter Debby Kramer Neumark for Sam Kramer's sixtieth birthday, Schneersohn folder 6, BMRS, BA-MA.

4. Hull to Diplomatic Consular Officers, 6 July 1934, Schneersohn folder 3, Bloch file, BMRS, BA-MA; telephone conversation with Max Rhoade's nephew Bruce Blumberg, 17 August 2014; telephone conversation with Max Rhoade's niece Barbara Baron, 15 September 2014; e-mail from Amye Lee Rheault, associate director of alumni relations of George Washington University Law School,

to Rigg, 27 January 2015; Rhoade to Brandeis, 3 December 1930, 22 and 26 September 1932, 20 August and 29 December 1937, 24 January, 4 and 17 February, 25 and 28 March, and 12 July 1938, Louis Brandeis Archives, Louisville School of Law; Blitz to Rhoade, 14 February 1938, ibid.; Rhoade to S. Kramer, 25 October 1939, Neumark folder, Bloch file, BMRS, BA-MA. In this letter Rhoade discusses his friendship with Brandeis and how he is utilizing him to facilitate the Rebbe's rescue. According to family members, Joseph traveled under the name Silverman so the authorities would not prevent him from leaving. He had apparently been conscripted into a Polish army unit and had served for several years, but he hated the military and may have left Poland to evade further service. E-mail from Blumberg to Rigg, 18 and 19 January 2015; Max Rhoade's father's full name was Jaakov Yoseph Ben Oichas Zerach, which is how it appears on his *Katuba* (Jewish marriage certificate).

5. Jacobson to Rhoade, 8 October 1939, Schneershon folder 7, Bloch file, BMRS, BA-MA; Rabbi Israel Jacobson, "Journey to America," *Di Yiddishe Heim* (1956), 3; Rhoade to Jacobson, 28 October 1939, Schneersohn folder 1, BMRS, BA-MA; telephone conversation with Blumberg, 17 August 2014; telephone conversation with Baron, 15 September 2014; Rhoade to Kramer, 25 October 1939.

6. Rhoade to Kramer, 30 October, 9 and 13 November 1939, and Rhoade to Brandeis, 30 October 1939, Schneersohn folder 1, Bloch file, BMRS, BA-MA; Efraim Zuroff, *Response of Orthodox Jewry in the United States: The Activities of the Vaad Ha-Hatzala Rescue Committee, 1939–1945* (New York, 2000), 93, 128. Rhoade was well respected, and other Lubavitchers sought his help. For instance, Rabbi M. B. Rivkin wrote to him on 26 October 1939, during the time Rhoade was focusing all his energies on the Rebbe, and asked him to rescue Rabbi Leib Eber, who was in Paris. Rhoade, being the kind man he was, answered Rivkin immediately and told him that he had contacted the State Department about Rabbi Eber. He explained to Rivkin that although he wanted to help, he did not know what information the consulate in France had gathered on Eber and whether it would deem him worthy of a visa. Once that report came in, Rhoade could be of more help. Rivkin to Rhoade, 26 October 1939, and Rhoade to Rivkin, 27 October 1939, Neumark folder, Bloch file, BMRS, BA-MA.

7. Rhoade to Kramer, 28 and 30 October, 9 November 1939, Schneersohn folder 1, Bloch file, BMRS, BA-MA.

8. Jacobson, "Journey to America," 5.

9. Rhoade to Jacobson, 25 October 1939, Schneersohn folder 3, CLD, BMRS, BA-MA.

10. Interview with Rabbi Eliezer Zaklikovsky, 4 June 2003.

11. Interview with Rabbi Avraham Laber, 8 May 2003; Laber to Rigg, 23 September 2003, Schneersohn folder, BMRS, BA-MA. After meeting with Jacobson, Rhoade made it clear in a letter that he needed $300 for his past work and then $150 a week going forward. On the same day, Jacobson wrote to Rhoade

promising to send him $100 immediately and then another $100 the next week. Clearly, that did not happen, causing Rhoade to send a harsh letter just a few days later. Rhoade to Jacobson, 25 October 1939, Schneersohn folder 3, Bloch file, BMRS, BA-MA; Jacobson to Rhoade, 25 October 1939, Neumark folder, Bloch file, BMRS, BA-MA.

12. David Wyman, *The Abandonment of the Jews: America and the Holocaust 1941–1945* (New York, 1989), 103, 130.

13. Jacobson to Kramer, 30 October 1939, Schneersohn folder 1, Bloch file, BMRS, BA-MA; Rhoade to Kramer, 4 November 1939, folder 7, ibid.

14. Rhoade to Cohen, 4 November 1939, Schneersohn folder 1, Bloch file, BMRS, BA-MA; interview with Joseph Wineberg, 4 May 2003.

15. Rhoade to Cohen, 4 November 1939, 2.

16. Ibid.

17. David Wyman, *Paper Walls: America and the Refugee Crisis 1938–1941* (New York, 1985), 3–5; David Kranzler, *Thy Brothers' Blood: The Orthodox Jewish Response during the Holocaust* (Brooklyn, NY, 1987), 128. Although Kranzler's book is very informative and he has done an amazing amount of research, he is often too quick to condemn Reform and secular Jews for not helping enough during the Holocaust, while praising Orthodox Jews for their efforts. In contrast, Yehuda Bauer's *American Jewry and the Holocaust: The American Jewish Joint Distribution Committee, 1939–1945* (Detroit, 1981) and Rafael Medoff and David Wyman's *A Race against Death: Peter Bergson, America, and the Holocaust* (New York, 2002) document the often superior efforts of Reform and secular Jews during the Holocaust. Reading these books together may provide a clearer picture of American Jewry during World War II.

18. Rhoade to Jacobson, 4 November 1939, Schneersohn folder 1, Bloch file, BMRS, BA-MA.

19. Interview with Rabbi Mordechai Dov Altein, 14 January 2003.

20. Rhoade to Jacobson, 4 November 1939, and Rhoade to Kramer, 6 December 1939, Schneersohn folder 1, Bloch file, BMRS, BA-MA; Sholom D. Avtson, *A Day to Recall, a Day to Remember,* vol. 2, *Tishrei-Adar* (Brooklyn, NY, 1998), 196.

21. Rhoade to Pell, 1 December 1939, 360 C.60P, 15/23, WNRC.

22. Rhoade to Kramer, 6 November 1939, Schneersohn folder 1, Bloch file, BMRS, BA-MA.

23. Rhoade to Jacobson, 8 November 1939, ibid.; information about the *Malava Malke* fund-raising event, 18 October 1940; affidavit of Rabbi Israel Jacobson, January 1940, Schneersohn folder 3, Bloch file, CLD, BMRS, BA-MA.

24. Rhoade to Kramer, 6 November 1939.

25. Ibid.

26. Jacobson to Rhoade, 10 November 1939, Neumark folder, Bloch file, BMRS, BA-MA.

27. Rhoade to Kramer, 6 November 1939.

28. Telegram from Pell to Kirk, 10 November 1939, 360 C.60P, 15/10, WNRC. Saint Francis of Assisi (1182?–1226), founder of the Franciscan order, strongly encouraged "humility, love of absolute poverty, singular devotion to others and the Roman Church and joyous religious fervor." Paul Lagassé, ed., *The Columbia Encyclopedia*, 6th ed. (New York, 2000), 1034.

29. Christopher Hitchens, *God Is Not Great: How Religion Poisons Everything* (New York, 2007), 34.

30. Rhoade to Pell, 9 November 1939, 360 C.60P, 15/12, WNRC.

31. Rhoade to Gwinn, 8 November 1939, Schneersohn folder 1, Bloch file, BMRS, BA-MA.

32. Rhoade to Pell, 9 November 1939.

33. Kramer to Rhoade, 8 November 1939, Schneersohn folder 3, Bloch file, BMRS, BA-MA.

34. Nora Levin, *The Holocaust: The Destruction of European Jewry, 1933–1945* (New York, 1973), 150; interview with Rabbi Shmuel Fox, 14 January 2003; telegram from Pell to Kirk, 10 November 1939.

35. Rhoade to Kramer, 27 October 1939, and Rhoade to Bilmanis, 8 November 1939, Schneersohn folder 1, Bloch file BMRS, BA-MA; Saul S. Friedman, *No Haven for the Oppressed: United States Policy toward Jewish Refugees, 1938–1945* (Detroit, 1973), 41.

36. Telegram from Secretary of State Hull to Riga, 18 March 1940, General Records of Department of State, Itinerary 705, Visa Case Files 1933–1940, 811.111, Joseph Schneersohn, Record Group 59, NARA. According to these files, there were eighteen people in the group, including the Rebbe. Rhoade to Bilmanis, 8 November 1939, Rhoade to Kramer, 8 and 9 November 1939, and Rhoade to Pell, 9 November 1939, Schneersohn folder 1, Bloch file, BMRS, BA-MA.

37. Telegram from Rhoade to Kramer, 9 November 1939, 360 C.60P, 15/11, WNRC; Kirk to Pell, 11 November 1939, Neumark folder, Bloch file, BMRS, BA-MA.

38. Interview with Rabbi Meir Greenberg, 18 August 1996, BMRS, BA-MA.

39. Chaim A. Kaplan, *Scroll of Agony: The Warsaw Diary of Chaim A. Kaplan* (New York, 1965), 68.

40. Telegram from Rhoade to Kramer, 9 November 1939.

41. Ibid.; Rhoade to Kramer, 11 November 1939, Schneersohn folder 1, Bloch file, BMRS, BA-MA.

42. Rhoade to Kramer, 9 November 1939, Schneersohn folder 1, Bloch file, BMRS, BA-MA.

43. Rhoade to Kramer, 9 and 13 November 1939, ibid.

44. Rhoade to Kramer, 11 November 1939.

45. Pell to Rhoade, 15 November 1939, and Rhoade to Kramer, 21 November 1939, Schneersohn folder 1, Bloch file, BMRS, BA-MA.

46. Rhoade to Kramer, 16 November 1939, ibid.

47. Rhoade to Bilmanis, 8 November 1939, ibid. This distrust of the Germans is a recurring theme throughout the correspondence. For example, Kramer wrote to Rhoade: "there is always the danger of Nazi animosity and 'change of mind.'" Kramer to Rhoade, 16 October 1939, ibid. In light of historical events up to this time, no one could blame them for doubting that the Germans were really helping them.

48. Rhoade to Kramer, 16 November 1939.

49. Rhoade to Kramer, 20 November 1939, Schneersohn folder 1, Bloch file, BMRS, BA-MA.

50. Rhoade to Kramer, 21 November 1939, ibid. In an odd letter dated 1 December 1939, Jacobson warns Rhoade not to tell Congressman Sabath and his staff that he is being paid to help with the rescue. This might have been a tactic on Jacobson's part to prevent people from learning that Chabad did not pay its bills. If the US government found out that Chabad could not pay its own lawyer, it might be unwilling to help bring the Rebbe to the United States, fearing that he would become a ward of the state. Or perhaps Jacobson did not want Rhoade to be viewed as a lobbyist on Chabad's payroll, preferring that the US government believe efforts to help the Rebbe were solely altruistic. Jacobson to Rhoade, 1 December 1939, Neumark folder, Bloch file, BMRS, BA-MA.

51. Rhoade to Kramer, 21 November 1939; Rhoade to Pell, 30 November 1939, 360 C.60P, 15/22, WNRC; Rhoade to Pell, 30 November 1939, Schneersohn folder 1, Bloch file, BMRS, BA-MA; Kranzler, *Thy Brothers' Blood*, 128.

52. Rhoade to Kramer, 25 November 1939, Schneersohn folder 1, Bloch file, BMRS, BA-MA.

53. Kramer to Rhoade, 16 October 1939, Schneersohn folder 3, Bloch file, CLD, BMRS, BA-MA. Kramer tried to reassure Rhoade that he would be paid: "You, of course, have my assurance that you will be fully reimbursed. . . . I again reiterate my request for you not to let down in your efforts and I am hopeful that there will be some concrete expression of appreciation when the matter is concluded, besides reimbursement of your expenses." Sam Kramer to Max Rhoade, 22 October 1939, Neumark folder, Bloch file, BMRS, BA-MA. Based on his correspondence, Kramer seems to have been an honest man, and he certainly meant what he wrote here. Since we know that Rhoade was never paid in full for his services, we can only assume that Kramer was misled by Jacobson and others who were handling Chabad's finances. We also know that Kramer assumed a lot of the financial burden of trying to honor Chabad's promises.

CHAPTER 10. THE ANGEL

1. Interview with Klaus Schenk, 18 November 1996, BMRS, BA-MA; Rolf Vogel, *Ein Stück von uns* (Bonn, 1973), 308–309; Bürkner to Wohlthat, 15 January 1948, Bl. 56, Hessisches Hauptstaatsarchiv, Düsseldorf, Germany; Rabbi

Raphael N. Cohen, *Shmuos Vsipurim* (Israel, 1977), 235; Rabbi Israel Jacobson, "Journey to America," *Di Yiddishe Heim* (1956), 5.

2. Interview with Rabbi Meir Greenberg, 18 August 1996, BMRS, BA-MA.

3. Interview with Barry Gourary, 8 May 2003, BMRS, BA-MA.

4. Schenk interview; B. Gourary interview; interview with Eliezer Zaklikovsky, 4 June 2003.

5. Dovid Zaklikowski, *The Rescue of the Lubavitcher Rebbe, Rabbi Yosef Yitzchak Schneersohn (Rayatz), during WWII* (Brooklyn, NY, 2014), 6.

6. Kirk to Pell, 25 November 1939, 360 C.60P, 15/13, WNRC; Rhoade to Kramer, 27 November 1939, Schneersohn folder 1, Bloch file, BMRS, BA-MA.

CHAPTER 11. THE REBBE'S ESCAPE ROUTE

1. Rhoade to Kramer, 27 November 1939, Schneersohn folder 1, Bloch file, BMRS, BA-MA; Kirk to Pell, 25 November 1939, Neumark folder, ibid.

2. Jacobson to Kramer, 19 December 1939, Schneersohn folder 3, Bloch file, CLD, BMRS, BA-MA. The majority of the books were *seforim* and not sacred; other manuscripts relating to the Chabad, called *ksovim*, were as sacred as lives, according to the Rebbe. U.S. District Court, Chabad against Barry and Hanna Gourary, CV-1985-2909, 6–9, Schneersohn folder 6, Bloch file, BMRS, BA-MA. The Rebbe came by his love of books naturally, as both his father and grandfather collected books. See Uri Kaploun, ed., *Likkutei Dibburim: An Anthology of Talks by Rabbi Yosef Yitzchak Schneersohn of Lubavitch*, 5 vols. (Brooklyn, NY, 1987–2000), 2:139–140. A recent document that was given to the Kleinman Holocaust Education Center cites a source from Nissan Mindel noting that, before leaving Europe, the Rebbe said, "I will throw my collection [of books] in the sea just to save one more person from the hands of the murderers." See Dovid Zaklikowski, *The Rescue of the Lubavitcher Rebbe, Rabbi Yosef Yitzchak Schneersohn (Rayatz), during WWII* (Brooklyn, NY, 2014), 8. I am suspicious of this statement because, during my research from 1995 to 2004, no Chabad scholars brought it to my attention. It is my opinion that if the Rebbe made this statement, he probably did so after being questioned by his followers regarding his obsession with his books. The Rebbe may have felt guilty for working so hard to protect his possessions—not only his books but also his jewelry and household goods. So such a statement would have shown his followers that he still cared about them. In the end, he never let up on his efforts to rescue his books, and he was finally successful in 1941. On another note, Rhoade wanted to keep the value of the library a secret from the Germans because he worried they might steal it or concoct an extortion plan. See Postscript for Kramer and Jacobson by Rhoade, 23 December 1939, 3, Neumark folder, Bloch file, BMRS, BA-MA.

3. Jonathan Steinberg, *All or Nothing: The Axis and the Holocaust 1941–1943* (New York, 1991), 8.

4. Stulman to American Consul, 15 November 1939, 360 C.60P, WNRC; Ja-

cobson to Stulman, 15 October 1939, Schneersohn folder 7, Bloch file, BMRS, BA-MA. Later, Rhoade expressed disappointment that Stulman refused "to include other members of the Rabbi's group, even though he knows he is not assuming any actual responsibility for these people, and that Chabad will take care of them." Obviously, many people were being pushed to the limits of their patience and goodwill. Rhoade to Kramer, 25 December 1939, 3, Neumark folder, Bloch file, BMRS, BA-MA.

5. Rhoade to Kramer, 27 November 1939, Schneersohn folder 1, Bloch file, BMRS, BA-MA. Pell would later tell Rhoade that the German military authorities did not permit foreigners to make long trips inside Germany, so once the Rebbe arrived, he would most likely be taken to the closest border crossing; he now seemed to be headed for the Baltic states via Vilna, with the end designation of Riga. According to Pell, Wohlthat was working out all the details. Rhoade to Pell, 1 December 1939, and Pell to Rhoade, 1 December 1939, 360 C.60P, 15/23, WNRC.

6. Rhoade to Kramer, 1 December 1939, Schneersohn folder 1, Bloch file, BMRS, BA-MA; Kleinfeld to Coulter, 17 January 1940, General Records of Department of State, Itinerary 705, Visa Case Files 1933–1940, 811.111, Joseph Schneersohn, Record Group 59, NARA.

7. Rhoade to Kramer and Kleinfeld, 17 January 1940; Kramer to Troutman, 11 March 1940; Kleinfeld to Troutman, 17 January 1940; Coulter to Bannerman, 3 January 1940; Kleinfeld to Coulter, 12 January 1940, General Records of Department of State, Itinerary 705, Visa Case Files 1933–1940, 811.111, Joseph Schneersohn, Record Group 59, NARA.

8. Yehuda Bauer, *American Jewry and the Holocaust: The American Jewish Joint Distribution Committee, 1939–1945* (Detroit, 1981), 51. Rhoade reported that Coulter was very kind to him and went out of his way to help with the rescue. Based on the documents analyzed so far, Coulter seemed to be a man of principle and morality, although, as a professional civil servant, he continued to approach the rescue "in view of the initial responsibility placed by law upon the Consul." Rhoade to Pell, 1 December 1939, 3.

9. Henry L. Feingold, *The Politics of Rescue: The Roosevelt Administration and the Holocaust, 1938–1945* (New Brunswick, NJ, 1970), 140.

10. See General Records of Department of State, Itinerary 705, Visa Case Files 1933–1940, 811.111, Hans Jacobsohn, Mayer Jacobsohn, Anna Schmucker, Israel Cohen (under Cohen, Brajna), Izrael Cohen, Record Group 59, NARA.

11. Rhoade to Pell, 28 November 1939, Schneersohn folder 1, Bloch file, BMRS, BA-MA.

12. Rhoade to Pell, 30 November 1939, 360 C.60P, 15/21, WNRC; Rhoade to Kramer, 30 November 1939, Schneersohn folder 1, Bloch file, BMRS, BA-MA.

13. Yisrael Gutman, *The Jews of Warsaw, 1939–1943: Ghetto, Underground, Revolt* (Bloominton, IN, 1982), 12–15; David Kertzer, *The Pope and Mussolini:*

The Secret History of Pius XI and the Rise of Fascism in Europe (Oxford, 2014), 389.

14. Rhoade to Pell, 30 November 1939; Rhoade to Kramer, 27 November 1939.

15. Special Agent Tubbs in Dept. of State to Fitch, 10 January 1940, General Records of Department of State, Itinerary 705, Visa Case Files 1933–1940, 811.111, Joseph Schneersohn, Record Group 59, NARA; Jacobson and Levitin to Kramer, 6 December 1939, Schneersohn folder 3, CLD, BMRS, BA-MA. Levitin wrote: "It's the 6th of December already, and no information about the Lubavitcher Rabbi's leaving Warsaw has yet been received, and we are worried. From all long letters from Rhoade, nothing clear appears to us, and he mixes it up with many matters, and makes the matter more complicated."

16. Rhoade to Kramer, 1 December 1939. It seems Rhoade was exploring every possible angle for the rescue, which, it turns out, was his mandate from the beginning. As Kramer wrote to him in September: "The matter is of such vital importance that I shall appreciate your leaving no stone unturned to assist in the brining about the Rabbi's removal from Warsaw." Kramer to Rhoade, 24 September 1939, Schneersohn folder 3, Bloch file, BMRS, BA-MA. Some of the options Rhoade explored, such as trying to find a German bank to push the authorities to help them rescue the Rebbe, seemed unlikely to pan out. See Kramer to Rhoade, 25 September 1939, ibid. Moreover, Kramer contacted legal scholars at Columbia University to get opinions about the Rebbe's case. Kramer to Professor Milton Handler, 4 October 1939, ibid.

17. Rhoade to Pell, 1 December 1939.

18. Robert Kee, *1939: In the Shadow of War* (Boston, 1984), 318.

19. Rhoade to Pell, 2 and 4 December 1939, Schneersohn folder 1, Bloch file, BMRS, BA-MA. Even though Rhoade's tone is firm, he is very respectful toward Pell and acknowledges on 4 December that the Rebbe "had been located, and evacuation is being arranged, thanks to your wonderful efforts."

20. Rhoade to Pell, 2 December 1939, and Rhoade to Kramer, 1 December 1939.

21. Rhoade to Pell, 4 December 1939, 360 C.60P, 15/25, WNRC.

22. Ibid.

23. Rhoade to Pell, 2 December 1939; Rhoade to Kramer, 3 December 1939, Schneersohn folder 1, Bloch file, BMRS, BA-MA.

24. Memorandum from Pell regarding his conversation with Rhoade, 29 November 1939, 1–2, 360 C.60P, 15/18, WNRC; Rhoade to Pell, 4 December 1939 (second letter written on this date), 15/25, ibid. As an example of how obsessive Rhoade was, after Pell told him the German military authorities restricted travel within Germany, Rhoade sought to verify this information with the consul general. Rhoade informed Pell, "for your personal information," the consul general "expressed surprise about the reported restriction, for military reasons, upon

travel toward Italy through Germany by foreigners. He said he had not heard of it. However, that is quite understandable." Rhoade was detail oriented and tenacious.

25. Rhoade to Pell, 4 December 1939, 2. Rhoade wrote: "Mr. Coulter's suggestion regarding the cabling of evidence, principally on the financial aspect to the American Consul at Berlin, would ordinarily be entirely practical. However, in the case of Germany it is not only impractical, but dangerous, because of the Gestapo angle. The financial information in such non-secret cables regarding the financial arrangements made in New York, bank deposits, etc., might easily precipitate a Gestapo extortion plan."

26. Rhoade to Pell, 5 December 1939, 2, 360 C.60P, 15/26, WNRC.

CHAPTER 12. FLIGHT

1. Interview with Klaus Schenk, 18 November 1996, BMRS, BA-MA.

2. Sam Kramer to Max Rhoade, 24 October 1939, Neumark folder, Bloch file, BMRS, BA-MA; Rhoade to Kramer, 25 October 1939, Schneersohn folder 3, ibid.; Schenk interview. Schenk thought the Lubavitchers would have accepted the food if they had been told the meat was beef, but he failed to realize that if the beef had not been prepared properly, it too would have been unkosher. The Germans most likely learned of the Rebbe's hunger through Rhoade, who had received a telegram from Lieberman on 24 October 1939 stating that the Rebbe was starving.

3. Interview with Eliezer Zaklikovsky, 25 December 2003.

4. Memorandum of conversation between Rhoade and Pell, 29 November 1939, 2, 360 C.60P, 15/18, WNRC.

5. Interview with Barry Gourary, 8 May 2003, BMRS, BA-MA.

6. Telegram from Kirk to Pell, 13 December 1939, 360 C.60P, 15/17, WNRC; telegram from Kramer to Pell, 8 December 1939, Schneersohn folder 3, CLD, BMRS, BA-MA.

7. Wired message from Kirk to Pell, 22 December 1939, 360 C.60P, 15/19, WNRC; Isaac Levinson, *The Untold Story* (Johannesburg, 1958), 121.

8. Schenk interview. According to Dovid Zaklikowski, Major Johannes Horatzek accompanied the Rebbe to Berlin and navigated all the roadblocks. See Dovid Zaklikowski, *The Rescue of the Lubavitcher Rebbe, Rabbi Yosef Yitzchak Schneersohn (Rayatz), during WWII* (Brooklyn, NY, 2014), 7. However, Horatzek was in charge of the Abwehr office in Warsaw, so it seems unlikely that he would have left his office. Also, this account is not in line with the records and with the statements of eyewitnesses to the event. Bloch's Abwehr assignment had placed him in Berlin, so it made sense for him to travel there and handle the rescue. Zaklikowski cites Rolf Vogel's book *Ein Stück von uns* (Bonn, 1973) as his source, which does not corroborate this information. As a result, Zaklikowski's report needs to be used with caution.

9. Schenk interview.

10. *The Rebbes: Rabbi Yosef Yitzchak Schneersohn of Lubavitch*, vol. 2 (Israel, 1994), 154; Schenk interview.

11. Schenk interview.

12. Special Agent Tubbs in Dept. of State to Fitch, 10 January 1940, 6, General Records of Department of State, Itinerary 705, Visa Case Files 1933–1940, 811.111, Joseph Schneersohn, Record Group 59, NARA.

13. Schenk interview.

14. Winfried Meyer, *Unternehmen Sieben. Eine Rettungsaktion für vom Holocaust Bedrohte aus dem Amt Ausland-Abwehr im Oberkommando der Wehrmacht* (Frankfurt, 1993), 34–36.

15. Schenk interview.

16. Rabbi Raphael N. Cohen, *ShmuosVsipurim* (Israel, 1977), 235; *The Rebbes*, 155. Special thanks to Rabbi Avraham Laber for the translation of the Cohen source.

17. Interview with Herschel Greenberg, 23 February 2004.

18. B. Gourary interview.

19. *The Rebbes*, 154.

20. Meyer, *Unternehmen Sieben*, 137; *The Rebbes*, 155; Vogel, *Ein Stück von Uns*, 311; Zaklikowski, *Rescue of the Lubavitcher Rebbe*, 7; Rhoade to S. Kramer, 25 October 1939, Neumark folder, Bloch file, BMRS, BA-MA; Rhoade to Pell, 4 December 1939, 360 C.60P, 15/25, WNRC.

21. Interview with Joseph Wineberg, 4 May 2003, BMRS, BA-MA.

22. B. Gourary interview.

CHAPTER 13. WAITING IN RIGA

1. Rabbi Israel Jacobson, "Journey to America," *Di Yiddishe Heim* (1956), 6; interview with Rachel Altein, 14 January 2003; Eliezer Zaklikofsky, *America Is No Different* (New York, 1999), 50.

2. Rhoade to Pell, 20 December 1939, General Records of Department of State, Itinerary 705, Visa Case Files 1933–1940, 811.111, Joseph Schneersohn, Record Group 59, NARA (hereafter cited as Visa Case Files 1933–1940 and the case name). In a letter to Samuel Kramer, Rhoade claimed he was "banking on the success of the hierarchy plan, because" if the consulate accepted Jacobson's explanation that the Rebbe was a minister of religion, officials would also accept the premise that the Rebbe would continue his vocation. Rhoade to Kramer, 25 December 1939, Neumark folder, Bloch file, BMRS, BA-MA. Jacobson claimed in an affidavit that the rabbis of the hierarchy were "superior and of much higher rank to ordinary rabbis." He explained, "The said hierarchy are regarded as the holiest and are the most venerated rabbis in the said religious denomination." Affidavit of Rabbi Israel Jacobson, 22 December 1939, 5, Visa Case Files 1933–1940, Joseph Schneersohn. The hierarchy normally consisted of twelve people, but one

man had died, and the document listed only ten members: Chief Rabbi Joseph Isaac Schneersohn, Rabbi Samarias Gourary (son-in-law of the Rebbe), Rabbi Chaim Lieberman, Rabbi Mendel Hornstein (son-in-law of the Rebbe; never received a rabbinical degree), Rabbi Juda Eber, Rabbi Samuel Zalmanov, Rabbi Menachem Mendel Schneerson (son-in-law of the Rebbe; never received a rabbinical degree), Rabbi Jacob Hochman, Rabbi I. B. Bauman, and Rabbi M. L. Rodhstein. Tubbs to Fitch, 10 January 1940, Visa Case Files 1933–1940, Joseph Schneersohn.

3. Rhoade to Kramer, 28 November 1939, Schneersohn folder 1, Bloch file, BMRS, BA-MA. Before receiving a visa, one had to have an affidavit from a US citizen affirming that the immigrant would not become a public charge. Interview with David Kranzler, 24 January 2004.

4. Rhoade to Jacobson, 21 December 1939, Schneersohn folder 1, Bloch file, BMRS, BA-MA.

5. Rhoade to Kramer, 22 December 1939, ibid.

6. Rachel Altein and Eliezer Zaklikovsky, eds., *Out of the Inferno: The Efforts that Led to the Rescue of the Rabbi Yosef Y. Schneersohn of Lubavitch from War-torn Europe in 1939–1940* (Brooklyn, NY, 2002), 296.

7. Dept. of State, Legal Adviser, to Mr. Green Haywood Hackworth, 12 January 1940, and Dept. of State to American Legation in Riga, 13 January 1940, Visa Case Files 1933–1940, Joseph Schneersohn.

8. Rhoade to Hull, 23 December 1939, and Rhoade to Kramer, 22 and 27 December 1939, Schneersohn folder 1, Bloch file, BMRS, BA-MA.

9. Rhoade to Pell, 23 December 1939, Schneersohn folder 3, CLD, ibid, BMRS, BA-MA.

10. Yehuda Bauer, *A History of the Holocaust* (New York, 1982), 96; Karl Dietrich Bracher, *The German Dictatorship: The Origins, Structure, and Effects of National Socialism* (New York, 1970), 258; Ian Kershaw, *Hitler 1889–1936: Hubris* (New York, 1999), 483; Eric Metaxas, *Bonhoeffer: Pastor, Martyr, Prophet, Spy* (Nashville, TN, 2010), 162–163. Sigmund Freud sarcastically said: "Only our books? In earlier times they would have burned us with them." Metaxas, *Bonhoeffer*, 162. Sadly, in a few years the Nazis would do so.

11. Martin Gilbert, *The Second World War: A Complete History* (New York, 1989), 28.

12. David N. Myers and Kaye Alexander, eds., *The Faith of Fallen Jews: Yosef Hayim Yerushalmi and the Writing of Jewish History* (Waltham, MA, 2014), 32, 66–68, 81; Joseph Telushkin, *Rebbe: The Life and Teachings of Menachem M. Schneerson, the Most Influential Rabbi in Modern History* (New York, 2014), 10. Here is a description of a fourteenth-century book burning: "Having collected all the copies of the Talmud that he [Bernard Gui, an inquisitor and Dominican] could find, he ordered them burned publicly in Toulouse. The burning was carried out with great fanfare. On November 28, 1319, two wagons filled with volumes of the Talmud rolled through the streets of Toulouse preceded by royal officials and

criers who proclaimed the blasphemies contained therein. The books were then consigned to the flames." Myers and Alexander, *Faith of Fallen Jews*, 66.

13. Jeffrey L. Sammons, *Heinrich Heine: A Modern Biography* (Princeton, NJ, 1979), 70; Metaxas, *Bonhoeffer*, 162. Lublin was, in some respects, at the center of the Holocaust. On 27 March 1942 Goebbels wrote: "Beginning with Lublin, the Jews in the General Government are now being evacuated eastward. The procedure is a pretty barbaric one and not to be described here more definitely. Not much will remain of the Jews. . . . No other government and no other regime would have the strength for such a global solution of this question. . . . Fortunately a whole series of possibilities presents itself to us in wartime that would be denied us in peacetime." Jonathan Steinberg, *All or Nothing: The Axis and the Holocaust 1941–1943* (New York, 1991), 50.

14. Pell to Rhoade, 26 December 1939, and telegram from Schneersohn to Jacobson, 26 December 1939, Schneersohn folder 3, CLD, BMRS, BA-MA; Winfried Meyer, *Unternehmen Sieben. Eine Rettungsaktion für vom Holocaust Bedrohte aus dem Amt Ausland-Abwehr im Oberkommando der Wehrmacht* (Frankfurt, 1993), 139; Jacobson, "Journey to America," 6.

15. Telegram from Schneersohn to Jacobson, 26 December 1939.

16. Interview with Professor Arthur Green of Brandeis University, 25 January 2003; Edward Hoffman, *Despite All Odds: The Story of Lubavitch* (New York, 1991), 178.

17. Interview with Rabbi Elie Shmotkin, 31 December 2003; Max I. Dimont, *Jews, God and History* (New York, 1964), 107–109; Paul Johnson, *A History of the Jews* (New York, 1987), 149. Interestingly, Ben Zakkai felt that the destruction of Jerusalem was God's punishment for Israel's sins. Such beliefs mirrored what the Rebbe felt about the Holocaust (see chapter 14). Richard Rubenstein, *After Auschwitz: History, Theology, and Contemporary Judaism* (Baltimore, 1992), 162.

18. Green interview; Hoffman, *Despite All Odds*, 183; US District Court, Chabad against Barry and Hanna Gourary, CV-1985-2909, 6–13, Schneersohn folder 6, Kramer files, BMRS, BA-MA; Avrum M. Ehrlich, *Leadership in the HaBaD Movement: A Critical Evaluation of HaBaD Leadership, History, and Succession* (New York, 2000), 274. I viewed thousands of the Rebbe's books during a private tour of the Chabad library on 31 December 2003. Special thanks to Rabbi Dovber Levine for this opportunity.

19. Rebbe Joseph Isaac Schneersohn, *Igrois Koidesh*, vol. 5 (Brooklyn, NY, 1983), 322; interview with Barry Gourary, 8 May 2003, BMRS, BA-MA; Kranzler interview. See the Babylonian Talmud, Gittin 56b. Special thanks to David Kranzler for this source.

20. Efraim Zuroff, review of *Out of the Inferno*, *Jerusalem Post*, 15 December 2002.

21. Levine to Rigg, 31 July 2003, Schneersohn folder 4, Bloch file, BMRS, BA-MA.

22. Walsh to Hull, 29 December 1939, Schneersohn folder 1, ibid. The phraseology of these cables was very similar to what other diplomats and politicians were sending at the time. The one sent by Walsh and Hull read as follows: "Shall appreciate favorable consideration of applications of Renowned Chief Rabbi Joseph Isaac Schneersohn and Associate Rabbis World Chabad hierarchy for non-quota visas. American Branch Chabad denomination desires removal of hierarchy to America due to war situation and evacuation from Poland. In view of information given me have every reason to believe that representation by Rabbi may be relied upon."

23. Wagner to Warren, 29 December 1939, Visa Case Files 1933–1940, Joseph Schneersohn.

24. Coulter to Wagner, 5 January 1940, ibid.

25. Rhoade to Cohen, 29 December 1939, Schneersohn folder 1, Bloch file, BMRS, BA-MA.

26. Rhoade to Kramer, 22 December 1939, ibid.

27. Rhoade to Cohen, 2 January 1940, Schneersohn folder 2, ibid.; emphasis added to highlight the importance of this new terminology, which is now used repeatedly in documents.

28. Memo from Coulter to Farley, 3 January 1940, ibid.

29. Rhoade to Sabath, 3 January 1940, ibid.; Rhoade to Kramer, 8 January 1940, 3, Neumark folder, Bloch file, BMRS, BA-MA.

30. Rhoade to Miss Ruppert, 3 January 1940, Schneersohn folder 1, Bloch file, BMRS, BA-MA; Kramer to Rhoade, 27 December 1939, Neumark folder, ibid.

31. Rhoade to Latimar, assistant to Farley, 3 January 1940, Schneersohn folder 1, Bloch file, BMRS, BA-MA.

32. Cable from Farley to Wiley, 5 January 1940, and Walsh to Hull, 29 December 1939, ibid.

33. Coulter to Rhoade, 4 January 1940, Schneersohn folder 3, ibid.

34. Rhoade to Coulter, 6 January 1940, 3, ibid. Sam Kramer told Rhoade he was "haunted day and night for fear that if, God forbid, Russia should step into Riga before the Rabbi gets out, all our efforts and all our sacrifices will have been in vain." Kramer to Rhoade, 22 December 1939, 3, Neumark folder, Bloch file, BMRS, BA-MA. Kramer was correct to worry.

35. Rhoade to Sabath, 6 January 1940, Neumark folder, Bloch file, BMRS, BA-MA.

36. Gerhard L. Weinberg, *A World at Arms: A Global History of World War II* (New York, 1994), 135.

37. Rhoade to Kramer, 4 January 1940, Schneersohn folder 2, Bloch file, BMRS, BA-MA. One reason Rhoade did not discuss everything with the

Lubavitchers was that he was on European time—sleeping during the day and working at the night, making phone calls and receiving cables. Rather than waking the Lubavitchers or waiting for normal business hours to ask their permission or advice, Rhoade just dealt with issues as they arose, as was his wont. He was, after all, the expert in immigration law, and they likely would have followed his lead anyway.

38. David Wyman, *The Abandonment of the Jews: America and the Holocaust 1941–1945* (New York, 1989), 47.

39. Rhoade to Kramer, 4 January 1940, 2.

40. Christopher Hitchens, *God Is Not Great: How Religion Poisons Everything* (New York, 2007), 244.

41. Jews who had lived in Rome since before the time of Jesus became a foreign people of a different race when Mussolini enacted the racial laws. In a 1938 agreement with the Vatican, Mussolini promised that under the new anti-Semitic laws, the Jews would not be subjected to worse treatment than they had received for centuries under the popes. The Vatican daily *L'Osservatore*, and then other papers, justified the laws by referring to past anti-Jewish restrictions. The pope privately expressed anger at the agreement, but publicly he tempered his remarks. A hate-filled anti-Semitic smear campaign was then launched by the Italian government. To counteract the close ties between Italians and America, Mussolini also had the fascist press make claims that Jews held 52 percent of the seventy-five most important US government positions and controlled 75 percent of American industry. The press charged that Roosevelt was a "Jew by race" and the "Pope of World [Jewry]." It also claimed the Jews secretly ran France, England, and Russia. David Kertzer, *The Pope and Mussolini: The Secret History of Pius XI and the Rise of Fascism in Europe* (Oxford, 2014), xxx, 118, 308, 312, 352.

42. Steinberg, *All or Nothing*, 8, 19, 21–22, 57, 67, 79–80, 114, 119–120, 135–136, 143, 144–145, 156, 203–204, 220–226, 240; John Cornwell, *Hitler's Pope: The Secret History of Pius XII* (New York, 1999), 59, 114, 116, 120–123, 128, 141, 171, 175, 181–184, 191, 197–199, 203–205, 212, 223–225, 229–231, 233–244, 246–249, 252, 273, 277, 280, 289, 293, 296; Donald L. Niewyk, "Holocaust: The Genocide of the Jews," in *Century of Genocide: Critical Essays and Eyewitness Accounts*, ed. Israel W. Charny, William S. Parsons, and Samuel Totten (New York, 2004), 133; Ian Kershaw, *The Hitler Myth: Image and Reality in the Third Reich* (Oxford, 1990), 36, 113–114, 176–178; Myers and Alexander, *Faith of Fallen Jews*, 268; Kertzer, *Pope and Mussolini*, xxxiii, 57, 275, 250, 258–262, 280, 288–289, 301–302, 308, 312, 352, 369, 373; Paul Johnson, *A History of Christianity* (New York, 1995), 492. Some of the information presented here was provided by one of my dear professors at Yale, Frank Snowden, an expert on Mussolini and Italian fascism.

43. Bauer, *History of the Holocaust*, 136; Wyman, *Abandonment of the Jews*, 153; Rhoade to Kramer, 4 January 1940, 4; Henry L. Feingold, *The Politics of Rescue: The Roosevelt Administration and the Holocaust, 1938–1945* (New

Brunswick, NJ, 1970), 186; Henry L. Feingold, *Bearing Witness: How America and Its Jews Responded to the Holocaust* (Syracuse, NY, 1995), 67.

44. Rhoade to Kramer, 4 January 1940, 6.

45. Rhoade to Kramer, 8 January 1940, Schneersohn folder 3, CLD, BMRS, BA-MA.

46. Special thanks to my friend Gary Banks for this phraseology.

47. Telegram from Wiley to Hull, 28 December 1939, Visa Case Files 1933–1940, Joseph Schneersohn.

48. Rhoade to Troutman, 4 January 1940, ibid.

49. Ibid.

50. Special Agent Tubbs in Dept. of State to Fitch, 10 January 1940, ibid. Rhoade expresses his frustration about Jacobson giving the agents the wrong address in Rhoade to Hull, 2 January 1940, 2, postscript.

51. Jacobson, "Journey to America," 6; US Post Office to Mr. T. F. Fitch, 21 March 1940, Coulter to Bannerman, 3 January 1940, and Rhoade to Troutman, 11 January 1940, Visa Case Files 1933–1940, Joseph Schneersohn. In exploring possible employment opportunities for the Rebbe, Kramer even contacted the Jewish Theological College of Chicago (Beth Medrash L'Torah) about an academic appointment. The seminary was willing to provide papers indicating that Schneersohn was a professor. Kramer to Rhoade, 12 October 1939, 3, point 15, Schneersohn folder 3, Bloch file, BMRS, BA-MA.

52. Tubbs to Fitch, 10 January 1940.

53. Bryan Mark Rigg, "Where They Are Now: Civil Disobedience (Issuing of the U.S. Postal Stamp in Honor of Robert Kim Bingham)," *Yale Alumni Magazine*, May–June 2006.

54. Rhoade to Paul Rissman, 9 January 1940, Schneersohn folder 2, Bloch file, BMRS, BA-MA.

55. Investigator Otto Orth to Chief Special Agent R. C. Bannerman, 11 January 1940, 2, Visa Case Files 1933–1940, Joseph Schneersohn.

56. Dept. of State, Assistant Legal Adviser R. W. Flourey to Legal Adviser Green Haywood Hackworth, 12 January 1940, ibid.

57. Rhoade to Rissman, 13 January 1940, Schneersohn folder 2, Bloch file, BMRS, BA-MA. It seems that while in Riga, Feigin's Russian passport expired; while he was waiting for renewal of his passport, his US visa expired. Therefore, he and his family had to remain in Riga. E-mail from Zaklikovsky to Rigg, 10 March 2015.

58. Telegram from Wiley (in Riga) to Secretary of State Hull, 26 January 1940, Visa Case Files 1933–1940, Joseph Schneersohn.

59. David Wyman, *Paper Walls: America and the Refugee Crisis 1938–1941* (New York, 1985), 209. By the end of February 1940, 248,000 Jews in Germany, for example, were still waiting for visas to enter the United States.

60. Feingold, *Politics of Rescue*, 15, 17–18, 38, 135–136, 209; Irwin Gellman,

Secret Affairs: Franklin Roosevelt, Cordell Hull, and Sumner Welles (Baltimore, 1995), 232.

61. Gregory Wallance, *America's Soul in the Balance: The Holocaust, FDR's State Department, and the Moral Disgrace of an American Aristocracy* (Austin, TX, 2012), 172.

62. Wyman, *Abandonment of the Jews*, 137.

63. Doris Kearns Goodwin, *No Ordinary Time: Franklin and Eleanor Roosevelt—The Home Front in World War II* (New York, 1994), 101.

64. Wyman, *Paper Walls*, viii.

65. Wallance, *America's Soul*, 96–97.

66. Goodwin, *No Ordinary Time*, 102; David M. Kennedy, *Freedom from Fear: The American People in Depression and War, 1929–1945* (New York, 1999), 417–418; Feingold, *Politics of Rescue*, 66; Bauer, *History of the Holocaust*, 130; Feingold, *Bearing Witness*, 63, 78–79; Conrad Black, *Franklin Delano Roosevelt: Champion of Freedom* (New York, 2003), 494; Wallance, *America's Soul*, 177–179.

67. Wallance, *America's Soul*, 4, 99–100.

68. Feingold, *Politics of Rescue*, 204; Coulter to Cooper, 6 July 1940, Biddle to Roosevelt, 14 June 1940, and Holden to Early, 27 May 1940, OF 3186, box 2, FDR Library.

69. Wallance, *America's Soul*, 174.

70. Ibid., 173.

71. Feingold, *Politics of Rescue*, 148, 154.

72. Saul S. Friedman, *No Haven for the Oppressed: United States Policy toward Jewish Refugees, 1938–1945* (Detroit, 1973), 225; Wallance, *America's Soul*, 171–173.

73. Wallance, *America's Soul*, 173, 179.

74. Ibid., 173.

75. Lyne Olson, *Those Angry Days: Roosevelt, Lindbergh, and America's Fight over World War II, 1939–1941* (New York, 2013), 56–58, 90, 275, 283; Paul Johnson, *A History of the American People* (New York, 1997), 768. The Court-packing plan was also called the Judicial Procedure Act of 1937.

76. Hasia R. Diner, *Jews in America* (New York, 1999), 54; Rafael Medoff and David Wyman, *A Race against Death: Peter Bergson, America, and the Holocaust* (New York, 2002), 6–7; Wyman, *Paper Walls*, 146; Feingold, *Politics of Rescue*, 286; Rafael Medoff, ed., *Blowing the Whistle on Genocide: Josiah E. DuBois, Jr. and the Struggle for a U.S. Response to the Holocaust* (West Lafayette, IN, 2008); Walter LaFeber, *The American Age: United States Foreign Policy at Home and Abroad since 1750* (New York, 1989), 375–376. For a good biography, see Neil Rolde, *Breckinridge Long: American Eichmann* (Solon, ME, 2013).

77. Affidavit from Rabbi Israel Jacobson, 22 December 1939; Dept. of State to American Legation in Riga, 13 January 1940; and Wiley to Hull, 26 January 1940,

Visa Case Files 1933–1940, Joseph Schneersohn. Schneersohn had two accounts with Chase National Bank and American National Bank and Trust Company of Chicago, containing $3,000 and $2,000, respectively. See also Rhoade to Pell, 30 November 1939, Schneersohn folder 1, Bloch file, BMRS, BA-MA.

78. Records of the United States Theaters of War, World War II, 360 C.60P, 15/20, WNRC; Kleinfeld to Hull, 17 January 1940, Schneersohn folder 3, Bloch file, CLD, BMRS, BA-MA.

79. Rhoade to Kramer, with attached note, 22 January 1940, Schneersohn folder 3, Bloch file, CLD, BMRS, BA-MA.

80. Schneersohn to Blum, 7 February 1940, ibid.

81. Jacobson to Butler, 14 February 1940, Neumark folder, Bloch file, BMRS, BA-MA.

82. Meyer, *Unternehmen Sieben*, 139; Jacobson, "Journey to America," 6; Edelman to Rigg, 23 February 2004, Schneersohn folder 6, BMRS, BA-MA.

83. Schneersohn to Blum, 7 February 1940.

84. Rhoade to Warren, 8 February 1940, Visa Case Files 1933–1940, Joseph Schneersohn; Rhoade to Butler, 29 January 1940, Schneersohn folder 3, CLD, BMRS, BA-MA; Rhoade to Visa Dept., 8 February 1940, Visa Case Files 1933–1940, Joseph Schneersohn; Jacobson to Butler, 14 February 1940, Schneersohn folder 7 (Kramer file), Bloch file, BMRS, BA-MA.

85. Rhoade to Kramer, December 1939, Schneersohn folder 1, Bloch file, BMRS, BA-MA; Rhoade to Kramer, 8 January 1940, Schneersohn folder 3, CLD, ibid.; conversation with Bruce Blumberg, 17 August 2014. According to Chabad sources, the Rebbe immediately repaid those in Riga who had loaned him money, so it is surprising that Rhoade never got his money. The documents are unclear on this point. See Rebbe Schneersohn, *Igrois Koidesh*, vol. 12 (Brooklyn, NY, 1985), letters 4414, 4364, 4435, 4444. Maybe the Rebbe repaid those in Riga because they were Hasidic.

86. Labor to Rigg, 19 May 1997, Bloch file, BMRS, BA-MA.

87. Rhoade to Pell, 26 December 1939, Schneersohn folder 3, Bloch file, CLD, BMRS, BA-MA.

88. B. Gourary interview.

89. Friedman, *No Haven*, 134.

CHAPTER 14. CROSSING THE PERILOUS OCEAN

1. John Keegan, *The Second World War* (New York, 1990), 49; Clay Blair, *Hitler's U-Boat War: The Hunters, 1939–1942* (New York, 1996), 145.

2. Rabbi Israel Jacobson, "Journey to America," *Di Yiddishe Heim* (1956), 6; Chaim Miller, *Turning Judaism Outward: A Biography of the Rebbe Menachem Mendel Schneerson* (Brooklyn, NY, 2014), 126; Dovid Zaklikowski, *The Rescue of the Lubavitcher Rebbe, Rabbi Yosef Yitzchak Schneersohn (Rayatz), during WWII* (Brooklyn, NY, 2014), 8.

3. Telegram from American Legation in Riga to Secretary of State Hull, 18 March 1940, General Records of Department of State, Itinerary 705, Visa Case Files 1933–1940, 811.111, Joseph Schneersohn, Record Group 59, NARA.

4. Ibid.

5. Handwritten note labeled Schneersohn et al., ibid.

6. Interview with Barry Gourary, 8 May 2003, BMRS, BA-MA; Jacobson, "Journey to America," 6; Eliezer Zaklikofsky, *America Is No Different* (New York, 1999), 61.

7. Jacobson, "Journey to America," 6; Records of the United States Theaters of War, World War II, 360 C.60P, 15/20, WNRC; Winfried Meyer, *Unternehmen Sieben. Eine Rettungsaktion für vom Holocaust Bedrohte aus dem Amt Ausland-Abwehr im Oberkommando der Wehrmacht* (Frankfurt, 1993), 138; Miller, *Turning Judaism Outward*, 126; interview with Rabbi Alex Weisfogel, 20 January 2004. With regard to the number of the Rebbe's stateroom, note that thirteen is not considered unlucky in Judaism.

8. Winston S. Churchill, *The Second World War*, vol. 1, *The Gathering Storm* (Boston, 1983), 433–436; Robert Kee, *1939: In the Shadow of War* (Boston, 1984), 307, 320; Blair, *Hitler's U-Boat War*, 67–68; Martin Gilbert, *The Second World War: A Complete History* (New York, 1989), 5.

9. Churchill, *Second World War*, 423, 434, 491; Kee, *In the Shadow of War*, 307, 320; http://www.hmsroyaloak.co.uk/index.htm; http://168.144.123.218/18thCenturyStottsEndnotes.htm. The German U-boat commander who sank the *Royal Oak*, Günther Prien, did so by sneaking into the harbor at Scapa Flow and hitting the ship at its moorings. This shows how skillful and daring the U-boat commanders were. Special thanks to graduate student Anthony Newpower for this information.

10. Blair, *Hitler's U-Boat War*, 118, 120, 124, 138–139, 141; Edgar McInnis, *The War: First Year* (New York, 1940), 67; http://168.144.123.218/18thCenturyStottsEndnotes.htm. Sinking neutral shipping was not unique to the Germans. The United States sank several Russian merchant ships and even a Japanese hospital ship during the war. Special thanks to graduate student Anthony Newpower for this information.

11. Interview with Rabbi Mordechai Dov Altein, 14 January 2003. Early in the war the Germans did abide by the Prize Regulations (*Prisenordnung*), which stated that any unarmed ship must be alerted to the presence of the raider (U-boat), stopped, and searched; all personnel were supposed to be lowered into lifeboats within safe reach of land prior to the ship's destruction. By November 1939, these rules were starting to be ignored, and in the late fall Admiral Karl Dönitz issued a new order: "Rescue no one and take no one with you. Have no care for the ships' boats. Weather conditions and the proximity of land are of no account. Care only for your own boat and strive to achieve the next success as

soon as possible!" Quoted in Peter Padfield, *War beneath the Sea: Submarine Conflict during World War II* (New York, 1996), 65. Obviously, neutral ships fell into a separate category, but it quickly became apparent that submarine warfare and the *Prisenordnung* were not compatible. Luckily for the Rebbe, the German U-boats were still abiding by the laws of war when he crossed the Atlantic.

12. McInnis, *War*, 67; Gilbert, *Second World War*, 29.

13. Zaklikofsky, *America Is No Different*, 51.

14. Blair, *Hitler's U-Boat War*, 146, 148.

15. Zaklikofsky, *America Is No Different*, 53; Lubavitch News Service, 1 March 1965; David Wyman, *Paper Walls: America and the Refugee Crisis 1938–1941* (New York, 1985), 152; B. Gourary interview; Weisfogel interview. It is difficult to ascertain how many times the ship was stopped. I tried to locate the ship's logs at the Marinmuseum in Karlskrona, Sweden, but was unsuccessful. Rabbi Weisfogel (interviewed 23 February 2004) remembers only one U-boat stopping them southwest of Iceland. He believes Chabad may have exaggerated the number of times to highlight God's divine intervention.

16. Kramer to Troutman, 11 March 1940, General Records of Department of State, Itinerary 705, Visa Case Files 1933–1940, 811.111, Joseph Schneersohn, Record Group 59, NARA.

17. Memorandum to the President from Warren and McDonald, 8 October 1940, OF 3186, box 3, FDR Library; Harry Rabinowicz, *Hasidism: The Movement and Its Masters* (New York, 1988), 303.

18. Jacobson to Risman, 8 March 1940, Neumark folder, Bloch file, BMRS, NA-MA. Remarkably, Schneersohn was supposed to pass two medical exams: one by the public health officer at the consulate and one at Ellis Island. Apparently, the exam at the consulate was never performed, although this was something Rhoade worried about. See Rhoade to Kramer, 25 October 1939, 6, Schneersohn folder 3, Bloch file, BMRS, BA-MA.

19. Sabath to Uhl, 14 March 1940, Neumark folder, Bloch file, BMRS, BA-MA.

CHAPTER 15. THE REBBE AND THE HOLOCAUST

1. Eliezer Zaklikofsky, *America Is No Different* (New York, 1999), 50–51; interview with Rabbi Eliezer Zaklikovsky, 4 June 2003.

2. David Wyman, *Paper Walls: America and the Refugee Crisis 1938–1941* (New York, 1985), 126; Clay Blair, *Hitler's U-Boat War: The Hunters, 1939–1942* (New York, 1996), 771.

3. Rabbi Israel Jacobson, "Journey to America," *Di Yiddishe Heim* (1956), 7. This is a common benediction when one has not seen a friend for more than twelve months. Interestingly, although Bloch and his team got seventeen or eighteen people out of Warsaw in 1939, only eleven of them traveled to the United States in March 1940. The Rebbe's secretary Haskell Feigin and his family and a

few other Lubavitchers did not get out of Riga. Zaklikofsky, *America Is No Different*, 58, 63; Edelman to Rigg, 23 February 2004, Schneersohn folder 6, BMRS, BA-MA. La Guardia, who had Jewish ancestors on his mother's side, hated Hitler and had once told a Jewish group that Hitler's picture should be "put in a chamber of horrors at the World's Fair." David Kertzer, *The Pope and Mussolini: The Secret History of Pius XI and the Rise of Fascism in Europe* (Oxford, 2014), 257.

4. Jacobson, "Journey to America," 7; interview with Rabbi Meir Greenberg, 18 August 1996; interview with Barry Gourary, 8 May 2003; Posner to Rigg, 8 January 2004, Schneersohn folder 6, all in BMRS, BA-MA.

5. Charles Rader, ed., *Challenge: An Encounter with Lubavitch-Chabad* (Brooklyn, NY, 1970), 54; Zaklikofsky, *America Is No Different*, 6, 54, 56, 58; *Time*, 1 April 1940, 46; *Newsweek*, 1 April 1940, 31; Winfried Meyer, *Unternehmen Sieben. Eine Rettungsaktion für vom Holocaust Bedrohte aus dem Amt Ausland-Abwehr im Oberkommando der Wehrmacht* (Frankfurt, 1993), 138; Avrum M. Ehrlich, *Leadership in the HaBaD Movement: A Critical Evaluation of HaBaD Leadership, History, and Succession* (New York, 2000), 101. According to Rabbi Zalman Posner, slightly less than 1,000 people were there. Interview with Posner, 3 May 2003. The Rebbe wore his *Shtreiml* (a hat of Russian origin) only on holidays and special occasions. Barry Gourary to Rigg, 11 January 2004, Schneersohn folder 6, BMRS, BA-MA; interview with David Kranzler, 8 February 2004.

6. Posner interview; Zaklikofsky, *America Is No Different*, 63.

7. Lubavitch News Service, 1 March 1965. See also Zaklikofsky, *America Is No Different*, 55, 57, 61, 63; *The Rebbes: Rabbi Yosef Yitzchak Schneersohn of Lubavitch*, vol. 2. (Israel, 1994), 157.

8. Lubavitch News Service, 1 March 1965. In this source, the word "holocaust" is used. It is unknown what word the Rebbe actually used for Hitler's systematic extermination, but it was clear he meant the Holocaust.

9. Ibid. There are some troubling concepts here about the religious sacrifice of humans. According to Chabad theology, the "communal sin offering" is a legal Talmudic expression, and it is used here as a metaphor to denote that all people in the world are part of one organism. What happens to one part of the "organism" affects the entire "body."

10. Ibid.; Uri Kaploun, ed., *Likkutei Dibburim: An Anthology of Talks by Rabbi Yosef Yitzchak Schneersohn of Lubavitch*, 5 vols. (Brooklyn, NY, 1987–2000), 3:222.

11. *Hakreah Vehakedusha* [Reading and Holiness] 1, 10 (July 1941): 2–4, 3, 37 (October 1943): 1. Others shared the view that American Jews were responsible for the Holocaust. See Alice Lyons Eckardt, "Suffering, Theology and the Shoah," in *Contemporary Christian Religious Responses to the Shoah*, ed. Rabbi Steven L. Jacobs (Lanham, MD, 1993), 46–47.

12. *Hakreah Vehakedusha* 1, 11 (August 1941): 2.

13. Christopher Hitchens, introduction to *The Portable Atheist: Essential*

Readings for the Nonbeliever (Cambridge, MA, 2007), xvii. See also Sam Harris, *The End of Faith: Religion, Terror, and the Future of Reason* (New York, 2004), 82.

14. Manfred Windfuhr, ed., *Heinrich Heine, Historisch-kritische Gesataus-gabe der Werke* (Hamburg, 1973–1997), 10:318; Christopher Hitchens, *God Is Not Great: How Religion Poisons Everything* (New York, 2007), 43.

15. George M. Marsden, *The Twilight of the American Enlightenment: The 1950's and the Crisis of Liberal Belief* (New York, 2014), 165.

16. *Hakreah Vehakedusha* 2, 17 (February 1942): 4.

17. Ibid., 1, 9 (June 1941): 6–8; 1, 10 (July 1941): 1; 1, 11 (August 1941): 2–3; 2, 14 (November 1941): 1–3; 2, 15 (December 1941): 1, 4–5; 2, 16 (January 1942): 1–2; 2, 17 (February 1942): 1; 2, 19 (April 1942): 4; 2, 23 (August 1942): 1–2; 3, 34 (July 1943): 1; 3, 35 (August 1943): 1; Zaklikofsky, *America Is No Different*, 36; Aviezer Ravitzky, *Messianism, Zionism, and Jewish Religious Radicalism* (Chicago, 1996), 194–195.

18. *Hakreah Vehakedusha* 1, 7 (April 1941): 16; 1, 10 (July 1941): 2, 6; 1, 11 (August 1941): 2; 1, 12 (September 1941): 3; 2, 15 (December 1941): 4; 2, 16 (January 1942): 1; 2, 23 (August 1942): 1; 3, 32 (May 1943): 1; 3, 34 (July 1943): 1; 5, 60 (August 1945): 1; Tractate Shivas Yamim (Yoma) 9b. For some of the Rebbe's pre–World War II thoughts on the end-time, see *Likkutei Dibburim*, 2:46.

19. *Likkutei Dibburim*, 3:101, 5:255–257, 313–314; *Hakreah Vehakedusha* 1, 8 (May 1941): 4; 2, 13 (October 1941): 2–4; 3, 27 (December 1942): 1; Zaklikovsky interview, 4 June 2003; Levine to Rigg, 9 March 2003, Schneersohn folder 4, BMRS, BA-MA; Meyer, *Unternehmen Sieben*, 138–139.

20. *Hakreah Vehakedusha* 2, 23 (August 1942); 2, 24 (September 1942): 1–2.

21. Ibid., 1, 1 (October 1940); 1, 7 (April 1941): 16; 2, 13 (October 1941): 1–4; 1, 9 (June 1941): 1–2, 5–6; 1, 10 (July 1941): 2; 1, 11 (August 1941): 2; 1, 12 (September 1941): 1, 6; 2, 18 (March 1942): 1; 2, 22 (July 1942): 1, 4; 2, 24 (September 1942): 1–2; 3, 27 (December 1942): 1; 3, 33 (June 1943): 1; 4, 38 (September 1943): 1; 4, 39 (December 1943): 1; 4, 40 (January 1944): 1; 4, 46 (July 1944): 1; 5, 53 (February 1945): 1; Levine to Rigg, 9 August 2003, Schneersohn folder 6, BMRS, BA-MA. The concept that the Jews were being punished for their sins was also espoused by other Jewish religious leaders. See Eckardt, "Suffering, Theology and the Shoah," 46–48; interview with Herschel Greenberg, 23 February 2004; interview with Eliezer Zaklikovsky, 13 January 2004. For more on the Rebbe's views about politics, see *Hakreah Vehakedusha* 1, 8 (May 1941).

22. *Hakreah Vehakedusha* 1, 9 (June 1941): 6.

23. Isaiah 2:4, 11:4–9, 50, 52, 53, 66:6–8; Ezekiel 4:16, 33:11, 37, 38:18–23; interview with Rabbi Moshe Kolodny, 4 September 2003; Matthew Black and H. H. Rowley, eds., *Peake's Commentary on the Bible* (New York, 1963), 586–587; *Hakreah Vehakedusha* 1, 12 (September 1941): 4; *Likkutei Dibburim*, 3:56–57, 62–64, 81, 85–86; 5:317–318.

24. *Hakreah Vehakedusha* 1, 10 (July 1941): 6–7; 1, 9 (June 1941): 1; 5, 52

(January 1945): 1; Kolodny interview; Rebbe Joseph Isaac Schneersohn, *Igrois Koidesh,* vol. 12 (Brooklyn, NY, 1985), 187–195 (letter 1988).

25. *Hakreah Vehakedusha* 1, 9 (June 1941): 7–8. Although this article is not signed by the Rebbe, he is obviously its principal author. Besides, nothing appeared in the Chabad newspaper without the Rebbe's approval.

26. Zaklikovsky interview, 4 June 2003.

27. The story of Haman, the king of Persia's anti-Semitic minister who tried to kill all the Jews, is found in the book of Esther.

28. Rachel Altein and Eliezer Zaklikovsky, eds., *Out of the Inferno: The Efforts that Led to the Rescue of the Rabbi Yosef Y. Schneersohn of Lubavitch from War-torn Europe in 1939–1940* (Brooklyn, NY, 2002), 290. Even earlier, on the day the Rebbe arrived in Riga from Berlin, he wrote a letter addressed to all Jews in the world in which he discussed the horrific situation of Polish Jewry under the Nazis and pleaded with the Jewish people, "regardless of sect or affiliation, to create special funds for Polish Jewry and to hand over all the collected funds." Rebbe Schneersohn, *Igrois Koidesh,* vol. 5 (Brooklyn, NY, 1983), 4–5.

29. Hasia R. Diner, *Jews in America* (New York, 1999), 48, 54.

30. Robert A. Divine, T. H. Breen, George M. Fredrickson, and R. Hal Williams, *America: Past and Present* (London, 1987), 561–573.

31. Michael Berebaum, *The World Must Know: The History of the Holocaust as Told in the United States Holocaust Memorial Museum* (Baltimore, 2007), 12, 53.

32. Schneersohn to Hull, 25 March 1940, General Records of Department of State, Itinerary 705, Visa Case Files 1933–1940, 811.111, Joseph Schneersohn, Record Group 59, NARA (hereafter cited as Visa Case Files 1933–1940 and the case name).

33. Memorandum for the President from Edwin M. Watson, Secretary to the President, 20 August 1940, OF 76c, box 7, FDR Library. The Visa Case Files in the National Archives show that McCormack was an avid fighter for the rights of Jewish refugees trying to enter the United States. Rabbi Dovid Rabinovitz gives most of the credit for the Rebbe's rescue to Brandeis, noting, "Before him all the gates opened up and even leaders of the Nazis obeyed him." Rebbe Schneersohn, *Igrois Koidesh,* vol. 12, 19.

34. Chaim Miller, *Turning Judaism Outward: A Biography of the Rebbe Menachem Mendel Schneerson* (Brooklyn, NY, 2014), 130–132; Shaul Magid, "America Is No Different," "America Is Different—Is There an American Jewish Fundamentalism?" Internet version, 9 September 2014, 79; Menachem Friedman and Samuel Heilman, *The Rebbe: The Life and Afterlife of Menachem Mendel Schneerson* (Princeton, NJ, 2010), 2.

35. *Toldois Chabad B-Artzois Ha'Bris: History of Chabad in the USA 1900–1950* (Brooklyn, NY, 1988), 323; *Hakreah Vehakedusha* 1, 9 (June 1941): 15; Rafael Medoff and David Wyman, *A Race against Death: Peter Bergson, America, and the Holocaust* (New York, 2002), 193; *Igrois Koidesh,* 5:44; Kranzler interview, 8 February 2004.

36. Lubavitch News Service, 1 March 1965; Rebbe Schneersohn, *Igrois Koidesh*, vol. 5, letters 1133, 1136.

37. Rebbe Schneersohn, *Igrois Koidesh*, vol. 5, letter 1237. This letter actually refers to fifty-two visas; since most of the other documents mention thirty visas, I believe this is a typo. See ibid., letters 1212, 1272, 1335, 1336, 1391, 1420; telegram from Schneersohn to Jacobson, 26 December 1939, Schneersohn folder 3, CLD, BMRS, BA-MA; *Hakreah Vehakedusha* 1, 6 (March 1941): 15; Kranzler interview, 8 February 2004.

38. *Hakreah Vehakedusha* 1, 9 (June 1941): 15; Medoff and Wyman, *Race against Death*, 193; Gregory Wallance, *America's Soul in the Balance: The Holocaust, FDR's State Department, and the Moral Disgrace of an American Aristocracy* (Austin, TX, 2012), 172. For information about the Rebbe's fund, see Ehrlich, *Leadership in the HaBaD Movement*, 64.

39. Efraim Zuroff, *Response of Orthodox Jewry in the United States: The Activities of the Vaad Ha-Hatzala Rescue Committee, 1939–1945* (New York, 2000), xvii. Even Rabbi Wise made special efforts on behalf of the wife and daughter of his assistant, Rabbi Emil B. Cohn. Wise wrote to Warren directly in 1940 and was eventually successful. So the Orthodox were not the only ones focused on their own. See Visa Case Files 1933–1940, Margarete Cohn.

40. Henry L. Feingold, *The Politics of Rescue: The Roosevelt Administration and the Holocaust, 1938–1945* (New Brunswick, NJ, 1970), 131, 160, 164–165; Posner to Rigg, 8 January 2004, Schneersohn folder 6, BMRS, BA-MA. It seems like this was a problem for many. See Vaad memorandum for the State Department, box 20, folder 123, YU-VHC.

41. Schneersohn to Roosevelt, 12 September 1941, OF 76c, box 7, FDR Library; the Rebbe's prayer is attached to Kaufman to Roosevelt, 2 December 1941, ibid.

42. Wallance, *America's Soul*, 204.

43. Martin Gilbert, *The Holocaust* (New York, 1985), 229–230; e-mail from Eliezer Zaklikovsky to Rigg, 7 February 2015; Wallance, *America's Soul*, 105.

44. See the excellent book by Mark Roseman, *The Villa, the Lake, the Meeting: Wannsee and the Final Solution* (New York, 2002).

45. *Hakreah Vehakedusha* 2, 17 (February 1942): 12.

46. Ibid.

47. Lyne Olson, *Those Angry Days: Roosevelt, Lindbergh, and America's Fight over World War II, 1939–1941* (New York, 2013), 28.

48. According to the National World War II Museum in New Orleans, 16 million Americans served during the war. Using the figures from Diner's *Jews in America*, 8 percent of US servicemen, or 1.28 million, were Jews. However, other sources, such as the Jewish virtual library, put the number of Jews who served in the US military at around 550,000. Diner reports that 40,000 died during the war and 36,000 received medals for distinguished service (ibid., 101). In addition to

combatants, there were 309 rabbis (Reform, Conservative, and Orthodox) commissioned as chaplains in the US armed forces, some receiving awards for valor
ranging from the Distinguished Service Cross to Bronze Star to presidential cita-
tions as they ministered to soldiers, sailors, airmen, and marines in North Africa,
Europe, Asia, and at sea as well as traumatized survivors in concentration camps.
Philip S. Bernstein, "Jewish Chaplains in World War II" in *Jewish Year Book*,
173 et. seq.

49. Bill D. Ross, *Iwo Jima: Legacy of Valor* (New York, 1985), 323. Sadly,
the three Protestant chaplains assigned to Gittelsohn's office tried to prevent him
from giving his eulogy, showing their latent anti-Semitism. Interview with Kenneth Roseman, 23 February 2015.

50. Jacob Rosenheim diary, 3 September 1942, KHEC.

51. Ibid., 4 September 1942.

52. Wallance, *America's Soul*, 115–116. The Jewish leaders pleaded with FDR
for action. Roosevelt responded, "We are dealing with an insane man—Hitler,
and the group that surrounds him represent an example of a national psychopathic case. We cannot act toward them by normal means." In short, Roosevelt
seemed to think that the only way to end the extermination was to destroy Nazi
Germany. Ibid., 121, 127.

53. Conversation with R. D. of KHEC, 13 February 2015.

54. Schneersohn to Roosevelt, 1 September 1942, OF 76c, box 8, FDR Library.

55. *Hakreah Vehakedusha* 1, 9 (June 1941): 5; 1, 11 (August 1941): 2; 2, 15
(December 1941): 1; 3, 27 (December 1942): 1; 4, 49 (October 1944): 1; 5, 51 (December 1944): 1; 5, 52 (January 1945): 1; 5, 55 (April 1945): 1. The Rebbe wrote
that American Jews were "nurtured with the sole hope that the Jewish people will
be saved through a victory of world-democracy," which he considered entirely
wrong. See also ibid., 2, 16 (January 1942): 1–2. The Rebbe's newspaper cited
what had happened to the Jews under Haman, which had also been a democracy,
and noted that the situation could change quickly. Therefore, the best thing for
Jews to do was to rely on God. Ibid., 2, 18 (March 1942): 3. With respect to the
Rebbe's claim about the "destroying angel," rabbis Simon and Yosef Jacobson
claim that this was not a "curse"; rather, it was a way of interpreting history
from a moral and spiritual perspective, a way of seeing how spiritual behavior
can affect human welfare. Spiritually speaking, the Torah and mitzvoth are to
the Jews like water is to fish. They are their link to life and fulfillment, mentally,
spiritually, and even physically. Simon and Yossi Jacobson to Rigg, 25 March
2004, Schneersohn folder 6, BMRS, BA-MA. The phrase "God helps those who
help themselves" is from Benjamin Franklin's *Poor Richard's Almanac*. See Walter Isaacson, *Benjamin Franklin: An American Life* (New York, 2003), 99.

56. Gershon Greenberg, "Menahem Mendel Schneersohn's Response to the
Holocaust," *Modern Judaism* 34, 1 (20 February 2014): 88.

57. Rebbe Schneersohn, *Igrois Koidesh*, vol. 5, letter 1498. For the Jewish experience in Shanghai during the war, see Astrid Freyeisen, *Shanghai und die Politik des Dritten Reiches* (Würzburg, 2000).

58. *Hakreah Vehakedusha* 2, 17 (February 1942): 40–41; interview with Joseph Wineberg, 4 May 2003, BMRS, BA-MA. One student died there, and many blame this on the Vaad's unwillingness to help Lubavitchers. Interview with Avraham Laber, 8 May 2003. Rabbi Laber is quick to point out that although many Lubavitchers have repeated this story, he should not be used as a source for its legitimacy. Many Chabad rabbis interviewed for this book heard similar stories, and most members of Chabad believe this about the Vaad, despite the lack of supporting documents. In fact, an oral tradition exists within Chabad that the Vaad was responsible for several Lubavitcher students dying in China. Interview with Rabbi Elie Shmotkin, 31 December 2003.

59. Horenstein never finished his rabbinical studies, even though he is referred as a rabbi in several documents. Rhoade probably did this to play up the hierarchy angle, hoping to convince government officials that Horenstein was necessary to the religious movement. He could not make this claim based on Horenstein's relationship to the Rebbe as his son-in-law, but he could cite Horenstein's value as the "custodian" of the library or a minister in Chabad.

60. Rhoade to Kramer, 24 January 1940, point 1, Neumark folder, Bloch file, BMRS, BA-MA.

61. B. Gourary interview. Soon after Menachem became the Rebbe, Samarius became a strong supporter of his brother-in-law. Chana is a difficult person to understand. According to Rabbi Elie Shmotkin, she was driven by hatred because she felt the Rebbe favored her sister and brother-in-law. For example, she never got over the fact that only a few people attended her wedding, whereas hundreds attended the wedding of her sister Chaya Moussia and Menachem Mendel Schneerson, and it was a great celebration. Shmotkin interview. Menachem's succession as Rebbe was not a foregone conclusion until 1951. In fact, it seemed that Samarius Gourary was being groomed for the position, traveling with Rebbe Schneersohn on most of his important trips throughout the 1920s and 1930s. See Ehrlich, *Leadership in the HaBaD Movement*, 3. Rabbi Zelig Slonim tells the following story about how Gourary was convinced to accept his brother-in-law as the Rebbe: A few years after Menachem became the Rebbe, Samarius approached him for some advice about a difficult issue. Menachem was unable to provide any guidance, but he said he would go to the grave of their father-in-law and ask for his help. Soon thereafter, Menachem gave Samarius an answer that he had received from their father-in-law. Gourary was very impressed and thereafter accepted his brother-in-law as the Rebbe. H. Greenberg interview.

62. Feingold, *Politics of Rescue*, 143; Edward Hoffman, *Despite All Odds: The Story of Lubavitch* (New York, 1991), 25; Miller, *Turning Judaism Outward*, 134–135.

63. Wallance, *America's Soul*, 82.

64. Altein and Zaklikovsky, *Out of the Inferno*, 328–331; interview with David Kranzler, 24 January and 8 February 2004.

65. Simon Jacobson, *Toward a Meaningful Life: The Wisdom of the Rebbe Menachem Mendel Schneerson* (New York, 1995), xxiv. According to Rabbi Zaklikovsky, the other candidate, Samarius Gourary, "could not sustain the movement . . . and in comparison to Menachem, was substandard. It was clear to everyone that Menachem was the only one with the skills to be a world leader of Lubavitch." Zaklikovsky interview, 4 June 2003. According to Rabbi Shmotkin, the Rebbe had actually written in his unpublished memoirs that he considered Samarius unfit for Chabad leadership. Shmotkin interview. According to Ehrlich, there was more competition than many Lubavitchers like to admit, but Menachem was indeed the best candidate. Ehrlich, *Leadership in the HaBaD Movement*, 340–350. Interestingly, Menachem worked for a while as an engineer after he arrived in the United States, so it is unclear how he was initially involved with the movement. Menachem's lack of a rabbinical degree was apparently not unusual for Rebbes. It seems that Rebbe Joseph Isaac Schneersohn could not register with the Polish authorities in 1939 because he could not provide documents proving that he was a rabbi. See S. Kramer to Rhoade, 16 October 1939, Neumark folder, Bloch file, BMRS, BA-MA. To show that the Rebbe viewed Menachem as the best choice for the next Rebbe, the following story is told: when a professor came to the Rebbe for a critique of a scholarly article, the Rebbe responded, "Show it to [Menachem Mendel Schneerson]. You'll be asking him all your questions soon." See Joseph Telushkin, *Rebbe: The Life and Teachings of Menachem M. Schneerson, the Most Influential Rabbi in Modern History* (New York, 2014), 21.

66. Zaklikovsky interview, 4 June 2003. Rabbi Yosef Jacobson has looked through the scattered archive of Samarius Gourary and found nothing of importance. He notes that the archive for 1940–1945 "has not been preserved properly." According to many, if there were documents proving the Rebbe's efforts with politicians, they would be in that archive. Yossi Jacobson to Rigg, 25 March 2004, Schneersohn folder 6, BMRS, BA-MA.

67. David Kranzler, *Thy Brothers' Blood: The Orthodox Jewish Response during the Holocaust* (Brooklyn, NY, 1987), 12–13, 34, 36–37, 92–93, 134–138; Zuroff, *Response of Orthodox Jewry*, 69; Yehuda Bauer, *American Jewry and the Holocaust: The American Jewish Joint Distribution Committee, 1939–1945* (Detroit, 1981), 308; Feingold, *Politics of Rescue*, 178; Michael Beschloss, *The Conquerors: Roosevelt, Truman and the Destruction of Hitler's Germany 1941–1945* (New York, 2002), 65, 251; Kolodny interview; Amos Bunin, *A Fire in His Soul: Irving M. Bunin 1901–1980—The Man and His Impact on American Orthodox Jewry* (New York, 1989), 126; Monty Noam Penkower, *The Jews Were Expend-*

able: Free World Diplomacy and the Holocaust (Chicago, 1983), 204; YU-VHC, box 3, box 20, folder 123, and box 21, folders 130, 132; Kranzler interview, 8 February 2004.

68. Efraim Zuroff, review of *Out of the Inferno, Jerusalem Post*, 15 December 2002; Penkower, *Jews Were Expendable*, 249; Feingold, *Politics of Rescue*, 270.

69. Altein and Zaklikovsky, *Out of the Inferno*, 244; interview with Chaskel Besser, 15 July 2003, BMRS, BA-MA. On 11 October 1939 Dr. Jonas Simon, chairman of the Jewish Community of New York, wrote to Senator Wagner about the Gerer Rebbe (Avraham Mordechai Alter) and rabbis Ben Zion Halberstam and Aaron Rokeach, asking for his assistance in rescuing these men. Wagner immediately sent Simon's letter to Avra Warren in the Visa Department and asked for his support. Warren answered Wagner on 20 October and advised him to look into the nonquota visas allowed for "ministers of religion" under section 4(d) of the Immigration Act of 1924. Warren told Wagner that the Visa Department could do nothing until these men applied to the general consuls where they resided, at which time their cases would be accorded "every consideration consistent with the restrictive features of the immigration laws." In addition to Wagner, Senator Bloom, Justice Brandeis, and even Secretary Hull attempted to help the Gerer Rebbe. Moshe Prager of the Joint Distribution Committee also helped with the escape and actually traveled to Warsaw to help Rebbe Alter. Eventually, the US politicians were able to facilitate an escape plan, with the help of German officials. In April 1940 two German officers (one may have been Bloch) accompanied the Gerer Rebbe and several family members to Italy, where they boarded a ship for Palestine. Gerer Hasidim is the largest Hasidic sect in Israel today. Simon to Wagner, 11 October 1939, and Wagner to Warren, 12 October 1939, Visa Case Files 1933–1940, Mordechai Alter; Zuroff, *Response of Orthodox Jewry*, 246; Besser interview, 15 July 2003; Ben Zion Klugman, *The Light Is Sown for the Righteous (Ohr Zoruah la Tzadik)* (Jerusalem, 2001). Many thanks to Professor Roseanne Schnoll for her analysis of this text, and thanks to Rabbi Chaskel Besser for providing this source. See also Tzvi Rabinowicz, *Hasidism in Israel: A History of the Hasidic Movement and Its Masters in the Holy Land* (New York, 2000), 9–10; Harry Rabinowicz, *Hasidism: The Movement and Its Masters* (New York, 1988), 269; Rebbe Schneersohn, *Igros Koidesh*, vol. 5, 326–327 (a review of the Belz's rescue can be read in Devar Chain); Yaffa Eliach, *Hasidic Tales of the Holocaust* (New York, 1982), 46–48; Chaim Shlomo Friedman, *Dare to Survive* (New York, 1991), 112–117; Gilbert, *Holocaust*, 555–556, 662, 701, 751.

70. Rebbe Schneersohn, *Igrois Koidesh*, vol. 5, 159–160 and vol. 6, 19.

71. Walter Laqueur, "The Failure to Comprehend," in *The Holocaust: Problems and Perspectives of Interpretation*, ed. Donald L. Niewyk (New York, 2003), 266; David Wyman, *The Abandonment of the Jews: America and the Holocaust 1941–1945* (New York, 1989), xiv, xiii; Henry L. Feingold, *Bearing Witness: How*

America and Its Jews Responded to the Holocaust (Syracuse, NY, 1995), 2–3, 226, 269; Feingold, *Politics of Rescue*, 10, 12–13, 15, 21, 218–221, 298–299, 301; Rebbe Schneersohn, *Igrois Koidesh*, vol. 5, 159–160 and vol. 6, 19.

72. Gilbert, *Holocaust*, 790.

73. *Hakreah Vehakedusha* 1, 1 (October 1940): 12; 1, 2 (November 1940): 16; Zaklikovsky interview, 3 May 2003.

74. M. Greenberg interview; Isaac Levinson, *The Untold Story* (Johannesburg, 1958), 121; Dina Porat, "The Holocaust in Lithuania," in *The Final Solution: Origins and Implementation*, ed. David Cesarani (New York, 1994), 167; Albert Seaton, *Russo-German War 1941–1945* (London, 1971), 10–11; Laber interview; Ehrlich, *Leadership in the HaBaD Movement*, 284 n. 3.

75. The people named were Mordechai Dubin, his wife Fanija, son Zalman, and daughter-in-law Edite; Leib Edelman; Majer Glikman; Benjamin Halberstam and several family members; Szyja Kac; Hirsz Kahn; and Szeine Levitan and his sons Gerszon, Szolom, and Abraham.

76. Memorandum for Eleanor Roosevelt, 18 March 1941, ER box 359, Papers of Eleanor Roosevelt, FDR Library; *Hakreah Vehakedusha* 1, 9 (June 1941): 15; *Toldois Chabad B-Artzois Ha'Bris*, 324; Pickett to Roosevelt, 5 March 1941, Secretary of Mrs. Roosevelt to Pickett, 15 March 1941, and Pickett to Roosevelt, 17 March 1941, ER box 359, Papers of Eleanor Roosevelt, FDR Library; Kranzler interview, 31 December 2003, 8 February 2004.

77. B. Gourary interview; Simon Jacobson to Rigg, 25 March 2004, Schneersohn folder 6, BMRS, BA-MA.

78. Welles to Roosevelt, 31 March 1941, Pickett to Roosevelt, 22 April 1941, ER box 359, Papers of Eleanor Roosevelt, FDR Library. Welles brought the refugee problem to Roosevelt's attention on several occasions. See, for example, Welles to Roosevelt, 21 December 1940, Counselor of Polish Embassy Jan Drohojowski, 2 December 1940, OF 3186, box 3, FDR Library; Warren to Besser, 31 January 1939, Visa Case Files 1933–1940, Lotte Jacoby. Mrs. Roosevelt seemed to be in regular contact with Warren. See Roosevelt to Warren, 21 September 1940, ER box 347, Papers of Eleanor Roosevelt, FDR Library; Visa Case Files 1933–1940, Hermann Gottlieb; John Morton Blum, *V Was for Victory: Politics and American Culture during World War II* (New York, 1976), 11, 174; Allida M. Black, *Courage in a Dangerous World: Political Writings of Eleanor Roosevelt* (New York, 1999), 109.

79. Interview with Holger Herwig, 10 January 2003.

80. Rebbe Schneersohn, *Igrois Koidesh*, vol. 5, 159–160 and vol. 6, 19.

81. Julian Jackson, *France: The Dark Years, 1940–1944* (Oxford, 2003), 362; Robert Paxton, *Vichy France: Old Guard and New Order, 1940–1944* (New York, 1972); Robert Paxton and Michael Marrus, *Vichy France and the Jews* (Stanford, CA, 1995).

82. Jackson, *France*, 358, 362; Paxton, *Vichy France*; Paxton and Marrus, *Vi-*

chy France; Edward Cody, "Rabbi, Three Children Shot Dead Outside Jewish School in France," *Washington Post*, 19 March 2012.

83. Files of Rabbi Shemaryohu Gurary and Rabbi Jacob Rosenheim, compiled by Dovid Zaklikowski, KHEC. In addition to these files, there is a short essay by Zaklikowski titled *The Rescue of the Lubavitcher Rebbe, Rabbi Yosef Yitzchak Schneersohn (Rayatz), during WWII* (Brooklyn, NY, 2014). Zaklikowski's research needs to be used with caution, however; he cites only a few sources, and it is clear he does not understand the structure of the Nazi government or the Wehrmacht. For instance, on page 5 he writes that Wohlthat was head of the Wehrmacht; in fact, General Wilhelm Keitel was head of the Wehrmacht at this time, and Wohlthat was in Göring's Four-Year Plan Department. Had Zaklikowski read my *Rescued from the Reich* or Meyer's excellent book *Unternehmen Sieben*, he would have known that. When Zaklikowski handed this document over to KHEC archivist Dovid Reidel, he said it had been written in response to my first book, *Rescued from the Reich*. Chabad and Zaklikowski intended to use this work to disprove my claim that the Rebbe did too little to rescue Jews during the Holocaust (discussion with Dovid Reidel, 29 December 2014). However, this document adds nothing to the understanding of what the Rebbe did or did not do during the Holocaust; Zaklikowski shows only that the Rebbe tried to send food and religious items to "religious Jews in Soviet-Russia." Jacob Rosenheim diary, 27 March 1942, 28 February 1944, KHEC.

84. Interview with Alex Weisfogel, 8 March 2004; Kranzler interview, 8 February 2004; Simon and Yosef Jacobson to Rigg, 25 March 2004, Schneersohn folder 6, BMRS, BA-MA.

85. Kolodny interview; Weisfogel interview, 8 March 2004; Milton Kramer, ed., *The Kramers: The Next Generation* (Brooklyn, NY, 1995).

86. Levine to Rigg, 9 March 2003, Schneersohn folder 4, BMRS, BA-MA; Kolodny interview; Kranzler interview, 8 February 2004; Simon and Yosef Jacobson to Rigg, 25 March 2004; Rebbe Schneersohn, *Igrois Koidesh*, vol. 6, 196, 252. Rabbi Aaron Kotler, a fierce opponent of Chabad for its focus on the Rebbe and the Messiah, did indeed write a letter of thanks to the Rebbe in 1932 (see *Algemeiner Journal*, Spring 1999, for a copy of this letter). However, by 1940, the Vaad had grown tired of Chabad's mission. The Rebbe's newspaper focused almost entirely on his religious crusade, as did most of the Rebbe's *farbrengen* [sermon] published in *Lukkutei Dibburim* from 1940 to 1941.

87. Petition to the President of the United States from Vaad Hahatzala, Emergency Committee, American Jewish Congress, Union of Orthodox Rabbis of the United States and Canada, Agudath Israel of America, Rabbinical Council of America, Union of Orthodox Jewish Congregations of America, Young Israel of America, Emergency Committee to Save the Jewish People of Europe, presented by Rabbi Aaron Kotler, Rabbi Baruch Korff, and Michael G. Tress to the Honorable Edward R. Stettinius, Undersecretary of State, for transmission to the

President, 10 July 1944, Michael Tress Collection, KHEC; Joseph Finklestone, "Obituaries: Rabbi Baruch Korff," *Independent*, 3 August 1995. For Welles's downfall, see Wallance, *America's Soul*, 93, 98–99, 187–190, 262.

88. National Emergency Campaign for the United Lubavitcher Yeshivoth Tomchei Tmimim, Rabbi S. Gourary, Chairman, Executive Committee, to Michael G. Tress, Agudath Israel, 29 November 1944, Tress Collection, KHEC.

89. Zuroff, *Response of Orthodox Jewry*, 244; Kranzler interview, 31 December 2003. Problems often arose between secular and Orthodox groups. See Bunin, *Fire in His Soul*, 105; memorandum on why the Joint [Distribution Committee] cannot take care of Orthodox Jews, box 20, folder 123, YU-VHC.

90. Kranzler, *Thy Brothers' Blood*, 12–13, 34, 36–42, 71, 92–93, 135, 136, 137, 138; Bunin, *Fire in His Soul*, 100, 126; Zuroff, *Response of Orthodox Jewry*, 39, 134, 195–197, 221, 251, 254, 286; Beschloss, *Conquerors*, 251; Kolodny interview; Weisfogel interview, 8 March 2004; Penkower, *Jews Were Expendable*, 204; YU-VHC, boxes 3 and 21, folders 120, 123, 132. The efforts of Kalmanowitz and Kotler helped bring about the War Refugee Board. Kranzler interview, 24 January 2004; Simon and Yosef Jacobson to Rigg, 25 March 2004.

91. Wallance, *America's Soul*, 87–90.

92. Stephen Wise, *Challenging Years: The Autobiography of Stephen Wise* (New York, 1949), 280, 283, 285, 288–289, 295.

93. Carl Hermann Voss, *Rabbi and Minister: The Friendship of Stephen S. Wise and John Haynes Holmes* (Buffalo, NY, 1980), 314; Wallance, *America's Soul*, 127–128.

94. Wallance, *America's Soul*, 131–132.

95. *Likkutei Dibburim*, 4:80–81. Even though the Rebbe did not agree with Rabbi Wise's Reform status or his movement, the Lubavitchers asked for his help with Schneersohn's rescue. They apparently wanted to utilize Wise's relationship with Senator Key Pitman, chairman of the Foreign Relations Committee. So, as demonstrated with the Quakers, Chabad was more than happy to use those they deemed inferior if it helped the cause. It is unclear from the documents what Wise did for Chabad, if anything. Pitman is rarely mentioned, so it seems he played little of a role. Memorandum of activities regarding Rabbi Schneersohn, 26 September 1939, 2, point 7, Schneersohn folder 3, Bloch file, BMRS, BA-MA.

96. *Hakreah Vehakedusha* 1, 12 (September 1941): 2; 3, 27 (December 1942): 1; 3, 35 (August 1943): 1; 5, 54 (March 1945): 1; 5, 55 (April 1945): 1; Simon and Yosef Jacobson to Rigg, 25 March 2004. Phraseology at the end of this paragraph is taken from Zuroff, who expresses the same sentiment about several Orthodox Jewish leaders. Efraim Zuroff, "Orthodox Rescue Revisited," *Jewish Action* 63, 3 (Spring 2003): 36.

97. Friedman, *Dare to Survive*, 129; *Likkutei Dibburim*, 4:79–80; *Hakreah Vehakedusha* 1, 9 (June 1941): 6; 1, 11 (August 1941): 1; 2, 15 (December 1941): 4.

98. *Hakreah Vehakedusha* 2, 16 (January 1942); 2, 17 (February 1942); 2, 23 (August 1942); Blum, *V Was for Victory*, 178; Wise, *Challenging Years*, 227.

99. Levine to Rigg, 9 March 2003, Schneersohn folder 4, BMRS, BA-MA. For the population figure of 160,000 see Kleinfeld to Farley, 27 September 1939, 360 C.60P, 15/4, WNRC; Special Agent Tubbs in Dept. of State to Fitch, 10 January 1940, Visa Case Files 1933–1940, Joseph Schneersohn; Meyer, *Unternehmen Sieben*, 129.

100. Wyman, *Abandonment of the Jews*, 78; Friedman, *Dare to Survive*, 130.

101. Zuroff, *Response of Orthodox Jewry*, 257–260; Medoff and Wyman, *Race against Death*, 11, 43, 113–114, 144, 154–156; David Kranzler, "Orthodoxy's Finest Hour: Rescue Efforts during the Holocaust," *Jewish Action* 63, 1 (Fall 2002): 34–35; David Kranzler, "Stephen S. Wise and the Holocaust," in *Reverence, Richteousness, and Rahamanut: Essays in Memory of Rabbi Dr. Leo Jung*, ed. Jacob J. Schacter (New York, 1992), 158, 186; Kranzler, *Thy Brothers' Blood*, 71, 100–101, 141; Bunin, *Fire in His Soul*, 127; Neil Rolde, *Breckinridge Long: American Eichmann* (Solon, ME, 2013), 230; Wallance, *America's Soul*, 240–242. The Rebbe certainly recognized the utility of approaching political personalities. In a moving letter from 1948, he pleaded with the queen of Holland to liberate Jewish children who were being raised by Christians and return them to the Jewish faith. Unfortunately, the queen did not answer or comply with the Rebbe's request. Protests, he believed, would not have helped the situation. Interestingly, a generation later, his son-in-law deeply opposed demonstrations on behalf of the liberation of Russian Jews. He too believed that quiet diplomacy was the best way to help Jews under the Soviets. Rebbe Schneersohn, *Igrois Koidesh*, vol. 13, 459.

102. See Nathan Stoltzfus, *Resistance of the Heart: Intermarriage and the Rosenstrasse Protest in Nazi Germany* (London, 2001).

103. Rebbe Schneersohn, *Igrois Koidesh*, vol. 7, 187–195 (letter 1988).

104. Right before Passover, all leavened bread is burned and the crumbs are swept away. Any crumbs that remain in the home are disowned and proclaimed to be "dust of the earth." Clearly, the Rebbe felt abandoned by the democracies. See *Hakreah Vehakedusha* 2, 23 (August 1942): 1; Rebbe Schneersohn, *Igrois Koidesh*, vol. 7, 187–195 (letter 1988).

105. Rebbe Schneersohn, *Igrois Koidesh*, vol. 7, 187–195 (letter 1988); Rebbe Schneersohn to Klatzkin, Agudath Archives of New York. Special thanks to Professor Roseanne Schnoll and Rabbi Avraham Laber for translating this letter and to Rabbi Eliezer Zaklikovsky for originally bringing it to my attention. See also *Hakreah Vehakedusha* 1, 9 (June 1941): 1–8; 1, 10 (July 1941): 1–4; *Likkutei Dibburim*, 3:56–57, 62–64, 81, 85–86, 5:317–318; Medoff and Wyman, *Race against Death*, 34; Shmotkin interview.

106. According to Hannah Arendt, many Jews, especially those who lived in

eastern Europe, had "no political traditions or experience." David N. Myers and Kaye Alexander, eds., *The Faith of Fallen Jews: Yosef Hayim Yerushalmi and the Writing of Jewish History* (Waltham, MA, 2014), 247.

107. *Likkutei Dibburim*, 5:311; Jacobson, "Journey to America," 7; Zaklikofsky, *America Is No Different*, 61, 65.

108. *Hakreah Vehakedusha* 2, 16 (January 1942): 1. In the Rebbe's worldview, divine punishments could be stopped by pleading with God. See Joseph I. Schneersohn, *On the Teachings of Chassidus (Kuntres Toras Hachassidus)* (Brooklyn, NY, 1965), 41.

109. Ehrlich, *Leadership in the HaBaD Movement*, 102, 266, 285 n. 17.

110. *Likkutei Dibburim*, 3:291, 1:111, 115; Posner interview; *Hakreah Vehakedusha* 1, 9 (June 1941): 4; Ehrlich, *Leadership in the HaBaD Movement*, 281; Kranzler interview, 23 January 2004; Aaron Wertheim, *Law and Custom in Hasidim* (Hoboken, NJ, 1992), 432 n. 53.

111. *Likkutei Dibburim*, 3:229; Altein and Zaklikovsky, *Out of the Inferno*, 308. Interestingly, the Rebbe's father had stated in his will that Joseph Isaac should become the next Rebbe if he adhered to the principles of Chabad and carried out his duties properly. The Rebbe probably had this in mind when he gave this statement, verifying, at least in his own mind, his authority. There had been some controversy about his leadership at the beginning. In his youth, one of Joseph Isaac's instructors, Avraham Ha-Malach, had apparently caught him reading secular literature and denounced him to his father. The Rebbe denied this, and when Avraham moved to the United States, he claimed that Schneersohn was a liar. Ehrlich, *Leadership in the HaBaD Movement*, 111, 269–271.

112. While researching this book, I repeatedly asked the Chabad community for documents that would paint a different picture from that presented here, but it was unable to provide such material. Around 1,500 pages of the Rebbe's speeches printed in *Likkutei Dibburim*, a few hundred pages of articles in the Rebbe's newspaper published from 1941 to 1945, several of the Rebbe's letters translated by the Lubavtichers, and countless books about Lubavitch accurately present the Rebbe's theological beliefs, which I have discussed in this chapter. According to Rabbi Elie Shmotkin, other documents regarding the Rebbe's beliefs exist, but he refused to reveal where to find such documents or how to obtain copies of them. Discussion with Shmotkin, 30 January 2004.

113. Zaklikovsky interview, 4 May 2003.

114. *Every Jew Has a Silver Lining: An Adaptation of the Public Addresses of the Lubavitcher Rebbe Rabbi Menachem M. Schneerson, on the Tenth of Teves and on Sahbbos Parshas Vayechi*, vol. 47 (Brooklyn, NY, 1990), 3 n. 8. Interestingly, many Lubavitchers do not see contradictions between Rebbes as a problem. Lubavitchers believe that each Rebbe knows what his society and his age are ready for, so he may react differently from his predecessor or successor, but

in essence, they all think the same. For the modern reader, this is a difficult concept to grasp and may appear to be an apologetic way of looking at their leaders and their different philosophies. Ehrlich, *Leadership in the HaBaD Movement*, 54–55; Shmotkin interview. For an excellent description of Rebbe Menachem Mendel Schneerson's take on the Holocaust, see Miller, *Turning Judaism Outward*, 392–394.

115. *Hakreah Vehakedusha* 1, 9 (July 1941): 2, 6; 4, 43 (April 1944): 1; 5, 56 (April 1945): 1; Greenberg, "Menahem Mendel Schneersohn's Response to the Holocaust," 87. Renowned historian and rabbi Richard Rubenstein has reached the same conclusion about the Rebbe's views. See Richard Rubenstein, *After Auschwitz: History, Theology, and Contemporary Judaism* (Baltimore, 1992), 160.

116. The Rebbe was horrified that many American Jews did not go to synagogue on the Sabbath, did not take ritual baths, did not wear religious garments (*Tzitzis*), and cut their beards. He was also upset that many worship services allowed mixed seating. The Rebbe said, "In a word, in America one is allowed to do whatever is forbidden in the rest of the world." *Likkutei Dibburim*, 3:83.

117. *Likkutei Dibburim*, 3:56–57, 62–64, 81, 85–86, 5:317–318; *Hakreah Vehakedusha* 4, 49 (October 1944): 1; Joseph I. Schneersohn, *The "Tzemach Tzedek" and the Haskala Movement (Ha "Tzemach Tzedek" Utenaus Hahaskolo)* (Brooklyn, NY, 1962), 99, 105. Rebbe Schneersohn described *teshuvah* as follows: "We can now understand the meaning of teshuvah, repentance, or preferably, return. Teshuvah means, *tashuv hai*, return the *hai*, the last letter of G-d's Name, the symbol of the Shechinah, and—as we have explained—this is the soul. Teshuvah then would mean returning the soul to the thoughts of G-d. Teshuvah is more than regret alone, repentance. 'The wicked are full of regrets,' we are told (*Nedarim* 9b). True teshuvah means to return to G-d, to be close to Him through Shema and Torah and mitzvot. Thus the Shechinah, the soul, is bound up with G-d and Torah." Schneersohn, *"Tzemach Tzedek" and the Haskala Movement*, 98–99. To read more on the Rebbe's thoughts on *teshuvah*, see *Likkutei Dibburim*, 2:1–2, 65; Joseph I. Schneersohn, *Saying Tehillim: Selected from Letters by the Late Lubavitcher Rebbe Rabbi Yoseph Yitzhak Schneersohn on the Subject of Reciting Psalms* (Brooklyn, NY, 1975), 31.

118. Roseman interview.

119. Karen Armstrong, *A History of God: A 4,000-Year Quest of Judaism, Christianity and Islam* (New York, 1993), 376. It seems that Armstrong borrowed her thoughts from an exploration of God by Epicurus, who wrote, "Is he [God] willing to prevent evil but not able? Then he is impotent. Is he able but not willing? Then he is malevolent. Is he both able and willing? Whence then is evil?" Hitchens, *God Is Not Great*, 267–268.

120. Harold S. Kushner, *When Bad Things Happen to Good People* (New York, 1981), 10. See also Eckardt, "Suffering, Theology and the Shoah," 38–57.

121. Besser interviews, 16 January and 15 July 2003. For an excellent biography of Besser, see Warren Kozak, *The Rabbi of 84th Street: The Extraordinary Life of Haskel Besser* (New York, 2004).

122. Discussion with Norman Lamm, 18 December 2004; Norman Lamm, *The Face of God: Thoughts on the Holocaust* (Yeshiva University Department of Holocaust Studies, 1986), 120–132.

123. Harris Lenowitz, *The Jewish Messiahs: From the Galilee to Crown Heights* (Oxford, 1998), 222, 264.

124. Zyklon B was developed using the research of Fritz Haber. Haber, a baptized Jew, helped manufacture munitions and explosives during World War I, organized the chemical warfare service, and personally directed gas operations on the battlefield. In addition, he and Professor Richard Willstätter "designed the first gas mask used by the German army." He also developed a method of manufacturing synthetic ammonia gas, which allowed Germany to make fertilizers and high explosives. Some claim that without Haber's inventions, the war would not have lasted as long as it did. Ironically, Haber's wife Clara "condemned his work as inhumane and immoral and demanded he stop," but he refused. Soon after the gas he helped develop was used at the battle of Ypres, Clara committed suicide. In 1918 Haber received the Nobel Prize for chemistry and was credited with "discovering a means of mining nitrogen from air," allowing scientists to "manufacture . . . cheap fertilizer—and, of course, gunpowder." When the Nazis came into power, Haber fled to Switzerland, where he died as a refugee. Erik Larson, *In the Garden of Beasts: Love, Terror, and an American Family in Hitler's Berlin* (New York, 2011), 77–79; Heinrich Walle, "Deutsche jüdische Soldaten, 1914–1945. Ein Rundgang durch die Ausstellung," in *Deutsche Jüdische Soldaten, 1914–1945*, ed. Militärgeschichtliches Forschungsamt (Bonn, 1984), 30; Jacob R. Marcus, *The Rise and Destiny of the German Jew* (Cincinnati, OH, 1934), 82; Walter Goerlitz, *The German General Staff, 1657–1945* (New York, 1971), 169–170; Fritz Klein, *Verlorene Größe* (Munich, 1996), 216, 241; David Vital, *A People Apart: The Jews in Europe 1789–1939* (Oxford, 1999), 649. Zyklon B allowed the Germans to kill people more efficiently and without "spilling any blood." The *Einsatzgruppen* personnel, who killed well over a million people, had a difficult time living with their actions; many became alcoholics and unfit for duty. The head of Auschwitz, Rudolf Höss, testified that using gas "set my mind at rest" because it was easier to kill. Höss went on to explain: "Our system is so terrible that no one in the world will believe it to be possible." Unfortunately, Höss was right. It took a long time for the Allies to acknowledge what the Germans were doing to the Jews. Wallance, *America's Soul*, 28, 30.

125. Elie Wiesel, *Night* (New York, 1982), 32.

126. Schneur Zalman, *Tanya* (Brooklyn, NY, 1969), chap. 25.

127. Jacobson, "Journey to America," 10; *Likkutei Dibburim*, 3:57, 80, 225; Berenbaum to Rigg, 28 February 2003, Schneersohn file, BMRS, BA-MA; *Likkutei Dibburim*, 5:276, 305–307, 311.

128. *Likkutei Dibburim*, 3:174, 203. See also ibid., 5:316.

129. Ibid., 3:125–126, 219–225, 230–232.

130. Victor J. Stenger, *God the Failed Hypothesis: How Science Shows That God Does Not Exist* (Amherst, MA, 2007), 208.

131. *Likkutei Dibburim*, 3:219–225; *The Rebbes*, 14; Hoffman, *Despite All Odds*, 26; Kramer, *The Kramers*, 71; M. Greenberg interview; Wineberg interview; Zaklikofsky, *America Is No Different*, 88; H. Rabinowicz, *Hasidism*, 399; Joseph I. Schneersohn, *Lubavitcher Rabbi's Memoirs: The Memoirs of Rabbi Joseph I. Schneersohn, the Late Lubavitcher Rabbi*, vol. 1 (Brooklyn, NY, 1961), xi; H. Greenberg interview; Friedman, *Dare to Survive*, 115.

132. Steven Smith, *Spinoza, Liberalism, and the Question of Jewish Identity* (New Haven, CT, 1997), 31.

133. Besser interview, 15 July 2003; Ehrlich, *Leadership in the HaBaD Movement*, 82, 84, 87, 108, 115–116, 373–374, 387–388; Zaklikofsky, *America Is No Different*, 93; Friedman and Heilman, *Rebbe*, 12, 14, 30–31, 35–36, 254; Telushkin, *Rebbe*, 20; David Berger, *The Rebbe, the Messiah and the Scandal of Orthodox Indifference* (Oxford, 2001), 7. The Rebbe died intestate, so there was a lot of confusion about who should be the next Rebbe, and it eventually came down to his two sons-in-law. Friedman and Heilman speculate that the Rebbe's strong belief in the Messiah's imminent arrival probably led him to defer writing his will or even considering what would happen if he died before the Messiah came. See Friedman and Heilman, *Rebbe*, 33–34. Interestingly, while Chabad was waiting for Menachem Mendel Schneerson to decide whether he would become the next Rebbe, many in the community "circulated a public letter (*pan klah*), which was read aloud at the yeshiva. It was a plea, addressed to all Chasidim, both those in the vicinity and those far away, to entreat the soul of the deceased [Rebbe Schneersohn] to intercede from the other side and influence Menachem Mendel Schneerson to become their leader." Telushkin, *Rebbe*, 34. Note the Lubavitchers' dependence on communing with the dead to make their decisions. For Schneerson's struggle with the decision whether to become the next Rebbe, see ibid., 26–27.

134. Ehrlich, *Leadership in the HaBaD Movement*, 3, 12, 108–109, 117, 259, 359; Sue Fishkoff, *The Rebbe's Army: Inside the World of Chabad-Lubavitch* (New York, 2003), 10–16, 261–284; Lenowitz, *Jewish Messiahs*, 215–223; Friedman and Heilman, *Rebbe*, 12. For a damning take on the Lubavitch community's response to the Rebbe's death, see Berger, *Rebbe*. Just like with his father-in-law's death, the "high hopes" that Menachem was indeed the Messiah "began to dissipate except with the hard-core *meshikhistn* [messianists]." Friedman and Heilman, *Rebbe*, 254; Lenowitz, *Jewish Messiahs*, 215–223; Myers and Alexander, *Faith of Fallen Jews*, 280. In the 1980s Rabbi Elazar Menahe Schach, "the venerable head of one of the major yeshivas in Israel and the rabbinical authority of a significant non-Zionist religious party," foresaw the coming storm if Lubavitch

continued to focus so heavily on the Messiah and the problems for the Rebbe if he continued to hint that he might be the next Messiah. Schach claimed Chabad was practicing *avodah zarah* (idol worship). Berger, *Rebbe*, 7.

CHAPTER 16. THE FATE OF THE RESCUERS

1. Interview with Martin Bloch, 13 October 1996, BMRS, BA-MA.

2. Pers 6/9887, Bl. 19, BA-MA. According to Bloch's military files, he did not become a lieutenant colonel until 1941, but during a trip in November 1940, his office referred to him as lieutenant colonel.

3. Julius Mader, *Hitler Spionagegenerale sagen aus* (Berlin, 1971), 57–66; interview with Ursula Cadenbach, 15 October 1996, BMRS, BA-MA; Pers 6/9887, Bl. 62, 72.

4. Pers 6/9887, Bl. 25; Lt. Col. Bloch to Commander of Abwehr I, Oberst G. Piekenbrock, 7 January 1943, Bloch file, BMRS, BA-MA.

5. Pers 6/9887, Bl. 27, 35, 42; Bloch interview; Cadenbach interview.

6. Heinz Höhne, *Canaris* (New York, 1979), 515–517, 527; Karl Heinz Abshagen, *Canaris* (London, 1956), 223.

7. John Keegan, *The Second World War* (New York, 1990), 468; Matthew Cooper, *German Army 1933–1945: Its Political and Military Failure* (New York, 1978), 458–459; David M. Glantz and Jonathan M. House, *The Battle of Kursk* (Lawrence, KS, 1999), 344–345.

8. Bloch interview; Cadenbach interview.

9. Adolf Ratjen to Bloch, 2 September 1943, Bloch file, BMRS, BA-MA; Ernst to Sabine, 23 and 26 September 1943, Bloch, Feldpost file, BMRS, BA-MA (all correspondence between Bloch and his wife are from this source).

10. Gordon A. Craig, *The Politics of the Prussian Army 1640–1945* (New York, 1964), 154–155; Guy Sajer, *The Forgotten Soldier* (New York, 1971), 302, 337, 373; Ernst to Sabine, 22 September 1943. This quote comes from *Faust*, part 1, "Night." The English translation is from http://www.bartleby.com/345/authors/193.html. See also Charles W. Eliot, ed., *Johann Wolfgang von Goethe: Christopher Marlowe Doctor Faustus*, trans. Anna Swanwick (Danbury, CT, 1982), 30. Bloch's use of this phrase reminds one of Ludwig Wittgenstein's study of the power of language and the importance of using the right words to get one's meaning across. As he wrote: "Most of the propositions and questions of philosophers arise from our failure to understand the logic of our language." *Tractatus Logico-Philosophicus* 4.03, cited in Carlos Muñoz-Suárez, "The Tractatus . . . Is It So Intractable," *Philosophy Now*, November–December 2014. Muñoz-Suárez writes that Wittgenstein introduced a "pioneering view regarding the complex relationships between thought, language and reality" and proposed that these complexities could be solved through "logical analysis of language." Bloch's division apparently took the following path: "Kiev, Yagotin, Rommy, Krolevets,

NOTES TO PAGES 267–272 [423]

Glukhov, Borzna, Nezhin, Nosovka, Chernigov, Zhitomir, Vasilkov." T315M, German Division 213, catalog 118, NARA.

11. Ernst to Sabine, 22 September, 29 October, and 8 December 1943; 24 April, 4 June, and 12 August 1944. General Hell was a highly decroated officer and received the Knight's Cross with Oak Leaves. In the summer of 1944 the Soviets would take him prisoner during the massive battles in Romania; he would finally be released in 1955. General Dostler executed fifteen American commandos in 1944; in 1945 the Allies would find him guilty of war crimes and execute him. http://www.lexikon-der-wehrmacht.de/Personenregister/H/HellEE.htm; http://www.lexikon-der-wehrmacht.de/Personenregister/D/DostlerAnton.htm.

12. Ernst to Sabine, 23 September 1943.

13. Sajer, *Forgotten Soldier*, 316. Although Sajer's work is cited throughout this chapter, it must be used with caution, as some have disputed his claims and his historical accuracy. However, he was indeed on the Russian front, and his often eloquent descriptions of warfare and the experiences of German soldiers in Russia ring true to the research conducted for this book. His book is used by the US Army Command and General Staff College and is on the recommended reading list of the commandant of the US Marine Corps. Moreover, British historian Alan Clark and American historian Stephen Fritz often rely on Sajer to describe the realities of war in Russia.

14. Ibid., 385.

15. 28 September, 2 and 3 October 1943, Bloch, Feldpost file, BMRS, BA-MA.

16. Sajer, *Forgotten Soldier*, 220–221.

17. Pers 6/9887, Bl. 35.

18. 1, 11, 14, and 20 November 1943, Bloch, Feldpost file, BMRS, BA-MA; Cooper, *German Army*, 470–471.

19. 11 November 1943, Bloch, Feldpost file, BMRS, BA-MA.

20. Ibid., 11 and 12 November 1943.

21. Ibid., 14 November 1943; Ian Kershaw, *The Hitler Myth: Image and Reality in the Third Reich* (Oxford, 1990), 211. Bloch got the date wrong in his letter; he said he was quoting Hitler's speech from 9 November 1943, but it was most likely the well-known speech from 8 November. One month earlier, Hitler had claimed, "The National Socialist Party has never allowed itself to be discouraged by setbacks. It is the hard fighting spirit that provides the German people again today with moral backing and support, particularly in the difficult hours of air attacks. We shall strike everywhere and never tire until our aim is reached. If our determination does not falter the war will end in a great German victory." "Hitler's Speech: Not Discouraged by Setbacks," *Kalgoorlie Miner*, 9 October 1943.

22. Kershaw, *Hitler Myth*, 211.

23. Sajer, *Forgotten Soldier*, 194.

24. Ernst to Sabine, 11 and 20 November 1943.

25. Sajer, *Forgotten Soldier*, 103, 110.

26. Ibid., 334; Alan Clark, *Barbarossa: The Russian-German Conflict 1941–1945* (New York, 1965), 181.

27. Ernst to Sabine, 24 November 1943.

28. Stephen G. Fritz, *Frontsoldaten: The German Soldier in World War II* (Lexington, KY, 1995), 31.

29. Ernst to Sabine, 12 November 1943; Cadenbach interview. In his letters from the front, Bloch often mentions the wonderful letters he received from Frau Cadenbach and how his department in the Abwehr is not the same without him.

30. Ernst to Sabine, 16 November 1943; Fritz, *Frontsoldaten*, 31.

31. Ernst to Sabine, 17 and 18 November 1943; Water Kaufmann, ed., *The Portable Nietzsche* (New York, 1968), 467. This phrase comes from *Twilight of the Idols*.

32. Ernst to Sabine, 18 November 1943.

33. Michael Burleigh, *Ethics and Extermination: Reflections on Nazi Genocide* (New York, 1997), 41.

34. Ernst to Sabine, 20 November 1943; Cooper, *German Army*, 470.

35. Ernst to Sabine, 21 November 1943.

36. Bloch mentions Harney often in his letters, and it is obvious Bloch thought a lot of him. He writes that the minister who gave the sermon on the parable will return, and since Harney visited the unit often, he was most likely the preacher in question. Interestingly, Harney was part of the Confessional Church, which broke with the Nazis and was led by men of conscience such as Martin Niemöller and Dietrich Bonhoeffer. See the Internet source "Rudolf Harney-Pfarrer in politisch und theologisch stürmischer Zeit," in *Verein für Rheinische Kirchengeschichte: Monatshefte für Evangelische Kirchengeschichte des Rheinlandes*, Band 57, Düsseldorf, 2008.

37. Philip Yancey and Tim Stafford, commentators, *The Student Bible, New International Version* (Grand Rapids, MI, 1986), 917.

38. Sajer, *Forgotten Soldier*, 203. Sajer also describes a Catholic chaplain who started to live in the moment and engaged in sex with prostitutes. War brought out the worst in some people's characters. Ibid., 219.

39. Matthew Black and H. H. Rowley, eds., *Peake's Commentary on the Bible* (New York, 1963), 837.

40. Alexander Balmain Bruce, *The Parabolic Teaching of Christ: A Systematic and Critical Study of the Parables of Our Lord* (London, 1900), 276, 400.

41. Ernst to Sabine, 21 November 1943.

42. Ibid., 24, 26, 28 November and 5 December 1943; Sajer, *Forgotten Soldier*, 345–346. After fighting around Zhitomir, Bloch's division traveled the following path: "Fastov, Verbov, Zhitomir, Vilsk, Kolodiyevka." T315M, German Division 213, catalog 118, NARA.

43. Ernst to Sabine, 24, 26, 28 November and 5 December 1943.

44. Ibid., 7 and 10 January 1944.

45. Ibid., 7 and 10 January, 2, 24, and 27 April 1944.

46. Sajer, *Forgotten Soldier*, 174.

47. Ernst to Sabine, 7 and 10 January, 2, 24, and 27 April 1944.

48. Gussmann an Hauptverbindungsamt, Pg. Spangenberg, 10 February 1943, NS 18/482, BA-B; Ernst to Sabine, 20, 23, 24 April, 25 May, and 4 June 1944; Reinhard R. Doerries, *Hitler's Last Chief of Foreign Intelligence: Allied Interrogations of Walter Schellenberg* (London, 2003), 105–107; Cooper, *German Army*, 541. Bloch's division took the following path: "Berdichev, Khmelnik, Derazhmya, Proskurov, Lyuboml, Brody." T315M, German Division 213, catalog 118, NARA.

49. Abshagen, *Canaris*, 92; Pers 6/9887, Bl. 35, 39; Cadenbach interview; Ernst to Sabine, 15 September 1943.

50. Hans Eduard Meyer to Sabine Bloch, 20 March 1950, Bloch file, BMRS, BA-MA; Pers 6/9887, Bl. 25; Ernst to Sabine, 11 June 1944.

51. Rotraut Nonnenmann to Sabine Bloch, 19 July 1944, Bloch file, BMRS, BA-MA.

52. H. W. von Goerschen to Sabine Bloch, 26 July 1944, ibid.

53. Ernst to Sabine, 27 July 1944.

54. Ibid., 30 July 1944. Bloch's division traveled from the region of Kovel along the following line: "Sokal, Nemirov, Bilgoraj, Zamosc, Chelm, Sandomierz, Ostrowiec, Kielce." T315M, German Division 213, catalog 118, NARA.

55. Lt. Col. Bloch to Sabine Bloch, 10 April 1945; Pers 6/9887.

56. Pers 6/9887, Bl. 41.

57. Uwe Adam, *Judenpolitik im Dritten Reich* (Düsseldorf, 1972), 331–332; Beate Meyer, *Jüdische Mischlinge. Rassenpolitik und Verfolgungserfahrung 1933–1945* (Hamburg, 1999), 100, 108, 153.

58. Rudolf Absolon, *Wehrgesetz und Wehrdienst 1935–1945. Das Personalwesen in der Wehrmacht* (Boppard, 1960), 119; Bormann an Lammers, 2 November 1944, R 43 II/599, BA-B; R 43II/603b, BA-B.

59. Suchanck to Burgdorf, 15 September 1944, Pers 6/9887, Bl. 41, BA-MA.

60. Burgdorf to Suchanek, 26 September 1944, ibid., Bl. 42 and 43.

61. Ibid., Bl. 44.

62. Anthony Beevor, *The Fall of Berlin 1945* (New York, 2002), 7.

63. Ernst to Sabine, 17 March 1945; Walther Brockhoff to Sabine Bloch, 31 October 1945, Bloch file, BMRS, BA-MA; Bloch interview.

64. Interview with Harald Ettheimer, 2 September 1995, BMRS, BA-MA.

65. Rolf Vogel, *Ein Stück von Uns* (Bonn, 1973), 262.

66. A *Frontführer* or *Bauführer* in the OT was a second lieutenant.

67. Interview with Horst Schmechel, 29 November 1994, BMRS, BA-MA. Schmechel was in several OT camps, including Hazebrouk, Watten, Vizernes, and Boulogne Sur-Mer in France.

68. Interview with Klaus Budzinski, 15 November 1994, BMRS, BA-MA.

69. Niedersächsischer Verband Deutscher Sinti, ed., *"Es war unmenschen möglich." Sinti aus Niedersachsen erzählen—Verfolgung und Vernichtung im Natio-nalsozialismus und Diskriminierung bis heute* (Hannover, 1995), 50, 87. This unit was named after SS Oberführer Oskar Dirlewanger, who was a sadist and a necrophiliac. Clark, *Barbarossa*, 391 n. 3; Keegan, *Second World War*, 482; Heinz Guderian, *Panzer Leader* (Costa Mesa, CA, 1988), 356; "Jews Seized in Nazi Army Ask for Scripture First," *Miami Daily News*, 25 September 1944.

70. Schreiben Chef des Heeres-Personalamts Burgdorf, 3 January 1945, H 6/172, BA-MA; Pers 7786, BA-MA.

71. B. H. Liddell Hart, *The German Generals Talk* (New York, 1979), 178.

72. Adam, *Judenpolitik im Dritten Reich*, 332–333.

73. Ian Kershaw, *Profiles in Power: Hitler* (New York, 1991), 165; Fritz Redlich, *Hitler: Diagnosis of a Destructive Prophet* (Oxford, 1998), 232–234, 275; Werner Maser, *Adolf Hitler. Legende Mythos Wirklichkeit* (Munich, 1971), 376, 394, 402; John Keegan, *The Mask of Command* (New York, 1987), 309.

74. Karl A. Schleunes, *The Twisted Road to Auschwitz: Nazi Policy toward German-Jews 1933–1939* (Champaign, IL, 1970), 3–4; Eberhard Jäckel, *Hitler's Weltanschauung* (Stuttgart, 1981), 78; Kershaw, *Profiles in Power*, 30.

75. Bloch interview. He spoke with Dr. H. Schneider, lawyer Westrick, and banker H. W. von Goerschen.

76. Ernst to Sabine, 10 April and 25 March 1945. For an excellent work on the Volkssturm, see David K. Yelton, *Hitler's Volkssturm: The Nazi Militia and the Fall of Germany 1944–1945* (Lawrence, KS, 2002).

77. Ernst to Sabine, 10 April 1945.

78. http://www.lexikon-der-wehrmacht.de/Personenregister/G/GoeschenAlex .htm; http://www.lexikon-der-wehrmacht.de/Gliederungen/LandschtzReg/Land schtzReg177-R.htm.

79. Beevor, *Fall of Berlin*, 27, 316.

80. Ernst to Sabine, 18 October 1944.

81. Ibid., 16 March 1945.

82. Beevor, *Fall of Berlin*, 1.

83. Bloch interview.

84. Beevor, *Fall of Berlin*, 11, 123, 127, 178, 247, 316.

85. James Megellas, *All the Way to Berlin: A Paratrooper at War in Europe* (New York, 2003), 252–253.

86. Ibid.

87. Beevor, *Fall of Berlin*, 3, 161, 173, 177.

88. Ibid., 11, 147, 155, 177, 346, 424.

89. Timothy Snyder, *Bloodlands: Europe between Hitler and Stalin* (New York, 2010), 416.

90. Ibid., 304; Beevor, *Fall of Berlin*, 28, 31, 107–108, 300, 410; Sajer, *Forgotten Soldier*, 415–416, 421. For an excellently researched book on the sex crimes of the Soviet army, see Ingo von Münch, *Frau, komm! Die Massenvergewaltigungen deutscher Frauen und Mädchen 1944/45* (Graz, Austria, 2009).

91. Interview with Albert Kerscher by historian Colin Heaton, 1985.

92. Beevor, *Fall of Berlin*, 158; Anton Gill, *An Honourable Defeat: A History of German Resistance to Hitler 1933–1945* (New York, 1994), 257; Winston S. Churchill, *The Second World War*, vol. 1, *The Gathering Storm* (Boston, 1983), 348. For information on General Heinrici, see Bryan Mark Rigg, *Hitler's Jewish Soldiers: The Untold Story of Jews and Men of Jewish Descent Who Served in the German Military* (Lawrence, KS, 2002), 166, 186.

93. Beevor, *Fall of Berlin*, 262.

94. Pfeiffer to Bloch, 6 April 1945, Bloch file, BMRS, BA-MA.

95. Bloch interview; Cadenbach interview; Register's Officer Berlin to Karl Preis, 1 November 1946, Bloch file, BMRS, BA-MA.

96. Beevor, *Fall of Berlin*, 335.

97. Karl Preis to Sabine Bloch, 24 October 1946, Bloch file, BMRS, BA-MA.

98. Beevor, *Fall of Berlin*, 431.

99. Höhne, *Canaris*, 465, 489, 524; Abshagen, *Canaris*, 84, 90.

100. Höhne, *Canaris*, 466; Abshagen, *Canaris*, 108, 122–123. For the number of Jews rescued, see Dept. of State to American Legation in Riga, 13 January 1940, General Records of Department of State, Itinerary 705, Visa Case Files 1933–1940, 811.111, Joseph Schneersohn, Record Group 59, NARA. This document indicates that at least thirty Jews were saved. See also Martin Gilbert, *The Righteous: The Unsung Heroes of the Holocaust* (New York, 2003), 184–185. For an excellent work about Canaris's efforts to help Jews, see Winfried Meyer, *Unternehmen Sieben. Eine Rettungsaktion für vom Holocaust Bedrohte aus dem Amt Ausland-Abwehr im Oberkommando der Wehrmacht* (Frankfurt, 1993).

101. Höhne, *Canaris*, 557–563, 569; Abshagen, *Canaris*, 11, 191, 238–239, 240.

102. Höhne, *Canaris*, 571, 583–584, 594, 596–598; Bürkner to Wohlthat, 15 January 1948, 100021/49193, Bl. 55F, Hessisches Hauptstaatsarchiv, Düsseldorf, Germany; David Kahn, *Hitler's Spies: German Military Intelligence in World War II* (New York, 1977), 235–236; Abshagen, *Canaris*, 246–257; André Brissaud, *Canaris* (London, 1986), 2; Gill, *Honourable Defeat*, 252, 258; Eric Metaxas, *Bonhoeffer: Pastor, Martyr, Prophet, Spy* (Nashville, TN, 2010), 529.

103. Interview with Hans Baur by historian Colin Heaton, 1985.

104. Höhne, *Canaris*, 571, 583–584, 594, 596–598; Bürkner to Wohlthat, 15 January 1948; Kahn, *Hitler's Spies*, 235–236; Abshagen, *Canaris*, 246–257; Brissaud, *Canaris*, 2; Gill, *Honourable Defeat*, 252, 258; Metaxas, *Bonhoeffer*, 529.

105. Telephone interview with Gisela Bauer, 27 September 2014; Gisela Bauer, *Graue Wahrheit: Schizophrenie—eine heilbare unheilbare Krankheit* (Frankfurt, 2004), 128–130; Gisela Bauer to Bryan Mark Rigg, 13 September 2014, Bloch

file, BMRS, BA-MA; Günter Schubert, *Der Fleck auf Uncle Sams weißer Weste: Amerika und die jüdischen Flüchtlinge 1938–1945* (Frankfurt, 2003), 96 n. 2.

CHAPTER 17. WHAT WOULD HAVE HAPPENED IF HITLER HAD WON THE WAR?

1. Ursula Büttner, "The Persecution of Christian-Jewish Families in the Third Reich," *Leo Baeck Yearbook* 34 (1989): 288.

2. *The Holocaust*, vol. 1, *Legalizing the Holocaust—The Early Phase, 1933–1939* (New York, 1982), 31.

3. Hans Globke and Wilhelm Stuckart, *Kommentare zur Deutschen Rassengesetzgebung* (Munich, 1936), 17.

4. A. Rüter-Ehlermann and C. F. Rüter, eds., *Sammlung deutscher Strafurteile wegen nationalsozialistischer Tötungsverbrechen* (Amsterdam, 1968–1981), Bd. 6, 406.

5. Karl A. Schleunes, *The Twisted Road to Auschwitz: Nazi Policy toward German-Jews 1933–1939* (Champaign, IL, 1970), 130.

6. Office of the United States Chief Counsel for Prosecution of Axis Criminality, ed., *U.S.A. Military Tribunals: Case No. 11.2* (Nuremberg, 1949), 125.

7. Hildebrandt to Himmler, 17 March 1943, NS 19/1047, Bl. 2–3, BA-B; Jeremy Noakes, "The Development of Nazi Policy towards the German-Jewish 'Mischlinge,' 1933–1945," *Leo Baeck Yearbook* 34 (1989): 339–340.

8. NS 19/1047, Bl. 10, BA-MA; Peter Adam, *Art of the Third Reich* (New York, 1992), 328.

9. Nathan Stoltzfus, *Resistance of the Heart: Intermarriage and the Rosenstrasse Protest in Nazi Germany* (London, 2001), 57.

10. *Akten der Parteikanzlei der NSDAP: Rekonstruktion eines verlorengegangenen Bestandes* (Munich, Bundesarchiv, Microfiches, hrsg. v. Institut für Zeitgeschichte, 1983), 107-00409-410.

11. Eichmann Prosecution Document, Police d'Israel Quartier General 6-ème Bureau No. 1102, Der Reichsminister für die besetzten Ostgebiete (Schmitz), 30 January 1942, IfZ; Hefte N-71-73, Dr. Feldscher, betr. "Verschärfung des Judenbegriffs," 13 August 1941, IfZ; NS 19/1772, Bl. 2, BA-B; *The Holocaust*, vol. 2, *Legalizing the Holocaust—The Later Phase, 1939–1943* (New York, 1982), 103; Noakes, "Development of Nazi Policy," 344–345.

12. Raul Hilberg, *Destruction of the European Jews* (New York, 1961), 309.

13. Noakes, "Development of Nazi Policy," 338; Kurt Pätzold, ed., *Verfolgung, Vertreibung, Vernichtung. Dokumente des faschistischen Antisemitismus 1933 bis 1942* (Leipzig, 1984), 249, 264–265.

14. Rüter-Ehlermann and Rüter, *Sammlung deutscher Strafurteile*, 15.

15. Victor Klemperer, *Ich will Zeugnis ablegen bis zum letzten, 1933–1945* (Berlin, 1996), 377, 475.

16. Hannah Arendt, *Eichmann in Jerusalem: A Report on the Banality of Evil*

(New York, 1964), 174. One half-Jew who escaped from Denmark was the famous scientist Niels Bohr, who later found his way to the United States and worked on the atomic bomb project.

17. Testimony of witness Charlotte Salzburger née Wreschner, in *The Trial of Adolf Eichmann: Record of Proceedings in the District Court of Jerusalem*, ed., State of Israel Ministry of Justice (Jerusalem, 1992), vol. 7, sess. 42, 752; Bernhard Lösener, "Als Rassereferent im Reichsministerium des Innern," in Das Reichsministerium des Innern und die Judengesetzgebung, *Vierteljahreshefte für Zeitgeschichte* 9 (1961): 299–302; Eichmann Prosecution Document, Police d'Israel Quartier General 6-ème Bureau No. 1102, Der Reichsminister für die besetzten Ostgebiete (Schmitz), 30 January 1942, Aufzeichnung, 2–3; Reichsminister für die besetzten Ostgebiete, 2 May 1942, NS 19/1772, Bl. 2, BA-B; Yehuda Bauer, *A History of the Holocaust* (New York, 1982), 229; Der Judenbegriff in den besetzten Gebieten, N 71–73, IfZ; Gideon Hausner, *Justice in Jerusalem* (New York, 1966), 256; Beate Meyer, *Jüdische Mischlinge. Rassenpolitik und Verfolgungserfahrung 1933–1945* (Hamburg, 1999), 9; H. G. Adler, *Der Verwaltete Mensch. Studien zur Deportation der Juden aus Deutschland* (Tübingen, 1974), 283–284; Mark Roseman, *The Villa, the Lake, the Meeting: Wannsee and the Final Solution* (New York, 2002), 83, 100.

18. See Stoltzfus, *Resistance of the Heart*; Marion A. Kaplan, *Between Dignity and Despair: Jewish Life in Nazi Germany* (New York, 1998), 149, 193.

19. Dieter Maier, *Arbeitseinsatz und Deportation. Die Mitwirkung der Arbeitsverwaltung bei der nationalsozialistischen Judenverfolgung in den Jahren, 1938–1945* (Berlin, 1994), 203; Dieter Rebentisch, *Führerstaat und Verwaltung im Zweiten Weltkrieg. Verfassungsentwicklung und Verwaltungspolitik, 1939–1945* (Stuttgart, 1989), 439.

20. Robert Jay Lifton, *The Nazi Doctors* (New York, 1986), 56.

21. Ian Kershaw, *Hitler 1936–1945: Nemesis* (New York, 2000), 486; Arendt, *Eichmann in Jerusalem*, 96.

22. Hilberg, *Destruction of the European Jews*, 296 n. 164. Müller became head of the Gestapo in 1939 under Himmler. Robert Gellately, *The Gestapo and German Society: Enforcing Racial Policy* (Oxford, 1990), 55.

23. David Roskies, ed., *The Literature of Destruction: Jewish Responses to Catastrophe* (New York, 1989); Chaim A. Kaplan, *Scroll of Agony: The Warsaw Diary of Chaim A. Kaplan* (New York, 1965), 446.

24. Stoltzfus, *Resistance of the Heart*, 184–186.

25. Ernst Klee, *Euthanasie im NS-Staat: Die Vernichtung lebensunwerten Lebens* (Frankfurt, 1985), 419; Noakes, "Development of Nazi Policy," 348; George Victor, *Hitler: The Pathology of Evil* (Dulles, VA, 1998), 172; Gerhard L. Weinberg, *Germany, Hitler, and World War II* (New York, 1996); Adler, *Der Verwaltete Mensch*, 16.

26. *Der Stürmer*, 9 November 1944.

27. Bauer, *History of the Holocaust*, 190–191; Büttner, "Persecution of Christian-Jewish Families," 289; Cynthia Crane, *Divided Lives: The Untold Stories of Jewish-Christian Women in Nazi Germany* (New York, 2000), 30.

28. *Trial of Adolf Eichmann*, vol. 2, sec. 42, 755; Hanns-Heinz Bauer file, BMRS, BA-MA; interview with Hanns-Heinz Bauer, 29 March 1998, BMRS, BA-MA.

29. Hans Kirchholtes file, Bl. 4, BMRS, BA-MA.

30. Wolf Zuelzer, "Keine Zukunft als 'Nicht-Arier' im Dritten Reich," in *Der Judenpogrom 1938: Von der Reichskristallnacht zum Völkermord*, ed. Walter H. Pehle (Frankfurt am Main, 1988), 154.

31. Interview with Hans Döppes, 19 May 1996; Bauer interview; interview with Friedemann Lichtwitz, 18 July 1997; interview with Rolf Schenk, 23 May 1997; Herbert Simon file, Bl. 11; Erik Blumenfeld file; Helmuth Rosenbaum file, Bl. 9; Werner Eisner file, all in BMRS, BA-MA; Meyer, *Jüdische Mischlinge*, 236, 251, 469; Hans A. Schmitt, *Quakers and Nazis: Inner Light in Outer Darkness* (Columbia, MO, 1997), 174–175; Adler, *Der Verwaltete Mensch*, 320; Alison Owings, *Frauen: German Women Recall the Third Reich* (New Brunswick, NJ, 1995), 48.

32. Ian Kershaw, *Hitler 1889–1936: Hubris* (New York, 1999), 487; Fritz Redlich, *Hitler: Diagnosis of a Destructive Prophet* (Oxford, 1998), 111; Norbert Frei, *National Socialist Rule in Germany* (Cambridge, 1993), 122; Lifton, *Nazi Doctors*, 27; Georg Denzler and Volker Fabricius, *Die Kirchen im Dritten Reich* (Frankfurt, 1984), 112–113.

33. Interview with Hans-Oskar Löwenstein de Witt, 6 December 1994, BMRS, BA-MA; Alfred Posselt, *Soldat des Feindes* (Vienna, 1993), 18–19.

34. Bier an Rigg, 26 March 2001, Gerhard Bier file, BMRS, BA-MA.

35. Bauer, *History of the Holocaust*, 206.

36. Interview with Fritz Steinwasser, 13 December 1994 and 7 February 1997, BMRS, BA-MA.

37. Ian Kershaw, *The Hitler Myth: Image and Reality in the Third Reich* (Oxford, 1990), 238–240, 250–251; Martin Gilbert, *The Holocaust* (New York, 1985), 73–75; William Sheridan Allen, "Die deutsche Öffentlichkeit und die 'Reichskristallnacht'—Konflikte zwischen Werthierarchie und Propaganda im Dritten Reich," in *Die Reihen fest geschlossen. Beiträge zur Geschichte des Alltags unterm Nationalsozialismus* (Wuppertal, Germany, 1981), 397–411; Hilberg, *Destruction of the European Jews*, 29; Kaplan, *Between Dignity and Despair*, 148.

38. Redlich, *Hitler*, 156; Jochen von Lang, *The Secretary: Martin Bormann* (New York, 1979), 221; Noakes, "Development of Nazi Policy," 354; Jeremy Noakes and Geoffrey Pridham, eds., *Nazism 1919–1945* (Exeter, UK, 1983), vol. 3, 1031–1043; Denzler and Fabricius, *Die Kirchen im Dritten Reich*, 98, 116–132; Rebentisch, *Führerstaat und Verwaltung*, 431; Victor, *Hitler*, 93, 172. More than 70,000 mentally ill and deformed patients were murdered under this program.

See Ian Kershaw, *Profiles in Power: Hitler* (New York, 1991), 141; Kershaw, *Hitler 1936–1945*, 261, 427–430; Redlich, *Hitler*, 154; Stoltzfus, *Resistance of the Heart*, 15, 145; Robert Gellately, *Backing Hitler: Consent and Coercion in Nazi Germany* (Oxford, 2001), 103. Gellately notes that Hitler might have thought it was a good time to stop the euthanasia program because the staff was needed for the extermination now taking place in the east.

39. In February 1943 Goebbels ordered about 2,000 Jews living with Aryan spouses arrested and deported. However, wives, children, family, and friends in Berlin protested day and night for a week—sometimes numbering close to 6,000 protesters. Amazingly, the Nazi regime relented under this pressure and freed the Jews in March. See Nathan Stoltzfus, "Widerstand des Herzens," in *Geschichte und Gesellschaft. Zeitschrift für Historische Sozialwissenschaft 21. Jahrgang/Heft 2 April–Juni 1995, Protest und Widerstand* (Göttingen, 1995), 218–247; Stoltzfus, *Resistance of the Heart*, xvi–xxii; Noakes, "Development of Nazi Policy," 354; Weinberg, *Germany, Hitler, and World War II*, 231; interview with Werner Goldberg, 17 October 1994, BMRS, BA-MA; interview with Elisabeth Behrend, 3 March 1997, BMRS, BA-MA; Meyer, *Jüdische Mischlinge*, 57; Schmitt, *Quakers and Nazis*, 175; Richard J. Evans, *Lying about Hitler: History, Holocaust, and the David Irving Trial* (New York, 2001), 84; Owings, *Frauen*, 462; Louis P. Lochner, ed., *Goebbels Diaries* (New York, 1948), 276, 288, 294.

40. Roseman, *Villa*, 53.

41. Arendt, *Eichmann in Jerusalem*, 159; Schmitt, *Quakers and Nazis*, 174.

42. Interview with Reiner Wiehl, 17 May 1996, BMRS, BA-MA.

43. Interview with Robert Braun, 10–14 October 1994, 7 January 1996, BMRS, BA-MA.

44. Wilhelm Dröscher file, BMRS, BA-MA.

CONCLUSION

1. Rhoade to Kramer, 17 January 1940, Schneersohn folder 2, Bloch file, BMRS, BA-MA.

2. Rhoade to Kramer, 25 October 1939, Neumark folder, Bloch file, BMRS, BA-MA.

3. Hasia R. Diner, *Jews in America* (New York, 1999), 90; Carl Hermann Voss, *Rabbi and Minister: The Friendship of Stephen S. Wise and John Haynes Holmes* (Buffalo, NY, 1980), 289; David Kertzer, *The Pope and Mussolini: The Secret History of Pius XI and the Rise of Fascism in Europe* (Oxford, 2014), 224, 249. Rabbi Stephen Wise was called a "Christ-Killer" and an "anti-Christ" for criticizing Father Coughlin. See Voss, *Rabbi and Minister*, 289.

4. David Wyman, *The Abandonment of the Jews: America and the Holocaust 1941–1945* (New York, 1989), 315.

5. Saul S. Friedman, *No Haven for the Oppressed: United States Policy toward Jewish Refugees, 1938–1945* (Detroit, 1973), 50.

6. John Morton Blum, *V Was for Victory: Politics and American Culture during World War II* (New York, 1976), 176–177; Henry L. Feingold, *The Politics of Rescue: The Roosevelt Administration and the Holocaust, 1938–1945* (New Brunswick, NJ, 1970), 15; Gregory Wallance, *America's Soul in the Balance: The Holocaust, FDR's State Department, and the Moral Disgrace of an American Aristocracy* (Austin, TX, 2012), 134.

7. Unsigned letter by a coward to Roosevelt, 1 September 1941, OF 76c, box 7, FDR Library.

8. Deborah E. Lipstadt, *Beyond Belief: The American Press & the Coming of the Holocaust 1933–1945* (New York, 1986), 2, 91–93, 97, 115.

9. Barringer to Roosevelt, 30 June 1941, and Early to Roosevelt, 29 July 1941, OF 76c, box 7, FDR Library.

10. Stephen Wise, *Challenging Years: The Autobiography of Stephen Wise* (New York, 1949), 228; Conrad Black, *Franklin Delano Roosevelt: Champion of Freedom* (New York, 2003), 156.

11. Wise, *Challenging Years*, 232; Feingold, *Politics of Rescue*, 15–18; Rafael Medoff and David Wyman, *A Race against Death: Peter Bergson, America, and the Holocaust* (New York, 2002), 45, 47, 187–188, 192, 195, 200; Feingold, *Politics of Rescue*, 180–1; Yehuda Bauer, *A History of the Holocaust* (New York, 1982), 316–317; Wallance, *America's Soul*, 120.

12. Wallance, *America's Soul*, 170.

13. Ibid., 245, 248.

14. Interview with Dr. David Woolner of the Franklin/Eleanor Research Institute, Hyde Park, New York, 18 September 2003.

15. Wyman, *Abandonment of the Jews*, 183; Wallance, *America's Soul*, 255.

16. Interview with Karl Wolff by Colin Heaton, 1984.

17. Dors Kearns Goodwin, *No Ordinary Time: Franklin and Eleanor Roosevelt—The Home Front in World War II* (New York, 1994), 396; Ted Morgan, *FDR: A Biography* (New York, 1985); Wallance, *America's Soul*, 128.

18. Wyman, *Abandonment of the Jews*, xv. Yerushalmi wrote less aggressively that the Allies basically "abandoned the Jews in Nazi Europe to their fate," claiming that leaders at this time were simply indifferent to the victims' fate. David N. Myers and Kaye Alexander, eds., *The Faith of Fallen Jews: Yosef Hayim Yerushalmi and the Writing of Jewish History* (Waltham, MA, 2014), 268.

19. Kertzer, *Pope and Mussolini*, 489 n. 12.

20. See James S. Corum, *The Roots of Blitzkrieg: Hans von Seeckt and German Military Reform* (Lawrence, KS, 1992).

21. Jonathan Steinberg, *All or Nothing: The Axis and the Holocaust 1941–1943* (New York, 1991), 180.

22. Wyman, *Abandonment of the Jews*, 103.

23. William Safire, "Truman on Underdogs," *New York Times*, 14 July 2003; Voss, *Rabbi and Minister*, 320.

24. See Wallance, *America's Soul.* The people listed in this paragraph are mentioned all throughout Wallance's book.

25. Friedman, *No Haven*, 143.

26. Based on countless talks with Lubavitchers, including Rabbis Zaklikovsky, Laber, and Shmotkin.

27. Efraim Zuroff, "Orthodox Rescue Revisited," *Jewish Action* 63, 3 (Spring 2003): 37.

28. David Kranzler, "Stephen S. Wise and the Holocaust," in *Reverence, Righteousness, and Rahamanut: Essays in Memory of Rabbi Dr. Leo Jung*, ed. Jacob J. Schacter (New York, 1992), 170, 191.

29. Wallance, *America's Soul*, 231, 274.

30. Medoff and Wyman, *Race against Death*, 12; Wyman, *Abandonment of the Jews*, 285; Pehle to Kalmanowitz, 8 and 19 December 1944, folder 132, box 21, YU-VHC; Feingold, *Politics of Rescue*, 269–270. Interestingly, William Rubinstein claims that Hitler would not agree to release any Jews after late 1940, but this document proves that this is indeed what happened. Rubinstein says Wyman's claim of the number saved by the WRB is exaggerated by "at least 90 per cent." However, he does not provide any data to support his position. William D. Rubinstein, "The Myth of Rescue," in *The Holocaust: Problems and Perspectives of Interpretation*, ed. Donald L. Niewyk (New York, 2003), 237. See Morgenthau to Vaad, 8 July 1944, box 130, YU-VHC; George Warren to the Vaad, 2 November 1944, folder 123, box 20, YU-VHC; Lipstadt, *Beyond Belief*, 263; Walter LaFeber, *The American Age: United States Foreign Policy at Home and Abroad since 1750* (New York, 1989), 368; Michael Berenbaum, *The World Must Know: The History of the Holocaust as Told in the United States Holocaust Memorial Museum* (Baltimore, 2007), 165; Wallance, *America's Soul*, 271.

31. Berenbaum, *World Must Know*, 165.

32. Kranzler, "Wise and the Holocaust," 182–183.

33. Zuroff, "Orthodox Rescue Revisited," 36–37; Michael Beschloss, *The Conquerors: Roosevelt, Truman and the Destruction of Hitler's Germany 1941–1945* (New York, 2002), 53.

34. *A Decade of American Foreign Policy: Basic Documents, 1941-1949.* Prepared at the request of the Senate Committee on Foreign Relations by the staff of the committee and the Department of State (Washington, DC: Government Printing Office, 1950); "War Crimes Trials Records of Case II, *United States of America v. Erhard Milch*" (National Archives and Records Service, General Services Administration, Washington, DC, 1975), 1; Kalmanowitz to Berle, 4 August 1944, box 20, folder 123, YU-VHC.

35. Wallance, *America's Soul*, 135–136.

36. Rhoade to Kramer, 17 January 1940, Schneersohn folder 2, Bloch file, BMRS, BA-MA.

37. Berenbaum, *World Must Know*, 53.

38. Wyman, *Abandonment of the Jews*, 184–185, 191. For example, in June 1941 ambassador of the Polish government-in-exile Jan Ciechanowski delivered a white paper to Hull "charging the Nazis with 'compulsory euthanasia' against the Jews," yet Hull did not act. Friedman, *No Haven*, 135. Hull would often have files related to the refugee issue "routed away" from his office. Irwin Gellman, *Secret Affairs: Franklin Roosevelt, Cordell Hull, and Sumner Welles* (Baltimore, 1995), 346.

39. Beschloss, *Conquerors*, 53. See also Neil Rolde, *Breckinridge Long: American Eichmann* (Solon, ME, 2013), 13.

40. Wallance, *America's Soul*, 77.

41. Schneersohn to Hull, 25 March 1940, General Records of Department of State, Itinerary 705, Visa Case Files 1933–1940, 811.111, Joseph Schneersohn, Record Group 59, NARA (hereafter cited as Visa Case Files 1933–1940 and the case name).

42. Wallance, *America's Soul*, 78.

43. Meeting of Officers of the Inter-Governmental Committee on Political Refugees, 17 October 1939, 5, OF 3186, box 2, FDR Library.

44. Feingold, *Politics of Rescue*, 166, 233, 295–296.

45. Donald L. Niewyk, "Holocaust: The Genocide of the Jews," in *Century of Genocide: Critical Essays and Eyewitness Accounts*, ed. Israel W. Charny, William S. Parsons, and Samuel Totten (New York, 2004), 139.

46. Friedman, *No Haven*, 83. See also Lipstadt, *Beyond Belief*, 95.

47. Bauer, *History of the Holocaust*, 281.

48. Feingold, *Politics of Rescue*, 49.

49. Henry L. Feingold, *Bearing Witness: How America and Its Jews Responded to the Holocaust* (Syracuse, NY, 1995), 68, 78.

50. Iris Chang, *The Rape of Nanking: The Forgotten Holocaust of World War II* (New York, 1997), 4, 6, 87, 91, 103, 155. Historian Richard Frank suggests that Chang's figure of 300,000 is too high for Nanking alone. He agrees that this number probably reflects all the Chinese citizens raped and killed by the Japanese, starting with their departure from Shanghai to their ultimate conquest of Nanking. He points out that the Japanese army was sent out on this campaign without any food or supply chain. Even though that is no justification for the crimes they committed, the fact that the soldiers had to pillage every town they entered for food and water only added to the brutalization by the Japanese troops. Conversation with Richard Frank at Iwo Jima, Japan, 21 March 2015.

51. Chang, *Rape of Nanking*, 222.

52. Dominic Green, "When Hitler Looked East," *Wall Street Journal*, 16 January 2015.

53. André Brissaud, *Canaris* (London, 1986), 153.

54. Primo Levi, *Moments of Reprieve: A Memoir of Auschwitz* (New York, 1995), 62.

55. Cadenbach to Martin Bloch, 16 November 1996, Bloch file, BMRS, BA-MA.

56. James Tent to Bryan Mark Rigg, 12 March 2003.

57. Anton Gill, *An Honourable Defeat: A History of German Resistance to Hitler 1933–1945* (New York, 1994), 37.

58. Ernst to Sabine, 14 November 1943, Bloch, Feldpost file, BMRS, BA-MA.

59. Nonnenmann to Sabine Bloch, 24 February 1950, Bloch file, BMRS, BA-MA.

60. Interview with Martin Bloch, 13 October 1996, BMRS, BA-MA.

61. Karl Heinz Abshagen, *Canaris* (London, 1956), 92.

62. Bryan Mark Rigg, *Hitler's Jewish Soldiers: The Untold Story of Jews and Men of Jewish Descent Who Served in the German Military* (Lawrence, KS, 2002), 272.

63. For short biographies on Milch and Rogge, see Bryan Mark Rigg, *Lives of Hitler's Jewish Soldiers: Untold Tales of Men of Jewish Descent Who Fought for the Third Reich* (Lawrence, KS, 2009), 171–192.

64. Walter Laqueur, "The Failure to Comprehend," in Niewyk, *Holocaust: Problems and Perspectives*, 260–262.

65. "Progressives and Disorder: The Next Two Years May Be the Most Dangerous since the Cold War Ended," *Wall Street Journal*, 31 December 2014.

66. This comes from the Talmudic Tractate *Sanhedrin* 37a or *Baba Batra*, 11-a; Medoff and Wyman, *Race against Death*, 115, 246 n. 17. See also George Robinson, *Essential Judaism: A Complete Guide to Beliefs, Customs, and Rituals* (New York, 2000), 200; Uri Kaploun, ed., *Likkutei Dibburim: An Anthology of Talks by Rabbi Yosef Yitzchak Schneersohn of Lubavitch*, 5 vols. (Brooklyn, NY, 1987–2000), 1:136.

67. Dept. of State to American Legation in Riga, 13 January 1940, Visa Case Files 1933–1940, Joseph Schneersohn. This document indicates that at least thirty Jews were saved: eleven rabbis and their wives and children. However, based on a document from Hull's office, only eighteen individuals boarded the *Drottningholm* in 1940, headed for America. For information about them, see telegram from American Legation in Riga to Secretary of State Hull, 18 March 1940, Visa Case Files 1933–1940, Joseph Schneersohn.

68. Discussion with Bruce Blumberg, 17 August 2014; e-mail from Ann Groer to Bryan Rigg, 6 September 2014.

69. Memorandum of conversion between Benjamin V. Cohen and Robert T. Pell, 3 October 1939, 360 C.60P, 15/4, WNRC.

70. Viktor Frankl, *Man's Search for Meaning: An Introduction to Logotherapy* (New York, 1984), 19.

71. Of course, Rhoade knew that immigration authorities worked with public health officers attached to consulates and that once the Rebbe arrived at Ellis Island, he would have to undergo another medical exam. However, there is no record in the National Archives that the Rebbe was ever examined. Clearly, Rhoade was worried about this, as indicated in a letter he wrote to Sam Kramer, but how they got around this obstacle and why it never came up in the State Department's investigations remains a mystery. Rhoade to S. Kramer, 25 October 1939, Neumark folder, Bloch file, BMRS, BA-MA. For other immigrants who were denied access due to medical issues, see Visa Case Files 1933–1940, Hans Jacobsohn, Mayer Jacobsohn, Anna Schmucker, Israel Cohen (under Cohen, Brajna), and Izrael Cohen.

72. http://www.uscis.gov/working-united-states/permanent-workers/employ ment-based-immigration-fifth-preference-eb-5/eb-5-immigrant-investor.

73. Burton Barton, "Hopper and Dropper, Musing from Entrepreneur and Investor Rich Barton: My Trip through the Clinton Global Initiative—America Meeting, 27 June 2014"; Daniel Gonzalez, "Paths to Immigration Reform Will Be Bumpy," *Republic*, 3 February 2013; AQOnline, "Mitt Romney Courts Latinos at Univision 'Meet the Candidates' Forum," *Americas Quarterly*, 20 September 2012.

74. Robert A. Divine, T. H. Breen, George M. Fredrickson, and R. Hal Williams, *America: Past and Present* (London, 1987), 563.

75. Bryan Mark Rigg, "Where They Are Now: Civil Disobedience (Issuing of the U.S. Postal Stamp in Honor of Robert Kim Bingham)," *Yale Alumni Magazine*, May–June 2006.

76. Levi, *Moments of Reprieve*, 128.

77. Berenbaum, *World Must Know*, xxi.

AFTERWORD
1. Sue Fishkoff, *The Rebbe's Army: Inside the World of Chabad-Lubavitch* (New York, 2003), 7.

2. Avrum M. Ehrlich, *Leadership in the HaBaD Movement: A Critical Evaluation of HaBaD Leadership, History, and Succession* (New York, 2000), 6, 61. Several Lubavitchers have claimed in public that they do not think Rebbe Menachem Mendel Schneerson is the Messiah, even though they privately believe that he is. According to David Berger, the majority of Chabad believes the Rebbe is indeed the Messiah. See David Berger, *The Rebbe, the Messiah and the Scandal of Orthodox Indifference* (Oxford, 2001), 2. One who agrees with Berger is Robert M. Price, "Jesus: Myth and Method," in *The Christian Delusion: Why Faith Fails*, ed. John W. Loftus (New York, 2010), 282. Lubavitchers also have different public and private views about non-Jews. Although many have distanced themselves from the belief that Gentile souls are inferior, their philosophy teaches that Gentiles are dramatically inferior to Jews. As the Rebbe's newspaper wrote in

December 1941, "But in general and as a nation, as a whole, we are always better than the other nations." It explained in June 1942 that the cause of anti-Semitism was that people "begrudged the Jew his enviable higher position." *Hakreah Vehakedusha* [Reading and Holiness] 2, 15 (December 1941): 2; 2, 21 (June 1942): 1. Chabad believes that Jews have both "animal" and "divine" souls, whereas Gentiles have only "animal" souls. According to historian Roman Foxbrunner, the Lubavitchers believe that Gentile souls are of an "inferior order" and "totally evil with no redeeming qualities whatsoever." These souls "were created only to test, to punish, to elevate, and ultimately to serve Israel (in the Messianic Era)." Roman A. Foxbrunner, *HABAD: The Hasidism of R. Shneur Zalman of Lyady* (Tuscaloosa, AL, 1992), 108–109. Lubavitch philosophy teaches that a divine soul takes man closer to God, while an animal soul drags him down. According to the founder of Chabad, Rebbe Schneur Zalman, only Jews have divine souls because they are the "descendants of the righteous patriarchs." Gentile souls die with the bodies, whereas Jewish souls are eternal. Most of these ideas come from Zalman's book *Tanya* (Brooklyn, NY, 1969). For example: "For in the case of Israel, this soul of the *kelipah* [animal soul] is derived from *kelipat nogah*, which also contains good, as it originates in the esoteric 'Tree of Knowledge of Good and Evil.' The souls of the nations of the world [Gentiles], however, emanate from the other, unclean *kelipot* which contain no good whatever. . . . 'The kindness of the nations is sin'—that all the charity and kindness done by the nations of the world is only for their own self-glorification." Ibid., 23–24. According to one rabbi, *Tanya* "is quoting the Talmud, basic Jewish law. It's not a question against Chabad, but against Judaism, as a whole. As is often the case, Chabad is now defending normative Jewish thought, a position it is comfortable with, but which requires a fair chance and adequate time to achieve properly." Eli S. to Rigg, 6 January 2004, Schneersohn folder 6, BMRS, BA-MA. When confronted with this debate, Rabbi Eliezer Zaklikovsky wrote that the claim that Gentiles have only animal souls "is absolutely absurd." Zaklikovsky to Rigg, 4 January 2004, ibid. Zaklikovsky's seems to be the prevalent view among Lubavitchers today. Many groups believe they are superior physically, intellectually, or spiritually, so Chabad philosophy on this matter is not unusual. See also Fishkoff, *Rebbe's Army*, 7; Louis Jacobs, *The Jewish Religion: A Companion* (New York, 1995), 205, 464.

3. Ehrlich, *Leadership in the HaBaD Movement*, 5–6, 292–295; interview with Herschel Greenberg, 23 February 2004.

4. Eli S. to Rigg, 6 January 2004. Although Eli S. helped me a lot at first, when he disagreed with some of the facts in my work, he declined to provide any further assistance and refused to show me documents he had found in the meantime that might have changed some of my conclusions in this book. He indicated that when this book was published he would use these document to "defend his movement." Although I repeatedly asked to see these "valuable" documents, he denied me access to them. Discussion with Eli S., 30 January 2004. Had he shown

me these documents and proved their merits, I would have used them. Since 2004, I have yet to see or hear anything about these documents.

5. Samuel Moyn, "History's Revenge: What Happened to Jewish Faith When a New Attitude toward the Past Emerged?" *Forward*, 9 January 2004. Moyn reviews David N. Myers's *Resisting History: Historicism and Its Discontents in German-Jewish Thought*.

6. Despite their earlier kindness, I am sure that if they read this book they would change their opinions, since it is not in line with their religious beliefs.

7. Christopher Hitchens, *God Is Not Great: How Religion Poisons Everything* (New York, 2007), 64.

8. Quoted in Richard Dawkins, *The God Delusion* (New York, 2006), 29.

9. Michael Berenbaum, *The World Must Know: The History of the Holocaust as Told in the United States Holocaust Memorial Museum* (Baltimore, 2007), 192.

10. John M. Barry, *Roger Williams and the Creation of the American Soul: Church, State, and the Birth of Liberty* (New York, 2012).

BIBLIOGRAPHY

ARCHIVAL SOURCES

Louis Brandeis Archives, Louisville School of Law, Louisville, Kentucky
  Max Rhoade Papers
Bundesarchiv, Berlin (BA-B), Germany
Bundesarchiv/Militärarchiv (BA-MA), Freiburg, Germany
Chabad-Lubavitch & Agudath Israel World Organization
Hessisches Hauptstaatsarchiv, Düsseldorf, Germany
Institut für Zeitgeschichte (IfZ), Munich, Germany
Kleinman Holocaust Education Center (KHEC), Brooklyn, New York
  Jacob Rosenheim Diary
  Michael G. Tress Collection
National Archives and Records Administration (NARA), Washington, DC
Nuremberg Trials Documents
Reichsgesetzblatt (RGBL), I (1935), BA-MA
Franklin D. Roosevelt Library, Hyde Park, New York
  Papers of Eleanor Roosevelt
Washington National Records Center (WNRC), Suitland, Maryland
Yeshiva University Archives, Vaad Hatzala Collection 1939–1963 (YU-VHC),
  New York, New York

INTERVIEWS

Bryan Mark Rigg Sammlung [Collection], BA-MA
  Heinz Günter Angreß, 10 December 1994
  Hermann Aub, 14 December 1996
  Hans B. [Bernheim], 29 October 1998
  Hanns-Heinz Bauer, 29 March 1998
  Elisabeth Behrend, 3 March 1997
  Chaskel Besser, 15 July 2003
  Dr. Martin Bloch, 13 October 1996
  Robert Braun, 10–14 August, 10–14 October 1994, 7 January 1996
  Klaus Budzinski, 15 November 1994
  Ursula Cadenbach, 15 October 1996
  Hans Döppes, 19 May 1996
  Harald Ettheimer, 2 September 1995
  Karin Falencki (née Tiche), 3 January 2003
  Werner Goldberg, 17 October 1994
  Barry Gourary, 8 May 2003
  Zalman Gourary, 18 May 2003

Rabbi Meir Greenberg, 18 August 1996
Michael Günther, 19 February 1997
Rabbi Zalman Gurary, 19 January 1997
Mrs. Johannes Hamburger, n.d.
Helmut Krüger, 27, 31 August 1994
Friedemann Lichtwitz, 18 July 1997
Hans-Oskar Löwenstein de Witt, 6 December 1994
Klaus Schenk (pseudonym), 18 November 1996
Rolf Schenk, 23 May 1997
Friedrich Schlesinger, 10 December 1994
Horst Schmechel, 29 November 1994
Fritz Steinwasser, 13 December 1994, 7 February 1997
Reiner Wiehl, 17 May 1996
Joseph Wineberg, 4 May 2003
Helmuth Wohlthat (by Rolf Vogel), 17 December 1974

Unrecorded Interviews
Mordechai Dov Altein, 14 January 2003
Rachel Altein, 14 January 2003
Sue Batzdorff, 21 November 2004
Gisela Bauer, 1, 27, 28 September 2014
Diedra Berger, 20 June 2014
Chaskel Besser, 16 January 2003
Bruce Blumberg, 16 August 2014
Adam Boren, 9 December 2003
Shmuel Fox, 14 January 2003
Arthur Green, 25 January 2003
Herschel Greenberg, 23 February 2004
Holger Herwig, 10 January 2003
Paula Hyman, 20 September 2003
Bernhard Klein, 9 September 2003
Moshe Kolodny, 4 September 2003, 21 January 2004
Hirsch Kotlarsky, 3 January 2003
David Kranzler, 31 December 2003, 24 January, 8 February 2004
Avraham Laber, 8 May 2003, 6 January 2004
Norman Lamm, 18 December 2004
Johnny Lee, 13 February 2015
Henri Lustiger, 30 December 2014
James Ponet, 23 May 2005
Zalman Posner, 3 May 2003
Dovid Reidel, 29 December 2014, 13 February 2015
Kenneth Roseman, 25 August 2003, 23 February 2015

Elie Shmotkin, 31 December 2003
Gerhard Weinberg, 2 September 2005
Alex Weisfogel, 20 January, 23 February, 8 March, 18 November 2004
David Woolner, 18 September 2003
Eliezer Zaklikovsky, 4 June, 25 December 2003, 13 January 2004
Unrecorded Interviews by Colin Heaton
Hans Baur, 1985
Albert Kerscher, 1985
Otto Kumm, 1985
Karl Wolff, 1984

WEBSITES
http://168.144.123.218/18thCenturyStottsEndnotes.htm
http://avalon.law.yale.edu/imt/judgoeri.asp
http://www.bartleby.com/345/authors/193.html
http://chgs.umn.edu/museum/exhibitions/rescuers/savingDiplomats.html
http://www.hmsroyaloak.co.uk/index.htm
http://www.kemstone.com/Nonfiction/Philosophy/Thesis/plague.htm
http://www.lexikon-der-wehrmacht.de/Personenregister/G/GoeschenAlex.htm
http://www.lexikon-der-wehrmacht.de/Personenregister/H/HellEE.htm
http://www.lexikon-der-wehrmacht.de/Gliederungen/LandschtzReg/Land
    schtzReg177-R.htm
http://www.lds-mormon.com/nibley4.shtml
http://www.uscis.gov/working-united-states/permanent-workers/emplo
    yment-based-immigration-fifth-preference-eb-5/eb-5-immigrant-investor

BOOKS AND ARTICLES
Abrams, Alan. *Special Treatment.* Secaucus, NJ, 1985.
Abshagen, Karl Heinz. *Canaris.* London, 1956.
Absolon, Rudolf. *Wehrgesetz und Wehrdienst 1935–1945. Das Personalwesen in der Wehrmacht.* Boppard, 1960.
Adam, Peter. *Art of the Third Reich.* New York, 1992.
Adam, Uwe. *Judenpolitik im Dritten Reich.* Düsseldorf, 1972.
Adler, H. G. *Der Verwaltete Mensch. Studien zur Deportation der Juden aus Deutschland.* Tübingen, 1974.
Akten der Parteikanzlei der NSDAP: Rekonstruktion eines verlorengegangenen Bestandes. Bundesarchiv, Microfiches, hrsg. v. Institut für Zeitgeschichte, 1983.
Allen, J. Michael, and James B. Allen. *World History from 1500.* New York, 1993.
Allen, John L., Jr. "Second UN Panel Criticizes Vatican on Sex Abuse." *Boston Globe,* 23 May 2014.

Allen, Matthew. "Ten Years after Swiss Banks Agreed to Pay Back Assets to Holocaust Victims, One of the Deal's Chief Architects Said It Helped Lift a Cloud over the Country." *Swiss News*, 11 August 2008.

Allen, William Sheridan. "Die deutsche Öffentlichkeit und die 'Reichskristall-nacht'—Konflikte zwischen Werthierarchie und Propaganda im Dritten Reich." In *Die Reihen fest geschlossen. Beiträge zur Geschichte des Alltags unterm Nationalsozialismus.* Wuppertal, Germany, 1981.

Altein, Rachel, and Eliezer Zaklikovsky, eds. *Out of the Inferno: The Efforts That Led to the Rescue of the Rabbi Yosef Y. Schneersohn of Lubavitch from War-torn Europe in 1939–1940.* Brooklyn, NY, 2002.

Amen, Daniel. *Change Your Brain, Change Your Life: The Breakthrough Program for Conquering Anxiety, Depression, Obsessiveness, Anger and Impulsiveness.* New York, 1998.

Arendt, Hannah. *Eichmann in Jerusalem: A Report on the Banality of Evil.* New York, 1964.

Aristotle. *Nicomachean Ethics*, trans. Martin Ostwald. New York, 1962.

Arlow, Oliver. "Kim Jong-il Keeps $4 Billion 'Emergency Fund' in European Banks." *Telegraph*, 20 February 2015.

Armstrong, Karen. *The Battle for God.* New York, 2000.

———. *A History of God: A 4,000-Year Quest of Judaism, Christianity and Islam.* New York, 1993.

Aschheim, Steven E. *Brothers and Strangers: The East European Jew in German and German Jewish Consciousness, 1800–1923.* Madison, WI, 1982.

Avtson, Sholom D. *A Day to Recall, a Day to Remember*, vol. 2, *Tishrei-Adar.* Brooklyn, NY, 1998.

"Banks and the Holocaust; Unsettling." *Economist*, 17 August 2000.

Barker, Dan. *Godless: How an Evangelical Preacher Became One of America's Leading Atheists.* Berkeley, CA, 2008.

Barry, John M. *Roger Williams and the Creation of the American Soul: Church, State, and the Birth of Liberty.* New York, 2012.

Barton, Burton. "Hopper and Dropper, Musing from Entrepreneur and Investor Rich Barton: My Trip through the Clinton Global Initiative—America Meeting, 27 June 2014."

Bar-Zohar, Michel. *Hitler's Jewish Spy: The Most Extraordinary True Spy Story of World War II.* London, 1985.

Basu, Moni. "Arrest Highlights Clergy's Role in Rwanda Genocide." CNN, 30 November 2009.

Bauer, Gisela. *Graue Wahrheit: Schizophrenie—eine heilbare unheilbare Krankheit.* Frankfurt, 2004.

Bauer, Yehuda. *American Jewry and the Holocaust: The American Jewish Joint Distribution Committee, 1939–1945.* Detroit, 1981.

———. *A History of the Holocaust.* New York, 1982.

Baynes, Norman H., ed. *The Speeches of Adolf Hitler*, vols. 1–2. Oxford, 1942.

Beevor, Anthony. *The Fall of Berlin 1945*. New York, 2002.

Below, Nicolaus von. *Als Hitlers Adjutant 1937–1945*. Mainz, 1980.

Ben-Sasson, H. H., ed. *A History of the Jewish People*. Cambridge, 1976.

Benton, Joshua. "National: David Duke Reverts to Unabashed Racism in Congress Run." *PG News*, 1 May 1999.

Benz, Wolfgang. *The Holocaust: A German Historian Examines the Genocide*. New York, 1999.

Berenbaum, Michael. *The World Must Know: The History of the Holocaust as Told in the United States Holocaust Memorial Museum*. Baltimore, 2007.

Berger, David. *The Rebbe, the Messiah and the Scandal of Orthodox Indifference*. Oxford, 2001.

Beschloss, Michael. *The Conquerors: Roosevelt, Truman and the Destruction of Hitler's Germany 1941–1945*. New York, 2002.

Bethell, Nicholas. *The War Hitler Won: The Fall of Poland, September 1939*. New York, 1972.

"Bill to Aid Britain Strongly Backed." *New York Times*, 9 February 1941.

Black, Allida M. *Courage in a Dangerous World: Political Writings of Eleanor Roosevelt*. New York, 1999.

Black, Conrad. *Franklin Delano Roosevelt: Champion of Freedom*. New York, 2003.

Black, Matthew, and H. H. Rowley, eds. *Peake's Commentary on the Bible*. New York, 1963.

Blair, Clay. *Hitler's U-Boat War: The Hunters, 1939–1942*. New York, 1996.

Blatt, Joel, ed. *The French Defeat: Reassessments*. Providence, RI, 1998.

Blum, John Morton. *V Was for Victory: Politics and American Culture during World War II*. New York, 1976.

Boteach, Shmuel. *The Wolf Shall Lie with the Lamb: The Messiah in Hasidic Thought*. Lanham, MD, 1993.

Bower, Tom. *Nazi Gold: The Full Story of the Fifty-Year Swiss-Nazi Conspiracy to Steal Billions from Europe's Jews and Holocaust Survivors*. New York, 1997.

Bracher, Karl Dietrich. *The German Dictatorship: The Origins, Structure, and Effects of National Socialism*. New York, 1970.

Brady, Brittany. "Babies' Herpes Linked to Circumcision Practice." CNN, 8 April 2013.

Braithwaite, Tom. "Credit Suisse Pleads Guilty to Tax Evasion." *Financial Times*, 19 May 2014.

Brant, Irving. *The Fourth President: A Life of James Madison*. Norwalk, CT, 1970.

Brewster, Todd, and Peter Jennings. *The Century*. New York, 1998.

Brissaud, André. *Canaris*. London, 1986.

Brodie, Fawn M. *No Man Knows My History: The Life of Joseph Smith.* New York, 1995.

Broszat, Martin, and Norbert Frei, eds. *Das Dritte Reich im Überblick.* Munich, 1989.

Brown, Andrew M. "Intelligence Squared Debate: Catholics Humiliated by Christopher Hitchens and Stephen Fry." *London Telegraph*, 19 October 2009.

Bruce, Alexander Balmain. *The Parabolic Teaching of Christ: A Systematic and Critical Study of the Parables of Our Lord.* London, 1900.

Buber, Martin. *The Way of Man: According to the Teaching of Hasidism.* New York, 1966.

Buckley, E. B. *Hitler's Austria: Popular Sentiment in the Nazi Era, 1938–1945.* Chapel Hill, NC, 2000.

Bullock, Alan. *Hitler: A Study in Tyranny.* New York, 1983.

Bunin, Amos. *A Fire in His Soul: Irving M. Bunin 1901–1980—The Man and His Impact on American Orthodox Jewry.* New York, 1989.

Burkett, B. G., and Glenna Whitley. *Stolen Valor: How the Vietnam Generation Was Robbed of Its Heroes and Its History.* Dallas, TX, 1998.

Burleigh, Michael. *Ethics and Extermination: Reflections on Nazi Genocide.* New York, 1997.

———. *The Third Reich: A New History.* New York, 2000.

Burns, Edward McNall. *Western Civilizations: Their History and Their Culture.* New York, 1954.

Burns, James MacGregor. *Roosevelt*, vol. 1, *The Lion and the Fox*. Norwalk, CT, 1956.

Büttner, Ursula. "The Persecution of Christian-Jewish Families in the Third Reich." *Leo Baeck Yearbook* 34 (1989).

Campbell, Joseph, with Bill Moyers. *The Power of Myth.* New York, 1991.

Cesarani, David, ed. *The Final Solution: Origins and Implementation.* New York, 1994.

Chanes, Jerome. "Give Me Liberty or the Tanakh: Michael Walzer Ponders the Meaning in God's World." *Forward*, 21 September 2012.

Chang, Iris. *The Rape of Nanking: The Forgotten Holocaust of World War II.* New York, 1997.

Chang, Jung, and Jon Halliday. *Mao: The Unknown Story.* London, 2006.

Charny, Israel W., William S. Parsons, and Samuel Totten, eds. *Century of Genocide: Critical Essays and Eyewitness Accounts.* New York, 2004.

Childers, Thomas. *A History of Hitler's Empire.* 2nd ed. Chantilly, VA, 2001.

Churchill, Winston S. *The Second World War*, vol. 1, *The Gathering Storm*. Boston, 1983.

Citino, Robert M. *The German Way of War: From the Thirty Years' War to the Third Reich.* Lawrence, KS, 2005.

———. *Quest for Decisive Victory: From Stalemate to Blitzkrieg in Europe, 1899–1940.* Lawrence, KS, 2002.

Clark, Alan. *Barbarossa: The Russian-German Conflict 1941–1945.* New York, 1965.

Cody, Edward. "Rabbi, Three Children Shot Dead Outside Jewish School in France." *Washington Post*, 19 March 2012.

Cohen, Patricia. "Yale Press Bans Images of Muhammad in New Book." *New York Times*, 12 August 2009.

Cohen, Rabbi Raphael N. *Shmuos Vsipurim.* Israel, 1977.

Cohn, Norman. *The Pursuit of the Millennium: Revolutionary Millenarians and Mystical Anarchists of the Middle Ages.* Revised and expanded ed. Oxford, 1970.

Cooper, Matthew. *The German Air Force 1933–1945.* New York, 1981.

———. *German Army 1933–1945: Its Political and Military Failure.* New York, 1978.

Cornwell, John. *Hitler's Pope: The Secret History of Pius XII.* New York, 1999.

Corum, James S. *The Roots of Blitzkrieg: Hans von Seeckt and German Military Reform.* Lawrence, KS, 1992.

Craig, Gordon A. *Germany 1866–1945.* New York, 1978.

———. *The Politics of the Prussian Army 1640–1945.* New York, 1964.

Crane, Cynthia. *Divided Lives: The Untold Stories of Jewish-Christian Women in Nazi Germany.* New York, 2000.

Crossan, J. D. *Jesus: A Revolutionary Biography.* New York, 1994.

Crovitz, L. Gordon. "Defending Satire to the Death." *Wall Street Journal*, 12 January 2015.

Dalfin, Chaim. *The Seven Chabad-Lubavitch Rebbes.* New York, 1998.

Dalton, Dennis. "Power over People: Classical and Modern Political Theory." In *The Great Courses.* Chantilly, VA, 1991.

Davies, Norman. *God's Playground: A History of Poland*, vol. 2, *1795 to the Present.* New York, 1982.

Dawkins, Richard. *The God Delusion.* New York, 2006.

Denzler, Georg, and Volker Fabricius. *Die Kirchen im Dritten Reich.* Frankfurt, 1984.

Dimont, Max I. *Jews, God and History.* New York, 1964.

Diner, Hasia R. *Jews in America.* New York, 1999.

Divine, Robert A., T. H. Breen, George M. Fredrickson, and R. Hal Williams. *America: Past and Present.* London, 1987.

Doerries, Reinhard R. *Hitler's Last Chief of Foreign Intelligence: Allied Interrogations of Walter Schellenberg.* London, 2003.

Dower, John. *War without Mercy: Race and Power in the Pacific War.* New York, 1986.

Ehrlich, Avrum M. *Leadership in the HaBaD Movement: A Critical Evaluation of HaBaD Leadership, History, and Succession.* New York, 2000.

Ehrman, Bart D. *Misquoting Jesus: The Story behind Who Changed the Bible and Why.* New York, 2007.

Eliach, Yaffa. *Hasidic Tales of the Holocaust.* New York, 1982.

Eligon, John, and Claudio Gatti. "Iranian Dealings Lead to a Fine for Credit Suisse." *New York Times,* 15 December 2009.

Eliot, Charles W., ed. *Johann Wolfgang von Goethe: Christopher Marlowe Doctor Faustus,* trans. Anna Swanwick. Danbury, CT, 1982.

Elster, Jeremy. "Twenty Years to the Baruch Goldstein Massacre in Hebron." *Jewish Journal,* 24 February 2014.

Ericksen, Robert. *Theologians under Hitler.* New Haven, CT, 1985.

Evans, Richard J. *Lying about Hitler: History, Holocaust, and the David Irving Trial.* New York, 2001.

Every Jew Has a Silver Lining: An Adaptation of the Public Addresses of the Lubavitcher Rebbe Rabbi Menachem M. Schneerson, on the Tenth of Teves and on Shabbos Parshas Vayechi, vol. 47. Brooklyn, NY, 1990.

Faiola, Anthony, and Michelle Boorstein. "U.N. Panel Blasts Vatican Handling of Clergy Sex Abuse, Church Teachings on Gays, Abortion." *Washington Post,* 5 February 2014.

Feingold, Henry L. *Bearing Witness: How America and Its Jews Responded to the Holocaust.* Syracuse, NY, 1995.

———. *The Politics of Rescue: The Roosevelt Administration and the Holocaust, 1938–1945.* New Brunswick, NJ, 1970.

Ferguson, Niall. *The War of the World: Twentieth Century Conflict and the Descent of the West.* New York, 2006.

Finklestone, Joseph. "Obituaries: Rabbi Baruch Korff." *Independent,* 3 August 1995.

Fischel, Jack R. *The Holocaust.* Westport, CT, 1998.

Fisher, Max. "Kim Jong Un Just Had His Own Uncle Killed. Why?" *Washington Post,* 12 December 2013.

Fishkoff, Sue. *The Rebbe's Army: Inside the World of Chabad-Lubavitch.* New York, 2003.

Fitzpatrick, Sheila. *The Russian Revolution 1917–1932.* Oxford, 1990.

"Former KKK Grand Wizard Living in Austria." *Telegraph,* 13 May 2009.

Fox, Robin Lane. *The Unauthorised Version: Truth and Fiction in the Bible.* New York, 1991.

Foxbrunner, Roman A. *HABAD: The Hasidism of R. Shneur Zalman of Lyady.* Tuscaloosa, AL, 1992.

Frankl, Viktor. *Man's Search for Meaning: An Introduction to Logotherapy.* New York, 1984.

Freedland, Jonathan. "Pope Benedict Has to Answer for His Failure on Child Abuse." *Guardian,* 15 February 2013.

Freedman, Samuel G. *Jew vs. Jew: The Struggle for the Soul of American Jewry.* New York, 2000.

Frei, Norbert. *National Socialist Rule in Germany.* Cambridge, 1993.

Freyeisen, Astrid. *Shanghai und die Politik des Dritten Reiches.* Würzburg, 2000.

Friedländer, Saul. *Nazi Germany and the Jews*, vol. 1, *The Years of Persecution, 1933–1939.* New York, 1997.

Friedman, Chaim Shlomo. *Dare to Survive.* New York, 1991.

Friedman, Menachem, and Samuel Heilman. *The Rebbe: The Life and Afterlife of Menachem Mendel Schneerson.* Princeton, NJ, 2010.

Friedman, Saul S. *No Haven for the Oppressed: United States Policy toward Jewish Refugees, 1938–1945.* Detroit, 1973.

Fritz, Stephen G. *Frontsoldaten: The German Soldier in World War II.* Lexington, KY, 1995.

Fullenkamp, Leonard, Stephen Bowman, and Jay Luvaas, eds. *Guide to the Vicksburg Campaign.* Lawrence, KS, 1998.

Gaster, Theodor H. *Myth, Legend, and Custom in the Old Testament.* New York, 1969.

Gay, Ruth. *The Jews of Germany.* New Haven, CT, 1992.

Gellately, Robert. *Backing Hitler: Consent and Coercion in Nazi Germany.* Oxford, 2001.

———. *The Gestapo and German Society: Enforcing Racial Policy.* Oxford, 1990.

Gellman, Irwin. *Secret Affairs: Franklin Roosevelt, Cordell Hull, and Sumner Welles.* Baltimore, 1995.

Gibbon, Edward. *The Decline and Fall of the Roman Empire*, vol. 1. New York, 1931.

Gibson, David. "Cardinal Raymond Burke: Gays, Remarried Catholics Are Just as Sinful as Murderers." Religion News Service, 27 March 2015.

Gilbert, Martin. *The Holocaust.* New York, 1985.

———. *The Righteous: The Unsung Heroes of the Holocaust.* New York, 2003.

———. *The Second World War: A Complete History.* New York, 1989.

Gill, Anton. *An Honourable Defeat: A History of German Resistance to Hitler 1933–1945.* New York, 1994.

Glantz, David M., and Jonathan M. House. *The Battle of Kursk.* Lawrence, KS, 1999.

Globke, Hans, and Wilhelm Stuckart. *Kommentare zur Deutschen Rassengesetzgebung.* Munich, 1936.

Goerlitz, Walter. *The German General Staff, 1657–1945.* New York, 1971.

Gonzalez, Daniel. "Paths to Immigration Reform Will Be Bumpy." *Republic*, 3 February 2013.

Goodstein, Laurie, Nick Cumming-Bruce, and Jim Yardley. "U.N. Panel Criticizes the Vatican over Sexual Abuse." *New York Times*, 5 February 2014.

Goodwin, Doris Kearns. *No Ordinary Time: Franklin and Eleanor Roosevelt—The Home Front in World War II.* New York, 1994.

Gordon, Sarah. *Hitler, Germans and the "Jewish Question."* Princeton, NJ, 1984.

Green, Dominic. "When Hitler Looked East." *Wall Street Journal*, 16 January 2015.

Green, Peter. *Ancient Greece: A Concise History.* New York, 1973.

Greenberg, Gershon. "Menahem Mendel Schneersohn's Response to the Holocaust." *Modern Judaism* 34, 1 (20 February 2014).

Gregory, Paul Roderick. "Want Putin's Attention on Ukraine? Follow His Money." *Forbes*, 3 March 2014.

Guderian, Heinz. *Panzer Leader.* Costa Mesa, CA, 1988.

Gutman, Yisrael. *The Jews of Warsaw, 1939–1943: Ghetto, Underground, Revolt.* Bloomington, IN, 1982.

Haffner, Sebastian. *The Meaning of Hitler.* Cambridge, 1979.

Halkin, Abraham S., ed. *Moses Maimonides' Epistle to Yemen: The Arabic Original and the Three Hebrew Versions*, trans. Boaz Cohen. Ann Arbor, MI, 1952.

Hall, John. "Hurled to His Death in Front of a Baying Mob: ISIS Barbarians Throw 'Gay' Man off Building in Another Sickening Day in Jihadi Capital of Raqqa." *Daily Mail*, 5 March 2015.

Harding, Luke. "Putin, the Kremlin Power Struggle and the $40 Billion Fortune." *Guardian*, 20 December 2007.

Harris, Lis. *Holy Days: The World of a Hasidic Family.* New York, 1985.

Harris, Sam. *The End of Faith: Religion, Terror, and the Future of Reason.* New York, 2004.

Hart, B. H. Liddell. *The German Generals Talk.* New York, 1979.

Hastings, Max. *All Hell Let Loose: The World at War 1939–1945.* London, 2012.

Hattaway, Herman, and Richard E. Beringer. *Jefferson Davis, Confederate President.* Lawrence, KS, 2002.

Hausner, Gideon. *Justice in Jerusalem.* New York, 1966.

Heaton, Colin D., and Anne-Marie Lewis. *German Aces Speak II: World War II through the Eyes of Four More of the Luftwaffe's Most Important Commanders.* Minneapolis, 2014.

Heeresadjutant bei Hitler 1938–1943. Aufzeichnungen des Majors Gerhard Engel. Hrsg. u. kommentiert v. Hildegard von Kotze. Schriftenreihe der Vierteljahreshefte für Zeitgeschichte Nr. 29. Stuttgart, 1974.

Heilbrunn, Jacob. "War Torn: 'Those Angry Days' and '1940.'" *New York Times*, 25 July 2013.

Heilman, Uriel. "Pew Survey of U.S. Jews: Soaring Intermarriage, Assimilation Rates." *JTA: The Global Jewish News Source*, 1 October 2013.

Heni, Clemens. "Why Prof. Wolfgang Benz Is Headed in the Wrong Direction." *Wissenschaft und Publizistikals Kritk*, 1 May 2009.

Herzstein, Robert Edwin. *Roosevelt & Hitler: Prelude to War.* New York, 1989.

Hilberg, Raul. *Destruction of the European Jews.* New York, 1961.

Hitchens, Christopher. *God Is Not Great: How Religion Poisons Everything.* New York, 2007.

———. *Hitch-22: A Memoir.* New York, 2010.

———. *Letters to a Young Contrarian.* New York, 2001.

———. *The Portable Atheist: Essential Readings for the Nonbeliever.* Cambridge, MA, 2007.

———. *Thomas Jefferson: Author of America.* New York, 2005.

———. "What I Learned about Hugo Chavez's Mental Health When I Visited Venezuela with Sean Penn." *Hugo Boss,* 2 August 2010.

———. "Yale Surrenders: Why Did Yale University Press Remove Images of Mohammed from a Book about the Danish Cartoons?" *Slate,* 17 August 2009.

Hitler, Adolf. *Mein Kampf.* Boston, 1971.

Hoffman, Edward. *Despite All Odds: The Story of Lubavitch.* New York, 1991.

Höhne, Heinz. *Canaris.* New York, 1979.

———. *Canaris: Patriot im Zwielicht.* Munich, 1976.

The Holocaust, vols. 1 and 2, *Legalizing the Holocaust—The Early Phase, 1933–1939,* and *The Later Phase, 1939–1943.* Introduction by John Mendelsohn. New York, 1982.

Höpfl, Harro, ed. *Luther and Calvin on Secular Authority.* Cambridge, 1991.

Horowitz, Elliott. *Reckless Rites: Purim and the Legacy of Jewish Violence.* Princeton, NJ, 2006.

Hosking, Geoffrey. *Russia: People and Empire 1552–1917.* Cambridge, 1997.

House, Jonathan M. *Combined Arms Warfare in the Twentieth Century.* Lawrence, KS, 2001.

Howell, Elizabeth. "How Many Stars Are in the Milky Way." *Space.com,* 21 May 2014.

Huberband, Shimon. *Kiddusch Hashem: Jewish Religious and Cultural Life in Poland during the Holocaust.* New York, 1987.

Isaacson, Walter. *Benjamin Franklin: An American Life.* New York, 2003.

Issa, Issam Abu. "Arafat's Swiss Bank Account." *Middle East Quarterly* (Fall 2004).

Jäckel, Eberhard. *Hitler's Weltanschauung.* Stuttgart, 1981.

Jackson, Julian. *France: The Dark Years, 1940–1944.* Oxford, 2003.

Jacob, Aaron. *The Campaign against Israel's Legitimacy: Answers to Israel's Critics.* New York, 2010.

Jacobs, Louis. *The Jewish Religion: A Companion.* New York, 1995.

Jacobs, Rabbi Steven L., ed. *Contemporary Christian Religious Responses to the Shoah.* Lanham, MD, 1993.

Jacobson, Rabbi Israel. "Journey to America." *Di Yiddishe Heim,* 1956.

———. *Zi Koron L'Beis Yisrael: Memories of Rabbi Israel Jacobson 1907–1939.* Brooklyn, NY, 1996.

Jacobson, Simon. *Toward a Meaningful Life: The Wisdom of the Rebbe Menachem Mendel Schneerson.* New York, 1995.

James, Susan Donaldson. "Baby Dies of Herpes in Ritual Circumcision by Orthodox Jews." ABC News, 12 March 2012.

"Jews Seized in Nazi Army Ask for Scripture First." *Miami Daily News,* 25 September 1944.

Jochmann, Werner, ed. *Adolf Hitler Monologe im Führerhauptquartier, 1941–1944.* Hamburg, 1980.

Johnson, Paul. *A History of the American People.* New York, 1997.

———. *A History of Christianity.* New York, 1995.

———. *A History of the Jews.* New York, 1987.

Josephus, Titus Flavius. *The Jewish War,* trans. G. A. Williamson. New York, 1981.

Kahn, David. *Hitler's Spies: German Military Intelligence in World War II.* New York, 1977.

Kaminetzky, Yosef Y. *Days in Chabad.* Brooklyn, NY, 2002.

Kammer, Hilde, and Elisabet Bartsch, eds. *Nationalsozialismus. Begriffe aus der Zeit der Gewaltherrschaft 1933–1945.* Hamburg, 1992.

Kantor, Jodi. "Disinvitation by Obama Is Criticized." *New York Times,* 6 March 2007.

Kaplan, Chaim A. *Scroll of Agony: The Warsaw Diary of Chaim A. Kaplan.* New York, 1965.

Kaplan, Marion A. *Between Dignity and Despair: Jewish Life in Nazi Germany.* New York, 1998.

Kaploun, Uri, ed. *Likkutei Dibburim: An Anthology of Talks by Rabbi Yosef Yitzchak Schneersohn of Lubavitch.* 5 vols. Brooklyn, NY, 1987–2000.

Karff, Samuel E., ed. *Hebrew Union College—Jewish Institute of Religion at One Hundred Years.* Cincinnati, OH, 1976.

Katz, Steven T. *The Holocaust in Historical Context,* vol. 1, *The Holocaust and Mass Death before the Modern Age.* Oxford, 1994.

Kaufmann, Walter, ed. *The Portable Nietzsche.* New York, 1968.

Kaylor, Brian. "Anniversary of Bailey Smith's Harmful Moment in Baptist-Jewish Relations." *Ethics Daily,* 23 August 2010.

Kee, Robert. *1939: In the Shadow of War.* Boston, 1984.

Keegan, John. *The Mask of Command.* New York, 1987.

———. *The Second World War.* New York, 1990.

Kennedy, David M. *The American People in World War II: Freedom from Fear Part Two.* Oxford, 1999.

———. *Freedom from Fear: The American People in Depression and War, 1929–1945.* New York, 1999.

Kennedy, Paul. *The Rise and Fall of the Great Powers.* New York, 1987.

Kershaw, Ian. *Hitler 1889–1936: Hubris.* New York, 1999.

———. *Hitler 1936–1945: Nemesis.* New York, 2000.

———. *The Hitler Myth: Image and Reality in the Third Reich.* Oxford, 1990.

———. *The Nazi Dictatorship.* New York, 1985.

———. *Profiles in Power: Hitler.* New York, 1991.

Kertzer, David. *The Pope and Mussolini: The Secret History of Pius XI and the Rise of Fascism in Europe.* Oxford, 2014.

Kirsch, Jonathan. *Moses: A Life.* New York, 1998.

Klee, Ernst. *Euthanasie im NS-Staat: Die Vernichtung lebensunwerten Lebens.* Frankfurt, 1985.

Klein, Edward. *The Kennedy Curse: Why America's First Family Has Been Haunted by Tragedy for 150 Years.* New York, 2003.

Klein, Fritz. *Verlorene Größe.* Munich, 1996.

Klemperer, Victor. *Ich will Zeugnis ablegen bis zum letzten, 1933–1945.* Berlin, 1996.

Klugman, Ben Zion. *The Light Is Sown for the Righteous (Ohr Zoruah la Tzadik).* Jerusalem, 2001.

Kors, Alan C., and Edward Peters, eds. *Witchcraft in Europe: A Documentary History 1100–1700.* Philadelphia, 1972.

Kozak, Warren. *The Rabbi of 84th Street: The Extraordinary Life of Haskel Besser.* New York, 2004.

Kramer, Milton, ed. *The Kramers: The Next Generation.* Brooklyn, NY, 1995.

Kranzler, David. *The Man Who Stopped the Trains to Auschwitz: George Mantello, El Salvador, and Switzerland's Finest Hour.* Syracuse, NY, 2000.

———. "Orthodoxy's Finest Hour: Rescue Efforts during the Holocaust." *Jewish Action* 63, 1 (Fall 2002).

———. *Thy Brothers' Blood: The Orthodox Jewish Response during the Holocaust.* Brooklyn, NY, 1987.

Krüger, Helmut. *Der Halbe Stern. Leben als deutsch-jüdischer "Mischling" im Dritten Reich.* Berlin, 1992.

Kugel, James L. *How to Read the Bible: A Guide to Scripture Then and Now.* New York, 2007.

Kushner, Harold S. *When Bad Things Happen to Good People.* New York, 1981.

LaFeber, Walter. *The American Age: United States Foreign Policy at Home and Abroad since 1750.* New York, 1989.

Lagassé, Paul, ed. *The Columbia Encyclopedia.* 6th ed. New York, 2000.

Lamm, Norman. *The Face of God: Thoughts on the Holocaust.* Yeshiva University Department of Holocaust Studies, 1986.

———. *The Religious Thought of Hasidism: Text and Commentary.* New York, 1999.

Lang, Jochen von. *The Secretary: Martin Bormann.* New York, 1979.

Larson, Erik. *In the Garden of Beasts: Love, Terror, and an American Family in Hitler's Berlin.* New York, 2011.

Lasser, William. *Bengamin V. Cohen: Architect of the New Deal.* New Haven, CT, 2002.

Lauren, Paul Gordon. *Power and Prejudice.* London, 1988.

Lenowitz, Harris. *The Jewish Messiahs: From the Galilee to Crown Heights.* Oxford, 1998.

Lerski, Jerzy Jan. *Historical Dictionary of Poland, 966–1945.* Westport, CT, 1996.

Levack, Brian P. *The Witch-Hunt in Early Modern Europe.* London, 1987.

Levi, Primo. *Moments of Reprieve: A Memoir of Auschwitz.* New York, 1995.

———. *Survival in Auschwitz: The Nazi Assault on Humanity.* New York, 1986.

Levin, Nora. *The Holocaust: The Destruction of European Jewry, 1933–1945.* New York, 1973.

Levinson, Isaac. *The Untold Story.* Johannesburg, 1958.

Lifton, Robert Jay. *The Nazi Doctors.* New York, 1986.

Lipstadt, Deborah E. *Beyond Belief: The American Press & the Coming of the Holocaust 1933–1945.* New York, 1986.

Lochner, Louis P., ed. *Goebbels Diaries.* New York, 1948.

Loewenthal, Naftali. *Communicating the Infinite: The Emergence of the Habad School.* Chicago, 1990.

Loftus, John W., ed. *The Christian Delusion: Why Faith Fails.* New York, 2010.

Lösener, Bernhard. "Als Rassereferent im Reichsministerium des Innern." In Das Reichsministerium des Innern und die Judengesetzgebung, *Vierteljahreshefte für Zeitgeschichte* 9 (1961).

Lowenthal, Marvin. *The Jews of Germany: A History of Sixteen Centuries.* Philadelphia, 1936.

Lucchetti, Aaron, and Jay Solomon. "Credit Suisse's Secret Deals." *Wall Street Journal*, 17 December 2009.

Machtan, Lothar. *The Hidden Hitler.* New York, 2001.

MacMullen, Ramsay. *Christianizing the Roman Empire A.D. 100–400.* New Haven, CT, 1984.

Madej, Victor, and Steven Zaloga. *The Polish Campaign 1939.* New York, 1985.

Mader, Julius. *Hitlers Spionagegenerale sagen aus.* Berlin, 1971.

Magid, Shaul. *"America Is No Different," "America Is Different—Is There an American Jewish Fundamentalism?"* Internet version, 9 September 2014.

Mai, Tram. "Pastor Calls for Killing Gays to End AIDS." *USA Today*, 6 December 2014.

Maier, Dieter. *Arbeitseinsatz und Deportation. Die Mitwirkung der Arbeitsverwaltung bei der nationalsozialistischen Judenverfolgung in den Jahren, 1938–1945.* Berlin, 1994.

Malone, Dumas. *Jefferson and His Time*, vol. 2, *Jefferson and the Rights of Man.* Boston, 1951.

Maltitz, Horst von. *The Evolution of Hitler's Germany*. New York, 1973.

Manstein, Erich von. *Lost Victories: The War Memoirs of Hitler's Most Brilliant General*. Novato, CA, 1982.

Marcus, Jacob R. *The Rise and Destiny of the German Jew*. Cincinnati, OH, 1934.

Marks, Dena. "Jewish Leaders Concerned Televised Sermon Could Fuel Antisemitism." *Jewish Herald-Voice*, 23 October 2014.

Marsden, George M. *The Twilight of the American Enlightenment: The 1950's and the Crisis of Liberal Belief*. New York, 2014.

Maser, Werner. *Adolf Hitler. Legende Mythos Wirklichkeit*. Munich, 1971.

Matthäus, Jürgen. "German *Judenpolitik* in Lithuania during the First World War." *Leo Baeck Yearbook* 43 (1998).

Maurer, Trude. *Ostjuden in Deutschland 1918–1933*. Hamburg, 1986.

May, Ernest R. *Strange Victory: Hitler's Conquest of France*. New York, 2000.

Mayer, Arno J. *Why Did the Heavens Not Darken: The "Final Solution" in History*. New York, 1988.

McClure, Marc Eric. *Earnest Endeavors: The Life and Public Work of George Rublee*. Westport, CT, 2003.

McGreal, Chris. "The Catholic Church Must Apologise for Its Role in Rwanda's Genocide." *Guardian*, 8 April 2014.

———. "Hiding in Plain Sight in France: The Priests Accused in Rwandan Genocide." *Guardian*, 7 April 2014.

McInnis, Edgar. *The War: First Year*. New York, 1940.

McJimsey, George. *The Presidency of Franklin Delano Roosevelt*. Lawrence, KS, 1999.

Medoff, Rafael, ed. *Blowing the Whistle on Genocide: Josiah E. DuBois, Jr. and the Struggle for a U.S. Response to the Holocaust*. West Lafayette, IN, 2008.

Medoff, Rafael, and David Wyman. *A Race against Death: Peter Bergson, America, and the Holocaust*. New York, 2002.

Megellas, James. *All the Way to Berlin: A Paratrooper at War in Europe*. New York, 2003.

Melson, Robert. *False Papers: Deception and Survival in the Holocaust*. Champaign, IL, 2000.

Melville, Herman. *Moby Dick*. Oxford, 2008.

Metaxas, Eric. *Bonhoeffer: Pastor, Martyr, Prophet, Spy*. Nashville, TN, 2010.

Metzger, Alter B. *The Heroic Struggle: The Arrest and Liberation of Rabbi Yosef Y. Schneersohn of Lubavitch in Soviet Russia*. Brooklyn, NY, 1999.

Metzmacher, Helmut. "Deutsch-englishe Ausgleichsbemühungen im Sommer 1939." *Vierteljahrshefte für Zeitgeschichte* 14, 4 (1966).

Meyer, Beate. *Jüdische Mischlinge. Rassenpolitik und Verfolgungserfahrung 1933–1945*. Hamburg, 1999.

Meyer, Winfried. *Unternehmen Sieben. Eine Rettungsaktion für vom Holocaust*

Bedrohte aus dem Amt Ausland-Abwehr im Oberkommando der Wehrmacht. Frankfurt, 1993.

Miles, Jack. *God: A Biography.* New York, 1995.

Militärgeschichtliches Forschungsamt, ed. *Deutsche Jüdische Soldaten, 1914–1945.* Bonn, 1984.

———. *Germany and the Second World War*, vol. 1, *Build-up of German Aggression.* Oxford, 1998.

Miller, Chaim. *Turning Judaism Outward: A Biography of the Rebbe Menachem Mendel Schneerson.* Brooklyn, NY, 2014.

Millett, Allan R., and Williamson Murray, eds. *Military Innovation in the Interwar Period.* New York, 1998.

Mindel, Nissen. *Rabbi Joseph I. Schneersohn, the Lubavitcher Rabbi.* New York, 1947.

Mooney, Alex. "Controversial Minister off Obama's Campaign." CNN, 15 March 2008.

Mooney, Alex, and Peter Hamby. "Clinton: Wright Would Not Have Been My Pastor." CNN, 8 April 2008.

Morgan, Ted. *FDR: A Biography.* New York, 1985.

Morison, Samuel Eliot. *The Oxford History of the American People.* New York, 1965.

Morris, William, ed. *The American Heritage Dictionary of the English Language.* New York, 1973.

Mosely, Leonard. *On Borrowed Time: How World War II Began.* New York, 1969.

Moyn, Samuel. "History's Revenge: What Happened to Jewish Faith When a New Attitude toward the Past Emerged?" *Forward*, 9 January 2004.

Münch, Ingo von. *Frau, komm! Die Massenvergewaltigungendeutscher Frauen und Mädchen 1944/45.* Graz, Austria, 2009.

Muñoz-Suárez, Carlos. "The Tractatus . . . Is It So Intractable." *Philosophy Now*, November–December 2014.

Myers, David N., and Kaye Alexander, eds. *The Faith of Fallen Jews: Yosef Hayim Yerushalmi and the Writing of Jewish History.* Waltham, MA, 2014.

Myers, John. *The Alamo.* London, 1948.

"New York Sues Credit Suisse over Mortgages." *New York Times*, 29 November 2012.

Nguyen, Tina. "Ultra-Orthdox Jewish Newspaper Edits Female World Leaders out of *Charlie Hebdo* March." *Mediaite*, 12 January 2014.

Niedersächsischer Verband Deutscher Sinti, ed. *"Es war unmenschenmöglich." Sinti aus Niedersachsen erzählen—Verfolgung und Vernichtung im Nationalsozialismus und Diskriminierung bis heute.* Hannover, 1995.

Niemöller, Wilhelm. *Die Synode zu Steglitz.* Göttingen, 1970.

Niewyk, Donald L., ed. *The Holocaust: Problems and Perspectives of Interpretation.* New York, 2003.

Noakes, Jeremy. "The Development of Nazi Policy towards the German-Jewish 'Mischlinge,' 1933–1945." *Leo Baeck Yearbook* 34 (1989).

Noakes, Jeremy, and Geoffrey Pridham, eds. *Nazism 1919–1945.* Exeter, UK, 1983.

"Obama Decries Pastor's Remarks." *Seattle Times,* 15 March 2008.

Obeidallah, Dean. "ISIS's Gruesome Muslim Death Toll: The Group's Killing of Westerners Gets Attention. But ISIS Has Killed Far More Muslims, and Publicizing That Fact Would Harm It More." *Daily Beast,* 7 October 1914.

Office of the United States Chief Counsel for Prosecution of Axis Criminality, ed. *U.S.A. Military Tribunals: Case No. 11.2.* Nuremberg, 1949.

Olson, Lyne. *Those Angry Days: Roosevelt, Lindbergh, and America's Fight over World War II, 1939–1941.* New York, 2013.

O'Neill, Robert. *The German Army and the Nazi Party, 1933–1939.* New York, 1966.

"1,000 Rabbis Greet Rabbi Schneersohn, Exiled Polish Leader." *New York Herald Tribune,* 20 March 1940.

Ostroff, Jonathan. "Why Haredim Don't Serve in the IDF." *Failed Messiah,* 21 March 2014.

Owings, Alison. *Frauen: German Women Recall the Third Reich.* New Brunswick, NJ, 1995.

Padfield, Peter. *War beneath the Sea: Submarine Conflict during World War II.* New York, 1996.

Paskuly, Steven, ed. *Death Dealer: The Memoirs of the SS Komandant at Auschwitz Rudolf Höss.* New York, 1996.

Pätzold, Kurt, ed. *Verfolgung, Vertreibung, Vernichtung. Dokumente des faschistischen Antisemitismus 1933 bis 1942.* Leipzig, 1984.

Paxton, Robert. *Vichy France: Old Guard and New Order, 1940–1944.* New York, 1972.

Paxton, Robert, and Michael Marrus. *Vichy France and the Jews.* Stanford, CA, 1995.

Pehle, Walter H., ed. *Der Judenpogrom 1938: Von der Reichskristallnacht zum Völkermord.* Frankfurt, 1988.

Penkower, Monty Noam. *The Jews Were Expendable: Free World Diplomacy and the Holocaust.* Chicago, 1983.

Picker, Henry, ed. *Hitlers Tischgespräche im Führerhauptquartier.* Stuttgart, 1976.

Plato. *The Trial and Death of Socrates: Apology.* Cambridge, 1975.

Plitnick, Mitchell. "Reclaiming Antisemitism." *Jews for Global Justice,* 20 July 2003.

Posselt, Alfred. *Soldat des Feindes.* Vienna, 1993.

Powell, Michael. "Following Months of Criticism, Obama Quits His Church." *New York Times*, 1 June 2008.

"Progressives and Disorder: The Next Two Years May Be the Most Dangerous since the Cold War Ended." *Wall Street Journal*, 31 December 2014.

"Rabbi from Warsaw." *Time*, 1 April 1940.

Rabinowicz, Harry. *Hasidism: The Movement and Its Masters*. New York, 1988.

Rabinowicz, Tzvi. *Hasidism in Israel: A History of the Hasidic Movement and Its Masters in the Holy Land*. New York, 2000.

Rader, Charles, ed. *Challenge: An Encounter with Lubavitch-Chabad*. Brooklyn, NY, 1970.

Randall, J. G., and David Donald. *The Civil War and Reconstruction*. Boston, 1961.

Rapoport-Albert, Ada, ed. *Hasidism Reappraised*. London, 1996.

Rashi. *The Torah: With Rashi's Commentary Translated, Annotated, and Elucidated*, vol. 1, ed. Yisrael Isser Zvi Herczeg. Brooklyn, NY, 1995.

Ravitzky, Aviezer. *Messianism, Zionism, and Jewish Religious Radicalism*. Chicago, 1996.

Raz, Hila. "Israel Orders Ultra-Orthodox to End Discrimination against Women: Attorney General Decrees Sweeping Changes in Public Services." *Haaretz*, 8 May 2013.

The Rebbes: Rabbi Yosef Yitzchak Schneersohn of Lubavitch, vol. 2. Israel, 1994.

Rebentisch, Dieter. *Führerstaat und Verwaltung im Zweiten Weltkrieg. Verfassungsentwicklung und Verwaltungspolitik, 1939–1945*. Stuttgart, 1989.

Redlich, Fritz. *Hitler: Diagnosis of a Destructive Prophet*. Oxford, 1998.

Reid, T. R. "Daughter's Denunciation of Historian Roils Mormon Church." *Washington Post*, 8 May 2005.

Rheins, Carl J. "The Verband nationaldeutscher Juden 1921–1933." *Leo Baeck Yearbook* 25 (1980).

Rich, Norman. *Hitler's War Aims*. New York, 1974.

Rigg, Bryan Mark. *Hitler's Jewish Soldiers: The Untold Story of Jews and Men of Jewish Descent Who Served in the German Military*. Lawrence, KS. 2002.

———. *Lives of Hitler's Jewish Soldiers: Untold Tales of Men of Jewish Descent Who Fought for the Third Reich*. Lawrence, KS, 2009.

———. *Rescued from the Reich: How One of Hitler's Soldiers Saved the Lubavitcher Rebbe*. New Haven, CT, 2004.

———. "Where They Are Now: Civil Disobedience (Issuing of the U.S. Postal Stamp in Honor of Robert Kim Bingham)." *Yale Alumni Magazine*, May–June 2006.

Rischel, Jack, and Sanford Pinsker, eds. *Jewish American Culture and History Encyclopedia*. New York, 1992.

Robinson, George. *Essential Judaism: A Complete Guide to Beliefs, Customs, and Rituals*. New York, 2000.

Ro'i, Yaacov, ed. *Jews and Jewish Life in Russia and the Soviet Union.* New York, 1995.

Rolde, Neil. *Breckinridge Long: American Eichmann.* Solon, ME, 2013.

Rose, Paul Lawrence. *German Question/Jewish Question: Revolutionary Anti-Semitism from Kant to Wagner.* Princeton, NJ, 1990.

Roseman, Mark. *The Villa, the Lake, the Meeting: Wannsee and the Final Solution.* New York, 2002.

Roskies, David, ed. *The Literature of Destruction: Jewish Responses to Catastrophe.* New York, 1989.

Ross, Bill D. *Iwo Jima: Legacy of Valor.* New York, 1985.

Rossino, Alexander B. *Hitler Strikes Poland: Blitzkrieg, Ideology, and Atrocity.* Lawrence, KS, 2003.

Rubenstein, Richard. *After Auschwitz: History, Theology, and Contemporary Judaism.* Baltimore, 1992.

Rubinstein, Richard E. *When Jesus Became God: The Struggle to Define Christianity during the Last Days of Rome.* New York, 1999.

"Rudolf Harney-Pfarrer in politisch und theologisch stürmischer Zeit." In *Verein für Rheinische Kirchengeschichte: Monatshefte für Evangelische Kirchengeschichte des Rheinlandes,* Band 57. Düsseldorf, 2008.

Rüter-Ehlermann, A., and C. F. Rüter, eds. *Sammlung deutscher Strafurteile wegen nationalsozialistischer Tötungsverbrechen.* Amsterdam, 1968–1981.

Sachar, Howard M. *The Course of Modern Jewish History: The Classic History of the Jewish People, from the Eighteenth Century to the Present Day.* New York, 1990.

Sadan, Tsvi. "Orthodox Jews Threaten to Quit Israel over IDF Draft." *Israel Today,* 2 March 2014.

Safire, William. "Truman on Underdogs." *New York Times,* 14 July 2003.

Sajer, Guy. *The Forgotten Soldier.* New York, 1971.

Sammons, Jeffrey L. *Heinrich Heine: A Modern Biography.* Princeton, NJ, 1979.

Schacter, Jacob J., ed. *Reverence, Righteousness, and Rahamanut: Essays in Memory of Rabbi Dr. Leo Jung.* New York, 1992.

Schapiro, Jane. *Inside a Class Action: The Holocaust and the Swiss Banks.* Madison, WI, 2003.

Scherman, Nosson, and Meir Zlotowitz, eds. *The Complete Artscroll Siddur.* Brooklyn, NY, 1984.

Schleunes, Karl A. *The Twisted Road to Auschwitz: Nazi Policy toward German-Jews 1933–1939.* Champaign, IL, 1970.

Schmidl, Erwin A. *Juden in der K.(u.) K. Armee 1788–1918, Studia Judaica Austriaca,* Band XI. Eisenstadt, 1989.

Schmitt, Hans A. *Quakers and Nazis: Inner Light in Outer Darkness.* Columbia, MO, 1997.

Schneersohn, Joseph I. *Igrois Koidesh.* Brooklyn, NY, 1983–1985.

———. *Lubavitcher Rabbi's Memoirs: The Memoirs of Rabbi Joseph I. Schneersohn, the Late Lubavitcher Rabbi*, vol. 1. Brooklyn, NY, 1961.

———. *On the Teachings of Chassidus (Kuntres Toras Hachassidus)*. Brooklyn, NY, 1965.

———. *Saying Tehillim: Selected from Letters by the Late Lubavitcher Rebbe Rabbi Yoseph Yitzhak Schneersohn on the Subject of Reciting Psalms*. Brooklyn, NY, 1975.

———. *The "Tzemach Tzedek" and the Haskala Movement (Ha "Tzemach Tzedek" Utenaus Hahaskolo)*. Brooklyn, NY, 1962.

Schneerson, Menachem Mendel. *Sichot Kodesh*. Unpublished transcript of Schneerson's talks from 1958.

Scholem, Gershom G. *Major Trends in Jewish Mysticism*. Jerusalem, 1941.

———. *Sabbatai Sevi: The Mystical Messiah 1626–1676*. Princeton, NJ, 1973.

Schubert, Günter. *Der Fleck auf Uncle Sams weißer Weste: Amerika und die jüdischen Flüchtlinge 1938–1945*. Frankfurt, 2003.

Seaton, Albert. *Russo-German War 1941–1945*. London, 1971.

Segal, Simon. *The New Order in Poland*. New York, 1942.

Shachnow, Sid, and Jann Robbins. *Hope and Honor*. New York, 2004.

Shelton, Dinah, ed. *Encyclopedia of Genocide and Crimes against Japan's National Shame*. London, 1999.

Shirer, William L. *Berlin Diary: The Journal of a Foreign Correspondent 1934–1941*. New York, 1941.

———. *The Nightmare Years 1930–1940*. New York, 1984.

Silver, Zachary. "The Excommunication of Mordecai Kaplan." *American Jewish Archives Journal* 62, 1 (2010): 21–48.

Singing the Living Tradition. Boston, 1993.

Sinmun/Yonhap, Rodong. "Kim Jong Un's Executed Uncle Was Eaten Alive by 120 Hungry Dogs: Report." *NBC World News*, 3 January 2014.

Smith, Steven. *Spinoza, Liberalism, and the Question of Jewish Identity*. New Haven, CT, 1997.

Snyder, Timothy. *Bloodlands: Europe between Hitler and Stalin*. New York, 2010.

Solomon, Aryeh. *The Educational Teachings of Rabbi Menachem M. Schneerson*. Lanham, MD, 2000.

Solomon, Lewis D. *The Jewish Book of Living and Dying*. New York, 1999.

Solomon, Robert C. *No Excuses: Existentialism and the Meaning of Life*. Chantilly, VA, 2000.

Spencer, Robert, ed. *The Myth of Islamic Tolerance: How Islamic Law Treats Non-Muslims*. New York, 2005.

Squires, David. "Rev. Jeremiah Wright Says 'Jews' Are Keeping Him from President Obama." *Daily Press*, 10 June 2009.

State of Israel Ministry of Justice, ed. *The Trial of Adolf Eichmann: Record of Proceedings in the District Court of Jerusalem.* Jerusalem, 1992.

Steinberg, Jonathan. *All or Nothing: The Axis and the Holocaust 1941–1943.* New York, 1991.

Stenger, Victor J. *God the Failed Hypothesis: How Science Shows That God Does Not Exist.* Amherst, MA, 2007.

Steyn, Mark. "Obama's Pastor Disaster." *Orange County Register,* 15 March 2008.

Stoltzfus, Nathan. *Resistance of the Heart: Intermarriage and the Rosenstrasse Protest in Nazi Germany.* London, 2001.

———. "Widerstand des Herzens." In *Geschichte und Gesellschaft. Zeitschrift für Historische Sozialwissenschaft 21. Jahrgang/Heft 2 April–Juni 1995, Protest und Widerstand.* Göttingen, 1995.

Stone, Kem. *The Struggle of Sisyphus: Absurdity and Ethics in the Work of Albert Camus—Moralist Camus—The Plague.* 2006. http://www.kemstone.com/thesis.html

Strzetelski, Stanislaw. *Where the Storm Broke: Poland from Yesterday to Tomorrow.* New York, 1942.

Stuckart Wilhelm, and Hans Globke. *Kommentare zur Deutschen Rassengesetzgebung.* Munich, 1936.

Sullivan, Andrew. "The Wright Post 9/11 Sermon." *Atlantic,* 22 March 2008.

Telushkin, Joseph. *Rebbe: The Life and Teachings of Menachem M. Schneerson, the Most Influential Rabbi in Modern History.* New York, 2014.

Templeton, Charles. *Farewell to God: My Reasons for Rejecting the Christian Faith.* Toronto, 1996.

Tenney, Merrill C., ed. *Pictorial Bible Dictionary.* Nashville, TN, 1966.

Tent, James F. *In the Shadow of the Holocaust: Nazi Persecution of Jewish-Christian Germans.* Lawrence, KS, 2003.

Tepper, Daniel. "Ultra-Orthodox Jews Are Refusing to Join the Israeli Army." *Vice,* 5 March 2014.

Thomson-DeVeaux, Amelia. "Study Shows That Mormons Are the Fastest-Growing Religious Group in the U.S." Public Religion Research Institute, 2 May 2012.

Tick, Ira. "Jesus the Hasid: A Review of Geza Vermes' 'Jesus the Jew.'" *Beacon,* 24 October 2011.

Toland, John. *Adolf Hitler.* New York, 1976.

Toldois Chabad B-Artzois Ha'Bris: History of Chabad in the USA 1900–1950. Brooklyn, NY, 1988.

Toras Menachem Hisva' Aduyos. Brooklyn, NY, 1992.

Totten, Michael J. "ISIS Exterminating Minorities in Iraq." *World Affairs,* 6 August 2014.

Trepp, Leo. *The Complete Book of Jewish Observance.* New York, 1980.

Trevor-Roper, H. R. *The European Witch-Craze of the Sixteenth and Seventeenth Centuries and Other Essays.* New York, 1967.

Troyer, John. "Hatemongers Try to Cleanse History. Gays: Forgotten Heroes of 9/11." *Counter Punch*, 3 May 2002.

Tschuy, Theo. *Dangerous Diplomacy: The Story of Carl Lutz, Rescuer of 62,000 Hungarian Jews.* Cambridge, 2000.

Tull, Charles J. *Father Coughlin and the New Deal.* Syracuse, NY, 1965.

Turner, Henry Ashby, Jr. *Hitler's Thirty Days to Power: January 1933.* London, 1996.

Vermes, Geza. *Jesus the Jew: A Historian's Reading of the Gospels.* Philadelphia, 1981.

Victor, George. *Hitler: The Pathology of Evil.* Dulles, VA, 1998.

Vital, David. *A People Apart: The Jews in Europe 1789–1939.* Oxford, 1999.

Vogel, Rolf. *Ein Stück von Uns.* Bonn, 1973.

The Von Hassell Diaries 1938–1944: The Story of the Forces against Hitler Inside Germany as Recorded by Ambassador Ulrich von Hassell—A Leader of the Movement. New York, 1947.

Voss, Carl Hermann. *Rabbi and Minister: The Friendship of Stephen S. Wise and John Haynes Holmes.* Buffalo, NY, 1980.

Vuletic, Aleksandar-Saša. *Christen Jüdischer Herkunftim Dritten Reich. Verfolgung und Organisierte Selbsthilfe, 1933–1939.* Mainz, 1999.

Waley, Arthur. *The Analects of Confucius.* Franklin Center, NY, 1980.

Wallance, Gregory. *America's Soul in the Balance: The Holocaust, FDR's State Department, and the Moral Disgrace of an American Aristocracy.* Austin, TX, 2012.

Walzer, Michael. *In God's Shadow: Politics in the Hebrew Bible.* New Haven, CT, 2012.

Warfield, Hania, and Gaither Warfield. *Call Us to Witness: A Polish Chronicle.* New York, 1945.

"War Front: Capitalism in Germany." *Time*, 7 April 1941.

Watt, Richard M. *Bitter Glory: Poland and Its Fate 1918–1939.* New York, 1979.

Weinberg, Gerhard L. *Germany, Hitler, and World War II.* New York, 1996.

———. *A World at Arms: A Global History of World War II.* New York, 1994.

Weinthal, Benjamin. "Berlin Professor Slammed for Defending Nazi." *Jerusalem Post*, 31 January 2010.

Weiss, Andrew S. "The Improviser." *Wall Street Journal*, 21–22 February 2015.

Wertheim, Aaron. *Law and Custom in Hasidim.* Hoboken, NJ, 1992.

Wheeler-Bennett, John. *The Nemesis of Power.* New York, 1980.

Wiesel, Elie. *Night.* New York, 1982.

Windfuhr, Manfred, ed. *Heinrich Heine, Historisch-kritische Gesatausgabe der Werke.* Hamburg, 1973–1997.

Wink, Walter. *The Powers That Be: Theology for a New Millennium.* New York, 1998.

Wise, Stephen. *Challenging Years: The Autobiography of Stephen Wise.* New York, 1949.

Wistrich, Robert. *Hitler and the Holocaust.* New York, 2001.

Wouk, Herman. *This Is My God: The Jewish Way of Life.* New York, 1959.

Wright, Lawrence. *Going Clear: Scientology, Hollywood, & the Prison Belief.* New York, 2013.

Wyden, Peter. *Stella: One Woman's True Tale of Evil, Betrayal, and Survival in Hitler's Germany.* New York, 1993.

Wyman, David. *The Abandonment of the Jews: America and the Holocaust 1941–1945.* New York, 1989.

———. *Paper Walls: America and the Refugee Crisis 1938–1941.* New York, 1985.

Yahil, Leni. *The Holocaust: The Fate of European Jewry.* Oxford, 1990.

Yancey, Philip, and Tim Stafford, commentators. *The Student Bible, New International Version.* Grand Rapids, MI, 1986.

Yelton, David K. *Hitler's Volkssturm: The Nazi Militia and the Fall of Germany 1944–1945.* Lawrence, KS, 2002.

Yukich, Grace. *One Family under God: Immigration Politics and Progressive Religion in America.* Oxford, 2013.

Zaklikofsky, Eliezer. *America Is No Different.* New York, 1999.

Zaklikowski, Dovid. *The Rescue of the Lubavitcher Rebbe, Rabbi Yosef Yitzchak Schneersohn (Rayatz), during WWII.* Kleinman Holocaust Education Center, Brooklyn, NY, 2014.

Zalman, Schneur. *Tanya.* Brooklyn, NY, 1969.

Zeleny, Jeff. "Obama Says He's Outraged by Ex-Pastor's Comments." *New York Times*, 29 April 2008.

Zuelzer, Wolf. "Keine Zukunft als 'Nicht-Arier' im Dritten Reich." In *Der Judenpogrom 1938: Von der Reichskristallnacht zum Völkermord*, Walter H. Pehle. Frankfurt am Main, 1988.

Zuroff, Efraim. "Orthodox Rescue Revisited." *Jewish Action* 63, 3 (Spring 2003).

———. *Response of Orthodox Jewry in the United States: The Activities of the Vaad Ha-Hatzala Rescue Committee, 1939–1945.* New York, 2000.

———. Review of Rachel Altein and Eliezer Zaklikovsky, eds., *Out of the Inferno. Jerusalem Post*, 15 December 2002.

INDEX

size in North America in 1939, 108
system of theology, 50–51
Lubavitch (city in Russia), 1–2, 45, 50, 64
Lubavitchers (members of Chabad), 29, 45,
52, 56, 61, 80, 83, 89, 92, 94, 95, 98,
99, 100, 101, 106, 111, 113, 132, 134,
136, 139, 141, 143, 146, 148, 149,
151–153, 155, 157–160, 162, 164,
165, 168, 171, 172, 174, 177–179,
182, 185, 188, 189, 191, 192, 194,
199, 200, 203, 205, 213, 215, 216,
218–220, 222, 232, 235–237, 240,
250, 252, 255, 256, 262, 314, 323,
328, 330–333, 347, 361n25, 362n30,
363–364n36, 365n48, 371n25, 375n4,
377–378nn22–23, 405n3, 411n58,
416n95, 418n112, 418n114, 421n134,
436–437n2
belief that only their community can
produce Messiahs, 261n25
crisis within the community because
Rebbe Schneerson is declared the
Messiah, 262, 421n134, 436n2
dishonesty with their history, 330–333,
364n48, 418n112
ex-members in anti-religious activities,
61
mission work of, 347n2
prejudice against atheists, 58
prejudice against Gentiles, 56–57,
436–437n2
prejudice against non-Orthodox Jews,
58
prejudice against socialists, 58
size of community in World War II,
377–378n23
speaking with the dead, 362n30,
421n133
unwillingness to fight, 177
unwillingness to pay their legal bills,
152, 159, 160, 189
unwillingness to serve in the military,
76, 77, 83
See also Chabad
Lublin, Poland, 398n13
Lublin's Jewish Religious Academy
(*Yeshiv Chachi Lublin*), 182

Luftwaffe (German air force), 79, 83, 87,
89, 92, 94, 96, 205
Luke (Biblical book), 274, 275
Luria, Rabbi Isaac (Arizal), 360–361n18
Lustiger, Cardinal, xii
Lustiger, Henri, 365n45
Luther, Martin, 47, 48
Luxembourg, 33, 297
Lychen, Germany, 294

MacArthur, General Douglas, 79
Madagascar, 114
Madej, Victor, 374n72
Magid of Mezerich, 50
Magog (ancient enemy of Israel), 252
Maimonides, 216, 252
Makeig-Jones, Captain William Tofield,
204
Malava Malke, 141, 387n1
Manhattan Project, 197
Mann, Thomas, 228, 273
Manstein, Field Marshal Erich von, 94
Marine Corps, xiii, 226
Marinmuseum in Karlskorna, Sweden,
405n15
Marseilles, France, xi, 132, 192
Masada (ancient battle of Jewish zealots
against the Romans), 290
Más a Tierra (World War I battle), 114–115
Massachusetts, United States, 185, 219
May, Earnest, xix, 33
McClure, Marc E., xix, 132
McCormack, Congressman John W., 219,
408n33
McDonald, James, 197, 206, 228
Medal of Honor, 365n49
Medicare, 307
Medoff, Rafael, 389n17
Mein Kampf, 6, 11, 22, 26–28, 43, 90, 133,
358n19
Meiser, Lutheran bishop Hans, 39
Melville, Herman, 84
Memelland, 13, 15
Mendelssohn, Moses, 182, 214
Mengel, Rabbi Nisson, 176
Menorah Society, 143
"Merchants of Death," 17